Guidance and Counseling in the Elementary and Middle Schools

Guidance and Counseling in the Elementary and Middle Schools

A Practical Approach

James J. Muro
University of North Texas

Terry Kottman
University of Northern Iowa

WCB Brown & Benchmark
PUBLISHERS

Madison, Wisconsin • Dubuque, Iowa

Book Team

Editor *Sue Pulvermacher-Alt*
Developmental Editor *Suzanne Guinn*
Production Editor *Kristine Queck*
Designer *Eric Engelby*
Art Editor *Tina Flanagan*
Photo Editor *Carol Judge*
Visuals/Design Freelance Specialist *Mary L. Christianson*
Marketing Manager *Steven Yetter*
Promotions Manager *Mike Matera*
Production Manager *Beth Kundert*

WCB Brown & Benchmark

A Division of Wm. C. Brown Communications, Inc.

Executive Vice President/General Manager *Thomas E. Doran*
Vice President/Editor in Chief *Edgar J. Laube*
Vice President/Marketing and Sales Systems *Eric Ziegler*
Vice President/Production *Vickie Putman*
Director of Custom and Electronic Publishing *Chris Rogers*
National Sales Manager *Bob McLaughlin*

Wm. C. Brown Communications, Inc.

President and Chief Executive Officer *G. Franklin Lewis*
Senior Vice President, Operations *James H. Higby*
Corporate Senior Vice President and President of Manufacturing *Roger Meyer*
Corporate Senior Vice President and Chief Financial Officer *Robert Chesterman*

The credits section for this book begins on page 484 and is considered an extension of the copyright page.

Cover image: Faces reprinted from posters with written permission from How Do You Feel Today Productions, PO Box 1085, Agoura, CA 91301.

Freelance Permissions Editor Karen Dorman

Copyedited by Nikki Herbst

Contents

In the mid 1960s at a meeting of the then American Personnel and Guidance Association (now the American Counseling Association) in Chicago, one of the authors of this text (Jim Muro) attended a session on developmental guidance and counseling. The attendance at the session was very small, but some of the pioneers of the modern elementary and middle school guidance movement were there. Harold Cottingham, Don Dinkmeyer, Van Faust, George Hill, and Bill Von Hoose, all of whom were instrumental in developing the elementary guidance movement, were grappling with some of the concepts that are now a major part of the literature in the field.

Part of the discussion that day was an attempt to identify the meaning of developmental guidance and counseling and how this concept applies to elementary and middle schools. As we near the twenty-first century, this concept is still evolving.

Developmental guidance and counseling is a concept that most counselors seem to understand and accept, yet no two counselors understand and accept it in the same way. We have written this text to help counselors and counselors-in-training clarify their ideas about what developmental guidance and counseling is and how it can be applied in elementary and middle schools.

The contents of this book were designed to provide the reader with the basic knowledge and skills needed to initiate and expand guidance and counseling programs in elementary and middle schools. At the present time in the United States, most school districts are expanding their elementary and middle school guidance and counseling programs. There is a trend toward mandated K–12 counselors for every school. Ten to fifteen states have already passed legislation putting such programs into place, and federal legislation designed to encourage elementary guidance and counseling programs on a nation-wide basis has been presented to Congress. In response to this trend, universities and colleges have begun to expand their course offerings in the area of elementary and middle school guidance and counseling.

The basic concept of this book is that guidance in the elementary and middle schools should be developmental in nature, while acknowledging that a remedial or problem-solving approach is sometimes necessary to provide services for the varied populations of children in school. We have stressed the fact that guidance and counseling are needed by all children, and should be as much a part of the life of the school as reading and language arts. At the same time, the book reflects our convictions that the counselor is a professional who must have the appropriate skills and understandings to work with children with special needs.

This book would be a valuable resource in graduate programs in Guidance and Counseling, School Psychology, or Human Development. In recent years, many counselors seeking master's degrees have not planned to work in schools. Instead, they choose to work in mental health agencies or private practices. This book could be valuable to them if they want to work with children and their families and consult with school personnel. This book could also be extremely helpful to counselors who are not currently enrolled in a university course, but wish to enhance and expand their skills and knowledge in the areas of school guidance and counseling and working with children.

Since some of the students enrolled in the courses using this book will not intend to work in schools, the book is broad enough in scope to be useful to them. It includes a discussion about normal human development—focusing on how these concepts can be practically applied in counseling children and adolescents. The material contains examples and illustrations to tie theory to practice. The authors have surpassed most books in the field in the scope of the coverage, for the book also contains chapters on working with families, using assessment instruments with children, providing consultation services, handling crises, and dealing with legal and ethical issues.

This book provides a comprehensive discussion of the actual counseling process with children, including a chapter on group counseling. In addition, we have also discussed play and activity techniques and creative and expressive arts techniques. We have provided material on many of the specific populations that counselors must deal with in their work, such as children of alcoholics, gifted children, children of color, children in stepfamilies and one-parent families, and children with Attention-Deficit/Hyperactivity Disorder. In fact, this book may well be considered a handbook for guidance and counseling with children. It could be used as a text for a course or as a ready reference for practicing counselors, whether they work in schools, agencies, or private practice.

This book is more practical than any other text in the field of elementary and middle school guidance and counseling because it contains a broad range of topics related to working with children. The authors have included specific, concrete examples of the concepts discussed to provide a framework for the practitioner, especially in the chapters related to individual and group counseling. Practicing counselors tend to be pragmatic, and this text will meet that need.

This text is also broader in scope and more comprehensive than any other text that deals with guidance and counseling in elementary and middle schools. To cover the material in this type of course, the instructor must usually have two or three textbooks. This book will address every aspect of counseling children in elementary and middle schools in a concrete manner designed to appeal to practitioners.

The supplementary material, the Instructor's Manual, contains chapter objectives, test questions, and suggestions for lecture enhancement and class projects.

The authors have designed this book and the ancillary materials to provide readers with everything they ever wanted to know about elementary guidance and counseling, but were (or were not) afraid to ask. The unifying theme is the concept of a developmental approach that stresses guidance and counseling for all children. However, the book also reflects the realities of elementary schools, in that there will always be a need to provide help for troubled children and their families. In a nutshell: guidance for all and special help for some.

Reviewers:

Reece Chaney
Indiana State University

Susan A. Anzivino
University of Maine at Farmington

Roger D. McCormick
University of Dayton

Donna Brown Evans
University of North Florida

Thomas W. Hosie
Louisiana State University

Peterann M. Siehl
Bowling Green State University

JoAnna White
Georgia State University

Guidance and Counseling in the Elementary and Middle Schools

Chapter One

*Introduction: An Overview of Guidance and Counseling
in Elementary and Middle Schools*

🌳 Over the years, both of the authors of this text have pondered the following
questions:

- What is school guidance, and why is it important?
- What is the role of counseling in the schools?
- What are the appropriate roles and functions of elementary and middle school
  counselors?
- Why is it important for a school counselor to have a "personal" theory of
  counseling?

1

We have designed this book to help students explore these questions. We do not suggest that we have completely answered all of these questions, and we are not sure that it is possible to definitively answer them, because the issues involved are extremely complex. The field of school counseling and guidance has continued to evolve since its inception, and we assume that it will continue to grow and change, keeping the answers to such questions ever in flux. We hope that students will learn something about guidance and counseling and about themselves in the process of reading and thinking about the contents of this volume.

The Evolution of School Guidance and Counseling

A brief description of some of the important elements in the evolution of school guidance and counseling may give students a historical perspective as they begin this journey of exploration and understanding. Until the early part of the twentieth century, there were no counselors in schools. Teachers gave students information and support in their personal, social, and career struggles, as well as providing academic instruction (Schmidt, 1993). The school guidance movement began to develop as a result of the Industrial Revolution and the influx of various types of students into public schools. In 1898, Jesse B. Davis, a class counselor in Detroit, began providing educational and vocational counseling to high school juniors (Schmidt, 1993). In 1907, Davis got a job as a high school principal in Grand Rapids, Michigan, and brought guidance into the schools when he mandated that guidance be included as an element of each English class taught in his school (Wittmer, 1993). The purpose of these guidance lessons was to "help students develop character, avoid problem behaviors, and relate vocational interests to curriculum subjects" (Schmidt, 1993, p. 8).

At the same time, other professionals were introducing guidance programs across the country. Eli Weaver organized widespread guidance services in New York City, and Frank Goodwin developed a systemwide guidance delivery system in Cincinnati, Ohio. Meanwhile, Frank Parsons, known by many counselor educators and counseling students as the "Father of Guidance," organized a vocational bureau in Boston, Massachusetts, to help young people choose a career based on a scientific selection process. Several years later, Parsons began training vocational counselors and vocational managers for business and educational facilities.

During both of the world wars, the armed services developed and used many new types of testing procedures in their screening and classification of inductees. After World War II, professional educators adopted some of the instruments developed during the war (Myrick, 1993; Schmidt, 1993), and the guidance and counseling movement expanded to include a measurement function.

In the 1940s and 1950s, in addition to this focus on testing, there was also an emphasis on "mental health" and "guidance counseling," especially in junior and senior high schools. E. G. Williamson developed a school guidance model that was extremely popular in the 1940s and 1950s—trait and factor (directive) guidance. In this model, the school counselor was to use information to solve students' problems, especially in the areas of vocational and interpersonal adjustment (Baker, 1992). The counselor's role was directive, with an emphasis on teaching skills and molding attitudes and behaviors.

The other important change that occurred in the 1950s was the launch of the Soviet satellite, Sputnik I. This launch frightened the people of the United States because they thought that it signaled Russian dominance in the fields of industrial technology and other scientific endeavors (Baker, 1992; Schmidt, 1993). In response to the resultant public outcry, Congress passed several pieces of legislation, including the National Defense Education Act (NDEA) of 1958. This law provided funds for training counselors at the middle and high school levels and for helping the states to develop and support testing programs, school counseling, and other guidance-related programs (Schmidt, 1993).

Many educational professionals felt that the directive approach to school counseling was too narrow and problem-focused. Carl Rogers developed a theory of client centered counseling, which helped shift the focus away from the problem and its solution to the relationship between counselors and their clients. Client centered counseling became the primary mode of interaction for many counselors—both in schools and in the field of mental health in the late 1960s and 1970s. However, this, too, seemed to be a rather narrow approach to school guidance and counseling. According to Wittmer (1993),

> Very little attention was being given to the co-equal emphasis on prevention and on environmental intervention techniques so desperately needed in schools. Little attention was being placed (in counselor education programs) on the consulting and coordination roles needed by effective developmental school counselors. (p. 3)

This dissatisfaction with a strictly client centered approach eventually led to the further evolution of the school guidance and counseling movement.

During the 1960s, 1970s, and 1980s, the role and function of school counselors began to evolve to its present expanse, which includes development, implementation, and evaluation of comprehensive guidance programs; provision of direct counseling services to students, parents, and teachers; educational and vocational planning; student placement; referral; and consultation with teachers, administrators, and parents (Schmidt, 1993). Part of this evolution led to the appearance of elementary school counselors, which began in the early 1960s. In 1966, a Joint Committee on the Elementary School Counselor (ACES-ASCA, 1966) issued a report that described the role and functions of elementary school counselors as falling into three distinct categories: counseling, consulting, and coordinating.

As time passed, counseling and guidance services continued to grow and change, especially at the elementary level. The Education Act for All Handicapped Children of 1975 (Public Law 94-142) provided federal funds for special education services for handicapped children. While this act did not specifically address the role of counselors with special education children, many districts included school counselors, particularly those at the elementary and middle school levels, in the process of program coordination and curriculum planning, teacher consultation, and parent counseling, as well as child counseling (Schmidt, 1993).

Another strong influence on the direction of elementary and middle school guidance and counseling has been the growth of professional organizations, including the American Counseling Association (ACA), the American School Counselor Association (ASCA), and the Association of Counselor Education and Supervision (ACES) (Wittmer, 1993). The efforts of members of these organizations have brought about a movement toward professional growth and regulation, in terms of program accreditation and certification. As the field of school counseling continues to evolve, we will move toward a more professional, integrated status in our schools and communities.

Approaches to Guidance and Counseling

Over the years, four basic approaches to guidance and counseling have developed: (a) crisis, (b) remedial, (c) preventive, and (d) developmental (Myrick, 1993).

In the crisis approach, the counselor waits until there is some type of crisis and then leaps into action to help the person in crisis deal with the problem. With this approach, quite frequently all parties involved expect the counselor to use crisis intervention techniques and "fix" the problem. For example, Sally Appleby comes into Ms. McMillan's office, crying about the fact that George Stormwinds knocked her down on the playground because she would not give him a toy he wanted. If Ms. McMillan was using the crisis approach to guidance and counseling, she might ask Sally to brainstorm a solution to her crisis with George. She might also ask George to come into her office and work with both of the children on coming to some sort of resolution to the problem.

When a counselor engages in the remedial approach, he or she focuses on measurable weaknesses and tries to remediate them (Myrick, 1993). The purpose of this intervention is to avoid a possible crisis in that particular area. Many of the strategies used in the remedial approach involve teaching students skills, such as study skills and social skills, they do not already have. If Ms. McMillan was using the remedial approach with Sally and George, she might decide to teach them negotiation skills, so that they could more equitably solve interpersonal problems.

In the preventive model of guidance and counseling, the counselor tries to anticipate generic problems and to prevent them from happening (Myrick, 1993). These problems might include drug abuse, smoking, eating disorders, dropping out of school, teenage pregnancies, and the like—problems that could potentially affect large numbers of students. The preventive model is based on the idea that if the counselor can educate students about the dangers of certain activities and the methods of avoiding them before they begin to indulge in these problem behaviors, the counselor will be able to prevent them from doing so. Most of the techniques used in the preventive model involve teaching and disseminating information. If Ms. McMillan was going to use the preventive model of counseling, she would have already taught Sally and George about asking for what they want and being assertive, in order to prevent them from using aggressive behavior to get what they want.

The developmental approach is more proactive than the other three approaches to guidance and counseling. The counselor who uses the developmental approach has identified specific skills and experiences that children need to have in order to be successful in school and in life (Myrick, 1993). Because a developmental guidance program is based on student outcomes, the counselor designs a guidance curriculum in which there are developmentally appropriate activities that provide information and practice so that students have the opportunity to acquire each of these skills. The counselor, the teachers, or some combination of school personnel can deliver the various elements of a developmental guidance curriculum (Reynolds, 1993). The intervention techniques used in this approach include teaching, sharing information, role playing, coaching, tutoring, and counseling. If Ms. McMillan's primary focus was on the developmental approach, she would have been working with Sally and George from the time they were in first grade, using instruction and experiential learning to give them the interpersonal skills they needed to effectively interact with one another.

A well-designed developmental guidance and counseling program will encompass a balance of the other three approaches, as well as the developmental approach. The counselor who chooses to employ the developmental approach will want to use elements of crisis intervention; skill-building; remedial work; prevention programs; and a comprehensive developmental guidance curriculum (Baker, 1992; Myrick, 1993). She or he will develop student outcomes and accompanying plans for how to attain those outcomes for the academic, social/personal, and career domains (Reynolds, 1993).

Components of a Guidance and Counseling Program

While there are many ways to design a guidance and counseling program, a model that many school districts around the country are using is based on the approach developed by Norman Gysbers and Patricia Henderson (1988). This model for comprehensive, developmental guidance and counseling programs has four components: (a) guidance curriculum, (b) responsive services, (c) individual planning, and (d) system support.

The guidance curriculum is the core of the developmental approach (Gysbers & Henderson, 1988; Texas Education Agency, 1990). It delineates the goals for guidance instruction and student competencies by grade level. This component addresses self-esteem, motivation for success, decision making and problem solving, interpersonal and communication skills, cross-cultural awareness, and responsible behavior. The counselor's role in the delivery of the guidance curriculum is to provide group or classroom guidance lessons to all children in the school and to consult with teachers and other school personnel so that they can provide additional guidance lessons. In schools where counselors do not deliver any of the guidance curriculum themselves, provision of guidance lessons to teachers and other school personnel is a primary role for the counselor. The counselor would also coordinate the implementation of the guidance curriculum and make sure that it is delivered to all the children in her or his school.

Responsive services include elements of the crisis approach, the remedial approach, and the preventive approach. The purpose of this component is to provide intervention services for students in crisis and for students who have made unwise choices or need help with specific areas of weakness and prevention services for students who are on the verge of making unwise choices (Gysbers & Henderson, 1988). This component addresses: academic problems; school-related issues, such as tardiness, truancy, the potential of dropping out, and misconduct; relationship issues; abuse; bereavement; substance abuse; family concerns; sexuality issues; and stress management (Texas Education Agency, 1990). The counselor's role in this component of the guidance program is multifaceted. The counselor would provide counseling services (both individual and group) to students experiencing difficulties; consult with teachers, administrators, other school personnel, and parents about devising crisis intervention, remedial, and preventive services for students, both at school and at home; and coordinate the various intervention strategies being carried out with such students. If the counselor felt that the school could not provide the necessary services, she or he would also refer students and their families to mental health agencies, counselors in private practice, tutors, physicians, social service agencies, and other resources that might be able to provide help for them.

The individual planning component provides assistance for all students in making and implementing personal, educational, and career plans (Gysbers & Henderson, 1988). The primary goal of this element of the guidance program is to help students learn to monitor and understand their own growth and development and to proactively take action on this information (Gysbers & Henderson, 1988; Texas Education Agency, 1990). This component addresses three major areas of concern: educational, career, and personal-social. Within the educational area, the important elements are:

- Learning and using study skills.
- Increasing awareness of educational choices.
- Selecting appropriate courses.
- Understanding the value of lifelong learning.
- Effectively using test scores.

Within the career area, the important elements are:

- Exploring career opportunities.
- Exploring possibilities for vocational training.
- Understanding the need for positive work habits.

Within the personal-social area, the important elements are:

- Developing a positive self-concept.
- Developing appropriate social skills.

The counselor's role in this component is primarily related to guidance. All of these elements can be covered in group guidance activities that are geared toward the developmental level of the students in the school. Some of these areas will also lend themselves to individual consultation with students, teachers, parents, and administrators. The counselor will need to use assessment skills and knowledge of measurement instruments and test results to help the students in the school effectively use assessment information.

The system support component provides support for the guidance staff in carrying out the other three components and for other school personnel in carrying out educational programs in the school (Gysbers & Henderson, 1988; Texas Education Agency, 1990). In service to the guidance program, the system support component addresses: guidance program development, including management of budget, materials, and facilities; staff development; parent education; consultation with teachers and administrators; community outreach; public relations; professional development of counselors; and research and publishing. In service to other educational programs, the system support component addresses: school improvement planning; site management assignments; guidance-related administrative activities; and cooperative ventures with special education and vocational education programs. The counselor's role in system support consists primarily of program management and consultation.

Role of the Counselor

"School counselor roles seem to have run the gamut: they're all things to all people; they're miracle workers; they're only record-keeping and scheduling clerks; they own the guidance program" (ERIC/CAPS, 1985a, p. 1). The American School Counselor Association (ASCA) defined the school counselor as "a certified professional educator who assists students, teachers and administrators. Three generally recognized helping processes used by the counselor are counseling, consulting, and coordinating" (ASCA, 1990, p. 1). According to the ASCA definition, the first step of counseling is to establish trust and a confidential working relationship—either in a small group or with individual students. The counselor then tries to help the student(s) with exploring and understanding personal meaning as it relates to learning and developing. This process should ultimately help the student(s) with problem solving, coping skills, and decision making. Hannaford (1991) suggested that counseling covers three areas: academic, career, and preventive/developmental. Academic counseling at all levels involves helping motivate students to learn and enjoy learning. On the middle school level, it also involves class selection and beginning to consider future education direction. Career counseling at the elementary and middle school levels involves increasing students' job awareness and helping them to learn the basic decision-making skills they will need to be able to pursue long-term goals. At the middle school/junior high school level, the school counselor will more actively expose students to a wide range of career information to deepen their awareness of potential life goals. He or she will actively help students examine their interests and aptitudes in order to enhance their career opportunities. At both the elementary and middle school levels, the counselor uses preventive/developmental counseling to teach students communication skills, coping strategies, problem-solving techniques, and interpersonal relationship skills.

Consultation involves a cooperative process through which the counselor helps other people, usually parents, teachers, or administrators, to more clearly understand their interactions with others (ASCA, 1990). The goal of the consultation process is that the consultees learn information and enhance skills that they can use to interact more effectively with others, especially with students. "Consultation is a process of working with a second party directly to indirectly help a third party, the student" (Perry, 1992).

The ASCA report defined coordination as "a leadership process in which the counselor helps organize and manage a school's counseling program and related services" (1990, p. 1). The coordination aspect of the counselor's job might involve serving as a liaison between the school and community agencies, organizing a mentor program, leading a child study team, and other similar activities.

What Elementary Counselors Do

In 1985, the Educational Resources Information Center/Counseling and Personnel Services (ERIC/CAPS) provided a "representative" list of role and function descriptions for elementary school counselors. The list included the following descriptions:

1. Counseling—helping students to better understand and accept themselves and to increase their level of self-responsibility.
2. Consultation—working with administrators, teachers, and staff to meet student needs.
3. Pupil appraisal—coordinating the information that goes into confidential student files and interpreting the information to help qualify students for special programs.
4. Parent help—meeting individually and in groups with parents and providing resource materials and information on child development, problematic behaviors, and other child-related topics.
5. Referral—providing referrals to appropriate professionals in the schools and in the outside community.
6. Program planning—coordinating work of various school personnel, parents, and other interested parties in implementation of the guidance program.
7. Career development—developing and implementing career awareness as part of the guidance curriculum and consulting with teachers about including career awareness as part of the academic curriculum.

8. Change agent—trying to change any elements of the school atmosphere that might negatively affect students and their affective or academic development.

9. Ombudsman—acting as a student advocate.

10. Disciplinarian—consulting with teachers or working directly with students whose behavior is disruptive or inappropriate.

11. Public relations—explaining the importance of guidance and counseling to the various consumers of guidance services, including students, parents, teachers, administrators, and members of the community.

12. Local research—coordinating local research, including student population characteristics, guidance program evaluation, student outcomes, and the like.

13. Curriculum planning—coordinating the adaptation of the academic curriculum for students with special needs. Planning the guidance curriculum to make sure that all student outcomes are addressed.

14. Screening—interviewing new students and their parents, coordinating screening and appraisal, and making sure that students are appropriately placed.

In an article exploring the role and function of the elementary counselor, Wilgus and Shelley (1988) added several other duties in their list of elementary counselor functions, as follows:

1. Parent education—teaching parents parenting skills by providing parent education classes.

2. Guidance and counseling-oriented meetings—attending meetings about the emotional, behavioral, and/or developmental concerns of students.

3. Nonguidance and counseling meetings—attending meetings about concerns other than the emotional, behavioral, and/or developmental concerns of students.

4. Individual counseling—assisting individual students to resolve conflicts.

5. Group counseling—helping students resolve conflicts through small group interaction.

6. Classroom programs—conducting guidance and counseling activities through interactions with classes of students.

7. Recognition programs—participating in organized efforts to identify and acknowledge students who merit special recognition.

8. Staff consultation—consulting with school personnel about the academic, social, or emotional well-being of students.

9. Individual testing—providing assessment of students on an individual basis.

10. Group testing—providing and coordinating assessment of students on a group basis.

11. Staff development—conducting in-service programs for school personnel.

12. Referrals—providing suggestions for community and school district resources and services.

13. Classroom observation—providing feedback to school personnel based on classroom observations.

14. Parent contact—discussing the particular needs of students with their parents.

15. Other—having other duties in addition to those described in the preceding list. This might include lunch room duty, playground duty, serving as a classroom substitute, and the like.

In her description of an elementary guidance counselor's role in managing the school guidance and counseling program, Snyder (1993) included many of the elements in these two lists. She added several other duties, including the training and coordination of a peer helping program, and administrative tasks, such as managing access to records, supervising clerical assistants and guidance program secretaries, organizing and participating in the guidance and counseling advisory committee, and conducting guidance program evaluation.

None of these descriptions include suggestions of how elementary counselors can distribute their time in pursuit of their various duties. Since each school will be different in terms of the needs of the students and the school personnel, it would be impossible to dictate the amount of time that counselors should devote to each of these tasks. However, Henderson (1987) recommended specific percentages of elementary counselors' time be dedicated to each of the four program components in order to attain an optimal balance in their elementary guidance programs. She suggested that elementary counselors spend 40 percent of their time on the Guidance Curriculum component, 25 percent of their time on the Individual Planning component, 25 percent of their time on the Responsive Services component, and 10 percent of their time on the System Support component. This would give the biggest priority in elementary guidance and counseling programs to student contact time.

What Middle School/Junior High Counselors Do

To a certain extent, middle school/junior high counselors do the same sorts of things that elementary counselors do. They do, however, have some additional duties, and their priorities are quite frequently different than those of elementary counselors. Miller (1986) listed the functions of middle school counselors in order of priority as follows:

1. Consulting with teachers on the developmental needs of students.
2. Giving students, parents, teachers, and other school personnel information about the guidance program.
3. Organizing and managing the guidance program.
4. Evaluating the efficacy of the services provided by the guidance program.
5. Providing one-to-one counseling for students about personal and social concerns.
6. Providing one-to-one counseling for students about educational concerns.
7. Providing small group counseling for students about educational concerns.
8. Providing small group counseling for students about personal and social concerns.
9. Assessing students, identifying those who need special services, and making related referrals.

The Educational Resources Information Center/Counseling and Personnel Services (1985b) suggested that middle school/junior high counselors must remember the rapid developmental changes that their students are undergoing and predicate their programs on the idea that young adolescents need programs that are flexible, exploratory, and transitional. This report stressed the importance of using group guidance, peer facilitation, and consultation with teachers to help students assume a higher level of responsibility for their own lives and education. Counselors at this level can use teacher in-service training, consultation, and team teaching to increase the possibility that subject area teachers will address developmentally appropriate, guidance-related issues, such as sexuality, relationships, and AIDS education. At the middle school/junior high school level, career guidance becomes much more concrete and extensive. One essential element of the guidance and counseling program is the organization and implementation of interventions that engage students in assessing their own career maturity and career planning. Counselors will also want to expose students to career information and help them use career information to make educational decisions about course selection and future academic paths.

Because peers are the most influential people in the lives of students in middle schools and junior highs, counseling students in groups and training and supervising peer facilitators become even more important tools for counselors at this level than they were for elementary counselors. Parents of students in middle school and junior high schools may also need more individual support and opportunities for parent education classes than they needed when their children were younger. This is due to that fact that sometimes adolescents are more difficult to understand and parent than elementary school children.

Since middle school/junior high students invariably have multiple teachers and usually have some limited choices in the classes they take, counselors at this level frequently have scheduling responsibilities (Henderson, 1987). They also help register students for classes in the first year of high school and help with high school orientation.

Because they have a separate set of responsibilities and level-specific priorities, Henderson (1987) suggested that middle school/junior high counselors have a different balance of their time than elementary counselors. She recommended that they spend 30 percent of their time on the Guidance Curriculum component, 30 percent of their time on the Individual Planning component, 25 percent of their time on the Responsive Services component, and 15 percent of their time on the System Support component. While contact with students is still a priority, middle school counselors who follow these guidelines would spend less time designing and implementing the guidance curriculum and more time with students planning their futures. Because the middle school program has more functions related to system support, these guidelines also shift some of the counselors' time into that area.

Deciding on Priorities

There are so many responsibilities involved in elementary and middle school counseling that school counselors could easily feel overwhelmed with what they are "supposed" to do. The counselor will obviously not be able to do everything on these lists of functions. One way to make the job manageable is to determine personal priorities, the priorities of the school and the district, and the needs perceived by students, teachers, parents, and members of the community. The counselor can then design a program to meet his or her own needs and the needs of a particular setting. It is essential for each counselor to formulate her or his own "job description" that defines what an elementary school counselor or middle school counselor should be doing. This will be based primarily on each individual's own values and beliefs about which components of the counselor's job are the most important in helping children. Each person will want to consider the "ideal" situation and the "real world" aspect of school counseling, stressing the duties that he or she believes are essential, but remembering that there are some things that will have to be done that seem unimportant. In this process each person should also evaluate his or her own strengths and weaknesses as a counselor. The counselor should design a job description to capitalize on the skills she or he possesses, at the same time working to improve areas in which she or he does not excel.

The counselor must also consider the priorities of the school administration—both on a building level and a district level. The counselor can discover what the principal and any guidance administrators believe are important duties through discussions with them. She or he should also conduct a needs assessment, asking children, teachers, parents, and members of the community what they believe the essential duties of a school counselor entail and what the important outcomes of a school counseling program are.

Counselors and Counseling Theory

Obviously counseling children—individually and in groups—is a major part of the duties of elementary and middle school counselors. In order to effectively deliver counseling services, the school counselor would do well to develop a personal process model or counseling theory (Muro & Dinkmeyer, 1977). To choose a personal process model or counseling theory, the counselor must synthesize academic information about the elements of the theory with his or her personal beliefs about people and the factors that influence behavior (Finch, Mattson, & Moore, 1993). The theory will provide a cognitive map that can help the counselor understand clients, their motivation, and how they change. It can also provide guidelines for possible counselor intervention strategies (Blocher, 1987). While some authors advocate an eclectic approach (Brabeck & Welfel, 1985; Norcross & Prochaska, 1983), others favor choosing one counseling theory as a basis for conceptualizing clients and planning interactions (Patterson, 1985; Smith, 1982). No matter whether you decide to approach counseling from an eclectic perspective, combining several counseling approaches, or from a unitary counseling perspective, you will need to develop a consistent, organized cognitive structure that reflects your own beliefs about people, the process of change, and your personality.

While none of the major counseling theories was specifically designed for application in school settings, most students in school counseling programs have taken at least one course in counseling theories. There is not room in this text to adequately examine each of the major counseling theories and discuss the implications for school counseling within each theory. However, because we believe that students will be more effective counselors if they have selected at least one of the major theories as a guide for their interactions with students, we would like to provide students with some suggestions for developing their own personal theory. We have adapted the following procedure for developing a personal theory of counseling (Watts, 1993) for application in a school counseling setting.

Exploration Phase

1. Examine your own personal values and your beliefs about people and life. You will need to consider how children grow and change, what elements combine to form their personalities, what causes behavioral, social, and academic problems for children, what you think are important goals for children in life, and other fundamental philosophical questions that have an impact on children and their families.
2. Examine the basic tenets of each of the major counseling theories to determine which of these process models most closely agrees with your personal values and beliefs about people and life. While all of the theoretical constructs are important, pay special attention to ideas that relate to children, families, and development. Choose one theory that most closely resembles your own personal belief system and begin the examination phase.

Examination Phase

1. In order to learn your chosen theory both intellectually and experientially, read extensively about the theory, finding specific points that coincide with or contradict your own belief systems. Think about why you agree or disagree with each of these points. If you have major disagreements with the basic tenets of the theory, you will probably want to discard this theory and begin the exploration phase again. Think about how you could apply the theory to particular situations in a school. If the theory will not meet your specific needs as a school counselor, you may want to discard this theory and begin again.
2. In working with children in your school, begin to test your comfort level in using the concepts and techniques that grow from this theory. Your personality and the natural way you interact with people should be compatible with the intervention strategies advocated by the theory. Your initial interactions may feel stilted, but if this theory is a "fit," it should gradually become more comfortable.

Integration Phase

Now that you have a thorough understanding of one specific theory, you may want to integrate selected elements from other counseling theories to complete your evolving personal theory. If you choose to add other techniques, you will want to consider how these strategies fit within the framework of your original theory. If you want to integrate theoretical elements from other theories, you must consider the philosophical compatibility of the new constructs with the original theory. Because integration is sometimes difficult, in order to make sure that you are being philosophically and theoretically consistent, you may want to discuss this integration with other counselors. This will help you to more fully explore your ideas and the ideas of each of the theories you want to incorporate into your own personal counseling process model.

Personalization Phase

During this phase, you will take the ideas that you have developed and begin to consistently apply them in your work with children in schools. You will want to polish your intervention strategies so that they become a natural part of your interactional style. You will want to relax in your sessions with children and let your personality become part of your counseling interactions. This is a process that will take time and patience on your part. As you begin to live your theory and apply it in your interactions with others, it will become a natural extension of who you are.

CONCLUSION

As students begin their process on the way to becoming elementary or middle school counselors or perfecting their skills in this area, they will want to remember that members of the counseling profession must always continue to grow in knowledge of self and others and in skills. They are beginning a process that will involve an ongoing examination of their own beliefs about school guidance, the role of school counselors, the functions of school counselors, and how people grow and change. They must remember that counseling is a process, an evolution, and so is the job of the school counselor.

REFERENCES

ACES-ASCA Joint Committee on the Elementary School Counselor. (1966). The elementary school counselor: Preliminary statement. *Personnel and Guidance Journal, 44,* 648–661.

ASCA. (1990). *Role statement: The school counselor.* Alexandria, VA: ACA Press.

Baker, S. (1992). *School counseling for the twenty-first century.* New York: Merrill.

Blocher, D. (1987). On the uses and misuses of the term theory. *Journal of Counseling and Development, 66,* 67–68.

Brabeck, M., & Welfel, E. (1985). Counseling theory: Understanding the trend toward eclecticism from a developmental perspective. *Journal of Counseling and Development, 63,* 343–348.

Educational Resources Information Center/Counseling and Personnel Services (ERIC/CAPS). (1985a). *The role of the school counselor: Elementary level.* Ann Arbor, MI: The University of Michigan.

Educational Resources Information Center/Counseling and Personnel Services (ERIC/CAPS). (1985b). *The role of the school counselor: Middle/junior high level.* Ann Arbor, MI: The University of Michigan.

Finch, J., Mattson, D., & Moore, J. (1993). Selecting a theory of counseling: Personal and professional congruency for counseling students. *TCA Journal, 21,* 97–102.

Gysbers, N., & Henderson, P. (1988). *Developing and managing your school guidance program.* Alexandria, VA: ACA.

Hannaford, M. (1991). *Counselors under construction.* Marietta, GA: Active Parenting.

Henderson, P. (1987). A comprehensive school guidance program at work. *TACD Journal, 15,* 25–37.

Miller, G. (1986). State guidance consultants' views of elementary and middle school counseling. *Elementary School Guidance and Counseling, 21,* 166–167.

Muro, J., & Dinkmeyer, D. (1977). *Counseling in the elementary and middle schools: A pragmatic approach.* Dubuque, IA: Wm. C. Brown.

Myrick, R. (1993). *Developmental guidance and counseling: A practical approach* (2nd ed.). Minneapolis, MN. Educational Media.

Norcross, J., & Prochaska, J. (1983). Clinicians' theoretical orientations: Selection, utilization and efficacy. *Professional Psychology: Research and Practice, 14,* 197–208.

Patterson, C. (1985). New light for counseling theory. *Journal of Counseling and Development, 63,* 349–350.

Perry, N. (1992). SCANS: Validation of comprehensive school guidance programs. *The ASCA Counselor,* February, p. 3.

Reynolds, S. (1993). Developmental school counseling: An overview. *The ASCA Counselor,* April, pp. 12 13.

Schmidt, J. (1993). *Counseling in schools.* Boston: Allyn & Bacon.

Smith, D. (1982). Trends in counseling and psychotherapy. *American Psychologist, 37,* 802–809.

Snyder, B. (1993). Managing an elementary school guidance program: The role of the counselor. In J. Wittmer (Ed.), *Managing your school counseling program: K–12 developmental strategies* (pp. 33–44). Minneapolis, MN: Educational Media.

Texas Education Agency. (1990). *A guide for program development pre-k to 12th grade: The comprehensive guidance program.* Austin, TX: Author.

Watts, R. (1993). Developing a personal theory of counseling: A brief guide for students. *TCA Journal, 21,* 103–104.

Wilgus, E., & Shelley, V. (1988). The role of the elementary-school counselor: Teacher perceptions, expectations, and actual functions. *The School Counselor, 35,* 259–266.

Wittmer, J. (1993). Developmental school guidance and counseling: Its history and reconceptualization. In J. Wittmer (Ed.), *Managing your school counseling program: K–12 developmental strategies* (pp. 2–11). Minneapolis, MN: Educational Media.

Chapter Two

Human Growth and Development

🌳 In order to counsel one should have some understanding of how humans grow and develop. Counseling theories are dependent on the theory author's view of development. For example, if one were to develop a theory of counseling that had a large number of Freudian concepts, then it would be necessary for one to understand how Freud viewed normal human development, and abnormal development. In Freud's theory, experiences early in life are significant and dictate or at least guide therapist behaviors in counseling sessions. If one were to utilize Glasser's Reality or Control Theory, then the past or the history of the individual counseled would be of much less importance than if one were of Freudian persuasion.

The education of the counselor should be just that—an education. There has been a tendency in some counselor education programs to "force a theory" or require that a student counselor become a Rogerian, an Adlerian, or a Glasserian. While knowledge about what each of these or others have to say about human development is important, the neophyte counselor should be broadly based in the disciplines of biology, psychology, sociology, and education. In addition, he or she should study the works of Freud, Adler, Sullivan, Horney, Miller and Dollard, Rogers, and others in some depth.

In this chapter we shall present some perspectives on human development as a brief introduction to those who would counsel. Of course, scholars have written volumes upon volumes of material on the topic of human development, and a complete discussion of all points of view in child development is beyond the scope of this book. We are particularly interested in the work of Gesell and Piaget in that they seem to have much to say to individuals studying developmental counseling. In particular, we are strong advocates of the concepts advanced by Gesell and his colleagues at the Gesell Institute of Child Development in New Haven, Connecticut.

Freud's Contributions to Counseling

Perhaps no elementary school counselor will describe himself or herself as "Freudian." Of course, this is appropriate, since Freudian analysis is not only inappropriate for elementary school work, it is also beyond the scope of training and education of most school counselors. The fact that one is not Freudian, however, does not mean that Freud's work should be ignored in the development of a personal theory of counseling.

While the uninitiated usually associate Freud's work with sexual concepts, they should also know that his contributions ranged far beyond the concepts he developed about human sexuality. Freud, in fact, was one of the pioneers in outlining the developmental aspects of personality. In his thinking, the early years of life are of key importance in the development of personality. He believed that the major components of personality are well developed by the time children reach the age of five. Theorizing that tension is a major component of personality development, Freud identified and elaborated on four major tension sources. They are: (1) psychological growth processes, (2) frustrations, (3) conflicts, and (4) threats (Freud, 1949). Since these tensions are present, the child must discover how to reduce them, and this process is considered key in personality development. What is important in this process is Freud's contention that personality does not develop in a random or haphazard way; rather, development may be traced through a series of well-defined stages.

Starting at birth, children enter into a series of stages that last until they reach young adulthood. Of these stages, the first three are characterized by periods of turbulence and stress. When the child enters the latency period at or about the time he or she enters school, personality dynamics become more stabilized. When the child reaches adolescence, turbulence is once more a key aspect of life.

It is the earlier stages of life that are most controversial, and perhaps his descriptions of these stages have been the most criticized part of Freud's work. The first of these, the oral stage, runs from birth to the end of the first year of life. During this phase, as the name implies, the child's chief source of pleasure and his or her chief way of interacting with the world is derived through the mouth. Eating involves tactile stimulation of the lips and oral cavity. The child will readily consume what tastes "good" and reject all that does not, even through immature taste buds probably do not allow for taste discrimination as it is found in adults.

This stage has been labeled the "mouth ego" and to those who follow Freud, this early ego is the prototype for behavioral characteristics that will be evident later in life. For example, Freudians might consider a gullible adult to be fixated at the oral incorporative stage of personality. Often, we hear the expression that certain individuals will "swallow anything they are told." Another example is that since the child is naturally dependent on others for survival during the oral stage, strong feelings of dependency occur at this time and are likely to reoccur throughout later life when a person feels anxious or insecure. "Freud believed that the most extreme symptom of dependency was the desire to return to the womb" (Nutten, 1962, p. 91). Concepts such as the one described here are those that have made Freud's work controversial.

Following the oral stage, which terminates around the end of the first year of life, the child enters into the anal stage of personality development, a period that lasts from one to three years of age. Critical during this period is the process of toilet training imposed. What possible meaning could this have on personality development? In Freudian thinking, it could have substantial impact. Suppose, for example, that the parents of the child are very restrictive and stern in their methods of toilet training. This could cause the child to hold back or retain feces and become constipated. As this mode of reacting then generalizes to other ways of behaving, the child will develop a retentive character, or one who is generally obstinate and stingy. This may also be the prototype for all kinds of explosive traits—cruelty, wanton destructiveness, and temper tantrums. On the other hand, if the mother praises the child for bowel movements, the child may get the idea that she or he is a productive person indeed. In Freudian thinking, this may be the basis for producing creative character traits.

The third stage of personality development, the phallic stage, occurs approximately between three and six years of age, when children become aware of their sex organs and learn that manipulation of them will produce pleasurable sensations. This discovery sets the stage for the oft-criticized Oedipus/Electra complex that is said to occur during this period. According to Freudian theory, male children want to possess their mothers and remove their fathers, and girls want to remove their mothers and possess their fathers. Since this is not possible, children become frustrated, angry, and confused. This period is particularly difficult for children, because they must resolve this problem in order to grow into mature, healthy adults. This is accomplished by a process of repression in which the situation is removed from the conscious thoughts of the individual (Freud, 1938). It is also during this turbulent time that children learn appropriate sex roles and the manner in which they are supposed to act. Freud and his associates thought that the events of this stage form a number of characteristics in the human personality.

From the age of seven until children reach puberty, they exist in what Freud labeled the latency stage of development. The sexual interests that were so prominent during the phallic stage lie dormant in the background of personality. As children grow, they are no longer governed by primary process thinking and they learn to curtail impulses If they have successfully resolved the Oedipal/Electra conflict, they will develop self-confidence and be able to meet the demands imposed by society in general and by school in particular.

From the relative tranquility of latency to the turmoil of puberty, children undergo a drastic change that some adults may find alarming. Although convinced that an individual's personality was well formed by the age of five, Freud did recognize the importance of adolescence (Freud, 1938) Three or four months prior to puberty the child, according to psychoanalytic theory, will become belligerent and uncommunicative. This is caused by a reawakening of the sexual drives that had been dormant since the end of the phallic stage. This period is marked by defiance of parents, a breakdown of emotional home ties, and long periods of frustration, all of which Freud felt are necessary in order for the child to complete formation of the self or ego. Before this stage, ego strength was not great enough to deal with such tensions, but at this age, the child should have the necessary strength to cope with problems of life. In fact, conflicts encountered at this stage may actually help individuals build ego strength.

From adolescence the child moves on to adulthood. According to Freudian theory, a child becomes an adult when there is a harmonious functioning among the Id, Ego, and Superego. The mature adult is able to control his or her drives and frustrations and is generally a "happy" person. A healthy adult personality is characterized by lack of turmoil. In a healthy adult the sexual and aggressive drives, which are prime motivators of behavior, are channeled into culturally acceptable patterns. In addition, the adult has developed adequate defense mechanisms and is able to live and work in the world.

Counseling Implications

Sigmund Freud is widely recognized as a pioneer in the development of a comprehensive theory of psychotherapy. While counselors in elementary schools do not practice psychoanalysis, they owe some of their operational behaviors to the work of Freud. His concept of how behavior is motivated, for example, is a forerunner of many of our modern concepts of human functioning.

It is true that very little of Freud's work was done with children, but almost every counselor accepts the idea of unconscious motivation for some behaviors, a concept that was very much a contribution of this creative thinker. From Freud, counselors also have a much better understanding of ego defense mechanisms, including repression, projection, displacement, denial, sublimation, regression, rationalization, and reaction formation. Regardless of the theoretical underpinnings that guide the counseling practice of modern school counselors, they frequently use these concepts in individual and group work with children.

While there is a tendency to consider Freud as one who was primarily interested in human biology, it should be noted that Freud was an early leader in calling attention to the environment rather than biology and heredity as a key factor in causing mental illness (Vander Zanden, 1989). While Freud did write extensively about biological urges (instincts) as an impelling cause of behaviors, he did not neglect the importance of the environment in his work.

It is probable that Freud's work seems distant to counselors, since his image of persons was basically negative. Few school counselors, especially those who are followers of Carl Rogers, Clark Moustakas, and Jessie Taft, are willing to accept children as beings who are driven by destructive animalistic forces. In addition, the contention that behavior initiates with a reservoir of negative energy in individuals has been frequently questioned by critics.

None of this should detract from recognizing what Freud gave to the modern counselor. It was Freud who called attention to the importance of the early years in human development. In fact, his daughter Anna made additional contributions through use of Freud's ideas in psychoanalytic play therapy. Almost all counselors now pay close attention to early patterns of development, and many employ play in their counseling of the young.

Perhaps more than any other individual, Sigmund Freud deserves credit for initiating the movement for the study of social experience in human development. The modern counselor who counsels a child and generates hypotheses about the home, parents, classroom, peer relations, and private inner world of the child, probably does not often think of Freud. Yet in a sense, Freud was one of the very early thinkers about children and, in a way, about counseling children.

Erikson's Contributions to Counseling

Erik Erikson, a Freudian disciple of Danish extraction, while admittedly borrowing from his mentor, developed his own views of human development. For the most part they were distinctly different from Freud's views. While Freud was convinced that the human personality was established during the first six years of life, Erikson argued that the human personality continues to develop throughout one's life. While Freud emphasized psychosexual development, Erikson emphasized psychosocial development.

In concepts reminiscent of Freud, Erikson theorized that humans develop their personalities by moving through a series of stages. Erikson hypothesized eight major stages of human development, each of which contains a unique developmental task that presents to individuals a crisis that they must solve. In his thinking, healthy personalities are the result of mastering life's tasks. All development follows the "epigenetic principle—anything that grows has a ground plan and out of that plan the parts arise, each having spent its time of special ascending, until all parts have arisen to form a functioning whole" (Erikson, 1968, p. 92).

While Erikson's work followed a Freudian pattern of developmental stages, his concepts were more broadly conceptualized. For example, both Freud and Erikson view the first year of life as an initial stage in personality development. To Erikson, the initial year of life is more importantly thought of as a time of what he called *trust vs. mistrust.* It is during this period that babies learn to trust (or to mistrust) that other individuals will meet their basic needs for food, sucking, warmth, cleanliness, and physical contact. If their needs are met, children will probably approach the world feeling safe and secure. If their needs are not met, children will probably incorporate fear and suspicion as part of their personalities (Vander Zanden, 1989).

Closely following Freud's creation of an anal stage, or the period of life at two to three years, was Erikson's stage of *autonomy vs. shame and doubt.* During this period, infants become more mobile; they face the conflict of whether or not they should assert their wills. Parents who display patience at this stage of a child's life will help their children have a greater chance of becoming self-sufficient in many activities such as walking and feeding. On the other hand, children who are thwarted may exhibit a sense of shame and doubt.

Erikson replaced Freud's oft criticized phallic stage with one that he labeled *initiative vs. guilt.* Rather than focus on genital organs as Freud suggested, Erikson theorized that children are more concerned with running, sliding, and bike riding than they are with sexual fantasies. At this stage, parents who give their children freedom will help them develop positive initiatives. Those who closely control their children may be molding passive recipients of whatever the environment will bring (Berger, 1988).

Erikson's fourth stage, that of *industry vs. inferiority,* runs roughly parallel to the period Freud called the latency period of development. This phase, if Erikson's views are accurate, may be of particular interest to elementary school counselors, since this age (approximately six to eleven) is when children are in elementary schools. Erikson indicates that during this time children who are recognized for their efforts will gain a sense of industry. To meet this task requires strong parental and teacher support. If, however, children are constantly rebuffed and labeled failures, they may well develop feelings of inadequacy and inferiority (Erikson, 1968).

During adolescence, children are interested in discovering "Who am I?" This is a period when young people attempt new roles, such as romance or choice of a career. At this time in their lives, it is essential that they develop a sense of self, or a "centered identity." Those who fail to meet this crisis could become delinquents or engage in criminal behaviors.

Erikson divides the adult portion of human life into three different stages, *young adulthood, middle adulthood,* and *old age.* In the first stage of adulthood, called the *intimacy vs. isolation stage,* young adults seek out companionship, love, and romance. They tie up their identities with those of others and learn to care for and love another. Because they fear rejection, some individuals do not seek out close relationships and as a result may withdraw or become isolated.

In middle adulthood, or the *generativity vs. stagnation stage,* Erikson theorized that individuals reach out beyond their own concerns to embrace broader societal issues. For some this means a period of selflessness and a desire to help others. Stagnation can produce individuals who are primarily concerned with their own material possessions (Berger, 1988).

The final stage of human personality development is called *integrity vs. despair.* During this period of their lives some individuals are pleased and happy with what they have accomplished. Others, however, develop feelings that life is too short and there is not enough time to attempt alternate pathways to integrity (Vander Zanden, 1989).

Counseling Implications

Erikson had a broader and much more positive view of human nature than Freud did. While retaining the concept of the importance of early childhood experiences in development, he extended what he had learned from Freud and presented a theory that states that personality development does not end at age five, six, or seven. Rather, for all of us there are significant events that shape who we are throughout our lives.

Counselors who read the original works of Erikson will soon discover a more positive view of humans. For many counselors this more positive view is generally more acceptable than that of Freud.

Erikson makes a strong argument for a positive, humanistic approach to education during the elementary school years. The comprehensive guidance activities discussed in Chapter 3 that are designed to help children feel good about themselves fit very well into Erikson's industry vs. inferiority stage. Also Erikson's language and phrases are very much a part of counseling and psychological literature. Terms such as "identity crisis," "identity," and "life cycle" are commonly used when Americans think about the young and beyond (Turkle, 1987).

Piaget's Contributions to Counseling

Among the best known of the cognitive theorists of human development is the Swiss psychologist Jean Piaget, who had a profound impact on American education and psychology until his death in 1980. Piaget, as a cognitive theorist, was very much interested in the structure and development of human thought processes and how these processes impact an individual's understanding of and expectations of his or her world. Piaget was also interested in how these understandings affect behavior, a concept of interest to elementary and middle school counselors as well as teachers.

Piaget's interest in human thinking stemmed from his work in the field of intelligence testing. While attempting to determine at what age children could answer certain questions, he became much more interested in their incorrect responses. What he found to be fascinating was the fact that children who were of the same age made similar mistakes in responding to questions. This suggested to him that there is a developmental sequence to intellectual growth. He deemed it more important to determine how children think rather than to simply tabulate what they know (Berger, 1988; Flavell, 1963; Cowan, 1978)

In 1970, Piaget reported that basic to the concept of cognitive development is the idea that each individual's knowledge of the world and its objects is the product of his or her operation on and with them (Watson & Lindgren, 1973). Acting on and transforming these phenomena enables the child to know them. At various stages in an individual's life, each person deals with similar phenomena in different ways.

In Piaget's thinking, cognitive development is a process that follows universal patterns. For each human being, there is a need for equilibrium, or a state of mental balance (Piaget, 1970). This means that each of us needs to make sense out of conflicting experiences and conflicting perceptions (Berger, 1988).

Piaget believed that there are four major stages of intellectual development. They are labeled the *sensorimotor stage* that lasts from the time of birth to the end of the second year of life, the *preoperational stage* that takes place between the ages of two and six, the *concrete operational stage,* the period of life between seven and eleven years, and the *formal operational stage* that takes place from the age of twelve on. These stages are continuous in nature, and each is built upon and derived from the earlier one. In Piaget's thinking, no stage can be skipped since later stages depend on the earlier ones.

In the *sensorimotor stage,* children are actively engaged in attempting to discover the relationships between sensations and motor behaviors. They may learn that their limbs are part of themselves and an object like a ball or a mobile is not. They learn how far they need to reach in order to grasp a toy. A key concept at this age is the mastery of object permanence or the notion that children have to learn that objects have an independent existence. For example, very young children will not seek out a ball that rolls away from them in play even though it remains in reach. At about the age of eighteen months, however, children begin to comprehend the fact of object consistency and will begin to search for objects that have disappeared from view. In sum, infants in this period of their lives begin to distinguish between objects and experiences and generalize about them. This ability provides the groundwork for the stages that are to follow (Vander Zanden, 1989; Elkind, 1978).

In the *preoperational stage* of development, children begin to develop the capacity to employ symbols, the most important of which is language. This enables children to manipulate the meaning of objects and events. A block becomes a car or truck, a stick an airplane, and a piece of wood becomes a house. The stage is called preoperational because the thought process representing actions is not yet reversible, and a child's knowledge is not yet systematized. Children may count objects and may be struck by similarities in the properties of objects, but they will not be engaged in logical-mathematical thinking until they discover—through their own actions—that the arranging and disarranging of objects can be ordered and related (Almy, 1961).

Piaget further divided the preoperational stage into two subdivisions, the *preconceptual subphase,* which takes place between the ages of two and four, and the *intuitive phase,* which lasts from about the ages of four to seven. One and two word phrases at age two become four and five word phrases at age four. This rapid language development results in a number of intellectual gains, including the ability to free children from a restrictive here-and-now orientation to a broader perspective that gives them access to the past and the future, a feat that could not have been accomplished without language symbolization (Vander Zanden, 1989).

In the *intuitive subphase,* children are able to think in terms of classes, numbers, and relationships. They can now respond on these bases, but they are unable to provide reasons for their responses. They may now, for example, understand simple relationships such as "the dog is bigger than the cat" but "smaller than Daddy." What they cannot do, in this preoperational period, is perform mental operations as part of a larger system. A child may understand that Mommy is Daddy's wife, but not that Mommy is also Mary's aunt. A child of this age cannot grasp the fact that his or her relationship with Mommy or Daddy is just one of a complex series of relationships. Mom is simply Mom. Another characteristic of this age is egocentrism, which in Piaget's thinking means that children of this age believe that their point of view is the only one possible. They are not yet capable of putting themselves in the place of another.

Between the ages of seven and twelve, children are in the stage of what Piaget calls *concrete operations.* It is here that one will be able to notice the beginnings of rational activities. Adding, subtracting, or placing an object in a classification system are examples in this stage. Since individuals cannot classify without some knowledge of what is being classified, the four and five year olds are considered preoperational.

Children in this stage are now capable of mental representations, conservation, relational terms, class inclusion, and serialization. They are capable of developing a mental plan and are able to have a mental image of a sequence of events, something that the same children could not do at the age of four. For example, if a child were to go to a store, she or he can not only follow a designated route and make the appropriate turns, but the child can now "map out" the route to follow.

With respect to conservation, children in the stage of concrete operations are now able to understand that liquids and solids may change shape without changing in volume or mass. An example frequently cited to illustrate this principle is that of presenting children two equal lumps of clay. The five year old will probably readily agree that both are equal. If one is flattened, like a pancake, the child will typically state that the two clay masses are no longer equal. A seven year old, however, may well relate that they are still equal in that the "pancake clay" is thinner, but it is also wider.

In addition, children in the stage of concrete operations can reason simultaneously between parts and wholes (class inclusions), a feat they could not accomplish during the preoperational period. Finally, children can now arrange objects according to some qualified dimension such as size and height (serialization), a necessary factor for the learning of arithmetic (Mussen, Conger, & Kagan, 1974).

From the age of twelve and beyond, children are considered to be in the stage of *formal operations*, a period characterized by the ability to think about abstractions and hypothetical concepts. They are also able to move in thought "from the real to the possible" (Berger, 1988, p. 48). They are able to consider the various ways a problem could be solved. Seven to eleven year olds have begun to deal with logical problems and organize what is real into a logical system, but secondary nonexistent relationships are still a fleeting thing. Thus the possible is not given systematic importance by preoperational children. In contrast, adolescents consider all possibilities and begin to consider all possibilities of a problem. No longer do children of this age always attempt to solve problems through trial and error as was the case when they were seven. Like adults, adolescents' thinking is more rational and systematic than is young children's thinking.

Counseling Implications

Piaget's work and that of other cognitively oriented theorists are important to counselors, since they have provided valuable insights into the mental structures of thought. Counselors and others can appreciate the limitations of thinking that are present at various ages and the ways these limitations and capacities can impact behavior (Berger, 1988). For example, counselors who deal with six-year-old children or perhaps even younger ones in kindergarten will need to understand that while children are using symbolic language and have been for some time, the world as they understand it is highly idiosyncratic. Thus children may have difficulty understanding the world as others see it. While language skills are developing almost daily, the use of play and play media in counseling as at least a part of the process may be recommended here. Play allows the counselor to capitalize on the flourishing imagination that is now evident in young children. Children who were egocentric at the beginning of this phase are starting to comprehend different points of view so that exercises that stress self-understanding and understanding of others may not be totally inappropriate. This may be particularly true for students who are in the latter months of grade one.

At age seven and beyond, there may still be a place for play and activity group approaches, but the development of mental representations means that children are capable of developing mental plans, that they may have sufficient language skills to engage in normal verbal individual and group counseling, as well as classroom guidance activities that are related to self and other acceptance. Children this age are able to become partners in the counseling process in working out solutions to personal concerns. If Piaget is correct, the more concrete the solutions, the better children will be able to implement them. Highly abstract concepts in the counseling sessions may not be as effective, especially for those at the early years of this stage.

Piaget, of course, was not without his critics, and as is the case with other theorists, counselors should view his work as a guide rather than as a definite road map. However, the study of cognitive factors in development continues to be of intense interest to psychologists and counselors. Mental processes sometimes called scripts or frames tend to function as selective mechanisms that influence the information individuals attend to, how they structure it, how much importance they attach to it, and what they do with it (Markus, 1977; Vander Zanden, 1987). In all counseling, it is essential to consider how individuals learn or relearn. Counseling sessions, though different from classroom learning, are concerned with an individual learning about self. In this context, Piaget has given the profession some guidelines to help counselors observe and evaluate children's thinking and their behavior.

Contributions of the Humanists

Humanistic psychologists believe that at the core of human development is the individual's strong drive to maximize his or her human potential. In addition, humanistic psychologists also view human growth and development from a holistic view, or the view that all humans are very much more than a collection of instincts or of past conditioning (Vander Zanden, 1989).

No single theorist or group of theorists, for that matter, has had as much impact on the counseling profession as have had two of the leading humanistic psychologists in the field, Abraham Maslow and Carl Rogers. These so-called "third force" individuals each spent a lifetime developing a humanistic point of view widely accepted by many mental health care workers. Their efforts have left a legacy for future generations of educators, psychologists, and counselors.

In 1959, in the early days of the NDEA Guidance Institutes, which many believe were the driving force behind the school counseling movement in America, the works of Maslow and Rogers composed almost the total curriculum for the basic study of counseling. Through the years, their stars remain undiminished in spite of critics who have been less than tolerant of humanistic approaches. One has only to study the works of such individuals as Clark Moustakas, Doug Arbuckle, Cecil Patterson, Don Dinkmeyer, Jerry Pine, Angelo Boy, Bill Van Hoose, George Hill, and Harold Cottingham to see the influence of Rogers and Maslow on the everyday work of both secondary and elementary school counselors.

Both Maslow and Rogers stressed the uniqueness of human beings as they grow and develop, and both called the attention of the mental health worker to the concept of individual differences. While Freud presented a picture of humankind as instinct driven, Maslow and Rogers presented humankind from a largely positive point of view. They theorized that humans react to the environment and modify it rather than being driven by pools of internal energies.

Maslow and Rogers also emphasized the importance of the individual's drive to maximize her or his potential as a primary motivating force. We are not, they contended, a mere collection of physical, social, and psychological components (Vander Zanden, 1989).

Widely quoted in the fields of psychology, counseling education, business, and human relations is Maslow's concept of a hierarchy of human needs. Maslow became convinced that each human being is motivated to meet a series of needs that are present in all humans. These needs are arranged in a hierarchy, and in order for one to meet higher-level needs, then one must first meet the needs at the lower levels.

At the bottom or the base of his need hierarchy (often depicted as a triangle of needs) Maslow identified the physiological needs, or the needs to satisfy hunger, thirst, threat, and sex drives. Once these basic needs have been satisfied, humans can then turn their attention to meeting the need for safety or for protecting the self from outside dangers. These are classified as fundamental needs.

If individuals successfully meet these basic needs, they are then ready to move on to meet their psychological needs, or the needs for love, belonging, acceptance, and affiliation with others. In addition, a second category of psychological needs are the esteem needs or the needs of individuals to be competent, to experience success, and to gain approval and recognition from others.

At the top of the needs hierarchy are the most abstract areas of needs, including the need for beauty and the need for self-actualization. The latter need is the individual's drive to become all that he or she is capable of becoming. Not all humans reach that level of functioning. Maslow did identify some that met his criteria for self-actualization, and these include Lincoln, Einstein, Eleanor Roosevelt, and Walt Whitman. These self-actualized individuals are self-acceptant and spontaneous. They also have a need for privacy and are independent, autonomous, sympathetic, and capable of establishing deep relationships (Maslow, 1955). Maslow also believed that scientific inquiry was at its very best when it was directed toward helping people achieve freedom, hope, and self-fulfillment (Maslow, 1955).

It was the work of Carl Rogers, however, that was perhaps even more influential on the guidance and counseling profession, particularly in the counseling process itself. His classic work, *Client Centered Therapy* (1951), is still required reading in virtually every university counseling program in America.

At the core of Rogers' thinking was the concept that the individual is at the center of all that is learned, and that individuals will learn only those things that have personal meaning to them. Learning also is enhanced in an atmosphere where there is an absence of threat, and where the learner experiences positive regard and acceptance. In other words children will develop into healthy adults when the atmosphere that they grow in is one of acceptance and positive regard. According to Rogers' theory, mounds of information and behavioral modification techniques are not essential, since individuals, by nature, are good and want to do good things. Growing individuals bring "values, that help them to select, filter, what they see and learn, and they bring attitudinal sets and learning styles that render each student unique and different from all the rest" (Hamachek, 1977, p. 156).

Like Maslow, Rogers believed that all individuals attempt to actualize their potential, a process he labeled as our human attempts to become *fully functional.* In order to achieve this, all persons need to have significant others in their lives. Children fortunate enough to receive unconditional positive regard will develop feelings of acceptance that will last a lifetime.

Counseling Implications

From the standpoint of human development, both Maslow and Rogers provided counselors and educators with the concepts of genuineness, congruence, empathy, and unconditional positive regard. In this context, human relationships are more important than therapeutic techniques in the promotion of fully functioning human beings.

In addition, from the humanists, we have learned the importance of the inner world of the individual. It is what a person perceives, rather than the counselor's description of external reality, that is of key importance. To individuals, their perceptions are in fact "reality."

Both theorists have had wide impact on public education as well as on counseling and therapy. Some must view humanistic approaches as being overly simplistic and optimistic in that most societies do not encourage or even allow for the development of full potential. Nonetheless, Maslow's and Rogers' positive views of personkind have made a profound impact on several generations of counselors and children.

Havighurst's Contributions to Counseling

Robert Havighurst's contributions to developmental guidance and counseling and to human development are a direct result of his work in the area of developmental tasks. He was very much interested in the study of how societal demands relate to individual human needs. A developmental task according to Havighurst is one that arises at a certain time in the life of an individual, achievement of which will lead to success and happiness. In addition, successfully completing developmental tasks will help individuals acquire the skills necessary to meet additional tasks that will occur in the future (Havighurst, 1948, 1952, 1953; Rice, 1992). These tasks include the knowledge, skills, attitudes, and functions that individuals have to acquire at certain points in their lives in order to eventually function effectively as mature persons. Children who are unsuccessful in mastering these tasks will, in all probability, experience poorer adjustments and be less prepared for the more difficult tasks to follow.

Havighurst believed that there were developmental tasks for infancy and early childhood (ages zero to five), for middle childhood (ages six to eleven), for adolescence (ages twelve to eighteen), for early adulthood (ages nineteen to thirty), and for middle age and late maturity. For the purposes of this book, the first two categories of developmental tasks, those of early childhood and of middle childhood, are of most importance.

While elementary school counselors rarely work directly with children under five years of age, they should be aware of the nine developmental tasks that occur in infancy and early childhood, since completion of these tasks will impact how children function when they enter school. The tasks at this level include learning to walk and talk, learning to eat solid foods, learning to control body wastes, learning about sex differences and modesty, and achieving physiological stability. Also children need to learn about social and physical reality, and learn to relate to parents, peers, and siblings. In addition, they need to learn to distinguish between right and wrong (Havighurst, 1948, 1952, 1953).

In middle childhood, or the period between the ages of six and eleven, the developmental tasks seem to fit nicely into a general guide for the creation of comprehensive programs of guidance and counseling in elementary schools. According to Havighurst (1953), the tasks at this stage are as follows:

1. Learning physical skills necessary for ordinary games.
2. Building wholesome attitudes toward oneself as a growing organism.
3. Learning to get along with age mates.
4. Learning appropriate masculine and feminine roles.
5. Developing fundamental skills in reading, writing, and calculating.
6. Developing concepts necessary for everyday living.
7. Developing conscience, morality, and a scale of values.
8. Achieving personal independence.
9. Developing attitudes toward social groups and institutions.

Havighurst has also provided developmental tasks for adolescents and adults, and his work has given educators and counselors excellent insights into their development. His works deserve reading in their entirety.

Counseling Implications

Havighurst (1952) suggested two reasons why his concept of developmental tasks is useful to educators. Gazda (1989) argued that this concept is equally useful to counselors. "First, it helps in discovering and stating the purpose of education (group counseling and life skills training) in the schools. The second use of the concept is in the timing of the educational efforts" (Gazda, 1989, p. 5).

The tasks suggested by Havighurst can provide a broad general map that the counselor may use to create both guidance and curriculum activities. The counselor will want to use the following questions: How does our guidance program reflect the developmental tasks of children in our schools? Is our school curriculum developmentally oriented, or is it an amalgamation of concepts designed by commercial book companies?

Obviously, few schools will be able to meet the needs of all of the children all of the time. Readers will recall from Chapter 1, that one task of counselors is that of attempting to determine if there are programmatic gaps in the guidance effort. Are there significant omissions? What skills and what understandings are present now? Which are not? To be able to provide comprehensive help for all children, the counselor's work must be measured against agreed upon standards. Havighurst's work provides counselors with some standards for evaluating overall guidance programs.

The Contributions of the Gesell Institute of Child Development

Muro and Dinkmeyer (1977) note that the field of child development in general and guidance in particular had not given significant attention to the contributions of the Gesell Institute of Child Development in New Haven, Connecticut. For years Arnold Gesell and Francis Ilg conducted significant research in the area of child development. Today that work is still being carried on by Dr. Louise Bates Ames, but it has not had, in the opinion of the authors, the attention it deserves. In the past, the work of the institute has been criticized for its "heavy biological emphasis" and for a perception that the norms used in their extensive studies were not inclusive enough to include children of different races and cultures. In spite of this the authors feel that an understanding of human development from the Gesell point of view is still valuable for counselors. Over a period of twenty-five years, one of the authors has extensively used their concepts as a guide for some aspects of counseling practice. Accordingly, we are including some aspects of the Gesell developmental profiles, as summarized in the books *School Readiness* (Ilg & Ames, 1965), *Child Care and Development* (Ames, 1970), *Youth: The Years from Ten to Sixteen* (Gesell, Ilg & Ames, 1958), *Child Behavior, The Child from Five to Ten* (Gesell & Ilg, 1946), *Your Six Year Old* (Ames & Ilg, 1979), *Your Seven Year Old* (Ames & Hober, 1980), *Your Eight Year Old* (Ames & Hober, 1989), *Your Nine Year Old* (Ames & Hober, 1990).

These profiles present a developmental as opposed to a chronological age of children. Readers need to understand that we are presenting behavioral ages. Once the behavioral age of a child is identified through individual assessment, then one works with that child as if he or she were at that chronological age. This means that not all children who have an assessed behavioral or developmental age of five or six will actually be that age. In addition, not all children who are chronologically six years of age will behave as the six year olds outlined in the Gesell profiles. Again, since behavioral ages are determined through the use of paper and pencil devices, the authors are aware of the uses and misuses of data obtained that way. We want to stress that test data from the Gesell tests as with test data from other psychological instruments is simply that, a single sample of behavior. We therefore want to stress once again that the profiles presented here are guides rather than absolutes.

Individuality and Biology

The developmental profile data presented here are not given in an attempt to provide the reader with a description of how individual children *will behave*. They will, however, give a good indication of what *may be generally expected* of a given age range.

The counseling profession prides itself in its concern with individual differences, as well it should. To some, assessments and the use of any kind of group norms are concepts that draw attention away from individuality. Most counselors, however, are professional enough to understand that individual differences do exist, and attempts should not be made to force children into any activities by using standardized test scores as a single determining criterion.

For most American children, the fifth birthday marks the start of what may well become thirteen to seventeen years of formal education. For a select few, formal education will reach well into adulthood. To those entrusted with the responsibility of educating these children goes the responsibility of doing all that is possible to ensure that each has a chance to reach maximum potential. In order to do so, those individuals must have some understanding of what children at a given behavioral age can and cannot do.

While some will argue that most children can be taught anything at any time, authorities such as Gesell believe that the body may dictate what can and cannot be learned at a given time. For example, there is mounting evidence to suggest that some educational processes may be harmful when the physiological makeup of children is ignored. At the University of North Texas, researchers at an innovative Center for Research on Learning and Cognition have been able to show the wide individual differences in the ways that the human brain operates. In studying the data they have gathered from brain mapping, one could easily reach the conclusion that the technique of forcing poor readers to spend additional time on reading tasks could well be harmful and of little use. With some children, reading as we understand it is not possible if we attempt to teach it in traditional ways through repetition and continued practice. Far better, perhaps, would be efforts to determine ways to teach reading that use different neurological pathways than those of the average child.

Brain mapping is an innovative way to look at human learning, and as such it holds great promise for working with both normal and learning disabled children. It also holds promise for counselors who work with children who have academic difficulties. Studying the biological basis for human behavior, which received little emphasis in our professional literature during the past three decades, can be valuable. The material presented here reflects that view.

At various developmental age levels, counselors should be observant of patterns of behavior. Most behavior is patterned and predictable and proceeds through a series of undifferentiated maneuvers from general to specific. At times schools require children to perform tasks that can cause unnecessary problems for young learners. For example, children who have not gained sufficient ocular muscle control to move their eyes across a horizontal plane should not have to acquire this coordination while they are learning to read at the same time. Yet, in many schools, the developmental levels of children seem to be ignored, and they are taught as if each one were at the exact same stage of development. The results of this can be an early sense of failure and a referral to the counselor at some later date for help. The point here is that school activities should be designed to fit the child rather than have the child fit the activities. By developing a thorough understanding of human development, counselors can help ensure that children are biologically and psychologically ready to do what is asked of them.

The Five Year Old from a Behavioral Age Standpoint

The psychological makeup of five year olds almost ensures them of success in the various school tasks required of them (Ames, 1979). Rarely do they attempt more than they feel that they can manage. If allowed to choose, they will frequently attempt to do only those things where success is a strong possibility. Too many parents, in an attempt to give their children every advantage, attempt to push children of this age into activities the children feel they are unable to do. While children will generally comply when pushed into tasks, the result of such pushing could well be frustration. One need only observe the overdemanding mother or father who insists that his or her preschooler learn to print right now to understand the frustration that some children face. When children can, they will protect themselves. Unfortunately many are not able to resist parents who insist that an early entrance into school is vital for future success. A significant percentage of later school failures can be traced back to parents who demand too much too soon (Ames, 1979). Counselors who are aware of maturity and the potential harm associated with pushing children beyond their maturational levels should actively work with parents to ensure that all who enter formal schooling are indeed ready to do so.

In general, five year olds may be described as "good." They readily respond to orders and commands and seem to feel at home in their own particular worlds. These worlds are very much "here and now" places. Children of this age enjoy the familiarity of the self-contained classroom. The majority relate well to parents and teachers (Ames, 1979).

Most five year olds will want to play with others of their own age. They tend to be helpful and will readily respond to teacher requests for almost any kind of help. They tend to need and actively seek immediate attention from adults. Waiting, for most children this age, is extremely difficult, and interruptions of adult conversations are not uncommon. They love "show and tell" activities that provide a forum with a vehicle for attention, approval, and affection. The basic needs for love and worth are fully operative in the five year old (Ilg & Ames, 1965).

Kindergarten teachers do not need to be told that children of this age are fidgety. They can, however, sit quietly and be "good" as good is generally described by adult standards. Most fives tend to like school, especially when skilled teachers do not start to "sort out" children based upon how they perform as opposed to who they are as young people. The structure generally present in most kindergartens is appropriate in that children of this age like structure. Short attention spans dictate activities of twenty to twenty-five minutes in length (Ames, 1979).

As counselors who are active users of play and play materials will readily attest, play is a major part of the world of children of this age. When asked what they like to do, most children will answer "play." Most like art activities that include the use of color, cutting and pasting, and drawing. They admire their creations and want to take what they have made home to show parents.

They thrive on encouragement, and even minor reprimands may produce tears. As children move closer to six, the smooth behavioral patterns now begin to break up. The child who was quiet and calm at the beginning of the year may now become combative. He or she may now become hesitant or indecisive. Often behavior patterns show extremes in that children who are shy at one moment may well become explosive the next (Ilg & Ames, 1965).

In general children will behave more calmly at school than at home. The frequent use of questions may be an indication of frustrations. "How do I make a G?" may be an expression of frustration rather than a request for a response.

Counseling Implications

1. Whenever possible, counselors should attempt to work with children of this developmental age directly in the classroom. Most of these children feel that the teacher is significant in their lives. This is the real world for these children, and although these children love to display their individuality, they prefer to do so as part of a group. Short counseling sessions, perhaps even brief talks at a child's desk while the total class is involved in group work, may be useful.

2. Guidance activities involving the total class work very well. Activities developed by the counselor are also appropriate at this level. Short-term group counseling sessions, particularly with the use of play or play media, may also be helpful.

3. Work with children at this developmental age must take into account the here and now orientation of these children. Little time should be spent delving into the child's past or in the use of approaches that are aimed at insight. Most children will react negatively to any problem-centered approach, and emphasis should be placed on the psychology of use. In other words, counselors should try to identify as many strengths as possible in children and then work with the child to help him or her use these strengths. For example, if a child is not completing tasks, counselors may want to create structured play sessions that include the completion of tasks. Once children begin to make changes, counselors and teachers should make a special effort to point out their successes. The counselor's attitude here should be "You can do it. You have the skill. I'm proud of you for completing the task." This approach will be far more effective than will one of discussing the child's problems.

4. It is important that children of this age know who the counselor is. Counselors should make frequent visits to the classroom and interact on an informal basis with as many children as possible. From time to time, the counselor should meet the morning bus or be present when the children are gathering to go home. The key point is that counselors must be viewed by children as a normal part of the school environment.

5. As noted, children's keen interest in play will allow counselors to initiate developmental play groups with as many children as possible. Play approaches are discussed in more detail in Chapter 8.

6. When children are to be removed from the room, counselors can use a creative approach to help children understand that counseling is not only for "bad" kids. The counselor can use a puppet or toy animal to announce that "Freddy Frog" or "Andy Tiger" is here to go with Jamie to talk with the counselor. It is important that the first children selected either for individual or group counseling be children who are popular and considered to be class "stars."

7. Other than the use of play, a liberal use of the encouragement process as outlined by Dinkmeyer and Dreikurs (1963) seems to work well with children of this developmental age. Counselors will notice positive growth through discussion of what children do well or by simply letting children experience the benefits of a warm relationship with an adult. For example, a very good opening technique is that of simply making a list of all the things the child does well. A copy of the list should be given to the child even if she or he is not able to read the contents. Verbalizing positive attributes to children can have a strong impact. Many children will carry the lists with them for several days, and in many cases the lists are taken home and placed on the refrigerator along with other "work" children have done in school.

8. Counselors should not hesitate to use the playroom for brief one- or two-session counseling to allow children normal tensional outlets, especially if this need has not been met in the classroom. Developmental groups designed to help children vent excess energy are useful in the earlier grades.

The Six Year Old from a Behavioral Age Standpoint

A developmental six year old is very much the center of the entire universe. As most first grade teachers will attest, children at this age could be classified as egocentric (Ames & Ilg, 1979).

In a manner similar to that of the five year old, these children are plagued by opposites. They will be compliant and rebellious, laugh and cry, smile and be sullen. Most children will want (even demand) to be at the center of almost everything. Each wants to be number one in any line, and to have the most colors, pencils, and snowballs. In the counseling technique described earlier, wherein the counselor and child compile a list of "what the child does well," the "typical" first grader will not encounter difficulty coming up with at least ten things at which he or she excels (Ilg & Ames, 1965).

The best way to describe these children is dynamic. They seem to express themselves with all parts of the body, and their hand movements can sometimes communicate what their vocabularies will not. Their energy seems to be boundless, and it is this activity level that bothers some teachers. More than one elementary school has had to dispense physician-prescribed Ritalin to help control "out-of-bounds behavior" in this age group. Unfortunately, though medical doctors seem to prescribe this medication freely to help children with self-control, the authors wonder if it is overprescribed. At least some of the excessive chair wiggling, sliding, and fingernail biting is more normal than many believe. One does not have to spend much time in a first grade classroom to discover that verbal sounds such as clicking noises, grinding of teeth, and clearing of throats often accompany body movements. Children frequently bite their lips, gnaw on pencils, and stuff a wide range of material into their mouths. Parents and teachers, sometimes at wit's end, seem to welcome the use of medication. It can be an obvious short-term solution to hyperactivity (Ilg & Ames, 1965).

Children of this age can often be silly, brash, fresh, and argumentative. Frequent crying spells and harsh arguments are not uncommon. Like the five year old, however, these children thrive on praise and encouragement (Ames & Ilg, 1979).

Counselors who work with these children in groups will notice that their strong egos cause a range of interpersonal problems. Sharing is difficult, and there is often an unwillingness to take turns in play or in the classroom. They can be very critical and are quick to point out the inadequacies of their friends and accuse them of misbehavior. They may be willing to cheat, and most will quickly accuse peers of cheating as well (Ames & Ilg, 1979).

Children's relationships with their teachers gradually become more personal, and this closeness is a key variable in the academic success of most young learners. A warm, caring teacher is far more valuable to learners than is the most sophisticated computer ever developed! Children of this age can also develop close relationships with counselors, although this process may be easier for them in later years. The word of the teacher is law, and even parents dare not challenge what the teacher has said!

Six year olds will encounter difficulty in making changes, especially if they have made up their minds. They may not always tell the truth, and at this age some minimal stealing (borrowing) should not be considered unusual. Most seem to "collect objects that do not belong to them," and parents may find toy cars, pencils, and erasers in their children's pockets. When confronted, many children are capable of fabricating tall tales about where they obtained the objects!

While six year olds are still very much here and now individuals, adults will notice that they are beginning to develop a sense of time and some interest in the future, particularly the near future. Still, most have only minimal understanding of the meaning of a month or a year.

These children will spend a considerable amount of time in fantasy. To them their fantasies are indeed real, although first and second graders begin to distinguish between reality and fantasy. Of note is the fact that fantasy is very much a part of the average child's development. For some children, however, fantasy may well become a way of creating a world that is much better than the real one. For these children, counseling may be one of the most significant occurrences in their young lives (Ilg & Ames, 1965).

Counseling Implications

1. From the viewpoint of the counselor, much of what has been written about five year olds is equally appropriate for six year olds. Whenever possible, counselors should work closely with classroom teachers in both counseling and guidance activities.

2. Play and play media approaches are still effective counseling tools at this developmental age. One difference may be that children at this age level may show a more pronounced amount of very active and aggressive behaviors when compared to developmental five year olds. The counselor's office must be solid and durable enough to withstand the onslaught of the very active six year old.

3. With the use of either play or verbal approaches, counselors should encounter little difficulty in getting children to talk about themselves. With some exceptions, the pronoun "I" will be very prominent. As the relationship with the counselor grows, the child may be willing to discuss a wide range of topics. However, as is the case in adult counseling, children of this age will almost always blame "others" in any instances of wrongdoing. They will persist, at least initially, in their claim that the source of all problems is way beyond their own myopic, self-centered world. Counselors attempting to provide insights via use of the tentative hypothesis or tentative analysis techniques (see Chapters 6 and 7) may find that these children either ignore or dismiss counselor verbalization designed to provide insight. On the other hand, these children will readily and energetically become involved in role-playing situations that require use of their exuberant speech and active body movements. A simple suggestion or lead might be, "Let's pretend we're playing kick ball, and I'm Harry and I kick you in the knee. What will you do?" Most children will move rapidly into such a role. They will also
readily discuss such a situation with a puppet such as a frog or toy bear. At times, it may seem to the counselor that she or he is not present in the room when children become so totally engrossed in speaking with puppets.

4. At times counselors will have all they can manage in controlling the frequent bursts of activity, brash behaviors, and loud speech. In play situations the use of limits (see Chapter 8) is essential to tie the process into reality. With some children simple behavioral contracts may help them work on controlling out-of-bounds behaviors.

5. Like five year olds, six year olds respond well to praise and encouragement. They will not generally respond well to criticism or reprimand and when confronted may respond with tears. The counselor may want to attempt the aforementioned tentative analysis and tentative hypothesis techniques even though the hypothesis may not be accepted. When a tentative hypothesis "hits the mark," children may not verbalize a response, but they will usually respond with a "recognition reflex" such as a broad smile.

6. For the most part "stealing" (or "borrowing" as some children like to call the process) need not be a serious counselor concern unless it becomes frequent and part of a child's life-style. The authors have used classroom guidance units conducted jointly by the counselor and teacher in conjunction with bibliotherapy readings with a reasonable degree of success.

7. Individual and group counseling with this age level should still be "present" and "here and now" oriented. These children are "now oriented," and regardless of the theoretical orientation of the counselor, little is to be gained by a discussion of events that took place last year or even last month.

8. Since these children tire easily, counseling should be done at a time early in the day if possible. Afternoons may be marked by restlessness and inattentive behaviors.

9. Counselors should be prepared for a wide range of perceived "crises" situations that may actually be normal developmental concerns.

10. As the year progresses, some children may refuse to come to school because of one or more unpleasant incidents in class or problems related to separation from parents. Counselors and teachers should provide time for children to discuss these and other concerns.

11. As a final note, the authors recommend that any group counseling situation be structured to have a minimum of two and a maximum of five children.

The Seven Year Old from a Behavioral Age Standpoint

Consistent with a cyclical pattern of human development, the child of seven (as opposed to six) is much more calm, organized, and quiet. While six is a very active doer, seven is much more of an active thinker. The ability to reason and arrive at conclusions is now more evident. Children can concentrate and reflect a quality that may have been absent a year earlier. From time to time, their reflections lead to moodiness and self-criticism. Rather than attack problems as a six year old would, a seven year old may choose to withdraw. Of course, not all seven year olds will choose to withdraw. Counselors must always be alert for individual differences. Many children seem to be lacking in self-confidence at this time in their lives, and "I can't do that" is a common phrase. Seven also seems to operate more in a world of feeling than she or he had done previously (Ames & Hober, 1980).

These children tend to be world-class worriers. They may internalize their feelings and be concerned about their health, about the fact that one of their parents might die, and about their school work. Not at all surprising is their tendency to blame others for all that they perceive as wrong (Ilg & Ames, 1963).

While children at six seemed to have great difficulty in sitting still, developmental sevens can and do remain quiet for longer periods of time. They will attentively listen to teacher and peer talk. Perhaps for the first time, children of this age begin to show small signs of self-criticism. This does not mean that they are ready to accept criticism from others. They enjoy groups, but they are not fond of being singled out, even for praise. Singling out these children for criticism can be harmful and damaging to their self-esteem. While there is less tendency to blame others for problems than there was at six, they do not want to be considered as a problem themselves (Ilg & Ames, 1965).

These children are also very demanding of teacher time. Many seek to form close relationships with their teachers. Some children will even force themselves to appear inadequate to command teacher attention.

These children also have more capacity than do younger children to concentrate and complete a wide range of tasks. In addition, seven year olds will be much less easily distracted than their younger peers.

Counseling Implications

1. Counseling a child who is developmentally seven years of age will usually be a very active process. While play and play media are still appropriate approaches to use with these children, counselors will discover that they can also use verbal techniques. Since they have an increased capacity to think and reason, children

can reach conclusions that would not have been possible a year earlier. Classroom guidance activities that require group discussion will work well with this age group.

2. If a proper relationship has been established, counselors will discover that these children can engage in surprisingly insightful self-analytic discussions. For example, they are now capable of listing strengths and weaknesses with minimal counselor direction. Most, however, will reject or deny counselor interpretations that place them in an unfavorable light. As with five and six year olds, seven year olds do not want to be considered someone's "problem."

3. With this age group, counselors may be able to use more leads that focus on affect, because children are more in tune with their feelings and are better able to label and discuss them. Again, in discussing problems, sevens will almost always describe others as the source of any difficulties.

4. Fantasy is very much a part of the seven year old's world, and counselors can expect to hear a wide range of "wild" stories. Counselors should carefully listen to these stories, since some may provide cues to fears, particularly those related to violence and death. It is not uncommon for some children to think that their fantasies are real, and indeed, for some children they are very real.

5. Commensurate with their developing maturity, these children may now be able to become involved in counseling for longer periods of time, although sessions that last longer than a half hour or forty minutes are probably too long. Counseling games such as the US Game described in Appendix H are useful in bothindividual and small group sessions.

The Eight Year Old from a Behavioral Age Standpoint

Children who are developmentally eight years of age will once again display explosive characteristics. While calm may describe seven, excitement is a good description of eight. Dramatic and inquisitive, eight year olds will willingly tackle a great deal more than they can handle. Enthusiasm and curiosity run high, and eights seemingly have a limitless reserve of untapped energy. Most will run, jump, dance, and tumble with courage and daring. Playgrounds, swings, high fences, puddles, and rough and tumble games pose no problems for these young people.

At this age, children will undertake almost anything. They anticipate and frequently assume a "know-it-all" attitude. Interests, however, may be short-lived, and impatience is common. They may be demanding of both parents and teachers. Some tend to be verbally "fresh." They will exaggerate and become critical of others, but they may also become self-critical (Ames & Hober, 1989).

The peer group now plays an ever more important part in the lives of these children. Teachers are still important, but there is ample evidence of the importance of peers. In addition, children at this age are able to assume more responsibility for their actions. If they blame others, there may now be a good reason to do so. Children who have done wrong will now be more ready to accept that blame.

Eight is still an active seeker of praise. Some children will "put down" their own efforts in an attempt to have adults state that what they have done is really good or excellent. Most have good communication skills, and self-expression seems to come easily. Children at this age are now beginning to understand that while they have needs, so do others (Ilg & Ames, 1965).

Counseling Implications

1. Eight is an excellent age for group counseling experiences and for larger group guidance activities in the classroom. Eight year olds are interested in what their peers feel and think about a wide range of topics. Group activities that were difficult at an earlier age are now much easier to conduct. A greater degree of self-control provides them with more self-discipline. For some this is the age where, for the first time, they are able to reason and change their minds about a given issue.

2. While play and play media approaches are still useful at this age, they are beginning to lose some of their impact. Counselors may wish to consider a modified activity group counseling approach.

3. Counselors can use a wide range of counseling leads, including tentative hypotheses, tentative analysis, and interpretation. They can now actively help children focus on the purposes of their behaviors and help them find more constructive behavior to meet these goals.

4. Most children are capable of assimilating information and evaluating what they do. Eight has an expanded universe, and relationships with others are important. Counselors must capitalize on this fact.

The Nine Year Old from a Behavioral Age Standpoint

A behavioral age of nine, like the ages of four and a half and fifteen, can best be described as an age of general confusion. Expressive behavior, so commonplace a year earlier, has now been replaced by a somewhat more placid existence. These children, for the most part, tend to live in the contexts of their own private worlds.

At this age, independent behavior emerges and distance between child and parent has begun to increase. The peer group replaces the parents as the key aspect of their world. Rather than form close relationships with adults, these children prefer to work with them on an activity level. Baseball, soccer, and softball become important, as well as scouting and outdoor expeditions. Both boys and girls seek independence, and they want to be considered mature and independent.

Nine year olds' activity level is extremely high. They will work and play hard for prolonged periods of time, and a full afternoon of baseball, biking, swimming, and hiking is not at all out of the question. Most love to test their strength, and team sports and games will usually generate a lot of interest.

Intellectually, nine has made great strides. Language now becomes a tool, and these children are capable of expressing a wide range of emotions. They are also able to think independently and critically.

Children will now show interest in the community. They are interested in problems of health, weather, seasons, holidays, and the like. They are also interested in cultures outside their own, and in this sense television viewing, blamed for so many problems, has actually expanded the geographical knowledge base of this age group. While still very much "here and now" oriented, nine year olds enjoy films and stories about prehistoric times.

Nines tell the truth with increasing frequency. This is an indication of growing moral development. While most children will not be above telling a "little" lie, much of this may be to support a friend who is perceived to be in trouble. As noted earlier, nines clearly see themselves as group members. They prefer groups and clubs to intimate relationships, and they attempt to test their self-concepts against peer standards.

Nines can exhibit a great deal of understanding and feeling for others. They are likely to rebel against authority and may choose pathways of either withdrawal or excessive complaint. This is an age of hypochondria, and aches and pains seem to occur almost weekly.

Counseling Implications

1. While lots of nine year olds can and do form personal relationships with adult counselors and teachers, they may do so at a slower pace than they did when they were younger.

2. Group counseling, especially if it is structured to include games such as the one included in Appendix G, will work very well with this age group. The behavioral and developmental contracts that are part of the game are readily carried out by students in this behavioral age. Nines especially seem to enjoy reporting their successes and in meeting goals that they have developed for themselves as part of the counseling group. Activity group counseling has also been used by one of the authors with good success.

3. Nines can and will participate in verbal counseling approaches. They can label their emotions and can readily express them. Clarification, tentative analysis, reflection, and "I message" confrontations are good counseling tools for this age group.

4. Classroom guidance activities, so much a part of the comprehensive guidance programs described in Chapter 7, are effective and enjoyable at this age. Children's increased interest in the community and other cultures make this an ideal age for guidance activities that promote multicultural and multiethnic awareness and sensitivities.

5. This age seems to be a critical time for an observable drop in self-worth. In one sense it is almost like a stage of separation, with some children rising to the top and the rest sinking into a feeling of lack of self-acceptance. Both classroom guidance activities and group counseling sessions should have the goals of developing a positive sense of self and building increased ego strength. Encouragement and verbal rewards are effective vehicles in this process. Empathic counselors and teachers can teach children to be empathic; through understanding, they can help the child feel understood. Through encouragement, they can assist in the development of positive self-images.

6. For those developmentally younger who are mixed in with nines, the world can and sometimes does become a very demanding place. Teachers and counselors will want to observe daily behavior and provide special help for these children. The authors feel that this age has a high potential for academic casualties, and some children who have entered school before they were developmentally ready to do so seem to find the fourth grade or its equivalent to be very stressful.

7. The use of play media may lose its impact at this age level, and the counselor will probably want to replace it with more activity group approaches. Although some children still show interest in some of the normal playroom toys, verbal counseling or activity counseling combined with verbal approaches seems to be most effective.

The Ten Year Old from a Behavioral Age Standpoint

Most adults find the behavioral age of ten rather delightful in comparison to some of the earlier ages. Life for children at this age is approached in a somewhat casual manner. Most children have a wide range of interests, and if parents permit it, they will spend large blocks of time viewing television. Many will identify with the characters portrayed on the programs, particularly those who represent the preadolescent life-style of the 1990s. Adults may well describe children of this age as obedient, good natured, and fun to work with in both teaching and counseling situations (Ilg & Ames, 1965).

Tens will exhibit an expanded sense of time that now includes minutes, years, and even centuries. Most children are mobile and can get from place to place on their own. They are also able to meet time commitments for meetings and for family meal schedules.

The tendency to be truthful will gradually increase, although "little white lies" and fibs are not uncommon. An occasional "whopper" is also not out of the question.

A more positive child generally means greater acceptance by adults; hence, the self-image of children this age is likely to show some improvement over the time that the child was nine. Of even more importance is the increase in self-acceptance and acceptance of others. These children enjoy life and are generally positive toward peers, school, and the home environment (Gesell & Ilg, 1946).

Most tens have made reasonable adjustments, and severe complications are not the rule. Children will smile readily and will usually show a good sense of humor. Sudden bursts of temper, though less common, are still possible.

Although tens can be and usually are verbal, they generally enjoy reading more than they do writing. Almost all of them enjoy talking!

These children can form close personal relationships with both teachers and counselors. If adults are perceived as warm and friendly, children will readily seek them out for assistance. Counselors can expect lots of self-referrals from this age group.

Counseling Implications

1. Group activities, including group counseling, will work well with this age group. Ten year olds are interested in many topics and will readily participate in structured classroom guidance and structured and nonstructured counseling sessions.

2. This age group can actively participate in verbal counseling, although activity group approaches are still possible. They are capable of arriving at their own insights and of understanding the insights provided by the counselor or their peers.

3. Bibliotherapy is useful with this age group, and counselors should have a list of books that deal with a wide range of developmental concerns. Discussions of some of these concerns, either in classroom guidance activities or in counseling groups, seems to work very well in that students can work on personal concerns through a discussion of the characters in the stories.

4. The fact that most schools now have VCR equipment can be a boon to counselors. Children love to see themselves on the screen, and you can tape simulated counseling sessions for orientation for the formation of future counseling groups. Children can learn that counseling is not just for "bad" kids by viewing role-played counseling tapes.

5. At times, counselors may want to spend time on the playground, because active play by both girls and boys can trigger sudden outbursts of temper. These situations, when they do occur, are a natural laboratory for the counselor to "teach" human relations skills on the spot!

6. Tens are able to recognize both their strengths and weaknesses, but they tend to overidentify their faults. Most need counseling help to also identify what they do well, since this is important in the development of positive self-images.

The Eleven Year Old from a Behavioral Standpoint

Elevens are rapidly moving toward adulthood. They are now becoming more assertive, more curious, and much more sociable. These children move rapidly and love to talk. They squirm and wiggle a great deal. Some teachers in grade six may wish for some form of restraining device to help with classroom control!

Eleven year olds' exuberance is sometimes matched by the intensity of their emotions. They may laugh quickly and loudly, or they may explode with sharp bursts of anger. There can be rapid shifts in mood. The happy child at ten in the morning may well be moody by lunch. However, they can also be thoughtful and sympathetic. Most have no difficulty in labeling their emotional states. They can relate their feelings to parents, teachers, and counselors (Gesell, Ilg, & Ames, 1958).

This is a very social age, and in school as at home, these children now want very much to be with others. This sociability does not prevent them from becoming competitive, even in social situations. Some will want to see how many friends they can make, others will strive for good grades or attempt to excel in sports.

This age group is often somewhat silly, and most laugh and giggle a lot. Off color words are not uncommon, although some of this behavior still does not have a sexual connotation. Almost any topic, however, including sex, will be sufficient to promote a loud laugh.

Elevens can engage in adult conversations. In fact, some are capable of formulating hypotheses and are capable of arguing hypothetically. They will readily interact with counselors and teachers (Ilg & Ames, 1965).

These children have positive peer interests and are sensitive to what takes place in groups. Most can make individual judgments, although peer pressures are starting to make this more difficult. At times they will get into fights and tussles with classmates and can be cruel to less fortunate peers. Verbal taunts such as "dumbo" or "fatso" can usually be heard as part of the playground interaction.

Counseling Implications

1. Working with eleven year olds requires a little more patience than working with younger children. In a counseling group, some may say things that are hurtful to others. The responses may seem to come out of the blue, and the speaker may not stop to consider the impact of what she or he has said to another group member. Counselors will want to insist that children learn to use "I" statements (see Chapter 7).

2. Counselors should not expect long introspective sessions from this age group. Since they will not sit still for long periods of time, they may not take the time to closely consider what they or their peers have said. If a topic is of interest, they may talk quickly and with animation, leaving little space for counselor interpretations. Most will do well in group counseling sessions. The use of tentative hypotheses and tentative analyses techniques are effective counselor tools.

3. Counselors and teachers may find increasing numbers of questions about bodily changes, particularly from girls who are concerned with these changes. Boys, for the most part, will be less willing to discuss sex with adults, preferring to seek information (or more likely misinformation) from peers. In some cases, this makes group counseling with mixed-sex groups a little difficult at this age. Some girls who were last year's teammate on the soccer team are now wearing some makeup and have exchanged soccer shorts for more dressy attire. Some immature boys find this "rapid" turnabout in girls confusing and threatening.

4. Almost all kinds of verbal counseling are now possible. When very brief counseling is necessary, rational emotive and reality approaches are useful. Eleven year olds will respond well to developmental behavioral contracts and enjoy working with counselors to set goals and to devise ways to meet these goals. As with earlier ages, counselors should spend little time assessing children's faults. Eleven year olds will respond well to empathic counselors who have a sense of humor. The counselor should consider many of the complaints of this age about overdemanding teachers and "bossy" parents as largely developmental concerns. Almost all children of this age consider teachers and parents to be overly demanding.

The Twelve Year Old from a Behavioral Age Standpoint

Twelve year olds, from a behavioral age standpoint, are best described as in-between individuals, as their behavior seems to flow from childlike to adult-like and back again. Children of this age are spirited and enthusiastic. When left to their own devices, they are capable of raising the noise level of the school considerably. Fortunately, enthusiasm is accompanied by a large measure of intuition and insight. They can read emotional expressions both in themselves and in others. They also have the capacity to comprehend the moods and emotions of peers. While adulthood is still in the future, twelve year olds have the potential for adultlike behaviors (Gesell, Ilg, & Ames, 1958).

Some of the excessive "moving around" behavior of earlier ages has modified, and twelve year olds can sit still for longer periods of time. The twitches and wiggles that were present at eleven, however, may still be in evidence.

This is a year when physical changes become important. Girls may have achieved a full 90 percent of their adult height. Their breasts have become fully developed, and if it has not occurred earlier, the menstrual cycle will probably begin. Casually accepted by some girls, menstruation can be a source of concern to others. Counselors will need to be alert to provide help for those who have not had good instruction in their homes.

Some boys at this age show marked sexual development, while others may show almost no change from how they were at eleven. Both boys and girls will almost always require privacy as they begin to understand the changes taking place in their bodies. In fact, open showers in junior high/middle schools may be inappropriate. Many students are willing to risk the wrath of the physical education teacher or principal rather than disrobe in front of their peers.

Emotionally, twelves may exhibit fewer disagreeable or moody periods of behavior than they did at eleven. In general, most twelve year olds seem to be good-natured a great deal of the time. While these children are obviously capable of anger, they are showing more and more self-control in the classroom and in peer relations.

In addition these children are becoming increasingly self-sufficient, self-reliant, and self-assured. They are also becoming more thoughtful, and many have a pleasant sense of humor.

Twelve year olds will discuss the future and even project themselves into situations such as college, the service, or a job. For most, however, time is no longer than the next party, dance, or football game. They should not be forced to make decisions that lock them into a particular career path or course of study at this age (Gesell, Ilg, & Ames, 1958).

Most twelve year olds like school, and peers are very important to them. There is a strong desire to be one of the group, and they feel that their clothing and language must not deviate too far from the perceived group norms. This fact has not escaped the jean manufacturers in our country!

Counseling Implications

1. A behavioral age of twelve is ideal for group counseling. In fact, counselors who work with this age group should have well-developed programs of developmental and if essential remedial group counseling. Mixed-sex and mixed-age groups are now very appropriate. While the girls in general are still more mature, the differences that were evident two years earlier have now lessened considerably. Most will eagerly participate in group counseling and seem to respond especially well to strength groups and "encouragement" laboratories. The counselor should design activities to help children discover their potentials and help identify the potentials in others.

2. Counselors may find an increased interest in discussion of sex and sexual activities if the children are allowed to introduce this topic. The fears associated with AIDS, almost unknown fifteen years ago, are now very much on the minds of young people, some of whom may be experimenting with sex. Girls may relate better to female counselors, but many boys tend to be hesitant about discussing sex, particularly if counselors are perceived as judgmental. If the school has a good sex education program, the instructor may answer many of the questions in this age group. If the school has no sex education program, be assured that some children of this age group will be seeking answers from the counselor about the meaning of the dramatic changes taking place in their bodies.

3. A wide range of counseling techniques can be effective with twelves. Client centered, Adlerian, Glasserian, developmental, and behavioral approaches have all been effective for counselors of different theoretical persuasions. In general, most of what applies to adult counseling, with the possible exception of time and environmental control, are applicable with this age level. Although twelve year olds are still not adults, they can easily be involved in verbal counseling sessions for half an hour or longer. Most are capable of using counselor insights and interpretations in a near-adult manner. If trust is present, counselor confrontations of an "I" message type are useful. Behavioral contracts, while still useful, need not be formalized as they were earlier. Verbal agreements between counselors and children for post-counseling "homework" are usually sufficient to judge how well children are progressing toward goals that they have agreed upon with the counselor.

CONCLUSION

In order to counsel, one must have some understanding of how human beings grow and develop, because counseling theories should flow from some conception of human behavior. Counselors who call themselves client centered, for example, will need to understand how the self and attitudes toward self have developed in an individual's life.

Volumes upon volumes about human development have been written, both by those who have developed systems of counseling and psychotherapy and by those who study human behavior for other reasons. We have only been able to include a small sample of the thinking on human development. Counselors should study human development in depth, and the introductions included in this book should be considered merely as a starting point.

We have included a brief discussion of Freud in this chapter, since this pioneer was and is a giant in the helping professions. Much of what one reads in the works of other theorists can be attributed to the brilliant thinking of this man. We have also included a discussion of Erikson to show how he expanded Freud's ideas and gave a broader interpretation. No counselor or educator can ignore the work of Piaget and his impact on cognitive theories of counseling as well as theories of teaching.

The works of Carl Rogers and Abraham Maslow should be studied in their entirety. These individuals, perhaps more than any others, have provided much of the foundation for modern guidance and counseling philosophy. Also included is the significant contribution of Robert Havighurst in the area of developmental tasks.

Finally we have included material on the developmental ages first developed by Arnold Gesell and later expanded by Louise Bates Ames and the late Francis Ilg. Much of this approach to human development has its roots in biology, and it is, in our opinion, timely for the 1990s. The years until the turn of the century and beyond will see a renewed interest in biology as part of overall human development, and counselors should study the biological antecedents of behavior in the same way they now study the environmental influences. Studying the work of the Gesell Institute is a good place to start.

REFERENCES

Almy, M. (1961). *Young children's thinking.* New York: Teachers College Press.

Ames, L. B. (1970). *Child care and development.* New York: Lippincott.

Ames, L. B. (1979). *Your five year old child.* New York: Dell.

Ames, L. B., & Hober, C. (1980). *Your seven year old.* New York: Bantam Doubleday.

Ames, L. B., & Hober, C. (1989). *Your eight year old.* New York: Bantam Doubleday.

Ames, L. B., & Hober, C. (1990). *Your nine year old.* New York: Bantam Doubleday.

Ames, L. B., & Ilg, F. L. (1979). *Your six year old.* New York: Bantam Doubleday.

Berger, K. S. (1988). *The developing person through the life span.* New York: Worth Publishers.

Cowan, P. A. (1978). *Piaget with feeling: Cognitive, social, and emotional disorders.* New York: Holt, Rinehart & Winston.

Dinkmeyer, D. C., & Dreikurs, R. (1963). *Encouraging children to learn: The encouragement process.* Englewood Cliffs, NJ: Prentice Hall.

Elkind, D. (1978). Erik Erikson's eight stages of man. *New York Times Magazine* (April 5), pp. 25 ff.

Erikson, E. H. (1968). *Identity: Youth and crises.* New York: Norton.

Flavell, J. H. (1963). *The developmental psychology of Jean Piaget.* Princeton, NJ: Von Nostromic.

Freud, S. (1938). *The basic writings of Sigmund Freud.* New York: Modern Library.

Freud, S. (1949). *The psychopathology of everyday life: Basic writings of Sigmund Freud.* New York: Norton.

Gazda, G. (1989). *Group counseling.* Boston: Allyn & Bacon.

Gesell, A., & Ilg, F. L. (1946). *The child from five to ten.* New York: Harper.

Gesell, A., Ilg, F. L., & Ames, L. B. (1958). *The years from ten to sixteen.* New York: Harper.

Hamachek, D. E. (1977). *Humanistic psychology: Theoretical-philosophical framework and implications for teaching.* In D. J. Treffinger, J. K. Davis, & E. E. Ripple (Eds.), *Handbook on teaching educational psychology* (pp. 221–243). New York: Academic Press.

Havighurst, R. J. (1948). *Developmental tasks and education.* Chicago: University of Chicago Press.

Havighurst, R. J. (1952). *Developmental tasks and education* (2nd ed.). New York: Longmanas Green.

Havighurst, R. J. (1953). *Human development and education.* New York: David McKay.

Ilg, F. L., & Ames, L. B. (1965). *School readiness.* New York: Harper & Row.

Markus, H. (1977). Self schemata and processing about the self. *Journal of Personality and Social Psychology, 35,* 63–78.

Maslow, A. H. (1955). Deficiency motivation and growth motivation. In M. R. Jones (ed.), *Nebraska symposium on motivation*. Lincoln, NE: University of Nebraska Press.

Muro, J. J., & Dinkmeyer, D. C. (1977). Counseling in the elementary and middle schools. Dubuque, IA: Wm. C. Brown.

Mussen, A. H., Conger, J. J., & Kagan, J. (1974). *Child development and personality*. New York: Harper & Row.

Nutten, J. (1962). *Psychoanalysis and personality*. New York: The American Library.

Piaget, J. (1970). *The child's conception of time*. New York: Basic Books.

Rice, F. P. (1992). *Human development*. New York: Macmillan.

Rogers, C. R. (1951). *Client centered therapy*. Boston: Houghton Mifflin.

Turkle, S. (1987). Hero of the life cycle. *New York Times Book Review* (April 5), pp. 36–37.

Vander Zanden, J. W. (1989). *Human development*. New York: Alfred A. Knopf.

Watson, R. I., & Lindgren, H. C. (1973). *Psychology of the child*. New York: Wiley.

Chapter Three

Developmental Guidance and Counseling

🌳 Perhaps the last real hope for a comprehensive program of developmental guidance and counseling rests with the programs that are emerging in the elementary and middle schools in our country. There are a number of factors that provide hope for developmental programs in the elementary school, including the fact that the ages of children who attend classes at this level provide opportunities for counselors to prevent problems that can otherwise become serious later.

School guidance *should be* developmental. Only through a developmental approach can we ever hope to meet the lofty goals of our profession. Only with a developmental approach will we be able to focus on human potential, on growth, on assets, and on the creation of conditions that help promote healthy, full-functioning human beings. If elementary and middle school guidance and counseling slip into a solely problem-centered mode, as has happened in some of our secondary schools, then guidance and counseling as it was envisioned in the 1950s, 1960s, and beyond may well disappear. We could well become one more arm of the profession of clinical psychology.

Assumptions About Elementary School Guidance and Counseling

In order to create a comprehensive approach to developmental guidance and counseling, one must understand the basic assumptions and needs that underlie this concept. Myrick (1987) notes that developmental guidance and counseling are based on the premise that human nature moves individuals sequentially and positively toward self-enhancement. Individuals have within them a force that seems to make them believe they are special and unique. This approach also assumes that individual potentials are valuable assets to humanity. This drive for personal expression can require compromise with other powerful forces in the environment. A growing human being must interact with individuals who live in a society of laws, regulations, and mutual values. At times these forces can and do clash with an individual's path to self-fulfillment (Myrick, 1987).

While there is some theory available to guide counseling practice, formal guidance theory still needs elaboration and definition. Guidance theory should suggest when guidance intervention might optimally occur, and for what reasons. For example, if guidance is to stress prevention, then program priorities should emphasize the creation of school environments that promote success rather than failure. In addition, guidance theory should be able to direct counselors where they could most effectively focus their energies.

Good guidance theory should also be able to provide guidelines about who could directly benefit from counseling services. Should teachers benefit from the skills of an elementary school counselor? Should parents? Should children? Should all three? Once the counselor has answers to these questions, she or he will be able to define a comprehensive program of guidance that will direct the counselor's efforts in daily practice. Counselors must be able to determine whether or not they wish to work with children directly (a counseling approach), indirectly (by consulting with teachers), or perhaps both. A comprehensive program of developmental guidance and counseling will provide the professional elementary school counselor with guidelines for responding to these important questions.

What Is Developmental Guidance?

Although there are a number of definitions of developmental guidance, most include some principles that are generally accepted by most professionals in the field (Gysbers & Henderson, 1988; Myrick, 1987; Worzbyt & O'Rourke, 1980). One can also discover a wide range of practices subsumed under the term "developmental guidance." Most guidance programs that could be labeled developmental in nature are organized around the following principles:

1. *Guidance and counseling are needed by all children.* In a developmental program, guidance and counseling activities are assumed to be needed by all children. Developmental programs, at times, must deal with troubled and troublesome children, but they are developed to serve all children.

   All children need to gain self-understanding, assume increasing responsibility for self-control, mature in their understandings of the world around them, and learn to make decisions. In addition, children need help in learning to solve problems and mature in their sense of values (Myrick, 1987). All individuals need to feel a sense of love and worth, all children need to succeed to the limit of their abilities, and all children need to know and accept their strengths.

2. *Developmental guidance and counseling has a focus on children's learning.* Modern elementary schools do not generally lack for specialists. There are specialists to help children read, play musical instruments, and develop physical skills. Counselors are specialists, but they specialize in human growth and development and in the study and understanding of the inner worlds of children.

   Counselors also operate under what Myrick (1987) calls an organized and planned curriculum that stresses cognitive, affective, and physical growth and development. This curriculum has particular emphasis on human learning and the human learner. Operationally this means that counselors are members of teams that include parents, teachers, administrators, and other specialists. Their task is to bring to bear their knowledge and skills to help children learn. A child in trouble must learn, and the slow learner must be helped to learn as much as possible, but *all* children are involved in the learning process. At times the counselor's role will be that of a teacher in a classroom guidance unit; at other times, counselors will work with children to remove or lessen the impact of situations that impede learning. A major purpose of school is learning. A major purpose of developmental guidance and counseling is helping learners learn.

3. *Counselors and teachers are cofunctionaries in developmental guidance programs.* The unique nature of elementary and middle schools is a key factor in promoting a developmental point of view for guidance programming. While some schools have a number of teachers working with children, the self-contained classroom is still very common. In such teaching situations, teachers tend to become involved with the whole child, and many teachers were doing "guidance" activities long before elementary school counselors were present. In addition, elementary school teachers, in general, seem to be less subject matter oriented and more child oriented than teachers of adolescents. For example, many elementary school teachers who see a child slipping into academic difficulty will not automatically refer the child for counseling. Often, they will work with counselors in collaborative ways to seek solutions that may not require that the child leaves the classroom. Teachers and counselors approach such situations with the goal of developing hypotheses that can be explored. For example, what is the child's attention span? Will he do better if I give him shorter assignments? How does she feel about herself? Can a positive guidance activity help him and others like him improve self-images? Will she do better if she works with one or more peers on an assignment? What is his maturity level? What do we know about her strengths and potentials? Can the counselor observe him and see if we can find clues to help him?

As a cofunctionary with the teacher, the counselor does not attempt to provide quick solutions. Nor does the counselor suggest that the first thing to be done is counsel the child. He or she is not the "expert" or the one with ready answers to complex situations. In this approach, the counselor is a co-investigator into the problem, listening closely to the teacher's feelings, clarifying, asking about approaches that have already been tried, and helping evaluate new courses of action. This is appropriate in that both teachers and counselors know that learning, like growth, is a *process,* and any single event must be considered as a point on a long continuum of learning. Teamwork between counselors and teachers is essential!

4. *An organized and planned curriculum is a vital part of developmental guidance* (Myrick, 1987). All developmental programs should contain a carefully planned and organized curriculum. In a manner similar to the regular school curriculum of mathematics, science, and social studies, the developmental curriculum contains goals and objectives that help children in their normal growth and development. The curriculum stresses cognitive, affective, and physical growth. Areas of study presented in a systematic way to students include activities designed to enhance self-esteem, motivation to achieve, decision making, goal setting, planning, problem-solving skills, interpersonal effectiveness, communication skills, cross-cultural effectiveness, and responsible behavior.

   These activities require the collaborative efforts of both teachers and counselors. In this sense, counselors must be able to teach as well as counsel.

5. *Developmental guidance is concerned with self-acceptance, self-understanding, and self-enhancement.* Whether working with children experiencing problems or with children involved in normal developmental concerns, developmental counselors will focus on activities designed to assist children to know more about themselves and to be more accepting of who they are and more aware of their strengths. For example, the counselor may want to organize counseling groups of one to three sessions that are designed specifically to have children discuss what they do well. The counselor can also use individual counseling sessions to focus on strengths. She or he may want to send letters home relating to parents all signs of positive progress. In the classroom, the counselor should display work for others to see whenever possible. Programmed materials such as DUSO II (Dinkmeyer, 1973) may also be used. In cases where children are not performing up to their own personal expectations, the counselor may need to work in individual and group counseling sessions to help reduce the gap between the actual and ideal self-images of the child.

6. *Developmental guidance and counseling focus on the encouragement process.* The process of encouragement, though it would seem to be self-evident in working with children, is more complex than most believe. It is insufficient that one wishes to encourage a child. In fact, the result of any corrective act depends less on what the counselor or teacher does than on how the child perceives and responds to the process (Dinkmeyer & Dreikurs, 1963, p. 4). The methods of encouragement as outlined by Dinkmeyer and Dreikurs stress that the person who encourages:

   1. Places value on the child as she or he is.
   2. Shows a faith in the child that enables the child to have faith in himself or herself.
   3. Has faith in the child's ability; wins the child's confidence while building self-respect.
   4. Recognizes a job "well done"; gives recognition for effort.

5. Utilizes the group to facilitate and enhance the development of the child.

6. Integrates the group so that the child can be sure of his or her place in it.

7. Assists in the development of skills sequentially and psychologically paced to permit success.

8. Recognizes and focuses on strengths and assets.

9. Utilizes the interests of the child to energize instruction. (p. 50)

Counselors using this approach will use statements such as "That was a great try!" more frequently than they will use statements like "Your reading needs lots of work."

7. *Developmental guidance acknowledges directional development rather than definitive ends.* Developmental counselors understand that children are in the process of becoming, that their physical and psychological growth will undergo multiple changes before they reach adulthood. Therefore, they design and evaluate activities for children with the idea that they do not expect any single activity to produce a final and unchanging result. They design activities based on developmental ages of children. Counselors should not expect that marked changes will take place in children after one or even ten counseling sessions. Rather than consider how a child has changed as a result of counseling, the counselor should concentrate on progress that has been made. Guidance and counseling at this level is truly a process, not a one act play.

8. *Developmental guidance, while team oriented, requires the services of a trained professional counselor.* As noted, successful developmental guidance programs require the efforts of all school personnel. In order to obtain maximum effectiveness of programs, schools must have access to the skills and knowledge of a trained counselor, who has specialized skills in individual counseling, group counseling, assessment, and child development. Otherwise comprehensive guidance programs are not possible. The counselor is a vital part of a dynamic process. The counselor's skills support and enhance the efforts of teachers and administrators in the schools.

9. *Developmental guidance is concerned with early identification of special needs.* Developmental guidance programs stress the early identification of the special needs of children. Counselors work with teachers to assess these needs which, if left unattended, could become problems requiring a remedial effort later in a child's life. Specialized child study efforts, the use of both large and small group approaches, and close relationships with parents are all integral parts of early identification.

10. *Developmental guidance is concerned with the psychology of use.* Educators have long been concerned with the assessment of intelligence, aptitudes, interests, and personalities of children and adults. While assessment remains a part of elementary school guidance, developmental philosophy is also concerned with how children utilize the qualities, abilities, and interests they possess. Developmental counselors are not only concerned with an assessment of a child's capacity to learn. They are also interested in how children use their abilities. Are there challenges for the gifted and talented? Do slow-learning children make maximum use of learning aids? Do children with musical talents have an outlet for creative expression? To a developmental counselor, what children do and do not do with their given abilities is equally as important as the abilities themselves.

11. *Developmental guidance has foundations in child psychology, child development, and learning theory.* The principles of developmental guidance listed here have roots in child psychology, child development, and learning theory. If guidance is to be truly developmental, then guidance programs must be designed to fit the child—children should not be made to fit the programs! Thus developmental guidance borrows from the concepts advanced by specialists in child psychology and human development. Our guidance practice is consistent with what we know about growing organisms. In addition, since a cornerstone of developmental guidance is helping children become competent learners, counselors at this level should be keen students of human learning.

12. *Developmental guidance is both sequential and flexible* (Myrick, 1987). To be effective, developmental guidance must be flexible enough to meet individual differences and planned so that what is accomplished by counselors is not done in a random, haphazard way (Myrick, 1987). Some activities (play in counseling for example) are appropriate for students in grade two but are inappropriate for students in grade seven. The counselor will want to design goals for specific developmental age levels, and guidance practice must follow these goals. Guidance at this level is proactive.

It is not enough to wait until students have problems in their classes or have misunderstandings with their teachers before they receive some guidance. Rather, students can benefit by identifying the kinds of behaviors that are related to achievement and then rating themselves or comparing ratings with teacher ratings (Myrick, 1987, p. 44). Many counselors and teachers who develop programs design them so they can be moved around and inserted into the curriculum to address particular needs or concerns. For example, the counselor should develop a unit dealing with traumatic events such as earthquakes if she or he lives in a region in which earthquakes commonly take place and are likely to be on the minds of children.

Differences Between Elementary and Middle School and Secondary School Guidance

To the neophyte in guidance, the concept of a developmental approach may seem obvious in that the principles of developmental guidance not only are consistent with sound educational practice, but they also reflect a philosophy that is goal and potential oriented, rather than remedial. There are, however, some important differences for counselors to consider in developing programs of guidance and counseling at the elementary school level, as follows:

1. In most cases, the elementary school environment is significantly different from that of the secondary school. Most elementary and middle school counselors do not see each child on a consistent basis; hence, counselors may be unable to significantly change the learning environment of a child even when such a change can lead to increased learning.

2. There will be numerous occasions when children will not utilize guidance services directly, but will experience them indirectly through teachers, parents, and other adults.

3. The concept of choice is central to guidance at any level, and it is especially true for developmental programs. However, in the elementary school, the opportunities for most choices, especially curricular ones, are very much limited.

4. Children in elementary schools are not able to assume self-responsibility as much as are those in secondary schools.

5. The development of all guidance programs at the elementary school level should initiate from the basic concept that guidance is primarily concerned with providing assistance to children as learners.

6. Elementary school guidance places relatively less emphasis on record keeping, testing, educational programming, problem-centered approaches, and extended long-term individual counseling and therapy.

Goals of Elementary and Middle School Guidance and Counseling

All children need to develop self-understanding and an understanding and appreciation of the individuals who live in this world. In a society that is rapidly becoming more pluralistic, individuals must be informed and responsible. Developmental guidance is based on the premise that a positive regard and respect for human dignity is essential in an interdependent society. In order to reach these objectives, everyone involved in elementary and middle school guidance and counseling programs will need to work toward the following goals. All children will:

1. Experience positive feelings from their interactions with peers, teachers, parents, and other adults.

2. Derive personal meaning from their learning activities.

3. Develop and maintain a positive sense of self, value their individuality, and be able to understand and relate to their feelings.

4. Become aware of the importance of their own values, and develop values consistent with those necessary to live in a pluralistic society.

5. Develop and enhance academic skills to the maximum of their ability.

6. Learn the necessary coping skills so that they will be better able to deal with the normal developmental concerns and problems that they will encounter.

7. Develop appropriate goal-setting, planning, and problem-solving skills.

8. Develop positive attitudes toward life.

9. Realize that they are responsible for their own behavior.

10. Work with parents in a variety of planned programs to assist them to develop attitudes and skills to enhance the child's academic and social development.

11. Work closely with classroom teachers to enhance learning activities.

Of these goals, perhaps the single most important one and the one that should be the cornerstone of a developmental guidance program is that the basic and major function of guidance in elementary and middle schools is the facilitation of learning. The purpose of the school is for learning, and if guidance is to be an integral part of the process, then all guidance activities should be directed toward learning. Children who are learning feel competent and confident about themselves as learners; children who grow in a climate that fosters learning about themselves and about the world around them have a much better chance of growing into competent, healthy adults. All schools are social laboratories, and the learning process has both psychological and academic components. If the counselor uses this overall goal of facilitation of learning as a guide for developmental practice, he or she can almost be assured that children will develop the ability to handle the demands and pressures of their environment with a high degree of success.

Implementing a Developmental Guidance Program in the Schools

Counselors who accept the principles of developmental guidance will need to be actively involved in the design and implementation of such programs. A hard, if unfortunate, lesson learned from the initiation of guidance in the secondary schools is that unless guidance professionals assume a proactive stance in the creation of programs, then others will determine the essential aspects of what is to be accomplished. Many secondary counselors are viewed as the one who "cures the problems" or the one who "sends kids to the right college." The principal and others who determine school policy are more often than not involved in deciding what the counselor would do. If a counselor is starting a new program and is not prepared to define her or his professional role in the schools, she or he can be certain that there are numerous others who will be pleased to define that role.

There are a number of approaches one can take to achieve program development in the schools. One of the most widely accepted models developed in recent years is that advocated by Gysbers and Henderson in 1988. The plan suggested by these authors is a four-phased approach that includes planning, designing, implementing, and evaluating. Many school districts in the country have used this model guide in the creation or the restructuring of guidance programs.

Planning a Developmental Program

Planning should not be done in isolation. Experience in educational institutions at all levels has taught us that individuals who have a say in the development of goals will be more likely to work toward those goals. A guidance program that is planned and implemented in the quiet confines of the counselor's office is almost certainly doomed to failure. A group effort is essential, therefore, to the individuals who will be involved in the process of guidance and to those who will be the consumers of what guidance has to offer. Organizing for guidance must involve key individuals in an organized, unified effort. If the plan is for a districtwide developmental guidance program, then the counselor should include personnel from the superintendent's office. If the district has a number of schools, then there needs to be active involvement by principals and other specialists from these schools. Individuals with expertise in special education, reading, and health are good candidates for a districtwide committee. If the guidance program is only for an individual school, the involvement of the building principal is essential.

At both the district level and the local building level, parent input is highly desirable. In a number of districts in the country at the present time, some fundamentally sound and widely utilized guidance approaches have come under attack from conservative parent groups who feel that any discussion of children's feelings and any group approaches are either antireligious or socialistic. While most consider these attitudes archaic, such groups tend to be vocal, active, and single-minded. Once organized, they target specific activities and place the counselor and the school in a defensive stance. It is far better to canvas the community and involve parents who are community leaders from the outset in the planning for guidance policy. Counselors who fail to involve parents from the beginning may well oppose them in altercations at some later date.

In order to plan, counselors must first organize a representative committee (Gysbers & Henderson, 1988). Such committees are often called steering committees, organizing committees, or simply guidance committees. Their task is the planning, designing, implementing, and evaluation of guidance. These committees may vary in size, from around eight to twelve members, but they should not be too large for active participation by all members. As noted, each committee should have building and district administrators, a principal or other specialist, teachers, and parents. The counselor is the organizer and the consultant to the committee, but the policy that emerges from the interaction must be the joint effort of all who are involved. A grass roots effort of this nature is absolutely essential for the initiation of the planning process.

The steering committee, charged with the task of revising or implementing a comprehensive program of guidance, will need to become involved in a number of important issues. Since no single model is appropriate for all schools and all districts, the committee will initially have to develop a comprehensive model as a guide for practice. This document should just be a guide, because the eventual curriculum will have content and goals that are locally developed.

A review by the authors of a number of guides for the development of comprehensive models reveals many similarities in programs initiated in most states. While there are a number of differences from state to state, the model developed in Texas is fairly representative of baseline planning goals that in turn will help determine guidance content. The Texas model includes the following goals for learners:

Self-esteem

Motivation to achieve

Decision-making, goal-setting, and planning skills

Problem-solving skills

Interpersonal effectiveness

Communication skills

Cross-cultural effectiveness

Responsible behavior

(Texas Education Agency, 1991, p. 70)

With these broad areas in mind, the guidance committee should next turn its attention to the development of locally appropriate statements of definition, rationale, and the underlying assumptions of the program. Program definition includes the identification of the populations to be served (students, parents, teachers, administrators), the basic content of the program (content areas and goals), and the organization of the program (delivery system, guidance curriculum, individual planning system, responsive services, and system support). The rationale for the program should result from an assessment of the needs of the students and the community. These may be either general in nature (at the district level) or specific (at the building level).

In addition, all the assumptions on which the program is based need to be made as clear as possible. These may include a description of the counselors' professional training, background, and professional experiences as they relate to the program. Assumptions should also include the contributions that guidance can make to normal healthy individual development. It is also of vital importance at this juncture to describe the conditions necessary for successful implementation, which include staffing, districtwide commitment, opportunities for program and staff development, budget, materials, supplies and equipment, and facilities for the program. All of these are essential components and must be included in the planning process (Texas Education Agency, 1991).

Designing a Developmental Program

The initial planning process will lead naturally into the design for a comprehensive guidance program. This stage of the process will require the committee to make a number of difficult decisions. The essential work of the committee will be to answer questions similar to those posed by Henderson (1987):

1. Which program component should have high priority for counselors?
2. Of the competencies that need to be learned, which should be emphasized at each grade level, or grade grouping?
3. Who will be served and with what priority: all students in a developmental mode, or some students in a remedial services mode? What are the relationships between services to students and services to adults in the students' lives?
4. What competencies and outcomes will have priority?
5. What skills will be utilized by the school counselors: teaching, guiding, counseling, consulting, testing, record keeping, coordinating, or disseminating information, and with what priority?
6. What school levels will benefit, and to what extent from the resources appropriated to the program: elementary, middle school/junior high school, or high school?
7. What is the relationship between the guidance program and staff and the other educational programs and staff? Is the sole purpose of guidance to support the instructional program? Does guidance have an identity and responsibilities of its own? Should it be a program or a set of services?

To guide thinking in the design of comprehensive guidance programs, Gysbers and Henderson (1988) have developed a seven-step process to establish the design of a program at either the building or district level, as described in the following paragraphs.

1. *Select the basic program structure.* The structural components contain: (a) program definition (mission statement, statement of centrality in the school, and the competencies the individual will possess as a result of involvement); (b) a rationale for program existence (guidance as an equal partner in the educational process); and (c) any assumptions (principles that shape the program). Program components include the guidance curriculum (goals and competencies to be developed in the program), individual planning (personal, educational, and appropriate grade-level career plans), responsive services (special help to students, counseling and remedial interventions), and system support (staff development, budget, community support, and individual planning activities).

2. *List student competencies.* In this process the counselor lists the competencies the guidance program will help students acquire. These include the knowledge, skills, and attitudes the students will develop as a result of their participation in the guidance program.

3. *Reaffirm policy support.* Starting with the building principal and working through the superintendent, the counselor will need to reaffirm the school district's support for the concepts in the design. With the help of the steering committee the counselor will next develop a policy statement. Again, the counselor will want the key individuals up through the school board to be part of the design. Since individuals work better toward goals that they have helped develop, working with key individuals along the way will simply help ensure program success.

4. *Establish parameters for resource allocation.* In this step the counselor is ready to define, in more concrete terms, the design of the program. This step is closely tied to the resources available. Will the design include only activities for which there is funding? In cases where existing programs are undergoing revision, some aspects of a comprehensive program may have to be delayed until additional resources are available. Also included in this process is the allocation of human resources. How much time can be allocated for counseling? for teachers? for other personnel?

    At this juncture the counselor will also need to define his or her own role. Discussions of the role of counselors at all levels has long been an issue in the field, and a move to comprehensive guidance programs will not make the issue go away. Gysbers and Henderson (1988) point out that a list of nine or ten duties will not suffice. They recommend instead that counselors develop position guides that describe the primary function of the job, its major responsibilities, key duties, organizational relationships, and performance standards. This description should include expectations of counselors' performance in teaching the guidance curriculum, counseling, consulting, referral, and other responses to specific needs and problems. It will also be important to define the role of all other individuals who work in the guidance program. As the program evolves, others such as teachers, parents, and volunteers should operate under role definitions. When the roles of others are not written down and agreed upon, then guidance can become whatever anyone in power in the school wishes it to be. More than one well-prepared counselor has been relegated to clerk status by a powerful principal who has his or her own view of what counselors should and should not do. The danger of this occurring in modern elementary and middle schools has not diminished. By dealing with the issue early on, the counselor may avoid pitfalls.

5. *Specify student outcomes.* A program based on specific student outcomes has, in the long run, a much greater chance of success than does one with a range of nebulous and largely unmanageable statements about hoped-for outcomes. Concepts such as understanding and respecting others, making wise choices, possessing problem-solving skills, and communicating effectively are appropriate outcomes. These goals should be stated in a manner that allows teachers, parents, and other professionals to understand them. A goal such as "all children will experience enhanced self-esteem and a more fluid way of relating to others" may well be understood by other counselors and by some teachers. To parents, however, it may say nothing. As the counselor's work progresses, she or he will want to develop specific *grade-level outcomes* and *school-level outcomes.* Once developed, everyone impacted by the outcomes and competences, including the guidance steering committee and the school administrative staff, should review them.

6. *Specify activities by components.* The next step in the process is to define the major emphases and the major activities in each component of the program. For each of the components of the guidance curriculum, these include the scope and sequence of the program and a restatement of the student outcomes expected for each. In the individual planning component, the task is one of defining the major activities that assist students to make individual plans. These plans may be educational and/or appropriate career plans. Individual planning activities are the ones that have been traditionally a part of most guidance programs. In the area of responsive services, counselors and others involved should identify the topics that students, teachers, and parents usually present. These will then allow for the development of a systematic means of addressing these concerns. An example would be a listing of the concerns that seem to impede normal personal, academic, social, or career development. Topics may include divorce, child abuse, causes of school failure, discipline, family situations, and peer pressures. Once identified, school personnel can develop a system for addressing each of these.

   System support is also important. This aspect has two parts: the support *needed* by the guidance effort and the support *provided* by the guidance effort. The support needed by the guidance program includes appropriate school policies and administrative procedures related to guidance. It also includes the areas of staffing, budget, facilities, and equipment. The support the guidance effort provides to other programs includes consulting, referrals, staff development, working with special populations, discipline, and curriculum.

7. *Write down and distribute the description of the desired program.* This is the final step in the design process. If the other steps have been completed, then the program in a unified form should be put in writing and shared with all who are concerned. The finished design should be reviewed in detail and revised by the steering committee, the school administration, teachers, and others it may impact. The school board should also review and approve final revision. In this way, the plan will have a better chance of "being owned" by the power structure. Gysbers and Henderson (1988) recommend that the final version contain five parts: the

structural components, the position guides, the program components, the recommended design/resource allocation for the program, and appendices. Note: The material for this section was both quoted and adapted from *Developing and Managing Your School Guidance Program* by Norman Gysbers and Patricia Henderson. The book should be consulted in its entirety for a complete discussion.

Implementing the Program

While careful planning and design are essential steps in guidance program development, the task of implementation also requires additional planning and a dedicated effort on the part of all concerned. Again, all counselors must remember that individuals work towards goals that they have had some say in developing. Hence, in this phase, as well as the others, all who are part of guidance or impacted by the process must be kept constantly informed and involved as much as possible. Lest we forget, teachers and administrators have additional agendas, and guidance may be only a part of what they deem important. Counselors, therefore, must be proactive in their implementation efforts.

A number of potential program improvements should come to the fore as a result of the organizing, planning, and designing process. The counselor can use guidelines developed in these components to decide on priorities and how they will be met. The counselor will use the goals that have been established to provide parameters for all improvement plans.

Implementation of a program works best when plans are developed for an entire school year. It will be helpful if the overall plan is broken down into monthly and weekly segments that direct the delivery of the guidance program as well as specialized counseling services.

Gysbers and Henderson (1988) suggest a transition planning stage as the school moves into a new program. Using Northside Independent School District in San Antonio, Texas, as a model, they recommend that counselors carefully analyze their present programs in order to gather appropriate data that will enable them to compare and contrast any elements in the present program with those that are not yet in place. This will provide counselors with an assessment of where programs overlap and where there are obvious gaps that require attention. By engaging in this discrepancy analysis, counselors will be able to determine the placement of resources. For example, if counselors are spending a small percentage of time in activities related to the guidance curriculum and an identified goal is the increase of time in that component, decisions that direct the counselor's attention to that component will probably need to be made. If additional resources are not available or forthcoming, counselors may decide to reduce the time spent in the responsive or individual planning aspects of the program in favor of more teaching of the guidance curriculum.

The discrepancy analysis process should be a positive experience for all involved with the program. With the help of teachers, parents, administrators, and others, the counseling staff should now be ready to create activities that it has been determined are of major importance. If, for example, a discrepancy analysis shows that very few students are ever counseled, you may want to study the responsive component of the program. Further analysis may reveal that the school offers little or no group counseling. In this instance, a newly created activity could be the initiation of developmental counseling groups for various grade and age levels. Other priorities calling for different activities could emerge in the support system aspect of the program or in the guidance curriculum.

It is perhaps redundant to suggest that all activities be carefully planned, but lack of planning has been a major historical weakness in many guidance programs, particularly those developed shortly after the inception of the NDEA Institutes and based on a problem-centered program of services model. All planning should be based on high-priority needs in the local school system as these needs relate to the overall developmental goals. A good plan will contain objectives linked to student guidance outcomes.

Program Evaluation

Gysbers and Henderson (1988) indicate that evaluation is not something done in the very last step of program revision. Rather, it is an ongoing process that provides continuous feedback during all phases of the program. The major purpose of evaluation is to provide data for the necessary decisions about program structure and future developments.

Trotter (1991) recommends a context-level evaluation which is used to describe current practice, characterize the student-client population, inventory human, financial, material, equipment, and political resources presently available to the program, and assess consumer needs. In this design, the counselor can assess current practices by using information from counselor logs that describes the nature and frequency of student-client contacts, job descriptions, student and consumer surveys, selected interviews with individuals from consumer groups, and the use of time and task analysis procedures. Assessment of the consumers of the program includes a gathering of facts about counselor- and teacher-to-student ratios, general achievement levels, socioeconomic status, ethnic composition, attendance and dropout figures, and the prevalence of exceptionality.

Consumer needs may be evaluated by gathering data from the advisory committee, using a qualified staff of outside observers (consultants) familiar with elementary guidance, presenting open forums for the community, conducting structured interviews with consumers (parents, teachers, students, administrators), and implementing record reviews, criterion-referenced surveys, and follow-up studies (Trotter, 1991).

Counselors should have an outline of an evaluation plan to guide their efforts in program review and change. They can choose from a number of approaches. A plan designed by a study group for the Texas Education Agency recommends the following eight steps:

1. State the evaluation question.
2. Determine the audiences/uses for the evaluation.
3. Gather data to answer the questions.

4. Apply the predetermined standards.
5. Draw conclusions.
6. Consider the context.
7. Make recommendations.
8. Act on the recommendations.

(Texas Education Agency, 1991, p. 93)

The evaluation process will require more than the counselor's efforts alone. Since comprehensive, developmental programs involve all children and other professional personnel, the evaluation of guidance must involve all who use guidance activities and all who may be impacted by these activities.

A natural starting point for evaluation of guidance is to examine the stated goals and objectives. In addition, it is essential to also examine the staff who are charged with the delivery of the services. All goals and objectives listed for the program should be turned into research questions for the evaluation process. For example, if the goals suggested earlier in the chapter were to be the basis for evaluation, the research questions would be as follows:

1. Are our children experiencing positive feelings from teachers, parents, and peers?
2. Is learning meaningful for our children?
3. Are our children developing positive self-images?
4. Are our children becoming more aware of their personal values and the values necessary to live in a pluralistic society?
5. Are our children developing the necessary academic skills?
6. Are our children developing planning, problem-solving, and goal-setting skills?
7. Are our children developing coping skills?
8. Are our children developing positive attitudes toward life?
9. Is there evidence that our children are developing responsibility for their own behavior?
10. How effective is our program for parents?
11. How effective are our efforts with teachers in the enhancement of learning?

Even the neophyte evaluator will be able to see that the evaluation of guidance cannot be a one-time, finished product. Many guidance activities are part of a long-term process and must be viewed as such. An assessment of a child's self-image done in September may be quite different from an additional assessment done in May, particularly if the child has been actively involved in the guidance program. Evaluators should also note that guidance goals are generally stated in broad terms, and a given goal may require two or more research designs in order to gather appropriate data for decision making. Again, it is essential that evaluation be considered a regular process that is part of the ongoing program in a manner similar to the guidance curriculum and the counseling program. The data needed will be related to the kinds of goals being measured. In some cases, the evaluation process may require a simple counting or a perceptual check of consumers' opinions. For example, the number of contact hours spent in group counseling or in the teaching of the guidance curriculum will provide quantitative data for evaluation purposes.

Qualitative data may be more difficult to measure. Assessing client satisfaction (teacher, parent, child) of various components of the counseling program is one way to determine the quality of a given effort. In a similar vein, the counselor may want to survey the children in the school to determine if they feel that they are generally receiving positive feelings from others (peers, teachers, parents). Then by simply computing frequencies and percentages of children who are and who are not experiencing positive feelings, the counselor can evaluate those aspects of the program designed to promote positive feelings. This review could cause the counselor to add, enhance, or delete some guidance activities. Based on these kinds of data, the counselor might decide to increase group counseling efforts, add new units to the guidance curriculum, or develop special programs for teachers and parents.

Counselors may also want to determine program effectiveness by measuring whether guidance programming has had any positive impact on consumers. For example, suppose counselors are concerned with enhancing the self-esteem of children in grades five and six. They could use a standardized instrument such as the *Children's Self-Concept Scale* or the *Coopersmith Self-Esteem Inventory* as a pretest measure. Once they have gathered and reviewed this data, counselors may want to design activities to improve the self-images of children. After they have implemented the activities, counselors could use the same instruments again, to determine whether or not the guidance activity conducted had any impact on the self-esteem of children. This simple design is widely used in numerous research designs in education and psychology.

In the evaluation process, counselors should not overlook single case studies. For example, suppose Mr. Radcliff, a teacher new to the school, seeks the counselor's help because he is encountering difficulties with classroom management. The new teacher feels the need to do a better job in "discipline" and indicates that much of his time is spent in attempts to control the class. He feels that the learning suffers because valuable teaching time is spent on "problem children." In a developmental program, Ms. Arnold, the counselor, may choose to observe the class, discuss her observations with the teacher, and help plan some activities to deal with Mr. Radcliff's concerns. She would not automatically begin by counseling the "problem kids," although this is an option that she might choose later. How does one evaluate this important counselor activity? A good starting point may be simply an assessment of how the teacher feels about the counselor interventions. Does he consider her work helpful? Why or why not? After the counselor interventions, are there fewer disruptions in class? Is the learning climate any better? By keeping careful records of what transpired between teacher and counselor, it is possible to make at least a subjective evaluation of one component of a developmental program. In a similar way, the counselor can use subjective evaluations of direct work with a parent or parents or with children for evaluation purposes. Counselors will not only want to maintain records on how many times consumers are seen, they will also want to keep records on progress of individuals.

Counselors should have a general plan or outline that includes local goals. The Texas Education Agency (1991) and other professional groups suggest four general areas of guidance evaluation:

1. How effective have program improvements been?
2. Does the program meet the program standards?
3. Have students become competent in the high-priority content areas?
4. How well are counselors performing their roles?

In the program improvement area, counselors should list objectives and strategies to be accomplished. These objectives should then be organized into a series of tasks that are to be accomplished in a given period of time. This will provide data on which objectives were met and which were not. Those not met may call for a change of strategy or a different process altogether.

Program standards have both a qualitative and a quantitative dimension. In the quantitative domain, counselors should note the numbers of contacts with parents, teachers, and children. Qualitative evaluations are those that show the outcomes or how well the standard was met. Stated another way, a quantitative evaluation might report, "The counselor met with 67 children in October and November." A qualitative statement may read, "Both parents and teachers generally expressed satisfaction with the program at two recent PTA meetings." While not all reports will be as positive as this one, counselors who take the time to evaluate may be pleasantly surprised about the impact of their work with individual children.

Student competencies may be evaluated by examining both cognitive and affective dimensions. Test scores, inventories, observations, case studies, pretest/posttest comparisons, goal attainment scaling, and follow-up interviews can all be used to assess competencies. For example, guidance directors may evaluate counselors by determining how well they are meeting job performance standards. Using a job description as a guide, directors employing performance evaluations can help counselors make maximum use of their professional skills. For example, one aspect of the counselor's job could be evaluated as follows:

Evaluation Question. Does the developmental group counseling meet local, state, and national standards for group work?

Target Audiences. Counselors, teachers, administrators, parents.

Data Gathering Methods. Interviews, reports, records, observations, professional peer review, self-reports, parent and teacher opinion data, and outside observer comments.

Standards. Indicators of performance, competencies.

Conclusions. Overall rating of the developmental group counseling program based on the data gathered for the evaluation.

Special Considerations. Experience level of the counselor, length of time the program was conducted, nature of the counseled groups (children with normal concerns or deeper problems), availability of children for balanced counseling groups.

Recommendations. Ratings to include the strengths and weaknesses of the program. Special emphasis on suggestions for improvement.

Plan of Action. All steps that are necessary for continued improvement. (For example, a workshop to increase group counseling skills for counselors.)

All aspects of the program may be evaluated using a plan similar to the one presented here.

A final step in evaluation is the determination of who will review the data gathered in the evaluation process. Obviously, all counselors and the director of guidance will want to review the findings. In some cases, it may be useful to have other professionals, such as teachers, review the findings and provide additional input. The school district administration or perhaps the building administrator are also likely recipients of evaluation studies.

It is worth repeating that the purpose of evaluation is for program improvement. Counselors who plan, organize, and implement a comprehensive program of guidance have little to fear from evaluations. In fact, most will probably enjoy learning that their efforts are generally perceived as being useful to guidance consumers. In reviewing data gathered for evaluations, counselors should focus on what they are doing well and then review the areas that need improvement.

One theme among authors who have developed comprehensive guidance programs is that new or expanding programs must not be considered as a group of loosely related adjunct services. In addition, there appears to be a high degree of consensus about how a new program or a revised one should proceed in making changes. For example, Jeanne Collet, writing in an *ERIC/CAPS Fact Sheet* (1983), proposes the following five guidelines for new comprehensive programs:

1. *Build on existing programs.* Evolution is not as costly as complete renovation.
2. *Use teamwork.* Parents, teachers, administrators, and members of the community all have skills and insights to offer guidance.
3. *Determine outcomes.* Counselors need to determine what are desirable student outcomes. Once a list of these has been developed, different guidance consumer groups (parents, teachers, administrators) should review it. Plans for priority outcomes may then be determined, and counselors will have valuable input data to determine priority outcomes.
4. *Program activities should be designed around desired student outcomes.* For each desired student outcome, counselors should design a model of the stages through which students must progress in order to reach the final outcome stage. The counselor should develop activities to help students reach that stage and include evidence that the students are mastering the skills and concepts inherent in these activities.
5. *Develop an ongoing evaluation system.* Evaluation is an ongoing process. (pp. 1, 2)

For the reader who may just be entering the counseling profession, the logic of Gysbers, Henderson, Collet, Hargens, the Texas Education Agency, and others may seem obvious. Neophytes may wonder how else a comprehensive program could be organized. Readers should be aware, however, that the ideas these authors are expressing represent an evolution from what was considered sound elementary guidance in the 1960s. During the 1960s and previously, very little was written about guidance curriculum, and individual planning was not suggested as part of the counselor's work in the elementary school (Muro, 1968; Faust, 1968; Hatch & Costar, 1961). Under the original "Three C" model for elementary and middle school guidance (counselors as consultants, coordinators, and counselors), most counselor functions were in the guidance component now called the responsive mode, primarily in the area of individual problem-centered counseling. While a modicum of systems support was generally provided by counselors, it was generally approached from the perspective of one problem or another in the lives of children.

Perhaps the greatest departure from the earlier elementary and middle school guidance programs is in the area of a guidance curriculum. As authors and writers began to embrace a developmental philosophy for elementary school, they began to conceptualize ways that would involve more adults in the guidance program. Dinkmeyer's *Developing Understanding of Self and Others* (*DUSO* and *DUSO II*) (Dinkmeyer, 1970, 1973) and Glasserian classroom meetings (Glasser, 1968) are examples of the movement to expand guidance beyond the counselor's office. New and improved materials are still very much a part of the modern guidance curriculum. *Grow with Guidance* (Radd, 1990) is an example of sequenced, prepared guidance activates.

One problem for counselors with limited budgets, however, is that much of the commercially produced material may be beyond the financial resources available to the school. In addition, some counselors prefer to create materials that focus on locally relevant issues or significant events. For example, Kline and Vernon (1986) suggested that commercially produced materials may not be useful for children in a given locale. A plant closing where parents of children lose jobs is an example of an event that will require the development of local materials.

Kline and Vernon (1986) outlined a six-step model for the creation of locally produced activities. Their plan involves developing, experiencing, publishing, processing, generalizing, and applying specific objectives.

For each activity counselors develop, they first should attempt to determine exactly what students are expected to learn from the experience. They list these outcomes in the form of behavioral objectives. If, for example, the activity deals with feelings, counselors may want to specify that students engaged in the activity will learn five new feeling words. For each twenty to forty minute activity, counselors should have two objectives.

Once the objectives have been determined, counselors move on to the experiencing stage. Children participate in activities that stimulate ideas related to the objective. Continuing the example above, the counselor would design activities that would help children explore ideas related to feelings. Role playing, reflection, and problem-solving and decision-making activities could be used to facilitate their experiences.

The publication phase has the goal of "bringing to the surface, thoughts, feelings, and behavioral reactions, about the experiencing phase" (Kline & Vernon, 1986, p. 24). This phase should also reflect the objectives of the exercise. At this point counselors ask appropriate questions, such as, "What were your feelings when you were playing the role of the teacher?" Part of this process is determining whether the reactions meet the objectives. There are a number of ways to determine this by written or oral responses or responses to specific items on an inventory. The counselor designs the activity so that all participants get the opportunity to display their ideas.

The next two steps involve process and generalization. In the process phase, the counselors may choose to summarize the responses and identify themes, particularly those that reflect universalization mechanisms in the group. Counselors may then ask additional questions to help students draw their own conclusions about the material.

The generalization phase includes counselor efforts to present concepts that will help students organize and understand the experiences. Themes about common experiences are also useful at this juncture. The counselor will summarize and cap discussion themes to bring about better self-understanding, awareness of more thoughts and feelings, and the learning of behavioral consequences.

In the final or application phase, students practice skills and learn how to apply these skills to individual situations. An example of a counselor intervention in this phase may be to ask, "How would you express your feelings if you were angry at a friend?" (Kline & Vernon, 1986, p. 26).

The range and scope of locally developed guidance activities are limited only by the imagination of the counselor. For illustrations of counselor-developed activities, see Appendix I.

Developmental Guidance and Significant Other Professionals

Myrick (1987) notes that it is a mistake to think of guidance and counseling as the private domain of counselors. If one accepts the contention that developmental guidance is for all children, then it follows that other professional and nonprofessional adults will have a role in the guidance process. Myrick provides a list that outlines a wide range of specific duties for principals, counselors, teachers, social workers, career or occupational specialists, school psychologists, and social workers. Of course, only the larger or the most wealthy districts will have the benefit of such a cadre of professionals, but if a district is lucky enough to employ this range of specialists, then it is essential to delineate the roles of each.

A word of caution, however, should be expressed here. Numerous guidance texts and articles in professional journals seem to focus on the roles of other professionals who may work with counselors. One concern, of course, is that guidance professionals who are suggesting role and function descriptions for other professionals rarely bother to consult with the other professional groups to determine whether they see their roles the same way. Counselors or the counseling profession simply cannot "lay on" a role description for a principal, teacher, or psychologist. The very best that can be done when two professionals seem to have concerns over who does what with whom is to talk directly with that professional to determine roles that are agreeable to all involved. To say that a principal should provide encouragement and support for guidance is a given, but all others who report to the principal also expect her or him to provide the same kind of support for their areas.

In the recent past, conflicts between counselors and principals were not uncommon, and not unexpected. One must remember that principals are prepared in departments of educational administration, and their views on guidance may well be influenced by professors of educational administration. Aspiring principals enrolled in graduate classes in supervision may be taught a very different version of guidance than aspiring counselors enrolled in departments of counselor education! In determining the counselor's role or the role of others at the building or district level, communication among groups is essential.

Counselors who are newly hired in a school or in a district would be wise to have a carefully structured discussion with the building principal or the superintendent or both before signing any contracts. The counselor may find it far easier to resolve problems at the contract negotiation stage than later, when he or she discovers that a program they may want to implement is not part of the principal's value system. In a similar vein, counselors have no more right to tell teachers, principals, psychologists, or social workers what their roles should be than other professionals do in determining the counselor's role!

Again, interaction, as early as possible, is the key to program harmony. A good starting point is to review the total school objectives and the objectives of guidance, psychology, special education, and other specialty areas. Next should come an assessment of what skills all individuals possess, what philosophies guide their practice, and what their strengths may be. For example, school psychologists who claim disruptive children as their chief concern will probably make most developmentally oriented counselors very happy.

Almost nothing will cause guidance personnel to become "persona non grata" in a school faster than the overexuberance of a well-meaning but unsophisticated counselor who delights in defining the role of all others in relation to the role of the counselor. In most cases, other professionals will have only a minimal understanding of guidance or counseling and almost no understanding of developmental guidance. Well-informed counselors will see their very first job in the school as one of interaction on an equal basis with all other professionals. Interaction, in turn, develops group cohesion, and group cohesion is essential if a mutuality of goals is to be reached. We are not implying that counselors should simply sit back and let others determine what the counselor should do, since almost certainly the counselor would be relegated to a heavy dose of problem children. Counselors must be proactive in describing their skills, but they must do so in a way that is not arrogant or condescending. Remember, many teachers, principals, and special educators have advanced degrees also, and they just may view the world through a different set of spectacles.

Principals

The very best thing that a principal can do for guidance is to be supportive of the program. In spite of the fact that counselors sometimes want to be considered as "positive agents of change," the reality of public education is that little takes place in most schools without principal approval. Principals can provide a great deal of support by enlisting faculty help with the guidance program, and in some cases becoming an active participant in some phase of the program. Of course the principal is the allocator of resources, both human and material, and he or she should work with the counselor to determine that the resources are wisely used. Evaluation of the program and the counselor's performance also involves the principal.

Even if the principal is not or will not be an active participant in some aspect of the guidance program, counselors should work hard to ensure that the principal is "the guidance voice in many chambers." Principals, by the nature of their jobs, interact with other principals, and perhaps with the superintendent in the district. They may also be part of an administrative council that makes key policy decisions. Principals who support guidance will understand it and may work with the counselor on the guidance team, but most of all they will be vocal supporters of the guidance program to all other inside and outside groups. Counselors need to remember that principals wear many hats and that there are many functionaries in the school who want to help them and the teaching staff. The most effective principals will be able to separate the contributions of the various specialists to meet the school goal of optimum student learning.

Teachers

Next to counselors, teachers are the most critical element in the implementation of a comprehensive guidance program. Their position in the classroom is such that they are a significant, and at times the most significant, adult to promote learning and positive self-development in students. Teacher effectiveness is clearly related to how open teachers are to individual needs of children and how highly they value the overall development of their students. At best, non-guidance-oriented teachers will only minimally participate in the guidance program; at worst, they may present serious hindrances.

Without teacher involvement, developmental guidance is simply one more good, but unworkable, concept. Teachers must see the importance of positive student self-images and respect individual student differences to become actively involved with the guidance program. Teachers are the first line of defense in the identification of special needs, the key advisors to children, and the best hope of providing personalization of learning. They are learning monitors and work closely with parents on academic matters. At times, teachers will refer children who need special help to the counselor. Other times, teachers and counselors will become a joint exploration team to try and discover ways to help the child without removing him or her from the classroom. Here again, counselors must speak *with* teachers, not *to* them. Teacher involvement in any guidance activities is directly related to their perception of the value of the guidance program and the competence of the counselors.

School Psychologists and School Social Workers

School psychologists have been labeled as diagnostic experts for decades, but some school psychologists view the development of elementary guidance as a direct invasion of "their" territory. This may be especially true in schools where the major focus of elementary and middle school guidance is problem-centered intervention.

In general, school psychologists are equipped, or should be equipped, to provide intensive individual and group counseling for children with serious concerns. They are also prepared to serve as referral agents for children who need the services of a mental health agency or the specialized help of a clinical psychologist or psychiatrist. Myrick (1987) also notes that the school psychologist should "organize, lead, and take an active role in child study teams, particularly those staffing regarding exceptional children, and their educational placement (i.e. P.L. 94–142)" (p. 49).

Clearly, from a guidance perspective, work with children with major problems and individual and group therapy (as opposed to individual and group counseling) are the domain of the school psychologist. Some school psychologists, however, reject the notion that therapy of any kind should be provided by schools. In addition, some school psychologists are developmentally oriented, are prepared in programs similar to those that prepare school counselors, and state that their major role is working with the "normal and less troubled child." One may see why the good interaction among professionals suggested earlier may be necessary. In some schools there may not be a school psychologist; in some communities, there may not be any mental health agencies. If so, the counselor may be the only trained person available to work with some troubled children.

Social Workers

Historically most social workers have worked with needy families and have coordinated guidance activities between the school and home. In addition they have served as a liaison between the school and public health and rehabilitation agencies. These professionals have also studied individual students and their family situations. In this work they provide some information that may be appropriate for guidance and counseling intervention (Myrick, 1987).

Social workers have always been perceived as individuals who may be school-based, but who work mainly outside the school with needy and troubled families. They tend to be well prepared in case study approaches and can gather and provide valuable information that may be of use in developing the guidance program.

In general, the roles of social workers and counselors have not experienced as much overlap as have the counselor-psychologist roles. However, some social workers also see elementary and middle school guidance as being in direct competition with what they do, even when the differences in goals and process may be different. Some social workers do individual and group counseling with children and parents. Some work directly with teachers in providing information gathered in home visits. In some states, such as Connecticut, social workers were employed by schools long before schools hired counselors.

As with psychologists, social workers have a contribution to make. The specifics of the contribution depend on the availability of other specialists, the history of specialists in a given school district, and the school and community perception of what is wanted from school specialists. In this context, it may not be useful to define the role of other specialists in books designed to be read by counselors. Rather it is essential that counselors begin and maintain a continued dialogue with their peers, both at the building level, and at the level of professional associations. There is much to be done. There is room for all.

CONCLUSION

Developmental guidance is not a new concept, but some of the practices associated with it are. Members of the guidance profession had long laid claim to the concept that our particular niche in the mental health world was with the normal child. Our goals were the development of the full potential, rather than any kind of remedial assistance.

Perhaps the last frontier for developmental guidance is in our elementary schools. Programs at this level were introduced into the schools relatively recently and, for the most part, are still evolving. In essence, developmental guidance reaffirms our professional commitment to guidance for all children, our interest in human learning, and our belief that other professionals must be involved in guidance. Developmental guidance should have a planned curriculum; it is strength and goal-oriented, and it is based on the view of children as in the process of becoming. Guidance, therefore, does not look for final conclusions, but rather it marks progress toward adulthood. It attempts to help all children derive personal meaning from what they are learning and to feel good about doing so. It stresses self-enhancement, a positive view of self, and the development of personal values. Guidance helps children cope with challenges, develop goals, plan, and assume responsibility for themselves. Implementation of developmental guidance in the schools involves organizing, planning, designing, implementing, and evaluating the overall program.

As guidance evolves, counselor roles may change, and in fact they have changed since the 1960s. Counselors now provide help in developing a guidance curriculum, engage in individual planning, work in responsive services, and provide systems support. Emerging guidance programs must maintain cognizance of the roles of other specialists in the schools as they evolve. In general, a developmental approach seems to be the very best vehicle for meeting our expressed goals.

REFERENCES

Collet, J. B. (1983). *Comprehensive program design.* Ann Arbor, MI: ERIC/CAPS.

Dinkmeyer, D., & Dreikurs, R. (1963). *Encouraging children to learn: The encouragement process.* Englewood Cliffs, NJ: Prentice Hall.

Dinkmeyer, D. (1970). *Developing understanding of self and others. (DUSO).* Circle Pines, MN: American Guidance Service.

Dinkmeyer, D. (1973). *Developing understanding of self and others. (DUSO II).* Circle Pines, MN: American Guidance Service.

Faust, V. (1968). *History of elementary school guidance: Overview and critique.* Boston: Houghton Mifflin.

Glasser, W. (1968). *Schools without failure.* New York: Harper & Row.

Gysbers, N. C., & Henderson, P. (1988). *Developing and managing your school guidance program.* Washington, D.C.: American Association for Counseling and Development.

Hatch, R., & Costar, W. (1961). *Guidance services in the elementary school.* Dubuque, IA: Wm. C. Brown.

Henderson, P. (1988). A comprehensive school guidance program at work. *Texas Association for Counseling and Development Journal, 15,* 25–27.

Kline, W. B., & Vernon, A. (1986). A design process for elementary school guidance activities. *Elementary School Guidance and Counseling, 21,* 23–26.

Muro, J. (1968). *The counselor's work in the elementary school.* Scranton, PA: International.

Myrick, R. (1987). *Developmental school guidance and counseling: A practical approach.* Minneapolis, MN: Educational Media.

Radd, T. (1990). *Grow with guidance.* Canton, OH: Grow with Guidance.

Texas Education Agency. (1991). *A comprehensive program for Texas public schools.* Austin, TX: Texas Education Agency.

Trotter, T. (1991). *Walking the talk: Developing a local comprehensive school counseling program.* Moscow, ID: University of Idaho.

Worzbyt, J. C., & O'Rourke, K. (1980). *Elementary school counseling.* Muncie, IN: Accelerated Development.

Chapter Four

Initiating Counseling

In their 1977 book, Muro and Dinkmeyer noted that counseling and the counseling profession were poorly understood by parents, teachers, administrators, and children. While understanding of the profession has improved, there is still a need to orient potential users of counseling to the nature of the process. In spite of intensive efforts by counselors to explain what they do and why, some potential users still view counseling as something that is somehow done with individuals who are "crazy" or severely troubled (Nugent, 1990).

In one sense, we have unwittingly fostered this image of counseling through our own professional literature. In most of our journals, the greatest percentage of articles are written about problem situations. One can find an abundance of material, for example, on working with individuals afflicted with AIDS or suggestions for working with people addicted to some form of chemical substance. Articles related to normal development, to fulfillment of potential and to enhancing the lives of others are more difficult to find. Even the programs at our regional and national conventions seem to stress the nature of the counselor's work in dealing with the troubled. This is not to argue that such topics are unimportant, for indeed they are. However, one could also argue that we have strayed far afield from the original purposes of our profession (Muro, 1991).

While counselors should and must work with troubled children in elementary and middle schools, they also have goals that are more broadly defined, and these goals include activities that are more developmentally oriented. If counseling is to remain as an integral and viable aspect of the counselor's job, counselors must continue their efforts to have others understand who they are. Children, teachers, parents, and administrators will not use the services of counselors if they do not understand the nature of counseling. Counselors, therefore, must be prepared to provide administrators, parents, teachers, and children with a clear and concise explanation of their services.

Orientation to Counseling

Establishing the Program with Administrators

The knowledge of guidance and counseling possessed by school administrators will vary. In general, school administrators do not enroll in graduate schools with extensive experience in counseling or related fields. The authors urge counselors to carefully develop plans to provide a process for informing the school administration of what is taking place in the counseling program and why (Nugent, 1990). Counselors should *not* assume that principals know about counseling or that they share counselors' views about counseling goals and outcomes. It is the fortunate counselor who works with a principal with an understanding of counseling.

If counselors' goals and those of the principal are divergent, conflict may result. Counselors who may be doing a thoroughly professional job may find that administrators have a different view of how well the counseling program is functioning. It is not uncommon, for example, for some principals to view counselors as those who handle all the difficult discipline cases. The expectation is that counselors will "cure" the behavioral disorders of disruptive children, or at least contain them so that they do not become major concerns for the principal.

Other administrators seek to use the counselor as a junior member of the administrative team. Some will readily assign counselors to bus duty, to teach classes, or to lunchroom monitoring and scheduling duties. Having spent a number of years in public education, the authors have learned that defining the counselor's role in isolation may not be fruitful. Unless counselors and administrators negotiate the job expectations, the role of counselors could well be decided by the principal. Counselors who do not develop a process to inform and guide administrative thinking should be prepared to accept some duties that they may consider to be outside their professional functions.

Counseling, if it is to be successful, *must have administrative support.* From time to time, you may read articles that call for an "activist counselor" to be the school's designated change agent, advocate for human rights, and champion of all that is good and necessary for children. All of these are lofty and honorable goals, but the reality of public education is that the climate in the school and the nature of the academic and counseling programs will most likely be impacted by the philosophical orientation of the administrator, not the counselor.

Administrators tend to make decisions based on information and data, or at least they should. It is the job of the counselor to provide the administrator with a continuous flow of "counseling" data. Failure to do so may result in an ineffective or weak counseling program (Muro & Dinkmeyer, 1977).

The first step in initiating a solid and professional principal-counselor relationship is a frank, honest exchange between the counselor and principal *before* the counselor actually accepts the position. During the job interview, the prospective counselor should attempt to clarify the principal's perception of counseling. What does the principal expect? Does she or he expect that the counselor will deal only with behavioral problems? Does he or she expect that the counselor will be able to "solve" these problems?

Neophyte counselors must pay close attention to what the principals say and how they say it. Do they talk more than they listen? Do they relate what is expected with little or no counselor input? What support will be provided? What are the expectations for work with teachers and parents? Is there any understanding of a developmental point of view, or is the counselor perceived as an "academic casualty" advisor who spends time placing band-aids on classroom problems? Do principals ask a series of "Don't you think" questions? This is a sure clue that they have already formulated answers and are seeking to discover if the counselor agrees with them.

A counselor should discuss the following items with administrators, preferably before taking a new counseling position. In fact, it is essential for counselors and principals to reach agreement on some basic issues prior to signing a contract. Counselors who are established should review job descriptions with the principal at least once each school year.

1. *Determine the budget for the overall guidance program.* Is it adequate to meet the goals of the program? Is it adequate to meet the expectations of the program? Determine details of the budget. Counseling facilities, working hours, and the availability of secretarial help are best negotiated at the initial meeting. Most school budgets become "set" soon after school opens, and counselors who do not prepare for their needs early may not be able to obtain support for key elements of their programs at a later time during the year (Muro, 1991).

2. *Be sure to present guidance in general, and counseling in particular, as vital parts of the total educational process.* Show how counseling is closely related to the primary objective of the school—that of student learning.

3. *Determine whether the principal accepts the concept of developmental guidance.* Stress the fact that while counselors do work with troubled children, counseling should be available for all children.

4. *Stress the active involvement of teachers in the program.* Show how teachers can be classroom "counselors" through the use of guidance techniques. Explain that counseling is most effective when it is a cooperative process involving teachers, counselors, parents, and administrators.

5. *Outline how counselors can work with parents and other individuals in the community to enhance the school's image as well as its learning activities.* Good guidance programs are one of the very best approaches to good public relations.

6. *Be certain to obtain a written agreement of the role and function of counselors in the total school program.* Prepare a description of how you perceive the role of counselor and try to obtain agreement from the principal. (In some instances the counselor may be required to negotiate some aspects of the role.) The counselor should be prepared to compromise on some issues, but she or he may need to remain firm on others. For example, the counselor should not have disciplinary duties as part of his or her job description.

7. *Be certain to develop a schedule for at least weekly meetings with the principal.* Working with the principal is a process that must be continuous throughout the year.

8. *Determine what kinds of reports will be required.* What kind of paperwork is involved in the job? Determine how frequently the reports will be required.

9. *Get specific details on how counseling is to be evaluated.* What results does the principal expect? Who does the evaluation? What are the evaluative criteria?

Orientation of Parents and the Public

Many parents still do not have an adequate understanding of guidance, and most have an even poorer conceptualization of counseling. Few of today's parents had the services of an elementary school counselor or any counseling at all. Teachers and principals did most of the counseling prior to the 1980s. Hence, many parents still have a perception of schools and school programs as they may have existed in the 1980s or earlier.

While one would hope that counseling, as a formal program, is not considered a strange idea, some parents still view schools solely as the place for obtaining such skills as reading, writing, arithmetic, and social studies. Some parents consider development of healthy self-concepts and self-acceptance to be the responsibility of the home and church. They may believe that attitudes, interests, and values are more properly learned at home or in Sunday school than in school. In fact, in recent years some parents and members of some religious groups have actively opposed the presence of concepts that seem to deviate from preconceived notions of what schools should be doing.

Orientating parents to counseling, then, may be a difficult process. Counselors have shown that cultural norms in some part of our society tend to view seeking help as a form of weakness (Brammer, 1988). Orientation, then, must be continuous and well planned. A single appearance by the counselor before a parent-teacher group once a year is simply not sufficient to gain parental support for the program.

The most effective way to explain counseling to parents is through one-to-one conferences. For the most part, parents who have children in elementary and middle schools have a deep interest in their progress, and most will welcome individual discussions of their children. Individual conferences allow counselors to personalize the process and explain in detail what counseling is and perhaps how it can be of assistance to children. Again, counselors should not make the mistake of conveying to parents that counseling is only for "bad" or "poor" students. In fact, a good way for counselors to obtain parent support is to hold parent meetings to explain how counseling can help "good" students do even better (Muro, 1991).

A key objective of parent conferences is to provide adults with factual information about counseling (as well as other guidance services). This is the time for counselors to try and correct any misperceptions that parents may have about the counselor as one who works only with children in trouble. Parents need to know that discussions of the mind, emotions, or self-images are not indications that a child has some form of mental disorder. Counselors should explain who they are, say a few words about their specialized training, and stress that their purposes are more developmental and educational than "therapeutic."

All parents should receive a written list of the goals of counseling. If the counselor has a simulated tape of a developmental counseling session, it may help to share this with parents. A ten-minute role-played video can do wonders to help parents accept the value of counseling.* (See Appendix A.)

It is also essential to ensure that the public knows about counseling programs. Experienced counselors have long utilized the PTA, Kiwanis, Lions, Masons, Knights of Columbus, or other similar groups to explain and gain support for school counseling. Each of these organizations generally has a program chair who schedules programs.

The media, particularly local papers and radio and television stations, are also outlets that can provide the public with information about counseling. For example, some counselors provide the media with reports that show how many children have been counseled and how guidance activities such as classroom career exploration units are part of their program. In addition, some counselors keep information on the number of community contacts including home visits with parents.

Counselors should volunteer to speak to church groups as well as service groups whenever possible. Since local media professionals like to get a "home town" slant on national news, counselors should send a list of the topics that they are prepared to discuss to local editors and station managers. For example, the media may be interested in how local children are reacting to events such as Desert Storm or the tragedy of the massacre in Killeen, Texas. In a word, counselors should take every opportunity to be available for commentary on a wide range of events that may impact schools and children.

When dealing individually with the parent of one of the children in school, counselors should make every effort to provide data on the child's needs, abilities, limitations, and current level of functioning. Always initiate meetings by focusing on the strengths of the child (Muro, 1991). Convey your interest in helping *all* children. Parents should leave individual conferences with the conviction that you have taken a special interest in their child.

*Note: Tapes of transcripts or recordings of actual situations cannot ethically be used without proper permission.

Some schools send home negative reports to parents that often outline some area or areas wherein the child is not doing well. While these so-called "warning slips" are probably necessary to inform parents of problems when they may still be minor, the authors recommend that deficiency slips not be sent from the guidance office. Rather, they should come from the main office with a copy to the counselor.

Negative reports almost always produce defensive reactions in parents, and if they come from the guidance office, they tend to convey the idea that the counselor is the "failure" person in school. A far more effective approach is to work with teachers to help identify what children are doing well. Short notes stating what a given child has done well are very effective. A simple note such as, "I wanted you to know that Joey was very helpful on the playground today. He organized a softball game for the third graders that all of them thoroughly enjoyed. He is showing real leadership!" will go a long way in gaining parent support.

Finally, counselors should consider the creation of a parental guidance committee. This committee should be designed to help develop guidance activities. Membership should come from a wide cross-section of parents from all racial and ethnic segments of the community, and the chair should be a parent who commands community respect. A major objective of a parental guidance committee is to review and evaluate all parts of the guidance program.

Each year a subcommittee of this overall group should work with the counselor to outline monthly guidance and counseling objectives for the total school year. Once these objectives have been determined, the subcommittee should present the objectives to the total guidance committee. The committee should send a copy to the building principals and the district superintendent. Almost any area of guidance may be included in this report, and when the final document is approved it should be released to the media for publication. (It is useful to have a "media parent" on the guidance committee.)

Parental guidance committees can be useful in giving parents in a community a sense of "ownership" of the overall guidance program. Nothing is more effective than having parents rather than the counselor sing the praises of the values of guidance and counseling. In addition, these groups can be very useful if and when controversial issues involving counseling occur.

Orientation of School Personnel

One could reasonably assume that modern teachers have a fair understanding of guidance and counseling and how counselors work with teachers to meet established goals in the elementary and middle school. Unfortunately, such is not the case. In a recent survey of over one hundred elementary school teachers (Muro, 1992), the data revealed that few understood guidance and even fewer had much understanding about the nature of counseling. While some of the more experienced educators in the survey had a better grasp of what guidance is supposed to accomplish, most still felt that the number one objective of counseling is to provide specialized help to teachers, particularly with children who are considered to be classroom problems (Nugent, 1990).

In this sense, one must wonder about all the books and articles that have been written about the teacher's role in guidance during the past two or three decades. It would appear that most of these books and articles were written *by* counselors *for* counselors. Perhaps no one has bothered to ask teachers to read the articles. Even those teachers who do read them may take objection to suggestions by counselors that seem to detail what teachers should and should not do. If anything, elementary and middle school teachers do not lack for advice!

Perhaps professional counselors should not be surprised to learn that classroom teachers are not always completely knowledgeable about guidance and counseling (Muro, 1991). One need only examine the content of most required undergraduate courses in the elementary certification sequence to understand that guidance and counseling are only two of numerous topics that prospective teachers are required to study. Since elementary and middle school courses are not generally taught by counselor educators, guidance and counseling are often treated in a perfunctory manner.

Unless counselors are extremely lucky, they must assume the task of orientation of most teachers to the concept of guidance and counseling. Counselors should not assume that the provision of information alone will be sufficient to enlist and maintain the support of teachers for guidance programs. Rather than look out the window and ask what teachers can do for counseling, the astute elementary school counselor is one who peers in the window and asks "What can counseling do for the teachers?"

Most individuals will behave in ways that support what they value. Unless teachers "own" the values typically expressed by counselors, they are not likely to be supportive of the program. Ownership of a concept does not come from being told what to do; thus teachers must have an active voice in the development of guidance policies if good programs are to be developed. Cohesion is indeed a function of interaction, and the first step in the orientation of teachers is to discover as many ways as possible for counselors and teachers to interact on the basis of equality (Muro, 1991).

A key initial step in the orientation process of school personnel is the formation of a guidance committee (Duncan, 1989). This committee should deal specifically with guidance policy and procedures. One of its major purposes is to involve teachers and administrators in the guidance program. While this concept is not new, it is not put into effect nearly as often as one would imagine. Most busy counselors support the idea of a guidance committee, but some seem to put the formation of one on a back burner. To do so may be a serious mistake. In fact, as early as 1974, Ohlsen recommended that counselors form guidance committees to deal with all decisions that may have an impact on the teaching staff. Of key importance here is the ego involvement of the faculty in being able to be a part of the decision-making process. The recent national movement to site-based management systems in public schools is an example of the necessity of involving people in decisions that impact them.

If possible, counselors should attempt to develop systemwide guidance councils. If the system is relatively small, the council should have representatives from each school. In very large districts, several committees may need to be formed, and one representative of each committee should be a delegate to a larger regional council. Some activities typically of concern to guidance committees include the provision of new guidance services, development of child study approaches, in-service education, provision of testing, and evaluation of the total guidance program. The committee should be officially appointed by the building principal for a single school or by the superintendent in a large district. Counselors, of course, should have input into the selection of membership, and such factors as age, educational philosophy, balance of gender, and years of experience of committee members should be considered.

At times, counselors tend to ignore teachers who have an "anti guidance" point of view for service on the committee. The authors suggest that the very best way to foster positive guidance attitudes is to deliberately appoint some "anti" faculty to the committee. The interaction of other "positive" members will eventually create a group norm of support for guidance. In such an atmosphere, the one-time guidance opponent may well become a staunch supporter.

Since it will not be possible for the entire staff of a school to serve on a guidance committee at one time, the orientation of teachers must include a number of other activities. If the school has in-service or preschool meetings, the counselor should ask for time to tell the "counselors' story." Counselors should spend time outlining what they will do in that school, particularly those guidance activities that will provide teacher assistance. The counselor should explain how she or he hopes to be working with teachers, and indicate openness to a discussion of ways that the working relationship may be made most effective. The counselor should refrain from "preaching and telling" and instead take the position of a support person for the teaching staff. The counselor should ask for teacher permission, visit classrooms, once again stressing the fact that visits will occur when it is convenient to the teachers.

Counselors must make a direct effort to interact with the staff at all given opportunities. If the school has departments, the counselor should ask to attend departmental meetings. He or she could take time to eat lunch with different teachers each day, or get out of the office and visit the playground and lunch room.

Counselors should always be conscious of teachers' time. They should schedule meetings and conferences during time slots that are identified by teachers as most appropriate. Many teachers have precious little time to themselves, and additional requirements assigned by counselors may not be well received.

While teachers will be able to understand the counselor's philosophy from orientation talks and demonstrations provided for the counseling orientation for children, counselors should also be prepared to design additional activities for teachers. They may want to prepare a handout that briefly outlines what counseling can and cannot accomplish. They could outline counseling goals and make a strong attempt to show that counseling is a *process* and that many children will need to be seen frequently over a period of time before they show evidence of change. If time permits, counselors may want to role play a short counseling session. Above all, they must make the point that counseling is available for all children, and that they, as counselors, will be dealing with many of the children in the school. Counselors should be sure to stress that what they do is part of a collaborative relationship with teachers in an attempt to meet common goals. As with parents and administrators, the orientation activities are a process and as such they must be continuous throughout the school year (Muro & Dinkmeyer, 1977).

Orientation of Children

Most adult clients will approach counseling with a wide range of misconceptions about the process. Some may expect counseling to resemble a visit to a medical doctor (Meier & Davis, 1989). Children may have similar misconceptions. A number of researchers (Orlinsky & Howard, 1978; Hoehn-Saric et al., 1964; Mayerson, 1984) suggest a process labeled role induction or the use of certain procedures such as describing the procedure and discussing its effectiveness (Meier & Davis, 1989).

Muro and Dinkmeyer (1977) noted that most elementary school children and many middle school children have little or no understanding about the nature of school counseling. Even though the number of professional counselors working in elementary schools has increased exponentially since the late 1970s, counselors will still find it essential to conduct ongoing orientation programs for children. Most younger children have had no exposure to a counselor, and it is probably safe to assume that for the most part, the parents of children who are in schools today did not have a counselor when they themselves were in elementary school.

In Chapter 7 we have outlined a process for orientating children to group counseling. We have suggested the use of a portable stage and puppets to tell "the group counseling story." This technique, which also uses a coloring book to help explain what counselors do (see Appendix B), is equally as appropriate for an orientation program as for individual counseling. As noted in the group counseling chapter, children relate very well to puppets, and with the help of a prepared script, sessions that explain counseling in a nonthreatening way are very useful for helping children understand that the counselor is indeed a person who is there to help. (See Chapter 7 for a discussion of the use of a puppet program with a portable stage for orientation programs.)

In developing orientation programs for individual counseling, the counselor should start with the assumption that children possess little readiness for counseling. In addition, if there is any awareness at all about counseling, it tends to be negative (Brammer, 1988). Even the most skillful of counselors must be alert to counter the remedial or problem-centered image that is all too often assigned to what they do by some parents and teachers. A common mistake that some counselors make is to enter a new school and ask for teacher referrals. As one may expect, those counselors who ask for referrals will surely get their wish and much more! Almost all teachers have a list of children who they will readily send to the counselor. Their expectation, of course, is that counseling will somehow provide a "behavioral cure" for whatever seems to be troubling a child. While it is not unreasonable for teachers to expect such specialized help from counselors, a long list of troubled youngsters sent for counseling can pose a difficult task. In addition, the expectations of the teachers for behavioral changes in these referred children are frequently unrealistic. Unfortunately, teacher attitudes toward guidance are often formed on how well they perceive counselors are successful at "fixing" troubled children. Of course, the children will also learn that those who go for counseling are in some form of difficulty. Even young children may then see the counselor as simply the resident "shrink" (Muro & Dinkmeyer, 1977).

The task of the counselor, then, is one of developing a plan that will include children other than just those referred by teachers. We have noted several times in this book that counselors may be well advised to initiate both individual and group counseling with "stars," or those children who are perceived by peers as among the best students in the school. It is worth mentioning here once more that we feel the initial perceptions of what the counselor does may well dictate the nature of the overall guidance program. Seeing only troubled children is an indication of a counseling program that is strictly remedial in nature.

There are a number of things a counselor should do in the area of student orientation to counseling. Whether or not counselors use the puppet and stage technique or make verbal presentations to older elementary school children, some form of discussion outline (similar to that used in group counseling) is necessary.

The Counseling Office

Working with practicing school counselors over the past two decades has provided the opportunity for the authors to observe a wide range of counseling settings. While an impressive number of newly built elementary and middle schools, particularly those constructed in the 1980s and early 1990s, have provided space for school counselors, many of the older structures call for a considerable degree of counselor ingenuity if they are to find space for counseling purposes. In addition some counselors work in systems where they are responsible for a number of different school buildings and must "roam" from building to building on a daily or in some cases a weekly basis. We have

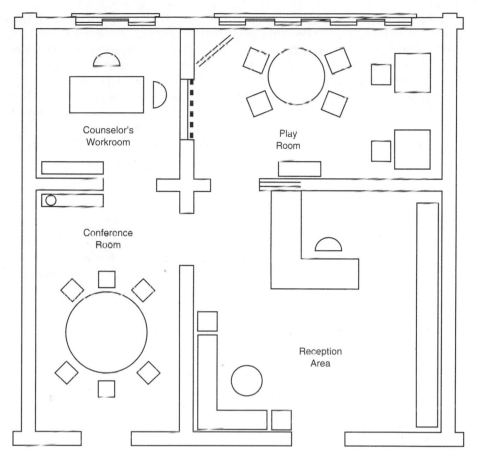

Figure 4.1
Ideal complex for
counseling

observed "guidance suites" that meet and exceed the model suggested in this book, and we have also watched counselors work in modified storage rooms or unused locker rooms. In some schools, hastily constructed partitions are the rule rather than the exception for counselor space.

With no end in sight for budget crunches, the suggestion of a guidance office like the one suggested in Figure 4.1 may be beyond the dreams of many counselors. However, we include the plan here, not because we are confident that all school counselors in the twenty-first century will enjoy such facilities, but rather to provide guidelines for an ideal situation.

The suggestions made by Muro and Dinkmeyer (1977) can still be used to guide counselors' thinking about what a counseling office should be. Ideally, an office should contain a minimum of at least 120 square feet, although 130 to 150 square feet is not unreasonable. The office should have at least one adjoining conference room of 160 square feet, and a playroom of 150 to 200 square feet for individual play sessions and an additional room of 300 to 400 square feet for group play and activity group approaches (Ginott, 1961).

If possible, counseling offices should be located in an area away from the principal's office. If the school has a vice principal who is the designated "disciplinarian," it is wise to keep the counselor at some distance from that office. Counseling should never be synonymous with discipline. Adequate lighting and the best soundproofing available should be primary considerations.

Office equipment should include a desk, chair, and appropriate furniture for both children and adults (Young, 1992). Other common essentials include a telephone, filing cabinets, a computer and printer, bookcases, paper and other supplies, and a large bulletin board. A tape recorder and a video camera and video cassette recorder are excellent tools that are widely used by elementary and middle school counselors.

Every effort should be made to keep the guidance office as bright and cheerful as possible. Children react well to bright warm colors and to a room where everything says "welcome." Counselors should actively solicit examples of children's art or other creative activities for placement on the walls. If the counselor uses children's art, she or he may want to send a short handwritten note to the parents of the young artists informing them of the fact that one of their children's creations was selected for display. This is a good public relations device.

Again, we are very much aware of the fact that the real and the ideal may never coincide. Yet, there are some counselors who do get the opportunity to have input into where they will work. It is in this spirit that the model in Figure 4.1 is presented.

The Initial Phase of Individual Counseling

Regardless of how well counselors have conducted their orientation programs for children, they can expect a wide range of differences about how children will react, especially during the initial stages of the counseling process. For example if Ms. Simpson refers one of her students for counseling and does not tell him or her why, this may pose a particular set of problems for the counselor. In this instance, the child may or may not have a concern. In fact, the child may be perfectly happy with the way he or she is now behaving in school. In other words the child does not "own" any problem, and indeed the problem may well lie with the one who referred the child (Brammer, 1988).

Acting-out children may well be behaving to meet their needs in ways that adults consider inappropriate, but if the child is obtaining peer recognition from classroom antics, he or she may be reluctant to give up that behavior, especially if it is their major way of feeling part of the classroom group (Thompson & Rudolph, 1992). In such cases, the counselor must be convinced that the child does indeed have a problem and get the child to agree that she or he has a problem. If this happens the counselor must then convince the child to change his or her behavior, presumably in the direction that the principal or the teacher wants the behavior to change. Obviously this is not the way most counselors want to work with children, but such situations are not uncommon. In fact, when teachers express disenchantment with counselors, it is generally because for one reason or another, counselors do not meet teacher expectations for change in children's behavior (Brammer, 1988).

On the other hand, children who seek counselor help of their own volition or agree to join a counseling group for a specific purpose tend to become enthusiastically involved in the process. At times, children will react to counseling based on their prior experience with counselors. If a child has had a positive experience with counseling, he or she will be likely to be a ready participant.

Much of the way children will react to initial sessions depends on how the student body perceives the counselor. If the general view of counseling is that it is something that is done to "bad" children, then the counselor may face a difficult task. There are a number of sources of conflict and disagreement in any interview. The counselor should attempt to recognize the source of these contradictions. Rich (1968, p. 16) lists the possibilities as follows:

1. The counselor and the student both agree to the purpose of the interview.
2. The counselor and the student both understand and accept the purpose of the interview, but either the student or the counselor may have reservations about the discussion.
3. The counselor and the student disagree on the function of the interview. Each is aware of how the other feels.
4. The counselor and the student may disagree on the purpose of the interview, but one or both of them may not recognize the disagreement.
5. Either the counselor or the student may have an unconscious motivation that differs from the conscious one.
6. The two individuals concerned may mean quite different things by the same words, and thus communicate something different than intended (Muro & Dinkmeyer, 1977; Rich, 1968, pp. 16–24).

This list of possibilities has been very beneficial to the authors in their work in university settings and in schools. The list can be copied and placed in the counselor's office for periodic review.

In many university programs, counselors are exposed to (some say imposed upon by!) a wide range of theoretical orientations. To hear discussions from beginning graduate students on the relative merits of the approach advocated by one theorist as contrasted to the theoretical tenets advanced by another can be stimulating. Our experiences have taught us that counselors approach children armed with a wide repertoire of techniques and theoretical orientations, but most will agree on the following essential counseling elements.

1. Establish an effective relationship. All counseling theorists agree that an effective relationship is an absolute essential aspect of the counseling process (Cottone, 1992; Hutchins & Cole, 1986; Kottler & Brown, 1992; Nelson-Jones, 1990; Nugent, 1990; Young, 1992; Brammer, 1988). While some would argue that a relationship is both a necessary and sufficient condition for producing positive changes in a counselee, others will only state that a relationship is necessary. None take issue with the fact that counseling is not possible if the relationship is flawed.

The nature of the counselor-child relationship is that it is one built on mutual trust and acceptance (Kottler & Brown, 1992). It is one wherein the counselor listens to the thoughts and concerns of the child and encourages the child to talk in an atmosphere free from external judgment. In fact, one of the reasons that counseling is effective is that the atmosphere of the counseling session may be unlike any that the child has experienced elsewhere. This respect entails an active adult who treats the child as a growing, dynamic person and not as an object to be manipulated to meet the expectations of others.

The counselor understands that the child is behaving to meet certain needs (described at various times by Maslow (1955) and Glasser (1989)), both physiological and psychological, with the latter including the needs for love, or belonging, power (achievement), freedom, and fun. In the first few sessions children may talk, play, or do both, but at least initially what the counselor says and does and what children in counseling say and do are perhaps less important than the fact that the child is in a situation where he or she feels respected and free enough to express his or her inner world without the fear of reprisal.

Why is this relationship necessary? Can a child be counseled in an atmosphere where mutual trust is not present? Perhaps, but successful outcomes are not probable when relationships are poor. By the time children reach school and meet teachers and counselors, they have usually had numerous experiences with adults that were not positive. Under the mantles of discipline, religion, child-rearing practices, or "good behavior" they may have been pushed, directed, guided, monitored, and punished many times over. Thus when the counselor indicates that counselees may say anything they want, the counselor may well expect children to be suspicious, because most children will not have experienced such freedom. In addition, if children suspect that what the counselor says is false or not genuine, they are likely to become defensive, sullen, or even silent.

Children as well as adults are at best reluctant to share anything with those they feel will somehow use such information to harm them. They will skip over information, ignore questions, or become angry. Which of us reacts any differently? Which of us is willing to share even a portion of our private world with any other human being if we feel that the person with whom we are sharing is going to use the information to push us in a direction we may not want to go? One thing is certain. Children are remarkably skillful in picking up counselors' hidden agendas or any direct attempts to change them. It is not uncommon to hear, for example, comments such as "I'll bet Mrs. Vacne sent me here to make me keep quiet more. Is that right?" or "Why do you want to help me? Nobody else does." Such statements indicate a lack of trust, a sense of doubt that the counselor really does care and want to help.

Thus warmth, empathy, positive regard, understanding, and therapeutic permissiveness are all conditions that describe the very first phase of counseling (Brammer, 1988; Kottler & Brown, 1992; Cottone, 1992). Counselors use all the skills and understandings at their disposal to assist the children they are counseling. Each of us is likely to want to do things with and for another person that we like and respect. Indeed, a positive, trusting relationship is a necessary condition for counseling, regardless of the theoretical orientation of the counselor.

2. Decide upon mutual goals. Counseling goals are generally directly related to the philosophical and operational views of the counselor. If, for example, the counselor believes that the root of children's concerns lies in a denial of self, then self acceptance on the part of children becomes a reasonable goal. If the counselor believes that children's concerns are rooted in unconscious mechanisms that impact functioning, then a counseling goal may be that of helping children achieve a greater degree of self-awareness. Other goals include behavioral changes, improved decision-making skills, better academic achievement, and the elimination of faulty or irrational thoughts. These goals and others are the foundation that provides guidelines for counseling practice. For example, counselors who consider themselves to be behaviorists will counsel differently than those who feel that a greater awareness of individual feelings is a major objective.

It is important for counselors to work with children to determine the goals for counseling (Young, 1992; Nugent, 1990; Gelso & Carter, 1985). As counselors attempt to establish the relationship just described, they must always keep in mind that counseling is indeed conversation with a purpose. Initial interviews with children can be difficult, particularly with children who have been referred for counseling by a teacher or a principal. Many will have no idea of why they were sent to see a counselor, and in this sense, they will have little, if any, understanding of what counseling is all about. With the very young child in play situations, it may be very difficult to communicate what counseling actually is.

Leona Tyler (1969) noted that any delay in getting to the reason for counseling can cause undue anxiety for children. Experienced counselors will be able to relate to the typical "picture" of a referred child standing in front of a counselor, with fingers in mouth and head hanging. In many cases the child will have no idea of why she or he was sent to a counselor. All that the child knows is that she or he is embarrassed and wants to leave the situation as soon as possible.

With children who refer themselves, the process is different and perhaps easier. The child may have listed concerns on a card at an orientation session, or he or she may directly state something such as, "I came to see you cause I don't have any friends." At any rate, it is important for the counselor and child to come to a mutual agreement of goals. The child, commensurate with his or her verbal and maturity levels, must have a response to the counselor question of "Can you tell me what brings you to see me?"

If children have been referred and seem to have no idea of why they are in counseling, counselors, after a short explanation of the fact that they are there to help children in any way that they can, should begin the session with statements similar to the following: "I've told you a little about me and what I do. I'm here to help boys and girls in any way that I can. I want to help you too if you need my help. Maybe we can start by making a little list of what is important to you or maybe we can also make a list of some of the things that you want or want to do. If we can come up with a list, then maybe you and I can decide on some ways that you can get what you want." Counselors should use their own words, but the general idea is to come to terms with the reasons for counseling. Not all children will be able to respond to what counselors may verbalize, but this should not be a major concern in attempts at getting started. There will be many times when counselors may need to remember the goals of the counseling interview.

Thus while we recommend that counselors and children develop personal goals for counseling, there are some general goals that the authors have utilized as an overall guide for a number of years. Within these broad counseling objectives, more specific goals can be delineated. General counseling goals for children are as follows:

1. To know and understand themselves, their assets and liabilities. Through self-understanding to develop a better understanding of the relationships among their own abilities, interests, achievements, and opportunities. To develop self-awareness.

2. To develop self-acceptance, a sense of personal worth, a belief in their own competence, a trust in themselves, and to develop an accompanying trust and acceptance of others. To integrate what they psychologically are and what they would psychologically like to be.

3. To develop methods of solving the developmental tasks of life with a resultant realistic approach to the tasks of life as met in areas of work and interpersonal relations.

4. To develop increased self-direction, problem-solving skills, and decision-making abilities.

5. To develop responsibility for their choices and actions; to be aware that their behavior is goal oriented; and to learn to consider the consequences when making a decision.

6. To clarify feeling so that they may develop attitudes and concepts of self and others; to be able to perceive reality as defined by others. (Dinkmeyer, 1964–1965; Muro & Dinkmeyer, 1977)

These goals developed by Dinkmeyer (1964–1965) have provided a useful guide to help structure counseling sessions and have stood the test of time. Naturally the broad general goals such as increased self-direction must be reduced to short-term goals that the counselor can discuss with children. For example, the general goal of increased self-direction may well become a counselor/child goal of finding some ways of improving school work without the everyday help of parents.

In addition to the goals just listed, we would like to add an additional one that has proven useful. We believe that individuals behave in ways that meet common needs. The works of Maslow (1954, 1955) and Glasser (1989) make a strong case that human motivation is driven by the needs for love and belonging, freedom, power, and fun. In this sense every child who enters the counseling office is behaving in some manner to meet these needs. When we ask a child to list what is important to him or her, we have a good picture of how that child is meeting a particular need or needs. If a child says "I want to make more friends," we know that the need to belong is a motivator of his or her behavior. Counseling, then, becomes a process of discovering what the child is presently doing to meet these needs and what kinds of additional things may be done to increase the probability of meeting these needs. It is not necessary to discuss the human motivation system with children; rather it is sufficient to understand what the child wants (needs) and help determine how to achieve what is desired. Thus a goal of counseling is to help children behave in ways that will help them meet their basic needs. If one can accept the contention advanced by the Adlerian school of thought and later expanded upon by Dinkmeyer (1964–1965), Glasser (1989), and others that behavior is indeed purposive and goal oriented, then a directional change of behavior is an appropriate counseling goal.

3. Provide structure. Counselors, in most cases, will still need to convey to children the nature of the counseling relationship when children come for a visit to the counseling offices. They must provide structure (Kottler & Brown, 1992; Corey, 1991). One major reason that counseling can be effective is that the situation is unique. Children must understand that the time spent with the counselor is different from time spent at home or in the classroom. The counselor will want to tell them that what they say in a counselor's office will not cause a loss of love or recognition. Above all, children must understand that there will be no punishment for anything that they say, or for what they may have done in the immediate or distant past. Moustakas (1964) suggests that messages similar to the following be conveyed to children in counseling: "In here you are free to do what you want." "I would rather know what your opinion is." "This is your time and place." "What you say here is between us and not anyone else's affair." "I can't decide for you; the only thing that matters is that you decide for yourself" (Moustakas, 1964, p. 105).

Statements such as those suggested by Moustakas or similar ones selected by the counselor will tell the child that counseling is something different than she or he has ever experienced before. Other structuring statements could include the following: "We have a half hour together that you can use any way that you wish." "In your homeroom and maybe at your house you are pretty much told what to do, but in here you and I will decide together what we should do."

During the early stages, counselor verbalizations should closely follow the leads provided by children as they seek to develop a collaborative relationship that includes the mutual agreement of goals, as discussed earlier in this chapter. Counselors need to provide time to explore children's expectations about how they will be working together. If children ask questions, counselors should be prepared to provide ready responses. While the climate suggested by Moustakas (1964) will put most children at ease, counselors should not attempt a completely "nondirective" approach in that it can cause frustration and anxiety in children. Empathy and warmth are essential. In fact, empathy was once described by Carkhuff as the "heavy ingredient of helping" (Carkhuff, 1969, p. 173).

The beginning counselor may attempt to give children a large dose of advice, persuasion, and quick solutions to concerns and problems. In fact, the easiest trap for the beginning counselor to slip into is the "advice and direction trap," wherein he or she knows exactly what is wrong with the child and exactly what needs to be done to "fix" the problem. Thinking for the counselee is, in effect, communicating that the counselor and not the child is the one responsible for solving problems. This also communicates that children are not capable of behaving in ways that meet their needs. Action-oriented approaches such as advice and direct intervention may be appropriate for later sessions but should not be part of the early sessions.

In summary, then, the initial part of counseling includes the formation of a relationship, goal setting, and structuring. Successful counselors provide warmth, empathy, respect, and caring. They refrain from quick judgments in order to provide time for children to become comfortable with them, the counseling process, and the direction that counseling will take. The counselor will frequently tell the child that he or she can decide how to use the time in the counseling session. The child must experience freedom, independence, and personal worth.

The relationship, however, is a necessary but not always sufficient condition for effective counseling. If two individuals are to work with one another for a period of time, they must develop a common purpose. Since at times the purpose may seem vague and ambiguous, especially with the very young who may have limited verbal skill, it is essential to review from time to time the nature of counseling and the agreed-upon goals. At times, counselors may have to help children express their goals. With some children, development of counseling goals may have to follow a period of discovering how the child is meeting basic needs and how she or he can meet these needs in ways that are self-enhancing.

Entering the World of Children

Once the counselor understands the importance of a proper relationship and the need for structure, as fundamental principles of counseling, then it is essential to discover ways to enter the child's world. No one approach is magic; no single technique will always work. Counselors must ask themselves, "How do I get involved with this child? What kinds of things can I do and say to let this child know that I do care, and that I want to help? What must this session look like to this child? How can we work together to meet the needs or help alleviate the concerns that brought this child here to see me?"

Through the years the authors have utilized a number of pragmatic approaches to enter the world of children. Counselors can employ play media, puppets, and a wide variety of homemade and commercial approaches to help children feel at ease as the relationship unfolds. A few examples will illustrate what seems to work for us and for some of our students. We would like to encourage the beginning counselor to be creative and experiment with other approaches.

Card games.   Children are used to playing card games. Games such as UNO, Old Maid, and a wide variety of other commercially produced card games (or games counselors make up) are excellent entries into the world of the young. Statements like, "Let's you and I play with these cards while we try and decide how we can help you do better in math" will help take the awkwardness out of the counseling situation for the very young and the frightened. Remember, self-exploration and self-revelation are not behaviors that children will ordinarily engage in during a normal day. Cards are a natural part of the child's world, have the element of play and "games," and will provide opportunities for helping structure the relationship. For example, if a child says, "I get in trouble for playing games at home unless I do my school work first," a counselor could respond with, "In here, we can play cards and talk about your work. You said you wanted to see me about doing better in school. We can play and help you work on what you want to do at the same time." Since cards are a normal part of children's worlds, and counseling is not, cards and other games will help initiate the process (Muro, 1991).

Stimulus pictures.   An excellent entre into the world of children is stimulus pictures (Muro & Dinkmeyer, 1977). Pictures are very much a part of what children see daily on television and in magazines and books. In fact, you can understand much of what is happening in the minds of the young through television programs or certain situations in a photograph. A picture, if stimulating and appealing enough, often suggests an emotional impact not readily expressed by words alone. Different children frequently read into the same pictures various feelings that reflect their unique perceptions.

The authors have long used Dinkmeyer's *Developing Understanding of Self and Others* (DUSO) (Dinkmeyer, 1973) to help children verbalize feelings and values. The stories and questions in this comprehensive approach have proved effective for over two decades.

The resourceful counselor can develop a stimulus file from a wide range of current periodicals ranging from some of the "home" magazines found at supermarket checkouts to those found in weekly newsmagazines. A convenient way to use these pictures is to create a file with three broad categories: pictures designed to develop rapport, pictures to help children to deal with their feelings and behaviors, and pictures to enhance growth.

In early sessions, counselors may want to find pictures that appeal to children's sense of humor or curiosity. In recent years, the daily "Calvin and Hobbes" comic strip is an excellent tool to use with children because the elements of fantasy, developmental concerns, and common school problems are very much a part of Calvin's comic strip world. Other examples are pictures showing people riding horses backward, a pet puppy chewing a huge shoe or boot, or a picture of someone falling in the mud or snow which will usually evoke a responsive chuckle from children. Since no single picture will develop "instant" rapport, you may want to experiment with a wide range of pictures and "weed out" those that do not seem to work well. A good "rapport-building" picture is one that encourages verbalizations that might otherwise not have been stated.

Counselors will also want to develop pictures for use with different age, maturity, personality, and language levels of children. In many cases, counselors will find that simply asking a child to pick out one picture "most like you" from a series of photos can be a very useful technique. The discussion that follows may focus on the child's perceptions. Did the child select a happy scene or person or a sad one? Did the child choose a picture that shows children in play with others or children who look sad and lonely? In addition, the counselor may ask the child to select pictures that show how teachers, parents, and other children seem to view the child. The discussion that follows can promote interaction and counselor/child cohesion and give insights into a child's world. Of course, the counselor must use caution in interpreting the child's choices and not attribute to the pictures more meaning than actually exists. With that in mind, stimulus pictures are an excellent way to initiate counseling.

Sally Long Hair. One of the most effective rapport builders with children has been a puppet called "Sally Long Hair" that one of the authors and many graduate students have used effectively for over twenty years (Muro & Dinkmeyer, 1977). Made of cloth taken from an old towel and a skein of yarn are four faces, one that is sad, one that is happy, one that is angry, and one that says "I need help." As can be seen in Figure 4.2, the yarn (Sally's hair) covers all four faces. We recommend that Sally (or someone like her) be placed on the counselor's desk within easy reach of all children who enter the counseling office. Either the child or the counselor can pick up the puppet.

To use Sally, counselors simply pick up the puppet and say something like, "I am glad you came in today, Anna. I feel good to see you." As you speak with children, simply part Sally's long hair to show the smiling face. In most cases, even the most shy children will smile. You may also say something like, "Yesterday, my car didn't start, and I was late for school. I felt a little angry and a little sad." (Show both faces.) "Maybe you would like to have Sally help you tell me how you feel today." At times, children will go through a number of faces to indicate how they were feeling when an event occurred. For example, Sally's sad face has been very much in evidence when the family pet dies or if a grandparent or parent passes away, and her angry face may appear too.

In addition to Sally we have created "Sam," who is a similar male puppet, "Scratch," who is our counseling dog who holds sad, happy, angry, and needs-help signs in his mouth, and "Clarence," a cat puppet, who performs

Figure 4.2
Sally Long Hair

similar tasks. Obviously there is no magic in the use of puppets in working with children. However, the sometimes somber world of adulthood is not the world of children, and the wise counselor is one who attempts to see the world as children see it. In this context, puppets as a vital part of children's play are a very important part of the world of young people.

Stick drawings and ambiguous figures.   Some counselors have found the use of coloring books with stick figures and ambiguous clay objects to be useful in establishing rapport (Muro & Dinkmeyer, 1977). Counselors can easily create stick figure coloring books by drawing a wide range of stick figure characters and photocopying them to hand out to children who are in individual or group counseling (see Figure 4.3). The counselor can simply ask children to "color how they feel." If no figure is present, children may create one of their own.

Ambiguous figures are objects of varying shapes and sizes made of any pliable material. Liquid rubber poured over clay is very good for creating these figures. Any number of figures can be made (we are presently using sixteen separate shapes). The counselor may place the figures on a small table in his or her office, or perhaps the figures will be on a shelf with other media in the playroom. Most children will pick up one of the objects and ask, "What's this?" To this question the counselor can reply, "It can be anything

Figure 4.3

How do I feel—
color me

"Sometimes I feel sad. When
I'm sad, Mom says I'm blue.
Color me blue."

"Sometimes when there's no
kids around to play, I feel
alone. Color me lonely."

"Some days we don't like
anybody. We're mad!
Color us mad."

"Today I'm happy, glad,
good! Color me good
and happy!"

you want it to be. It can be a magic rock, an elf, a good luck charm, or a personal friend." Children with good imaginations will generally create something out of the figures. Those who do not may lose interest in the clay figures and return them to the shelf. Nonetheless, enough children will spend time with them to make them a worthwhile and inexpensive addition to the counselor's play materials.

Some Early Counseling Leads

What counselors say and perhaps deliberately do not say to children are frequently labeled "counseling leads." To be effective, counseling should not be reduced to a stereotyped set of verbalizations that are preplanned and adhere to a rigid, unbending point of view. We believe that effective counseling needs to have a degree of spontaneity wherein each counselor uses his or her own natural language. While some counseling leads may be more effective than others at different stages of the counseling process, we feel that the important concept for counselors is to be aware of how their leads may impact the interaction. For example, a whole series of counselor questions may cause children to think and respond, and thus counselors run the risk of not learning what the concerns of the counselee may be. Note how the interaction process changes when counselors use different leads:

Child: "Boy, it was a rough night! My mom made me do all my homework before I could watch TV."

Counselor: "What did she make you do?"

Child: "I had to do all my math and make a chart for science."

In this case the counseling lead is a question, and the child responds to the counselor's request for information. While this lead should not be considered "wrong," it implies that the counselor needs additional information in order to help the child. The risk for the counselor here is that the child may have wished to go in a different direction rather than respond to the question. Now consider what may take place with a different lead.

Child: "Boy, it was a rough night! My mom made me do all my homework before I could watch TV."

Counselor: "Mm hmm. It seemed pretty rough to you last night."

Child: "Yes, it did. I got real mad and slammed the door to my room. Like always she's on my back."

In the latter example, the counselor used a simple reflection of content to respond to the child. The child, in turn, began to explore some of his feelings toward his mother. The point to remember is that what the counselor says will have an impact on both the content and process of interviews. The following sections describe types of leads and their possible consequences.

Acceptance.   Acceptance involves respect for the child and empathy with what the child says (Kottler & Brown, 1992; Nelson-Jones, 1990). It does not, as some beginning counselors seem to think, indicate that counselors necessarily *agree* with all statements children make. Acceptance is stimulated by active listening and encouraging children to continue to explore and feel heard. For example, if a child in counseling states that "Most of the kids don't like me. At least they never seem to pick me on any of the teams," a counselor may simply reply, "Yes, I see" or "Mm hmm, I think I understand." This is an effective statement, since both the counselor and child are getting to know each other, and in the process of establishing mutual trust and defining goals, counselors should encourage the child to speak. Undue probing of problems will not encourage children to speak freely, and the information that is volunteered may be extremely important later on in counseling.

Reflection.   Reflection is a technique for mirroring the key element of a child's communication (Hutchins & Cole, 1986). Reflection of feeling and content and action will enable children to feel deeply understood and will also demonstrate that what they discuss is important.

A reflection is also a way of validating what the child has said to the counselor. Although this seems like a very simple process, this is not the case. In most cases, children have not had their feelings validated; hence, reflection is a powerful clinical tool. Among the verbal techniques counselors use, reflection may be the most powerful in encouraging children to continue to explore and discuss their unique self-perceptions. For example, suppose a fifth grade boy offers the following statements:

Child: "I have to do all the chores at home, and it doesn't seem right that my sister won't help. She gets good grades; I get yelled at. I babysit my little brother; she plays tennis. Sometimes I'd like to bop her with her racket."

The child has expressed a number of thoughts and feelings in what he has said to the counselor. Depending on the direction the counselor may wish to take, any of the following reflections can be used:

"It doesn't seem fair to you that she won't help with the chores."

"You seem to do all the work, and she spends time playing."

"Sometimes you feel that you want to hit her."

"You're feeling disappointed and angry."

All reflections should attempt to feed back to the child the meaning of what he or she has said. Unfortunately, in some cases counselors tend to become stereotypical in their use of reflection and tend to endlessly "parrot" the exact words children have spoken. At other times, however, a reflection may go beyond what the child has said and can communicate that counselors truly do comprehend how the child feels. Reflective statements that include evidence of a counselor's comprehension of a concern or problem are probably closer to the counseling technique of interpretation (Teyber, 1989).

Silence.   There may be times when counselors simply say nothing in response to what children have verbalized (Hutchins & Cole, 1986; Corey, 1991; Young, 1992; Meier & Davis, 1989). Counselors may simply maintain good eye contact and add a nod of the head. Silence in itself may be either accepting or rejecting. It is accepting when counselors can convey to children that what they say is very important, so important in fact that it should not be interrupted with questions, interpretations, or premature solutions.

Children's silence can occur for a number of reasons. The most obvious is that silence occurs when there is nothing else to say. Silence can also occur when the child is frightened by the counselor, is uncertain about what to say, is fearful of being punished or reprimanded, or is afraid that what is said will be rejected (Corey & Corey, 1993).

A word of caution with respect to counselors' use of silence with children: in situations outside the counseling office, teachers and other authority figures frequently use their silence to punish children or to help control their own anger. Parents who are angry with their children often use "the silent treatment" to let them know that they have done something wrong. In counseling, counselors need to communicate that silence is not intended to be harmful. Statements such as, "It's OK to be quiet in here if you like" or "I didn't answer your question because I thought you were thinking some more about what you said. I just didn't want to interrupt you" can help to convey that message.

Clarification.   Counselors can use clarification at any stage of counseling, and it is especially appropriate for use in early sessions (Young, 1992; Hutchins & Cole, 1986). When using clarification, counselors do not attempt to add additional meaning to what children are saying (that is, they do not render interpretations); rather they attempt to tie in related verbalizations that may have been expressed but not necessarily understood. The following is an example of clarification:

Child: "I finally got picked by the guys. I got three hits in the game. One was a double."

Counselor: "You mean you got picked because you are playing pretty well?"

Summarizing.   At times, even in the early sessions of counseling, it is useful to pause and try to pull together the various thoughts and feelings that the child may have expressed (Hutchins & Cole, 1986; Kottler & Brown, 1992). The best time to summarize is when counselors feel that the major areas of a given topic have been discussed. When finished with a summarization, the counselor will want to provide time for children to agree or disagree with what has been said. In summarizing, the counselor may want to seek out recurring conflicts and expressions of affect noted during the session or during several sessions, as in the following example:

Child: "I had a fight with my brother over who owns the bike. My dad told me it was Joe's bike, and I was not to ride it. Today Mr. Simms told me to sit down and keep quiet. Like usual I got mad."

Counselor: "Let's see if I can understand what is happening to you. Earlier today you said your brother tells you what to do; then your dad tells you what to do, and today your teacher gives you an order. Each time you got angry. Seems like you get angry when someone forces you to do something you don't like."

In this instance, the theme of the discussion was related to the child's perception of being directed into certain behaviors. Feeling powerless, in each of these instances the accompanying affect was that of anger. The point to remember is that themes of affect, conflict, and content do occur in counseling. If the counselor can tie together such themes, it helps make children feel understood (Teyber, 1989).

Approval.   When using approval, counselors are communicating that they are in agreement with something children have said or done (Muro & Dinkmeyer, 1977). Approval is different from acceptance in the sense that acceptance shows counselor understanding of what may have been said or done. Approval, on the other hand, is a verbal reinforcement that is intended to help children continue on a path to a positive goal.

Wubbolding (1989) and Glasser (1989), while not discussing approval as a technique per se, are very much in favor of having counselors make positive approval statements to individuals. Verbalizations such as, "I want you to do it, since you do it well," or "I think you are making good progress" are not uncommon in the practice of Control Theory (Glasser, 1989) and Reality Therapy (Wubbolding, 1988, & Glasser, 1980).

Laughter.   Children's "real" worlds are often punctuated with laughter (Young, 1992). It seems strange that when individuals write or speak of counseling, there is little mention of laughter. Obviously counselors must not laugh at children who have presented concerns, and in a sense laughter cannot be really considered a counseling lead; however, throughout counseling and especially in early sessions a smile or an outright laugh when it is appropriate can go a long way to help children understand that counselors are human and capable of laughing at humorous situations that children reveal. For example:

Child: "That big kid on the playground didn't want to fight me today."
Counselor: "How come? What did you do?"
Child: "I stayed in my room" (smiles).
Counselor: (Laughing) "You didn't give him a chance, did you?"

While counselors must always be cautious and not laugh when the laughter would be offensive, there will be ample opportunities as illustrated here to bring laughter into the counseling office.

An example of counseling in its initial stages is illustrated in the material that follows.

The Initial Phase of Counseling

Phase I (A fourth grade girl)

COMMENT

Counselor: "Hi, Anna. I'm glad Mrs. Birchard could free you up today. I did get the card you sent to her asking to see me. I'm sorry that I couldn't see you on Friday."

Anna: "That's OK. Remember when you came to our class in the fall and said that we could come in to see you if we needed help with anything?"

Counselor: "I sure do remember. In fact, about nine of your classmates have been in to see me."

Anna: "I know. That's kinda why I came."

Counselor: "I see. They told you to come."

Anna: "Not exactly, but they said you were a good person."

Counselor: "Well, that is nice to know."

Anna: "Well, they are, at least most of the time."   Concern is expressed.

		COMMENT
Counselor:	"Mm hmm, they are usually good people."	Reflection of content.
Anna:	"Well, I don't mean that they are bad, but lately they have not been too nice to me."	
Counselor:	"Oh, I see. You still think they are good kids, but somehow they have not been nice to you."	Reflection. Another reflection of content.
Anna:	"Yes, I guess so."	
Counselor:	"Can you tell me a little more about what you mean?"	Clarification.
Anna:	"Well, you see, Mary, Helen, and me are usually best friends. We go to the mall, and the movies on Saturdays. Now they—" (pauses, as her voice trails off).	
Counselor:	"Go on, Anna."	
Anna:	"Well, I think they don't like me anymore."	
Counselor:	"Oh, I see. All three of you were best friends, and recently, Mary and Helen have kinda ignored you."	Summary.
Anna:	"Yes, and it makes me feel—" (voice trails off again).	
Counselor:	"I understand, you are feeling upset about what is happening."	Note the reflective stance. The counselor wants the child to continue to explore.
Anna:	"Yes, pretty soon, I'll have no friends at all."	
Counselor:	"I could be wrong, but I gather that you are not only upset about Helen and Mary, but you think that others could possibly do the same kind of things to you."	Here, the counselor actually goes beyond the data provided by the child and interprets what he thinks may be happening. Note that the interpretation is soft-pedaled in order to allow the child to reject any statement that is too frightening.
Anna:	"Yes, I was wondering if you could do something about it."	At times, children will make direct requests to counselors to "solve" what they perceive as a problem.
Counselor:	"I see, you want me to do something?"	
Anna:	"Yes, maybe you could talk to them and find out what's wrong?"	

		COMMENT
Counselor:	"Well, Anna, I suppose I could talk to them, but I guess I would rather help you figure out a way for you to talk to them. Maybe you and I can think of some things together that you can do to find out why the girls are not including you."	Here the counselor is helping Anna own the problem, and he is working toward the formation of a short-term goal. The counselor knows that Anna is expressing a need to belong and be a part of an important group. Somehow she has now been excluded. A short-term counseling goal here is to help Anna deal with the immediate situation and clarify to her satisfaction what may be happening.
Anna:	"Well, you will at least help?"	
Counselor:	"I surely will. I want to help you because I know that you feel your friends are important and they matter to you."	Counselor expresses acceptance and willingness to help. No attempt is made here to provide solutions.
Anna:	"OK."	
Counselor:	"OK, let's you and I see if we agree. We are going to try and figure out some ways to see what may be causing Mary and Helen to kinda ignore you, and if they are, we may see what we can do about it. I guess from what you said you still want them to be your friends."	
Anna:	"Yes. And I want them to ask me to go places."	
Counselor:	"OK. Let's see if we can start. Can you think back when you first noticed that they were not including you?"	
Anna:	"About three weeks ago."	
Counselor:	"What happened?"	
Anna:	"They ate at another lunch table with some other girls."	
Counselor:	"I gather you were not invited, and you felt a little bit sad."	Counselor interpreted and missed the depth of the feeling.
Anna:	"A lot sad!"	
Counselor:	"OK, a lot sad. What did you do then?"	
Anna:	"Nothing. I just went back to my room. I didn't talk to them that day."	

COMMENT

Counselor: "I see. You were feeling low, and simply ignored them."

Anna: "Yes, and I didn't talk to them for the next three days."

Counselor: "Mm hmm. You were upset enough to ignore them for a few days. You were not going to call them? Could it be you wanted to get even with them for not including you?"

Counselor attempts a tentative hypothesis. Use of this technique is to provide insight into concerns.

Anna: "Well, yes. I was mad at them."

Counselor: "I see. I'm mad at you and if you don't talk to me, I am not going to talk to you."

Anna: "You got it. In fact, I haven't talked to them even once since that happened."

Counselor: "Oh, I see. You have not attempted to talk to them at all about what happened in the lunch room."

Anna: "No, and I am not going to."

Counselor: "OK, let's see where we are. You say you still want them as friends, and you and I have agreed to figure out what you can do to see what has happened and what we may do to help you keep them as friends."

Goal is repeated.

Anna: "Yes."

Counselor: "Now if you want them to know what is wrong, but you are not talking to them, how are the girls going to find out? How is not talking to them helping you?"

Confrontation.

Anna: "I'm afraid they will tell me that they don't like me anymore."

Counselor: "I guess that could be, but do you have any other ways of finding out if they do or not?"

Anna: "Not unless you ask them."

Counselor: "Anna, I know you would like me to, but I think that you will have to do the talking. Are you willing to try?"

Anna: "I'm not sure. I feel dumb and nervous now."

Counselor: "Maybe we could practice what you will say, but first let's try and decide how and when you will go back and talk to Mary and Helen. OK?"

Anna: "OK, do you think they still like me?"

Counselor: "I don't know, but I want to help you find out."

In this initial session, the counselor attempted to establish a relationship with Anna. He listened, reflected, and allowed Anna to discuss her concerns from her viewpoint. Making friends is very important to elementary school children, and the counselor did not try to downplay this normal developmental concern. At the same time, he communicated to the child that she, not the counselor, must take the initiative to solve her problem. Thus he resisted Anna's efforts to have him do it for her. While refusing to act in her behalf, he still communicated his willingness to help. Also it is important to note that the counselor did not promise that a resolution satisfactory to Anna would occur. This would be providing false hope in that the girls in question may have decided, at least for this period of time, that Anna was not welcome. Anna, however, was making a large assumption that it was something that they (the girls) were doing *to* her. At this juncture she did not view the fact that she was also ignoring her friends and that they may have had a different perception of the situation.

Along with a developing relationship, the counselor attempted to set workable goals that were mutually agreeable. Once these were set, then counseling could move forward. Anna may have additional concerns, and in fact she may not relate well to peers, but these are topics that would probably be saved for additional sessions if necessary.

CONCLUSION

The field of elementary and middle school guidance and counseling has matured and expanded rapidly during the past two decades, but most counselors will still need to orient parents, teachers, administrators, and children to the nature of counseling. Counselors need to carefully define what counseling is and what kinds of assistance it can and cannot provide for children. It is important to demonstrate that counseling is at least available for all children, and that it is a vital aspect of the total educational process. Guidance committees formed with both parent and teacher groups are effective ways to help with orientation.

The counseling of school personnel and parents may be done through prepared talks and with video demonstrations of individual counseling sessions. In providing orientation to children in the primary grades, it may be useful to develop visual materials such as puppets and coloring books to explain counseling. Verbal orientation techniques are appropriate for older elementary and middle school children.

For an effective overall guidance program, counselors need adequate office space, including a play and conference room. Inadequate space, particularly in older structures, can make individual and group counseling difficult.

Counselors work with children from a variety of different philosophical orientations and use a wide range of counseling techniques. Almost all counselors, however, initiate counseling through the process of establishing a positive relationship with children. This relationship includes mutual trust, caring, and the counselor's willingness to allow the child to explore and come to grips with his or her concerns. Counseling goals are both long- and short-term, and counseling is most effective when counselors and children agree upon mutually acceptable goals. Among the techniques used by counselors in initial sessions are verbal and visual structuring approaches, and a variety of leads that include reflection, clarification, approval, acceptance, summarizing, and laughter.

REFERENCES

Brammer, L. (1988). *The helping relationship: Process and skills.* Englewood Cliffs, NJ: Prentice Hall.

Carkhuff, R. (1969). *Helping and human relations, Vol. I.* New York: Holt, Rinehart & Winston.

Corey, G. (1991). *Theory and practice of counseling and psychotherapy.* Pacific Grove, CA: Brooks/Cole.

Corey, M. S., and Corey, G. (1993). *Becoming a helper.* Pacific Grove, CA: Brooks/Cole.

Cottone, R. R. (1992). *Theories and paradigms of counseling and psychotherapy.* Boston: Allyn & Bacon.

Dinkmeyer, D. C. (1973). *Developing understanding of self and others. (DUSO II).* Circle Pines, MN: American Guidance Service.

Dinkmeyer, D. C. (1964–65). *Towards a theory of child counseling at the elementary school level.* Moravia, NY: Chronical Guidance.

Duncan, J. (1989). The school guidance committee: The counselor's support group. *The School Counselor, 36,* 192–197.

Gelso, C. J., & Carter, J. A. (1985). The relationship in counseling and psychotherapy: Components, consequences, and theoretical antecedents. *The Counseling Psychologist, 13,* 155–243.

Ginott, H. G. (1961). *Group psychotherapy with children.* New York: McGraw-Hill.

Glasser, W. N. (1980). Reality therapy. In W. N. Glasser (Ed.), *What are you doing,* pp. 48–60. New York: Harper & Row.

Glasser, W. N. (1980). *Stations of the mind.* New York: Harper & Row.

Glasser, W. N. (1989). Control theory. In W. N. Glasser (Ed.), *Control theory in the practice of reality therapy,* pp. 1–16. New York: Harper & Row.

Hoehn-Saric, R., Frank, J., Imber, S., Nash, E., Stone, A. D., & Battle, C. (1964). Systematic preparation of patients for psychotherapy. I. Effects on therapy behavior and outcome. *Journal of Psychiatric Research, 2,* 267–281.

Hutchins, D. E., & Cole, C. G. (1986). *Helping relations and strategies.* Pacific Grove, CA: Brooks/Cole.

Kottler, J. A., & Brown, R. W. (1992). *Introduction to therapeutic counseling.* Pacific Grove, CA: Brooks/Cole.

Maslow, A. H. (1954). *Motivation and personality.* New York: Harper.

Maslow, A. H. (1955). Deficiency motivation and growth motivation. In M. R. Jones (Ed.), *Nebraska symposium on motivation.* Lincoln, NE: University of Nebraska Press.

Mayerson, N. (1984). Preparing clients for group therapy: A critical review and theoretical formulation. *Clinical Psychology Review, 4,* 191–213.

Meier, S. T., and Davis, S. R. (1989). *The elements of counseling.* Pacific Grove, CA: Brooks/Cole.

Moustakas, C. E. (1964). Structuring the relationship. In M. Haworth (Ed.), *Child psychology.* New York: Basic Books.

Muro, J. J., & Dinkmeyer, D. C. (1977). *Counseling in the elementary and middle schools.* Dubuque, IA: Wm. C. Brown.

Muro, J. J. (1991). Guidance for all. Paper read at the Texas Personnel and Guidance Conference, Austin, Texas. May 12, 1991.

Muro, J. J. (1992). Elementary teachers view guidance. Paper read at the Texas Elementary School Guidance Conference, Austin, Texas. May 13, 1992.

Nelson-Jones, R. (1990). *Human relationships.* Pacific Grove, CA: Brooks/Cole.

Nugent, F. A. (1990). *An introduction to the profession of counseling.* Columbus, OH: Merrill.

Ohlsen, M. (1974). *Guidance services in the modern school.* New York: Harcourt Brace Jovanovich.

Orlinsky, D., & Howard H. (1978). The relation of process to outcome in psychotherapy. In S. Garfreed and A. Bergin (Eds.), *Handbook of psychotherapy and behavior change: An empirical analysis.* New York: Wiley.

Rich, J. (1968). *Interviewing children and adolescents.* London: St. Martin's Press.

Teyber, E. (1989). *Interpersonal process in psychotherapy.* Pacific Grove, CA: Brooks/Cole.

Thompson, C. T., & Rudolph, L. B. (1992). *Counseling children* (3rd ed.). Pacific Grove, CA: Brooks/Cole.

Tyler, L. E. (1969). *The work of the counselor* (3rd ed.). New York: Appleton-Century-Crofts.

Wubbolding, R. E. (1988). *Using reality therapy.* New York: Harper & Row.

Wubbolding, R. E. (1989). Pictures in conflict. In Naomi Glasser (Ed.), *Control theory in the picture of reality therapy,* pp. 239–254. New York: Harper & Row.

Young, M. E. (1992). *Counseling methods and techniques.* New York: Merrill.

Chapter Five

Middle Phase of Counseling

The counseling process has been divided into three stages in this book in order to help students understand that counseling is a process that may involve a number of stages. This is a rather arbitrary division, however. Sessions one, two, and three, for example, cannot be classified absolutely as the initial sessions and then sessions four, five, and six arbitrarily considered the middle sessions, because in some cases the initial stage of counseling may take more than three weeks. Factors such as the child's perceptions of counselors and counseling, the child's resistance, and whether or not the child has volunteered or been referred may all have an impact on the process of counseling (Muro & Dinkmeyer, 1977).

There may be, however, some marked differences in the interaction patterns with a child who is seen only once by a counselor as compared to one who has made a number of visits to the counseling office. For example, children who are reluctant to speak in initial counseling visits may readily share thoughts and feelings once they fully understand that the counselor is a helper.

If sessions go well, after several meetings the counselor and the counselee have come to an agreement with respect to counseling goals. If not, every effort should be made in the middle stages of counseling to determine what the expected outcomes may be. The counselor should continue to communicate in a variety of ways— through words, attitudes, facial expressions, and intent listening—that counseling is a special relationship that helps children make decisions about goals that they, the children, deem important.

Process in the Second Stage of Counseling

What actually transpires during the middle stages of counseling will depend on a number of factors. Counseling style and philosophical beliefs will play a large part in determining the nature of the interaction. For example, counselors who follow an Adlerian point of view may operate differently from those who work under the tenets of Rational Emotive Therapy. In broad terms, however, all counselors are concerned with obtaining a deeper understanding of the child and his or her concerns. They also seek to help children come to a greater understanding of those concerns and a greater understanding of themselves in relation to those concerns. The process is what Nugent (1990) calls a deeper exploration and analysis.

Understanding the Child's World and Style of Life

As the counselor and child interact, the counselor seeks to get a better understanding of the child's self-image, particularly in terms of how this image is related to the nature of the concern and the counseling goals. For example, children who see themselves as poor students will have a poor or even distorted image of themselves as learners. Some may even have given up as learners before they reach the fourth or fifth grade! Thus if a child expresses a wish to do better in school, the counselor must have some understanding of the child's present level of functioning in the context of that concern. Repeated poor grades, negative comments by teachers, and pressures by parents may result in a behavioral pattern that is almost certain to result in continued failure. Daydreaming, acting out, skipping school with "fake" illnesses, and a refusal to complete assignments may be the present life-style of the child.

The counselor listens closely to whatever the child has to say, to his or her complaints and reasons for not doing well. In many cases these complaints will be expressed in terms of "others are at fault for my problems." It is the rare child who has a grasp of how his or her behaviors and attitudes are contributing to the nature of the expressed concern that brought the child to counseling. Rather, the child will describe how the teacher, parents, siblings, friends, or some other peer or adult is at fault for problems. "She makes me mad; so, I talk back" or something to that effect is not an unusual verbalization. Like adults, most children quickly learn to blame others, as if finding a good excuse for self-defeating behaviors is a way of justifying any action. Blaming others, of course, is a good way for children to control anxiety.

As a child begins to explore, the counselor should listen carefully to discover the purposes of the child's behavior. Counselors should frequently ask themselves questions such as, What purpose did that particular behavior serve the child? Which of her needs were being met? Is the behavior consistent with what the child says he wants to improve? Is the child meeting needs to belong? Does he seem to be suffering from a lack of love? Is she expressing a need for power, for fun, or for freedom? (Muro & Dinkmeyer, 1977; Glasser, 1988).

Many counselors believe that a basic understanding of the life-styles of children is vital to counseling success. A life-style guide developed by Dinkmeyer is presented in Appendix D. This guide is useful in helping counselors obtain answers to some of the questions posed in the preceding paragraph. It is designed to assist counselors in gathering data about the present family atmosphere, including the relationship between parents and children. Additional techniques to use along with the guide to help determine the child's private logic include the technique of three wishes, asking the child what type of animal he or she would like to be, and the use of incomplete sentences (see Chapter 7). Counselors who use these techniques are not simply gathering information. Rather, they are seeking to understand the individual's development, logic, subjective point of view, strengths, weaknesses, and perhaps faulty assumptions (Muro & Dinkmeyer, 1977).

Dreikurs (1957) recognized the importance of knowing the life-style of an individual. In their thinking, all individuals will find special ways to attempt to complete plans. Out of an individual's life play, a style of life emerges that seems to characterize all the person does. With children and adolescents, one can observe their immediate goals as one sees them make a strong effort to find a place in the group. Even though this effort provides a strong motivational pattern, children are often not aware of their goals. The use of the tentative analysis and tentative hypothesis techniques (discussed later in this chapter) are useful approaches to helping children obtain insights into their behavior. As one would expect, children's behavioral patterns are consistent with the ways they meet needs and attempt to meet goals. Thus it is possible to infer the goals of children from an analysis of their behavior (Muro & Dinkmeyer, 1977).

Since most children in elementary and middle schools are still very much involved with parents and siblings, the family constellation can also provide important clues for the counselor. While the child's birth order may be of importance, his or her perceptions of family life are even more important. If an older sister is highly successful in school activities such as drill team or varsity athletic squad membership, a young sister may attempt to do the same things. If, however, the younger sibling does not meet with success in her efforts, she may tend to withdraw from these and similar activities. Most teachers are aware of the pressures placed on the younger brother or sister of a good athlete. In many cases, such children feel unable to compete and may develop a style of life completely void of games and physical activity (Muro & Dinkmeyer, 1977).

Another interesting approach to help determine a child's style of life is the use of early recollections. This is a historical as opposed to a present-oriented approach to understanding the child, but it can be very useful. Some psychologists, especially Adlerians, believe in the selective factor in memory that seems to remain consistent with the life-style of the individual. Out of the many experiences that all children have growing up, the ones that are retained tend to be those consistent with their life-styles. These experiences may not necessarily be negative or traumatic; rather they are experiences that reflect the perceptual framework in which children interpret these experiences. Thus early recollections are a type of protective technique that can provide counselors with information that is useful in knowing how children understand themselves and their worlds.

For example, Mosak (mimeo, no date) provides an interpretation of the following early recollection of a client: "We had a cookie jar on the top shelf of the kitchen. I couldn't reach it by myself, so my uncle lifted me up, and I got the cookie jar." This memory suggests that the child feels small. In order for her to obtain the "goodies" of life, she must rely on the assistance of larger people. The recollection may also be suggestive of a generalized dependency with respect to others (Mosak, no date; Muro & Dinkmeyer 1977). Of course, the interpretations of such early recollections must be done with caution, since the margin for error or misinterpretation can be high.

Helping Children Progress Toward Goals

Other than determining the life-styles or self-images of counselees, the second phase of counseling should also include some discussion of the things children feel are important to them, or, stated another way, children's values. In many cases, children in elementary and middle schools are still in the process of determining values, and counselor assistance in this area can be an important part of counseling. In fact, the development of "responsible" values can be considered an aspect of meeting counseling goals.

Simple understanding of the child and his or her concerns is not sufficient. Counseling must progress to the point of assisting children to develop greater social interest, cooperation, and concern for others. In this process, counselors attempt to help children understand and interpret their lives. To do this it is sometimes necessary to confront children and to help them gain insight and self-understanding through the use of tentative analysis and tentative disclosure (Muro & Dinkmeyer, 1977).

The tentative analysis and disclosure techniques are useful at this point in counseling in that very often children are attempting to meet their needs for fun, belonging, power, and freedom (Glasser, 1988), in what Dinkmeyer and Caldwell (1970) and Dreikurs (1957) describe as the goals of misbehavior. These goals are often subjective and may even be unconscious. Children seek approval and acceptance (attention getting), the ability to do exactly as they wish (power), to hurt others (revenge), and to withdraw and express hopelessness (display of inadequacy) as ways of meeting their needs. In many cases, however, they behave in ways that are perceived by adults as misbehaviors. The child who seeks attention, for example, prefers to receive it in positive ways, but will accept it negatively as this is preferable to being ignored (Dinkmeyer & Caldwell, 1970). Children who seek power will continue to behave in ways that cause them problems even when they are controlled and defeated in that their private logic convinces them that all they need to do is find a more effective method to get what they want.

Counselors who understand the basic need structure, life-style, and value system of counselees can help them to understand any mistaken or inappropriate goals and, of most importance, any dissonance between their expressed goals and their behaviors. For example, if Jim says that he wants the teacher to like him better, this can be considered both a value and a counseling goal. With proper rapport, Mr. Jamison and Jim begin to focus on what the child is doing to meet that goal. It is useful to determine the "what" of children's behavior as well as helping them understand the "why." In the example just given, Jim states that he wants the teacher to like him, but he also notes that he is continually out of his seat in almost every class. Thus there appears to be a discrepancy between what Jim says he wants and how he is behaving to meet this goal. At this juncture, Mr. Jamison could say, "Tell me a little more about what you are doing." If the behaviors Jim describes seem ineffective, Mr. Jamison could say, "Jim, you say you want Mrs. Holmes to like you, but you also said that you will not remain in your seat. Is that right?" If Jim agrees, Mr. Jamison could ask, "How is running around the room all the time helping you to get Mrs. Holmes to like you?" The objective of this dialogue is to have the child make a value judgment, in this case, about the merits of his behavior in terms of what he says he wants.

Also in this dialogue, the counselor may perceive that the child is misbehaving in his or her attempts to reach the goal of acceptance, but may only dimly perceive what his or her goals really are. In this case, Mr. Jamison may offer a tentative hypothesis (discussed later in this chapter) such as, "Jim, is it possible that you run around the room so much because you want Mrs. Holmes to be busy with you?" By interpreting children's goals, counselors are providing them with insights into the "why" of their behavior. Some theorists (Glasser, 1988) focus on the "what" of behavior as opposed to the "why." In working with children, both the what and the why may be important. The "why" helps children with self-understanding, and the "what" requires children to make value judgments about their behavior.

The time focus in this phase of counseling should be present and future oriented. While use of the life-style guide has elements of the child's past in it, it is important that counselors obtain an understanding of how the child perceives the world. In addition, counselors should help uncover as many positive aspects in the life of the child as possible. In other words, the most important part of any review of the child's past life is that of looking for positive and/or successful events or incidents.

Beyond looking for positives that have occurred in the past, most of the discussions between children and counselors should focus on what counselees are doing now and what they intend to do next week or beyond. Children, of course, will want to discuss the past, and will relate incidences of negative past events. Counselors must listen to these and be willing to discuss past perceptions, but in the final analysis all boys and girls must act within the limits and restrictions of the world as it is. Few would argue that there are many things that need to be changed in our schools and in the ways we interact with children. Counselors may have a role to play in such changes, but in the context of the counseling session it is more important to understand how the child sees his or her world. Environmental changes are more appropriately considered in guidance activities other than counseling (Muro & Dinkmeyer, 1977).

In summary, the second or middle stage of counseling is characterized by a transition from development of rapport and a mutual agreement of counseling goals to a stage characterized by attempts to help children explore, discover, and gain a measure of self. Counselors help children to express values and goals and make decisions about what they are doing to meet these goals. In the process, counselors attempt to obtain some understanding of the children's style of life, including their perceptions and private logic. Counselors tend to be present and future oriented and deal in the past for purposes of understanding children and discovering positive aspects of their lives. As in earlier sessions, counselors remain warm and empathic, but as counseling progresses, interpretations of children's behaviors and helpful confrontations may also be useful.

Techniques of the Middle Stages of Counseling

As noted earlier, no one technique is used exclusively in a given stage of counseling. The counselor could use a tentative hypothesis or tentative analysis in the middle stages or even in the ending stages of the process. In general, however, some leads such as acceptance and reflection, while they may be used at any time during counseling, are very effective in the initial stages of a relationship. Other leads may be more useful in the middle stages of counseling. Some examples are described in the following paragraphs.

Reassurance. In the description of the initial stages of counseling, the lead of approval or the communication by counselors that they are in agreement with something children have said or done was discussed. Related to approval is the technique of reassurance. Reassurance goes beyond approval in that it is an approach of verbally relating to children about the consequences of their behaviors and feelings. It is used to help reduce stress, build confidence, and promote expectations of future rewards. Examples include "You can do it," "You know how to solve the homework situation," and "You can find a way to get on the team." Reassurance often includes the expression of approval, as in, "I think that was a good idea," and is intended to build confidence, mobilize positive strengths, and help reduce stress and anxiety (Brammer, 1988).

Additional uses of this skill are for predicting outcomes ("You probably won't get an A on the exam, but I'll bet you will pass") and for providing factual assurance ("You will read at least a little better if you can follow the steps in this workbook"). However, counselors must be aware that use of reassurance can be limited if it is overused or is perceived by children as an attempt to minimize their concerns. In addition, assurance can come across as sympathy and can in some cases create dependency feelings in children (Brammer, 1988).

Suggestions.   Most counselors, especially beginning ones, love to give advice and suggestions. Being asked for advice and suggestions is flattering to most individuals, and advice givers ranging from garden experts to family counselors are replete in popular magazines and newspapers. To some lay people, the very essence of counseling is perceived to be that of one person who is more knowledgeable about some area of human behavior providing someone who is less mature with advice and suggestions about how to proceed and solve the problem. Counselors who are former teachers often seem to want to dispense advice freely. After a number of years in front of a classroom helping and telling children how to do certain things, it seems inevitable that they want to do the same kinds of things in the counseling office.

Brammer (1988) suggests that counselors formulate their own opinions about giving and receiving advice. He feels that all who counsel should ask themselves how *they* feel when others advise them and in what cases has advice been helpful in their lives. He further notes that advice is a controversial topic in the therapeutic literature because some view it as arrogance on the part of the counselor. Others, however, find it useful, particularly if it is given by a trusted person based on solid knowledge of a supporting field (included in such fields are law, medicine, and child rearing). He further notes that advice is often appropriate in crisis situations where several people must cooperate to help others make major readjustments in their lives (divorce, imprisonment), but it is wholly inappropriate for dealing with major individual choices (career selection, choice of a mate). Other problems with advice are that it is often not accepted by clients, creates dependency in clients, and shifts the focus to the counselor to provide solutions. Those who take an "If I were you" approach are probably projecting their own needs (Brammer, 1988).

Because many children seem immature and are perceived by adults as incapable of making decisions, adults, counselors included, may fall into the "If I were you" advice trap quite easily. If counselors do choose to use advice, they should probably not dispense it freely, especially in early sessions, and should use it with caution in the middle and ending sessions.

A somewhat less directive lead is that of suggestion, defined as a technique wherein counselors present alternatives to children that involve a number of courses of action without specifying which course is actually correct. In suggesting alternatives, counselors are providing children with the freedom and the opportunity to reject an alternative. For example:

Counselor: "John, I know you want to get this assignment done. Can you do it at lunch?"

John: "I don't think so."

Counselor: "Have you asked your dad if you can clean up the garage on Saturday?"

John: "No, not yet."

Counselor: "Can you get any help from your friends with the garage cleanup?"

By responding with suggestions, the counselor *may* have glossed over John's concerns and elected instead to provide alternative courses of action. In so doing, the counselor runs the risk of missing what may be a concern for John related to his overall school work or his relationship with his father. On the other hand, if the counselor is reasonably certain that what the child is relating is indeed a specific concern, then the provision of help by offering possible alternatives may be appropriate. It is worth mentioning once again that one of the major problems with suggestion is the tendency to overuse it in helping relationships (Muro & Dinkmeyer, 1977).

Information. The provision of information is related to the counselor's use of advice and suggestion. Brammer (1988) suggested the sharing of simple facts that helpers possess may be among the most useful things that they do. Counselors, particularly at the middle school and high school levels, may be called upon to provide information about intelligence, aptitude, or interest inventories to counselees.

Obviously, if children are seeking information and the counselor has the information requested, the counselor will want to provide it without hesitation. As in many aspects of counseling, counselors should understand that the key point with information is how children perceive and use it rather than the information itself. Can children use information that is provided to gain insight, self-understanding, and clarification of a course of action? The counselor should be careful not to dispense information in large amounts simply on the requests of children. Experienced counselors know that, at times, the presenting concern for a visit to seek information may be a facade that covers a more serious concern. Nonetheless many requests for information are simply that a child wants to know fact, policy, or procedure. For example:

Andy: "If I take Algebra I in grade eight next year, will that be all the math I need to take in junior high school and in high school?"

Mrs. Lamm: "No, Andy, our school board requires at least one unit of math in high school. If you are thinking at all about college, you will want to consider taking at least Algebra II and Plane Geometry in addition to Algebra I."

This interchange included a simple statement of fact in that the counselor felt that Andy was seeking factual information and it was provided. Counselors must be careful not to dominate the discussion and provide more information than is required. Of course, Andy's question may be something more than is obvious on the surface. It could, for example, be Andy's way of wanting to discuss his problems with math, or Andy may simply be seeking support for what he already knows or believes. Counselors must decide when to respond to requests for information directly and when to pause and try and determine if children are requesting data as a cover for some more serious concern.

Interpretation.   "Interpreting is an active helper process of explaining the meaning of events to helpees so that they are able to see their problems in new ways" (Brammer, 1988, p. 88). The use of interpretation is a way of offering an alternate view of some informative feeling or behavior (Hammer, 1968; Muro & Dinkmeyer, 1977).

Interpretation is a key technique for those practicing therapy in hospital and clinical settings, but it can be a useful tool for counselors also. At times the counselor gives an interpretation from a historical perspective in order to provide individuals with new or fresh insights from something that may have occurred in the past. The counselor can also use interpretation to help clarify the goals of behavior or some aspect of an individual's current level of functioning. What is interpreted and how it is actually utilized as part of the counseling interaction are dependent on whichever school of counseling philosophy is guiding a counselor's approach.

Generally, interpretations are given in forms of hunches or best guesses. In this sense a tentative analysis or tentative hypothesis could be considered a type of interpretation. Some prominent theorists, among them the late Carl Rogers, felt that interpretations, whether tentative or not, tended to slow the process of therapy and in some cases could be threatening to clients (Rogers, 1961). Others feel that counselors who use interpretations freely are actually taking over the process of the interview at the expense of the counselee.

Interpretations, like other counseling leads, are neither "good" nor "bad" per se. Their value depends upon when they are used, what is interpreted, and what the counselee can gain from the interpretation. Deep and probing interpretations in early counseling sessions can be rather threatening to children, while a similar interpretation in later sessions may be beneficial (Muro & Dinkmeyer, 1977).

In using interpretation as a counseling lead, counselors should have some idea of why they use this technique. In addition, since interpretation involves translating children's words into a new perspective, the possibility of a misinterpretation always exists. Thus the counselor should use "soft" words or those that suggest possibility rather than certain probability. Examples of "soft" words are: "Perhaps," "Maybe," "Is this a thought?", "I wonder if," or "Would you buy this?"

Some examples of counselor use of interpretations are as follows:

Jennifer:	"I'm having trouble with Mrs. Jones again. I hate to think that I have to go back into that class."
Mr. Lee:	"I know you are concerned about going back into Mrs. Jones' class. You've told me that you don't like her telling you what to do all the time. Last year you had some concerns about Mrs. Miller and Mr. Hart. Yet you get along well with Mr. Henry and you know how he gives directions for students to follow. Would you buy this? Is it possible that you have a lot more trouble taking directions from some teachers than you do with taking directions from others?"
Linda:	"I know that we talked about some new ways to make friends, but I just can't stand Helen. Today, I tripped her in line."
Mr. Lee:	"I may be wrong, but I get the feeling you still want Helen to like you. Is it possible you tripped her to kind of get her to pay a little more attention to you?"

Any interpretation can be perceived in various ways by children. They may accept what the counselor says, reject it, or simply be indifferent to it. At times when interpretations "hit close to home," children can become frightened that an adult seems to know so much about them. In such cases, vigorous denials or protests may follow, particularly if the child feels threatened or frightened.

Brammer (1988) also suggested the use of fantasy and metaphor interpretations, and experienced counselors have found these to be useful with some children. In this case the interpretation is put in the form of a daydream or fantasy. An example is: "I have a fantasy about you. When you go into Mrs. Stone's class, you enter like a warm summer breeze. As soon as she tells you to do an assignment and complete some work, you become a howling March wind, and you want to blow away all that bothers you. Is that a little like how you feel?" Brammer also suggests that counselors employ the same language patterns as counselees. For example, if children employ visual images in what they say, then counselors should use the same modalities. A statement such as "I see the light" by a child could be followed by a counselor statement such as "The light bulb just came on!" (Brammer, 1988).

The following excellent set of guidelines for interpreting have also been developed by Brammer:

1. Look for the basic message(s) of the helpees.
2. Paraphrase these to them.
3. Add to your understanding of what their messages mean in terms of your theory or your general explanation of motives, defenses, needs, styles.

4. Keep the language simple and level close to their messages. Avoid wild speculation and statements in esoteric words.

5. Introduce your ideas with statements that indicate you are offering tentative ideas on what their words or behaviors mean. Examples are: "I wonder if," or "Is this a fair statement?" or "Try this one on for size."

6. Solicit helpee reactions to your interpretations.

7. Teach helpees to do their own interpreting. Remember, we can't give insight to others; they must make their own discoveries. (Brammer, 1988, p. 91)

Incomplete Thought. The incomplete thought technique is used by counselors to help "draw out" an individual, or have them further verbalize or discuss additional aspects of a thought or topic. Incomplete thought approaches are particularly useful when counselors feel that children may gain increased self-understanding from a longer discussion of the topic at hand. An excellent way to know when counselors and children are "in tune" with each other is when they complete sentences or thoughts that the other has initiated.

In using the incomplete thought technique, the counselor comes to a deliberate pause in the discussion, with the expectation that the counselee will complete the statement. This technique may be used after a child has expressed a single thought, but it is more effective after some self-exploration has taken place. In this sense, this technique may be more appropriate in the middle stages of counseling than it is in earlier sessions (Muro & Dinkmeyer, 1977).

An example of the use of the technique is as follows:

Todd: "Of all the things I've tried, I feel good about at least two of them. I'm wondering if I can't get some other things to work for me."

Ms. Simms: "I see. At least two things seem to be working. You're now wondering if some new things will help you. . . ."

With this statement, the counselee is expressing some progress in meeting a goal. He is also suggesting that he has made a decision on some additional approaches. Upon hearing this, the counselor pauses and offers an incomplete thought to allow the counselee to continue to explore additional thoughts.

Projection (Interpersonal and Time). A technique not often discussed in great detail in professional counseling literature is that of having children project thoughts and feelings into some future time period and also having children try to view a given situation from the perspective of another individual. We have found this technique discussed by Miller (1962) to be very useful with children, particularly those who seem to insist that the source of all concerns is outside themselves.

In using this approach, counselors may employ active role playing, or they may simply ask the individual to discuss a concern from the perspective of another individual. Experienced counselors will recognize this role reversal approach as similar to that developed by Moreno (1957) and his associates. An example of this technique is as follows:

Lisa: "I don't know why Mary always does that. She never seems to want to take suggestions from anyone."

Mrs. Jordan: "What I am going to ask you to do may seem a bit hard, but maybe you and I can get a better idea of why Mary does things if you could pretend to be Mary. I'll pretend to be you. Can we figure out something that she has done recently and start from there?"

The counselor may have to use this approach a number of times for it to become effective, but with a little counselor help and direction, it is very powerful.

Related to the use of role reversal is the projection time technique. This lead is designed to have children project themselves into the future (some counselors have used a projection into the past) to obtain a different perspective on a concern. It is often used when counselors mistrust some of the decisions of children and seek to have them take a closer look at their present behavior in terms of future consequence. In general this technique is more effective with older elementary school and junior high school children in that young counselees are even more "now" oriented than are high school students. It may have to be used several times to be effective. For example:

Alexander: "I don't want to dress to play basketball at noon. I'm so skinny that the kids will laugh at how I look. I just won't do it."

Mr. Sidney: "Let's see, the game is on Friday, isn't it? That's a few days off, but what will you do when all your friends are playing and you won't be?"

Silence.   We have noted in Chapter 4 that children can perceive silence in counseling as both accepting and rejecting. If children feel that counselors are silent because they are allowing children the freedom to talk and explore, then silence may be accepting.

In the middle stages of counseling, counselors may find that periods of silence are now less threatening to children, particularly if counselors and counselees have established good rapport. It is permissible to remain quiet if the child wants to do so. If children have engaged in lengthy periods of self-exploration, then they may feel a need to pause and reflect on what they have said. This is what Comier and Comier (1991) and Young (1992) have labeled *attentive silence,* and as such it becomes a powerful incentive to encourage elaboration.

Brammer (1988) noted that silence may be a concern at any time during counseling, but it may be of particular significance during the relationship and exploratory phases of counseling (the beginning and middle stages in this text). He suggested that silence has a number of meanings. If, for example, the silence is perceived as resistive, then a discussion of the counselor/counselee relationship may be warranted. If the counselee is blocked, then the quiet time is needed to allow the child to collect his or her thoughts. If the child has come to an end of a thought, then the counselor and counselee may want to work out a new topic direction.

Additional potential benefits of silence during the middle stage of counseling include the fact that accepting silences can pace an interview and, for some children, an accepting silence can mean that one need not be necessarily "bubbly" and outgoing to be liked and accepted. It is not uncommon for children engaged in counseling using play media to play silently for fifteen minutes or more with few if any verbalizations to the counselor. All they seem to need at such times is the presence of an accepting adult.

Questions.   Above all else, beginning counselors seem to want to ask questions. Most supervisors of students new to counseling will probably agree that the natural thing to do when counselors are unsure of what to say next is to ask children questions. While the use of questions is not necessarily wrong in counseling, overuse of questions can be counterproductive. Young (1992) notes that questioning in initial sessions is unproductive because questions tend to strain the relationship between the counselor and child. However, once the process has reached the middle stages, the counselor can use questions to signal the transition into the "assessment phase" of the process. Young suggested the following:

> "How can I help you?"
>
> "Where would you like to begin?"
>
> "What prompted you to make today's appointment?"
>
> "Has something happened in the last few days or weeks that persuaded you that help was needed?"
>
> "What is it that you want to stop doing less of ?"
>
> "What is it you want to begin to do more of ?"
>
> (p. 89)

If counselors use questions, they should understand that questions are more than simple requests for information. For example, Tomm (1987) has suggested a model for questioning that is based on the intent of the counselor. This intent may be investigative, exploratory, corrective, or reflective. In exploratory questioning, counselors seek information: "How does your work in Miss Smith's class differ from what you do for Mr. Jones?" Investigative questions ask who, why, when, and where: "How did you feel, when you were not picked for the lead in the play?" Corrective questions, as the name implies, seek to have children pursue a different course of action: "What is keeping you from doing your assignments on time?" Reflective questions are a counselor's attempts to come up with his or her own solutions: "Would you do better in class if you felt Miss Jones liked you better?"

Brammer (1988) took a somewhat more cautious view of counselor questioning in that he feels that counselees often feel as if they are being interrogated. He noted that counselees may view a questioning session as similar to a visit to a physician in which, following a discussion of symptoms and complaints, a prescription is forthcoming. In his view, counselors should limit questioning, because the goal of psychological help is to discourage any passive-receptive discourse and engage in active listening and reflecting. He also noted that "why" questions are generally unproductive, although it is tempting for many counselors to ask them.

While accepting Brammer's cautions, we feel that there is a place for questioning in counseling, especially in the middle and ending phases of the process. In general, the use of questions should either help children to expand on their points of view or perhaps lead them to different points of view (Nelson-Jones, 1990). Counselors should be aware of why they are asking questions (Tomm, 1987a, 1987b) and be cautious not to overuse them (Brammer, 1988). In most cases, open-ended questions, or those that allow children to express internal points of view, are preferable to closed questions. For example, an open-ended question or one that seeks an elaboration from the child (Meier & Davis, 1989) could be, "How do you feel about what is happening in your class?" A closed question would be, "Do you like your class?" Closed questions are less useful in information gathering and may sometimes be answered in one or two words, thus ending communication unless one asks an additional question. Asking several questions is little more than interrogation (Nelson-Jones, 1990).

Two final notes on questions are appropriate here. First, counselors should understand that questions from counselees are generally not queries to seek information. Rather, they are generally expressions of feelings and thoughts. In most cases children are seeking counselor support and agreement rather than data. Frequently such questions take the form of "Don't you think I should go out for the team?" What the child is saying is that she thinks she should go out for the team, and the purpose of the question is to see if the counselor agrees and approves.

Second, there will be times when children will "push" counselors to give a personal opinion about some topic. When this occurs, counselors may want to "sandwich" personal views between reflective statements that are "fed" back to the counselee. For example:

Sharon: "I do not like our new principal. I hear the teachers don't like her either. Do you like her?"

Mr. Strunk: "Well, the important thing is how you feel about her, but yes, I think she is a really fine person. However, what is really important is what you think."

Tentative Analysis and Tentative Hypothesis.   Tentative analysis and tentative hypothesis (also discussed in Chapter 11 as a group counseling technique) can also be employed effectively in the middle stages of counseling. Counselors can use this type of lead to help children understand the purposes of their behavior. In the middle stages of counseling, children may well disclose several behaviors or thoughts that provide counselors with what the purposes of those behaviors (or misbehaviors) may be. The counselor responds in a tentative way, much as he or she does with interpretations, with a statement similar to, "Johnny, I could be wrong, but is it possible the kids on the playground are not picking you for any of the teams because you always want to be boss and set the rules?" Since the use of this technique is a kind of interpretation, "soft" statements are useful. "Could it be" or "Is it possible that" are good introductions to the use of this lead. (See also the discussions of interpretation in this chapter, and the use of this lead in group counseling, Chapter 7).

An Example of Counseling in the Middle Stages

In the preceding chapter, we discussed the initial stages of a counseling relationship. In the early sessions the emphasis was one of establishing a relationship and coming to a mutual agreement on counseling goals. Counseling leads or techniques during this period included reflection, approval, acceptance, clarification, silence, summarizing, and the use of humor. These techniques can of course be employed at any time during counseling, but they are usually effective in early sessions.

As counseling progresses, counselors should turn their attention to developing a deeper understanding of the student, to include his or her views, values, style of life, and goals. Counselors should also be interested in helping children better understand themselves, their concerns, and their behaviors. At this juncture, counselors will still employ some of the more passive leads noted in the previous chapter, but they will also work with some of the more active leads as they move toward meeting counseling goals. The following interaction is a sample of counselor student interaction during the fifth counseling session.

		COMMENT
Counselor:	"Mary, last week we talked about how you were going to find some ways to do better in school so your mom would let you go to athletic camp this summer. Anything to report?"	Counselor starts with a discussion of last session.
Mary:	"Not much. I'm still worried about my grades. I'll be in seventh grade in the fall, and unless I have a B average, no camp at North Texas, and no chance to make the squad."	Mary expresses the concern that led her to counseling.
Counselor:	"Let's see. We decided the area you were going to concentrate on was math. We had made a little plan for you to do all your homework for two nights in a row. Did you do that?"	Brief summary.
Mary:	"Just once. I went to see 'Batman Returns.' I had a free ticket from the garage that does my dad's car."	

Counselor:	"I see. You went to the movie. I could be wrong, but I gather you didn't finish your math."
Mary:	"No."
Counselor:	"I see. Let me see if I understand. We said that a big thing in your life right now is the summer athletic camp. To go to camp, your grades need to come up, at least some, so your mom will let you go. Right?"
Mary:	"That's about it."
Counselor:	"Mary, you say you want to make better grades. I believe you. Help me out a little. How is not doing your math helping you get better grades?"
Mary:	"I guess it isn't."
Counselor:	"Tell me a bit more about class. You noted you were going to try and pay more attention."
Mary:	"I try, but I just can't. I can't stand her anyway. Yesterday, Jack started to hum, you know, a hum with his mouth closed. I went along with him and hummed too."
Counselor:	"I could be wrong Mary, but I know you are angry at Miss Anderson because of your low grades. Are you cutting up just a little to get even with her?"
Mary:	(Smiles) "Maybe. I know I should not do things. It's just that I get so mad. Do you think she will pass me anyway?"
Counselor:	"What I hear is that you hope you will pass, but you're not sure."
Mary:	"Well, I don't want another D or E on my report card. Any chance Miss Anderson will call mom? I'm grounded if she does!"
Counselor:	"I suppose there is always a chance, but she will tell me first if she is going to call your parents. She hasn't said anything yet."
Mary:	"I sure hope she doesn't call."
Counselor:	"You're worried that she will though?"
Mary:	"Wouldn't you be?"
Counselor:	"Well, what's important is what you think. I guess I would be too, but right now the important thing is what you think."

Comments (right column):

Counselor discusses goals with Mary.

Counselor asks her to make a judgment with respect to her behavior and student goals.

Counselor reviews one aspect of Mary's present style of life.

Tentative hypothesis.

A smile is a recognition reflex. The counselor's "hunch" was correct.

Reflection.

A "sandwich" response.

		COMMENT
Mary:	"Well now what? Got any new ideas?"	
Counselor:	"Maybe you and I can figure out some new plans. Let's start with what you said you wanted to work on with me. You want to go to camp, and to do so means you need better grades. But you are not doing your work and you are fooling around a bit in class. Are there other things you are doing?"	
Mary:	"Just playing my music when I should be reading."	
Counselor:	"OK, you seem to be doing things that are not helping you a lot. How will you feel if your friends go to camp and you have to stay home?"	Projection time.
Mary:	"I'll die!"	
Counselor:	"It seems that what we tried last week is not working. You need better grades to get to camp, but you did not do your homework one night, you were a bit out of line in class, and you are listening to music rather than concentrating on reading. Am I on target?"	
Mary:	"I guess. . . ."	
Counselor:	"OK, Mary, let's start again. Do you still want to try and get better grades?"	Rediscussion of goals.
Mary:	"Yes. No grades, no camp."	
Counselor:	"Can we take a new look at what you are doing, and see if we can take a look at you and what you want to do? Maybe we can start by taking a new look on why last week's plan did not work. Is that OK with you for starters?"	Reexamination of present style of life.
Mary:	"Yes, I think so."	

In this session, the counselor was using more active leads. He discussed the goals that he and the child had agreed upon in earlier sessions, and asked the child to examine her behavior in terms of her expressed goals. Through questioning, he helped to uncover her present level of functioning by examining those parts of her life-style that relate to this functioning. At times he interpreted and used tentative analysis techniques. At this stage, the behaviors of the child and her expressed goals were not in harmony. Either the desire to go to an athletic camp was not powerful enough for her to choose to do the things that would enable her to meet this goal, or other more immediate needs were being met with her seemingly self-defeating behaviors. Continued counseling was necessary at this point. Note that Mary seems to accept the counselor and will speak freely in this accepting climate.

CONCLUSION

As noted, it is perhaps somewhat artificial to arbitrarily divide counseling into three distinct stages, since in reality counseling is an evolving process that tends to blend and overlap from the very first session until termination. Given that fact, it is still useful for students to think of counseling in terms of stages, since the nature of the interaction can be different in the middle and ending stages than it is in the beginning ones.

As counseling progresses and counselors are successful in establishing a relationship and agreeing upon goals, the counselor and the child may want to engage in discussions of how the child views the world, his or her values, and his or her style of life. In broad terms, counselors are concerned with obtaining a deeper understanding of children and their concerns and helping children

come to a greater understanding of self in relation to those concerns. For the most part, children's present level of functioning is more important than what may have occurred in the past. As counselors interact with children, they tend to look for psychological movement and seek to understand the purpose of children's behavior. If children are behaving in ways that do not seem to help them reach expressed goals, these "misbehaviors" are brought to their attention in order that they may examine them and, if they wish, replace or change them.

Counselor leads or techniques during the middle stages of counseling include reassurance, suggestions, information, interpretation, thoughts, interpersonal and time projections, silence, questions, and tentative hypotheses.

REFERENCES

Brammer, L. P. (1988). *The helping relationship.* Englewood Cliffs, NJ: Prentice Hall.

Comier, W., & Comier, L. S. (1991). *Interviewing strategies for helpers: Judgmental skills and cognitive behavioral intervention.* Pacific Grove, CA: Brooks/Cole.

Dinkmeyer, D. C., & Caldwell, C. E. (1970). *Developmental counseling and guidance: A developmental approach.* New York: McGraw-Hill.

Dreikurs, R. (1957). *Psychology in the classroom.* New York: Harper.

Glasser, W. N. (1988). Control theory. In W. N. Glasser (Ed.), *Control theory in the practice of reality therapy.* New York: Harper.

Hammer, E. J. (1968). Interpretation: What is it? In E. J. Hammer (Ed.), *Use of interpretation in treatment.* New York: Grune & Stratton, pp. 1–4.

Meier, S. T., & Davis, S. P. (1989). *The elements of counseling.* Pacific Grove, CA: Brooks-Cole.

Miller, L. L. (1962). *Counseling leads.* Boulder, CO: Pruett Press.

Moreno, J. L. (1957). *The first book of psychotherapy.* New York: Beacon House.

Mosak, H. H. (no date). *Early recollections as a projective technique.* (Mimeo).

Muro, J. J., & Dinkmeyer, D. C. (1977). *Counseling in the elementary and middle schools.* Dubuque, IA: Wm. C. Brown.

Nelson-Jones, R. (1990). *Human relationships.* Pacific Grove, CA: Brooks/Cole.

Nugent, F. A. (1990). *An introduction to the profession of counseling.* Columbus, OH: Merrill.

Rogers, C. R. (1961). *On becoming a person.* Boston: Houghton Mifflin.

Tomm, K. (1987). Interventive interviewing. Part I: Strategizing as a fourth guideline for the therapist. *Family Press, 26,* 3–13.

Young, M. E. (1992). *Counseling methods and techniques.* New York: Merrill.

Chapter Six

Ending Phase of Counseling

🌳 Once children have progressed through counseling to the point that they now possess a greater understanding of self and their concerns, they may be ready to move forward to the action phase of counseling or what Carkhuff (1969) so aptly called the phase of *emergent directionality*. Carkhuff's term seems particularly appropriate for use with children. Rather than thinking of counseling of the young as a one-time process, it may be more useful to think of a given session or series of sessions as simply a part of a process. Children are in the process of growing and becoming, and the concern of a given day or week may not be present next month or next year. Thus counselors should help children along the path to maturity with the full knowledge that there may be many other counseling sessions during their elementary and middle school years.

When, then, is counseling complete? To parents, it may be complete and successful when their child begins to make the kind of academic progress that they expect. To teachers, successful counseling may mean that children who are counseled stop some objectionable behaviors and replace these with ones that are not causing classroom difficulties. In most cases those outside of counseling generally expect that when children work with counselors, some sort of behavioral change will take place. Most counselors, however, have a somewhat broader view of successful counseling, citing changes in self-acceptance and self-understanding and improved methods of problem solving as acceptable counseling outcomes (Muro & Dinkmeyer, 1977).

Different counseling theorists, as one may expect, have a range of expected outcomes for counseling and therapy. For example, those who practice psychoanalysis attempt to reconstruct the individual's personality by bringing the unconscious into the conscious (Freud, 1949). Joseph Wolpe (1973) has demonstrated that changing emotionally debilitating behavior through a process of systematic desensitization is an appropriate counseling outcome (Nugent, 1990). The existentialists, among them May (1961), Frankel (1963), and Van Kaam (1967), feel that counseling may be complete when individuals have found meaning in their lives. Still others, such as Albert Ellis (1973), see the changing of irrational thought as a counseling goal, while Glasser (1989) suggests that counseling should result in a change of behavior.

Regardless of their philosophical orientation, counselors, at some point, must terminate the counseling process, even if the termination is only for the particular concern that initially brought the child to counseling. In fact, once children in elementary and middle schools have benefited from counseling, there is a high probability that they will return for additional help at a later date.

No matter what their theory, school counselors should operate on the assumption that a major aspect of their work with children and adolescents is predicated on the concept of helping individuals gain self-confidence and become ever more independent of adult control. As a result of counseling, children should be perceiving themselves, their concerns, and their behaviors in a new light (Muro & Dinkmeyer, 1977).

Goals of the Final Stage of Counseling

The goals in the middle stage of counseling included those of understanding children and their styles of life and of helping children understand themselves and their concerns. In the ending stages of counseling, counselors turn their attention to helping children act or behave in ways that are constructive to themselves and others. This phase has been described as one of implementation of goals through action (Nugent 1990), as a time when children learn specific procedures, develop plans, and put them into action (Blackman, 1977). Glasser (1980) described the final stage of counseling as a time for action-oriented plans.

Termination of Counseling

In this stage, accomplishments toward meeting goals are summarized and any progress is evaluated (Brammer, 1988, p. 63). Termination of a single interview is, of course, less difficult than a termination of counseling that has occurred over a period of weeks. In terminating single sessions, counselors may want to summarize what took place in counseling, refer to the future, or help children make simple plans (Muro & Dinkmeyer, 1977; Brammer & Shostrom, 1960).

For sessions that have gone on over a period of time, counselors may want to ask themselves the following questions, suggested by Sciscoe (1990), to determine the state of readiness for termination:

Is the presenting problem under control?

Has the client reduced the level of stress by developing better coping skills?

Has the client achieved greater self-awareness and better relationships?

Are life and work more enjoyable for the client?

Does the client now feel capable of living without therapy?

As noted, the word "termination" may not be appropriate for the ending of counseling, in that it implies something that is final and complete. Termination of counseling sessions requires sensitivity on the part of the counselor. The counselor must take care to ensure that children do not view termination as outright rejection, especially with children who have few friends. The counselor must assess the level of understanding the child has of his or her concern and the relative ability to act upon that concern. When the counselor is satisfied that the interaction with the child has provided the best possible course of action, then this may be the proper time for termination. Of course if the plan or plans developed by counselor and child are to take place over a period of time, the counselor should make arrangements to see the child to further determine progress. One good signal that children are ready to end a counseling relationship is their willingness to actively participate in the development of plans. During this time, it is important for counselors to communicate to children that they are available to help in the future.

Techniques for Action Orientation

A number of counseling techniques are appropriate at this juncture, and how they are used will depend on the point of view of the counselor and the purposes for which each technique is used. Again, some of these techniques may be used at any time during counseling. They are presented here because they are useful in the later stages of counseling.

Values Survey and Reinforcement.   In the course of counseling, children will express numerous values and beliefs that may not be congruent with their stated goals and observable behaviors (Muro & Dinkmeyer, 1977). In all probability, counselors will be aware of these discrepancies and able to point them out to children through the use of interpretation or the tentative analysis technique. In using this approach in the final stages, counselors work with children to examine what children are doing, and these discussions are always kept in the context of the child's expressed values (Glasser, 1980). The counselor may propose suggestions or alternatives, but the responsibility for any action always rests with the child. Children should never be forced into any behaviors that they do not deem appropriate. While the counselor's role in this process may be a very active one, he or she does not seek to impose ironclad solutions, direct the child's behavior into specific channels, or impose any controls. The objective goal of this technique is to have children assume as much personal control over their own behavior as possible.

Use of this approach can extend beyond the counseling session and at times is a trial and error process. For example, the counselor and counselee may agree on a plan to try out a new behavior for a period of time and then meet to evaluate any progress. In using the trial process, it is important that the behaviors selected have a high probability of at least a small measure of success. Children sometimes get excited over what has transpired in counseling and will suggest behaviors that may well be impossible. Statements such as "I will not talk out in class for the next six months" may well be beyond what can be accomplished. "I will try to remain quiet for the next three days" may be a better goal.

A key aspect of the use of this approach is the use of reinforcement by the counselor for any effort and positive steps that children make. Children should be freely praised for even the most minute progress toward goals that they have selected. At the same time counselors should withhold encouragement for any actions that are self-defeating or irresponsible. Even when children fail miserably in their attempts to move toward a goal, counselors must make every attempt to avoid any blaming or reprimanding. Children, like adults, are behaving the very best they can to meet inherent human needs, and the counselor's job is to help them meet these needs in a positive manner (Glasser, 1980).

Older children who have learned to write should be encouraged to write out their plans and progress regarding a slip of behavior in a small "diary" so the counselor can discuss that progress or lack of it in future sessions. Most children seem to enjoy reporting progress to counselors, particularly if the progress has brought about positive changes in their lives. An example follows:

Steve: "I really do want Miss Andrews to like me. I really do!"

Ms. Maybe: "Yes, I know you do. Let's take a look at what is happening. Start with this morning. What did you do when you came into the room?"

Steve: "Well, not much. I came in, took my seat, and talked with Helen a little."

Ms. Maybe: "OK. That seems like a good start. I assume that talking is OK when you come in the room."

Steve:	"Mostly, but today she was taking role, and asked us to be quiet."
Ms. Maybe:	"I see. I gather you were not supposed to be talking while she was taking role."
Steve:	"I wasn't talking loud."
Ms. Maybe:	"I know you probably weren't. Let's get one thing a little bit clearer. Is there a class rule that everyone should be quiet while she is taking attendance?"
Steve:	"Yes."
Ms. Maybe:	"I gather you know about this rule."
Steve:	"Yes, we voted on it earlier in the year."
Ms. Maybe:	"OK. I could be wrong, but I guess you broke the rule, even though you were not talking very loudly."
Steve:	"Yes, I guess so."
Ms. Maybe:	"What happened then?"
Steve:	"She yelled at me."
Ms. Maybe:	"And I gather you got upset. Now let's take a look at what you just said. You want the teacher to like you better. [Note: this is the counseling goal.] You knew about the no talking rule, and you kinda broke it, even though you were not talking very loud. Let me ask you to think about this a bit. If you want Miss Andrews to like you better, how is talking when she is taking role going to help? Will she like you better if you interrupt what she is doing?"
Steve:	"I don't know. I guess not."
Ms. Maybe:	"What can you do to help at attendance time tomorrow?"

This interaction assumes that the counselor and child have explored the concern, agreed upon a goal, and engaged in some exploration of self and of the expressed concern. The counselor's approach is one of restating the goal, examining what is occurring in relation to the expressed goal, making an evaluation of the behavior as helpful or not, and finally making a small plan that will help the child make positive steps (Glasser, 1980).

Confrontations.   Confrontation as a counseling technique is also discussed in Chapter 7 as one of the techniques of group counseling. It may also be used in individual counseling as part of the process of helping children assume self-responsibility (Muro & Dinkmeyer, 1977). It is, as Taylor suggests (in Chapter 10 of Young, 1992), an advanced technique that involves discussing with children the inconsistencies between expressed emotions, behaviors, and thoughts. It is also labeled by Egan (1990) as a challenge in that this term is less suggestive of a battle between the counselor and the child (Young, 1992).

Nelson-Jones (1990) suggests that confronting be used to help others expand and explore their perceptions. In using confrontations, he indicates that counselors should confront inconsistencies. For example, "On the one hand you say you are doing fine, but on the other I hear a little bit of worry in your voice." In addition, he notes that counselors should also use confrontations for possible distortions of reality such as, "You say that you are turning in your work, but I have not seen any of it yet." His guidelines for how to confront include the following:

1. Start with reflective responding.
2. Help speakers confront themselves.
3. Don't talk down.
4. Use a minimum of muscle.
5. Avoid treating voice and body messages.
6. Leave the responsibility with the speaker.
7. Don't overdo it.

                                                             (pp. 114–115)

In a similar vein, Brammer (1988) notes that constructive confrontation involves a complex cluster of helping skills consisting of the following:

1. Recognizing feeling in oneself as a helper.
2. Describing feelings in oneself and sharing them with the helpee.
3. Feeding back reactions in the form of opinions about his or her behavior.
4. Meditating as a form of self-confrontation.
5. Repeating as a form of emphasizing and clarifying.
6. Associating as a method of getting in touch with feelings.

                                                             (p. 80)

Among the most important points suggested by Brammer and Nelson-Jones is that of the counselor understanding his or her own feelings in the process. Confrontations that are done in anger or even annoyance are counterproductive in the counseling process.

Young (1992), in an excellent discussion of the technique of confrontation, notes that counselor statements in confrontation usually take one of the following forms:

> You said _____ but acted _____.
> You said _____ but also said _____.
> You acted _____ but also acted _____.
> You said _____ but I see _____.

                                                             (p. 277)

Young's approach to confrontation also includes a four-step process of using clarification and reflection to understand the child's message, gaining the child's acceptance of a confrontation, using the child's response to confrontation to reinforce the confrontation or require the child to explore and synthesize, and finally following up the confrontation with action. For example:

Lyle: "I want the other boys to quit making fun of me."
Mr. Bryl: "You are upset because they make fun of you?"

Lyle: "Yes, they seem to be OK friends sometimes, but when they want to they really pick on me."

Mr. Bryl: "You think they pick on you, yet you say that they are OK friends sometimes. You seem to like them, but you're upset with them sometimes?"

Lyle: "Well, I guess so."

Mr. Bryl: "Help me out a little bit here. You are telling me you are upset with them, but you still want them as friends."

Lyle: "Yes, I do. You know they all live in my neighborhood. If I don't have them for friends, I won't have anyone to play with."

Mr. Bryl: "OK. Let's see what we can decide to do now that may help you."

In this interchange the counselor used reflection of the child's feeling, pointed out the incongruence in what the child was saying, gained the child's acceptance of the confrontation, and started to follow up the process with a course of action (Young, 1992).

Immediacy. Immediacy in a counseling relationship refers to what is occurring between the counselor and child at the present moment (Muro & Dinkmeyer, 1977). It is a transition or a bridge between the softer empathic response of the counselor in the early sessions and the more confrontive ones that may be used as counseling is drawing to a close. In some respects it is closely related to the "here and now" aspect of group counseling. In essence, whenever two individuals interact, feelings are always involved. While they may be only dimly perceived or even neutral, individuals respond to each other with emotions as well as with spoken words. For example:

Tracy: "You said if I kept quiet in class, Miss Andrews would like me a little better. You were wrong. I shut up and she still does not like me."

Mrs. Mays: "I gather what we decided to do didn't work too well. I'm sorry about that, and maybe we need to try something else. Let me try something else out on you. I could be way off base, but I'm feeling that maybe you are a little angry with me because the plan did not work. Am I wrong?"

In this exchange, the counselor responds to what the child has verbalized, but she has also picked up the child's anger in her voice. In a tentative way she communicates the immediacy of the situation back to the child in an attempt to keep the relationship open and honest.

Encouragement. All individuals need to feel a sense of worth. In fact, Glasser (1988) suggested that a sense of worth is a part of the need to belong, which is a basic human need for all individuals. Absence of this sense of worth may cause individuals to engage in self-defeating behaviors or perhaps withdraw from the pains of feeling worthless in life. As indicated in the discussions of relationships in Chapter 4, part of the counselor's efforts must be directed toward helping children feel loved, respected, and worthy. The use of encouragement throughout counseling is one of the very best ways to help children meet this need, and it may be especially important as children terminate counseling and attempt new behaviors on their own. Its importance was eloquently stated by Dreikurs, Corsini, Lowe, and Sonstegard over thirty years ago:

> At present, children are exposed to a sequence of discouraging experiences. Deliberate encouragement is essential to counteract them. The child misbehaves only if he is discouraged and does not believe in his ability to succeed with useful means. Encouragement implies your faith in the child. It communicates to him, our belief in his strength and ability, not in his potentiality. Unless you have faith in him as he is, you cannot encourage him (Dreikurs et al., 1959, p. 23).

Unfortunately the notion that "at present, children are exposed to a sequence of discouraging experiences" has changed little in the past three decades. Discouragement is still experienced by numerous children in today's classrooms.

As a technique, encouragement is among the most popular tools available to counselors, although it does not follow a precise set of steps (Young & Feiler, 1990). In addition to the encouragement process outlined by Dinkmeyer and Dreikurs (1963) and described in Chapter 1, Young (1992) has identified the following fourteen encouraging behaviors from the writings of Dinkmeyer & Losoncy (1980), Losoncy (1977), Witmer (1985), and Sweeney (1989) as effective interventions:

1. Acknowledge efforts and improvements.
2. Concentrate on the present capacities, possibilities, and conditions rather than on past failures.
3. Focus on client strengths.
4. Show faith in the client's competency and capabilities.
5. Show an interest in the progress and welfare of the client.
6. Focus on the things that interest or excite the client.
7. Ask the client to evaluate his or her performance rather than comparing it to another standard.
8. Show respect for the client and the client's individuality and uniqueness.
9. Involve the self through honest disclosure.
10. Offer assistance as an equal partner in the counseling process.
11. Use humor.
12. Provide accurate feedback on deeds rather than on personality.
13. Confront discouraging beliefs.
14. Lend enthusiasm and ask for commitment toward goals.

(p. 237)

The types of encouragement in Young's list involve the use of both verbal and nonverbal procedures. As children move from the counselor's office to the classroom and home to attempt new and perhaps frightening behaviors, they feel confident of the support of the counselor. In many cases, growth requires that children engage in these new behaviors, and often the help of another human being is essential in helping them to attempt what may be new and different ways of interacting in their worlds.

Behavioral Contracts.   Behavioral contracts (sometimes called developmental contracts) are agreements between two individuals (or among three or more individuals) to behave or act in certain specified ways as indicated in the terms of the contract. Contracts range from what Glasser (1989) simply refers to as making a plan to more elaborate approaches that border on contracts used in the legal profession. Regardless of how simple or sophisticated the contract may be, we have found them to be very effective in counseling elementary and middle school children. In some cases, children keep worn and overly folded contracts in their possession long after they have ceased visits to the counselor!

In general, more formal contracts should include specifying the observable steps to be followed, developing a way to record the behaviors, establishing a reference point to compare observations, identifying the reinforcement for change, deciding on a reinforcement schedule, and identifying a time dimension in which change may be expected to occur (Hackney, 1974; Muro & Dinkmeyer, 1977).

We have found that for most elementary and middle school children, contracts which simply list the behaviors the child agrees to attempt to meet the goals he or she has established work well. The counselor might want to include a timetable for completing these agreements.

Self-Recording or Behavioral Diaries.   Counselors and children want to keep a record of what children do beyond the counseling session. In some cases the counselor can record behaviors, but most children will want to personally record what they are doing. This process may be a very simple one wherein a child records the number of times he or she engages in desirable behaviors between counseling sessions. (These are behaviors that have been mutually agreed upon by the counselor and child.)

A variation of this approach is the "cartoon" method of self-recording or the use of stick figures, one depicting the student engaging in behaviors that are helping him or her meet counseling goals and the other showing the child operating in a self-defeating manner. For example, one cartoon may have a child playing with others on the playground, and the other may show a group of children playing while the counseled child stands off alone. When a child "joins in" with others, she makes a mark under the picture of the stick figure who is playing with the other children. When she does not "join in," she marks the lonely figure. Children are requested to bring the tally sheets to the next counseling session because they provide an excellent start for a discussion of how well a child is moving toward goals (Muro & Dinkmeyer, 1977).

Homework.   Related to behavioral contracts is the technique labeled homework by a number of writers who feel that assignments given to children to be completed between sessions is very important for successful counseling outcomes (Last, 1985; deShazer, 1985; O'Hanlon & Weiner-Davis, 1989). An example of the use of this technique would be that of the counselor suggesting that the child create situations that are troubling rather than waiting for them to occur. A shy girl may be asked to introduce herself to at least one person a day for three or more days. A child who is deeply fearful that the teacher will call on him when he does not know an answer is asked to prepare a response to something the teacher may ask in class and then ask the teacher to call on him to respond to the question armed with the prepared material. As children gain confidence, they may then ask teachers to call upon them twice or three times a day and perhaps at a later date at any time during the day. With careful planning, psychological homework can be a very effective counseling tool (Muro & Dinkmeyer, 1977).

An Example of the Termination Stage of Counseling

The following discussion is an example of a counseling session that took place after seven previous counseling sessions. Note that at this point the child seems willing to attempt some different approaches to reaching her goals.

		COMMENT
Mary:	"I did what we talked about last week. I went out and talked to three people in the lunch room. I felt kinda nervous."	
Mrs. Bolger:	"Good. You are trying hard. I bet it feels good knowing that you are making some progress."	Encouragement.
Mary:	"Yes, but I did not do anything after lunch. I just watched the other kids."	
Mrs. Bolger:	"I see. Your goal is to make more friends. I believe that is what we said. Now how is your standing around after lunch helping you make more friends?"	Confrontation. Discrepancy between expressed goal and behavior of child.
Mary:	"I guess it isn't, but I get scared!"	
Mrs. Bolger:	"I understand. You feel uneasy about approaching other kids. Maybe we can figure out some way to make it easier. Do you have any ideas?"	Reflection.
Mary:	"Maybe, I could get Mr. Blake to help me. He could help me get started with one of the girls I want to meet. Think I can ask him?"	Plan.
Mrs. Bolger:	"I believe you think you can, and yes, I think you can too. Let's go over exactly what you will do."	Encouragement.
Mary:	"When I come in tomorrow, I'll ask Mr. Blake if he can think of something to say to Krista. I know, we are going to do a Christmas play, and Krista is one of the best singers. I'm going to play the piano. Maybe we can talk about the music."	

Mrs. Bolger:	"Sounds good to me. Can you do it all right?"
Mary:	"Yep, I think I can. I'll at least give it a try."
Mrs. Bolger:	"Good, Mary. In fact, very good. I feel you can do this. I know how hard this is for you, but I do believe you can do it. You're on the right road. Will you check with me tomorrow and let me know if it is working?"
Mary:	"OK. I have a few minutes before my bus comes. I'll let you know."

Note that this may not seem like a very serious problem to adults, but to this child, friends or lack of them are very important. In fact, in this particular case, Mary referred herself for counseling in order to find ways to meet new friends. This is a normal developmental concern and is fairly typical of the "problems" children bring to counseling. This is probably not the final counseling session, but progress has been made in that Mary is willing to attempt some new behaviors to meet her goals. In future sessions, they may discuss other new behaviors, perhaps role played and evaluated. In a sense, discussion of this concern is part of the very essence of developmental counseling.

CONCLUSION

When children have come to some understanding of themselves and of their concerns, they may be ready to enter the final phase of counseling wherein they gradually separate themselves from counseling. They may now be ready to use any newly developed insights and skills to begin to solve concerns and meet goals. If goals are not met, then counseling may continue with a new plan of action. If counseling is successful, the process will help children gain new strengths to help solve other concerns that may occur in the future.

The definition of successful counseling, of course, depends on one's theoretical point of view, but we believe that counseling is successful when children are able to reach reasonable goals that they have determined to be important. Termination of a session or of a series of sessions may take place when they have met expressed goals.

Techniques used in the final stage of counseling include values surveys, confrontations, immediacy, encouragement, behavioral contracts, self-recording, and psychological homework.

REFERENCES

Blackman, G. J. (1977). *Counseling theory, process and practice.* Belmont, CA: Wadsworth.

Brammer, L. M., & Shostrom, E. L. (1960). *Therapeutic psychology.* Englewood Cliffs, NJ: Prentice Hall.

Brammer, L. M. (1988). *The helping relationship.* Englewood Cliffs, NJ: Prentice Hall.

Carkhuff, R. R. (1969). *Helping and human relations, Vol. 1.* New York: Holt, Rinehart & Winston.

deShazer, S. (1985). *Keys to solutions in brief therapy.* New York: Norton.

Dinkmeyer, D. C., & Dreikurs, R. (1963). *Encouraging children to learn.* Englewood Cliffs, NJ: Prentice Hall.

Dinkmeyer, D. C., & Losoncy, L. E. (1980). *The encouragement book.* Englewood Cliffs, NJ: Prentice Hall.

Dreikurs, R., Corsini, R., Lowe, R., & Sonstegard, M. (1959). *Adlerian family counseling.* Eugene, OR: University of Oregon Press.

Egan, C. (1990). *The skilled helper* (4th ed.). Pacific Grove, CA: Brooks/Cole.

Ellis, A. (1973). *Humanistic psychotherapy: The rational emotive approach.* New York: Julian Press.

Frankel, V. (1963). *Man's search for meaning.* New York: Washington Square Press.

Freud, S. (1949). *An outline of psychoanalysis* (J. Strachey, Trans.). New York: Norton. (Original work published in 1940).

Glasser, W. N. (1980). Reality therapy. In W. N. Glasser (Ed.), *What are you doing?* (pp. 48–60). New York: Harper & Row.

Glasser, W. N. (1989). Control theory. In W. N. Glasser (Ed.), *Control theory in the practice of reality therapy* (pp. 1–15). New York: Harper.

Hackney, H. (1974). Applying behavioral contracts to chronic problems. *The School Counselor, 22,* pp. 23–29.

Last, C. G. (1985). Homework. In A. S. Bellack & M. Hersen (Eds.), *Dictionary of behavior therapy techniques* (pp. 140–141). New York: Rawson.

Losoncy, L. E. (1977). *Turning people on: How to be an encouraging person.* Englewood Cliffs, NJ: Prentice Hall.

May, R. (1961). *Existential psychology.* New York: Van Nostrand Reinhold.

Muro, J. J., & Dinkmeyer, D. C. (1977). *Counseling in the elementary and middle schools.* Dubuque, IA: Wm. C. Brown.

Nelson-Jones, R. (1990). *Human relationships.* Pacific Grove, CA: Brooks/ Cole.

Nugent, F. A. (1990). *An introduction to the profession of counseling.* Columbus, OH: Merrill.

O'Hanlon, W. H., & Weiner-Davis, M. (1989). *In search of solutions.* New York: Merrill.

Siscoe, M. (1990). The termination of therapy. (Unpublished manuscript). Quoted in M. Young, *Counseling methods and techniques.* New York: Merrill.

Sweeney, T. J. (1989). *Adlerian counseling: A practical approach for a new decade.* Muncie, IN: Accelerated Development.

Van Kaam, A. (1967). Counseling and psychotherapy from the viewpoint of existential psychology. In D. Arbuckle (Ed.), *Counseling and psychotherapy: An overview* (pp. 20–32). New York: McGraw-Hill.

Witmer, J. M. (1985). *Pathways to personal growth.* Muncie, IN: Accelerated Development.

Wolpe, J. (1973). *The practice of behavior therapy* (2nd ed.). New York: Pergamon.

Young, M. E., and Feiler, J. (1989). *Theoretical trends in counseling: A national survey.* Unpublished manuscript.

Young, M. E. (1992). *Counseling methods and techniques.* New York: Merrill.

Chapter Seven

Group Counseling

 Readers may be surprised to discover that for some counselors, group work with children is considered less than beneficial. In a recent tour of twenty elementary schools in Texas, Arkansas, and New Mexico, the authors found only three elementary school counselors who were actively engaged in group counseling on a daily basis. Many expressed a dislike for group work because of the management problems associated with groups, some doubted that group counseling works well with children, and some indicated that they were so busy with individual counseling that time for the formation of groups was simply not available. Others cited the problems associated with forming groups in schools that operate with self-contained classrooms.

In spite of these objections by practicing counselors, the authors feel that group counseling is a necessary and potentially vital part of all comprehensive guidance programs. Muro and Dinkmeyer (1977) note that children are social beings and as a result their actions have a social purpose. As with adults, the life-styles of children are expressed in their transactions with other individuals in their lives, as is their psychological movement. In this context, the counseling group is an ideal social laboratory (Nugent, 1990).

Rationale for Counseling in Groups

The behavior of children serves certain purposes. They want to belong, they actively seek acceptance, and they want to gain an understanding of themselves and others (Glasser, 1989). In spite of better methods of individualization of instruction, groups are still very much a way of life in most schools. Young people are taught in groups, they play and eat in groups, and their worth or lack of it is unfortunately often expressed in terms of how well they meet local or national norms on achievement and learning ability tests applied to large groups.

The transition from home to school can be a crucial aspect of a young person's life. For the vast majority of children, acceptance by parents is predicated on who the child is. Children receive love and affection and experience positive feelings of worth because of the fact that they are "special" to mommy and daddy. Once they enter the formal process of schooling, however, the love and worth that was so much a part of their lives is now, at least in part, contingent on what they can produce. Children no longer are assured of positive feedback from significant adults in their lives simply because they are present in a schoolroom.

Since most of the concerns of young children are interpersonal in nature, the counseling group with its focus on interpersonal relationships can be a most effective counselor tool for the promotion of optimum human growth (Ehly & Dustin, 1991). In a group, even very young five- or six-year-old children can express both verbally and nonverbally their hopes and fears and gain a growing awareness of how they impact others. In a group, under the watchful eye of the counselor, children are able to test and try out new behaviors they may not be able to attempt in other more structured situations. In a group, children may be able to learn numerous developmental tasks, including those of delaying gratification, controlling emotions, and dealing with abstractions.

While few children understand the abstract concept of universalization, this powerful group mechanism operates in such a way that children feel less isolated and learn that they are not alone in their fears and concerns. As they participate and help others, they come to understand that they, too, will have an opportunity to receive the help of their peers and that of an understanding, caring adult. Berg and Landreth (1990) echo and expand this rationale for using groups with children as follows:

> In group counseling relationships, children experience the therapeutic releasing qualities of discovering that their peers have problems too, and a diminishing of the barriers of feeling all alone. A feeling of belonging develops, and new

interpersonal skills are attempted in a real life encounter where children learn more effective ways of relating to people through the process of trial and error. The group then is a microcosm of children's everyday world. (p. 25)

While individual counseling is good and sometimes necessary, the value of group approaches should not be ignored. The counseling group may provide what the classroom cannot.

The Nature of Group Counseling

As indicated, growing children are very much involved in the process of establishing, understanding, and maintaining positive interpersonal relationships. Group counseling is an interpersonal process led by a professionally trained counselor and conducted with individuals who are coping with typical developmental problems. It focuses on thoughts, feelings, attitudes, values, purposes, behavior, and goals of the individual and the total group (Dinkmeyer & Muro, 1979).

What is important in this definition is the term "process." Group counseling is just that—a process as opposed to an activity that may be conducted only once or twice in a child's school career. In a comprehensive guidance program, counselors are working with developmental groups at each grade level. These could include play groups, activity groups, verbal or "talking groups," or some combination of these. For example, a child may be in a counseling group in grade three to deal with a particular developmental concern at that level. She or he may also be in developmental groups in grades four, five, or six to provide help with other developmental concerns. Since the purpose of group counseling is not to remediate severe problems, but rather to help a child along the path to maturity, it is possible that a given child may be in numerous groups throughout his or her tenure in elementary school.

Some children need intensive group and individual therapy. When counselors encounter such children, their job should be one of seeking appropriate referrals. However, for the most part, the children in counseling groups in school will be boys and girls who do not have severe problems. The counselor seeks out strengths, potential, and ways children are using their skills and talents for a productive life that is appropriate to their maturational level. Above all, elementary and middle school counselors should never lose sight of the fact that their chosen profession grew from the concept of promoting optimal human growth. At times, counselors work with children who are encountering difficulty in overcoming hurdles that seem to block normal development. In so doing, however, counselors always have in mind the importance of viewing children as vital, growing organisms rather than as beings who are beset by major concerns and problems.

Orientation of Children to Group Counseling

While groups are a way of life for elementary school children, counseling groups are not. Counselors should not expect, for example, that a group of second graders will remain still for periods of a half hour or longer and discuss topics, relationships, personal activities, or the group itself. Prior to initiating any kind of group counseling, the counselor will need to engage in orientation activities that will enable children to understand what a counseling group may be. The authors have personally used a number of approaches to orient children to the concepts of both individual and group counseling.

One of the approaches we have found most effective at the elementary level was an orientation process that utilized a small stage built from a packing box that could be easily transported from room to room and periodically was displayed in the lunch room in order that the children would see the stage as part of the normal school environment. The stage has a small curtain in the manner of the old Punch and Judy stages that may have been a part of the childhood of some counselors. If the counselor is skillful and a bit artistic, she or he can make hand puppets that represent a given grade level and are also representative of the ethnic makeup of the school from paper bags, socks, or the like. If the school has an adequate budget, there are a number of commercial companies that sell puppets, but our experience has been that most counselors do not have extensive materials budgets. If this is the case, then the counselor should either make his or her own puppets or seek the assistance of a friend who can provide inexpensive help. The stage and handmade puppets used by one of the authors are shown in Appendix H. The total cost of the stage and puppets shown was less than eight dollars.

Once the stage is complete, counselors will need to develop a series of scripts for each grade level. Obviously, for very young children, the scripts should be short and easy to understand. As the children get older, the counselor may want to limit the use of the stage for an oral presentation to all the classes. We have found the puppet stage to be very effective for use through grade three and sometimes we have used it with grade four (Muro & Dinkmeyer, 1979).

The dialogue for the puppets is limited only by the counselor's imagination. One of the authors' students made up a series of special "little plays" that she used for specific groups. For example, she developed special dialogues to help children understand what group counseling was all about, and she also had material prepared for when she wanted to create groups for children with special concerns (divorce, death, serious illness). In some instances, she found that she needed to have a series of stories about a given topic for children of different ages. Counselors would not inform sixth graders about the creation of a counseling group for dealing with death in the same way that they present ideas to second graders. Armed with scripts, the counselor and teacher can work together to find an appropriate time to enter a classroom and give the play. It is most effective if the counselor actively participates with the puppets and becomes one or more of the voices of the puppets. When the presentation is complete, the counselor should provide time for the children to talk directly to the puppets. Children are fascinated with this process and will readily interact with the puppets as if they were living beings.

Beyond third or fourth grade, the orientation to group counseling may be a simple discussion between the counselor and the children and the classroom teacher. At times, some teachers seem reluctant to give up class time for counseling orientation, but most teachers have children engage in small group work, and when the children are working in groups of five or six, they may not object to efforts to provide an orientation to both group and individual counseling. It is important to note that counselors will receive a much better reception during their attempts at orientation if they are present in the classroom during the course of a normal day. With teacher permission, the counselor should be visible in the classroom, perhaps participating from time to time in musical or other activities, and making every effort to form a personal relationship with as many children as possible. This is important because counselors want to be viewed as a part of the school and not as special people who are assigned to the school to work with troubled children. In fact, counselors would be wise to initiate group counseling by creating developmental groups of children who are generally considered to be the "stars" of the class. Once children learn that all children see counselors, the stigma that is too often associated with counselors may disappear.

In developing a program for an oral presentation, counselors should prepare materials that identify the process and benefits of group counseling for students and, if appropriate, for parents and teachers. The authors have used the guideline questions prepared by Ohlsen (1974) to structure the orientation sessions. The material for each question is presented here as a guide, and counselors will want to modify the material to meet the needs of a given school. In general, there are a number of questions commonly asked by children and adults about group counseling, as follows:

1. Why should I join a group?

   Groups are places where we can talk with each other about how we feel and think about things. Sometimes we can discuss what we can do to make more friends, get better grades, or discover what we do really well.

2. Who is in the group? Are groups for kids in trouble?

   No, groups are for all children. We hope that at some time all the boys and girls in the school can get the chance to be in a group. There will always be a counselor in the group. In this school, I am the counselor and I will be with you.

3. Who decides who is going to be in this group?

   Your teacher, Mr. Avery, and I will decide who will be in the first group. You may want to give us some suggestions. Is there anyone you would like to be with you in the group?

4. What do students do in the group?

   Students should be willing to share thoughts and feelings with others, to listen to others, to help others, and to come to all meetings. (The counselor makes this statement to try and have children make a commitment to the group. The counselor is seeking involved, committed members. With younger children, the counselor may say, "We will talk with each other, we will play sometimes, and we will try and help each other in any ways that we can." More details than this are not necessary with K–3 children.)

5. What do counselors do?

   I start the group, and I help students listen to each other. I help students learn about new things and learn about themselves, especially the things you do well.

6. What can I say in the group?

   We will talk about what we want to say in the group. Other groups that I have had talked about what they do well, what they hope to do when they grow up, how they can do better in what they want to do, and what they can do to make new friends. We can talk about other things too. We can decide on that when the group meets for the first time.

7. What do the rest of us do if someone is talking?

   We listen, and, from time to time, we share our thoughts with the other students.

8. Do you tell our teachers or our parents what I say?

   Generally, what we say in the group will stay there. Of course, if you told us something that needed to be shared with another adult, you and I would discuss it. I would involve you in what I was going to say. (Confidentiality issues must be consistent with the Ethical Guidelines developed by the Association for Specialists in Group Work.)

9. Will my friends or my brothers or sisters be in the group?

   Some of your friends may be, but in school here we will not usually put you in a group with family members.

10. How will I know my friends won't tell what I say?

    I think we can talk about that at our first meeting. If one of us does not trust someone else, we should know about it. Each of us is responsible for what we say and do.

11. Where will we meet?

    We may meet in my office (playroom) work area, or in an empty classroom. At times we may be able to use part of the lunch room. After we set up the group, I'll tell each of you where we will meet.

12. If I join, when will we meet?

    I'll be discussing that with your teacher. We will try and meet at a time when you will not miss any important class work.

13. Do I have to come all the time?

    Yes, we will be meeting for about six weeks. I'll need you to be there every day that you are in school.

Not all children will require answers to all questions. They are presented here since they seem to be common concerns of children who have never been a part of a counseling group. The counselor may want to prepare a brief talk in his or her own words to provide answers to these. Younger children, of course, will not be concerned with and will not generally ask some of the more mature questions. From about fifth grade on and sometimes even earlier, these thoughts will be on the minds of potential counselees. Once the counselor has completed the orientation speech, she or he should distribute sheets of paper to all students to have them write their name and degree of interest in joining a group (no, maybe, contact me, and yes). With younger children, counselors may use the puppets to have the children raise their hands if they would like to become members (Ohlsen, 1974).

With the very young, of course, counselors will not need to go through an elaborate explanation. A simple three to five minute puppet play, where the puppets explain what a counseling group is, will suffice. Teachers can be valuable allies in helping the counselor balance groups.

The authors have also found it helpful to provide each child with a coloring book (see Appendix B) that explains in simple terms what a counselor is and what a counselor does. The coloring book may be used in conjunction with the puppet play to further explain the overall guidance program and particularly the individual and group counseling components.

Group Composition

Counselors should give careful consideration to the composition of their groups in order to make them as beneficial as possible for all concerned. Factors such as sex, age, maturity, prior acquaintance, type of concerns, and personality factors should be considered (Nugent, 1990).

With middle school children, determining group composition should start with a brief interview between the children who are candidates to be in the group and the counselor. The purpose of this interview is to allow the counselor to explain group counseling, talk about the purposes of a specific kind of group (for example, to support children who have lost a parent), and explain any ground rules for the group. The interview is also useful to the counselor in making determinations about the readiness of children for a group experience. Counselors can clearly state their individual expectations of group members, such as possessing a willingness to share with the group, an understanding of the necessity of listening to others, and a desire to help others whenever possible. Of course, during the life of most groups, these rules will be forgotten and perhaps violated. They do, however, provide the counselor with a reference point which he or she may want to keep in mind for interventions in the group as it progresses. For example, a child who has difficulty listening may profit from an intervention such as, "Johnny, I know that what you tell us is very important to you. I believe Marty may want to say something to you that you may want to hear. What did you think about what Marty said earlier about his work in school?" Chances are Johnny did not hear Marty, and if he did, he soon forgot what Marty said in the group. However, by stating "What do you think about what Marty said?" you are teaching children that they should listen to others. As those who work regularly with children know, such interventions may have to be repeated a number of times in the life of a group. It is also appropriate to refer to the group contract discussed in the initial interview.

Approaches to Group Composition

Counselors should give careful consideration to the composition of children's counseling groups in order that each child who elects to participate will receive maximum benefit from the process. In composing groups, counselors need to consider the factors of age, sex, prior acquaintance, nature of concern, and personality factors.

Prior to initiating group counseling, counselors should hold individual interviews with each prospective group member. In the interview, children should learn the purposes of the group, any ground rules, and the expectations for group members. In addition, counselors should determine what specific concern or challenge each child is willing to share with the group, and to reinforce the concept that a group task for all members is a willingness to help others.

An interview prior to initiating a group is essential (Corey & Corey, 1992; Thompson & Rudolph, 1992) in order for counselors to develop groups that are balanced or groups where members have a remedial or developmental effect on each other. For example, groups could be composed of children who are very outgoing and children who are shy. Groups could also be composed of aggressive and shy children, and children who do well in academic areas with those who are having difficulty. The interview is also the time to get a commitment from each child as to his or her intent to operate within the purposes of the group. Even with the best of orientation programs, children will enter group counseling in various states of readiness and understanding. The interview session will enable children to be better prepared for group counseling.

In the early grades of elementary school, homogeneous groups in terms of age and sex are preferable. However, as children progress to the intermediate grades and junior high school, there are advantages in having mixed-gender groups, particularly in those instances when children are seeking new ways to relate to members of the opposite sex.

A frequent approach to composing groups, that of placing children in a group who have common problems, may be counterproductive. For example, if all children in a group are "rebellious," "constantly tardy," or "underachievers," then members may lack the resources and skills to help other members with similar concerns (Muro & Dinkmeyer, 1977). Thus the authors prefer the balanced concept noted previously.

In composing balanced groups, several techniques are available as guides for counselors, including use of the following:

1. Inclusion lists. Types of children to be included for good group conditions:
   a. Compulsive children
   b. Effeminate boys
   c. Restricted children
   d. Constant do-gooders—children with pseudo assets
   e. Children with specific fears
   f. Children with conduct problems

   Children who may be excluded for good group conditions:
   a. Children who have experienced a severe trauma
   b. Children who are experiencing severe sibling rivalry
   c. Children who steal
   d. Children with low affect, little conscience, and a poor sense of right and wrong (Ginott, 1961; Dinkmeyer & Muro, 1979; Harries, 1980)

2. Incomplete sentences. The child is asked to complete the following sentences. "I am _____." "Other members in school think I am _____." Counselors may use any number of incomplete sentences to obtain the information they want to use to compose groups. For example, if a child says "I am a poor student" and another says "I am a good student," both may be good group candidates in the sense of structuring for good group balance. (Harries, 1980, Dinkmeyer & Muro, 1979)

3. Children's drawings. A child is asked to draw a self-portrait. From what the child draws, a counselor may be able to obtain a rough estimate of how the child sees herself or himself. For example, is the figure a happy one? A sad one? A large one?

4. Teacher observations. Classroom teachers are in a good position to help counselors form groups. Since they spend the most time with children, they are able to judge who is shy, who is immature, who has behavioral problems, and so on. By discussing proposed group members with teachers and combining this data with the inclusion-exclusion lists, counselors can make a reasonable assessment of how a group may be composed for counseling purposes. (Harries, 1980)

5. Children's interaction matrix. In Appendix E there is a complete discussion of the Hill Interaction Matrix, one of the relatively few conceptual models of group counseling derived from empirical research. The model provides a guide for understanding the two basic dimensions of group interaction. These dimensions are content style (topics the group discusses) and work style (the emotional tone of the group).

Using the matrix as a guide, Hill also developed the HIM-B, a psychometric inventory that determines what topic and emotional styles are preferred by group members. Use of this inventory allows counselors to determine each individual's preference mode of interacting and use this information to compose groups. For example, individuals who prefer to discuss topics rather than relationships could be grouped in a single group. (Hill, 1965)

Hill's work was the basis for the development of the Children's Interaction Matrix (Drummond, McIntire, Muro, & Brown, 1975). This instrument contains both intermediate and primary forms and is useful in composing children's groups in the elementary and middle schools. A copy of both instruments is included in Appendix E.

Goals of Group Counseling

Some general goals are appropriate for group counseling experiences (Siepker & Kandaras, 1985; Nugent, 1990). The concept of group counseling goals, however, must always be considered in terms of the individual goals that are appropriate for a given child. The objective of group counseling is to produce more competent individuals, not to produce better groups. Dinkmeyer and Muro (1979) and Muro and Dinkmeyer (1977) developed a list of goals for group counseling with children, as follows:

1. To help each member of the group to know and understand himself or herself. To assist with the identity-seeking process.

2. As a result of coming to understand the self, to develop increased self-acceptance and feelings of personal worth.

3. To develop social skills and interpersonal abilities which enable one to cope with the developmental tasks in personal social areas.

4. To develop increased self-direction, problem-solving, and decision-making abilities, and to transfer these abilities to use in regular classrooms and in social contacts.

5. To develop sensitivity to the needs of others, which results in increased recognition of responsibility for one's behavior. To learn to identify with feelings of significant others in the world as well as develop a greater ability to be empathic.

6. To learn to be an empathic listener who hears not only what is said, but also the feelings that accompany what has been said.

7. To be congruent with self, really able to offer accurately what one thinks and believes. To say what one means, to be a congruent "sender."

8. To help each member formulate specific measurable goals that can be behaviorally observed.

Group Organization

Group Size.   As part of group organization, counselors must make decisions regarding group size, meeting schedules, setting, whether a group will be open or closed, and whether participation will be voluntary or required. The size of a counseling group should be a function of the age and maturity levels of the children in the group (Nugent, 1990). Gazda (1989) sees group size with children in terms of counselor control. He feels that since young children have not developed the social graces of listening and taking turns, it is incumbent upon the counselor to assert controls, especially with respect to safety issues. Group size should not exceed five for children who are in grades one, two, and three (Siepker & Kandaras, 1985). Larger groups, especially if they are conducted in wide open spaces such as an available gym or all-purpose room, can be extremely difficult to manage. With children in grades four through eight, six is an appropriate number. With eighth graders, the authors have found that eight is a workable number.

Group Meeting Schedules.   While there is no concrete evidence to support any given length of time that a group should meet as ideal, the authors feel that the frequency of meetings is directly related to the development of group cohesion. Thus if counseling is to be conducted for six weeks, we feel that at least two or three sessions of a half hour duration each week are preferable to six one-hour sessions.

The length of an individual session may also vary. Counselors working in secondary schools will find that individual sessions of an hour or even an hour and a half are workable. With children in elementary schools, groups that last an hour or forty-five minutes are preferable in that counselors must deal with reduced attention span (Siepker & Kandaras, 1985).

Since these are counseling as opposed to therapy groups, the authors recommend relatively short-term group counseling of no more than six to eight weeks at any one time. Of course, this does not preclude children enrolling in another group at a later date. These groups are developmental in nature and are not formed for the purpose of providing prolonged therapy. Most children will work well in a six to eight week framework with individual sessions that range from 30 to 45 minutes.

Setting for Group Counseling.   If counselors are lucky enough to have a well-equipped play room (see Chapter 14), then younger children may become part of a counseling group in that facility. If a playroom is not available, counselors should try and find one room in the school for group counseling purposes. (The authors know that this is easier said than done.) The room should be relatively free from distraction, and if media are used, the same media, arranged the same way on shelves, should be available at each session.

The small table techniques suggested by Foulkes and Anthony as early as 1965 are an excellent approach with younger children if a play room is not available, and a small room is very good with older elementary school children. If possible, counselors should stay away from large rooms that allow the children to be physically remote from the counselor. Not only does this prevent the counselor from helping some individuals with insights and behavioral changes, it also reduces counselor control. The authors are fully aware that most elementary schools, especially the older buildings, were not designed with either counselors or counseling in mind. Some counselors must "make do" with whatever space is available.

Open and Closed Groups.   A closed group is one that is formed with a specific number of children, and once the counseling process has started, no new children are admitted to the group. An open group is a more flexible approach wherein counselors add new members as some children complete counseling. In one sense, closed groups are easier for counselors to handle in that the presence of new group members will require that counselors attend to new behavioral patterns and perhaps different attitudes. It is also difficult to maintain good group balance if new members are added to an ongoing group. Thus short-term closed groups with specific purposes are generally a good workable setup for the organization of a group counseling program in an elementary school.

Having said that, the authors have also found that open groups with young children are very workable, especially in those groups where play and play media are central to the group communication process. One major concern of young children is their desire to get along better with peers. For example, when the authors have used sociometric techniques to identify isolated children, the adding of a "star" or popular child to the group to interact with the isolated children has worked well. Since the purpose of some groups is to help children form relationships with a greater number of children, the changing group structure was ideal for this purpose. In most cases, however, closed, well-balanced groups will probably be the core of the school's group counseling program.

Voluntary or Required Participation.   Older children and adults frequently volunteer to become members of a counseling group. While some younger children will seek the help of a counselor on their own, many will enter counselors' offices because they have been referred by teachers and parents. Obviously, children who want assistance are much better candidates for group counseling in that they may see the group as a way of getting help and be more willing to join.

Children who are referred may present some difficult problems. They may or may not feel that they have concerns and may or may not want to engage in counseling. Far too often, children who are referred are there because the teacher or the parent has a problem with the child. Many referred children, for their part, think that they are doing "just fine," which gives them little motivation toward change.

Counselors should expect resistance from involuntary clients. The issue should be approached directly. Counselors should state that they are aware that some members are reluctant to participate and that some do not wish to interact, to share, and to help others. However, since those referred are required to attend for the length of the group sessions, they should know that while those members are in the group, the counselor is willing to help in any way possible. Such a statement will not produce any magic, but warm, accepting counselors may be able, through skillful use of the group, to persuade such children that counseling can indeed be helpful. After all, if counseling is for all children, then all children should benefit. Again at this juncture we want to stress the importance of including nontroubled and nontroublesome children in the groups. During the course of a year if the children see that many children have been involved in group counseling, they may be less hesitant to become members (Dinkmeyer & Muro, 1977).

In recent years, some counselors have had to defend what they are doing in counseling to groups of irate parents who do not want their children to be involved in any type of self-exploration or any kind of group activity. Even some widely used approaches designed to help children feel good about themselves and some to help children understand the dangers of drugs have come under fire. Perhaps the counseling professionals brought this on themselves in that they have done a less than adequate job of explaining the nature of counseling. Parents object to counseling for a number of reasons, and some have sincere objections to the school's involvement in any aspect of a child's personal life. Corey and Corey (1992) suggest that counselors may be better served by keeping parents informed about the counseling program and, if necessary, obtaining parental permission before placing children in some groups. With widely used classroom approaches of an affective nature, the community should be informed in advance. Some schools have taken the approach that a certain kind of program is good, and if parents do not want to have their children involved, then other learning activities will be offered.

It is probably prudent to carefully explain the counseling program to the community at every opportunity. For example, the authors have conducted "mock" developmental group counseling demonstrations for parents and PTA meetings to show that our goals and objectives are to enhance and promote learning, not to modify values and concepts taught in the home. We feel that some of the parents who object to having their children counseled are fearful that children may reveal something that will embarrass the parents. Be this as it may, if some parents for whatever reasons object to counseling, then their children should probably not be included in groups. Our challenge as a profession is to do a better job of explaining who we are and what we do. If we are ever able to communicate that our goal is to help, not harm, then few parents will be fearful of counseling. Until we do so, we can expect challenges.

Group Leadership Competencies

Some of the skills commonly utilized in individual counseling are equally appropriate for use in counseling groups (Ehly & Dustin, 1991). The use of reflection, clarification, and questioning techniques, for example, may well be part of the repertoire of group counselors. However, group counseling is not individual counseling in a group setting, and some techniques are unique to groups. These techniques, in part, are related to the uniqueness of the group situation.

Effective group leadership requires individuals who are capable of holistically understanding the group experience. The group leader, while thoroughly understanding individual psychodynamics, must use this and additional knowledge to grasp the sometimes complex transactions, group interactions, and group dynamics principles that impact group life. Through skillful facilitation, group leaders should be able to create the climate and conditions that foster personal growth and development. Simply placing children in a group does not ensure that all children will have positive experiences. In fact, the group with a potential for great good can also be a place where serious harm can be done. Counselors should not and must not give up their responsibility to ensure that the group is beneficial to all.

Leaders must be involved in the development of group norms. They must provide structure, monitor interactions, make meaningful comments, interpret process, protect, encourage, and ensure nonjudgmental acceptance. Counselors are, above all, models, and what they say and do in groups provides a powerful learning experience for children. In fact, the reason some standard counseling techniques such as reflection are so powerful is that children (or adults, for that matter) rarely experience a reflection of their feelings in normal human discourse. Throughout the life of the group, many of the competencies described in the following paragraphs will be useful to counselors.

Structuring. Defining goals, communicating the purpose of the group, and setting limits are all part of the structuring process (Corey & Corey, 1992; Berg & Landreth, 1990; Kottler & Brown, 1992). While the authors are firm believers in the concept of interviewing each potential group member and perhaps consulting with a child's teacher before forming groups, we feel that counselors should repeat what has been discussed during screening interviews in the initial group session. Counselors should stress the importance of individual sharing of strengths and weaknesses and of a willingness to help others with their concerns. Through direct "teaching" and through modeling, counselors should look for ways to encourage good listening habits. In fact, if a child is paying close attention to what another child in the group is saying, counselors may appropriately say (in their own words), "Mary, I could tell that you were listening to Andy when he was telling about how sad he feels over losing his dog. I was pleased to see you listen so closely, and I was also pleased to see how you were trying to help Andy by telling him what you did when you lost your pet." Such verbalizations tell children that counselors are listening and watching and also indirectly teach children about listening and helping others.

In preparing for an initial session of a counseling group, counselors may want to prepare a brief "structure talk" to be used in the group. The use of any verbal intervention technique will be more effective if it is natural and free of stilted textbook, stereotypical jargon. Thus the following example of a "structure talk" is just that, an example. Counselors should use their own wording. A "structure talk" may be similar to the following:

> I have met with each of you individually, and all of you said that you were interested in joining our counseling group. For a moment, I would like to remind you of what we discussed when I met with each of you in my office. Remember this is your group. What we say in here will stay in here, and I will not be discussing this meeting with your teachers and parents. I asked each of you if I could talk to your parents. I have discussed this group with at least one of your parents, and they do know that you are a member.
>
> I believe I told you why we are here. Each of you feels that you are doing pretty well in school, but all of you told me you want to do better. So the purpose in our meeting is to share our concerns and to help each other. We will meet twice a week for a half hour starting at 2:30 in my office. Is this what each of you understands to be the purpose of the group? (Here the counselor should pause and scan the group.) Have I missed anything? (pause again) Does anyone else have anything to add?

Universalizing.   Universalizing is both a group mechanism and a leadership technique. In the opinion of the authors, universalization is the single most powerful mechanism used in groups, and it is also unique to the group situation. As a group mechanism, universalization refers to the concept that group members, by listening to others in the group, soon learn that they are not alone in what they are feeling or in their concerns. Many children (and adults, for that matter) feel that they are the only ones dealing with specific issues. Of course this is not so, but it is not uncommon for children in a group to look surprised and actually verbalize something like, "I thought I was the only one who felt that way." As a leadership technique, the counselor, after hearing one or more children express a concern, may interact in the following way:

Student: No matter how hard I try, I just can't make my mom happy. She wants all A's cause she says I'll need all A's to become a doctor or something like that. I can't do it!

Counselor: I'm hearing you say several things. One is you're upset because you
              can't seem to do what your mom expects. Secondly, you don't feel you
              are going to be able to make those kinds of grades. I think what you
              have just said is important. Has anyone else experienced this problem?

By asking if others have similar concerns, the counselor is attempting to
show the child who voiced the concern that he or she is not alone in his or
her thoughts and feelings. If other members share their concerns, the potential positive impact on a child who is feeling isolated can be substantial.

Linking.   Linking is a skill not usually learned in individual counseling.
Counselors who link student statements are attempting to point out both
similarities and differences in student thinking (Berg & Landreth, 1990;
Corey & Corey, 1992; Kottler & Brown, 1992). Counselors may link both content and feeling statements, which at times involves the ability to detect hidden meanings. By carefully scanning the group, counselors may also elect to
link or tie together nonverbal feelings and thoughts. Linking is an effective
technique to promote interaction and subsequent cohesion. In some instances, the links verbalized by counselors will allow some counselees to experience universalization. An example of linking is as follows:

Jessica: Every time I ask for the ball during our soccer games, the big kids kick
              it to someone else. I've decided I'm not going to play anymore.
Paula: Yeah, and speaking of plays, the teacher told us we could add our own
              stuff to the Mary Poppins play. I gave the kids a whole sheet of things I
              thought we could add, but when I saw the final copy none of my things
              were used. I may not go to the play this year.
Ms. Prebish: I hear both of you saying that you are disappointed with the ways your
              friends have been treating you. Rather than continuing to stay with
              them, you just may give it up and drop out. What do either of you feel
              about that right now?

In this example, the counselor ties together or links the similar thoughts
of two group members. Although the incidents are separate, the chosen behavior of both students is to withdraw. While the counselor's objective is not
that of trying to make them continue with a project, the desirability of
exploring it and thinking through it can be beneficial. In a similar note, if a
child expressed anger at his friends and another child seemed to agree by
making an angry expression, the counselor could link the feelings of the two,
one expressed verbally and one nonverbally, as follows:

Joey: I get mad when I am not allowed to play!
Harry: (Nods head, tightens lips.)
Mr. Ivey: Joey is telling us that he gets angry when he is not allowed to play the
         game. I could be wrong, but I think Harry is also angry. Can either of you
         tell the group any more about this?

Confronting.   Much of the fear that some children (and lots of adults) have
about group counseling stems from the erroneous perception that much of
what happens in groups is one or more persons singling out an individual

and telling him or her all the negative things about who he or she is, how he or she relates, and what is inadequate about the individual (Kottler & Brown, 1992; Hutchins & Cole, 1986; Young, 1992; Nugent, 1990; Brammer, 1988; Muro & Dinkmeyer, 1979). Some of this comes from movie or television drama about group therapy. The ways group work is usually presented on television are so poor that one should not be surprised that groups are negatively viewed by a segment of our population. In addition, the encounter group movement of the 1960s and 1970s, a movement often involving poorly trained leaders, has done little to enhance the use of group approaches as a constructive force.

A confrontation is not an attack on another, nor is it some form of cathartic experience. A confrontation is a statement that allows an individual to know and understand the impact of his or her behavior on another (Corey & Corey, 1992). Thus a statement such as "I don't like the way you act" is more akin to scapegoating than it is to a confrontation. If a counselor confronts a child, the counselor should always soft pedal the confrontation and attempt to help the child better understand the counselor's intentions. For example:

Lottie: Mom and dad won't let me go to the hockey games on school nights. So, when they look for me to clean the snow off the walk, I won't be there. I just won't show up to do the work. Let them shovel it!

Ms. Lester: Is it possible that you are trying to get even with your mom and dad for not letting you do what you want?

In this example, the counselor "confronts" the child in a soft way and attempts to have the child comprehend the purposes of her behavior. The verbalization is soft and provides an opportunity for the child to consider what she has just said.

Most negative confrontation in the group will generally be from child to child and will usually occur in the early or middle (transition) stages of group life. Often children do not mince words, and at times a child will blurt out a negative and hurtful confrontation before the counselor can intervene. Counselors must then attempt to have the confronting child "own" his or her feeling and send an "I" as opposed to a "you" message. For example:

Jimmy: Joe, you're a wimp. You whine all the time. That's why the kids don't like you.

Mrs. Evans: (To confronter) Jimmy, could you start again and tell Joe what you just said, but start with "I feel." Try and say, "Joe, I feel _____ when you _____." Can you do that?

Use of the "Here-and-Now" Interaction.   We have noted in this chapter our belief that the use of here-and-now interaction (Yalom, 1985) is important in all group counseling. The authors believe that long, involved discussions of events that took place in the near or distant past can squeeze the very life out of the group. In addition, long discussions of the past are frequently used by some people to resist the interaction of the group. Again, we have no quarrel with counselors who want to use historical data in the group. Such data is best used when it is brought into the context of the here-and-now of group life. All problems and concerns that children bring to the group must, in the final analysis, be solved in the present. Thus one skill or competency needed by counselors is to bring the individual or group focus to what is happening in the group at the present moment. For example:

Andy: I did not like math last year, and now I'm in sixth grade and I do not like it any better. When I have work to do at home, I hide my book in my gym bag and forget about it. I did the same thing when I was in second grade and in third and fourth too.

Ms. Hurly: Andy, it is clear you do not like math, and you seem to go to great lengths to avoid doing it when you can. Can you share with the group how you are feeling about what you just told us right now?

In this instance, the counselor conveyed to the child that she heard the message and added a mild interpretation. The key point, however, is that the concern over math, although it is part of the child's learning history, must be solved at the present time.

Blocking. Blocking involves intervening in any communication that is destructive to the group or to the growth of individual members (Berg & Landreth, 1990; Corey & Corey, 1992; Kottler & Brown, 1992). Blocking checks communication that hinders individual growth. Blocking can take on a variety of forms, from blocking questions to asking members to make statements that clarify a stated position. Blocking gossip, "there and then" discussions, and statements from group members that are judgmental and harmful are other uses of this skill. An example of a block follows:

Leon: Peter is a snitch. He tells Miss Adams when someone pushes him on the playground.

Harold: I know. He even tells the cooks if someone bumps him in the lunch line.

Sally: (To counselor) Can't you tell him to grow up a little?

Mr. Timms: I think you want me to do your work for you. I believe all three of you should speak directly to Peter, only I would like to have you start what you say with these words: "Peter, I feel. . . ."

In this case, the counselor blocked or stopped the three children who were gossiping about one other member in the group without talking directly to him. Not only did the counselor block the interaction which could become more intense, but he also taught the group to own their feelings and send "I" messages.

Paraphrasing and Clarifying. From time to time in the life of a group, the leader may want to paraphrase or clarify some part of the group's interaction. When counselors are able to effectively summarize and paraphrase the content and affect in the group, they help counselees gain a better understanding of how they are being perceived by other group members. Members can then be requested to clarify their values and assumptions.

Counselors should also be alert to use paraphrasing and summarizing at the end of discussions of specific topics or themes. There will be instances in the life of most groups when a topic has had maximum discussion and nothing more needs to be said. At such junctures, counselors should intervene with such statements as, "All of us have expressed relief that exams are all over, and now we can look forward to summer. I gather that all of you are happy about that, and a few of you are a bit concerned over possible grades. Does anyone want to say anything else about that?" In this case, the counselor summarized the recent discussion and followed it with an overhead question to the group as a whole to help ensure that members had examined this issue to their satisfaction. Another example of paraphrasing and clarifying is as follows:

Hannah: I really aced it today! For the first time this marking period, I feel that I made it through the exam. Also, I did not panic.

Brian: Isn't that something. I did the same thing you did. We talked about how to take tests in here and I used that stuff. For once I did good!

Ms. Tinsley: Both of you are excited and happy at the same time. Not only do you think you did well, but you are glad that the exam is over. Both of you seem to feel you learned something in this group.

In this case, the counselor paraphrased the discussion of two group members and also linked or brought their thoughts together. This could also be followed by an overhead question or by a sponsorship of some other group member.

Encouraging Positive Feedback.   While there seems to be a general perception that much of group interaction dwells on the negative, this is far from accurate. In most groups, counselors will encounter multiple opportunities to provide positive feedback to members themselves, and to teach and encourage group members to do the same (Egan, 1990). Counselors look for strengths and encourage group members to do likewise in that strong peer responses of a positive nature can be very powerful in helping children make progress in the group. One example of positive feedback is as follows:

Carrie: I have a hard time making friends. I don't know how to go up and talk to people if I don't know them.

Mrs. Ebert: I understand that talking to people you do not know is hard for you. However, I've noticed that when you came in the group you did a good job talking to everyone here.

Another example might be as follows:

Sarah: I am not a good athlete. I can't hit the ball.

Joey: Well, you can run pretty fast, and that's good.

Ms. Medler: I've seen you run too, Sarah, and I agree that you are one of the better runners in your class. Also, Joey, I heard you trying to help Sarah by telling her what she did well.

In this case the counselor provides positive feedback to one student and also uses the situation to provide positive feedback to another student who is attempting to help. This technique is effective in establishing the norm of members helping each other in positive ways.

Use of Nonverbal Cues. The facilitator is one who is concerned about having contact with the whole person, that is, the person's thoughts, feelings, purposes, and actions (Dinkmeyer & Muro, 1979). In this context, counselors should constantly scan the group to look for body language that reveals what is happening in the inner world of the child. Counselors should look for emotional cues, such as blushing, or other body language that might reveal tension, boredom, anger, restlessness, and resistance.

For example, if a child has his arms crossed and his legs crossed, he may be showing defiance or lack of interest in what is going on in the group. Since the margin for error is potentially very large when one attempts to identify nonverbal behavior, the counselor should interpret any such behavior in a tentative manner. If the counselor sees a child leaning forward on her chair and peering intently at another group member, the counselor may elect to intervene as follows:

Mr. Maxie: Mary, I could be wrong, but you seem to be very interested in what Helen is saying.

In this example, the counselor interpreted Mary's behavior as an expression of keen interest in what another group member was saying. While Mary was not verbalizing anything at the moment, her body language seemed to indicate interest. Again, the authors want to caution group leaders that while body language is generally closer to an individual's true feelings than what he or she may verbalize, one cannot always be certain that a given body posture is an indication of a specific emotion or thought. With that in mind, the authors feel that the following nonverbal cues may be an indication of what a child is thinking or feeling:

1. Openness: Holds hands open, palms facing up.
2. Defensiveness: Has arms crossed on chest, leg thrown over chair, uses chair as a shield, has legs crossed, hand in front of head, palm out, fingers curled.
3. Evaluation: Sits on edge of chair, stares with unblinking eyes, places hand on cheek, puts hand to face with chin in the palm of the hand, tilts head, strokes the chin.
4. Suspicion, Secretiveness: Puts hand over mouth, glances sideways, turns feet and entire body toward exit, touches or rubs the nose. (These are sometimes called "left-handed gestures.")
5. Happiness: Looks into counselors' eyes and the eyes of others. (Unhappy children will not usually do this.)
6. Uncertainty: Looks away while talking.
7. Special interest: Eyes dilate.
8. Anxiety: Plays with ring, watch.
9. Frustration: Has jerky body movements.

10. Reflective: Has intent gaze, wrinkled forehead.
11. Showing authority: Wags finger at person.
12. Guilt: Covers mouth.
13. Confidence: Makes steeple configuration with fingers.
14. Depression: Has no animation, no humor, is droopy.
15. Rejection: Sits back in chair.

Sending "I" Messages.   An "I" message in group counseling is one that is sent from the speaker to some other member of the group or the counselor. When individuals send an "I" message, they are attempting to convey how another's words and behaviors affect them. The sender of such a message must own the feeling that she or he is expressing. It is the job of counselors to model "I" messages and to intervene in the group when children send a "you" message. "I" messages may also be used by counselors when children use questions. For example, the counselor may want to intervene when one child asks another, "Why do you always act that way?" He or she may say, "Mary, can you say again what you just asked Harry, but this time start with 'I feel' or 'I think'?" An example of intervention when a "you" message is sent is as follows:

Joey: You always want to be first in everything. You are first in line, first to use the stuff on the playground, and first to try and answer every question Miss Aherns asks!

Mr. Eichner: Joey, could you talk directly to Mike and start by saying "I feel"?

Joey: I don't know what you mean.

Mr. Eichner: Let me help you. Say, "Mike, I feel (angry, sad, annoyed) when you always try to be first in everything."

In this example, the counselor is helping the child to own his feeling, rather than verbalize a judgmental "you" statement. This process will encourage children to verbalize their feelings and deal with them in a way that does not subject another child to a negative confrontation.

Tentative Hypotheses.   A tentative hypothesis is a verbalization by counselors designed to help children develop insight into their behavior, either in the here and now of group life or in nongroup situations (Muro & Dinkmeyer, 1977). When used in the group setting, it allows all the members to better understand the reason for a certain act or behavior. Tentative hypotheses must be offered in a warm friendly way by the counselor. They are designed primarily to provide children with an understanding of the purposes of what they do and say. In many cases, it is appropriate to ask children "Would you like to know why you do that?" If there is agreement, then counselors should begin what they say with "Is it possible. . ." or "Could it be. . ." or "I wonder. . . ." An example of counselor use of a tentative hypothesis is as follows:

Andy: Every time Jimmy talks in here today, I am going to laugh out loud. Every time!

Ms. White: Andy, would you like to know why you are doing that?

Andy: Well, I guess so.

Ms. White: I could be wrong, but could it be you are trying to get even with Jimmy for calling you names on the playground this morning?

The hypothesis is offered in a tentative manner, and the use of "could it be" provides the child with an insight that may be accepted as a positive statement rather than an accusation.

Task Setting and Obtaining Commitment.   While group goals may be general in nature, the purpose of group counseling is to help individual members. Individual development, not group development, is the most important outcome of any counseling. Thus while a general goal of a group may be that of self-understanding, each group member should have individual goals that she or he would like to accomplish within the framework of the overall group goal. It is the job of counselors, therefore, to help children verbalize individual goals and make commitments to those goals as part of group life (Muro & Dinkmeyer, 1977). An example of one approach to this is as follows:

Amy: I know we are all in this group because we want to do better in school, but I'm not sure what that means for me. How am I going to do better if all I do is listen to these other kids talk?

Mr. Miner: I understand what you may be feeling. You are wondering if this group can help you, and perhaps you may even be a bit unhappy about the way I have set up the group. If you were to pick out one area that you would like to work on, what would it be?

Amy: Well, if you listen to my mom, I need a lot of work in a lot of areas, but my major problem is I can't seem to keep my mind on my homework. I have my own room, and my own desk, but I sometimes just stare out the window or think about other things. I don't always get my homework done, and then, bingo, more trouble.

Mr. Miner: Well maybe we could start with that. Are you willing to discuss with the group some of your concerns and perhaps some of the ways you could deal with them?

Amy: Yeah, I guess I can at least try that out.

In this example, the counselor recognized that the student may have been discussing her dissatisfaction with the group and perhaps with the counselor as one more powerful adult. By allowing the child to express a personal goal, the counselor may have helped make the experience more meaningful to the student. In addition, the counselor, by not judging the child's concern, conveyed acceptance and was thus able to obtain a commitment or goal for the child to work toward.

The Counselor in the Group

In the Beginning

Counselors new to group counseling should not be surprised to note that in the initial stages of group counseling, children may be preoccupied with expectations from each other and from the counselor (Johnson & Johnson, 1987; Siepker & Kandaras, 1985). Group leaders should also expect mild anxiety from the children. Depending on the age of the children, it is not unusual to discover rapid talking and a quick movement from topic to topic. The talk will be topic-centered and non-group oriented. One should not expect young children to become deeply introspective or to provide ready feedback to each other. Most children will have some fears about the group and perhaps wonder why they, as opposed to others, were selected, and some will fear being ridiculed or teased.

If the orientation to group counseling has been good, most children will become very active in groups. Once initiated, counseling groups become as much a part of school as recess. Counselors who make a special effort to present counseling in a positive light will find that these efforts will result in very positive dividends (Ehly & Dustin, 1991).

In the first session, it is important that counselors structure the group and clearly state the purpose of counseling in terms understandable to the age and grade level of the children in the group (Johnson & Johnson, 1987; Siepker & Kandaras, 1985). If a goal of the group is to help members understand themselves better, not only should that be stated to members, but in the course of the life of the group, it should be repeated. Structuring occurs not only in the early stage of group life—it may also be used when the group wanders from its purpose. Young students have not read books on group counseling, so they do not know what they're "supposed to do." Thus the counselor must not only provide structure, he or she must "teach," via modeling, desired group behaviors.

For example, if a group of sixth graders has been organized to allow members to share concerns, the leader may need to focus on one or more of these concerns if the group begins to wander. At times a simple "Could someone help us? What seems to be happening in the group right now?" may bring the group back into focus. After a few blank gazes and perhaps a "What do you mean, Mrs. Avery?", some group member may say, "We are not talking about what we're supposed to be talking about." If this happens, the group leader can be certain that at least one member of the group is aware of its purpose.

As the group unfolds, there may be lots of nervous laughter and a lack of group purpose. Children, particularly the dependent and those lacking in confidence, may work hard to get and keep the attention of the counselor. If counselors are supportive and group oriented, they should be able to teach children how to interact with each other and with the counselor. Most early verbalizations will be directed to the counselor and not to other members of the group (Siepker & Kandaras, 1985). Since one of the first tasks of the leader is to promote group cohesion, and since group cohesion is a function of member to member interaction, the counselor should actively reflect, link, and summarize to get members to speak to one another.

Counselors should expect children to try them out, to test the limits. This may be especially true if "acting out" children are group members. Younger children may bang a toy on the floor or push another group member, acts that are frequently followed with a glance toward the counselor to see what she or he is going to do. With sixth, fifth, and sometimes fourth graders, one can expect an off-colored joke, a "taboo" word. As the children grope for structure, they soon sense the permissiveness of this situation. Thus they want to try and see if this is "for real" or if they will quickly experience the kind of discipline commonly used in the classroom. There are, and of course, there should be, limits in the group sessions, since limits are essential to tie the process into reality. However, the testing of these limits and the way counselors handle them are important to the development of the group. If, for example, counselors show profound shock at a curse word uttered by a child, group members may very well refrain from expressing other feelings. The testing of the group atmosphere, if successfully handled by the counselor, will allow the group to move on to other significant topics.

One of the first tasks of the counselor in early sessions is to reduce the tension and anxiety that will almost certainly be present in the group (Johnson & Johnson, 1987; Siepker & Kandaras, 1985). If, for example, a child expresses a fear of tests, counselors should bring that fear out into the open. Even a superficial discussion has the effect of reducing anxiety and providing structure. Counselors need to be emphatic, to model behaviors, without trying to be the "expert" in the manner of a domineering parent. Counselors should not attempt to respond to every question that the group raises, because then the children may feel that this is a group for adults and not for children.

Middle Stages

As the group develops, there are a number of matters that require the attention of the counselor (Siepker & Kandaras, 1985). The first of these is that the counselor must have an appropriate level of control. The counselor should listen closely to what the children are saying to the counselor and to each other. He or she should try to observe the nonverbal cues (squirming, dropped eyes, leg shaking, smiles, judgmental glances, and so on) and make a note of which children seem especially nervous and preoccupied in the event that this information could be used at some later time.

Second, counselors should be aware that topics in the group may simply be a "front" for real issues. The true meaning of the topic discussed may be something to do with the group itself. For example, a young boy who is talking about the terrible time he had at recess may well be wondering about how he is being accepted in the group. In many cases what children discuss has meaning in the group, and at times the child who discusses the topic may be unaware of the true meaning of what he or she has just uttered. As group members begin to talk to each other more, counselors should try to closely follow the interaction and, when appropriate, softly interpret what has been said for the benefit of the group. These interventions should always be done gently, with a tentative hypothesis such as, "Could it be, Johnny, that you didn't feel part of the group at recesses and maybe you're wondering if you will be part of this group?" The counselor may choose not to make such interventions, but the authors believe that very often the topics discussed have some meaning to the individuals discussing them and perhaps to the group as a whole.

In primarily verbal (as opposed to play) groups, counselors should be alert for group themes or focal points of discussion. The theme may be one of homework, the upcoming holiday, or how brother at home "bugs" me. These themes may last anywhere from a few minutes to a whole group session, and counselors should be alert to identify these themes and help explain them. For example, the counselor may say, "As I listened to you today, all of you seemed to be concerned with the fact that it is time once again for report cards. Some of you seem concerned about them, and some of you seem to think your parents will not be too pleased. All of you seem to think that this is important. Is there anything else anyone in the group wants to say?" In this case, the counselor "capped" the theme, or provided a summary. It was followed by an overhead question, or a question to the group as a whole. It is appropriate for the counselor to summarize and cap themes from time to time, and it is also appropriate to have the group summarize by answering "What have we discussed today?" Another good ending technique is to pause ten or fifteen minutes before the group is to close and ask, "What did you learn or relearn today?"

Later Stages of Group Life

In many cases, counseling groups in elementary schools do not meet for as many sessions as do groups composed of adolescents or adults. Thus the fairly typical stages of group development are not always as apparent when counselors work with elementary school children. Nevertheless, we have found that counseling groups who remain together for a period of weeks develop in approximately the same way as do groups of older persons, particularly if the groups are closed (membership is constant) and the interaction of the members has been high. As with adults, children in counseling groups will tend to become more cohesive, will engage in some rudimentary leadership functions (reflections, sending "I" messages), and will show a sustained interest in the thoughts and concerns of others.

Also during this stage, more children are willing to attempt "try out" behaviors such as attempting to be less shy with peers, or being willing to offer an opinion in class. Behavioral contracts, developed by children and shared with the counselor and the group, can also be very much a part of the final stages of group life.

In the final stages of the life of a group it is useful to spend some time with children to review what they have learned in the course of working with others. "Going around statements" wherein each child states what "I learned in this group" or "I relearned in this group" are effective counseling leads.

Some children, very much like adults, will express a feeling of sadness when they know the counseling group is coming to an end. This seems to be particularly true for children who experienced rejection either at home or in the classroom or both. In deciding what new behaviors they may try as a result of the group experience, some children will express feeling such as, "If it works, who can I tell now?" Such statements indicate that loss of the support of the counseling group is a concern. Children frequently ask to continue the group. Most will eagerly volunteer to join any newly forming groups.

Counselors need to deal with any feelings of anxiety that may be present over the ending of the group and indicate that they will be present if any of the children wish to come to the office for an individual session. Counselors should also be supportive, provide positive feedback when appropriate, and freely use encouragement as a technique. Thus some techniques that may have been used earlier in the life of the group are still useful in the later stages of group life (Johnson & Johnson, 1987; Siepker & Kandaras, 1985).

CONCLUSION

Group counseling is probably not as widely practiced in the public schools as it should be. Some counselors do not enjoy working with children in groups, some feel that they lack the necessary skills, and others have different and higher priorities in the guidance program. However, since groups are very much a way of life for most elementary school children, all guidance programs should have a group counseling component.

Counseling groups are formed to help children deal with normal developmental concerns that include self-understanding, development of social skills, increased self-direction, sensitivity to others, self-acceptance, and enhanced problem-solving and decision-making skills. Groups also help children to become empathic listeners, to become congruent with self, and to formulate and work on specific self-enhancing goals.

Group counseling is not always well understood and accepted by some children, parents, and teachers. It is necessary, therefore, for counselors to design and carry out comprehensive orientation procedures.

The formation of a counseling group is not a random activity. Counselors must initiate groups with the concept of group balance in mind. Each child in the group should have a positive impact on the other children. Factors such as age, sex, interaction styles, and maturity are some of the considerations necessary to achieve good group balance.

Group counseling with children requires that the counselor operate somewhat differently with children than she or he does with adolescents or adults. Counselors must be active and observant and utilize approaches and techniques appropriate to the age levels of the children. In some cases play, play media, and activity approaches are especially useful. Verbal techniques include summarizing, universalizing, sending "I" messages, linking, confronting, use of the here-and-now, blocking, paraphrasing and summarizing, encouraging positive feedback, interpretation of nonverbal cues, and the use of tentative analysis and task setting.

Pragmatic concerns such as the length of group session, the duration or life of a group, whether or not to have open or closed groups, how and when to use play media, group size, group rooms, composition, and ways to orient parents, teachers, and children must also be considered by counselors who wish to initiate groups.

REFERENCES

Berg, R., & Landreth, G. (1990). *Group counseling: Concepts and procedures.* Muncie, IN: Accelerated Development.

Brammer, L. M. (1988). *The helping relationship: Process and skills.* Englewood Cliffs, NJ: Prentice Hall.

Corey, M., & Corey, G. (1992). *Group process and practice* (4th ed.). Pacific Grove, CA: Brooks/Cole.

Dinkmeyer, D. C., & Muro, J. J. (1979). *Group counseling: Theory and practice.* Itasca, IL: Peacock.

Drummond, R., McIntyre, W. G., Muro, J. J., & Brown, D. B. (1975). The children's interation matrix. In D. Dinkmeyer & J. Muro, *Group counseling: Theory and practice.* Itasca, IL: Peacock.

Egan, G. (1990). *The skilled helper* (4th ed.). Pacific Grove, CA: Brooks/Cole.

Ehly, S., & Dustin, D. (1991). *Individual and group counseling in the schools.* New York: Guilford.

Foulkes, S. H., & Anthony, E. J. (1965). *Group psychotherapy.* Baltimore, MD: Penguin Books.

Gazda, G. (1989). *Group counseling: A developmental approach.* Boston: Allyn & Bacon.

Ginott, H. G. (1962). *Group psychotherapy with children.* New York: McGraw-Hill.

Glasser, W. N. (1989). *Control theory.* In W. N. Glasser (Ed.), *Control theory in the practice of reality therapy.* New York: Harper.

Harries, F. (1980). *Group composition.* Personal communication of a presentation made at an ASCA Workshop in Group Procedures. Pembroke, NH.

Hill, W. F. (1965). *Hill interaction matrix.* Los Angeles: University of Southern California.

Hutchins, D. E., & Cole, C. G. (1986). *Helping relations and strategies.* Pacific Grove, CA: Brooks/Cole.

Johnson, D., & Johnson, F. (1987). *Joining together: Group theory and group skills* (3d ed.). Englewood Cliffs, NJ: Prentice Hall.

Kottler, J. A., & Brown, R. W. (1992). *Therapeutic counseling.* Pacific Grove, CA: Brooks/Cole.

Muro, J. J., & Dinkmeyer, D. C. (1977). *Counseling in the elementary and middle schools.* Dubuque, IA: Wm. C. Brown.

Nugent, F. A. (1990). *An introduction to the profession of counseling.* Columbus, OH.: Merrill.

Ohlsen, M. (1974). *Guidance services in the modern school.* New York: Harcourt Brace and Jovanovich.

Siepker, B., & Kandaras, C. (Eds.) (1985). *Group therapy with children and adolescents.* New York: Human Sciences Press.

Thompson, C., & Rudolph, L. (1992). *Counseling children* (3rd ed.). Pacific Grove, CA: Brooks/Cole.

Yalom, I. P. (1985). *The theory and practice of group psychotherapy* (4th ed.). New York: Basic Books.

Young, M. (1992). *Counseling methods and technique.* New York: Merrill

Chapter Eight

Play and Activity Techniques

🌳 Counselors who work with children have long used play techniques as a way to understand and communicate with children. In the early part of the twentieth century, Hermine Hug-Hellmuth (1921) introduced play into child analysis. Hug-Hellmuth visited children's homes and observed and participated in their spontaneous play. She interpreted the activities of these children in the conceptual framework of psychoanalytic theory.

Anna Freud (1946) advocated the observation of children's play as a way for the counselor to form an emotional attachment with them. Since children are usually not voluntary clients, she felt that it was necessary to entice them into cooperation. She used play and toys to get children interested in the process of therapy. Freud suggested that children's spontaneous play was an excellent method of communicating with them in an environment that was safe and familiar to them. She did not employ direct interpretation of play, and she suggested that the counselor could not always view actions and situations in play as symbolic (Landreth, 1991). As her young clients became more personally invested in therapy and in herself, Freud gradually switched the focus from the play to more verbal forms of interaction (O'Connor, 1991).

In contrast to Freud's belief that the value of play was strictly confined to building a relationship with the child, Melanie Klein (1932) advocated play as being the equivalent of the adult's language. She used spontaneous play as a substitute for free association. In Kleinian play therapy, the counselor makes direct psychoanalytic interpretations of the play to the child (O'Connor, 1991).

Levy (1939) pioneered an approach to play therapy, called release therapy, which combined psychoanalytic conceptualization of children and their problems with a more structured, goal-oriented orientation. He used this approach to treat children who had experienced some traumatic event. Levy gave children specific toys and play media chosen to allow them to play out the traumatic situations. In release therapy, the counselor offers little or no interpretation. The principle underlying this approach is that, given a safe environment and the proper toys, children will act out difficult situations, discharging harmful thoughts and emotions, until the past event no longer holds any threat (Muro & Dinkmeyer, 1977; O'Connor, 1991). Building on the ideas of release therapy, Hambridge (1955) set up play situations with the exact specifics of the traumatic events and guided children through a reenactment of the situations.

Taft (1933) and Allen (1934) adapted the work of Otto Rank (1936) to use with children. In the resulting "relationship" play therapy, the counselor focuses on the relationship with the child as a means of growth and transformation for the child. The counselor does not investigate past experiences, but simply stresses current feelings and reactions (Landreth, 1991). This rather existential position was also explored by Moustakas (1959), who suggested that given a strong, nurturing relationship with the counselor, the child would move toward mental health and individuation (O'Connor, 1991).

Virginia Axline (1947) built upon the foundations laid by these play therapy pioneers and upon the ideas of Carl Rogers' person centered theory. Her work on play therapy established this approach as a treatment of choice for children experiencing emotional and behavioral difficulties. Axline (1969) presented the following eight basic principles of child-centered, nondirective play therapy:

1. The therapist must develop a warm, friendly, genuine relationship with the child in order to build a solid therapeutic rapport.

2. The therapist must be totally accepting of the child, without wishing to change any aspect of the child.

3. The therapist must establish an atmosphere of permissiveness that allows the child to freely explore and express feelings.

4. The therapist must stay alert to the child's feelings and reflect them in a way that helps the child gain insight and self-understanding.

5. The therapist must always maintain respect for the child's ability to solve his or her own problems if given a chance to do so. The child is responsible for making decisions and may choose whether to make changes or not.

6. The therapist should never take the lead in therapy. The child leads and the therapist follows.

7. The therapist must never try to hurry the therapeutic process. It is a gradual course that the therapist cannot and should not attempt to alter.

8. The therapist should establish only those limits that are necessary to anchor the therapy to reality and to return responsibility back to the child for his or her role in the relationship.

Recently, other authors have expanded the application of play therapy to many different therapeutic approaches. Violet Oaklander (1969) explained how to use play and other activity-based strategies from the perspective of Gestalt therapy. John Allan (1988) has applied the principles of Jungian counseling to play therapy for practitioners in schools and clinics. Terry Kottman (1993a, 1993b, in press a; in press b; Kottman & Warlick, 1990, 1991) combined the concepts and techniques of Adler's Individual Psychology and the practice of play therapy in her development of Adlerian play therapy. Stanley Kissel (1990) made a case for an eclectic, "strategic" approach to play therapy that matches the particular strategy to the child's situation. Kevin O'Connor (1991) has expanded ideas from several theoretical orientations, including psychodynamic theory, "release" therapy, and "relationship" therapy, in ecosystemic play therapy.

There are also contemporary authors who have written books about play therapy designed to help counselors work with specific populations of children. Marvasti (1989) and Gil (1991) have both written about ways to use play therapy with sexually abused children. Webb (1991) edited a book of case studies focusing on play therapy with children in crisis—children who have experienced abuse, foster care, parental death, parental suicide, and divorce situations. Kottman and Schaefer (1993) edited a book of case studies that represent the various approaches to using play therapy in working with children with a wide range of presenting problems including the death of a parent, parental divorce, custody battles, abuse, and elective mutism.

While there are many clinical and anecdotal reports to substantiate the claim that play therapy helps children, there are few empirical findings to support the efficacy of play therapy (Phillips, 1985). The Center for Play Therapy at the University of North Texas has recently started an ambitious effort to provide more quantitative evidence to support the effectiveness of play therapy as an intervention for helping children.

Over the past several decades, many authors (Alexander, 1964; Kottman & Johnson, 1993; Landreth, 1987; 1993, Nelson, 1966) have suggested that various forms of play therapy are viable tools for elementary school counselors. However, there are also those who have contended that the traditional forms of play therapy are not particularly suitable for use in elementary school settings (Golden, 1985). The critics of play therapy in the schools have suggested that it takes a longer period of time than is available to most school counselors in working with an individual child. In response to this criticism, a special issue of *Elementary School Guidance and Counseling* (Campbell, 1993) described several innovative "brief" methods of applying play techniques in elementary schools.

Another objection has been that "therapy" is not usually considered to be within the purview of most school counselors (Golden, 1985). The authors believe that even if school counselors do not want to label their intervention strategy as play "therapy," a counseling with toys program can be a very helpful approach for many school counselors.

If school counselors choose to use play and play media as one method of working with children, they must be sure that they have the proper training and supervised experience. Many universities and colleges are adding training programs so that counselors in the field can obtain the appropriate coursework and supervision. The Center for Play Therapy (1993) at the University of North Texas has published a director of institutions that offer play therapy training. The Association for Play Therapy has recently established procedures for national credentialing of professionals who are qualified to use play approaches with children and to supervise other play therapists.

The Meaning of Play

Most counselors who have worked with young children believe that play is children's innate mode of self-expression (Axline, 1947; Landreth, 1991; Muro & Dinkmeyer, 1977). Play comes naturally to children and is a spontaneous expression of emotions and thoughts. Play is the method most children use to explore the world and relationships, to understand the past and prepare for the future (Frank, 1982). Play is the universal language of all children, both those who are experiencing difficulties and those whose progress through life is relatively smooth.

In addition to being a form of communication, play can also have other significance to a child. Erikson (1963) suggested that play may represent condensed portions of the child's life that the child uses to work through traumatic events, confess to some kind of transgression, or master a difficult life situation. Piaget (1962) believed that play was the child's way of assimilating new information into his or her view of the world and adapting to new situations.

Play is not a uniform activity, and there is no "standard" meaning of play. The significance of each child's play is unique to that child and to that moment in the child's life. An adult—whether a counselor trained in play therapy, a concerned parent, or a passing stranger—observing the child's play may have some idea about what the play means or may have no idea at all about the significance of the child's behavior. However, the counselor does not have to know exactly what each activity means to be able to use the play to communicate with the child and help the child enhance self-esteem, increase self-understanding, and move toward self-acceptance.

Developmental Aspects of Play

Between the ages of two and eight, children engage in dramatic or symbolic play (Muro & Dinkmeyer, 1977). During this representational period of development, children use play to "shape" reality to meet their own individual egocentric view of the world (Piaget, 1962). They use "make believe" to control the world and to reveal their images, thoughts, feelings, and fantasies.

As children develop, their play adapts and becomes more reality oriented (Muro & Dinkmeyer, 1977). Children eight and older, in the "concrete operational" stage of development, use play to practice cooperation with peers and adults (Piaget, 1962). Their play is characterized by logic, rules, and structure.

As counselors work with children using play media, they will want to take these developmental considerations into account when they are trying to understand the structure of the play and the types of toys used in the interaction. Counselors should expect more fantasy play with younger children. When working with children under the age of eight or nine, counselors should provide play media that capitalizes on the "make-believe" aspect of play. When working with older children, counselors will probably use an adapted form of interacting with children, activity therapy. Activity therapy employs play media that incorporates the developmental needs of children eight or nine and older for order and regulations. Games and toys with rules and set procedures work well with this age group.

Using Play Media in School Settings

Until children reach a level of facility and sophistication with verbal communication that allows them to express themselves fully and effectively to others, the use of play media is mandatory if significant communication is to take place between child and counselor. It would seem then that it is not a question of whether the elementary school counselor, psychologist, or social worker should use play therapy, but rather how play therapy should be utilized in elementary schools. (Landreth, 1983, p. 201)

The primary duty of the school counselor is to help children in the school to be able to benefit from the learning opportunities provided by the school. The elementary counselor can use play media as "an adjunct to the learning environment, an experience which assists children in maximizing their opportunities to learn" (Landreth, 1983, p. 201). This approach works with children who are experiencing emotional distress, academic difficulties, and behavior problems. It can also be a part of an ongoing developmental guidance program for children with normal developmental issues or no concerns whatsoever. As school counselors, individuals can even use play media to introduce themselves to children and to explain their role in the school. They can also use play as a part of their developmental guidance curriculum, to help children learn relationship skills, enhance self-esteem, practice assertive behavior, and so forth.

Introducing the Program to Administrators and Teachers

For the school counselor who wishes to use play media in the school setting, the first step in the process is to gain the support of the building administrator (Landreth, no date, 1991). The counselor must explain the rationale for counseling with toys and present an overview of how the process works. The discussion should include a brief description of the techniques used in working with children with this approach and the expected results of such a program. If the counselor is going to use play counseling as a diagnostic or intervention strategy with children experiencing some type of difficulty that is interfering with their functioning in school, she or he may want to provide administrators with a list of the types of problems that are amenable to change through this approach. The counselor may want to discuss the political ramifications of what to call the program—"counseling with toys," "counseling with play media," "play counseling," or (in some areas of the country this would be perfectly acceptable) "play therapy" (Landreth, 1983, 1991). For the purposes of this chapter, the authors have decided to use these terms interchangeably.

In discussing the possibility of using play media in the elementary school, the counselor will also want to introduce practical considerations, such as space and financial support for materials such as shelves and toys

(Landreth, no date). Ginott (1961) described the ideal play room as a sound-proofed space of 150 to 200 square feet. For a group approach to the counseling with toys program, the ideal space would need to be much bigger: 300 to 400 square feet. However, there may not be access to such a spacious area. This difficulty should not prevent counselors from using this approach in the elementary school—the setting does not have to be perfect to be helpful to the child. Landreth (1983) suggested that play sessions can occur in the nurse's office, the library, a closet, or a corner of the cafeteria or the auditorium. Whatever space is available for the play sessions should be sturdy and able to stand considerable wear and tear (Muro & Dinkmeyer, 1977). If the counselor cannot be sure that the space will be secure and free from interruptions, he or she should let the children know about the limitations to confidentiality (Landreth, 1983).

The next step in the process of establishing a program of using play media to counsel children in elementary schools is to conduct an in-service with teachers (Landreth, no date, 1991). During the initial meeting with teachers, the counselor will explain the counseling with toys process, its rationale, and objectives. The counselor will need to give teachers a set of general criteria for referring to the counselor for this type of assistance. The following are examples of behaviors that the authors have observed can adversely affect children's school performance and are frequently amenable to play intervention:

1. Behaving inappropriately in the classroom.
2. Having poor self-confidence and/or self-concept.
3. Having difficulty making decisions.
4. Being unwilling to take turns or delay gratification.
5. Being unwilling to cooperate with others.
6. Being unwilling or unable to follow directions.
7. Having poor social skills.
8. Being overly anxious or fearful.
9. Being unwilling to take responsibility for behavior.
10. Underachieving in school.
11. Worrying excessively about school achievement.
12. Seeming depressed and/or uninvolved in school.
13. Getting into power struggles with authority figures.
14. Clinging to parents and/or teachers.
15. Having temper tantrums.
16. Having few friends.

There are many other behaviors that could fit into this category. Landreth (no date) has developed several lists of such behaviors. School counselors who want to use play strategies should probably generate a list of behaviors they have observed in their schools that would warrant referral for play intervention.

The following situations are life events that may adversely affect school performance:

1. Death of someone close to the child: parent(s), grandparent(s), close friend, pet.
2. Hospitalization or chronic illness of the child or a person close to the child.
3. Divorce or separation of parents.
4. Abuse of the child or sibling (emotional, physical, sexual).
5. Adoption of the child or sibling.
6. Parent(s) or sibling in prison.
7. Foster care placement of the child or sibling.
8. Violence in the home.
9. Birth of sibling.
10. Drug addiction or alcoholism of family member.
11. Moving.
12. Gang involvement of the child or family member.

There are, of course, other life events that will adversely affect children. Each school counselor must generate a list of situations appropriate to his or her setting.

One purpose of this in-service is to help teachers to understand that each of these classroom behaviors and problematic interactions exists on a continuum, from slightly annoying to debilitating. Children will also have different reactions to each of these stressful life events. Some children will be devastated by stressful situations, whereas other children will not be distressed at all by the exact same set of circumstances.

School counselors are most helpful with situations from the middle of the continuum. If the behavior or life event is minimally affecting the child's learning, the teacher can probably handle the situation without any direct intervention from the counselor. If the behavior or life event is having a disabling effect on the child, the disturbance may be beyond the training and expertise of the school counselor. Even if the counselor has the prerequisite background, if the problem is long term and severe, the counselor may not have the time necessary to effectively help the situation. Since the counselor's responsibility is to *all* the children in the school, devoting a disproportionate amount of time and energy to one child would be counterproductive. In these cases, the school counselor will probably choose to refer the child to appropriate agencies or counselors in private practice where a more long-term, intensive intervention can occur. However, problems that are interfering with the child's performance in school, but are not chronic or pervasive in nature, are frequently amenable to intervention by the school counselor using play media.

Counselors will want to provide concrete examples of different aspects of the continuum for selected problems from this list. They may wish to engage teachers in brainstorming in order to clarify the types of problems they feel can be helped with this approach. During this discussion, counselors should explain the protocol for teacher referrals and for child self-referrals (Landreth, no date). This would be an appropriate time to discuss the procedure for working with the parent(s), to reiterate the policy on confidentiality, and to discuss ways that counselors can use the information and patterns gained through the play process to consult with teachers. Counselors should give the teachers a chance to ask any questions about the program during this meeting, and let teachers know that they want and need teacher support for the counseling with toys program to be successful.

About a week after the presentation to the teachers, counselors may want to consolidate the introduction to the counseling with toys program by distributing follow-up material (Landreth, no date, 1991). Counselors could include a summary of the ideas covered in the in-service meeting and a list of the brainstormed ideas of classroom behaviors and stressful life events that might prompt a referral. They might also want to include several articles discussing counseling with toys or a bibliography of information about play media in elementary counseling (Landreth, no date).

Difficulties in Using Play Media in Schools

One difficulty in using play as an intervention approach in an elementary school is that parents and teachers may have a preconception that play therapy is a process used exclusively with severely disturbed children (Muro & Dinkmeyer, 1977). In answer to this objection, counselors can stress the fact that they frequently work with children who exhibit very normal developmental concerns. They can also stress the communication and relationship-building aspects of play, rather than the psychological aspects. In this context, counselors would probably be wise to use the phrase "play media" or "counseling with toys," rather than the potentially ominous-sounding "play therapy." Usually a simple explanation of the fact that the counselor uses play and toys because they are a natural part of children's lives will be sufficient to allay colleagues' and parents' concerns (Muro & Dinkmeyer, 1977).

Another problem in using play media in an elementary counseling program is that many times teachers and/or administrators may object on the grounds that the play will be noisy and disturb others in the school (Landreth, 1983). While studies have shown that the majority of play during a play counseling experience is neither noisy nor destructive (Hendricks, 1971; Landreth, 1983; Withee, 1975), this is a legitimate concern for school personnel. Landreth (1983) suggested that the best way to handle this difficulty is to make sure that school personnel are prepared for the possibility of noise. One way counselors can help alleviate objections is to explain the potentially positive outcome of allowing children to actively release tension, anger, frustration, or aggression in an appropriate time and setting (Landreth, 1983). Expressing these feelings in the counselor's office using the play media quite frequently prevents children from expressing them in the classroom or on the playground in an unacceptable fashion.

The lack of funds for supplying and maintaining the equipment for a play media program may also handicap some school counselors (Landreth, 1983). Many times the elementary school budget simply does not contain money for buying toys or shelves for a play setting. Some school counselors find the means to obtain the initial toys and other materials, but they have difficulty with the ongoing expense of resupplying such essentials as paper, paint, and paste. Neither of these obstacles is insurmountable (Landreth, 1983). Counselors can obtain most of the toys and materials needed for this process with limited amounts of money from parent donations, community sources such as local companies, and garage sales. Many times local businesses, such as newspapers, telephone companies, and office supply stores, will donate newsprint, old telephones, and shelves. The school parent-teacher organization and/or local service organizations, such as the Optimist's Club or the Rotary Club, may be willing to sponsor a counseling program designed to help children.

Toy Selection and Arrangement

Some elementary counselors worry that they will not be able to establish a counseling with toys program because they do not have a "fully equipped" play room facility. It is important to remember that a counselor can accomplish a great deal with just a few carefully chosen toys (Landreth, 1983). The toys and materials in the counselor's office should meet all of the following criteria (Ginott, 1961; Landreth, 1987, 1991):

1. They should be sturdy and resistant to breakage with repeated use.
2. They must provide opportunities for success and channels for children to build self-esteem and self-confidence.
3. They must be interesting to children.
4. They should facilitate exploration and expression without requiring verbalization.
5. They should provide possibilities for expressing a wide range of emotions.
6. They should allow the counselor chances to build a positive relationship with children.
7. They must provide children with opportunities to explore both real-life situations and fantasies.

Some of the toys used in a counseling with toys program will also need to allow children to test limits and provide the counselor with a way of redirecting inappropriate behaviors (Landreth, 1987). This will encourage children to develop self-control and increase responsibility (Landreth, 1991).

No matter whether the counselor sets up a permanent play room with the "ideal" set of toys or carries toys from school to school in a suitcase, the selection of toys needs to include a combination of real-life toys, acting-out/aggressive toys, and expressive/creative toys (Landreth, 1987, 1991).

Real-Life Toys

Some examples of real-life toys are: a baby doll, a bendable doll family; a doll house; furniture for the doll house; play dishes, pots, pans, and utensils; a telephone; and transportation toys, such as cars, trucks, and airplanes. One of the authors (T.K.) has found that it is essential to have some representative of each of these types of materials for children to act out situations that occur at home. Especially important are the doll house and the kitchen ware. Children will frequently play through family problems with these toys. Even children who deny that there are difficulties at home may show the counselor what is really happening between various family members with the bendable doll family.

Children who have very little structure or order in their family lives may spend many sessions simply rearranging the furniture in the doll house. The baby doll and the kitchen utensils both give children an opportunity to ask for and provide nurturing. Children who feel trapped or unable to run away from intolerable situations in their lives may use the transportation toys to symbolically escape.

Children can use the telephone as a method of communication. Many times children will use the telephone to "tell" the counselor things they have been wanting to confide but are afraid to reveal directly. Sometimes children use the telephone as a channel of communication with other people in their lives, who are either absent or otherwise "unreachable." The authors have found that this works even better if the counselor has a "real" telephone instead of a plastic toy version. The local telephone company will quite frequently be willing to provide counseling programs with old retired "real" telephones. The best way to approach the company is to call and let them know of the opportunity to help children in the community, and they will usually respond quickly and positively.

If possible, it is best to have bendable family figures who can be easily dressed and undressed without destroying their clothing. Many children who have been sexually abused spend a great deal of time taking clothes off the dolls and putting them back on. If taking the clothes off destroys them, counselors may have to spend more money than they are willing or able to spend on new clothes or new dolls.

Aggressive Toys

Although this may be potentially controversial (Guerney, 1983), the authors believe that one of the essential elements in a counseling with toys program is play media that children can use to act out aggression in a symbolic manner. All human beings, including children, feel angry, aggressive, and fearful some of the time. The play setting gives children a place to express these feelings in a safe environment and to learn to control when and how they vent them. Some parents may complain that providing aggressive toys will increase aggression and encourage hostility. However, the authors disagree with this position. In working with children in play settings for years, they have not observed this to be the case.

This category would include weapons such as a pistol with a holster, a rubber knife, a machine gun or other noise-making weapon, a dart gun, handcuffs, and toy soldiers. If there is room, a punching bag/bop bag is also a useful toy for expressing aggression. With the pistol and the rubber knife, children can fantasize about defending themselves from danger and destroying their enemies and those who might threaten them in some way. Children use the toy soldiers and the punching bag/bop bag for all sorts of aggressive play, rescue scenarios, defensive fantasies, and fantasies of escaping from dangerous situations. They can use the noisy weapon for this kind of activity, or they can use it to drown out any comments the counselor might make that they do not particularly want to hear. Children, unlike adults, very seldom have the power to communicate that they do not wish to participate in a conversation or to ask an adult to be quiet. Loud, noise-making weapons provide them with a socially acceptable way of doing this without encouraging them to be defiant or rude. They can use the dart gun to attack or protect. In addition, it will frequently give the counselor a chance to set limits. The darts should not endanger property or people, and the counselor may need to remind children of this fact and redirect their "fire" to a more appropriate target.

Children can choose to use the handcuffs on themselves to demonstrate their own feelings of powerlessness and inadequacy. They may also want to use them on the counselor to practice feeling powerful or in control. The counselor should only allow this if she or he feels relatively comfortable being handcuffed. I (T.K.) only allow children to handcuff me with my hands in front of my body or to some stationary object like a chair. I feel uncomfortable with my hands behind my back, so I limit this. The handcuffs should have some kind of safety release that can be activated without a key, because the keys to the handcuffs usually vanish without a trace soon after they appear in the play room.

Another component in this category is the "scary" toys, such as monsters, spiders, other bugs, rats, and snakes. With these toys, children can act out their fears and nightmares. They can also protect themselves and others from things, real or imaginary, that frighten them. They can even attack and defeat their fears before these specters have a chance to menace them.

Children who have been sexually abused frequently use the snakes to act out various fears and fantasies. The best kind of snakes are the pliable rubber ones that can be twisted, stretched, draped, and otherwise manipulated vigorously. The pliable nature of this type of snake gives children the freedom to demonstrate that they can control the snake and decide what will happen to it. In working with counselors who use play media, the authors have heard many stories about children who stabbed, shot, stamped on, spit on, and buried snakes in sand. Some of these children are acting out their reactions in the aftermath of sexual abuse, and others are simply mastering their fears and frightening fantasies.

Expressive and Creative Toys

A play setting must also include toys that encourage children to express creativity and imagination (Landreth, 1987, 1991). Some of the toys in this category would be art materials such as crayons, paper, scissors, pipe cleaners, Play-Doh or clay, pencils, markers, tape, glue, finger paint, watercolors, and tempera paint. The counselor can use these art materials to help children express their feelings, explore family dynamics, investigate classroom interactions, practice new skills, and build self-esteem.

Also in this category are toys that the children can use to pretend. This would include a small plain mask, hats, purses, high-heeled shoes, jewelry, and other items that could be used as disguises. These materials provide children the chance to pretend to be someone else.

This category would also include puppets. Children can act out different scenarios from both school and home situations using the puppets as different characters. They can also use the puppets to talk for them. Many times children who are afraid to express themselves directly will use puppets to voice their thoughts and feelings. When buying puppets, the authors have found that the most efficient use of money is to buy puppets that can serve a dual purpose. The counselor might want to buy a "scary" puppet, such as an alligator or a lion, constructed from soft fur. This way, depending on their mood and the situation, children can use the same puppet to express both "negative" emotions such as anger or fear and softer emotions such as caring and nurturing.

The counselor should avoid using structured material and mechanical toys when working with younger (K–3) children (Landreth, 1987, 1991). Any type of game or toy with a prescribed set of activities involved in its operation or that can only be used in one way could easily inhibit creativity and expression of feelings. For example, the authors have found that it is extremely counterproductive to have video games in a counseling office. These toys do not encourage spontaneity or interaction with others. Rather, they inhibit individual expression of thoughts and emotions.

Arranging the Toys

If there is a permanent location for the counseling with toys program, counselors should place the toys on open shelves attached to the walls (Landreth, personal communication). This will prevent children from either purposely or accidentally upsetting the shelves. The best way to arrange the toys is to group them by category, with all the real-life toys together, the aggressive toys together, and the creative/expressive toys together (Landreth, 1983, 1991). This arrangement makes it easier for children to find certain toys because their order makes sense. It also provides children with a sense of safety and consistency because the toy placement is predictable and structured (Landreth, 1983, 1991).

Counselors who move from location to location or do not have a permanent area for the counseling with toys program can use portable play materials (Landreth, no date, 1983, 1991). These toys can usually travel in a suitcase or trunk of some kind. However, whenever these materials are needed, counselors will need to find a way to display them openly in a location where children can see and touch them (Landreth, 1983). Every time children are going to use the toys, counselors should arrange them according to theme or category in a predictable, structured pattern.

At the end of the session, the toys need to be placed back where they belong. This will provide a sense of security and continuity for the children using them (Landreth, 1983, 1991). Some authors suggest that the counselor is responsible for cleaning up the play area and replacing the toys (Axline, 1969; Landreth, 1991). Other authors suggest that the child help clean the play setting and put the toys where they belong (Kottman & Warlick, 1990, 1991). This is a matter of choice, depending on the counselor's philosophical beliefs and theoretical orientation.

Goals of Play Counseling

In keeping with the primary objectives of school counseling and guidance programs, the goals of play counseling revolve around helping children to learn about themselves and the world (Landreth, 1987). Children who are struggling with learning problems, out-of-control emotions, poor self-esteem, family problems, lack of social skills, and/or negative relationships with teachers and other authority figures are going to have difficulty learning in school. Even children who do not have any major emotional or behavior problems may be contending with normal developmental issues that could easily interfere with their acquisition of knowledge. A counseling with toys program can help free children from worries, fears, self-doubt, and other extraneous feelings and circumstances that might prevent them from taking full advantage of educational experiences. In the process of the play counseling, regardless of his or her theoretical orientation, the school counselor must accomplish the following objectives (Landreth, 1987):

1. Establish an atmosphere of safety and security for children by responding to the child in a warm, consistent manner.
2. Understand and accept children and their view of the world by showing real interest in their words and actions in the play room. Try to see relationships and interactions from children's perspective, and always acknowledge their viewpoint.
3. Encourage children to express their emotions by accepting their feelings without any kind of judgment.
4. Encourage self-responsibility and decision making by establishing an atmosphere of relative permissiveness in which children make choices for themselves about what to play with, how to play with it, the direction of role plays, and other decisions that commonly occur in the counseling process.
5. Provide children with chances to develop a sense of control over themselves and events by encouraging them to do things for themselves and by making sure they control as many of the unfolding events and interactions in the play setting as possible. Another method of helping children learn what they can and cannot control is to point out times in the play room when they are exercising power and/or mastery—over self, others, and materials.

6. Verbalize for children by putting into words the counselor's experiencing and observation of the children's feelings and actions. This verbalization by the counselor teaches children an emotional language and helps them gain insight into their motivations, underlying emotions, and patterns of interaction.

Basic Skills for Counseling with Toys

There are certain basic skills used by counselors in a counseling with toys approach, regardless of their theoretical orientation. These generic skills include tracking, restatement of content, reflection of feelings, returning responsibility to the child (Landreth, 1991), using the child's metaphor, pointing out patterns of behavior, and limiting.

Tracking

Tracking is describing the child's behaviors to the child. The purpose of tracking is to let the child know that whatever the child is doing is important and worthy of notice. This technique builds the relationship with the child because the child feels special and cared for. The following are examples of tracking responses:

Christine: (Picks up a gun and looks at it.)

Ms. O'Meara: You're picking that up and checking it out.

Christine: (Goes over to the doll house, sits down, and begins to rearrange the doll furniture.)

Ms. O'Meara: You're putting those just where you want them to be.

Christine: (Puts a hat on. Goes over and looks in a mirror and makes faces.)

Ms. O'Meara: You wanted to see how you look with that on.

Notice that the counselor in these examples avoided labeling objects. She also kept her descriptions of the child's behavior relatively vague. This is an important element in the art of tracking. By not labeling the toys or pinpointing the child's actions, the counselor encourages creativity and individual interpretation by the child (Landreth, 1991). That way, in the first interaction, the gun may be a gun to Christine, but it may also be a starship launcher, a laser, a telescope, or anything else the child wants it to be. In the third interaction, Christine could be making faces in the mirror or she could be scaring a monster, trying to be a different person, or an infinite number of other possibilities. By using purposefully vague language, the counselor allows the child to determine the course of the session.

Some children do not really need this "permission" to be self-determining. However, the authors have noticed that many children feel inhibited or challenged when the counselor forgets and labels or uses specific language. Children whose primary motivation is pleasing others, especially authority figures, will look to the counselor for approval and may never disagree or assert their opinions about what they are doing or the identity of toys. They are afraid that if they have their own interpretation of events or materials that they will displease the counselor, and the counselor will stop liking them.

Children whose primary motivation is control will use every chance they get to try to get into a power struggle with the counselor. Every time the counselor labels a toy or an action is a prime opportunity to quibble and argue. By using vague language and not labeling, the counselor can avoid both of these traps.

Restating Content

When the counselor tells the child what the child has said, this is restatement of content. Again, the purpose of this technique is to build the relationship with the child by letting the child know that whatever he or she has to say is important. The following are some examples of restating content:

Hillary: (Picking up the baby doll.) I'm this baby's mommy. I'm going to take good care of this baby.

Mr. Ruso: You're going to be the mommy and take care of that baby.

Hillary: (Punching the bop bag.) I'm going to punch this guy out. He can't even hit me because I'm so big and tough.

Mr. Ruso: You're about to beat him up, and he won't have a chance because you're so strong and powerful.

When counselors restate the content of the child's message, it is important to use words on the same level of vocabulary as the child's, but not necessarily to use the exact words of the child. They should try to paraphrase, rather than simply parroting the child's words. When counselors parrot too often, the child may ask, "Why do you always say exactly what I say?" An answer that most children will accept is, "What you say is important to me, and I wanted to let you know that I was listening to you."

Most counselors use tracking and restatement of content quite frequently during the first phase of counseling in order to build the relationship with the child. However, after the connection is established, these two strategies are less valuable because they do not really deepen the relationship or help the child gain insight. As time passes, the counselor will usually decrease the number of tracking and restating responses and increase some of the other types of responses.

Reflection of Feelings

Reflection of feelings is probably the most valuable of all the generic play counseling skills. It provides opportunities for deepening the counseling relationship, for the expression of emotions, for increased self-awareness and self-understanding, and for an expanded affective vocabulary. The following are examples of reflections of feeling:

Thomas: (Ripping up a picture he has drawn.) I hate this picture. It didn't turn out like it was supposed to.

Mrs. Fair: You're disappointed with the way you drew that picture, so you're tearing it up and getting rid of it.

Thomas: Is my teacher still in our room? How do I get back to the room?

Mrs. Fair:	I can tell that you're kind of worried that you might not be able to find your way back to your room.
Thomas:	Yeah. I am. Will you walk with me back to my room?
Mrs. Fair:	You seem a little confused and scared about getting around the school building.
Thomas:	(Moving the child doll figures behind some furniture while the parent doll figures yell at each other.)
Mrs. Fair:	It's kind of scary when the mom and dad yell at each other like that.

When the counselor reflects feelings, it is essential to note both the obvious, surface feelings and any less obvious, deeper feelings. In the first interaction, Mrs. Fair simply reflected the obvious feelings that Thomas had expressed. In the second interaction, she reflected the surface feelings and some less obvious, deeper feelings. If the child expresses feelings at a distance through characters or toys, like the third interaction, the counselor should reflect the feelings expressed by the characters or toys. When the child is ready to "own" those feelings, he or she will do so. Until that point, the child must be able to express the feelings without being pushed by the counselor to acknowledge ownership of them.

Again, it is important to use vocabulary that the child can understand. Most kindergartners and first graders recognize four primary feelings: sad, mad, scared, and glad. In order for children in the lower grades to relate to the reflection of feelings, it may be necessary, at least initially, to translate more subtle emotions to one of these four. Second and third grade children have a much wider range of feeling vocabulary, but they still do not recognize many of the more subtle emotions. They understand words like frustrated, disappointed, and jealous, but they may not regularly use these words themselves. This is the perfect opportunity for the counselor to expand their affective vocabulary by using these words that they understand but do not ordinarily employ in conversation. With most fourth, fifth, and sixth graders, depending on their developmental level, the counselor will want to use more sophisticated language and substitute a combination of activity counseling and discussion for the play counseling.

Returning Responsibility to the Child

In order to foster self-reliance and independence in children, the counselor can use various strategies to return responsibility to them within the session (Landreth, 1991). Most of the time, this involves not making decisions for them and not doing things for them that they can do for themselves. The purpose of this technique is to enhance self-confidence and decision-making skills. It also gives children a sense of accomplishment and affirms them as being "in control" of the situation. The following are examples of returning responsibility to the child:

Garren:	(Picking up a toy from the shelf.) What is this?
Miss Price:	In here, it can be anything you want it to be.
Garren:	(Painting a picture.) Do you know what I'm painting?

Miss Price:	That's for you to decide.
Garren:	No. I want you to guess.
Miss Price:	Since it's your picture, you're the only one who can know. The only way I will know what that picture is will be if you decide to tell me.
Garren:	Will you please tie my shoelaces? My mommy always ties them for me, but Mr. Jones, my teacher, makes me tie them myself.
Miss Price:	It sounds like that's something you can do yourself.
Garren:	Can you open this jar for me? I can't do it.
Miss Price:	Let's see if we can do it together. What do you think is the first thing we should try?

Part of returning the responsibility to the child is making sure that the child can actually accomplish the action. Notice the difference between the third and fourth interaction. In the third interaction, Miss Price knew that Garren could succeed in the endeavor, so she told the child that she had confidence that the child could do it. In the fourth interaction, because Miss Price was not sure that Garren could successfully carry out the action, she offered to work on it together. An alternative solution to situations in which the counselor is not confident that the child can carry out the action and to situations in which the child refuses to try, would be to ask the child to direct the counselor in the action. This could be accomplished by saying to the child, "Tell me how you want me to do it." This effectively gives the responsibility and the control back to the child.

Using the Child's Metaphor

Most of the communication that takes place in a play counseling session is indirect and metaphoric. The counselor must remember to attend to the child's actions and nonverbal behavior, because much of what the child does in the counselor's office with the play media represents struggles, triumphs, and relationships that occur outside the play setting. Sometimes the counselor will understand the metaphors, and sometimes they will be incomprehensible. This does not really matter because the most important skill to master in dealing with the child's metaphor is a willingness to "go" with the metaphor without needing to interpret it. There is no need to interpret the metaphor to the child. Rather, the authors contend that the best course in play counseling is to use the child's metaphors to communicate with the child without interpreting them.

Several years ago, one of the authors had a student who was working with a child who had a twin brother. Darwin, the child who was coming to the play sessions, had been labeled as the "bad" child in the family, and Jessie, his twin, had been labeled as the "good" child. Darwin consistently played out scenes in which a "bad" superhero was constantly punished even though he had done nothing to warrant punishment and the "good" superhero was rewarded even though he had done nothing to deserve reward. Darwin used this metaphor to work through his feelings of inferiority and his anger at Jessie. Instead of interpreting the metaphor, the counselor used the story to help Darwin explore feelings by making comments like, "I bet that 'bad' superhero feels sad when he gets punished and no one even seems to notice when he does things like he's supposed to do" and "The 'bad' guy seems really mad when the 'good' guy gets all the credit even though he helped too." By not interpreting the metaphor, the counselor allowed Darwin to deal with a situation indirectly that he was not willing to examine directly. The relationship with his brother and the attitude of the other members of his family was too painful for him to acknowledge without the distance of the metaphor. We believe that if the counselor had not used Darwin's metaphor, he would have shut down and stopped communicating about this pivotal relationship. Instead, through the metaphor he was able to resolve much of his ambivalence about this situation. In consulting with the mother of the twins, the counselor was able to suggest some changes in the way the family treated both of the twins. The "bad" twin's behavior and attitudes changed dramatically for the better after five or six sessions of play counseling and parent consultation.

Limiting

At some time in almost any counseling relationship with a child, it will be necessary for the counselor to limit the child's behavior (Muro & Dinkmeyer, 1979). Ginott (1961), Moustakas (1959), and Bixler (1982) all argued that limits are essential to the play counseling relationship. Limits help the counselor to maintain an attitude of empathy and acceptance toward the child, and they ensure the physical safety of the child and the counselor in the play room, strengthen self-control, and encourage social responsibility (Ginott, 1961). Moustakas (1959) emphasized that all relationships contain, by necessity, certain limits and that limits define the boundaries and rules of the relationship and tie it to reality. Bixler (1982) contended that "limits are therapy" (p. 173). The general consensus on limiting is that the counselor should limit:

1. Physical attacks on self, other children, and the counselor.
2. Destruction of the play setting or play materials.
3. Removal of toys or play materials from the play setting.
4. Staying beyond the time limit of the session.

Other limits are more controversial. While Moustakas (1959) suggested that the child should have to leave the room if she or he insists on repeatedly transgressing the rules, Ginott (1982) believed that the child should never have to leave the room. In a school setting, the authors believe that it would seem to make more sense to follow the dictums of Moustakas. A school counselor would be ill-advised to allow an out-of-control child to continue to escalate his or her behavior in a setting in which many other children are present. Since the mandate of the school counselor is not to conduct in-depth therapy or personality restructuring, the elementary school counselor should probably refer a child who repeatedly violates play room rules to a mental health professional outside the school.

The authors agree with Ginott (1982) that the counselor does not need to come into the relationship with a long list of regulations for the play room. The counselor can state the limits as the need arises. Otherwise, the counselor may simply be presenting the child with a challenge and a perfect set of strategies for getting into power struggles with the counselor.

There are many strategies for limiting in the play room. Ginott (1961) described one viable alternative for school counselors using play counseling. This procedure is a four-step process as follows:

1. Recognize the child's feelings and desires.
2. Clearly state the limit in a nonjudgmental way, using passive voice. In passive voice, "You can't shoot me" becomes "I am not for shooting." Other examples of passive voice would be: "The mirror is not for hitting," "Howie is not for throwing the markers at," "People are not for hitting."
3. Redirect the child to a more acceptable action.
4. Help the child express feelings of resentment involved in having the limit invoked.

The following sequence is an example of this type of limit-setting:

Kathy: I hate you, and I'm going to shoot you with this dart gun.

Mr. Omani: You're really angry at me right now.

Kathy: Yeah. I'm going to shoot you and you will be sorry.

Mr. Omani: I am not for shooting. You can pretend that the bop bag is me and you can shoot it if you want to.

Kathy: I don't want to do that. I want to shoot you.

Mr. Omani: I am not for shooting. I can tell you're even angrier at me than you were before because I told you that you can't do something you want to do.

Another form of limiting that could be extremely effective for school counselors using play media is a strategy described by Kottman (in press b) and Kottman and Johnson (1993). The first several steps resemble the limit-setting posited by Ginott, but the final steps are very different:

1. State the limit in a nonjudgmental way. Sometimes the counselor will choose to use passive voice, but other times the counselor will simply state the play room rule in a neutral, matter-of-fact way, such as, "In the play room, it's against the rules to shoot darts at people."
2. Reflect the child's feeling and the purpose of the behavior. For instance, if the child is testing the counselor to see how the counselor will react if physically threatened, the counselor can say, "You want to see what I will do if you tell me that you're going to shoot me with the dart gun."
3. Engage the child in redirecting the behavior. In this step, the counselor asks the child to come up with acceptable alternatives to the unacceptable behavior. This is a negotiation process in which the counselor and the child share the control, but in which the counselor has the final word.
4. If the child chooses not to abide by the agreement reached in step three, set up logical consequences that the child can enforce.

The following interchange is an example of this type of limit-setting:

Kathy:	I hate you, and I'm going to shoot you with this dart gun.
Mr. Omani:	It's against the rules of the play room to shoot people with guns.
Kathy:	I don't care. I'm going to do it anyway. You can't tell me what to do.
Mr. Omani:	You're really angry, and you're going to show me that I can't control you.
Kathy:	You think you're the boss of this place and you're not.
Mr. Omani:	I bet you can think of something else you could shoot that wouldn't be against the rules of the play room.
Kathy:	Nope. I only want to shoot you.
Mr. Omani:	Maybe you could pretend something else in the room is me and shoot that.
Kathy:	I could draw your face on the marker board and shoot it. That way I could shoot you and you couldn't stop me.
Mr. Omani:	Then you could pretend to shoot me, and that would show me that I can't tell you what to do.

If Kathy had persisted in insisting on shooting Mr. Omani or had actually gone ahead and shot the dart at him, Mr. Omani would have needed to engage her in generating logical consequences for that behavior. The counselor can set up the logical consequences in two different ways. In one approach, the counselor presents the consequences as a choice ("If you choose to shoot me, you choose to put the dart gun in the closet and not get to play with it for the rest of the session"). In the other method, the counselor collaborates with the child in generating the logical consequence in advance of any future transgressions ("What do you think should happen with the dart gun the next time you choose not to follow the rules?"). By including the child in the decision-making process which gives him or her a certain degree of power in the situation, the counselor can use this type of interaction to encourage self-control and self-responsibility. Dr. Kottman and her students have used this method of limit-setting extensively with children. This approach works well because it returns to the child much of the responsibility for following the limit and enforcing any consequences. It also teaches the child how to generate alternative behaviors that are more socially acceptable with very little adult direction. We have found that this process helps children generalize this skill and increases the transfer of self-control and self-responsibility to settings other than the play room.

Application of Various Theoretical Approaches

Psychodynamic Approach

The authors believe that very few, if any, school counselors will use a psychodynamic approach to working with children. They will not usually have the extensive training necessary to do in-depth, long-term therapy. Psychodynamic play therapy is extremely time-consuming and energy-intensive. It is usually used to facilitate major personality restructuring with children who have severe problems, intrapsychically and interpersonally. This approach would not be an appropriate treatment modality for a school counselor whose philosophical focus is developmental.

Release Therapy

The authors suggest that the basic format of release therapy (Levy, 1939) would be quite helpful for many elementary school counselors. It is usually relatively quick and problem-specific; it does not attempt to restructure the child's personality. The primary focus is to help the child deal with a particular situation in a short period of time. In talking to elementary counselors, it seems clear that much of their work involves letting a child vent feelings about a specific problem or relationship and then helping him or her to learn new ways of handling it. By using play media and toys, the school counselor has a very effective way of using the techniques of release therapy to help with this process. The counselor gathers information about the particular situation or relationship from the child, the teacher, and/or the child's parent(s). The counselor then sets up the situation using the toys in his or her counseling office. The child uses the toys to play through the situation several times. After the counselor feels that the child has gotten a sufficient grasp on the emotional content of the incident, she or he then uses the toys to help the child generate new and different ways of dealing with the problem.

Client Centered, Nondirective Play Therapy

Garry Landreth (1991, 1993) presented a current application of client centered, nondirective play therapy. Barlow, Strother, and Landreth (1985) make a case for school counselors using nondirective play therapy to work with students who demonstrate a lack of self-control, regressive behavior, dependency, reading failure, socially inappropriate habitual behaviors, school phobia, and social skills deficiencies. The primary goal of nondirective play therapy is to help a child grow as a person (Landreth, 1987). Nondirective play therapists do not believe in focusing on specific problems. Instead they concentrate on building a relationship with the child based on unconditional positive regard, personal warmth, respect for the child's ability to solve problems, and communication of empathic understanding.

This philosophy is a wonderful way to interact with others, but it may present difficulties for some school counselors. While the authors believe that few would disagree with the contention that nondirective play therapy is a marvelous way to build a relationship with a child, there are those (Nelson, 1967; Golden, 1985) who have challenged the efficacy of nondirective play therapy as a viable approach in the elementary school. Nelson (1967), while he advocated the use of play media in school counseling settings, noted that the nondirective play therapy process is time-consuming and does not necessarily lead to positive behavior change. Golden (1985) also suggested that nondirective play therapy takes too much time to be an effective tool for school counselors. Although Barlow, Strother, and Landreth (1985) acknowledged that time is a problem for school counselors and advocated limiting sessions to a small number, Golden (1985) contended that this would violate Axline's dictum that the play therapist never hurry the process (Axline, 1969). Golden (1985) also criticized the fact that nondirective play therapy does not usually involve other members of the child's family. He suggested that school counselors must include parents and other family members as part of the intervention process. Golden (1985) also challenged the notion of school counselors as "therapists." He asserted that "therapy" is a long-term procedure designed to eliminate serious emotional problems and that this is not within the responsibilities of the school counselor.

Despite the objections presented by Golden and Nelson, the authors believe that there is a place for child centered, nondirective play therapy in the schools. It is an excellent approach for building relationships with all children, no matter what their age. It is also an effective method for encouraging children to explore themselves and the world and to express their feelings. It is especially helpful with children in kindergarten through third grade whose verbal skills and abstract reasoning abilities are still in the early stages of development. It can also be an effective strategy for providing unconditional positive regard to children whose low self-esteem and self-confidence are adversely affecting their performance in the classroom.

Adlerian Play Therapy

Adlerian play therapy is an integration of the theoretical principles and therapeutic strategies of Alfred Adler's Individual Psychology and the techniques of play therapy (Kottman, 1993a, 1993b, in press a, in press b; Kottman & Johnson, 1993; Kottman & Warlick, 1990, 1991). The authors, while admittedly prejudiced, believe that Adlerian play therapy is well suited to application in schools. Dr. Kottman has trained a number of elementary school counselors to use this approach, and they have reported much success.

Adlerian play therapy has four phases: (a) building an egalitarian relationship with the child; (b) exploring the child's life-style; (c) helping the child gain insight into his or her life-style; and (d) reorientation/reeducation. During the first phase, the counselor uses a combination of the generic basic play therapy skills already discussed and several Adlerian techniques to establish a relationship in which the counselor and the child are equal partners. The counselor uses encouragement, answers the child's questions, and actively interacts with the child in both play and role play situations to make a trusting and warm connection with the child.

During the second phase of the counseling, the counselor uses questioning strategies, drawing techniques, observation, and consultation with the parent(s) and teachers to investigate the child's life-style and to form an understanding of the child's characteristic way of viewing self, the world, and others. The counselor explores the family constellation and family atmosphere to develop a sense of the child's method of gaining significance and belonging. The counselor also begins to formulate hypotheses about whether the goal of the child's behavior is attention, power, revenge, or proving inadequacy.

During the third phase of the play therapy, the counselor makes tentative hypotheses and shares inferences about the child's goals and beliefs about self, others, and the world. Based on patterns observed in the child's play and verbalizations and from consultation with the parent(s) and teachers, the counselor begins to make guesses about what the child thinks and feels. The counselor makes connections between what happens in the play sessions and the child's behavior at home and in the classroom. The counselor's purpose during this phase is to help the child understand his or her own feelings, attitudes, motivation, thoughts, and behaviors. After this has begun to happen, the counselor can also begin to help the child make decisions about what she or he wants to change and what is acceptable as it is.

The counselor uses the fourth phase, the reorientation/reeducation phase, to help the child bring about any desired changes. In this phase, the counselor uses role playing, storytelling, drawing, visualization, and other techniques to help the child generate alternative attitudes, goals, and behavior. The counselor may also teach the child new skills and behaviors and provide him or her with a forum to practice these new skills. The counselor uses encouragement to point to any changes in action, self-image, and philosophy as this process unfolds.

Throughout the entire sequence of the play counseling sessions, the counselor consults with the child's parent(s) and teachers. The counselor uses the adults in the child's life as sources of information about the child and as change agents. The counselor teaches them about goals of behavior, logical consequences, communication skills, and encouragement, and helps them put their new information and skills into practice with children.

Gestalt Therapy

Violet Oaklander (1969) pioneered the application of Gestalt therapy with children and adolescents. Her classic book, *Windows to Our Children,* provides instructions on ways of using Gestalt techniques with children. She discussed ways to use drawings and fantasy to help children explore their feelings and interactions. Oaklander also detailed methods of using storytelling, poetry, and puppets to allow children to express themselves. Her approach is extremely practical and down-to-earth. While she provided a model for ongoing, in-depth therapy with children, she also seemed to encourage practitioners to try the various ideas described in her book without necessarily involving themselves in a long-term therapeutic relationship. The authors believe that many of the strategies described by Oaklander would be helpful and feasible for application by school counselors, no matter what their theoretical orientation. Using these techniques would not require a specially designed space or difficult to acquire materials. The school counselor can use many of these activities with supplies easily available in today's schools.

Jungian Play Therapy

John Allan has made a case for using play therapy based on Jungian principles in elementary schools (Allan, 1988; Allan & Brown, 1993). He discussed specific strategies for using both spontaneous and directed drawings, visualizations, fantasy enactments, creative dramatics, serial story writing, and sandplay. He also gave Jungian interpretations for the common symbols in children's art and fantasy. While the authors agree that many school counselors could use the specific practical strategies suggested by Allan, they believe that most elementary school counselors do not have the extensive background necessary to be able to conveniently and accurately interpret the hidden symbolic significance ascribed to many of the drawings and imaginings in Jungian psychology.

Termination

As the child grows and changes, the counselor will begin to contemplate termination of the play counseling sessions. This will not, however, mean an end to the counselor's relationship with the child. Nor does it mean that the child will never need play sessions in the future. Counselors who take a developmental stance will realize that the same child, even though he or she has gotten more skillful at recognizing and expressing feelings and has an enhanced self-image, may experience renewed difficulties at a future development period (Muro & Dinkmeyer, 1977).

In deciding whether a child is ready for termination, the counselor must consider two factors: (a) Has the child's behavior in the play room changed significantly? (b) Has the child's behavior at home and in the classroom related to the presenting problem changed? In the play room, a child who is ready to terminate may express boredom or a decreased desire to interact with the play media (Landreth, 1991). This child may also act uninterested, listless, cranky, or whiny. He or she may simply express a belief that coming to the play room and/or working with the counselor is no longer necessary or helpful. Usually the counselor will notice that the child has changed for the better in counselor-child interactions. As the child grows and changes, she or he should exhibit reduced levels of inappropriate, irresponsible behaviors in the play sessions, such as overdependence, power struggles, inability to express feelings, and temper tantrums.

The counselor should also investigate the child's behavior at home and at school. Even if the child is acting perfectly during play sessions, he or she is probably not ready for termination if the presenting problem has not improved. This is a good time to enlist the help of the parent(s) and/or teachers. When asking them to report on progress or changes, counselors should request concrete factual information. For example, they should not just ask, "Is the presenting problem better?" Counselors should ask them the average number of times per day the child got into a power struggle before the play sessions started, and then ask how many times per day the child gets into a power struggle at the present time. If the counselor asks for observable, measurable data, she or he will get a much more precise and helpful idea of how the play counseling has impacted the presenting problem.

Counselors should be sure to notify the child several sessions before the actual termination. It is helpful to use the "notification" session to discuss changes the counselor sees and changes reported by the parent(s) and teachers. The counselor can also use this session to solicit the child's opinion on ways that he or she has changed since the beginning of the play counseling. This early warning will give the child a chance to consolidate any changes that have occurred in the play counseling. It will also give the child an opportunity to replay the major themes and patterns that have been important in the play sessions. The child can use the time between the notification and the final session to emotionally prepare to end this phase of his or her relationship with the counselor and with the materials in the play area.

Many times, the child will revert to some of the old, inappropriate behaviors and attitudes (Landreth, 1991). Often this is related to the child's anxiety about losing an important support network. It may also be related to the child's feelings of abandonment, anger, and unwillingness to change the relationship with the counselor. The child may simply be testing to see the difference between how people react to the "new" set of behaviors versus the "old" set of behaviors. The best way for the counselor to prepare for this eventuality is to remember that this is a natural part of the termination process. It would probably be helpful to warn the parent(s) and teachers to expect a possible reversion and to suggest that they not take it personally or overreact. The most helpful approach to this type of "back-sliding" is to reflect the child's underlying feelings and purposes. This helps the child to realize that this, too, will pass.

Activity Therapy

While play counseling works well with children in the primary grades, children in the intermediate grades or middle school may not respond quite so readily to the toys and play materials used in a counseling with toys program (Guerney, 1983; Kottman, Strother, & Deniger, 1987; Nickerson, Maas, & O'Laughlin, 1982). Activity therapy is an adaptation of the techniques and strategies of play therapy that frequently appeals to older children. In activity therapy, the counselor engages the child in "nonverbal modes of relationship—be they games, free play, movement, drama, music, art, or other activities—as the chief therapeutic media in which conflicts are sorted out and resolved and through which intellectual and emotional energies are freed for more adaptive and creative living" (Nickerson et al., 1982, p. 4).

Toy Selection

One of the primary differences between play therapy and activity therapy is the selection of the materials. Although there should be some toys representing each of the three major categories of play therapy media (real-life toys, aggressive toys, and creative/expressive media), the actual material chosen for each category will differ from those media found in a play room. The real-life toys might include some of the toys used in the play room, such as the doll family, but the majority of the toys in this category should reflect the fascination of older children with competition, realistic play, and game playing (Guerney, 1983). The activity area should have target games, a miniature bowling set, a Nerf basketball hoop, and board games. The board games can be the usual commercial, competitive games (such as checkers, Chutes and Ladders, Life) or noncompetitive, cooperative games (Sleeping Grump, Rescue the Princess), or specially designed therapeutic games (The Talking, Feeling and Doing Game; Conversations; The UnGame). If the counselor chooses to use competitive games, the authors have found that it is frequently better to use games that do not require any skill on the part of the players. While others (Crocker & Wroblewski, 1975; Gardner, 1969) advocate using games such as checkers and Monopoly, in the experience of the authors, it is easier to engage children in games that they can win based on chance, rather than skill.

Other real-life materials that could be helpful in activity therapy are stethoscopes and other medical equipment, tape recorders, and office supplies and equipment. Quite frequently, physicians, local companies, and other community resources are willing to donate these types of materials.

The toys for expressing aggression will, for the most part, resemble those used for play therapy. In buying these toys for older children the counselor may want to obtain toys that look more realistic than those intended for K–3 children. Since more mature children may also be stronger and more physically powerful than younger children, the counselor must be sure that none of these toys have sharp edges or are dangerous in any way. Counselors may also need to limit the use of the aggressive toys more often and more creatively than in play counseling. Older children are frequently less willing to abide by the rules and are more likely to "test" the counselor. However, children in this age group usually respond well to a counselor who is firm, fair, and consistent.

Most of the creative and expressive media for activity therapy are the same materials used for play therapy. However, the older children will have the potential for more varied applications. Activity therapy can also include more crafts, carpentry, model-making, collages and other artistic endeavors that require relatively advanced manual dexterity.

Goals in Activity Counseling

Nickerson and O'Laughlin (1982) suggested that the counselor can use games and activities with children to help investigate behavior patterns present in their interactions with others. Games and activities can also serve as tools for children to work through excessive anxiety, feelings of inadequacy, and overemphasis on competition and winning. Elementary and middle school counselors can use games to help children learn more about social skills, responsibility, and conforming behavior. In activity therapy, children can exhibit their natural playfulness and ability to fantasize (Crocker & Wroblewski, 1975). They can also use the activity situation to practice new behaviors in a safe environment. Therapeutic game playing helps children learn more adequate coping strategies, such as winning and losing gracefully; dealing with aggression in an appropriate manner; and receiving criticism, anger, or rejection from others and surviving the experience (Nickerson & O'Laughlin, 1982).

Basic Skills and Strategies

Many of the specific skills and strategies used by the counselor in activity therapy depend upon his or her theoretical orientation. However, some of the techniques used in working with children in this age group are basic and generic. These skills are similar to those used in play therapy. The counselor using an activity approach will probably not track or restate content very often. If the counselor does choose to use these techniques, he or she must be very careful to use them sparingly. In restating content with children in this age range, it is extremely important to paraphrase and not parrot their language. Children in the intermediate grades and middle school are constantly on guard to the possibility that others are making fun of them. In the authors' experience, these children frequently interpret tracking and restatement of content as a subtle form of ridicule.

The primary tools in activity counseling will be reflection of feelings, returning responsibility to the children, using children's metaphors, and limiting. However, in working with older children using activities and games, counselors will be able to use a broader range of feeling words and more abstract reasoning skills. Because of the developmental level of the children, they are able to engage in more decision-making activities, higher levels of verbal interchanges, and more complicated metaphors.

CONCLUSION

Play and activity counseling are both valuable approaches for school counselors. Children naturally engage in play and activities, and they easily use these modalities for communication and as avenues for self-exploration and new learning. There are many different counseling techniques including tracking, restatement of content, reflection of feelings, returning responsibility to the child, communication through metaphor, and limiting that counselors can use to help children learn about self, others, and the world. School counselors can use carefully selected play and activity media to help children who are experiencing academic, emotional, and behavioral difficulties to solve problems and maximize their learning. They can also use these tools to help children who are simply struggling with normal developmental processes deal with these situations more effectively and efficiently.

REFERENCES

Alexander, E. (1964). School centered play therapy program. *Personnel and Guidance Journal, 43,* 256–261.

Allan, J. (1988). *Inscapes of the child's world: Jungian counseling in schools and clinics.* Dallas, TX: Spring.

Allan, J., & Brown, K. (1993). Jungian play therapy in elementary schools. *Elementary School Guidance and Counseling, 28,* 30–41.

Allen, F. (1939). Therapeutic work with children. *American Journal of Orthopsychiatry, 9,* 737–742.

Axline, V. (1947). *Play therapy: The inner dynamics of childhood.* Boston: Houghton Mifflin.

Axline, V. (1969). *Play therapy* (rev. ed.). New York: Ballantine Books.

Barlow, D., Strother, J., & Landreth, G. (1985). Child-centered play therapy: Nancy from baldness to curls. *The School Counselor, 32,* 347–356.

Bixler, R. (1982). Limits are therapy. In G. Landreth (Ed.), *Play therapy: Dynamics of the process of counseling with children* (pp. 173–188). Springfield, IL: Charles C Thomas.

Campbell, C. (1993). Play therapy in elementary schools: Special issue. *Elementary Guidance and Counseling, 27.*

Center for Play Therapy. (1993). *Directory of play therapy training.* Denton, TX: Author.

Crocker, J., & Wroblewski, M. (1975). Using recreational games in counseling. *Personnel and Guidance Journal, 53,* 153–158.

Erickson, E. (1963). *Childhood and society.* New York: W. W. Norton.

Frank, L. (1982). Play in personality development. In G. Landreth (Ed.), *Play therapy: Dynamics of the process of counseling with children* (pp. 19–32). Springfield, IL: Charles C Thomas.

Freud, A. (1946). *The psychoanalytic treatment of children.* London: Imago.

Gardner, R. (1969). The game of checkers as a diagnostic and therapeutic tool in child psychotherapy. *Acta Paedopsychiatrica, 38,* 253–262.

Gil, E. (1991). *The healing power of play: Working with abused children.* New York: Guilford.

Ginott, H. (1961). *Group psychotherapy with children.* New York: McGraw-Hill.

Ginott, H. (1982). Therapeutic intervention in child treatment. In G. Landreth (Ed.), *Play therapy: Dynamics of the process of counseling with children* (pp. 160–172). Springfield, IL: Charles C Thomas.

Golden, L. (1985). Response to "Child-centered play therapy: Nancy from baldness to curls." *The School Counselor, 33,* 88–90.

Guerney, L. (1983). Client-centered (nondirective) play therapy. In C. Schaefer & K. O'Connor (Eds.), *Handbook of play therapy* (pp. 21–64). New York: Wiley.

Hambridge, G. (1955). Structured play therapy. *American Journal of Orthopsychiatry, 25,* 601–617.

Hendricks, S. (1971). *A descriptive analysis of the process of client-centered play therapy.* Unpublished doctoral dissertation: University of North Texas.

Hug-Hellmuth, H. (1921). On the technique of child analysis. *International Journal of Psychoanalysis, 2,* 287.

Kissel, S. (1990). *Play therapy: A strategic approach.* Springfield, IL: Charles C Thomas.

Klein, M. (1932). *The psycho-analysis of children.* London: Hogarth Press.

Kottman, T. (1993a). Billy, the teddy bear boy. In L. Golden & M. Norwich (Eds.), *Case studies in child counseling* (pp. 75–88). New York: Merrill.

Kottman, T. (1993b). The king of rock and roll. In T. Kottman & C. Schaefer (Eds.), *Play therapy in action: A casebook for practitioners* (pp. 133–167). Creskill, NJ: Jason Aronson.

Kottman, T. (in press a). Adlerian play therapy. In K. O'Connor & C. Schaefer (Eds.), *Handbook of play therapy, vol. 2.* New York: Wiley.

Kottman, T. (in press b). *Partners in play: An Adlerian approach to play therapy.* Alexandria, VA: American Counseling Association.

Kottman, T., & Johnson, V. (1993). Adlerian play therapy: A tool for school counselors. *Elementary Guidance and Counseling, 27,* 42–51.

Kottman, T., & Schaefer, C. (Eds.), (1993). *Play therapy in action: A casebook for practitioners.* Creskill, NJ: Jason Aronson.

Kottman, T., Strother, J., & Deniger, M. (1987). Activity therapy: An alternative therapy for adolescents. *Journal of Humanistic Education and Development, 25,* 180–186.

Kottman,T., & Warlick, J. (1990). Adlerian play therapy: Practical considerations. *Journal of Individual Psychology, 45,* 433–446.

Kottman, T., & Warlick, J. (1991). Adlerian play therapy. *Journal of Humanistic Education and Development, 28,* 125–132.

Landreth, G. (no date). *Play therapy class laboratory book.* (Available from University Bookstore, University of North Texas, Denton, TX.)

Landreth, G. (1983). Play therapy in elementary school settings. In C. Schaefer & K. O'Connor (Eds.), *Handbook of play therapy* (pp. 200–212). New York: Wiley.

Landreth, G. (1987). Play therapy: Facilitative use of child's play in elementary school counseling. *Elementary School Guidance and Counseling, 21,* 253–261.

Landreth, G. (1991). *Play therapy: The art of the relationship.* Muncie, IN: Accelerated Development.

Landreth, G. (1993). Child-centered play therapy. *Elementary School Guidance and Counseling, 28,* 17–29.

Levy, D. (1939). Release therapy. *American Journal of Orthopsychiatry, 9,* 713–736.

Marvasti, J. (1989). Play therapy with sexually abused children. In S. Sgroi (Ed.), *Vulnerable populations: Sexual abuse treatment for children, adult survivors, offenders, and persons with mental retardation.* Lexington, MA: D. C. Heath.

Moustakas, C. (1959). *Psychotherapy with children: The living relationship.* New York: Harper & Row.

Muro, J., & Dinkmeyer, D. (1977). *Counseling in the elementary and middle schools: A pragmatic approach.* Dubuque, IA: Wm. C. Brown.

Nelson, R. (1966). Elementary school counseling with unstructured play media. *Personnel and Guidance Journal, 45,* 24–27.

Nelson, R. (1967). Pros and cons of using play media in counseling. *Elementary School Guidance and Counseling, 2,* 143–147.

Nickerson, E., Maas, J., & O'Laughlin, K. (1982). An introduction to the theory and practice of action-oriented approaches. In E. Nickerson & K. O'Laughlin (Eds.), *Helping through actions: Action-oriented therapies* (p. 108). Amherst, MA: Human Resource Development.

Nickerson, E., & O'Laughlin, K. (1982). The therapeutic use of games. In C. Schaefer & K. O'Connor (Eds.), *Handbook of play therapy* (pp. 174–187). New York: Wiley.

Oaklander, V. (1969). *Windows to our children.* Highland, NY: Center for GestaltDevelopment.

O'Connor, K. (1991). *The play therapy primer: An integration of theories and techniques.* New York: Wiley.

Phillips, R. (1985). Whistling in the dark? A review of play therapy research. *Psychotherapy, 22,* 752–760.

Piaget, J. (1962). *Play, dreams, and imitation in childhood.* New York: Rutledge.

Rank, O. (1936). *Will therapy.* New York: Knopf.

Taft, J. (1933). *The dynamics of therapy in a controlled relationship.* New York: Macmillan.

Webb, N. (1991). *Play therapy with children in crisis: A casebook for practitioners.* New York: Guilford.

Withee, K. (1975). *A descriptive analysis of the process of play therapy.* Unpublished doctoral dissertation: University of North Texas.

Chapter Nine

Creative and Expressive Arts Techniques

🌳 When I (T.K.) was a school counselor, some of the most exciting and powerful work I did with the children in my school did not "look" very much like counseling. I used many creative and expressive arts strategies that were fun for the children, and at the same time they afforded me with an opportunity to better understand the children in my school.

Just as play is a natural medium of expression for children in counseling, creative and expressive arts techniques can have unique value for counseling work in schools. Most children are quite comfortable using art, drama, stories, or books as a way to connect with the counselor and with other children. Quite frequently, the creative and expressive arts give children a concrete method of exploring who they are, what kinds of relationships they have, and how they would like to change their thoughts, feelings, and/or behaviors (Case & Dalley, 1990; Furrer, 1982; Jacobs, 1992; Warren, 1984). Because the processes involved in these strategies are fun and usually non-threatening, the school counselor can use them to help children enter into the counseling relationship. Even those children who would have uniformly resisted other forms of counseling may be willing to engage in some of the creative and expressive techniques, primarily because they do not look like that "scary counseling stuff."

Since these techniques have a concrete component—the picture the child draws, the finished story, the book the child reads—the school counselor can use these techniques to help children, families, and school personnel gain insight into self-concept and relationships. Unlike the more abstract "talk" counseling, the very tangible nature of any product created in this type of counseling reduces the likelihood of continued denial or avoidance (Gladding, 1992; Jacobs, 1992).

While there are many different kinds of creative and expressive arts appropriate for counseling interventions, we have decided to highlight some techniques from the areas of art and drawing, creative drama, storytelling and metaphor, and bibliocounseling. We have chosen these particular strategies because they are especially appropriate for counseling children and adolescents. We have tried to choose methods that are easy to learn and do not take too much space, time, or money, so that they will serve as viable tools for school counselors.

Art and Drawing Techniques

The school counselor can use art and drawing techniques to stimulate and encourage children "to reach their highest functioning level. . .and enrich their lives through the use of the creative process" (Furrer, 1982, p. viii). Doing art activities can enhance "awareness of self (feelings, sensations, thoughts, intuition) and of others and of the environment" (Furrer, 1982, p. viii). The process of creating an art product can also facilitate both verbal and nonverbal communication and provide an avenue for stress reduction and expression of emotions. The school counselor can use drawing as (a) a diagnostic tool for exploring interpersonal relationships at home and school and intrapersonal issues and (b) an intervention strategy for helping children discover potential solutions to problem situations in their lives.

Most elementary school children are willing to participate in art and drawing projects because they have not yet decided that they "cannot draw." Since they have not developed this attitude, it is usually relatively easy to engage these children in producing art products. Sometimes this is more difficult with junior high/middle school students because they have frequently decided that they cannot "do art" due to their insecurity about their products. When this is the case, the counselor will have to make extra efforts to emphasize that the counseling relationship is not evaluative and the art is simply a way of communicating—that she or he is not going to be critical or focus on the appearance of the finished product. Counselors may also want to engage in the art or drawing activity themselves to help the children feel less threatened by the process of art production.

Materials

Furrer (1982) suggested that the counselor gather the following art supplies for use with children: pencils, erasers, thin black markers, thin and thick colored markers, colored pencils, crayons, scissors, white glue, rubber cement, a ruler, watercolor paints and brush, a stapler, tape, and a hole punch. She also suggested that counselors provide cover-up smocks if they are asking children to work on messy projects. Phillips (1991) included these items and several additional materials in her list of counseling art supplies: newsprint rolls, a pencil sharpener, modeling clay, chalk (both white and colored), and tempera paint cakes and brushes. She noted that she prefers tempera paint cakes to premixed tempera paints because they take less space in an office, and they are less messy.

While, of course, counselors do not need to have all this material to use art as a counseling tool, the more potential media on hand for children to use, the more avenues of expression available to them. Children who think they cannot draw may be willing to use clay because it is less precise; children who are afraid of the permanence of markers may be willing to use a pencil and eraser; and so on. If there is enough space, the counselor will probably want to openly display all of the art materials available on a shelf or table to allow the child to explore the possibilities. However, if there is limited space or the counselor has to travel from school to school, she or he may just want to store art materials in a box or suitcase that can be transported or put away in a closet.

Role of the Counselor

The counselor will, of course, tailor the interaction with the child using art media according to the needs of the child, the counselor's own personality, and the theory of counseling he or she follows. However, there are certain basic tactics typically used in art therapy that counselors may want to consider as they determine their role in this process (Phillips, 1991). As the counselor explains the process of using art and drawing techniques to the child, she or he will need to emphasize that there are no concrete rules in the process, no right or wrong way of doing the activities. It is important that instructions are kept to a minimum, letting the child decide for himself or herself the best way to approach the project. This allows for greater creativity and the freedom for the child to tailor the project to his or her own personal needs and issues. The counselor should observe the child's physical movement, his or her use of space, the expression of emotion, and the choice of media. Even if the child is struggling, the counselor will still need to refrain from becoming directive. By letting the child solve the problem in his or her own way, the counselor will reinforce the idea that there are no right or wrong ways of doing the activity. The counselor can also provide the child with an empowering experience in which he or she can make mistakes without criticism or correction and perhaps even work out a resolution. The only time to offer technical information is when the problem is directly connected to the art media, and it does not appear possible for the child to remedy the problem. For instance, if the child is working with clay that is too dry, the counselor might suggest that the problem is with the clay and not with the child and then help the child generate a solution to this technical dilemma.

One of the most important decisions to make in using visual arts techniques in counseling is whether, how, and when to discuss the experience and the art product with the child. Some counselors let the art techniques stand on their own. They do not discuss either the process or the product with the child unless the child initiates a discussion. They simply rely on their observations and the child's experiencing the process to help them understand the child and to help the child make any necessary changes. Some counselors choose to discuss the experience with the child (how the child felt when he or she was creating the art, what he or she was thinking about as the product developed, and other process-oriented questions), but they do not ask the child to discuss the actual artwork. Other counselors choose to discuss the art product—what it is, who the subjects are, what they are doing, and other product-oriented questions. Some counselors combine these two different techniques, depending on the child and the situation.

If the counselor decides that discussion is helpful and has chosen the focus of the discussion (process or product), she or he must also decide when to have the discussions, either as an ongoing conversation while the child is producing the art or after the product is complete. Since it is relatively easy to influence children and their artwork, if the counselor decides to have an ongoing conversation, he or she will want to be very careful and intentional in choosing the direction of the discussion so as to avoid affecting the process or the product.

General Principles in Interpreting Drawings and Art

Most school counselors will not have training as art therapists or in the more esoteric methods of analysis of drawings and art products. The authors do not believe this is necessary, as school counselors will not be conducting indepth therapy designed to restructure children's personalities. There are some general principles that can help the school counselor apply some commonsense ideas in discerning the meaning in a child's artwork. These concepts will allow the school counselor to use art and drawing as a method of understanding the child's self-concept, relationships with others, and views of the world. They may also provide some means for the school counselor to use art as an intervention strategy.

As the counselor observes the child begin work on the art project, the counselor can probably assume that the child approaches this assignment in a similar way to the way he or she approaches other school assignments. If the child "dives" into the project, beginning without visible consideration of how to go about doing the work, the counselor can probably assume that this is the way the child usually goes about doing things in the classroom. If the child repeatedly asks for clarification, permission, and approval, the counselor will probably be able to predict that this is a child who is unsure of himself or herself and who frequently seeks acceptance and expects some type of punishment or disapproval. If the child constantly erases or starts over, voicing a steady stream of dissatisfied comments, or destroys or criticizes the finished product, the counselor can guess that this is a child who has a tendency toward expecting perfection from self and others. All of these interpretations are based on common sense and a basic knowledge of children and how they act. Personal observations will help the counselor begin to understand the interpersonal and intrapersonal dynamics of the child that are affecting his or her performance in school and will suggest possible directions for interventions.

Looking at the actual art product, the counselor will want to consider the media the child chose to use, the subject of the product, and the size of the product (Kaufman & Wohl, 1992). As we suggested in the Materials section, the media chosen may be emblematic of the child's personality. For instance, a very self-confident child may select permanent markers and boldly begin drawing without much advance consideration. A rather shy child who is not at all sure of himself may decide to use modeling clay for his project, think for a long time before starting, and then continually flatten his creation and begin again.

What the child chooses to construct may also tell the counselor something about the child. For instance, a child who is sent to the counselor because she has a tendency toward aggression might draw a superheroine beating up "bad guys," or she might use clay to model a gun. A withdrawn child, on the other hand, might draw a picture of a little mouse being chased by a dog, or she might use the clay to build a fence with a child behind it.

The size of the product is also sometimes important, as there seems to be a correlation between the size of the product and the artist's self-esteem (Kaufman & Wohl, 1992). Products that seem to be average size (for example, human figure drawings that are about nine inches in height) are typical of children who are not experiencing major interpersonal or self-image difficulties. Products that are much larger or much smaller than this frequently indicate that the artist is experiencing some type of problem.

In interpreting drawings, the counselor will want to consider his or her global impression, the placement of figures on the page, details, erasure, line quality, shading, and symmetry (DiLeo, 1983; Hammer, 1980; Kaufman & Wohl, 1992; Ogdon, 1977). The global quality or tone of the picture will give the counselor some clues about the child and his or her self-concept and interactions. In thinking about the global impression of the drawing, the counselor should look at whether the drawing is sad or happy, elaborate or simple, organized or chaotic, peaceful or turbulent (DiLeo, 1983). The counselor will also want to consider how quickly and carefully the child drew the picture. The counselor may also learn something about the child if he or she drew a representational picture from memory, a fantastic picture from the imagination, or a copied picture from some other source.

When looking at the paper on which the child has drawn a picture, the counselor should observe how the child has placed the figures on the page. Children usually draw in the center of the page, indicating security, self-direction, self-centeredness, and a tendency to live in the here and now (Hammer, 1980; Jolles, 1971; Kaufman & Wohl, 1992; Ogdon, 1977). A child who draws at the top of the page may have a tendency to strive for unattainable goals, and a child who draws at the bottom of the page may have a tendency toward insecurity or depression (Kaufman & Wohl, 1992). A child who draws on the right-hand side of the page may tend to focus on the future, and a child who draws on the left hand side of the page may tend to focus on the past (Jolles, 1971). In a family drawing, the relative placement of each member of the family may signify how the child views the interactions between the various family members—those near one another in the drawing may have closer relationships than those placed farther away (Burns & Kaufman, 1972).

The details in drawings can also be significant. The counselor should look at the amount of detailing, the types of details, and the way the details are organized (Jolles, 1971; Kaufman & Wohl, 1992; Hammer, 1980). The drawings of well-adjusted individuals have some details, indicating that they are aware of and interested in the world. People who draw hardly any details may be very self-absorbed, not paying attention to the rest of the world. They may be introverted, depressed, or have a low energy level. People who draw excessive details may have an unusually high need to control their environment, or they may be overly interested in minutia.

The kind of details and the way they are drawn may give clues about the types of things that the individual believes are important. For instance, Donald draws a house with limited details except for the doors and windows. On the doors and windows, Donald carefully draws several locks that have elaborate decorations on them. One possible interpretation would be that Donald has a need to control or limit his accessibility. There are, of course, other interpretations, and it would be important to check this out with Donald and to integrate any drawing interpretation with other data about Donald.

Erasures may also be important in analyzing drawings (Hammer, 1980; Kaufman & Wohl, 1992; Ogdon, 1977). A well-adjusted person will frequently have a moderate number of erasures, resulting in an improved quality in the drawing. This usually indicates that the individual is flexible and able to be appropriately self-critical. If the person draws, erases, draws, erases, and so on, resulting in a deteriorated drawing, there is a possibility that the individual feels a certain degree of conflict or ambiguity about the subject or is so perfectionistic as to be self-defeating. Sometimes when an individual uses erasures excessively it may mean that the person is indecisive or insecure.

The counselor can use line quality and pencil pressure as additional indicators about the artist and his or her personal characteristics (DiLeo, 1983; Hammer, 1980; Kaufman & Wohl, 1992; Ogdon, 1977). Determination, persistence, and security are frequently traits of a person who draws with a firm stroke. Flexibility and willingness to deviate from traditions are possible attributes of a person who uses curved lines. Steady, moderate pencil pressure is usually a sign of good mental health. Sketchy lines and/or light penciling can indicate uncertainty, shyness, fearfulness, and insecurity. Lines that look like the person used a ruler to draw them sometimes suggest compulsivity. People who draw with extremely heavy strokes are frequently very forceful and may act in an aggressive manner.

Many experts in the field of drawing interpretation (Hammer, 1980; Jolles, 1971; Ogdon, 1977) consider shading to be of significance. These authorities suggest that shading indicates a high degree of anxiety or agitation. They believe that the area shaded in the drawing is the usual source of the internal conflict. For instance, Johnny, a child who was sexually abused, might draw a picture of a person with a heavily shaded genital region, but no shading in other parts of the drawing. This could be a picture of himself or of his abuser, and the heavy shading would indicate a focus of his anxiety.

After the age of seven, children's drawings should have a certain degree of symmetry (Hammer, 1980; Kaufman & Wohl, 1992; Ogdon, 1977). If their drawings are extremely asymmetrical, it may mean that they lack balance in some area. This unbalance might include being poorly coordinated, impulsive, aggressive, or insecure. If their drawings are almost perfectly symmetrical, however, it may mean that they lack flexibility, warmth, and the ability to be close to others. An excessive concern with balance may lead to depression, obsessive-compulsive behavior, or overintellectualization.

Before applying any of these principles to derive meaning from children's artwork, the counselor must take into consideration the child's age, developmental stage, cognitive abilities and weaknesses, and any potential neurological impairments (Kaufman & Wohl, 1992). It is also essential that the counselor consider any important environmental factors, such as the time of year, the weather, and such, and anything the counselor knows about the child's history and family structure. All of these elements will have an impact on the child, the child's artwork, and the meaning inherent in that artwork. The counselor should never base a diagnosis or make conclusions about a child or a child's family or school situation on one or two pieces of artwork without verification from some other source. After all, as Sigmund Freud once said, "sometimes a cigar is just a cigar."

In order to assess the developmental characteristics of children's drawings, the counselor must understand how artistic development takes place. While this topic is beyond the scope of this volume, there are many sources of information about this maturational process (DiLeo, 1970; Dubowski, 1990; Kellogg, 1969). By learning about the developmental aspects of children's drawings, the counselor will be more able to assess the maturational level of the drawing, as compared to the chronological age of the child. This may be a key to helping the counselor understand the child's interpersonal interactions and any kinds of traumatic situations that could have affected the child's developmental process. For instance, quite frequently children who have experienced trauma of some type, such as physical or sexual abuse, may produce drawings that appear to be considerably less mature than one would expect, given their chronological ages (Kaufman & Wohl, 1992).

Specific Techniques

While there are hundreds of possible visual arts strategies, we have chosen the following procedures as a representative sample that could be used in an elementary or middle school. Counselors can use these strategies in individual counseling, in group counseling, or in classroom guidance. Counselors will want to tailor the instructions to their specific purpose and target population.

Kinetic Family Drawing (KFD). Many times it is helpful for the school counselor to understand the child's perception of his or her family and the relationships among family members. Family tensions, rules, and interactions may be adversely affecting the child's school performance. The Kinetic Family Drawing (KFD) (Burns & Kaufman, 1972) is an instrument that can help a school counselor gain a clearer comprehension of family dynamics. The counselor can also use this family portrait to help the child learn more effective coping skills and reduce any negative fallout from family situations.

The usual instructions for completion of the KFD are: "Draw a picture of everyone in your family, including you, DOING something. Try to draw whole people, not cartoons or stick people. Remember, make everyone DOING something—some kind of action" (Burns & Kaufman, 1972, p. 5). Sometimes children may ask who they should include in their drawings. This frequently happens with children whose parents share custody, children with blended families, children who live with their grandparents, and so on. When this happens, the counselor may want to tell them to draw whoever they think of as a part of their family.

Burns and Kaufman (1970) supplied a list of potential questions that the counselor can ask the child to help understand the drawing and the relationships among family members. These questions include queries about the name of each person in the drawing, his or her age, his or her relationship to the child, what the person is doing in the picture, and other important personal characteristics. The following list of questions is a sample of the types of questions adapted from this list that would be appropriate for the school counselor to ask:

What is this person thinking?

What is this person feeling?

What do you like about this person?

What don't you like about this person?

How does this person get along with others?

What will happen to this person in the future?

What would you like to change about this family?

What do the people in this family do for fun?

What happened to this family right before this picture?

What will happen to this family right after this picture?

These questions can be adapted to the child and the situation. The child's answers will help the counselor gain a better understanding of how the child's family affects his or her self-concept, behaviors, attitudes, and feelings.

While there are several scoring procedures available for interpreting the KFD (Burns, 1982; Knoff, 1985; Reynolds, 1978), these may be more formal and analytical than most school counselors will need or want. A common-sense approach combines the general principles described in the section on interpretation of artwork with some concepts specific to the KFD. Knoff & Prout (1985) suggested that the counselor examine the people, the objects, and specific areas of interest, including actions between figures; individual figural characteristics; position, distance, and barriers; style; and symbols. When looking at the people it is important to consider interactions, facial expressions, and individual activities. The actions of each person quite frequently depict how the artist views that person gaining importance in the family. For instance, Ronnie "Reader" Roberts would probably draw himself studying or reading a book, his brother James "Jock" Roberts playing baseball, his mother Connie "Clean" Roberts washing dishes, and his father Harold "Handy" Roberts fixing the lawnmower.

An examination of the objects can reveal what material possessions have special significance to the child. The counselor should look at the positions of objects in relation to the people in the drawing, the emphasis the child has placed on the object by using shading or making it disproportionately large or small, and the uses of each object. Usually the person located closest to the object is the individual that the child associates with the object. For instance, in the Roberts family portrait, Ronnie probably would have drawn a book next to himself, a baseball bat next to James, a dishcloth next to Connie, and a lawnmower next to Harold. If he had, instead, drawn a football by himself, this might have meant that he was perceiving pressure to be more athletic.

As the child draws the picture, he or she will place more emphasis on objects that are important or threatening to him or her. If Harold is a harsh disciplinarian who uses his belt to carry out corporal punishment, Ronnie might shade his father's belt with heavy pencil pressure.

The uses of objects are also important, in a sort of negative way. The counselor should look for strange or unexpected uses of objects in drawings; this might have special significance for the child, and the counselor should ask about it. For example, if Ronnie had drawn his father with a flyswatter stuck in his back pocket, the counselor would want to ask Ronnie why his father kept that object in such a place. The counselor might find out that Mr. Roberts uses a flyswatter in corporal punishment, or that the Roberts family lives in a place where there are a lot of flies.

One specific area of interest is the actions between figures (Knoff & Prout, 1985). The counselor should pay careful attention to what happens among family members. For instance, if Ronnie were to draw his parents having a sword fight, the counselor might want to investigate the relationship between his parents to determine how conflictual it was.

Another specific area of interest is individual figural characteristics. Knoff and Prout (1985) provided a list of significant characteristics included in figure drawings and what they mean. Some examples of this would include: (a) a large drawing of self might mean that the artist has aggressive tendencies; (b) a small self drawing might mean that the artist has a poor self-concept; (c) similarity between self drawing and another figure might signify that the artist admires the other person; (d) omission of a certain member of the family might indicate hostility toward that person.

Position, distance, and barriers are also important elements in understanding KFDs (Knoff & Prout, 1985). Counselors should explore the significance of placement (where each of the figures is placed relative to the other figures), integration (how the figures are oriented in terms of the other figures), ordering (the arrangement of the figures), distance (how closely the figures are placed to one another), and barriers (the types of barriers placed between figures, the placement of barriers, and the figures separated by the barriers). All of these factors can be important to the child, and the counselor may want to ask questions about each of them.

The style elements of KFDs include encapsulation, compartmentalization, lining at the bottom, lining at the top, underlining individual figures, and edging (Knoff & Prout, 1985). Encapsulation involves drawing a line or circle around one or more of the figures. If the encapsulation involves self, this may mean that the artist feels a need to be protected or isolated from other family members. If the encapsulation involves other members of the family, it may mean that the artist feels a need to isolate that particular member. If Ronnie and his brother were involved in negative sibling rivalry, Ronnie might encapsulate his brother.

Compartmentalization involves drawing lines between the various members of the family or otherwise separating them from one another. Most of the time when a child draws a compartmentalized family, he or she feels closed off or a need to be closed off from other family members. If Ronnie had drawn lines separating the members of his family from one another, it might indicate that his is a disengaged family in which members seldom interact with one another. However, it might also have exactly the opposite meaning—that Ronnie's family is enmeshed and that he has no privacy, but desperately wants it.

When a child draws a lot of lines or does excessive shading at the top or bottom of the page, it may signify some type of anxiety. "Lining" at the top usually suggests that the child feels worried about something. "Lining" at the bottom may mean that the child feels as though his or her world needs more foundation or support than it currently has. If the Roberts family has financial problems, Ronnie might draw them as a gloomy raincloud that constantly casts a shadow over the family, or he might draw an elaborate stage to support the family.

When a child underlines specific figures in the drawing, he or she is usually worried about some aspect of the relationship between or among those people. If Ronnie felt insecure about his relationship with his mother, he might heavily shade spaces underneath his drawings of himself and his mother.

Edging is drawing all of the figures around the edges of the paper. Usually edging means that the child has a tendency to stay on the sidelines and observe life without becoming a part of the interactions. If Ronnie used edging in his drawing, one would probably expect him to be very uninvolved in relationships with other people. Since Ronnie drew himself reading a book, the counselor might make the prediction that Ronnie was much more invested in his reading than he was in the interactions with other members of his family.

Symbols may also be important to the understanding of drawings. However, there can be many different interpretations of the meaning of each symbol. There are entire books that discuss the analysis of symbolism in drawing (Burns & Kaufman, 1972; DiLeo, 1983; Kellogg, 1969; Koppitz, 1968), so those interested in pursuing this aspect of using art in counseling will probably want to investigate these sources.

The school counselor can effectively use the KFD for both diagnostic and intervention purposes. The counselor can explore how the child gains a place in the family, how he or she views self, other family members, and relationships among family members, and how the family atmosphere affects him or her. The counselor may also choose to use the discussion of the drawing to try to help the child gain insight into self-concept, family relationships, attitudes, family values and beliefs, world view, and so forth. In discussing the KFD or other pictures related to the family, the counselor can also explore the child's goals for change; help him or her consider alternative behaviors, attitudes, feelings, and thoughts; examine possible ways of resolving conflict; and measure the child's progress in counseling. For example, the counselor could ask the child to draw a picture of how the family would look if the members were just the way the child would like them to be. Or the child could be asked to draw a family conflict and then draw possible ways that family members could resolve the conflict. Using the KFD as a springboard, the possibilities for intervention strategies are limited only by the counselor's imagination.

Kinetic School Drawing (KSD).   Another helpful art technique for school counselors is the Kinetic School Drawing (KSD) (Knoff & Prout, 1985). To administer the KSD, the counselor says to the child:

> Draw a school picture. Put yourself, your teacher, and a friend or two in the picture. Make everyone doing something. Try to draw whole people and make the best drawing you can. Remember, draw yourself, your teacher, and a friend or two, and make everyone doing something (Knoff, 1985, p. 1).

The counselor can use questioning strategies similar to those described for the KFD, but related to school situations. In addition to asking about each figure, the counselor might ask:

> What would you like to change about this class?
> How would you like to be different in school?
> How would you like school to be different?

How do the people in this class get along?

What do they do that is fun for them?

What do they do that gets them into trouble?

What happens when they get into trouble?

The school counselor can use this tool for diagnostic purposes in understanding how the child views school, teachers, other students, and his or her academic achievement. To gain a complete picture of the child's perception of school, the counselor should also observe the child in various settings in the school, such as the classroom, the playground, and the cafeteria. This, combined with an interpretation of the KSD, will give the counselor a more complete picture of the child's attitudes toward school, his or her relationships with teachers and other students, his or her relationships with other school personnel, and how the child responds to being in school and the school atmosphere.

The interpretation of the KSD for diagnostic purposes uses the general principles of drawing analysis (Burns & Kaufman, 1972) and the specific principles of KFD/KSD analysis (Knoff & Prout, 1985). The primary focus is on actions between figures; figural characteristics; position, distance, and barriers; and style. For instance, a child who is engaged in an ongoing power struggle with her teacher may draw herself as a very tiny figure and her teacher as a very large figure. A child who is struggling in reading may draw a picture of his teacher holding a book on one side of the page, himself on the other side of the page, with a wall in between them. A child who sees herself as gaining significance in athletics rather than academics may draw a picture of herself playing softball during recess. These are rather commonsense interpretations, but they can be very helpful to school counselors who usually have limited time to gather information about a child's difficulties.

The counselor can also use the KSD as an intervention tool to help children make changes in attitudes, thoughts, and feelings about school, teachers, and other students; in academic self-concept; and in school behavior and academic performance. With some children, the counselor will want to begin any intervention by using the KSD to help them gain insight into their attitudes toward school and relationships with teachers, students, and school authority figures. Many times, children will be unaware of how their attitudes toward school are contributing to making school an unpleasant place for them. By pointing out different aspects of the KSD, sometimes the counselor can help children understand the dynamics of what is happening in school. This may lead to changes in thoughts, feelings, and behaviors.

Other times the child already understands what is happening between him or her and the other people in school, but is not sure what to do about it. This would be a situation in which the counselor could use drawings and discussion as a springboard for further explorations into possible alternative behaviors, changing relationships and attitudes, and conflict resolution. The counselor can ask the child to draw other pictures to provide direction and impetus for change.

Body outline drawings.   Steinhardt (1985) suggested the technique of body outline drawings as a versatile way of working with children. In this strategy, the child lies on the floor on a large piece of paper and the counselor (or another child if this is a group activity) draws around the child's body. The counselor then asks the child, "Who do you want this to be?" The child can finish the drawing any way he or she chooses. Quite frequently, the child will decide to use the body outline drawing as a self-portrait, which will give the counselor information about how the child sees himself or herself. The child may also choose to make the body outline drawing represent someone else— it will sometimes be a hero character or some fictional person or a real person the child admires or fears. Whoever the child chooses, this decision will also give clues about the child's views of self, others, and the world.

As the child draws, the counselor can suggest that the child pretend that the various parts of the body can talk and ask the body parts what they would say (Steinhardt, 1985). This may help the child voice concerns that he or she would not normally express.

The counselor can also use the body outline drawing to help children with boundaries. Children who have weak boundaries may draw very faint lines around the body outline. Children who have boundaries that are too impermeable may heavily reinforce the lines around the outline. This would be a valuable opportunity for the counselor to explore the possible ramifications of different approaches to boundaries and to make suggestions of other ways to draw the outline that might indicate changes in the status of boundaries.

With adopted children, the counselor can use the body outline drawings to help children examine their biological and environmental heritage. As they draw, they can list the physical, emotional, and mental attributes that they think they inherited from their birth parents and the attributes that they think came from their adoptive parents. This gives adopted children a chance to realize that they have qualities from each set of parents in their makeup.

The counselor can also ask children to add a favorite place, other people, pets, and so forth to the background of the body outline (Steinhardt, 1985). This will afford the counselor an opportunity to explore what and who is important to the children and give the children an opportunity to express themselves to a person who will listen to them and who thinks what they have to say is important.

Cartoons.   Crowley and Mills (1989) outlined several techniques that engage children in drawing cartoons to help them deal with their fears and worries. One of these strategies is a three-step process in which the child first draws a fear, worry, or pain on a sheet of paper. In the second step, the child draws a picture of a cartoon helper who could help with the problem. On the third sheet of paper, the child draws how the problem would look when it is solved. In another strategy, after the child draws the fear, worry, or pain, the counselor asks him or her to draw a gift that the cartoon helper could give the child that would transform the problem into something positive. The child then draws how the problem looks after "it is all better."

Feeling art.   Another art technique that works well with younger elementary children is feeling art (Gerler, 1982). The counselor can use this strategy in classroom guidance or in group or individual counseling. The directions are simply to use art materials to create different feelings—how various emotions appear to the students. The counselor can choose the specific feelings for children to explore or let them choose their own feelings. The counselor can use this activity as a way of teaching feeling vocabulary, learning to communicate about feelings, or exploring the types of situations that evoke certain feelings.

Counselors can also use feeling art to help reduce fears. Kissel (1983) developed the Erase-A-Fear game, in which the counselor asks the child to write the sentence "I am afraid of _____" on a piece of paper and fill in the blank. The counselor tells the child to erase the last word of the sentence and crumple up the paper. On another piece of paper, the counselor asks the child to write, "I am afraid of," then erase "afraid of" and crumple up the paper. On the next piece of paper, the counselor asks the child to write, "I am," erase "am," and crumple up the paper. On the final piece of paper, the counselor asks the child to write "I," draw a circle around the word, and add two eyes and a smile. The counselor then tells the child, "It is difficult to worry or feel afraid with a smile on your face!" The counselor can use this with children to give them the idea that they can control the kinds of feelings that they feel.

Squiggle drawing.   Another drawing technique that works well with young children is the Squiggle Game (Winnicott, 1971). In the original version of this game, the counselor draws a squiggle (a curved, wavy, or zigzagged line) and asks the child to make the squiggle into a picture. Claman (1980) elaborated on the original technique by asking the child to use the squiggle to draw a picture and then tell a story about the picture. According to Kissell (1990), it is important to observe the degree of elaboration of the story and the content of the story. Children who tell overly elaborate, rambling stories are frequently too "loose"—they may have difficulty with impulsivity, predicting consequences for their behavior, and respecting the rights of others. Children who refuse to tell a story or simply tell very short, simple stories are frequently too "tight"—they may be fearful, anxious, perfectionistic, and have difficulty expressing themselves. By noticing these responses to the Squiggle Game, the counselor can diagnose the "looseness" or "tightness" in children and plan appropriate interventions.

Other Techniques

The preceding descriptions are simply a sample of possible visual art techniques that school counselors can use. Other strategies include making masks and puppets, making collages, creating group drawings or group sculptures, drawing fantasy representations of self and others (rosebushes, gardens, animals), using symbols to represent the child and important people in the child's life, making board games, and so forth. The following are resources that provide concrete descriptions of therapeutic art techniques:

1. *Art Therapy Activities and Lesson Plans for Individuals and Groups* (Furrer, 1982)
2. *Art Therapy for Groups* (Liebmann, 1986)
3. *Windows to Our Children* (Oaklander, 1992)
4. *Cows Can Be Purple* (Dreikurs, 1986)
5. *The Anti-Coloring Book* (Striker & Kimmel, 1978)
6. *Make Beliefs* (Zimmerman, 1987)

Counselors interested in pursuing this avenue of exploration and intervention with children in the schools will want to examine these books and others like them.

Using Drama for Counseling Children

While there has not been much information in the literature about using drama as a tool for counseling children in schools, this modality can offer many possibilities for the school counselor (Gladding, 1992; Irwin, 1987; Renard & Sockol, 1987). Drama in counseling helps children learn safe ways to express feelings and thoughts. It increases children's ability to concentrate, listen, observe, and discuss their ideas. Participating in dramatic interactions gives children a chance to take on other roles, which allows them to change perspectives, learn to understand other people's perceptions, and practice new behaviors. It also encourages their spontaneity, creativity, imagination, and visualization. Working in a group on creative dramatics fosters cooperation, decision-making, and problem-solving skills. As an intervention strategy, creative drama can help children increase their sense of belonging, power, and uniqueness, as well as providing them with positive role models (Renard & Sockol, 1987). The school counselor can also use drama as a diagnostic instrument to explore children's issues and concerns (Irwin, 1987).

Developmental Considerations

Just as with other counseling techniques, the counselor will want to tailor the use of drama in counseling to the developmental age of the child (Gladding, 1992). Children in kindergarten and first grade should be provided with toys or puppets to help them act out their dramas. Younger children tend to do more concrete, solitary kinds of play and may not be willing to engage in group drama, fantasy playing, or taking on the roles of others. Older elementary children, from second grade on, may also be interested in using toys and puppets to express themselves. They are frequently more willing than are younger children to engage in role playing, staged guidance plays, and writing and producing their own plays. With middle school/junior high school students, the counselor may want to use videotaped or audiotaped improvisational drama and role-playing situations.

Process/Structure

Renard and Sockol (1987) suggested that the counselor follow an organized format in order to provide structure when using drama in group counseling or guidance activities. They provided the following outline of a possible format:

1. Focus: Decide on the key concepts and learning objectives that you want to cover in this activity. You can use objectives from the academic curriculum, the guidance curriculum, or some combination of the two.

2. Introduction: Choose the specific activity and consider the guidance and/or counseling rationale for using this activity. You will want to ask yourself, "How does this activity help children gain in self-esteem or enhance their ability to succeed in school?"

3. Preparation: Before you start a drama experience with the children, gather any materials that you need and decide on a warm-up activity.

4. Directions and Activities: Decide how you are going to structure the activity, including the directions, rules, and grouping (single individual, dyads, entire class, or small groups).

5. Discussion: Consider the kinds of questions you will ask in order to help the children ponder both the content and the process of the drama activity. You will want to be sure to include all of the children involved in some type of analysis and synthesis of information designed to facilitate generalization of the concepts they have explored in the activity.

6. Summary: Remember to integrate the concepts the children have learned and the thoughts and feelings they have experienced and expressed with your objectives and the guidance and counseling rationale.

Resources for Drama Activities

Specific drama strategies appropriate for use with children in schools are limitless. Counselors need only exercise their imaginations to generate ideas they can use in their interaction with children. The following are resources that can provide counselors with some concrete suggestions for integrating drama into the guidance and counseling program:

Theater Games for the Classroom (Spolin, 1986) has a multitude of suggestions for acting out objects, characters, and situations. While the author is not a counselor, she describes many drama activities that the counselor could use with children in elementary and middle schools to increase their awareness of their own thoughts and feelings, enhance their ability to express themselves, and learn new behaviors for interacting with others.

Creative Drama: Enhancing Self-Concepts and Learning (Renard & Sockol, 1987) contains warm-up and cool-down exercises, as well as activities designed to enhance children's sense of belonging, power, and uniqueness. It also has activities to help children discover the positive role models in their lives and to help children explore interactional processes, decision making, and problem solving.

Creative Counseling Techniques: An Illustrated Guide (Jacobs, 1992) contains descriptions of strategies that use props, chairs, fantasy, and movement to actively explore thoughts, feelings, and behaviors. While this book is aimed at counselors who work with adults, the school counselor could easily adapt the activities to use with children.

Put Your Mother on the Ceiling (de Mille, 1973) is full of "imagination games." These are games that the counselor can use as guided imagery or as a stimulus for a creative dramatic activity.

Spinning Inward (Murdock, 1987) also contains guided imagery exercises. Since many parents object to relaxation or guided imagery activities, the school counselor can adapt the ideas contained in this book for more active interactions that use art, drama, and role playing.

Using Metaphors and Storytelling[1]

Young children naturally think and act in metaphor. They also tell stories and listen to stories—about themselves, their friends, their families, and imaginary creatures—as a normal part of their interacting with others. The school counselor can use metaphors to help children master new ways of expressing their feelings, coping with conflict, interacting with people, and behaving in difficult situations (Lankton & Lankton, 1989; Mills & Crowley, 1986). The use of metaphor helps children create a bridge of personal connection between themselves and the counselor, thus helping children feel more comfortable in communicating. Through their understanding of the therapeutic story, children develop a sense of identification with the characters and events portrayed. This sense of identification experienced by the children contains the transformational power of the metaphor (Gordon, 1978). As children identify with the story, they realize that they are not alone or without support (Brooks, 1985). Elementary and middle school counselors can capitalize on children's natural inclination to communicate through story and metaphor by incorporating these techniques in their interactions with children.

Developmental Considerations

Lankton and Lankton (1989) discussed several developmental considerations that affect children's understanding of metaphors and stories. The school counselor must remember to use age-appropriate or grade-appropriate vocabulary in the story. The counselor should also take age and grade into account when deciding on the length of the story and the amount of detail included in it. Since the attention span of younger children is shorter than the attention span of older children, metaphors and stories need to be less detailed and shorter when the counselor is working with younger children. It is easier to engage the interest of younger children if the counselor uses "story voices" for different characters and delivers the story slowly and deliberately. Younger children seem to be more interested in stories that

[1]The authors would like to thank Leslie Baughman, a doctoral student at the University of North Texas for her input to this section.

feature animals, and older children seem to be more interested in stories that feature people. It is easier to capture the attention of younger children if the counselor uses props such as puppets, dolls, or animal figures to tell the story. Older children do not necessarily need this visual input to stay involved in the story.

Specific Strategies

One method of using metaphors and stories in counseling with children is to simply continue their metaphors. Other strategies are designing therapeutic metaphors for specific children and engaging children in mutual storytelling.

Continuing the child's metaphor. To continue the child's metaphor, the counselor simply avoids interpreting any metaphor the child is using to communicate about his or her life. If Julian is telling a story about a family of bears and it seems that this animal family symbolizes Julian's family, the counselor refrains from suggesting that the bears are really Julian's family. The counselor makes guesses and asks questions about the bear family, rather than about Julian's family. Children usually use metaphor to communicate about issues or situations that they are not comfortable discussing in their "real" form. By refraining from making interpretations or "breaking" the metaphor, the counselor can demonstrate respect for the child and a desire to communicate in the child's natural, comfortable format.

Designing therapeutic metaphors. There are two basic types of therapeutic metaphors for children: those designed to help children express and resolve emotions and those designed to help children change their behaviors (Lankton & Lankton, 1989). Before designing a therapeutic metaphor for a specific child, the counselor must decide whether to focus on expression of feelings or evolution of behaviors. Since some children need to work on both emotions and behaviors, the counselor may choose to combine elements from the two different protocols.

Lankton and Lankton (1989) suggested the following steps for designing a therapeutic metaphor focused on helping children express or explore their emotions:

1. Select and describe a main character for the story.
2. Select and describe other characters and the setting.
3. Establish a relationship between the main character and the other characters or elements of the story. This relationship must involve some kind of evident emotion, such as sadness, confusion, anger, or love. You will want to consider which particular emotions you want the child to explore or express and incorporate them into your narrative.
4. Describe some type of change or movement that alters the relationships among the characters. This can be either a positive or negative change. You may want to include some details of the struggle to overcome whatever problem the main character faces. You will also describe the resolution of this conflict and any

changes in the feelings or behavior of the main character. It is important to include some sort of celebration to acknowledge any changes in a character's feelings and self-image.

5. Throughout the telling of the story, focus on the feelings of the main character and other characters. You might want to even describe physical changes and facial expressions that you notice in the child during the telling of the story.

The following story is an example of a therapeutic metaphor that a counselor tells to Rick, a fifth grade boy who believes that he must always be tough and must never express his more vulnerable feelings:

Once upon a time, there was a young wolf—he wasn't still a pup, but he wasn't a grown-up wolf yet either. This wolf's name was NoHowl, because no matter how cold or tired or hurt he was he never howled like the other wolves did. NoHowl ran in a pack with his mother, Little Ear, his father, Far Runner, and his uncle, Wise One. He liked to listen to the stories that his uncle, Wise One, told about other wolves and about adventures that the pack had before NoHowl was born. He especially liked the story about the day when Little Ear had gotten caught on an ice floe and she yipped and yipped and Far Runner and Wise One had come to help her jump to safety. NoHowl also liked to play and wrestle with other wolves from different packs, but he always came back to his own pack at the end of the day.

Late one day, in the middle of a very cold winter, NoHowl started running in the forest to find his mother, father, and uncle, but he couldn't find their scents on the wind. He ran and ran, but he still could not find them. The evening was getting darker and colder because night was falling, and NoHowl was getting very frightened. He had never spent the night by himself, and he had no way to get food or to stay warm. He wanted to find his pack very badly, but he didn't know what to do. Finally, he remembered the story that Wise One had told him about the time his mother had gotten into trouble, and he decided that he would need to make some noise and see if the other members of his pack could find him. He yipped and yipped, but no one came. He was getting very scared and feeling lonely. One time he thought that he heard a wolf howling way off in the distance, but when he listened he couldn't hear anything. He yipped some more, but still no answer.

Finally, NoHowl decided that he needed to make as much noise as he possibly could to try to contact his family, so he opened his mouth and he let out a great big loud HOWL. He kind of liked how that sounded—he was really loud when he wanted to be—so he let out another HOWL. Just then, from the other side of the forest, he heard an answering howl. NoHowl was so excited and relieved that he let out several more big howls, and he heard more howls, coming closer and closer through the forest. He kept making his big noises until up trotted his mother, father, and uncle. They were very happy to see him because they were afraid that something might have happened to him during the night if he had spent it by himself. NoHowl was so excited to see them and so glad they had heard his howls that all through the night, whenever he woke up, he gave a happy little howl.

The next day, Wise One told NoHowl that he was no longer NoHowl. He had done such a good job of letting the other members of the pack know he needed help that he had earned a new name—Mighty Howler.

The purpose of the behavior-related metaphor is to illustrate a desired behavior change. Lankton and Lankton (1989) outlined the following steps for metaphors designed to change children's behavior:

1. Select and describe a main character for the story.
2. Select and describe the other characters and setting of the story.
3. Explain the metaphorical conflict, and describe the main character's behavioral goals. You will want these goals to be parallel to the behavior you want the child to develop.
4. Describe how the main character responds to the metaphorical dilemma. You will want to focus on the main character's struggle to overcome the problem and the *actions* he or she takes to do so.
5. You may want to detail some of the internal dialogue and nonobservable behaviors of the main character during the struggle to deal with the problem. It will help children more closely identify with and understand any behavioral changes if you describe the character's thoughts, feelings, and decision-making processes.
6. If possible, include several repetitions of the desired behaviors within the story. One effective way of doing this is to have the main character observe someone else use the behaviors. Another character can also observe the main character taking part in the goal behaviors, or the main character may remember using these behaviors at some other time.
7. After the main character has successfully used the goal behaviors to solve the conflict, he or she should engage in some type of ceremony or party to celebrate having learned new behaviors and having overcome the obstacles.

The following metaphor is designed to help change the behavior of Suzi, a fourth grader who is having difficulty making friends because she has poorly developed social skills:

> I want to tell you a story about a bunny named Hopper. Hopper wanted to be friends with the other animals in the forest, but she wasn't sure how to go about making friends. When Hopper saw another animal, like Brownie the deer and Fuzzy the raccoon, she jumped out from behind a tree and yelled, "Hi!" This startled the other animals, and they always ran away whenever they saw her coming. Hopper felt very sad and wondered why the other animals didn't want to be her friends. She decided that she wanted to learn how to make friends a new way. As she was sitting there thinking about this, Juniper the frog jumped up and stopped in front of her. He smiled a great big smile (you know how frogs have those BIG mouths) and said, "Nice to see you today." Hopper smiled back, and they had a little chat about the weather and Juniper's new pond. After Juniper left, Hopper went back to thinking about how she could learn to make friends. Just then, Bartlet the beaver walked up and asked Hopper if she would help him drag a tree branch he had just felled down to the stream. Hopper said, "Sure!" and they pulled the branch to Bartlet's dam. After Bartlet had thanked Hopper for her help, Hopper went back to her hutch to think about her day.
>
> The next day, Hopper hopped over and stood close to Fuzzy the raccoon. She smiled a great big smile and said, "Nice to see you today." Fuzzy looked kind of surprised, but he smiled back and asked Hopper how she was doing, and they had a nice talk about how hot the summer had been. Later that day, Hopper

hopped over by Brownie the deer and asked Brownie if she could help Hopper find some small tender leaves for dinner. Brownie knew just exactly where a whole bush of leaves was, and they went off together to find them. They ate dinner together, and it was the end of the day before Hopper noticed that she hadn't been sad or lonely or hopped on anyone all day long.

Mutual storytelling.   Mutual storytelling is another method of using metaphors in counseling with children. This technique was developed by Richard Gardner (1986). In mutual storytelling, the counselor asks the child to tell a story with a beginning, middle, and end. The counselor retells the story with a more appropriate or adaptive ending. Because mutual storytelling requires that the child be able to tell a story with a certain amount of narrative flow, this strategy seems to work best with children in the second or third grade or older. Younger children do not usually understand the idea of a story having a beginning, middle, and end.

To use mutual storytelling in the counseling setting, consider the following set of instructions as a guide (Gardner, 1986):

1. Set the scene. The child can be the guest of honor on a television or radio show featuring storytelling or can choose a puppet or a set of animals to use to tell the story.
2. Set up rules of the storytelling:

   a. The story must be made up. It cannot be something that the child has seen in television shows or movies, read in books, and so forth.
   b. The story needs to have a beginning, a middle, and an end.

3. Listen to the story metaphorically. The story might illustrate the child's intrapersonal dynamics, various issues in the child's life, or the child's relationships with significant others. Use your own theoretical orientation to understand the underlying meaning in the story and to plan a retelling of the story. Consider:

   a. Which character represents the child and which represents other important people in the child's life?
   b. What is the overall affective atmosphere of the story? How is this representative of the child's views of self, others, and the world?
   c. What are the themes and patterns of interaction present in the story? How are they typical of the child's issues and usual way of behaving?
   d. What is the primary method of conflict resolution or problem-solving strategy expressed in the story? How is this representative of the child's usual strategies?
   e. What would be a more appropriate way of resolving the conflict or situation in the story, and how can you present that to the child in the retelling?

4. Retell the story, using the same characters, setting, and beginning as the child's story. You will change the middle and the ending of the story. The altered story can illustrate (a) a more appropriate resolution of the story conflict; (b) alternative ways of viewing self, the world, and others; (c) different ways of building relationships and getting along with others; and (d) varied interpretations of personal issues that may be interfering with the child's ability to function.

5. Invent a moral or lesson for the retold story, or ask the child to develop one. (This is optional. It seems to work better with older children than it does with younger children.)

The counselor can adapt this technique in any way that would be appropriate for his or her style and the children in his or her school. Gardner's original interpretations were psychoanalytic. However, we believe that other theoretical interpretations of the stories are equally valid (Kottman & Stiles, 1990).

An example of a mutual storytelling would be the following interaction between Miss McNamara and Jason, a sixth grade boy who solves conflicts with his fists:

Miss M: Jason, I would like you to pretend that you are making up a plot for a new movie and tell it to me. Remember that a movie has a beginning, a middle, and an end.

Jason: OK. Well, this really tough guy named Mike has a friend that he hangs out with at the mall. Two other guys come up to them and go, "What are you guys doing here?" Mike and his friend go, "This is where we hang out." The other guys go, "You can't hang out here because we were here first." Mike and his friend go, "So what? We're here now and we're staying here." The other guys go, "You can't stay here!! We won't let you." Mike goes, "How are you going to stop us?" The other guys go, "We'll make you leave." Mike goes, "You and what army?" Then the other guys step up real close to Mike and his friend, so Mike hits one of them, and his friend jumps on the other guy and beats him up. The security guy comes and makes them all leave the mall.

Miss M: Well, I am going to tell another story about Mike and his friends. The next week, Mike and Johnny went to the mall and they were hanging out at the corner by the shoe store. Two other boys came up and said, "Hi, we're James and Lenny. What are you guys doing?" Mike said, "This is where we hang out." James said, "You can't hang out here. This is our space to hang out, and we were hanging out here yesterday and we want to hang out here today." Johnny was thinking to himself, "We got kicked out of the mall for fighting last week, and we don't want to have to leave again." He said, "I wonder if we could work something out so we don't all get kicked out of the mall." Lenny said, "Well, we have been hanging out at this corner for the last few days, and we think it's our corner. This is a big mall though. There are lots of corners in it, and you guys could go to another corner." Mike said, "We want to hang out at this corner. We don't want to go to another corner." James said, "Well, how about if you guys hang out at that corner down the corridor today, and then you guys can have this corner tomorrow and we'll hang out down there tomorrow." Johnny said, "You guys are kinda cool. Why don't we all hang out together?" Mike said, "Yeah—sounds like a great idea." James and Lenny said, "OK. That would be cool."

Jason may not think that Miss McNamara's ending is more satisfactory than his, but this approach illustrates some other possibilities in addition to violence. The counselor can choose to discuss what happened in the two different approaches to the situation and let the child come to his or her own conclusion about what happened. Most of the time, the counselor will want to let the story stand on itself and not point out the parallels in the child's life and style of interacting. However, sometimes the counselor may want to interpret the metaphor and explore the child's usual patterns of interaction that are symbolized in his or her story.

Bibliocounseling

Bibliocounseling is another creative method of interacting with children. It is "a natural and easy way to enter the tentative, sometimes fantasy-laden, world of the child" (Muro & Dinkmeyer, 1977, p. 256). In bibliocounseling, the counselor either reads a book to a child, the child reads a book alone, or they read a book together, with the idea that the ideas presented in the book and any ensuing discussion can change the child's outlook or behavior.

Goals of Bibliocounseling

There are four primary goals when a counselor uses books as a tool in the counseling process: identification, catharsis, insight, and universalization (Hynes & Hynes-Berry, 1986; Shrank, 1982). Through identification, the child identifies with character(s) in the book and is able to gain insight, consider a different perspective, or learn a new way of behaving from the interactions in the book. An example of identification would be when a child who has been having a bad day reads *Alexander and the Terrible, Horrible, No Good, Very Bad Day* (Viorst, 1972) and realizes that Alexander can live through an awful day and so can he or she.

It is a catharsis when a child experiences release of emotions because of his or her involvement in a book character's life. An example of catharsis would be a child who has recently had a pet die reading *The Tenth Good Thing About Barney* (Viorst, 1971) and crying about Barney dying.

A child may also gain insight into self, problem situations, or relationships based on a book character's struggles. The child may try to apply or adapt the character's solution and change his or her personal behavior or attitudes to bring them into alignment with the character in the book. Thus a child whose parents are getting a divorce might learn something about his or her own situation from *Dinosaurs Divorce* (Brown & Brown, 1986).

Through universalization, a child may recognize that his or her difficulties are not unique and that others face similar problems and struggles. Reading *Boardwalk with Hotel* (Mills, 1985), an adopted child may realize that other adopted children have feelings that are the same as his or hers.

Steps to Follow in Applying Bibliocounseling

Counselors who want to use bibliocounseling as a tool with the children in their schools may want to follow these suggestions as outlined by Hynes and Hynes-Berry (1986) and Shrank (1982):

1. Select an appropriate book. The book you choose needs to:

    a. Be appropriate for that particular child and his or her situation and specific issues.

   b. Be appropriate for that child's developmental level and vocabulary—either listening or reading.

   c. Be well written, exciting, and evocative. It should encourage imagination, creativity, and engage the child's cognitive, affective, and sensory systems.

2. Read the book carefully. Pay attention to theme, plot, attitudes, and character development. Avoid books with characters who are stereotypical and messages that you do not support.

3. Use introductory activities to involve the child in the story, and begin to make a connection between the story and the child's life.

4. Read the book to the child, have him or her read it alone, or read the book together.

5. Allow the child time to think about the story and his or her feelings and reactions.

6. Discuss the story and the child's feelings and reactions. You can also do other follow-up activities, including art, role playing, writing, and so forth.

Finding Appropriate Books

The following is a list of different resources that contain annotated descriptions of books appropriate for use in bibliocounseling. These guides are usually organized by topic, author, and title and contain information about the plot of the books and the age range for which they are appropriate.

1. *The Elementary School Library Collection: A Guide to Books and Other Media* (Brodart, 1984)

2. *The Bookfinder: When Kids Need Books* (American Guidance Service, 1985)

3. *Subject Guide to Children's Books in Print* (Bowker, published annually)

The school librarian and the children's librarian at the local library can also be tremendously helpful in helping counselors search for the perfect book for a specific child.

Making Books with Children

Another way of using books for counseling children is to make homemade books for and with children. Robert Ziegler wrote a book entitled, *Homemade Books to Help Kids Cope: An Easy-to-Learn Technique for Parents and Professionals* (1992) that outlines this process. This text contains practical suggestions for constructing books about everyday life, feelings, growing up, illness and death, divorce, adoption, parental injury, and many other topics. It also has examples of the text of books about each of these topics and illustrations to accompany the texts. A counselor could successfully use this technique with younger children by either composing a book designed specifically with them in mind or by writing the book as they dictate the text. Some older children may enjoy having the counselor write a book designed to deal with their own particular problems, but they will usually want to have a more active role in the process. The counselor may want to let them write and illustrate their own book, or the counselor may just write the narrative and leave any illustrating to them.

CONCLUSION

Creative and expressive arts techniques provide school counselors with unlimited possibilities for diagnosis and intervention with elementary and middle school children. Children in this age range are frequently more willing to engage in these exciting and interactive experiences than they are to simply sit in the counselor's office and talk about their struggles. These activities are appropriate for working with children who are experiencing normal developmental concerns and children who are experiencing crises or other serious problems. They will work in individual counseling, group counseling, and classroom guidance situations. By using their imaginations, counselors can use art, drama, storytelling and metaphors, and bibliocounseling to expand their repertoire of counseling skills. These activities can be easy to use and inexpensive, which is essential to most modern school counselors. Counselors do not need extensive training or experience to use these techniques in their schools. Counselors just need their own creativity and a willingness to take risks, experiment, and have fun with children.

REFERENCES

Brooks, R. (1985). The beginning sessions of child therapy: Of messages and metaphors. *Psychotherapy, 22,* 761–769.

Brown, L., & Brown, M. (1986). *Dinosaurs divorce: A guide for changing families.* Boston: Atlantic Monthly.

Burns, R. (1982). *Self-growth in families.* New York: Brunner/Mazel.

Burns, R., & Kaufman, S. (1970). *Kinetic family drawings (KFD): An introduction to understanding children through kinetic drawings.* New York: Brunner/Mazel.

Burns, R., & Kaufman, S. (1972). *Actions, styles and symbols in kinetic family drawings (K-F-D): An interpretive manual.* New York: Brunner/Mazel.

Case, C., & Dalley, T. (Eds.). (1990). *Working with children in art therapy.* New York: Tavistock/Routledge.

Claman, L. (1980). The Squiggle Drawing Game in child psychotherapy. *American Journal of Psychotherapy, 34,* 414–421.

Crowley, R., & Mills, J. (1989). *Cartoon magic: How to help children discover their rainbows within.* New York: Magination.

de Mille, R. (1973). *Put your mother on the ceiling.* New York: Penguin.

DiLeo, J. (1970). *Young children and their drawings.* New York: Brunner/Mazel.

DiLeo, J. (1983). *Interpreting children's drawings.* New York: Brunner/Mazel.

Dreikurs, S. (1986). *Cows can be purple: My life and art therapy.* Chicago, IL: Alfred Adler Institute.

Dubowski, J. (1990). Art versus language (separate development during childhood). In C. Case & T. Dalley (Eds.), *Working with children in art therapy* (pp. 7–23). New York: Tavistock/Routledge.

Furrer, P. J. (1982). *Art therapy activities and lesson plans for individuals and groups.* Springfield, IL: Charles C Thomas.

Gardner, R. (1986). *The psychotherapeutic techniques of Richard A. Gardner.* Creskill, NJ: Jason Aronson.

Gerler, E. (1982). *Counseling the young learner.* Englewood Cliffs, NJ: Prentice Hall.

Gladding, S. (1992). *Counseling as an art: The creative arts in counseling.* Alexandria, VA: American Association for Counseling and Development.

Gordon, D. (1978). *Therapeutic metaphors.* Cupertino, CA: Meta.

Hammer, E. (1980). *The clinical application of projective drawings.* Springfield, IL: Charles C Thomas.

Hynes, A., & Hynes-Berry, M. (1986). *Bibliotherapy: The interactive process.* Boulder, CO: Westview.

Irwin, E. (1987). Drama: The play's the thing. *Elementary School Guidance and Counseling, 21,* 276–283.

Jacobs, E. (1992). *Creative counseling techniques: An illustrated guide.* Odessa, FL: Psychological Assessment Resources.

Jolles, I. (1971). *A catalogue for the qualitative interpretation of the H-T-P* (rev. ed.). Los Angeles, CA: Western Psychological Services.

Kaufman, B., & Wohl, A. (1992). *Casualties of childhood: A developmental perspective on sexual abuse using projective drawings.* New York: Brunner/Mazel.

Kellogg, R. (1969). *Analyzing children's art.* Mountain View, CA: Mayfield.

Kissel, S. (1983). Self-talk for children. *RETwork, 2,* 8–9.

Kissel, S. (1990). *Play therapy: A strategic approach.* Springfield, IL: Charles C Thomas.

Knoff, H. (1985). *Kinetic drawing system for family and school: Scoring booklet.* Los Angeles, CA: Western Psychological Services.

Knoff, H., & Prout, H. (1985). *Kinetic drawing system for family and school: A handbook.* Los Angeles, CA: Western Psychological Services.

Koppitz, E. (1968). *Psychological evaluation of children's human figure drawings.* New York: Grune & Stratton.

Kottman, T., & Stiles, K. (1990). The mutual storytelling technique: An Adlerian application in child therapy. *Journal of Individual Psychology, 46,* 148–156.

Lankton, C., & Lankton, S. (1989). *Tales of enchantment: Goal-oriented metaphors for adults and children in therapy.* New York: Brunner/Mazel.

Liebmann, M. (1986). *Art therapy for groups.* Cambridge, MA: Brookline.

Mills, C. (1985). *Boardwalk with hotel.* New York: Macmillan/Collier.

Mills, J., & Crowley, R. (1986). *Therapeutic metaphors for children and the child within.* New York: Brunner/Mazel.

Murdock, M. (1987). *Spinning inward.* Boston: Shambala.

Muro, J. J., & Dinkmeyer, D. C. (1977). *Counseling in the elementary and middle schools.* Dubuque, IA: Wm. C. Brown.

Oaklander, V. (1992). *Windows to our children.* Highland, NY: The Gestalt Journal Press. (Original work published in 1969).

Ogdon, D. (1977). *Psychodiagnostics and personality assessment: A handbook* (2nd ed.). Los Angeles, CA: Western Psychological Services.

Phillips, J. (1991, July). *Art therapy with children.* Paper presented at the University of North Texas Center for Play Therapy Summer Institute, Denton, TX.

Renard, S., & Sockol, K. (1987). *Creative drama: Enhancing self-concepts and learning.* Minneapolis, MN: Educational Media.

Reynolds, C. (1978). A quick-scoring guide to the interpretation of children's Kinetic Family Drawings (KFD). *Psychology in the Schools, 15,* 489–492.

Shrank, F. (1982). Bibliotherapy as an elementary school counseling tool. *Elementary School Guidance and Counseling, 16,* 218–227.

Spolin, V. (1986). *Theater games for the classroom: A teacher's handbook.* Evanston, IL: Northwestern University.

Steinhardt, L. (1985). Freedom within boundaries: Body outline drawings in art therapy with children. *The Arts in Psychotherapy, 12,* 25–34.

Striker, S., & Kimmel, E. (1978). *The anti-coloring book.* New York: Henry Holt.

Viorst, J. (1971). *The tenth good thing about Barney.* Chicago: Atheneum.

Viorst, J. (1972). *Alexander and the terrible, horrible, no good, very bad day.* New York: Atheneum.

Warren, B. (Ed.). (1984). *Using the creative arts in therapy.* Cambridge, MA: Brookline.

Winnicott, D. (1971). *Therapeutic consultations in child psychiatry.* New York: Basic Books.

Ziegler, R. (1992). *Homemade books to help kids cope.* New York: Magination.

Zimmerman, B. (1987). *Make beliefs.* New York: Guarionex.

Chapter Ten

Counseling Specific Populations

🌳 During the course of an average day, elementary and middle school counselors work with many different children. They help children cope with their thoughts and feelings about parental divorce, stepfamily issues, alcoholism in the family, handicapped siblings, and adoption. They work with children who have academic, emotional, and behavioral problems related to Attention Deficit Hyperactivity Disorder (ADHD), depression, eating disorders, chronic illness, disabilities, and giftedness. School counselors may talk to elementary children who are not yet aware of their developing sexual orientations, but who feel different from other children without knowing why. They may work with middle school/junior high school children who, as they mature and become more aware of their own sexuality, need information and someone to talk to about what it means to be gay or lesbian. School counselors also provide services to students who are members of minority cultures and races and need help with self-esteem, learning to find a significant place for themselves, understanding what it means to be a part of a certain race or culture, and other related issues.

All of these factors can affect how children get along in schools, socially, emotionally, and academically. In order to provide the most appropriate and effective services for *all* children, school counselors need to understand the issues and concerns of many specific populations of children. They must know about how different concerns affect school performance and behavior. School counselors must also have information about specific intervention strategies they can use to help the children in their schools survive, learn, and flourish.

In this chapter we have described some specific characteristics, counseling issues, school problems, and intervention techniques for children of divorced parents, children in stepfamilies, children whose parents are alcoholics, children with ADHD, and gifted children. We have made suggestions for using multicultural counseling strategies to better serve the needs of children of color. We realize that we have not discussed all of the populations of children that counselors will have in their schools. Because of the limited space in this volume, we have chosen to address only a few of the many populations in elementary and middle schools. It was difficult to choose which populations of children to include in this volume because we believe that all children are important and deserve help. We decided to include the populations described here based on their prominence in the school counseling literature and our own belief that these groups of children are struggling with issues that affect their learning in schools. We also believe that school counselors have the experience and the level of training required to help them. For some other populations of children in schools not included in this chapter (for example, handicapped children, children with learning disabilities, children with handicapped siblings, depressed children, children with eating disorders, adopted children), we have listed resource references in Appendix J. Even with an appendix, we cannot cover all of the possible groups of children who need help from the counselor in elementary and middle schools. Counselors with children in their schools who are struggling with specific problems will need to take the time to investigate potential issues and intervention strategies that they can use to help those children.

Children of Divorced Parents

Divorce has become more widespread over the last several decades, and the number of children in elementary and middle schools whose parents are divorced is increasing rapidly. According to figures gathered by the Children's Defense Fund (1982), there are more than ten million children in the United States (one in every five students) attending schools and living with a single, divorced parent. Their figures also indicated that approximately one-third of the children born during the 1980s are going to live with a single parent for at least part of the time before they are eighteen years old.

While not all children are adversely affected by the divorce of their parents and subsequent single-parent living situation, many of them manifest social and emotional difficulties (Cantrell, 1986; Hall, Beougher, & Wasinger, 1991). Those children who have strong economic and social support, minimal environmental changes, positive self-concepts, and parents with effective parenting skills seem to have optimal divorce adjustment (Hall et al., 1991; Hetherington, Stanley-Hagan, & Anderson, 1989). For other children, parental divorce may profoundly affect their lives and relationships (Thompson & Rudolph, 1992).

During the first year after the divorce, many parents have difficulty making parenting a top priority (Hall et al., 1991). They are reacting to the stress of personal and financial hardship and may not have the mental or emotional energy to provide the appropriate support and structure for their children. This creates difficulties for children because this can be an extremely stressful time for them, and they need more support and love than usual (Wallerstein & Kelly, 1980). Children may have to cope with moving, meeting new friends, starting in a new school, having limited financial support, living in a place that is smaller, and so on (Hall et al., 1991; Stolberg, Camplair, Currier, & Wells, 1987). They may also have been hurt by custody battles, conflicting parenting styles, divided loyalties, and a need to "replace" the absent parent (Thompson & Rudolph, 1992).

Developmental Considerations

Between the ages of six and eight, children do not yet have the ability to separate their own needs from the needs of their parents (Cantrell, 1986; Wallerstein & Kelly, 1980). Most children in this age range react to their parents' divorce with feelings of sadness and loss. They are usually frightened by the uncertainty of the situation, and they may generalize their anxiety to the point of having frightening nightmares or fantasies. As a result of this pervasive sense of fear and loss, some children may become disorganized and have difficulty with school work.

Children this age may also feel abandoned and unloved by the absent parent and may be angry because they are feeling rejected (Cantrell, 1986). Many children do not know how to appropriately express their anger, so they may misdirect it at the custodial parent, other children, or their teacher. Sometimes young children feel lonely and miss the noncustodial parent, even if that parent does spend time with them. Even when the parents share custody, just the fact that time with one or both of their parents is rationed and must be planned in advance can create a feeling of loss and abandonment.

Young children also feel a sense of divided loyalties. They frequently believe that they must "choose sides," even when the parents are not asking them to do this. When either or both of the parents actually tries to enlist the children in an ongoing conflict, it creates a terrible tension within the children because they cannot possibly please both parents. Sometimes their attempts to reconcile these divided loyalties may involve developing fantasies or plans about their parents reuniting.

In school, some children in the six to eight age bracket have difficulty organizing their work and their desks. They will probably have problems concentrating on their school work or sitting still for even short periods of time. They may burst into tears with very little provocation, testing the patience of peers and teachers. These children may also be easily provoked into angry outbursts by small incidents that would not have bothered them before the divorce. They will need an extra degree of support because quite frequently their sense of abandonment and rejection affects their self-confidence and their sense of competence. Sometimes young children even generalize their feelings of divided loyalties and think that they must "choose sides" in school situations. As a result of this, children who are not usually "pleasers" may sometimes try to anticipate what others want from them and try to provide it. Occasionally these children attach themselves to some other adult, like a teacher or a counselor, to try to gain a sense of stability they feel is lacking in their families.

The response of older children (ages nine to twelve) is somewhat different than that of younger children, because older children can sometimes separate their own needs and desires from those of their parents (Cantrell, 1986; Wallerstein & Kelly, 1980). However, they still feel a sense of loss, rejection, helplessness, fear, and loneliness. They may also feel ashamed or embarrassed that their parents are getting a divorce and/or powerless because they cannot control their parents' behavior. As a result of these feelings, children this age frequently manifest psychosomatic symptoms, such as headaches and stomachaches.

In contrast to the sadness of younger children, the predominant feeling of children in the nine to twelve age group is anger (Cantrell, 1986). They usually blame one parent for the divorce and focus their anger on that parent. This scapegoating of one of the parents may help these children cope with their feelings of mixed loyalties, loneliness, or depression.

In school, children in this age range may also have difficulty concentrating and staying on task, which will probably adversely affect their school work. Occasionally, students feel that they must replace the lost sense of stability from home by devoting extra time to their school work. Because these children may have psychosomatic symptoms, they frequently ask to go to the school nurse. They may use these trips to gain the attention and support currently absent in their families. Because the predominant feeling in this developmental level is anger at one or both of their parents, these children may indulge in negative comments about their mothers or fathers. They may displace their anger and get into an increased number of conflicts with teachers and peers. In order to gain a certain level of control to compensate for their feelings of powerlessness about the divorce situation, children at this age sometimes provoke power struggles with authority figures at school.

Most teenagers who have negative responses to the divorce of their parents express those reactions through acting-out behavior, including alcohol or drug abuse, delinquency, and promiscuity (Wallerstein & Blakeslee, 1989).

Adolescents who have a sense of distance from the crisis involving their parents and who have extra-familial support systems of peers and other adults seem to cope very well with their parents' divorce. While middle school and junior high students will experience some of the same problems in school as younger children do, they seem to present fewer concerns than do elementary school children (Schlesinger, 1982).

Counseling Issues

Thompson and Rudolph (1992) suggested that factors such as the amount of tension and conflict in the family before the divorce, the length of time this tension and conflict went on, the parents' reaction to the conflict, and the parents' adjustment to the divorce may be more important than the developmental considerations. We believe that all of these factors are important and that in a developmental guidance and counseling program counselors will need to understand all of the elements that might influence how children will react to having their parents divorce.

Strangeland, Pellegreno, and Lundhold (1989) developed the following self-report questionnaire as a way of measuring children's attitudes, beliefs, and behaviors toward their families, friends, school, health, and their parents' divorce. This instrument can help counselors explore the counseling issues for a particular child. The counselor reads each statement and asks the child to decide if the statement describes a person "like me" or "not like me."

Questionnaire

1. I am hardly ever sick.
2. I often feel lonely.
3. I have trouble sitting still.
4. I don't like to be with other kids so much right now.
5. I know I will always have someone to take care of me.
6. I am usually happy.
7. I can take care of myself.
8. I have some good friends.
9. There is at least one adult I can talk to about problems.
10. I often get into trouble with teachers at school.
11. I help a lot at home.
12. I often yell at people.
13. I do well in school.
14. I would like to be held or hugged more often.
15. I daydream most of the time.
16. I wish I had more time with my dad.
17. Most grown-ups can be trusted.
18. I often feel angry at Dad.

19. I feel loved.

20. I don't worry much about my parents' problems.

21. I hardly ever have trouble sleeping.

22. Most of the time I feel sad.

23. I get in a lot of trouble at school.

24. I spend as much time as possible playing with my friends.

25. I often feel afraid.

26. I feel like crying a lot.

27. I feel helpless.

28. I have at least one friend I talk to when I am upset.

29. I can't keep my mind on school work.

30. There are a lot of fights between my parents.

31. I get along with both my parents.

32. I often feel like hitting.

33. I have trouble with school work.

34. I worry that there won't be enough money for things that I need.

35. I like being alone.

36. I wish I had more time with Mom.

37. I plan to get married some day.

38. I often feel angry at Mom.

39. My parents fight a lot.

40. I am embarrassed when teachers or friends ask questions about my parents.

41. I don't like to sit still.

42. I worry a lot.

43. I am sure both my parents love me.

44. I often wake up in the night.

45. I get a lot of stomach aches.

46. I have a lot of time for my own things.

47. I laugh a lot.

Questions About Divorce

48. I can easily talk about divorce with other kids.

49. I think Mom and Dad may get back together sometime.

50. Things are better for my parents since the divorce.

51. I can talk to Mom about divorce.

52. I sometimes worry that I did something that made my parents divorce.

53. I help at home more than I did before the divorce.

54. I know my parents will never live together again.

55. Things are better for me since the divorce.

56. I understand why my parents divorced.

57. I worry about being left alone.

58. I can talk to Dad about the divorce.

(Strangeland, Pellegreno, & Lundhold, 1989, pp. 172-173)

As the counselor looks at the replies individual children make to this instrument or others that are used to assess reactions to divorce, she or he may want to put answers in the context of the following list of "psychological tasks" (Wallerstein & Blakeslee, 1989) for children whose parents have divorced:

1. Acknowledging that the divorce has happened, that their parents are no longer married, and that they must deal with that fact.
2. Disengaging from any remaining conflict between their parents and refocusing on their own concerns and the business of "being a kid."
3. Resolving the losses—of a parent, of familiar surroundings and friends, of a more comfortable way of living.
4. Resolving angry and self-blaming feelings.
5. Accepting that the divorce is a permanent arrangement and that their parents are not going to reconcile.
6. Evolving realistic expectations and hope about relationships. This is especially important for adolescents, whose developmental tasks involve learning to establish and maintain love relationships.

Intervention Strategies

Each child has a different perception of the process of divorce. The best way for school counselors to help children is to provide a way for them to adapt to changes caused by the divorce. To do this, school counselors may want to work with children, school administrators, teachers, and parents (Counseling and Personnel Services Clearinghouse, 1986).

Children.   After they have assessed the individual child's issues and concerns, counselors will want to plan an intervention strategy. For some children, this will simply involve consultation with school administrators, teachers, and/or the parent(s). For other children, counselors will be able to choose from several modalities that seem to help children. The first thing counselors will need to decide is whether to use individual counseling, group counseling, or classroom guidance as the mode of delivery. While there are anedoctal data supporting the use of individual counseling and classroom guidance with children whose parents are divorcing (Counseling and Personnel Services Clearinghouse, 1986; Crosbie-Burnett & Pulvino, 1990), most of the literature on intervention with children of divorce suggests that group counseling is the treatment of choice with this population (Burke & Van de Streek, 1989; Cantrell, 1986; Crosbie-Burnett & Newcomer, 1989; Yauman, 1991). Peer counseling seems to work especially well for middle school/junior high school children (Sprinthall, Hall, & Gerler, 1992).

While there are various designs for group counseling with children of divorce, there seem to be several common elements. They usually combine discussion with experiential work (for example, games, bibliocounseling, puppetry, watching movies and filmstrips, art therapy exercises, role playing, and storytelling). Some of the discussions center on how the children felt and what they thought during the experiential aspects of the group, and some of the discussions center on how the children are reacting to the changes in their lives. The children also may discuss coping strategies, changing any negative ways of thinking and feeling about the divorce and their families, and gaining emotional and behavioral support from other children who are in similar situations.

When leading this type of group, counselors should make sure that the group gives children opportunities to: (a) increase their ability to understand and express their feelings about the divorce, (b) see that other children have similar experiences and feelings, (c) learn more about how the divorce process occurs and how it usually affects individuals and families, (d) acquire problem-solving skills that will help them cope with the changes in their lives, and (d) improve their self-images and their attitudes toward their parent(s) (Cantrell, 1986). With counselor help, children can effectively cope with this potential crisis situation in their lives, and it will have minimal negative effects on their school behavior and learning.

School administrators.   Drake (1981) listed ten major concerns school principals and central office personnel have with regard to children whose parents have divorced. These officials want to know: (a) Which school does the child legitimately attend? (b) How should they deal with parents' access to school records? (c) How should they handle the release of the child from school? (d) Which home should be visited on school visits? (e) Who should they contact in a medical emergency? (f) Who is financially responsible for the child? (g) What surname should school personnel call the child? (h) Who should they consult about possible retention? (i) How can they ensure confidentiality of records? (j) Who should attend school functions?

In order to make the transition easier for the child, counselors will want to consult with their administrators when they make policy decisions about these issues. With counselor input, school administrators can take the child and his or her feelings and concerns into account in making decisions.

Teachers.   When parents divorce, teachers can provide a certain amount of continuity in children's environments and help children to learn new coping skills (Cantrell, 1986). The primary intervention strategy that the school counselor can use with teachers is to conduct in-service classes on how divorce affects children and how teachers can best give children the support they need during this time of turmoil (Cantrell, 1986; Counseling and Personnel Services Clearinghouse, 1986). In-service classes should cover the typical emotional reactions and behaviors of children at each developmental level. Counselors might also include a section that emphasizes the need for special one-to-one times for children who are feeling insecure or who need a chance to talk about what is happening in their lives. Teachers also need to know how to recognize a severe reaction to parental divorce and how to refer children to the school counselor or other helping professionals. As part of in-service classes, it would be helpful for teachers to learn how to include "nontraditional" families (for example, single parent families, stepfamilies, families headed by grandparents, families headed by gay or lesbian couples, and the like) in the curriculum so that children who live in these families will not feel excluded.

Parents.   It is especially important for the school counselor to work with parents who are divorcing so that the parents can help minimize potentially negative effects of the divorce (Cantrell, 1986; Counseling and Personnel Services Clearinghouse, 1986). The counselor can help parents become aware of children's expected emotional and behavioral reactions to the divorce and how best to support their children. Parents need to know how to talk to their children about the divorce without exacerbating feelings of guilt or divided loyalties. In a consulting role, the school counselor can serve as a resource person for parents to contact about the specific divorce-related problems of family members. Parents need to keep their own issues and concerns separate and not burden children with inappropriate confidences or responsibilities. The school counselor can frequently offer brief counseling or consultation services to parents wanting help with their own issues about the divorce or suggest community resources such as divorce support groups. It is essential that parents deal with their own emotions and reactions so that they can provide the maximum amount of understanding and structure for their children at this time.

Children in Stepfamilies

A stepfamily is a family unit formed "as a result of a marriage between two partners, at least one of whom has been married previously, and includes at least one child who was born before the two partners married" (Walsh, 1992). These families are also known as blended families and remarriage families. According to census information reported in 1985, there are about 6.8 million children living in stepfamilies in the United States (Kantrowitz & Wingert, 1990). The research concerned with the effects of living in blended families on children has been contradictory (Ganong & Coleman, 1984; Skeen, Covi, & Robison, 1985). Some of the studies indicated that children in stepfamilies have significantly more problems than do children in first-marriage families (e.g., Bowerman & Irish, 1962; Touliatos & Lindholm, 1980). Other studies (e.g., Amato & Ochiltree, 1987; Ellison, 1983; Santrock, Warshak, Lindbergh, & Meadows, 1982) found that there was no difference in the attitudes, self-concepts, or behaviors between children in stepfamilies and children in first-marriage families.

Regardless of whether they have more problems than other children, children living in stepfamilies do have a distinct set of issues and concerns that may interfere with their performance in school. They can certainly use the support of the school counselor for what are becoming normal developmental concerns of a large section of the elementary school and middle school/junior high school population.

Counseling Issues and Intervention Strategies

Walsh (1992) identified twenty major issues that affect members of stepfamilies. All of these concerns can adversely affect the children in the family and their performance in school. We will make suggestions about intervention strategies that school counselors can use to help children cope with these issues and to minimize any problems that adversely affect learning and school performance.

1. **What should the children call the new parent?** Because there is no clear labeling system for determining how to address the new parent, many times children struggle with this issue. While counselors cannot resolve this for the family, they can discuss the situation with children, and they can offer to have the parents come in to school to talk about what will be the most comfortable solution for this family.

2. **How do the children express affection for both the new parent and the absent parent, without being disloyal?** Children frequently struggle with the notion that they can love two people in a similar role. They may not believe that they can love the stepparent at the same time they continue to love their birth parent. Counselors can sometimes resolve the tension created by this sense of divided loyalty simply by talking about the fact that this idea is a myth—that they can, indeed, love both their stepparent and their birth parent.

3. **Some children may feel that the remarriage signifies that they have lost their birth parent, which may set off a grief reaction.** This sense of loss can greatly decrease children's ability to function and learn in school. The counselors's job may be simply to reassure the child that the birth parent is not lost and to help the child maintain physical and emotional contact with the birth parent and grandparents. However, sometimes the birth parent and other members of his or her extended family truly are lost. If this is the case, the counselor will need to treat this situation as a type of mourning process and support the child through the stages of grief.

4. **Family members may have the unrealistic expectation that members of the blended family will immediately form close relationships with one another.** If the child believes this, he or she will be disappointed when this does not happen. It will be the counselor's job to help the child explore these feelings and to reassure him or her that an initial period of getting to know one another is a normal, natural part of the formation of a new family. If the parent(s) believe this myth, it will be the counselor's job to help the child deal with pressure from them. The counselor can also educate the parent(s) about the natural evolution of affection in blended families. Counselors should acknowledge to the family members that there may never be strong positive feelings between a stepparent and a stepchild (Gardner, 1984). It is important for family members to realize that just because a man and a woman love one another, they may not ever love one another's children, and their children may never love the new spouse.

5. **Quite frequently children fantasize about their birth parents reuniting.** There could be considerable conflict within the blended family if the child is not willing to give up the idea that she or he can bring about the reconstruction of the dissolved family. Since this conflict can permeate the child's life, counselors may want to use some cognitive strategies to help the child take a "reality check" on these fantasies. If the child is spending a lot of time daydreaming about a reconciliation, counselors will want to talk about the purpose these fantasies serve and ways for the child to learn to cope more appropriately with the here-and-now family situation.

6. **The blended family must work out a way for the stepparent to participate in the discipline process.** The research shows that children function better when stepparents do not assume an authoritarian role, but gradually develop a friendship with the child (Kirkwood, 1986; Stern, 1978). There is some evidence to show that if the mother supports the stepfather in setting consistent limits, the child will be more comfortable and discipline will proceed smoothly (Hetherington, Cox, & Cox, 1982). Counselors may want to consult with parents to make sure that they have a conscious, intentional plan that they jointly carry out in a consistent and fair way. This will help the child adjust to the new family configuration and prevent family tensions from escalating.

7. **In blended families there is frequently confusion over family roles.** Because roles were already established in the first-marriage family, the new family must renegotiate duties and relationships. If the counselor can help the family discuss the various conflicts about roles, she or he may be able to help family members quickly understand what their functions in the family will be. By making sure that the confusion dissipates, the counselor can help children feel more comfortable with the altered arrangement.

8. **Conflict between stepsiblings can be a problem in blended families, especially when the children have not yet resolved their feelings about a divorce.** It is important that the new siblings learn to coexist in a harmonious manner, because continued conflict can negatively affect individual children and the entire family. The best way for counselors to intervene with these problems is to work with the entire family. If counselors have access to several stepsiblings, they can conduct conflict resolution sessions with them. However, if it is only possible to see one child in the family, the counselor can work on resolving the child's feelings about the divorce and remarriage. The counselor can also help the child explore ways of gaining significance in the reconfigured family without continuing to struggle with stepsiblings. It also might be helpful to point out the possible advantages of having additional companionship and help with family chores (Gardner, 1984).

9. **It is inevitable that there is a certain amount of competition for time in blended families.** Children may divide their time between two custodial parents, or they may divide their time between a custodial and a noncustodial parent. When the blended family is formed, there will be more demands on both the parent's time and the child's time. The child may feel that he or she has to choose between parents, which exacerbates the feelings of divided loyalties. The child may also feel jealous because he or she now has to share the parent with the stepparent. Counselors can help children explore their feelings if the children have concerns about time, and they can provide children with a forum for expressing these feelings, through individual counseling, group counseling, or family work. If counselors work with the family or consult with the parents, they can help family members reduce conflicts and tension through family meetings and conscious planning.

10. **Remarriage can create a complex and confusing extended kinship network.** Children may be adversely affected by having different sets of extended families with conflicting expectations and rules. They may also have a difficult time understanding their continued relationship with the extended family of the noncustodial family. Counselors might want to use family drawing activities and genograms to help children explore these relationships. *This is Me and My Two Families* (Evans, 1986) is an awareness scrapbook/journal designed to help

children gain a concrete understanding of their extended kinship network. Teachers and counselors can help children explore these relationships in units about family. It is essential that the curriculum provide ways for children in stepfamilies to explore the various configurations of relationships in their families and to see that they are not alone (Prosen & Farmer, 1982).

11. **Sexuality is always a difficult issue for blended family members to resolve.** There seems to be a "loosening of sexual boundaries in remarriage families that is different than there is in biological families" (Walsh, 1992, p. 712). This sexually charged environment may lead to members, especially adolescents and adults, having sexual fantasies about one another. Family members are not usually comfortable about these fantasies, and there is a resultant elevation of tension and distancing behaviors among family members. There is also potential for the family members to act on their sexual feelings for one another, which also creates anxiety and conflict in the family. The counselor's role, especially in middle school, will be to help the family learn to deal with the sexual tensions and to tighten up the sexual boundaries. If there is sexual interaction occurring between a stepparent and a stepchild or between stepsiblings, the counselor will have to report this to the child protective authorities.

12. **It takes time for a blended family to run smoothly.** Generally speaking, it takes two years for a remarried family to develop a sense of cohesion. Counselors may want to remind children and their parents that the family structure will gradually evolve. The more patient they are with themselves and with each other, the more likely the family will survive and develop as a family unit.

13. **Moving back and forth between two separate families may adversely affect children.** Children frequently experience a sense of disruption when they change living arrangements. There is no simple solution to this problem, but Lutz (1983) suggested that the parents can ease the exit-entry situation somewhat by maintaining a cordial relationship with one another. If the counselor can help parents establish and maintain amiable interaction patterns between the two living situations, it may help minimize the Friday afternoon "pre-visitation jitters" and the Monday morning "post-visitation blues." Counselors might also want to conduct an in-service for teachers on how they can help children in stepfamilies adjust. One method is for them to make sure that they do not have vigorous school work planned for Monday mornings, so that children who are experiencing "post-visitation blues" can ease back into the academic stream. By simply being aware of potential problems, teachers can frequently help children avoid serious negative consequences.

14. **Society has a generally negative concept of blended families.** Children, especially early adolescents, are extremely sensitive about what other people think of them and their families, and they may feel hurt and angry about the negative myths about stepfamilies. Counselors can help families be aware of the possible impact of this prejudice, and they can help children realize that there is nothing wrong with the structure of their family. They may want to give the family information about what is "normal" for a stepfamily (Lutz, Jacobs, & Masson, 1981) in order to counter negative societal myths. Counselors can also encourage teachers and other school personnel to make accommodations for stepparents when they are planning teacher conferences, family picnics, honors ceremonies, and the like. Again, including blended families as one possible family configuration in the curriculum will also help children realize that they are not alone and that there is nothing wrong with the way their family is organized.

15. **Sometimes family members believe that the blended family is "different, inadequate, or deficient"** (Walsh, 1992, p. 713). If a negative familial self-concept is interfering with a child's ability to learn, the counselor can help the child explore thoughts, attitudes, and feelings. In the process of this exploration, the counselor may be able to provide accurate information about remarried families and counteract some of this negativity.

16. **Some members of blended families have negative personal self-concepts.** There is mixed research data about the self-images of members of stepfamilies, but Amato and Ochiltree (1987) stated that if family members have stable, positive interactions with one another, they will have a greater chance for positive self-esteem, no matter how their family is organized. Counselors can share this information with family members, and they can help build the self-concepts of the discouraged individuals.

17. **Conflicts over parenting can frequently have a negative impact on the new marital relationship in a blended family, which can adversely affect children's performance and behavior in school.** Since this is the case, counselors may want to provide parent consultation or parent education classes designed specifically for stepparents. Turnbull and Turnbull (1983) listed the "Ten Commandments of Stepparenting" for helping blended families avoid many potential conflicts in this area.

18. **Many stepfamilies have financial problems.** Money problems can create tensions in children who take on the worries of their parents. Children may not be able to buy material things that they could have had before the divorce, and the resulting sense of deprivation may evoke anxiety, anger, or disappointment. Counselors will have to remain aware of these concerns when working with children and help them avoid taking on parental problems as their own. Counselors may want to work with the entire family to establish some type of family council that provides a forum for discussing these kinds of problems (Bettner & Lew, 1990).

19. **The parents in the family may have unresolved conflicts with their former partners.** When ex-spouses cannot solve their own issues with one another, they sometimes draw the children into the continuing hostility. Counselors need to communicate to the parent(s) how important it is to avoid involving children in unresolved issues from the previous marriage. If they cannot work with the parent(s), counselors will want to work with the child to help him or her establish boundaries to keep from being co-opted into the ongoing struggle. It may also help to explore ways for the child to refuse to participate in parental conflict.

20. **Frequently the noncustodial parent engages in a competition for the time and affection of the children.** This may contribute to an unrealistic assessment of how life should be due to the " 'everyday is Disneyland' state of affairs" (Walsh, 1992, p. 714). This level of intensity does not usually continue for long after the remarriage. While it lasts, children may try to play "both ends against the middle," exploiting the atmosphere of competition. When the intensity fades, they sometimes feel abandoned and discouraged because the level of attention they are getting is significantly decreased. Counselors can help them cope with both of these eventualities by exploring feelings, clarifying values, and discussing relationships with children in individual, group, and family sessions.

Children of Alcoholics

According to the American Academy of Child and Adolescent Psychiatry (1991), there are at least seven million children in the United States who have an alcoholic parent. This translates to four to six children in each elementary classroom (Brake, 1988). Because growing up with a parent who abuses alcohol can have a profound negative impact on children's school performance, school counselors, especially those at the elementary and middle school levels, should be providing some kind of active intervention program with children in this population.

Characteristics of Children of Alcoholics

Children of alcoholics usually have low self-esteem, external locus of control, problems in learning, and feelings of being unloved and unworthy of love (Callan & Jackson, 1986; Werner, 1986). They have difficulty trusting other people and frequently do not relate well to their peers. They may feel angry and hostile toward both of their parents and toward other adult authority figures (Brake, 1988; Buwick, Martin, & Martin, 1988). They are angry at the alcoholic parent for drinking and for any negative behavior that results from the drinking, at the nonalcoholic parent for not stopping the drinking, and at other authority figures for not knowing about the situation and preventing it. These children are frequently confused and insecure because there is no consistency or predictability in their homes. Children of alcoholics may be highly anxious because they worry constantly about the situation in their families. Sometimes they also feel guilty because they are not preventing it from happening (American Academy of Child and Adolescent Psychiatry, 1991).

The three rules of an alcoholic family ("don't talk," "don't trust," "don't feel") (Black, 1981) may preclude the child from confiding in anyone about the problems in the family. This code of silence makes it difficult for school personnel to identify these children. There are some characteristic behaviors that occur at school and may be indicators that there is an alcohol problem in the family (American Academy of Child and Adolescent Psychiatry, 1991; Wilson & Blocher, 1990), including the following:

1. Difficulty in academic performance in school.
2. Truancy.
3. Social isolation and/or withdrawal from peers.
4. If the child does have friends, refusal to invite other children to his or her house.
5. More than average number of somatic complaints, such as headaches and/or stomach aches.
6. Aggressiveness and hostility toward peers; bullying.
7. Mood swings.
8. Evidence of child abuse, including physical marks, flinching, and such.
9. Evidence of child neglect, including poor hygiene, complaints of hunger, and such.

10. Expression of sadness at parent(s) missing ball games, birthday parties, holidays, and so on.

11. Acting out behaviors, including temper tantrums, lying, and disruptive behavior.

12. Distortions in level of responsibility taking—either overly responsible to the point of grandiosity or under responsible to the point of blaming others for personal behavior.

13. Delinquent behavior, including stealing, vandalism, and violence.

14. Evidence of alcohol or drug abuse.

All of these factors are indicators of alcohol or drug abuse in the home. They may, obviously, also be indicators of other family problems, but the school counselor should investigate the family situation further if a child evidences one or more of these. It would also be helpful if the counselor can conduct an in-service for teachers so that they can be alert to the signs and symptoms of an alcoholic parent and can help contravene the family rules that prevent disclosure and requests for support and assistance.

Counseling Issues and Intervention Strategies

There are some generic counseling issues that all children in alcoholic families have as a result of the "don't talk," "don't trust," and "don't feel" rules. Children of alcoholics need help learning to express themselves, trust others, and allow themselves to experience emotions. In order to help them do these things, counselors will need to encourage children to trust them by being consistent, making sure that their words and behavior are congruent , and asking children's permission if they are going to consult with others about them (Brake, 1988). Counselors will want to be sure to have a set routine and time schedule to follow when they work with these children to assure them of security and structure (Wilson & Blocher, 1990).

Since most children of alcoholics are not in touch with their feelings, one of the primary tasks will be to help them explore feelings, learn feeling vocabulary, and learn to express emotions. Counselors should incorporate decision-making skills as part of the counseling process, and be sure to build in opportunities to practice making choices, in the counseling office and in the classroom (O'Rourke, 1990; Wilson & Blocher, 1990). Counselors can also provide information about alcohol and alcoholism and how they affect family members (O'Rourke, 1990). Counselors should be able to obtain appropriate materials from their state commission on alcoholism.

Cognitive behavior therapy has proven effective in intervention with children of alcoholics (Webb, 1993). Counselors can use this method to model appropriate behavior, teach thought stopping, and help children restructure faulty cognitions.

Group counseling seems to work well for children of alcoholics because this venue allows them to recognize that they are not alone in their situation (Brake, 1988; O'Rourke, 1990; Wilson & Blocher, 1990). In group counseling, the counselor can continue to build trusting relationships, enhance self-esteem, practice social skills, explore and express feelings, and provide group support and understanding. Wilson and Blocher (1990) suggested that counselors use the following techniques in group counseling with children:

1. Bibliocounseling using books such as *My Dad Loves Me, My Dad Has a Disease* (Black, 1982), *Cages of Glass, Flowers of Time* (Culin, 1979), *Take My Walking Slow* (Norris, 1970), *Different Like Me* (Leite & Espeland, 1987), and *My Mom Doesn't Look Like an Alcoholic* (Hammond & Chestnut, 1986). Counselors can even structure their entire group around the workbook *An Elephant in the Livingroom* (Hastings & Typpo, 1984).

2. Role-playing situations that occur in the family and brainstorming ways to deal with them.

3. Rational emotive techniques that help children learn to assess the reasonableness of their own behavior and reactions.

4. Gestalt and awareness activities designed to help children become aware of their own thoughts and feelings. Techniques like the empty chair help children explore other people's perceptions and experiences.

5. Assertiveness work helps children learn to take care of themselves in stressful situations.

6. Relaxation techniques help children learn to appropriately deal with stress and anxiety.

It is inevitable that counselors will not be able to help all of the children of alcoholics in their school. However, there are also community resources available to these children. Support groups in the community like Alateen and Alanon can also help students learn to cope with their family situations.

Black (1981) suggested that children in alcoholic families usually fall into the role of hero, scapegoat, lost child, and mascot. Each of these roles has certain characteristic counseling issues and potential intervention strategies for counselors.

Hero children.   Hero children are quite frequently the oldest children in their family. They believe that they are responsible for anything negative that happens in the family (Brake, 1988; Buwick, Martin, & Martin, 1988; Fisher, 1989; Webb, 1993). Heroes develop a sense of grandiosity, trying to prevent negative things from happening. They sometimes believe that if they could only be "good enough" then their parents would stop drinking. Their duty in the family is to compensate for the alcoholic's behavior or to overshadow any negative behavior on the part of the alcoholic with their positive behavior. They believe that they must try to keep everyone happy by attending to everyone else's needs.

In school, heroes are frequently perfectionistic and set unreasonably high standards for themselves in academics, behavior, and extracurricular activities. These are children who cry if they miss one word on a spelling test or if they do not beat all the other children in a race. They may also spend a lot of energy "parenting" other children. These are children who are the first to console an upset classmate or first to try to cheer up a depressed friend.

Hero children often do not get referred for counseling because their behavior is actually the kind of behavior most teachers want to encourage. They do everything well, so no one notices that they are highly anxious, overly responsible, and not taking care of their own needs. Counselors can help these children in several ways (Fisher, 1989; O'Rourke, 1990; Webb, 1993; Wilson & Blocher, 1990). The first way to support hero children is to educate teachers to look for signs of overachievement, perfectionism, and overresponsibility as indicators that a child may be a hero child who needs counseling help. Counselors can also suggest to teachers and to the nonalcoholic parent that they need to reduce the load of responsibility and leadership these children are carrying. They will need to encourage heroes to let others take the lead and assume the burden of responsibility sometimes.

Teachers and parents can help hero children act like children instead of miniature adults. They can encourage them to be silly and whimsical and remind them to "lighten up" when they are being overly serious or parental. Sometimes it is hard for teachers and parents to do this because hero children are frequently very helpful to adults and many times the adults in their lives do not wish to have them relinquish their heroic qualities and behaviors. In their consultation and education, counselors will need to explain to adults how these characteristics can ultimately harm hero children, and counselors may want to explore what the adults are gaining by having the children continue in adult roles.

When hero children actually come to the counseling office, either as self-referrals or teacher-referrals, the counselor's primary job will be to help them to recognize and meet their own needs (Fisher, 1989; Webb, 1993). These children have usually been so hypervigilant to the needs of others they do not know how to take care of themselves. They may also need help learning to follow instead of lead and to trust that they can count on other people to be responsible. They may need help setting realistic goals and coping with imperfection—in themselves and in others. Hero children need to learn to relax and have fun. The counselor may have to help them practice relaxation skills and brainstorm ways to balance work with pleasure. Hero children also need help managing stress and anxiety and learning to believe that others will like them simply for themselves, not just for what they can do for them.

Scapegoats.   Scapegoat children in an alcoholic family are always in trouble for something (Black, 1981; Fisher, 1989; Webb, 1990). Their behavior is usually problematic, and they act withdrawn, sullen, hostile, and/or defiant. It is the scapegoat's job to distract from the parent's alcoholism by drawing negative attention to his or her own behavior. Scapegoats mask their feelings of hurt and rejection by engaging in self-destructive behavior like running away, abusing drugs and alcohol, being promiscuous, and/or getting in trouble with the law.

In school, these children have behavior problems. They are disrespectful, argumentative, and refuse to cooperate with teachers and other authority figures. Scapegoats frequently refuse to do their school work, and even when they turn it in, it is usually of inferior quality.

These children are often referred for counseling, and the counselor will be seeing a lot of them. In their consultation with teachers, counselors will want to stress the necessity for teachers to avoid personal power struggles with these children. Teachers should use logical consequences and choices with scapegoats, holding them responsible for their actions in an unemotional, firm, nonjudgemental way. Any time these children act in appropriate, responsible ways, teachers and other adults should encourage them.

In working directly with scapegoats, counselors will want to help them verbally express their pain and feelings of rejection. It is helpful to point out times when they act out those feelings instead of verbalizing them and to encourage children to practice what they could have said instead of acting out. Counselors will reinforce the work of the teachers in talking about being responsible and making wise choices, at the same time they encourage scapegoats to follow rules and avoid power struggles. If the counselor can find a constructive way for scapegoats to gain attention, this will provide them with a method of substituting positive behavior for negative behavior. Counselors may also want to teach scapegoat children social skills and work with them on making appropriate friends, because most of the time scapegoats are friends with other scapegoats which can lead to trouble. In schools where counselors have an effective mentoring program, they can match a scapegoat child with a positive role model—either a teacher or an older child. Peer counseling can also be highly effective with these children because they basically want to "fit in," but they do not yet know how to go about doing this in a socially appropriate way.

Lost children.   Lost children are usually loners, daydreamers who drift through life without purpose. They may be shy, withdrawn, scared, lonely, and confused. Sometimes these children may serve as a source of relief in their families because they can be ignored and they are undemanding (Wegscheider-Cruise, 1985). Lost children do not usually ask for help because they do not know how.

In school, these are frequently children who fall through the cracks because they do not get in trouble and their school work is usually adequate, but not outstanding. Teachers may not notice these children and their need for support, because lost children do not stand out in any way. In consultation with teachers, counselors might want to alert them to pay close attention to any children in their class that they find themselves ignoring. The best way for teachers to help these children is to pay attention to them when they are interacting and being active in the class. They should encourage lost children to participate in class discussions and activities and to avoid daydreaming. If lost children are spending an inordinate amount of time by themselves, the teacher may want to promote interaction with others and social skills by including these children in small group exercises. However, since lost children tend to be overly dependent on others, teachers should also try to keep other children from being too protective or doing too much for them (Fisher, 1989; Webb, 1993).

Counselors can provide direct services to lost children by building their self-esteem and their sense of worth and competence. Quite frequently when counselors pay attention to these children and act interested in them, they will blossom. These children can gain social skills and the ability to interact with others through group counseling, but it is important for counselors to establish a caring, personal relationship with them in which they feel comfortable before asking them to join a group. If counselors suggest that they participate in group counseling before they are ready, lost children may refuse to participate or drop out of the group. Counselors will need to remember that most of the time being "lost" is the way these children have always gained significance, and they may not feel comfortable being "found."

Mascots.   Most of the time, youngest children in the family find themselves in the role of the family mascot, the one who is cute, entertaining, and/or mischievous (Fisher, 1989; Webb, 1993). Mascots may manifest unusual degrees of anxiety, hyperactivity, and fragility (Wegscheider-Cruise, 1985). They serve the family by drawing attention to themselves with silly behavior that breaks tension between family members and distracts from the alcoholic's behavior.

In school, mascots are frequently class clowns. They like to be the center of attention, and in order to make sure that everyone attends to them they may engage in disruptive and inappropriate behavior. Sometimes mascots have difficulty focusing on their school work, and their short attention spans may cause problems with successful completion of school work. In working with teachers, counselors will want to help them learn to ignore mascots' inappropriate behavior. Teachers will need to work with the other children, encouraging them to ignore disruptive behavior. In order to build the idea that mascots can be sensible and responsible, teachers should give them duties and leadership roles in the classroom. Teachers can also point out times when mascots try to relieve tensions by diverting with humor or silliness.

When working with mascots, the counselor's primary task will be to teach them appropriate ways of expressing their feelings and getting their needs met. Counselors will want to teach them constructive ways to gain attention and approval. If possible, counselors should work with these children on learning to shift their locus of control so that they can evaluate their own behavior realistically and not depend on the attention of others for their significance. In order to help mascots deal with their anxiety, counselors might teach them relaxation exercises. By helping mascots relax more, counselors may also have a positive effect on their ability to concentrate and complete school work. Because mascots frequently make impulsive choices, counselors may also want to include decision-making and problem-solving skills in their work with mascots.

Children with Attention-Deficit/Hyperactivity Disorders

According to the *Diagnostic and Statistical Manual of Mental Disorders* (DSM-IV) (American Psychiatric Association, 1994), there are three types of Attention-Deficit/Hyperactivity Disorders (ADHD): Attention-Deficit Hyperactivity Disorder,

Predominantly Inattentive Type; Attention-Deficit/Hyperactivity Disorder, Predominantly Hyperactive-Impulsive Type; and Attention-Deficit/Hyperactivity Disorder, Combined Type. Individuals with the Inattentive Type primarily have difficulty paying attention. Individuals with the Hyperactive-Impulsive Type are frequently impulsive and hyperactive. Individuals with the Combined Type are inattentive, impulsive, and hyperactive.

While most authorities agree that ADHD is a physiological disorder, there is much disagreement about what causes it (Barclay, 1990; C.H.A.D.D., 1992). There is some evidence to suggest that ADHD is due to a chemical imbalance or a failure in neurotransmitters. There is other evidence to show that brain consumption of glucose may also be a factor in ADHD. Some individuals with ADHD have a genetic predisposition toward the disability, while in others the disability is due to prenatal or perinatal complications, brain damage, toxins, or infections. There is little scientific evidence to indicate that "true" ADHD is due to social or environmental causes, diet, or inadequate parenting (Barclay, 1990). However, there are some children who are diagnosed as having ADHD who do not seem to have the physiological component, but who are responding to something in their environments with symptoms similar to those of children with ADHD.

Experts estimate that 3 percent to 5 percent of the school-age population have problems due to ADHD (C.H.A.D.D., 1992). While this is not an overwhelmingly large group of children, we chose to address this population because these children usually have significant problems functioning in school.

Characteristics and Concerns of Children with ADHD

Children and adolescents with ADHD have problems in many different areas: (a) behavior, (b) social relationships, (c) cognitive functioning, (d) emotional functioning, and (e) physical functioning (American Psychiatric Association, 1994; Barclay, 1990; Gordon, 1991). They also have difficulty in academic performance and functioning in the classroom, which can significantly interfere with their learning.

Most of the behavior problems of children with ADHD relate to their distractibility and impulsivity. These children are restless and unable to stay in one place for even short periods of time. They may be extremely loquacious, to the point of teachers and parents reporting, "He just won't shut up! He's driving me crazy with this constant talking about nothing." Children with ADHD are extremely demanding because they have difficulty delaying gratification—they want what they want, and they want it now. They cannot take turns, and they have difficulty sharing. These children also take more risks than do other children, resulting in frequent accidents or injuries.

In terms of social relationships, children with ADHD have difficulty making friends and abiding by social rules. They seem to be unable to remember to act on social "dos" and "don't." Even when they can say what the rules are (and they frequently do not know, even when someone just told them), they may not follow them. These children have trouble complying with requests and/or prohibitions. Many times, right after the counselor asks them to do something they will do exactly the opposite thing, even though the counselor is standing right next to them. Children with ADHD have difficulty tolerating changes in routine or structure. If the teacher decides to do something special in their classroom—whether it be a surprise treat or a rearrangement of the furniture—these children will have trouble adjusting. ADHD children seem to have deficits in self-control, social problem-solving skills, peer relations, and respecting the feelings, rights, and property of others. They frequently are extremely aggressive, domineering, and demanding with other children and with adults. This behavior causes social problems, because other people simply do not like to be around individuals who act this way.

The difficulties in cognitive functioning involve deficits in attention span, short-term memory, and ability to focus. Frequently these children cannot pay attention long enough to have information register, and they cannot concentrate long enough to communicate about the things they do know. Children with ADHD seem to have more difficulty processing aurally than they do visually. They frequently learn best through the kinesthetic/tactile modality, but few teachers use this as a major component in their instruction. Many ADHD children have delayed speech development and/or learning disabilities that also make cognitive functioning difficult.

Attention-Deficit/Hyperactivity Disorder also affects children emotionally. These children may be excessively excitable and/or depressed. They are extremely emotionally labile, switching rapidly between various moods without external provocation. They can move from expressing uncontrollable outrage to extreme bursts of warmth for no apparent reason. They also seem to have extremely low tolerance for frustration, and their immature emotional control contributes to many temper tantrums. Perhaps as a result of their interpersonal difficulties and poor emotional control, children with ADHD frequently have very low self-esteem and lack feelings of competence and worth.

Children with ADHD sometimes have physical symptoms such as high numbers of ear infections, upper respiratory infections, and allergies. They may have immature bone growth and/or physical immaturity that manifests itself as smallness or thinness. Many of these children have short sleep cycles that make it difficult for them to sleep undisturbed and undisturbing through the night. Their unusually high tolerance for pain combines with their risk-taking behavior to put them into many physically dangerous situations.

As a result of all of these traits, ADHD children usually have difficulty in school. They have elevated levels of out-of-seat and off-task behavior because they cannot focus on their work. They may be disruptive and noncompliant in the classroom because of their behavior and social problems. Their academic work is plagued by problems due to a high level of learning disabilities, their difficulty paying attention, and their weakness in auditory processing. This especially becomes a problem in fourth grade and beyond, because many teachers in the intermediate grades and middle school/junior high school expect children to learn with limited visual or kinesthetic/tactile input.

Many children with ADHD get very discouraged in school. They know that they are trying to pay attention in class, focus on their work, complete their assignments, learn new information, remember what they learned previously, get along with other children, and cooperate with teachers and other authority figures. They also recognize that they succeed at very few of these and only sporadically. Many other children and the adults who encounter ADHD children do not believe that they are truly disabled and cannot succeed at many of these things. This, too, is very discouraging and disheartening. By the time they have gotten to the upper elementary grades and middle school, many children with ADHD have given up on trying and are rebellious and/or severely depressed. The counselor's job is to prevent this from happening by educating children, parents, and teachers about the problems associated with ADHD and the possible intervention alternatives that can help them, their teachers, and their families.

Intervention Strategies

Intervention strategies with this population can include working directly with the child, parent consultation and education, and/or teacher consultation. Most of the time counselors will be the most effective if they can combine elements of each of these delivery systems.

Working with the child. There are several choices for ways to intervene directly with the child. The most common treatment is stimulant medication (Barclay, 1990; C.H.A.D.D., 1992; Gomez & Cole, 1991). In some cases, physicians choose to administer antidepressants or other drugs instead (Gomez & Cole, 1991). Because this is a medical rather than an educational intervention, school counselors are not involved in deciding upon or carrying out this treatment. However, counselors may be instrumental in the decision to seek medical intervention and in monitoring the effects of the medication after it is prescribed. Because of this potential role, it is important for counselors to know about the various medications prescribed for ADHD and their possible side effects. Counselors should also know the kinds of questions that are important in determining whether to use medication as a treatment for ADHD.

According to research studies, stimulant medication (usually Ritalin or Cylert) is the most effective intervention strategy for intervention with ADHD (Gomez & Cole, 1991; Henker & Whalen, 1989). A significant majority (70 percent to 80 percent) of the children who receive stimulant medication respond favorably, with improved social interaction and behavior (Gomez & Cole, 1991). Although the findings on improved academic performance are mixed, research has demonstrated that stimulant medication reduces motor activity, disruptive behavior, aggressive behavior, and argumentativeness, while improving concentration, ability to focus and attend, and goal-directed behavior (Abikoff, 1985; Gomez & Cole, 1991; Johnson, 1988).

Physiological side effects of stimulant medication are usually mild and short-lived (Barley, 1990; Gomez & Cole, 1991). They consist of poor appetite, insomnia, headaches, stomach aches, moodiness, and tics. Most of the time these symptoms can be reduced or eliminated by reduction of the dosage. There are some concerns that stimulant medication can also slow growth. Stimulant medication may not be the treatment of choice with children who experience this. Some children suffer from a "rebound effect" in which their behavior deteriorates as the medication wears off. This can create problems for teachers at the end of the day or for parents after children arrive home. One potential solution for this problem would be for children to take an additional dose later in the day. This would ease transition to home and might improve family relationships.

The other major drug treatment used with children with ADHD is antidepressant medication (for example, Tofranil, Norpramin, and Prozac). While these drugs have some advantages over stimulant medication (for example, they last longer in the body so the child does not have to take them as often, they do not produce a rebound effect, and they can be monitored by blood tests), they do not work with as many children as do stimulant medications. They seem to be most widely used with children who have not responded to Ritalin and other stimulants (Biederman, Baldessarini, Wright, Knee, & Hermatz, 1989).

Other potential problems with medication are more psychological in nature (Gomez & Cole, 1991). Some people have expressed concerns that children may become dependent on the drug as the only way they can interact effectively. Others worry that using this medication might predispose children to future drug abuse or addiction. Still others are afraid that using a drug to control behavior sends a message to the child that he or she is incapable of controlling his or her behavior without drugs. While these concerns are not without substance, careful monitoring of the medication and education of children, parents, and teachers about the nature of medically based interventions would seem to be an appropriate method of countering any psychological side effects.

In deciding whether the counselor or the child's teacher should recommend that parents take the child for a medical evaluation for medication, counselors should consider the following set of questions (Goldstein & Goldstein, 1990; Gordon, 1991; Ingersoll, 1988):

1. What is the family's previous treatment history? If the family has a history of asking a number of different professionals for help and not following their suggestions, they will probably not be consistent in their follow-through with medication.

2. Is the child anxious or fearful? With some children who manifest these symptoms, stimulant medication makes this problem worse, so these children may not be good candidates for this treatment.

3. What is the age of the child? With children under six, there is a higher incidence of side effects, so it may not be appropriate to refer children in kindergarten. Their behavior could also be due to lack of maturity rather than ADHD, so it may be better to wait with young children to see how the passage of time affects their behavior.

4. Is there anyone to assist parents in an ongoing effort to monitor medication? It is essential that professionals (the physician, a nurse, teachers, and/or the counselor) help parents determine if the medication is having the desired effect.

5. What is the severity of attentional problems? With less severe cases of ADHD, other treatments may be effective without the potential side effects of medication.

6. What kind of financial resources does the family have? Medical evaluations, monitoring, and medication all cost money. If the family has limited funds, the counselor will need to refer them to a place with a sliding scale or other affordable services.

7. Has the child had thorough physical and psychological evaluations to eliminate the possibility of other causative factors? Sometimes the symptoms that serve as warning signs for ADHD are due to some other cause. Counselors need to help families get the services they need to investigate this possibility.

8. Is there a history of tics, psychosis, or thought disorders? Since there are rare occurrences of these difficulties as side effects of stimulant medication, if the child or other members of the family have experienced them, it would probably be advisable to find a different treatment.

9. What resources can the school district provide for the family, and what resources will they have to seek elsewhere? If there are services the district cannot provide, counselors may need to help the family access other systems.

Another effective intervention for children with ADHD is behavior modification (Barclay, 1990; C.H.A.D.D., 1992; Gomez & Cole, 1991). Counselors may want to work directly with the child on the behavior program, or they may want to serve as a consultant to the child's teacher. Since most teachers and counselors have training in the implementation of behavior modification, we will not spend a great deal of time describing how to go about doing this. In designing a behavioral program for a specific child, it is important to remember to follow these steps (C.H.A.D.D., 1992):

1. Define the target behavior in observable, measurable terms.
2. Identify the behavioral antecedents.
3. Identify the behavioral consequences.
4. Consider how the antecedents and consequences affect the target behavior.
5. Develop interventions that alter either the antecedents or the consequences.
6. Assess the effects of the interventions on the target behavior.

Counselors interested in setting up behavior intervention programs for ADHD children may want to further investigate texts that specifically describe how to do this. Some helpful examples of this were written by Barclay (1990), Goldstein & Goldstein (1990), and Gordon (1991).

While there is little empirical evidence to show that any type of talk therapy or play therapy is effective with children with ADHD (Barclay, 1990; Gomez & Cole, 1991), the authors have worked with children from this population effectively with both of these modalities. While these types of therapy do not reduce impulsivity or hyperactivity or increase attention span, they can help children understand what ADHD is and how it affects their behavior. One bibliocounseling resource for providing this type of information is *Putting on the Brakes: Young People's Guide to Understanding Attention Deficit Hyperactivity Disorder* (Quinn & Stern, 1991). You can use another bibliocounseling resource, *Eagle Eyes: A Child's View of Attention Deficit Disorder* (Gehret, 1991), to reframe some of the difficulties experienced by children with ADHD and their families by focusing on the positive qualities of these children. We have used talk therapy with older children and play therapy with younger children to help ADHD children enhance their self-esteem and reduce discouragement. Sometimes these children need just one person in their lives who is not critical and not demanding that they change their behavior. Counselors who choose to take on that role can make a big difference in their lives.

Since many children with ADHD have deficits in social skills, counselors may want to offer social skills training for them (C.H.A.D.D., 1992; Guevremont, 1990). The most effective way of doing this seems to be to include several ADHD children in a social skills group with several other children who have social deficits and several children who have adequate social skills. The plan for the group should include lessons on conversational skills, conflict resolution and problem solving, and anger control (Guevremont, 1990).

Working with parents.   As one part of an overall intervention plan with ADHD children, counselors should be sure to consult with the parents (Lavin, 1991). Parents of ADHD children need a great deal of support and understanding from educational professionals. By providing parents with parent training, information about ADHD, information about possible treatments, emotional support, and help in learning to communicate with teachers and other school personnel, counselors can be a positive influence in the lives of these children and their families (Kottman, Robert, & Baker, in press).

In working with the parents on parenting skills, counselors may want to include instruction on communication skills (for example, "I" messages, reflective listening), how to effectively give commands to their children, how to set up consequences and time out, how to give encouragement and support to their children, and how to set up a behavior modification program at home.

It is also important to work with parents on their ability to form a working alliance with teachers and other school personnel. Because these children frequently have difficulty in school, many parents of ADHD children develop an adversarial attitude about teachers and other school authorities. This is usually counterproductive, because it tends to alienate the people who could provide the most help for their children. In order to foster a positive relationship with the teacher, parents need to try to understand the classroom from the teacher's perspective and avoid blaming the teacher for the child's difficulty or automatically taking sides with the child in any dispute with the teacher. Parents need to remember that just as they get worn out and discouraged living with their children, so do teachers get tired working with their children. A little encouragement and appreciation goes a long way to solidifying a positive relationship between teachers and parents.

After parents have begun to build this working alliance, then they can start to educate teachers about how ADHD affects their child and what works and does not work with this particular child. If parents try to convey this information before they have established rapport with the teacher, they will probably be wasting their time because the teachers may be feeling defensive and may not be listening.

Counselors may want to help parents to temper their role of child advocate with realistic attitudes about their child. Some parents of ADHD children tend to be overprotective and unwilling to have their children take any consequences for their behaviors. Overprotectiveness is actually harmful to children with ADHD, because they come to believe that they are not responsible for their decisions and behaviors. By using empathy, warmth, and gentle confrontation with parents, counselors should be able to convey their support at the same time they teach parents that this behavior could harm, rather than help, their child.

Sometimes another aspect of counselors' work with parents will be to help parents gain access to available school resources. Although ADHD is not recognized as a distinct handicapping condition under P.L. 94-142, the United States Department of Education has acknowledged that many ADHD children need special education services (C.H.A.D.D., 1991). Some children with ADHD can qualify for special help under the "Other Health Impaired" category of P.L. 94-142. However, many school districts do not realize this fact, nor are they eager to offer these services. Without being disloyal to his or her school district, a counselor can educate parents about their rights and how to request special education services from the district.

Working with teachers.   Tolerant and supportive teachers are a key to school success with ADHD children. Consultation with teachers will probably be the most helpful service that counselors can provide for these children. The first thing counselors will want to do is to educate teachers about the typical behavior of ADHD children and about the fact that the child is not doing those 4,000 annoying behaviors a day on purpose. It is also important to stress to teachers that, with their help, ADHD children can learn to control their behavior more effectively. We believe that there is a fine line between (a) understanding that many of these children's behaviors and interactional styles are a function of their disorder and (b) letting these children use their "disorder" as an excuse for inappropriate behavior that they have no desire or intention to change. The counselor's job is to help teachers find a balance in their relationships with ADHD children and a way to adapt their own attitudes and classroom management style to optimize the learning of ADHD children without detracting from the learning of the other children in the classroom.

The following is a list of ways teachers can help ADHD children in the classroom. We adapted these suggestions from our own experiences with these children and from the recommendations of Barclay (1990), Goldstein and Goldstein (1990), Gordon (1991), Ingersoll (1988), and Wender (1987):

1. Make sure that the classroom has maximum structure and routine (e.g., clearly defined rules and consequences, consistent daily schedule, set class traffic patterns).

2. Minimize distractions in the classroom (e.g., good soundproofing, carrels for children to sit in, blinds on the windows).

3. Break assignments into small, manageable units to accommodate the need for short-term gratification and limited attention spans.

4. Arrange seating for minimal distraction or provocation.

5. Be encouraging and optimistic in order to counteract discouragement and low self-esteem.

6. Assign simple responsibilities in order to build leadership skills, self-confidence, and ability to follow simple instructions.

7. Design many classroom activities to focus on individual and small group assignments, because large group work is problematic, both behaviorally and academically.

8. Give feedback for inappropriate behavior and redirect to more acceptable activities.

9. Allow for sanctioned movement. Since these children are going to need to move around the classroom anyway, make sure they do so at your suggestion.

10. Keep instructions short and simple. If possible, build in both verbal and visual cues.

11. Work to include the kinesthetic modality in your instruction and in the learning assignments.

12. Alternate difficult/easy and fun/tiresome tasks to encourage going on to the next assignment and not getting "stuck" on one piece of work.

13. Warn children in advance before transitions occur in order to avoid disruptions or lack of compliance.

14. Take advantage of any way of making assignments into a game or challenge (e.g., racing the clock, seeing whether the child can beat the old record).

15. Communicate with the parent(s) frequently, both when the child is doing well and when the child is struggling. The teacher may be able to use the parent(s) as a resource about what works and does not work with the child. This will also build a cooperative working relationship with the parent(s) that can provide support for them and for the teacher in times of stress.

16. Keep a sense of humor, and focus on the fun parts of having a ADHD child in the classroom. Appreciate their creativity and spontaneity and join in whenever possible.

Gifted and Talented Children

In the last several decades, schools in the United States have responded to the needs of gifted and talented children by expanding the academic programs designed for them, but educators have done very little about giving them special support in the areas of personal and social functioning (Barnette, 1989; Blackburn & Erickson, 1986). Recent studies have shown that gifted and talented students seem to have more adjustment problems than do other students (Betts, 1986; Janos & Robinson, 1985; Levine & Tucker, 1986). This being the case, it is important that school counselors begin to work to alleviate the social problems and personal stress of this group of children.

Characteristics and Concerns of Gifted and Talented Children

One of the difficulties in understanding gifted and talented children is that there are many sides to giftedness (Kaplan, Madsen, Gould, Platow, & Renzulli, 1979). Because many people think of high intelligence as the only criterion for giftedness, there are many talented and gifted children who are overlooked. The National/State Training Institute on the Gifted and Talented (Kaplan et al., 1979) suggested that there are at least six different kinds of giftedness, as follows:

1. General intellectual ability. These children have a high IQ and a preference for complex and challenging tasks. They are usually curious, inventive, and creative.
2. Creative or productive thinking ability. These children produce highly original solutions to problems. They can hold many ideas at once, juggling them to find unusual or interesting combinations. They have a high tolerance for ambiguity and like the idea of a question not having a "right" answer. They are divergent thinkers, and they like to improvise, never following the same path twice. These children are extremely self-confident, and they enjoy explaining their ideas and expressing their opinions.
3. Visual and performing arts ability. These children show special talent in expressive or performing arts. They have a wealth of knowledge and information about their chosen field, and they have a high level of sustained interest in one or two specific areas. They set high standards for themselves in expressing their ability, and they expect to receive recognition and rewards for their talents.
4. Specific academic aptitude. These children are particularly adept at one or two specific subjects and/or skills. They have an unusual level of achievement in a narrow field of expertise. They usually spend the bulk of their time and energy focused on the specific subject(s) and/or skill(s) in which they excel.
5. Leadership ability. These children are particularly skilled socially and interpersonally. They have a high degree of charisma and organizational skills. They are almost always responsible and reliable. They seem to be genuinely concerned for and interested in others. In their interactions with others, they almost always assume a leadership position.
6. Psychomotor ability. These children have manipulative skills and manual dexterity beyond what is normally expected. They show evidence of exceptional motor skills early in life, and they usually excel in athletics. Most of these children have high standards of performance, striving toward perfection.

There are other classifications of giftedness, but this description seems to make sense to the authors for the purposes of understanding and explaining different ways of looking at giftedness to children, parents, and teachers.

Despite the positive qualities that accompany being gifted and talented, many of these children experience specific concerns related to their being gifted (Blackburn & Erickson, 1986; Brown, 1993; Rice, 1985). Many gifted and talented children seem to have a difficult time relating to other children. They want to fit in, but they know they are different. In order to compensate for this, some children pretend that they do not possess the knowledge and ability that would make them appear different. Other children overcompensate and gain their significance solely by being "superior" to their classmates. Other children simply shut down and withdraw. They believe that they cannot fit in, so they do not even try. Children who manifest this reaction may become overly involved in computers, videogames, or reading.

Another typical concern of gifted and talented children is their high standards and need for perfection. This comes partly from the expectations of others and partly from self-expectations. Quite frequently this quest for the impossible creates tension and anxiety in these children. They may have somatic symptoms such as headaches or ulcers.

One area of concern for many gifted children is a lack of good academic work habits. Many times school work comes easily for these children, and they may take success in school for granted. As a result of this, gifted children frequently neglect to learn how to apply themselves. They also do not learn effective study skills. When and if they encounter challenging and difficult work, they frequently struggle because of this lack.

Some gifted and talented children get into problems in school because they are divergent thinkers. Although it is sad to say, there are many classrooms, even at the elementary and middle school level, in which teachers feel threatened by children who have different ideas and opinions. While teachers want to encourage creative thinking, they also want children to conform to a certain extent. When this becomes a contradiction, what usually gets sacrificed is children's freedom to be inventive and divergent.

Many gifted and talented children lose interest in school at an early age. The lack of challenge and intellectually engaging work creates a sense of boredom and discouragement. Because these children frequently feel that they have nothing to learn in school, they may drop out or persist in being disruptive and disrespectful in the classroom.

Quite frequently, children who are gifted and talented also have difficult relationships with their parents and other family members (Conroy, 1987; Lester & Anderson, 1981; West, Hosie, & Mathews, 1989). Some parents feel uncomfortable that their child is "different." Some parents are overconcerned and overprotective, pressuring their child to be the "best." These parents may need special information, understanding, and support to be able to meet their children's needs and feel positive about their ability to parent.

Intervention Strategies

Just as with most other groups of children, with gifted and talented children counselors can intervene directly with the children, they can consult with or provide direct services to parents, or they can consult with teachers. Depending on the needs of the children and the job description, counselors will probably want to choose some combination of these various service delivery systems.

Working with children. "The most effective counseling for gifted students will continue to be that which can be internalized and become part of their own value systems" (Brown, 1993). Counselors will probably want to offer services to help children cope with the concerns and issues listed earlier in this section. They can offer social skills training and/or group counseling to practice ways to enhance interpersonal relationships. They can also offer relaxation training to help children with their drive for perfection and their resultant stress. A study skills group designed specifically for gifted children in which counselors discuss effective time management, assessment of study skills, and other related topics could be invaluable to gifted and talented students who are struggling because of deficits in this area.

Another valuable contribution that counselors could make to these children would be to provide a support group for them. In this group, the children could talk about the difficulty with being "different" and how they are handling their feelings of isolation. Counselors might also want to help them find a mentor who could support them in their area of interest (Kaufmann, Harrel, Milam, Woolverton, & Miller, 1986). Both of these situations would give these children an avenue for expressing themselves and for getting social and emotional support.

With children who like to read, counselors might also use a bibliocounseling approach, emphasizing fiction that focuses on gifted and talented children and biographies of famous individuals who were gifted and talented (Brown, 1993). Many children in the intermediate grades and middle school/junior high can also benefit from journal writing. This activity allows them the opportunity to express their thoughts and feelings and encourages them to explore more deeply.

Working with parents. Having a gifted and talented child in the family "(a) alters normal family roles, (b) affects parents' feeling about themselves, (c) requires the family to make several adaptations, and (d) often produces special family-neighborhood and family-school issues" (West et al., 1989). In work with parents of gifted and talented children, it might be helpful to discuss the social/emotional needs that are usually concerns for this group of children (Lester & Anderson, 1981). Counselors will want to help parents stop pressuring or overprotecting their children. They may also teach parents to help their children deal with being "different" and to learn ways of fitting in without sacrificing what makes them unique and special.

If the family is experiencing tensions between the siblings, counselors can give the parent(s) some guidance about this issue (Lester & Anderson, 1981). It is essential that parents avoid comparing the children with one another and encourage each child to gain significance in a different way. Parents can convey acceptance to each of the children in the family for just being themselves and not get overly invested in their accomplishments.

Conroy (1987) outlined a three-session parent education group for parents of gifted children. During the first session, the group discussed definitions of giftedness and methods of identifying gifted children. The second session covered the social/emotional needs of gifted children, their cognitive needs, several ways of meeting those needs, and typical difficulties faced by gifted individuals. In the third session, the group explored resources that were available locally and their personal areas of successful parenting. This group afforded the school counselor a way to communicate with the parents of gifted children and give them some tools to help their children as well as providing social/emotional support for the parents.

Working with teachers.   In consulting with teachers about optimizing the learning experience for gifted and talented students, counselors will want to help teachers create a responsive atmosphere in their classrooms by assisting them in the implementation of the following ideas for interacting with students. Teachers should:

1. Accept and expand upon students' ideas in a supportive and enthusiastic way.
2. Let students know that they hear and understand their feelings.
3. Give the students freedom to make choices.
4. Encourage students instead of criticizing them.
5. Build opportunities for success into the curriculum.
6. Stop and listen to students.
7. Allow time during instruction for student discussion.
8. Be accepting and enthusiastic about divergent and innovative ideas and methods of getting things done.
9. Build opportunities for social interaction and practicing relationship skills into the daily activities.
10. Accept mistakes in themselves and in others as opportunities for learning and for demonstrating the "courage to be imperfect."
11. Allow ambiguity and not demand immediate closure.
12. Gauge expectations of students so that they are challenged, but not overwhelmed.
13. Help students make goals and practice problem-solving and decision-making skills.
14. Be authentic and "real" with the students, not put up a facade.

If teachers follow these basic guidelines, it will help all the children intellectually, emotionally, and socially, not just the gifted children.

Counselors might also help teachers with an in-service on (a) the different types of giftedness; (b) the social and emotional concerns of gifted and talented students, especially their feeling of being "different"; (c) the problems with study skills and underachievement; and (d) family and parenting concerns. It is essential to clarify that, despite the fact that these children have strong native abilities, they need just as much (or more) help and support as do the other children in the school.

Some teachers will have emotional reactions to gifted children that can interfere with their interactions with these students. Many teachers feel challenged and/or threatened by children who are more talented or more knowledgeable in certain areas than the teachers are. These teachers may react with belligerence, trying to embarrass or humiliate the students to show that they have power over them. They may be intimidated by these students and allow the children to control the class. There are other teachers who believe that gifted and talented children must "live up to their potential" and proceed to pressure the children beyond reasonable expectations.

In these situations, counselors will need to explore the underlying personal issues of the teacher and help him or her to stop letting these issues interfere in their interactions with students. Sometimes these intrapersonal and interpersonal difficulties may be so deep-seated that counselors will want to refer the teacher to private counseling. If this solution is not possible and the counseling/consultation has not resulted in a change in the situation, counselors would probably want to avoid scheduling gifted and talented students in this teacher's class.

Children of Color

"Minority children and adolescents are the most rapidly growing segment of the youth population in America; yet, very little literature is available to enlighten clinicians, educators, health professionals, and social workers about their problems and needs" (Gibbs, Huang, & Associates, 1989, p. xv). Because there has not been very much written about counseling children of color, it is difficult for school counselors to find out about the concerns of members of the various ethnic and racial minorities and about intervention strategies that work. However, it is essential that counselors learn to better address the needs of children of color because they "face daily challenges to their success and self-esteem" (Miller, 1989, pp. xi).

Space limitations in this section prevent us from discussing intervention strategies for every group of racially, ethnically, or culturally different children. We have chosen to address some generic concerns and strategies for working with children from cultural and ethnic minorities. We recognize that each child is a unique and special individual with issues and concerns that may have nothing to do with the "group" he or she belongs to. However, we have tried to do the best we can given the limited space and small number of resources available that concern children of color.

Sue (1978) suggested that to be culturally effective, counselors must:

1. Gain an understanding of their own values and philosophical beliefs about the nature of people and their behavior. They must also recognize and accept that some other people have beliefs that differ from theirs.

2. Realize that counseling theories are not politically or morally neutral.

3. Recognize that many forces (sociological, political, economic) have strong influences on forming the personalities and interactional styles of people of racial and ethnic minorities.

4. Be able to project themselves into the world view of their clients and break out of their own cultural encapsulation.

5. Have the experience and training to allow themselves to select techniques and methods of counseling that fit the culture and specific issues of each of their clients.

We have adapted the following guidelines for enhancing the self-concepts of children of color from a list of suggestions developed by Locke (1989) designed to foster the self-esteem of African-American students:

1. Be open and honest in your interactions with children. Invite discussions about culturally and ethnically different attitudes and behaviors, and be open to input from students and parents about their culture.

2. Be aware of your own cultural background, since it is more likely that you will be able to be excited about other people's backgrounds if you are excited about your own.

3. Learn to truly value and respect other people's cultural beliefs, attitudes, and actions. Show that you believe other cultures are valuable and important.

4. Try to participate in as many experiences related to minority cultures as possible. Involve people from the African-American, Latin-American, Asian-American, Native-American, and other minority communities in activities in your school. This fosters a connectedness between the school and various cultural and ethnic communities.

5. Remember to give equal weight to the fact that the minority children in your school are members of a specific ethnic/cultural group and that they are also unique and special individuals who are not the same as any other human being in the world.

6. Extinguish any personal behaviors that might convey racism or bigotry, and do not tolerate any prejudiced behavior in other adults or children.

7. Try to encourage the participation of other school personnel in activities that celebrate a variety of cultures. It is important to ensure that this is a schoolwide effort.

8. Avoid negative self-fulfilling prophesies by having high standards for *all* students.

9. Ask the students and other people who are knowledgeable about different cultures about the culture. As you learn, introduce the ideas and information that you gain in your conversations with other people.

10. Institute programs that foster multicultural awareness, and use materials and strategies that address the psychological development and specific needs of children of color.

In a position paper on cross-cultural and multicultural counseling, the American School Counselor Association (1988) advocated the following strategies for school counselors:

1. Include parents from a variety of different cultures and ethnic groups in curriculum planning committees, guidance and counseling advisory boards, and other school projects.

2. Offer workshops designed to orient parents from cultural minority groups to the school's educational philosophy and services available for them and their children.

3. Sponsor in-service workshops for faculty and other school personnel on multicultural issues and strategies for working with children of color and their families.

4. Work to include culturally varied personnel and resources in the educational system and the guidance and counseling curriculum.

5. Support schoolwide experiences that celebrate differences and contributions of various minority groups.

6. Coordinate liaison services that work to improve the communication among different groups in the school and the community.

7. Eliminate resource materials, both in the academic and the guidance and counseling curricula, that contain cultural or ethnic biases or stereotypes.

We recognize that we have barely touched the surface of the issues involved in counseling children of color. In order to be able to begin to meet the needs of these children, counselors will need much more information about specific minority groups. They will also need information about explicit counseling issues and strategies that are effective with different groups of people. While the resources are limited, there are sources that counselors can use to begin to gather this information. In 1989, Gerler edited a special issue of *Elementary School Guidance and Counseling* on cross-cultural counseling with children in schools. Parker (1989) wrote an annotated bibliography in cross-cultural counseling for elementary and middle school children that can help counselors find more information in this area. Vargas and Koss-Chioino (1992) edited a book that addresses psychotherapeutic interventions with ethnic minority children and adolescents. Gibbs, Huang, and Associates (1989) wrote a book that describes psychological interventions with minority youth. While both of these books were written with mental health practitioners in mind, they can still be valuable resources for learning about ways to work with children of color in the schools. These resources will at least start counselors on their way to learning more about working to optimize the educational experiences of children of color. As counselors open their hearts and minds to this topic, they will grow both personally and professionally.

CONCLUSION

We have stressed throughout this volume that elementary and middle school counselors should be working with *all* children. As time passes, and the changes in our society continue to affect more children's lives, the need for knowledge about specific populations of children will also grow. The children described in this chapter and in the articles and books listed in Appendix J are rapidly becoming the majority of the students in today's elementary and middle schools. As we move into the beginning of the next century, school counselors will need personal and professional resources that enable them to equip themselves with the information and the training they need to work with a rapidly expanding variety of children.

We have designed this book as a kind of roadmap to help counselors begin to gather these resources. Good luck and remember to have fun along the way.

REFERENCES

Abikoff, H. (1985). Efficacy of cognitive training interventions in hyperactive children: A critical review. *Clinical Psychology Review, 5,* 479–512.

Amato, P., & Ochiltree, G. (1987). Child and adolescent competence in intact, one-parent, and stepfamilies: An Australian Study. *Journal of Divorce, 10,* 75–96.

American Academy of Child and Adolescent Psychiatry. (1991). Children of alcoholics. *Facts for Families, 17,* 9–10.

American Psychiatric Association. (1994). *Diagnostic and statistical manual of mental disorders* (4th ed.). Washington, DC: Author.

American School Counselor Association. (1988). Position statement on cross/multicultural counseling. Alexandria, VA: Author.

Barclay, R. (1990). *Attention Deficit Hyperactivity Disorder: A handbook for diagnosis and treatment.* New York: Guilford.

Barnette, B. (1989). A program to meet the emotional and social needs of gifted and talented adolescents. *Journal of Counseling and Development, 67,* 525–528.

Bettner, B., & Lew, A. (1990). *Raising kids who can.* New York: Harper/Collins.

Betts, G. (1986). Development of the emotional and social needs of gifted individuals. *Journal of Counseling and Development, 64,* 587–589.

Biederman, J., Baldessarini, R., Wright, V., Knee, D., & Hermatz, J. (1989). A double-blind placebo controlled study of desipramine in the treatment of ADD: I. Efficacy. *Journal of the American Academy of Child and Adolescent Psychiatry, 28,* 777–784.

Black, C. (1981). Innocent bystanders at risk: The children of alcoholics. *Alcoholism: The National Magazine, 1*(3), 22–26.

Black, C. (1982). *My dad loves me, my dad has a disease.* Denver: MAC.

Blackburn, A., & Erickson, D. (1986). Predictable crises of the gifted student. *Journal of Counseling and Development, 64,* 552–556.

Bowerman, C., & Irish, D. (1962). Some relationships of stepchildren to their parents. *Marriage and Family Living, 24,* 113–121.

Brake, K. (1988). Counseling young children of alcoholics. *Elementary School Guidance and Counseling, 23,* 106–111.

Brown, L. (1993). Special considerations in counseling gifted students. *The School Counselor, 40,* 184–190.

Burke, D., & Van de Streek, L. (1989). Children of divorce: An application of Hammond's group counseling for children. *Elementary School Guidance and Counseling, 24,* 112–117.

Buwick, A., Martin, D., & Martin, M. (1988). Helping children deal with alcoholism in their families. *Elementary School Guidance and Counseling, 23,* 112–117.

Callan, V., & Jackson, D. (1986). Children of alcoholic fathers and recovered alcoholic fathers: Personal and family functioning. *Journal of Studies on Alcohol, 47,* 180–182.

Cantrell, R. (1986). Adjustment to divorce: Three components to assist children. *Elementary School Guidance and Counseling, 20,* 163–172.

C.H.A.D.D. (Children and Adults with Attention Deficit Disorders). (1992). *Educators manual: Attention Deficit Disorders.* Plantation, FL: Author.

Children's Defense Fund. (1982). *America's children and their families: Key facts.* Washington, DC: Author.

Conroy, E. (1987). Primary prevention for gifted students: A parent education group. *Elementary School Guidance and Counseling, 22,* 110–116.

Counseling and Personnel Services Clearinghouse. (1986). *Helping children cope with divorce: The school counselor's role.* Ann Arbor, MI: Author.

Crosbie-Burnett, M., & Newcomer, L. (1989). A multimodal intervention for group counseling with children of divorce. *Elementary School Guidance and Counseling, 23,* 155–166.

Crosbie-Burnett, M., & Pulvino, C. (1990). Children in nontraditional families: A classroom guidance program. *The School Counselor, 37,* 286–293.

Culin, C. (1979). *Cages of glass, flowers of time..* Scarsdale, N Y: Bradbury.

Drake, E. (1981). Helping children cope with divorce: The role of the school. In I. Stuart & L. Abts (Eds.), *Children of separation and divorce: Management and treatment.* New York: Van Nostrand Reinhold.

Ellison, F. (1983). Issues concerning parental harmony and children's psychosocial adjustment. *American Journal of Orthopsychiatry, 53,* 73–80.

Evans, M. (1986). *This is me and my two families.* New York: Magination.

Fisher, G. (1989). Counseling strategies for children based on rules and roles in alcoholic families. *The School Counselor, 36,* 173–178.

Ganong, L., & Coleman, M. (1984). Stepparent: A pejorative term? *Psychological Reports, 52,* 919–922.

Gardner, R. (1984). Counseling children in stepfamilies. *Elementary School Guidance and Counseling, 19,* 40–49.

Gehret, J. (1991). *Eagle eyes: A child's view of Attention Deficit Disorder.* Fairport, NY: Verbal Images.

Gerler, E. (Ed.) (1989). Special issue on cross-cultural counseling. *Elementary School Guidance and Counseling, 23.*

Gibbs, J., Huang, L., & Associates. (1989). *Children of color: Psychological interventions with minority youth.* San Francisco, CA: Jossey-Bass.

Goldstein, S., & Goldstein, M. (1990). *Managing attention disorders in children: A guide for practitioners.* New York: Wiley.

Gomez, K., & Cole, C. (1991). Attention Deficit Hyperactivity Disorder: A review of treatment alternatives. *Elementary School Guidance and Counseling, 26,* 106–114.

Gordon, M. (1991). *ADHD/Hyperactivity: A consumer's guide.* DeWitt, NY: GSI Publications.

Guevremont, D. (1990). Social skills and peer relationship training. In R. Barkley (Ed.), *Attention Deficit Hyperactivity Disorder: A handbook for diagnosis and treatment* (pp. 540–572). New York: Guilford.

Hall, C., Beougher, K., & Wasinger, K. (1991). Divorce: Implications for services. *Psychology in the Schools, 28,* 267–275.

Hammond, M., & Chestnut, L. (1986). *My mom doesn't look like an alcoholic.* Pompano Beach, FL: Heath Communications.

Hastings, J., & Typpo, (1984). *An elephant in the living room.* Minneapolis, MN: CompCare.

Henker, B., & Whalen, C. (1989). Hyperactivity and attention deficits. *American Psychologist, 44,* 216–223.

Hetherington, E., Cox, M., & Cox, R. (1982). Effects of divorce on parents and children. In M. Lamb (Ed.), *Non-traditional families* (pp. 233–288). Hillsdale, NJ: Erlbaum.

Hetherington, E., Stanley-Hagan, M., & Anderson, E. (1989). Marital transitions: A child's perspective. *American Psychologist, 22,* 303–312.

Ingersoll, B. (1988). *Your hyperactive child: A parent's guide to coping with Attention Deficit Disorder.* New York: Doubleday.

Janos, P., & Robinson, N. (1985). Psychological development in intellectually gifted children. In F. Horowitz & M. O'Brian (Eds.), *The gifted and talented: Developmental perspectives* (pp. 180–187). Washington, DC: American Psychological Association.

Johnson, H. (1988). Drugs, dialogue, or diet: Diagnosing and treating the hyperactive child. *Social Work, 33,* 349–355.

Kantrowitz, R., & Wingert, P. (1990, Winter–Spring). Step by step. *Newsweek Special Issue, 114,* pp. 24–28.

Kaplan, S., Madsen, S., Gould, B., Platow, J., & Renzulli, J. (1979). *Inservice training manual: Activities for identification/program planning for the gifted/talented.* Ventura, CA: National/State Leadership Training Institute on the Gifted and Talented.

Kaufmann, F., Harrel, G., Milam, C., Woolverton, N., & Miller J. (1986). The nature, role and influence of mentors in the lives of gifted adults. *Journal of Counseling and Development, 64,* 576–579.

Kirkwood, G. (1986, January). Blended families: America's confusing phenomenon. *Colorado State Magazine,* 41–43.

Kottman, T., Robert, R., & Baker, D. (in press). Parental perspectives on Attention-deficit Hyperactivity Disorder: How school counselors can help. *The School Counselor.*

Lavin, P. (1991). The counselor as consultant-coordinator for children with Attention Deficit Hyperactivity Disorder. *Elementary School Guidance and Counseling, 26,* 115–120.

Leite, E., & Espeland, P. (1987). *Different like me.* Minneapolis, MN: Johnson Institute.

Lester, C., & Anderson, R. (1981). Counseling with families of gifted children: The school counselor's role. *The School Counselor, 29,* 147–151.

Levine, E., & Tucker, S. (1986). Emotional needs of gifted children: A preliminary phenomenological view. *The Creative Child and Adult Quarterly, 11,* 156–165.

Locke, D. C. (1989). Fostering the self-esteem of African-American children. *Elementary School Guidance and Counseling, 23,* 254–259.

Lutz, P. (1983). The stepfamily: An adolescent perspective. *Family Relations, 32,* 367–375.

Lutz, P., Jacobs, E., & Masson, R. (1981). Stepfamily counseling: Issues and guidelines. *The School Counselor, 28,* 189–194.

Miller, G. (1989). Foreward. In J. Gibbs, L. Huang, & Associates, *Children of color: Psychological interventions with minority youth* (pp.xi–xii). San Francisco, CA: Jossey-Bass.

Norris, G. (1970). *Take my walking slow.* New York: Atheneum.

O'Rourke, K. (1990). Recapturing hope: Elementary school support groups for children of alcoholics. *Elementary School Guidance and Counseling, 25,* 107–115.

Parker, L. (1989). An annotated bibliography in cross-cultural counseling for elementary and middle school counselors. *Elementary School Guidance and Counseling, 23,* 313–321.

Prosen, S., & Farmer, J. (1982). Understanding stepfamilies: Issues and implications for counselors. *Personnel and Guidance Journal, 60,* 393–397.

Quinn, P., & Stern, J. (1991). *Putting on the brakes: Young people's guide to understanding Attention Deficit Hyperactivity Disorder.* New York: Magination.

Rice, J. (1985). *The gifted* (rev. ed.). Springfield, IL: Charles C Thomas.

Santrock, J., Warshak, R., Lindbergh, C., & Meadows, L. (1982). Children's and parents' observed social behavior in stepfather families. *Child Development, 53,* 472–480.

Schlesinger, B. (1982). Children's viewpoint of living in a one-parent family. *Journal of Divorce, 5,* 1–23.

Skeen, P., Covi, R., & Robinson, B. (1985). Stepfamilies: A review of the literature with suggestions for practitioners. *Journal of Counseling and Development, 64,* 121–125.

Sprinthall, N., Hall, J., & Gerler, E. (1992). Peer counseling for middle school students experiencing family divorce: A deliberate psychological education model. *Elementary School Guidance and Counseling, 26,* 279–294.

Stern, P. (1978). Stepfather families: Integration around child discipline. *Issues in Mental Health Nursing, 1,* 326–332.

Stolberg, A., Camplair, C., Currier, K., & Wells, M. (1987). Individual, familial, and environmental determinants of children's post-divorce adjustment and maladjustment. *Journal of Divorce, 11,* 51–70.

Strangeland, C., Pellegreno, D., & Lundhold, C. (1989). Children of divorced parents: A perceptual comparison. *Elementary School Guidance and Counseling, 23,* 167–173.

Sue, D. (1978). Counseling across cultures. *Personnel and Guidance Journal, 55,* 422–425.

Thompson, C., & Rudolph, L. (1992). *Counseling children* (3rd ed.). Monterey, CA: rooks/Cole.

Touliatos, J., & Linholm, B. (1980). Teachers' perceptions of behavior problems in children from intact, single-parent and stepparent families. *Psychology in the Schools, 17,* 264–269.

Turnbull, S., & Turnbull, J. (1983). To dream the impossible dream: An agenda for discussion with stepparents. *Family Relations, 32,* 227–230.

Vargas, L., & Koss-Chioino, J. (1992). *Working with culture.* San Francisco, CA: Jossey Bass.

Wallerstein, J., & Blakeslee, S. (1989). *Second chances: Men, women, and children a decade after divorce.* New York: Ticknor & Fields.

Wallerstein, J., & Kelly, J. (1980). *Surviving the breakup: How children and parents cope with divorce.* New York: Basic Books.

Walsh, W. (1992). Twenty major issues in remarriage families. *Journal of Counseling and Development, 70,* 709–725.

Webb, W. (1993). Cognitive behavior therapy with children of alcoholics. *The School Counselor, 40,* 170–177.

Wegscheider-Cruise, S. (1985). *Choice-making.* Pompano Beach, FL: Health Communications.

Wender, P. (1987). *The hyperactive child, adolescent, and adult: Attention Deficit Disorder through the life span.* New York: Oxford University.

Werner, E. (1986). Resilient offspring of alcoholics: A longitudinal study from birth to age 18. *Journal of Studies on Alcohol, 47,* 34–41.

West, J., Hosie, T., & Mathers, F.N. (1989). Families of academically gifted children: Adaptability and cohesion. *The School Counselor, 37,* 121–127.

Wilson, J., & Blocher, L. (1990). The counselor's role in assisting children of alcoholics. *Elementary School Guidance and Counseling, 25,* 98–106.

Yauman, B. (1991). School-based group counseling for children of divorce: A review of the literature. *Elementary Guidance and Counseling, 26,* 130–138.

Chapter Eleven

Working with Families

🌳 Several years ago, I (T. K.) was presenting a workshop on at-risk children to a group of school counselors and school administrators at a conference. One of the main points I made was that it was absolutely essential for school counselors—especially those at the elementary and middle school levels—to learn the skills and gain the confidence and experience necessary to work with families. A member of the audience raised his hand and explained that, with all of the other duties he performed as a school counselor (and he had a very long list of valid and appropriate tasks that could have easily taken 80 hours a week to accomplish), he simply did not have time to add one more responsibility to his job. He ended his comments with the words, "As much as I'd like to counsel the families, I just can't afford the time." Another counselor in the group stood up and said in a very firm voice, "I do all of those things too, but even if I can't afford the time to provide counseling for families, I can't afford not to." With that verbal volley these two combatants drew the battle lines, and the entire group got involved in a heated discussion about the need for school counselors to use family therapy interventions with families. I never did get a chance to finish my "prepared remarks."

This scenario seems to represent the continuing struggle within the profession. Palmo, Lowry, Weldon, and Scioscia (1984) explained the crux of this dilemma:

> School counselors have often addressed the problem of attempting to work with the child but not having access to other family members. Family counseling may not always be a viable alternative for the school counselor, but family counseling has often been considered necessary for treating the child in the school setting. (pp. 272–273)

There is no one "right" answer to the debate about whether school counselors should provide family therapy for the children in their schools. Each individual school counselor, based on his or her job description, work setting, and student population, will have to decide whether it is appropriate and/or imperative to offer some form of counseling intervention with families.

We have written this chapter as a resource for those school counselors who decide that it is important to incorporate family therapy into the list of services they offer. This chapter consists of (a) a rationale for including some type of family therapy service through the schools, (b) several perspectives on how well-adjusted families function, (c) a description of the three primary delivery systems used to provide family therapy services in schools, (d) an outline of important general family systems theory concepts and techniques, and (e) a description and examples of elementary and middle school applications of several selected family systems approaches.

Why School Counselors Should Know and Use Family Therapy Theory and Techniques

Elementary or middle school counselors cannot ignore the impact of families on children. Since family dynamics have such a tremendous impact on children's academic, social, and emotional behavior, counselors need to learn about family systems and how they affect children so that they can better understand children's behaviors in school (Golden, 1993; Goldenberg & Goldenberg, 1988; McDaniel, 1981). Counselors can use general systems theory to help them gain a new perspective as they evaluate and conceptualize children's classroom behavior. Systems theory provides "a means of understanding classroom behavior by shifting one's perspective from the individual child to include the child's family. A child's classroom behavior may then be understood in the broader context of family interactions" (Worden, 1981, p. 178). Even if counselors choose not to provide family therapy, they can still use family therapy theories to better understand family dynamics and motivation and family therapy strategies to communicate with parents and other family members and to bring about changes in family interactions and children's behavior (Golden, 1993; Goldenberg & Goldenberg, 1988; Peeks, 1993; Thompson & Rudolph, 1992; Turnbull & Turnbull, 1990).

The case for including some type of family intervention as part of the counseling and guidance program stems from a number of different perspectives. Goldenberg and Goldenberg (1988) contended that "intervention at the family level, especially in a dysfunctional family, may be the most effective way to change the child's behavior and help the family gain (or regain) coping skills" (p. 28). Amatea and Brown (1993) suggested that school personnel frequently overlook families as a resource that they can access to bring about better understanding of students and motivation for change.

Nicoll (1984) believed, based on the constantly increasing demands on school counselors' time, that "counseling strategies demonstrated to be more effective and economical—such as family counseling—need to be increasingly developed and employed in school counseling programs" (p. 280). He summarized many of the reasons for providing some type of family counseling services through the school guidance and counseling program as follows: (a) greater communication and coordination among the significant adults in a child's life, (b) the ability of the school counselor to be a child advocate who helps parents and/or teachers better understand child behavior and motivation, (c) significant monetary savings on the part of families who need help, but cannot afford private counseling services, and (d) enhanced efficacy of school counseling services in the form of significantly increased changes in child behavior and family functioning.

Characteristics of Well-Adjusted Families

In order to help families improve their interpersonal interactions and the behavior and attitudes of family members, the counselor needs to be able to recognize a healthy or "functional" (Golden, 1993) family. There are, of course, many different definitions of the healthy family. Each family systems theory has its own list of traits that characterize a functional family, as do most counselors who work with families. Families exist on a continuum that ranges from very troubled and chaotic to relatively problem-free. Counselors will have to evaluate the various descriptions to determine which characteristics they believe are important in a happy, supportive family that provides a safe and encouraging environment for children. These are the characteristics that counselors will want to encourage in families, no matter how they decide to work with them.

Each major family systems therapy model has a vision of the ideal family and of the dysfunctional family. In Virginia Satir's model (Green & Kolevzon, 1984; Satir, 1972; Thompson & Rudolph, 1992), healthy families are characterized by congruent communication in which family members can "say what they feel and think in undisguised ways without fear of retribution, retaliation, or rejection by other family members" (Green & Kolevzon, 1984, p. 11). Unhealthy families communicate in incogruent modes, disguising or ignoring true feelings. In healthy families, the rules are flexible and subject to alteration, depending on the situation. Rules are clearly articulated, and the members of the family understand how rules evolved and why they are important. In dysfunctional families, rules are inflexible and covert. Members do not know how or why rules were formulated, nor do they understand how to change them when needed. According to Satir (1972), individuals from functional families have strong and satisfying links to people outside their families, whereas individuals from dysfunctional families have disturbed and unhappy relationships with society.

Murray Bowen's (1978) model of family health is based on differentiation and family boundaries (Friedman, 1991). The more differentiated the family members, the healthier the family. In functional families, members have distinct boundaries, demonstrate empathy for others, have positive interpersonal relationships, and are logical and rational (Goldenberg & Goldenberg, 1991; Green & Kolevzon, 1984).

In the structural model of family therapy, counselors look at boundaries, rules, and flexibility (Colapinto, 1991; Minuchin & Fishman, 1981; Nichols & Schwartz, 1991). Minuchin (1974) used family subsystem boundaries as a measure of family functioning. He described healthy families as having appropriate, but flexible boundaries, with closeness between subsystems changing in response to different circumstances and the life cycle of the family (Green & Kolevzon, 1984). Families with problems exhibit either enmeshment, characterized by excessive closeness, or disengagement, characterized by a lack of cohesion. Healthy families have well-defined structures of authority and clearly defined rules (Colapinto, 1991). They respond to changes in life situations and normal family development with flexibility. Members of healthy families are also willing to abandon unsuccessful problem-solving strategies and to try new solutions to difficulties.

Ponzetti and Long (1989) reviewed the research on healthy functioning families. They found that the most consistent characteristic of healthy families was a strong marital relationship between the parents. They also found that healthy families typically share mutual interests, have effective communication patterns, can effectively adapt to change, have a sense of mutual respect, are capable of engaging in problem solving and decision making, are willing to share household responsibilities, and enjoy each others' company and have fun together.

Curran (1985) listed fifteen traits of healthy families. According to her, members of well-functioning families:

1. Communicate and listen.
2. Affirm and support one another.
3. Teach one another respect for others.
4. Trust other people.
5. Have a sense of humor and play.
6. Show a sense of shared responsibility.
7. Teach one another a sense of right and wrong.
8. Have a strong sense of family in which tradition and shared rituals are important.
9. Have a sense of balance in their interaction with one another.
10. Have a shared religious or spiritual core.
11. Respect one another's privacy.
12. Value service to others.
13. Foster time together at meals for sharing and conversation.
14. Share leisure activities.
15. Recognize and acknowledge difficulties and seek help—from one another and from resources outside the family.

Family Systems Intervention Delivery Systems

When school counselors decide that it is important and necessary to include parents and other family members in the process of trying to help children, they have several options in terms of service delivery. The school district could create positions for professionals specifically trained in family therapy who would come into the school and provide therapy for children and their families, but would not have any of the other duties of a school counselor. The district could also make some type of arrangement for a family therapy clinic to provide family therapy to the families within the school district at no cost, as an adjunct to the district's guidance and counseling services. In the real world of financial woe and belt-tightening, however, these options are relatively rare.

In a more realistic vein, counselors could (a) use their knowledge of family systems to help them refer students and their families to family therapists in agencies and private practice (Amatea & Fabrick, 1984; Whiteside, 1983), (b) arrange for some type of consultation relationship with a family therapist in which the counselor works with the family based on suggestions from the consultant (Golden, 1988, 1993; Goodman & Kjonaas, 1984; Green, 1985), or (c) provide a systems-based intervention program themselves (Amatea & Brown, 1993; Amatea & Fabrick, 1981; Kern & Carlson, 1981; Mullis & Berger, 1981; Nicoll, 1984; Steele & Raider, 1991; Stone & Peeks, 1986). Some counselors will combine these three different approaches, depending on the family and the situation. Whether or not they choose to refer or to provide some kind of school-sponsored family therapy may depend on the district policy, their level of comfort and training in family therapy, and the population of families that their school serves.

Referring

Referring families for family counseling is a delicate operation (Amatea & Fabrick, 1984; Whiteside, 1993). No matter that the counselor is not trying to blame or shame them, most families assume that a referral for family therapy suggests that the family is part of or even the cause of the child's problems (Haley, 1990). Although parents frequently realize that they are involved in the dynamics of the problem, they may be afraid that counselors are going to tell them that they are bad parents and, perhaps, bad human beings. Counselors will need to use their best counseling skills when they make a suggestion to parents that family therapy would be the best option for helping their child.

The referral process usually follows a predictable pattern. The school counselor (a) collects information about the child, the family, and the situation; (b) makes a decision that referral is the most appropriate option; (c) actively assists the family in following through on the referral; and (d) provides continuing support for the family and serves as a liason between the family therapist and the school (Amatea & Fabrick, 1984). Before counselors can decide whether a family needs help and might be willing to take advantage of family counseling services, they will have to build a relationship with the various members of the family so that they can gather data. They must look at the severity of the difficulty, and the needs, strengths, and weaknesses of the family system (Amatea & Fabrick, 1984). One model of assessing families for referral was formulated by Golden (1988). He suggested that school counselors restrict the families they attempt to help to those within the "functional" range on the continuum of family health and refer families from within the "dysfunctional" range on the continuum. Golden (1993) listed five variables that distinguish a functional from a dysfunctional family: (a) parental resources, (b) time frame of problem behavior, (c) type and amount of communication, (d) hierarchy of authority, and (e) rapport between helping adults. School counselors can gather data about family performance on each of these variables in order to determine whether to refer the family to family therapy.

In assessing parental resources, the counselor examines the parent(s)' ability to provide for the child's basic needs and the ability to follow through on behavioral plans. Factors such as a supportive extended family, financial stability, and a strong marriage contribute to a family's ability to function. According to this model, if the family has strong parental resources, the counselor might want to intervene rather than refer. The time frame of the problem behavior is important because children and/or families with chronic difficulties are harder to help than those with short-term difficulties. Counselors would be more likely to refer a family with a chronic problem.

The counselor examines communication patterns to determine whether the family members can communicate well enough to solve problems. Families on the well-adjusted end of the continuum of functioning have more open communication patterns, even when the members are under stress, than do families on the poorly adjusted end of the continuum, and they would be accessible enough for direct intervention by the school counselor.

The counselor also assesses the hierarchy of authority in the family. In more functional families, the parent(s) hold the "executive" authority and the children have age-appropriate responsibility and freedom. The final important factor in Golden's model is the rapport between the parent(s) and helping professionals. In more functional families, the parent(s) demonstrate reliable and responsive behavior toward the helper and the counseling process. If the hierarchy of authority is unbalanced or the parents do not seem open and amenable to the family therapy process, counselors will probably want to refer them.

Even after counselors have made the decision to refer a family for family therapy, they must continue to develop a collaborative relationship with both the parents and the children (Amatea & Fabrick, 1984). Family members are much more willing and able to hear potentially painful suggestions from a person they trust who conveys respect and support. In order to demonstrate this collaborative attitude, counselors should continue to solicit the parent(s)' perceptions and thoughts about the problem, possible solutions, and alternative strategies for intervention.

Counselors may want to tailor their approach to referral based on the family dynamics and the amount of cooperation they anticipate receiving from the family. Whiteside (1993) characterized families as having three different levels of cooperation: maximum, intermediate, and minimum. Families who demonstrate the maximum level of cooperation discuss with counselors their belief that the family needs outside help. Quite frequently parents of families in this category approach the school counselor and request help, acknowledging that there is a family problem and asking for a referral. In this case, counselors can do some educating about family systems. Their primary job is to help the family choose an appropriate therapist. It is important to remember that even those families who realize that all the members of the system have some level of responsibility for the problem and the solution are experiencing pain and embarrassment that they cannot solve their own problems. Counselors will need to demonstrate empathy, respect, and support in their interactions with these families (Whiteside, 1993).

In referrals with intermediate cooperation, the counselor knows that the family wants to help the child but may not be aware of or willing to acknowledge the family system's role in the problem (Whiteside, 1993). The counseling approach with these parents will need to be more subtle. Counselors will need to contact the parent(s), stress the seriousness of the problem, and suggest that family therapy could be beneficial for all members of the family. In order to short circuit the defenses of the family, counselors should restrain themselves from teaching about systems thinking and allow families to continue to think that the child is the main problem and that their primary role in the family therapy will be to provide support and guidance in helping the child work out his or her difficulty.

With families who show minimal cooperation, counselors suspect from the start that family members, especially the parent(s), will have a negative reaction to any suggestion that might have a part in the child's problem. The best approach seems to be to simply inform them that they need to seek outside help with the child without emphasizing the system component and then hope that they follow through and that the therapist they choose can involve the rest of the family in treatment (Whiteside, 1993). Counselors can sometimes disarm a family's defensiveness by being very matter-of-fact about the child's problems and stressing the fact that everyone involved, parent(s) and school personnel, want the best for the child. They may have to try to convince these parents of the severity of the problem and the lack of impact other solutions have had on the problem (Amatea & Fabrick, 1984).

It sometimes helps with resistant families to ask other school personnel, such as the principal and the school psychologist, to reinforce to the parent(s) the recommendation of therapy and to suggest to them that they have the most significant power to influence the child and his or her motivation and behavior (Amatea & Fabrick, 1984; Whiteside, 1993). However, in the authors' experience, bringing in reinforcements sometimes intimidates parents and evokes their defenses. Counselors may want to consider this possibility in planning their referring strategy with uncooperative families.

When giving parents a list of (at least three) possible therapists, counselors may want to make comments on the style, personality, and strengths of each of them. It is helpful to suggest therapists with whom counselors have a mutually respectful professional relationship and who are skilled at communicating and working cooperatively with schools (Whiteside, 1993). Counselors should make the suggestions in a clear, firm, and professional manner, conveying to the parents that they, as an expert in the field, have confidence that this is the right approach to helping the child (Amatea & Fabrick, 1984). Counselors must not undermine the authority of their recommendations by being tentative or conditional, because by being hesitant they might give parents an excuse for not acting upon this frightening and potentially painful decision.

After the family starts in therapy, counselors should disengage from the family so that they come to rely on the family therapist for support and suggestions on how they make changes in the system (Amatea & Fabrick, 1984). The counselor's primary function in the ongoing therapeutic process is to provide feedback to the parents and (with parental permission) to the family therapist about the child's school performance. If the family therapist makes suggestions about implementing changes in the classroom, the counselor may want to serve as a liason between the therapist and the teacher and as a consultant to the teacher for ways to operationalize the therapist's recommendations.

Consultation

Various authors have described projects in which schools provide family therapy to children and their families through a consultation model (Golden, 1988, 1993; Goldman & Kjonaas, 1984; Green, 1985). There are different ways to arrange the delivery of services with this model. In one brief family consultation model, school counselors serve as consultants to teachers, parents, and children, making concrete suggestions for behavior change (Golden, 1993). In another model, a school-based counselor provided family therapy while being observed by a consultant who provided supervision and suggestions for the process, using an intercom system, consulting breaks, and written messages (Goldman & Kjonaas, 1984). Green (1985) suggested a consulting model in which the school counselor serves as a therapist/consultant to both the school and the family, using a strategic systems-oriented approach. The goal of the therapist/consultant is to encourage a collaborative relationship between school personnel and family members in which they learn to communicate directly and appropriately, focusing on specific problems and system assets.

Direct Delivery of Family Therapy Services by School Counselors

One advantage to direct delivery of family therapy services by school counselors is that the logistics of this approach are less complex than those of consultation. Consultation arrangements can be awkward or complicated to set up, and some families are not comfortable with being observed by a consultant/supervisor, nor are they always eager to work with an unfamiliar person even in the school setting. Parents also seem to be more willing to seek services offered in a familiar setting by a known professional. They are less likely to follow through with referrals to outside agencies or private practitioners. Only 30 percent of referred families make any contact with outside resources, and 92 percent of those who do make the contact drop out of therapy in less than three sessions (Conti, 1971).

Training.   If school counselors want to provide family therapy, they must obtain the training and supervised practice necessary to learn how to apply systems-oriented intervention strategies in their schools (Goldenberg & Goldenberg, 1988; Hinkle, 1993; Nicoll, 1984; Palmo et al., 1984; Wilcoxon & Comas, 1987). More recent graduates may have already taken at least one course in family counseling, because many counselor education programs have begun to include these courses as either part of the core curriculum or as an elective offering (Wilcoxon & Comas, 1987). Quite a few practicing school counselors will need to return to graduate school or attend in-service training programs to take an introductory-level course in family counseling, an advanced course in specific family systems intervention strategies, and a supervised practicum or internship in working with families (Hinkle, 1993; Wilcoxon & Comas, 1987). If school counselors want training in specific theoretical orientations, they will probably need to seek out programs that specialize in a particular approach (Goldenberg & Goldenberg, 1988; Nicoll, 1984; Palmo et al., 1984).

Logistics.   If a counselor has the training, experience, and desire to provide short-term family therapy as a part of the guidance and counseling program, his or her school district will have to make several important adjustments to support the integration of these services (Palmo et al., 1984). The counselor will need administrative support for flexible hours, changes in the physical setting, the ability to accommodate special-needs families, expanded programs for parents, and year-round employment (Palmo et al., 1984). The counselor will have to have a flexible schedule so that she or he can meet with families at times when school is closed—evenings, summers, and such. The counselor will need to be able to have easy access to the school building during off hours. Depending on the size and layout of the counseling office, the counselor may want expanded space or more furniture, so that there is comfortable seating for an entire family.

Counselors may need more resources or personnel so that they can provide family counseling services for the families of the special-needs students in their school. Families of gifted, handicapped, and behavior disordered/emotionally disturbed students need specially designed programs. Counselors will also want to arrange for the district to offer a wide range of programs designed to educate and support parents and their involvement with their children's emotional and educational development. Counselors may want to provide those services, or they may want other school personnel to conduct programs such as parent support groups and parenting classes. If counselors want to continue to work with parents during the summer, they may want to be employed year-round, at least on a part-time basis. If the administration is willing to make these changes, counselors can stop talking about how important it is to be able to provide direct family therapy services to students and their families and just do it.

Family Systems Theory and Techniques

In order to begin to deliver family therapy as a function of the guidance and counseling program, the school counselor must understand the basic tenets of systems theory. He or she will also need to be able to use a wide variety of family therapy strategies when working with families.

Basic Tenets of Systems Theory

"Systems theory does not view the individual as having a fixed personality, or fixed traits, but as acting and reacting in response to contextual cues" (McDaniel, 1981, p. 216). According to systems thinking, an event or situation that affects one member of the system has reverberations in the entire system. In trying to understand individuals, counselors must always consider them in relationship to their role and function in the family system (Goldenberg & Goldenberg, 1991; Nichols & Schwartz, 1991; Worden, 1981). All members of the system are interrelated in "a circular causal chain with a constantly recurring pattern of actions and reactions" (Amatea & Fabrick, 1981, p. 225).

As counselors conceptualize the family as a living social system, they will examine the relationship of the subsystems, the goals, and the rules (Goldenberg & Goldenberg, 1991; Worden, 1981). The component parts of the family are the subsystems—the parental subsystem, sibling subsystems, spousal subsystem, and extended family subsystem (Steele & Raider, 1991; Worden, 1981). The family system has the capacity to formulate goals and to modify its structure and its goals to protect its stability. In order to achieve a homeostatic balance, the system uses feedback to limit stress to tolerable levels (Amatea & Fabrick, 1981; Goldenberg & Goldenberg, 1991). The system also uses family rules, both overt and covert, to protect the balance and stability of the family.

Generic Systems Treatment Strategies

While each theory of family therapy has its own particular intervention techniques, there are several systems-oriented strategies that are appropriate within most of the theories. Generally, the counselor's role in family therapy is more directive than the counselor's role in many individual counseling relationships (Amatea & Fabrick, 1981). Using family systems therapy, the counselor is an active and directive therapist prescribing specific behaviors, asking probing questions, and challenging family members to make behavioral changes. For example, in family therapy, the counselor would focus on making systemic changes. He or she might formulate a ritual in which the various members of the family must listen without talking to Sally for ten minutes during a session, then repeat the essence of what she has said to her to check out how well they had listened. The counselor might give the family a homework assignment that each member of the family must repeat this ritual on an individual basis with Sally each day during the course of the week. Family members would then report back to the counselor about what had happened.

In family therapy, it is usually important that the counselor find out the details of the specific presenting problem and of the solutions that the family has tried (Goldenberg & Goldenberg, 1991; McDaniel, 1981). The counselor asks questions about the problem and probes for each family member's perception of the problem and of attempted solutions. In family therapy, counselors believe that frequently attempted solutions become part of the problem. For instance, the Martinez family comes in complaining about their son, Paul, a first grade boy who is retreating into the bathroom and screaming and refusing to do his school work. The family therapist/school counselor would ask questions about when this behavior started, how often it occurs, how all of the family members feel about the problem, and how they are affected by it (Love, Chappell, & Boorheim, 1987). Exploring the attempted solutions, the school counselor would find out that Paul's mother comes to school several times a day to check on his behavior, to make sure that he is not "doing that embarrassing thing," and that his father does not feel that this behavior is a problem because, "after all, boys will be boys." In looking at the various family members' behavior and the interaction between the subsystems, the school counselor might begin to see patterns in the interactions within the family system.

In order to further understand these patterns, the school counselor may ask family members to describe a typical day. The Martinez family might describe their routines in getting up, having breakfast, getting Paul to school, what happens while he is at school, for both the parents and him, what happens after school, and so forth. This recital would help the counselor check out patterns of responsibility, power, support, discipline, and rules. The counselor might also ask the family to act out their usual interactions. He or she would ask this mother and father to act out their usual conversations about discipline and acceptable versus unacceptable child behavior.

The counselor might also direct family members to practice new communication patterns during a session (Amatea & Brown, 1993; Amatea & Fabrick, 1981). After teaching the family different ways of interacting, the counselor would provide the family with a chance to try out their new skills in a session before attempting to use them at home. With the Martinez family, the school counselor might teach Paul new ways of getting what he wants without screaming and yelling. The counselor might also put the father in charge of helping Paul act in an appropriate manner. Another approach to using session time to practice restructuring communication patterns would be for the counselor to suggest to the parents that they are using Paul and his behavior as a battleground in order to avoid directly confronting conflicts in their marriage. The counselor would ask them to honestly and directly talk about marital issues without using Paul and their disagreements about discipline as a way of covertly communicating their displeasure with one another.

The counselor may try to escalate the family's level of stress to see how the system's homeostatic mechanisms work to keep the system in balance, or she or he may introduce a different, more adaptive way of handling system stress (Amatea & Brown, 1981). One way to do this is for the counselor to ask family members to discuss a topic that will generate controversy among them. As members begin to use their usual ways of dealing with system stress, the counselor can observe these homeostatic maneuvers and may comment on or even divert these attempts to lower tension and prevent change. Eventually the counselor will want to teach the family more appropriate and productive ways to handle stress and to make changes in the family system when appropriate.

In the Jackson family, every time there is potential conflict in her family or classroom, thirteen-year-old Suzanne makes a joke to break the tension. This behavior consistently gets her into problems with teachers, and she has been labeled as a troublemaker and a disruptive clown in school. In order to assess the family dynamics involved in this process, the school counselor could introduce a conversation about Lynette, Suzanne's sister, and her postgraduation plans. Everyone in the Jackson family has an opinion on this topic, and none of them agree about it. As tension escalates, Suzanne starts making jokes to try to defuse the system stress.

The school counselor could stop the family right there and make suggestions for other ways that the family could handle stressful situations and lead them through some practice in communicating more directly. The counselor also might want to work on restructuring and reinforcing the interpersonal boundaries in the family so that Suzanne does not feel obliged to act out any time conflict centers on another family member. Boundary restructuring would also help the family learn the idea that each member has the right to make independent life decisions, without input or pressure from other members.

Reframing the problem so the family can begin to consider it from a different perspective is also helpful in family therapy (Hinkle, 1993; Nichols & Schwartz, 1991; Stone & Pecks, 1986). In the situation with the Jackson family, the counselor could reframe Suzanne's actions to both her teachers and her family as showing how smart and quick-witted Suzanne is. This reframing might help the adults in Suzanne's life to see her clowning from a more positive perspective. Using reframing, the counselor can also illustrate to family members ways in which problem behaviors may be serving the family in a positive way. With the Martinez family, the counselor could point out how much Paul's school behavior has served to keep the parents from expressing their anger toward each other. They have been so busy squabbling over whether Paul's behavior is a problem, they have not had to think about their marital problems.

Many times the counselor will assign homework to the family (Hinkle, 1993). This may be in the form of a ritual that they are to do with one another, such as the mother and father taking five minutes after work to tell one another three positive things that happened during the day. It may also take the form of an "ordeal" set up as a consequence for some target behavior that family members want to change, such as having the father supervise his son in digging a hole and burying a record album any time the son misbehaves in school (Stone & Peeks, 1986).

Family Therapy Theories

"There are as many different theories about treatment in family therapy as there are family therapists, perhaps because the system can be viewed from different perspectives" (McDaniel, 1981, p. 217). Because the field of family therapy is so varied, it would be impossible in this chapter to cover adequately all of the theories currently in vogue. We will briefly outline several of the more widely held perspectives on family therapy theories described in the counseling literature as being appropriate for application in schools: Adlerian family therapy, Bowen's family systems therapy, Minichin's structural family therapy, Satir's communication model, and strategic family therapy.

Adlerian Family Therapy

Alfred Adler was one of the first proponents of the family counseling movement, and this model has shown promise as a school-based intervention strategy for working with children and families (Christensen, 1993; Fenell & Weinhold, 1989; Kern & Carlson, 1981; Nicoll, 1984; Nicoll, Platt, & Platt, 1983). Adlerian theory is based on four component ideas that are important in understanding of Adlerian family counseling (Kern & Carlson, 1981; Thomas & Marchant, 1993), as described in the following paragraphs.

1. All behavior exists within a social context, and the counselor must examine the social meaning of problems. The family is an interconnected system, and the counselor views family members' problems as a result of the interaction and relationships within the family system (Kern & Carlson, 1981). A school counselor must also consider the classroom as one of the child's social contexts. This means that the school counselor also examines the interconnections within the classroom in order to determine how the elements of each system affect the child.

2. All behavior is goal-directed. Adlerians examine the purpose served by the behavior of each member of the family. Dreikurs and Soltz (1964) posited four goals of children's misbehavior: attention, power, revenge, and proving inadequacy. If the school counselor understands how children use their behaviors to reach these goals within the family and classroom, the school counselor can design effective interventions to help children shift to more positive, constructive purposes.

3. Reality is subjective, and all members of a family have their own individual filters through which they perceive themselves, others, and the world (Kern & Carlson, 1981; Thomas & Marchant, 1993). The school counselor must remember that each person in the family and each other person in a child's life, including teachers and peers, will have an individual way of looking at the child. It is important for the counselor to solicit each family member's unique perception of various family situations and interactions. As the counselor explores these viewpoints, he or she may be able to help the members of the family learn to increase their understanding of one another. It will also be helpful for the counselor to explore the perceptions of the other people who interact with the child.

4. People have a need to belong and to gain significance (Kern & Carlson, 1981; Thomas & Marchant, 1993). They first learn how to gain a place for themselves in their families. The child's behavior at school and the way he or she gains significance in the classroom will be a reflection of how the child gains significance in the family. By gaining a better understanding of the ways the child belongs in the family, the school counselor will enhance his or her comprehension of how the child fits into the school.

After building a relationship with the various members of the family, the school counselor who is using Adlerian family counseling will explore the family constellation and family atmosphere (Thomas & Marchant, 1993). Family constellation, the birth order of the children in a family, greatly influences the personal identity, self-concept, and world view of each family member. The counselor can use an understanding of birth order positions to help family members explore their own assets and liabilities and to enhance their understanding of self and others.

Ms. Mills, Liza Kinder's school counselor, could use family constellation to help her understand Liza and how she gains significance in her family and how that affects her behavior in school. Knowing that Liza is the oldest child of three could give Ms. Mills some insight into how Liza will probably view herself, others, and the world. Liza's presenting problem of being a tattletale and bossy in her classroom fits into the profile of the typical oldest child. Ms. Mills could explore the possibility that, like most oldest children, Liza tends to take on responsibility for things going smoothly in the family and in her classroom. She may want to help Liza build on this potential strength, while helping her understand that being responsible does not necessitate being overly involved in other people's business. Ms. Mills might want to work with Liza's parents to make sure that they do not expect her to be responsible for her siblings' behavior and that they do not encourage her to be a junior parent.

Family atmosphere is the prevailing affective tone within the family system (Thomas & Marchant, 1993). It usually stems from the relationship of the parents, their attitudes toward their children, family values, and discipline procedures. One goal of Adlerian family therapy is the improvement of the family atmosphere, moving it toward a democratic atmosphere of mutual respect. Depending on what he or she finds out about the family discipline strategies, the counselor may teach the parent(s) Adlerian parenting skills, such as logical consequences and democratic conflict resolution. By teaching parents to be more empathic and understanding of their children, to understand interpersonal dynamics, and to use more appropriate methods of discipline, the school counselor can enhance parent-child relationships and change behaviors that negatively affect children's school performance.

Ms. Mills, in working with Liza's family, might find that Mr. and Ms. Kinder have established a high-standards family atmosphere, in which they take a judgmental stance any time one of the children, especially Liza, does not live up to their expectations. They punish Liza if she or her brothers do not behave appropriately, and they expect Liza to monitor her brothers' behavior and either correct problems herself or come to them with a negative report. Ms. Mills would want to explore the parents' purpose in supporting this type of family atmosphere. Depending on the parents' attitudes, Ms. Mills would design her interpretations of the family atmosphere and her parenting suggestions in a way that would optimize the possibility that the parents would be likely to hear and accept them.

Some typical therapeutic interventions in Adlerian family counseling are the initial interview, role playing, watching for a recognition reflex, disclosure and interpretation, information giving and teaching, action-oriented techniques, minimizing mistakes, and encouraging family fun (Christensen & Marchant, 1993; Fenell & Weinhold, 1989). Many Adlerian family therapists use an initial interview that gathers information about the presenting problem, the family constellation and family atmosphere, and a typical day. The counselor might ask the family to use role playing to act out a particular sequence of events and to demonstrate their usual interactions. The counselor can use these enactments to gain a more accurate picture of relationships and communication patterns within the family and to teach the family new ways of viewing themselves and each other. Role plays can also provide a vehicle for the counselor to teach new ways of interacting and new communication skills. The Adlerian counselor always watches the various family members, especially the children, for a recognition reflex. These are usually involuntary, unconscious reactions, such as a smile, a nod, or a shrug, that can give the therapist clues about how that family member is thinking and feeling.

One technique that all Adlerian counselors use is disclosure and interpretation. In this strategy, the counselor makes guesses and states opinions about the intrapersonal and interpersonal dynamics within the family. Many times these are interpretations about goals of behavior or how individual members gain their significance within the family. The counselor may use these interpretations and disclosures to try to motivate clients to make changes in relationships and perceptions or to teach alternative behaviors. They may actually provide clients with new information or teach them specific skills for interacting. Many of the skills that they teach in family counseling involve parenting techniques, such as limit setting, logical consequences, and reflective listening. Adlerians also use action-oriented techniques, such as homework, family councils, and rituals, to help family members practice the skills and perceptions they have learned in the therapy process.

Encouraging the family members by minimizing mistakes and emphasizing effort and progress, Adlerian counselors frequently serve as cheerleaders for the family as it grows and changes. An important component of Adlerian family counseling is promoting family fun—most families, especially those who are struggling, seem to forget to have fun. School counselors can teach families to include having fun *together* in their lives.

Bowen's Family Systems Therapy

Murray Bowen, one of the first family systems theorists, developed a psychodynamic theory based on the idea that each family is a system of emotional relationships. Bowen usually approaches a family by concentrating on one member of the family and how he or she relates to the rest of the family. Bowen's theory consists of eight interlocking concepts: (a) differentiation of self, (b) triangles, (c) nuclear family emotional system, (d) family projection process, (e) emotional cutoff, (f) multigenerational transmission process, (g) sibling positions, and (h) societal regression (Friedman, 1991; Goldenberg & Goldenberg, 1991). While all of these concepts are important to a true understanding of Bowen's work, due to limited space in this chapter, we have chosen to elucidate the four concepts unique to Bowen's theory: differentiation of self, triangles, nuclear family emotional system, and multigenerational transmission.

The primary focus in Bowen's approach to family therapy is the opposing forces within the system that encourage family togetherness and move each member toward individuality (Goldenberg & Goldenberg, 1991). The family therapist's primary role is to help each member of the family in the continuous process of separation from the "undifferentiated family ego mass (intense interdependence or symbiosis within the family)" (Goldenberg & Goldenberg, 1988, p. 31). As family members become more differentiated, they are less vulnerable to family stress, they take more responsibility for their own behaviors, and they are more resistant to peer and family pressure (Goldenberg & Goldenberg, 1991; Mullis & Berger, 1981). They can think for themselves, and they base their judgements primarily on empirical evidence, rather than on emotional reactions (Mullis & Berger, 1981; Worden, 1981).

An example of how a school counselor could help a child to gain increased levels of differentiation might be Mr. Riley working with Janette Leonard, a sixth grader who comes to his office complaining of not being able to get her math work done. Janette reports that she tries to do her math, but she "just can't understand it." As Mr. Riley asks Janette about her family and a typical day, he begins to get a picture of a child who is undifferentiated from her family. Janette has three younger sisters who go everywhere and do everything with her. The entire family goes to Janette's maternal grandparents' house to spend almost every weekend with them. Janette reports that she has never had a babysitter because her parents never "go away and leave us with some stranger." Mr. Riley asks Mr. and Mrs. Leonard to come in and talk to him about Janette's problem with math. Mrs. Leonard tells him there is no reason for them to come in because they do not expect Janette to do well in math, since neither she nor her husband nor any of their assorted relatives had ever done well in math. Mr. Riley decides to work with Janette on increasing her differentiation from the undifferentiated, we-just-can't-do-math ego mass of her family.

According to Bowen, all living creatures, especially human beings, exist in a state of chronic anxiety (Friedman, 1991). This anxiety increases when people have significant relationships that have only two participants. Since two-person relationships are basically unstable, they go through alternating periods of distance and closeness (Goldenberg & Goldenberg, 1991). By bringing in a third person and creating a triangle, a more stable interaction, people can use three-person relationships to try to keep their anxiety under control (Goldenberg & Goldenberg, 1991). However, triangles are counterproductive to individuation, because when people are part of a triangle, they function emotionally rather than cognitively (Mullis & Berger, 1981).

Triangles can affect children in their families or in their relationships in schools. In families and in the classroom, triangles are constantly shifting to include different members. In a family, children quite frequently get triangulated into the two-person marital relationship of the parents. This can be dangerous to the child because it may inhibit his or her process of individuation. The triangulated child may also serve as a scapegoat for the parents' marital tensions. In a classroom, pairs of children frequently use triangles to bring in a third individual to stabilize their relationship. Initially the third child might feel flattered that the other two children are including him or her. However, when the original pair no longer need a third individual to lower the relational tension, the third child is frequently dropped and may feel devastated.

A school counselor using Bowen's theory of family therapy might look at the typical triangles formed in a child's family or in the classroom. John Chung seems to cry very easily in the classroom. When Mr. Sims asks John to come in to the counseling office and talk, he discovers that while John's parents seldom argue, they go through long periods of time where they do not speak to one another and they use John as a go-between to pass their communication to one another. John feels responsible for the conflict in their marriage because he is constantly in the middle.

Mr. Sims suggests that Mr. and Mrs. Chung come in and talk with him about John's emotional outbursts. When they come in, he makes some suggestions about ways that they can communicate without using John as a conduit. After several couple sessions, in which Mr. Sims replaces John in the

Chung family triangle, Mr. Sims feels as though he has built a strong enough rapport with the parents to suggest that they might want to begin to work with a marriage counselor.

Bowen believed that people choose to marry individuals with a level of differentiation similar to their own (Goldenberg & Goldenberg, 1991; Nichols & Schwartz, 1991). A person who is fused to his or her family of origin will be attracted to people who are equally fused to their families of origin. This pattern creates unstable nuclear family emotional systems. Families that are fused have a set of relatively standard methods for reducing the chronic tension that haunts the system. The greater the fusion in the nuclear family emotional system, the greater the possibility for emotional distance in the marital dyad or overt marital conflict, one of the spouses developing physical or emotional problems, or a projection of the problem onto at least one of the children, resulting in physical or emotional problems (Goldenberg & Goldenberg, 1991; Nichols & Schwartz, 1991).

One of the ways a school counselor could apply Bowen's theory of nuclear family emotional system is to examine the child's parents and their differentiation from their own families. While it is more effective and efficient to do this in person talking to the parents, if counselors do not have access to the parents, they can question the child about relationships in the family. Jamie Gatlin, a fourth grader, gets into trouble for fighting on the playground and being verbally aggressive to other children. Jamie has consistently demonstrated these behaviors since he entered kindergarten and was placed in a special education classroom in second grade with a diagnosis of severely emotionally disturbed. When his parents came in for the Annual Review and Dismissal (ARD) meetings, they refused to look at one another and constantly contradicted each other. Mr. Gatlin always tells school personnel that he does not understand why Jamie acts like this and requests that every time Jamie transgresses a school rule that they call him so that he can "whip the tar out of him, just like my daddy did to me." Mrs. Gatlin gives school personnel a list of behavioral consequences that she has brainstormed with two of her sisters who also have aggressive children. Mrs. Lang, the school counselor, has taken several family therapy courses and has had a practicum in applying family systems therapy. She has studied Bowen's theories and believes that Jamie's behavior is due to the nuclear family emotional system and his parents' lack of differentiation from their own families of origin. She asks the entire family to come in to see if she can help the parents in their differentiation process, which she believes will have a positive impact on Jamie's attitudes and behavior.

The concept of multigenerational transmission process is related to the idea of the nuclear family emotional system. Bowen suggested that severe psychological problems are due to the combined effects of several generations of undifferentiated individuals. According to this conceptualization of dysfunctional individuals and families, the members of each generation of the family have progressively weaker differentiation, resulting in increasing levels of anxiety and fusion (Goldenberg & Goldenberg, 1991).

Applying the idea of the multigenerational transmission process to the Gatlin family, Mrs. Lang may discuss family of origin issues with Mr. and Mrs. Gatlin when they come to visit with her. She will begin to examine the differentiation of each proceeding generation in her effort to understand the Gatlins' present functioning and to devise a plan to increase the level of differentiation in Jamie's nuclear family. She will not discuss her beliefs about the multigenerational transmission process with the Gatlins. It would not be helpful or professional in this situation to encourage the Gatlins to "blame" someone else for the current problems.

In Bowen's family therapy, the counselor usually works with the parents, instead of with the children or the entire family (Nichols & Schwartz, 1991). Although the identified patient might be a child who is manifesting behavioral or emotional problems, the counselor frequently suggests that the parents must accept the idea that the primary difficulty lies in them and in their relationship (Goldenberg & Goldenberg, 1991). He or she joins with the couple, and the three of them become a therapeutic triangle. The counselor remains objective, calm, and emotionally detached, avoiding emotional involvement in the triangle, which forces the couple to work on themselves and their relationship. In this counseling relationship, the counselor serves as a coach or consultant, helping each member of the couple move toward self-differentiation—from the spouse and from the family of origin (Goldenberg & Goldenberg, 1991; Nichols & Schwartz, 1991).

In a session, Bowenian family counselors use questioning strategies, asking both of the spouses to acknowledge their part in relationship problems (Goldenberg & Goldenberg, 1991). They may teach the couple about the theoretical constructs of emotional systems and differentiation and ask them to examine their relationships in their families of origin. As a vehicle for this process, counselors may use genograms, which are diagrams that the clients use to illustrate and explore their families (Nichols & Schwartz, 1991). They may also use displacement stories—that is, using films, videotapes, and storytelling to help families learn about family systems without evoking their defenses about their own families.

School counselors can use all of these techniques with families from their schools. They can also apply Bowen's work in other ways in their schools in: (a) parent conferences, (b) classroom activities, and (c) group counseling or consultation (Mullis & Berger, 1981). In parent conferences or consultations, school counselors can use their understanding of differentiation and the nuclear family emotional system to help them plan how to involve parents in their children's school process. It is important for the counselor to use these opportunities with parents to gather data about the nuclear family and about previous generations. This information will be useful to school personnel in their efforts to understand and help children.

The counselor can also train teachers to use particular techniques in staff development or classroom activities. Subject area teachers could use exercises that help children explore their nuclear and extended families. Children could interview parents about their childhoods and their relationships to their parents. Children could write letters to extended family members requesting information about their parents as they were growing up. The possibilities for involving children in exploration of their families and the process of relationships is endless. The counselor can also use group counseling or consultation to help children explore relationships and emotional systems of peers. Children can draw genograms to help them understand their own families and to learn that each family operates in unique ways. This study will ultimately help children to avoid fusion with others and to maximize their own differentiation.

Minuchin's Structural Family Therapy

Minuchin (1974) explained the main ideas of structural family therapy when he wrote:

> In essence, the structural approach to families is based on the concept that a family is more than the individual biopsychodynamics of its members. Family members relate according to certain arrangements, which govern their transactions. These arrangements, though usually not explicitly stated or even recognized, form a whole—the structure of the family. (p. 89)

There are four basic constructs essential to the understanding of structural family therapy: structure, subsystems, boundaries, and hierarchy (Colapinto, 1991; Goldenberg & Goldenberg, 1991; Nichols & Schwartz, 1991). Family structure is the organized way in which the members of the family consistently interact with one another. This structure involves predictable patterns that make up the family relationships. Most of the time, the rules governing the interaction are unspoken, and the family members may not even be aware of the rules. For instance, in the Green family, when Ms. Green serves fish for Friday dinner, Mr. Green will get angry and leave the house, coming home late at night, usually in a drunken condition. This is the only time he drinks, and Ms. Green knows this. However, once or twice a month she still serves fish on Friday night, and the same sequence of events occurs.

The family does not usually remember how the structure was formed, and the patterns only change through conscious decision and determination on the part of family members (Nichols & Schwartz, 1991). The best way for the counselor to understand the family structure is observation. In order for this to happen, the family must act out the structure in a session. Structural family therapists may simply observe families interacting, and they may ask them to act out certain sequences of events in order to gain an understanding of the family structures.

According to structural family therapists, each family is composed of a myriad of subsystems: each individual, the marital dyad, sibling subsystems, gender subsystems, common interest subsystems, and the like (Goldenberg & Goldenberg, 1991). Each member of the family has a place in several different subsystems. Depending on the subsystem, the individual will have certain roles or functions that he or she must perform in that subsystem. Individual behavior and attitudes vary according to the prevailing subsystem. For instance, the Targents have five children. Stacy is the middle child of the five, but there is a ten-year gap between her and her next oldest brother. Based on this configuration, Stacy has a place in two different sibling subsystems. She is the middle child in the subsystem that includes all the children. In her role as the middle child, she tries to involve all the children in activities. She serves as the peacemaker and placater at times, but at other times she tends to be independent and rebellious. Stacy is also the oldest child in the younger sibling subsystem. When her two older siblings are not present, Stacy takes on the role and function of the oldest child, bossing the other children, being super-responsible and trying to make sure that everyone does what is "correct."

Interpersonal boundaries separate the various subsystems and surround each member and the entire family (Goldenberg & Goldenberg, 1991; Nichols & Schwartz, 1991). Boundaries regulate contact and define individuality and autonomy. Boundaries exist on a continuum that ranges from rigid to clear to diffuse. In families that have rigid boundaries, members have little contact with one another or with outside systems. They are disengaged from one another and from the rest of the world. The weakness of disengaged families is that members are so autonomous that they seldom provide support or nurturing for one another. They cannot usually rely on any type of warmth or affection within the family. The strength of disengaged families is that they encourage independence and self-reliance.

The Winnets are a disengaged family with rigid boundaries. This family never eats meals together, never goes on vacation together, never does any type of activity at the same time. Each of their three children refuses to involve themselves in group sports or community activities. The oldest son, a junior in high school, is involved on the school golf team. The two girls, one in elementary school and one in middle school, have done some gymnastics, but neither parent ever comes to watch their meets. The youngest daughter's teacher has reported to the school that she seems to be a "loner." When the counselor consults with the counselors of the other two children, they report that the other two children seem to have few friends and have made no close ties with their teachers.

In the family with clear boundaries, there is a flexible range of interpersonal contact and autonomy (Nichols & Schwartz, 1991). The parents have supportive relationships with one another and with their children, but all members of the family are accorded age-appropriate independence.

The Linggs are a family with clear boundaries. They do not always eat every meal together, but they make an effort to eat most dinners with one another. When their children have sports activities, one or both of the parents tries to be there to provide support. However, when this is not possible, Ms. Lingg makes arrangements for the younger child, a third grader, to have a ride to her games. The older child, who is in middle school, makes her own carpool arrangements with her friends.

Families with diffuse boundaries sacrifice autonomy and freedom for closeness and support. In these families, members are enmeshed with one another—there is no clear line of demarcation where one member ends and another begins. The weakness of enmeshed families is that they have difficulty relating to people outside the family and they tend to be overly dependent on one another. They very seldom have individual interests, ideas, or feelings. The strength of enmeshed families is that they provide maximum support and togetherness for members. The parents in these families are frequently overly involved in their children's activities and school work.

The Gladstones are an enmeshed family. They go everywhere and do everything together. Sam, the eldest child, a sixth grader, frequently gets in trouble at school for beating up other children for having "picked on" his two little brothers. Every time Sam gets punished for fighting in school, both of his parents call the teacher, the principal, and the school counselor. His mother, father, or maternal grandmother visits school "to find out how things are going" at least once a week.

Another important concept in structural family therapy is hierarchy. The hierarchy determines who has the decision-making power in the family (Colapinto, 1991; Goldenberg & Goldenberg, 1991). This power usually shifts from individual to individual, from subsystem to subsystem, depending on the particular context or situation. Sometimes various members of the family form an alliance to shift the power in the hierarchy (Goldenberg & Goldenberg, 1991). While there are many configurations of power that work for different families, most high-functioning families have a hierarchy in which the parents have more power than the children. In these families, children have age-appropriate power, but the parents are ultimately responsible for providing family leadership (Colapinto, 1991). There are usually problems in families where the children have too much power or one or both of the parents have abdicated power.

The Leeks have a balanced hierarchy that works well. Their mother, who is single, makes most of the major decisions about family functioning with input from the children. Depending on their ages, the children make decisions about themselves and their activities with help and guidance from their mother. The older children make more decisions with less input from their mother than the younger children do.

The Sikes have an unbalanced hierarchy that causes some family problems. Lester Sikes, who is a seventh grader, makes all of the decisions in the family. He decides when he is going to bed, what movies and television shows he is going to watch, when he is to come in from outdoors, what the family is going to have for dinner, and so on. If Mr. and Mrs. Sikes suggest that they disagree with Lester's mandates, Lester throws a temper tantrum. Both of his parents greatly value calm and quiet, and they give in to Lester's demands rather than having their peace disturbed. In working with the Sikes family, the school counselor would want to help them reorganize the hierarchy and have the parents assume more power and control over decision making.

The process of structural family therapy depends on an understanding of the structure, subsystems, boundaries, and hierarchy. In order to make changes in these elements of the family functioning, the counselor first builds a trusting relationship with the family (Thompson & Rudolph, 1992). The second step is to engage the family in describing the presenting problem and their daily routine until the counselor recognizes the patterns that make up the family structure and the role of each subsystem. The counselor may ask the family to reenact certain typical interactions so that he or she can understand the dynamics of the relationships. The third step is the examination of boundaries, family rules, and hierarchy. The counselor is active and directive, asking questions in a manner designed to encourage family members to think about relationships and interactions. Rather than asking, "Why doesn't your son ever look at you?" the counselor would say, "See if you can get your son to look at you." In order to help the family make shifts in the structure, boundaries, and hierarchy, the structural family therapist uses active intervention strategies such as asking family members to move to different places in the room to establish new subsystems, stand on chairs to change the power structure, or act out certain scenes in which family members establish new boundaries.

School counselors can use structural family therapy to help them understand children's problems in the context of their family organization and to facilitate reorganization in family structure (Goldenberg & Goldenberg, 1988). When working with families, they will investigate the boundaries, subsystems, and hierarchy in the family and examine how these factors affect children and their performance in schools. They will watch for ways children apply their understanding of relationships based on these elements of family structure to interactions in their classrooms. School counselors can help families begin to recognize and rearrange the family structure and to learn new ways of interacting with others.

Satir's Communication Approach to Family Therapy

Virginia Satir pioneered a method of working with families that focuses on family communication. She believed that family members could learn to communicate more honestly and effectively. They could learn to "get in touch with their feelings, listen to one another, ask for clarification if they do not understand, provide feedback to one another regarding their reactions to what is taking place, and negotiate differences that may arise" (Goldenberg & Goldenberg, 1988, p. 32). Counselors who follow Satir's model examine four components in the family situation: (a) family members' feelings of worth, (b) the family communication patterns, (c) the mechanics of the family system, and (d) the family rules (Goldenberg & Goldenberg, 1991; Seligman, 1981; Thompson & Rudolph, 1992).

The counselor using this approach to family therapy examines the self-worth of each member of the family. Satir believed that one of the primary reasons families come to therapy is the low self-esteem of the members (Fenell & Weinhold, 1989). The counselor spends a great deal of the time in sessions, especially at the beginning of the relationship, helping family members build self-esteem. As they gain a more positive perspective about themselves, they are better able to relate appropriately and to communicate honestly. The counselor uses the following strategies (Fenell & Weinhold, 1989) to help family members gain confidence in themselves:

1. Making comments to family members that indicate that the counselor has high regard for their personal worth.
2. Pointing out family members' assets.
3. Asking family members' input in areas in which they have expertise.
4. Suggesting that family members can ask for clarification when the counselor's communication is unclear.
5. Asking family members how they can contribute to one another's happiness.
6. Presenting the idea that changes in the family will come about as a result of the counselor and the family cooperating as a team to make family changes.

One of the primary goals of the Satir model of family therapy is the restructuring of the family's communication patterns (Fenell & Weinhold, 1989; Goldenberg & Goldenberg, 1991). Satir described the following communication styles as ineffective: (a) the *placater* tries to make sure that no one in the family ever gets angry or upset; (b) the *blamer* tries to find fault with other members of the family and never takes responsibility for any problems; (c) the *computer* avoids emotion and tries to keep communication on a strictly cognitive plane; and (d) the *distractor* changes the subject any time a conflict appears imminent (Fenell & Weinhold, 1989; Thompson & Rudolph, 1992). These communication styles prevent open, congruent, direct communication. Satir also described the *leveler,* who uses a communication style that consists of straightforward and consistent communication of honest thoughts and feelings (Satir, 1972; Thompson & Rudolph, 1992).

Counselors using the Satir method would teach the family about the various communication styles and encourage them to discover which of the styles each member typically uses (Fenell & Weinhold, 1989; Thompson & Rudolph, 1992). School counselors can help family members begin to catch themselves when they use these ineffective methods of communication and try to teach them to substitute the leveler approach. They can encourage family members to openly disagree; share hopes, fears, and expectations; seek clarification without threat; provide nonjudgmental feedback to one another; understand other positions and use reflective listening to convey that understanding; and maintain congruence in communication and diminish hidden messages.

In order to help the family, Satir believed that the counselor must understand the system of that particular family—how the interconnectedness of all of the members of the family works in this unique collection of individuals (Thompson & Rudolph, 1992). She maintained that it is important to examine the significance of the identified patient's presenting problem within the family structure and to observe any formations of triangles, especially ones that include the parent(s) and one or more of the children (Satir, 1972; Seligman, 1981).

As counselors begin to comprehend these elements of the family system, they teach the family about the interrelatedness of the family—how all of the members are connected to one another and how an action on the part of one member will have an impact on all the other members of the family. Counselors who follow this model help families analyze their own interactional patterns and make conscious decisions about changing certain patterns and trying to make personal adjustments so that every member of the family can be happy and satisfied without negatively affecting other members of the family (Thompson & Rudolph, 1992).

Satir believed that the rules in the family were also important in the process of family change (Thompson & Rudolph, 1992). She contended that most distressed families have unwritten rules that members do not respect or understand. These covert rules may prevent members from communicating clearly and directly. They may limit individual members' freedom to express what they are thinking or feeling, to agree or disagree, or to ask for clarification (Satir, 1972).

In exploring these rules, counselors try to help family members make the covert overt by asking them to describe what they believe the family rules are. They may use role playing, games, family sculpting, or other active interactional counseling techniques to help members recognize and decide to change formerly unspoken rules that hamper family functioning (Thompson & Rudolph, 1992).

LaJoy Jackson is a third grade girl who is overly anxious. She does extremely well in her school work, but she bursts into tears unless she gets a perfect score on every assignment. Mr. Hines, her school counselor, asks her parents to bring LaJoy's two younger brothers, one in second grade and one in kindergarten, and come to several sessions of family counseling. Mr. Hines, in exploring the self-esteem of all of the family members, determines that all of the members lack self-confidence. Mr. and Mrs. Jackson have both attended some junior college classes, but feel badly about their level of education, especially since they are the only members of their families of origin who did not complete a four-year college degree. They want their children to achieve this goal, and they put a great deal of emphasis on success in school, especially with LaJoy because she is the oldest child. LaJoy feels as though she can never meet their expectations, which tends to hamper her feelings of self-worth. Mr. Hines helps the parents look at ways in which they can increase their own self-concepts and can work to improve the children's self-esteem.

As Mr. Hines watches the family interact, looking for communication patterns, he realizes that Mr. Jackson tends to use the computer approach, Mrs. Jackson usually uses the blamer approach, LaJoy almost exclusively uses the placater approach, and her two brothers usually distract the others. By teaching the family members about the different types of communication and explaining and demonstrating the leveler approach, Mr. Hines starts to help the family members change how they communicate with one another. He can use communication games, family sculpting, and other active strategies to diagnose the old communication patterns and to help the family learn and practice new communication patterns.

Mr. Hines can also use these same types of interactional counseling techniques to explore the family system and the family rules. Many times, the school counselor who is using Satir's model will ask the family to role play or to play some type of game in order to be able to observe their interactions. Because the system and the rules are usually covert and may be out of the family members' awareness, active techniques are more effective in getting at the dynamics than talk therapy or questioning strategies.

Strategic Family Therapy

In strategic family therapy, the primary goal of therapy is the resolution of the presenting problem (Goldenberg & Goldenberg, 1991; Nichols & Schwartz, 1991). Systemic therapists do not believe that family members need to gain insight into the family dynamics or the function of the presenting problem. In order to make changes in the problem, the therapist is directive, authoritative, and manipulative (Haley, 1976). The primary proponents of this theory, Madanes and Haley (1977), suggested that the first step in eliminating family problems is for the counselor to help the family clearly define the problem. When the therapist understands the presenting problem and its function in the family, she or he provides the family with a series of directives that shifts the organization of the family system. The therapist designs the directives so that this shift eliminates the systemic function served by the presenting problem, thereby changing the aspect of the family system that supports the problem (Goldenberg & Goldenberg, 1991). In order to design a successful directive, the strategic family counselor must understand the previously applied solutions. The therapist asks the family to describe various attempts at solving the problem and the outcomes of these attempts.

When the identified patient is a child with behavioral or academic problems, strategic family therapists usually see the core issue as conflict between the parents resulting in a disturbance in the family hierarchy with the child or children having an inappropriate degree of power (Stone & Peeks, 1986). The goal of the resulting directive is to put the parents back into control in the family. This is the type of directive that would usually be appropriate for school counselors who are using strategic family therapy for children with school problems (Stone & Peeks, 1986).

For example, Lester Carol is having temper tantrums in his classroom and at home. Mr. Arbuckle, the elementary counselor, asks Lester's parents to come in for several family sessions. When he asks them to describe the presenting problem and the subsequent attempts to correct it, he discovers that Mr. Carol frequently travels on business and Lester's tantrums coincide with these business trips. Mrs. Carol is Lester's step-mother, and the way she deals with the home and the school tantrums is to threaten Lester with punishment when his father comes home. The time that Lester spends with his father during the discipline talks when Mr. Carol comes home are the bulk of their private time together. Mr. Arbuckle believes that the basic issues in the presenting problem are that Mrs. Carol does not believe that she is strong enough to handle discipline and that Lester wants to spend more time with his father, even if it means getting punished. In prescribing a directive, Mr. Arbuckle wants to correct both of these elements of the problem. Without making any type of interpretation, he directs the family to make the following changes:

1. Any time Lester has a temper tantrum, either at home or at school, Mrs. Carol is to take him to the back yard, where he is to dig a hole two feet deep and bury one of his favorite toys. He is allowed to pick the toy that he is going to bury. Mr. Carol is not to involve himself in any discipline process around the tantrums.

2. Any time Lester does not have a tantrum while Mr. Carol is away on a business trip, Mr. Carol is to spend an uninterrupted hour with him on his return, doing something that they both agree is fun.

Counselors who apply strategic family therapy techniques also use reframing, suggesting that problematic behavior serves a reasonable and helpful function within the family system (Goldenberg & Goldenberg, 1991). For instance, with a child who chases other children around the playground, the school counselor using a strategic approach might suggest that the child is just trying to get close to the other children.

Strategic family therapists sometimes "prescribe the symptom," asking a family member to purposely manifest the presenting problem. Using this type of paradoxical intervention (Goldenberg & Goldenberg, 1991) gives the identified patient permission to continue the behavior, but usually at a specified time and place. In this type of approach, the school counselor would first use a reframe to suggest a positive function for the presenting problem.

Kaitlin Smith is a second grade child who is constantly using profanity. Ms. Brown, the school counselor, discusses the problem with the family and discovers that the parents have many conflicts about discipline and other family issues. Since Mr. and Mrs. Smith agree that the profane language is a problem, but seldom agree on anything else, Ms. Brown might suggest that Kaitlin is using the profanity to get her parents to agree on something. Ms. Brown could reframe the problem by pointing out that Kaitlin's behavior is a way to help the parents work out their differences. In prescribing the symptoms, Ms. Brown would tell the family that together both of the parents must spend a half an hour a day with Kaitlin, supervising her to make sure that she includes at least one profanity in each of her sentences. If Kaitlin says a sentence without a profane word, the parents must generate some consequence that involves all three of the family members, such as holding hands and jumping up and down three times. This intervention would serve two purposes: forcing the child to do something that has been formerly prohibited, thus taking the power of the forbidden away from the activity, and forcing the parents to work together to bring about a behavior change in the child.

Strategic family therapy sounds relatively simple, but it involves a great deal of training and skill—in understanding the presenting problem from a systemic perspective and in designing appropriate interventions. If school counselors intend to use strategic techniques, they should obtain extensive training and supervision in the proper application of the technique. Strategic interventions, as should be apparent from these examples, can be rather controversial. This theory is not straightforward or easy for lay people to understand. The manipulative aspect of this approach may render strategic interventions inappropriate or inadvisable in many school settings. If counselors choose to apply strategic family therapy in their schools, it is essential that they first obtain the understanding and support of their administration, at the district and the building levels.

CONCLUSION

Considering the number of family problems affecting children and their behavior and performance in schools, it is not surprising that there is currently strong interest in applying family systems theory and counseling techniques in schools. All school counselors will not be able to provide comprehensive family therapy for students. However, they should understand the factors that contribute to family health and how different elements in family functioning can affect children in schools (Wilcoxon & Comas, 1987). They should also be informed about the various systems concepts and strategies and the many specific family therapy theories. This information will help them appropriately refer families with severe problems to family therapists in agencies and private practice. With proper training and supervised experience, school counselors can also provide time-limited family interventions for those families who could benefit from them.

REFERENCES

Amatea, E., & Brown, B. (1993). The counselor and the family: An ecosystemic approach. In J. Wittmer (Ed.), *Managing your school counseling program: K–12 developmental strategies* (pp. 142–150). Minneapolis, MN: Educational Media.

Amatea, E., & Fabrick, F. (1981). Family systems counseling: A positive alternative to traditional counseling. *Elementary School Guidance and Counseling, 15,* 223–236.

Amatea, E., & Fabrick, F. (1984). Moving a family into therapy: Critical referral issues for the school counselor. *The School Counselor, 31,* 285–294.

Bowen, M. (1978). *Family therapy in clinical practice.* Creskill, NJ: Jason Aronson.

Christensen, O. (Ed). (1993). *Adlerian family counseling* (rev. ed.). Minneapolis, MN: Educational Media.

Christensen, O., & Marchant, W. (1993). The family counseling process. In O. Christensen (Ed.), *Adlerian family counseling* (rev. ed.) (pp. 27–56). Minneapolis, MN: Educational Media.

Colapinto, J. (1991). Structural family therapy. In A. Gurman & D. Kniskern (Eds.), *Handbook of family therapy: Vol. 2* (pp. 417–443). New York: Brunner/Mazel.

Conti, A. (1971). A follow-up study of families referred to outside agencies. *Psychology in the Schools, 8,* 338–340.

Curran, D. (1985). *Stress and the healthy family: How healthy families control the ten most common stresses.* Minneapolis, MN: Winston.

Dreikurs, R., & Soltz, V. (1964). *Children: The challenge.* New York: Hawthorn.

Fenell, D., & Weinhold, B. (1989). *Counseling families.* Denver, CO: Love.

Friedman, E. (1991). Bowen theory and therapy. In A. Gurman & D. Kniskern (Eds.), *Handbook of family therapy: Vol. 2* (pp. 134–170). New York: Brunner/Mazel.

Golden, L. (1988). Brief family interventions in a school setting. In W. Walsh & N. Giblin (Eds.), *Family counseling in school settings* (pp. 51–57). Springfield, IL: Charles C Thomas.

Golden, L. (1993). Counseling with families. In A. Vernon (Ed.), *Counseling children and adolescents* (pp. 271–290). Denver, CO: Love.

Goldenberg, I., & Goldenberg, H. (1988). Family systems and the school counselor. In W. Walsh & N. Giblin (Eds.), *Family counseling in school settings* (pp. 26–38). Springfield, IL: Charles C Thomas.

Goldenberg, I., & Goldenberg, H. (1991). *Family therapy: An overview* (3rd ed.). Monterey, CA: Brooks/Cole.

Goodman, R., & Kjonaas, D. (1984). Elementary school family counseling: A pilot project. *Journal of Counseling and Development, 63,* 255–257.

Green, B. (1985). Systems intervention in the school. In M. Mirkin & S. Koman (Eds.), *Handbook of adolescents and family therapy* (pp. 193–206). New York: Gardner.

Green, R., & Kolevzon, M. (1984). Characteristics of healthy families. *Elementary School Guidance and Counseling, 19, 9–18.*

Haley, J. (1976). *Problem-solving therapy.* San Francisco, CA: Jossey-Bass.

Haley, J. (1990). *Master founders series.* Interview conducted at the American Association of Marriage and Family Therapy, Washington, DC.

Hinkle, J. S. (1993). Training school counselors to do family counseling. *Elementary School Guidance and Counseling, 27,* 252–257.

Kern, R., & Carlson, J. (1981). Adlerian family counseling. *Elementary School Guidance and Counseling, 15,* 301–306.

Love, P., Chappell, G., & Boorheim, H. (1987). Guidelines for a family interview. *TACD Journal, 15,* 77–80.

Madanes, C., & Haley, J. (1977). Dimensions of family therapy. *The Journal of Nervous and Mental Disease, 165,* 88–89.

McDaniel, S. (1981). Treating school problems in family therapy. *Elementary School Guidance and Counseling, 15,* 214–222.

Minuchin, S. (1974). *Families and family therapy.* Cambridge, MA: Harvard University.

Minuchin, S., & Fishman, H. (1981). *Family therapy techniques.* Cambridge, MA: Harvard University.

Mullis, F., & Berger, M. (1981). The utility of Bowen's theory of family therapy for school counselors. *The School Counselor, 28,* 195–201.

Nicoll, W. (1984). School counselors as family counselors: A rationale and training model. *The School Counselor, 31,* 279–284.

Nicoll, W., Platt, J., & Platt, A. (1983). Adlerian programs in the schools. In O. Christensen & T. Schramski (Eds.), *Adlerian family counseling: A manual for counselors, educators and psychotherapists* (pp. 317–348). Minneapolis, MN: Educational Media.

Nichols, M., & Schwartz, R. (1991). *Family therapy: Concepts and methods* (2nd ed.). Boston: Allyn & Bacon.

Palmo, A., Lowry, L., Weldon, D., & Scioscia, T. (1984). Schools and family: Future perspectives for school counselors. *The School Counselor, 31,* 272–278.

Peeks, B. (1993). Revolutions in counseling and education: A systems perspective in the schools. *Elementary School Guidance and Counseling, 27,* 245–251.

Ponzetti, J., & Long, E. (1989). Healthy family functioning: A review and critique. *Family Therapy, 14,* 43–49.

Satir, V. (1972). *Peoplemaking.* Palo Alto, CA: Science and Behavior Books.

Seligman, L. (1981). An application of Satir's model to family counseling. *The School Counselor, 29,* 133–139.

Steele, W., & Raider, M. (1991). *Working with families in crisis: School-based intervention.* New York: Guilford.

Stone, G., & Peeks, B. (1986). The use of strategic family therapy in a school setting: A case study. *Journal of Counseling and Development, 65,* 200–203.

Thomas, C., & Marchant, W. (1993). Basic principles of Adlerian family counseling. In O. Christensen (Ed.), *Adlerian family counseling* (rev. ed.) (pp. 7–26). Minneapolis, MN: Educational Media.

Thompson, C., & Rudolph, L. (1992). *Counseling children* (3rd ed.). Pacific Grove, CA: Brooks/Cole.

Turnbull, A., & Turnbull, H. (1990). *Families, professionals, and exceptionality: A special partnership.* Columbus, OH: Merrill.

Whiteside, R. (1993). Making a referral for family therapy: The school counselor's role. *Elementary School Guidance and Counseling, 27,* 273–279.

Wilcoxon, S., & Comas, R. (1987). Contemporary trends in family counseling: What do they mean for the school counselor? *The School Counselor, 34,* 219–225.

Worden, M. (1981). Classroom behavior as a function of the family system. *The School Counselor, 28,* 178–188.

Chapter Twelve

Consultation

🌳 Brown, Kurpius, and Morris (1988) note that consultation is still very much in its infancy in both theory and practice. Many counselors view consultation simplistically, when in fact the process is complex. To effectively practice consultation requires special training, because there are numerous knowledge bases from which to draw and a wide range of skills involved.

Consultation, as a special aspect of counselor education, now receives careful attention in most preparation programs. For example, the counseling faculty at the University of North Texas in Denton, Texas, compiled a list of skills that counselors should possess for consultation purposes. They note that counselors should be able to:

1. Maintain attitudes that form the core conditions necessary for effective consultation relationships.
2. Demonstrate interpersonal skills needed to create and maintain consultation relationships, goals, and desired behavioral change.

3. Demonstrate communication skills.
4. Demonstrate problem-solving skills.
5. Demonstrate the knowledge base necessary for consultation.
6. Demonstrate skill in working with organizations.
7. Demonstrate the interactive skills necessary for the consultation process.
8. Provide consultative expertise collaboratively.
9. Interpret and explain concepts and new information effectively.
10. Advocate for individual consultees.
11. Maintain ethical professional behavior.

(Engels and Dameron, 1990, pp. 135–141)

Readers will note that the skills considered necessary for consultation are also skills needed for effective counseling. In this sense, the acquisition of counseling skills will be useful for counselors in those instances that require them to function as consultants. One should not assume, however, that all counselors will automatically become good consultants as a result of counselor training alone. Additional skills and understanding are necessary.

Consultation Defined

Defining consultation is difficult because of its newness and complexity and because of the range of approaches that individuals use in the consultation process. Consultation has been defined in various places as the provision of "expert advice" and in others as a special relationship wherein the consultant helps others to define and solve their own problems (Brown et al., 1988).

Most professionals will, however, agree on what consultation is not—it is not or should not be simple advice giving, nor is it purely "teaching," "counseling," or "supervision." In each of these approaches, helpers are engaged in providing direct help to students or clients to assist in bringing about certain changes. Consultation, on the other hand, is a "triadic" process between one individual (the consultant) and a consultee working to bring about a desired change in a third individual, a group, or an organization that is outside the consultant-consultee relationship (Brown et al., 1988).

Dougherty (1990) defines consultation as "a process in which a human services professional assists a consultee with a work-related (or caretaking-related) problem with a client system, with the goal of helping both the consultee and the client system in some specified way." Another widely quoted definition was offered by Caplan (1970) over two decades ago and is still considered by many to reflect the essence of the consultation process. Caplan described consultation as a voluntary, nonhierarchical relationship between two professionals who may be from different professions or groups. The process is initiated by the consultee to improve the consultee's function with individuals or groups.

Brown, Pryzwansky, and Schulte (1991) saw Caplan's definition as too restrictive, and they have defined consultation in the following way:

> Human services consultation is defined as a voluntary problem-solving process that can be initiated and terminated by either the consultant or the consultee. It is engaged primarily for the purpose of assisting consultees to develop attitudes and skills that will enable them to function more effectively with a client which can be an individual, group, or organization for which they have responsibility. The goals of the process are twofold: enhancing services to third parties, and improving the ability of consultees to function in areas of concern to them. (p. 12)

This definition seems particularly appropriate for elementary and middle school counselors, because in many cases the request for consultation may be initiated by administrators, parents, or teachers. Usually those who seek the help of the consultant (counselor) are requesting some form of aid to deal with a third party or condition—a disruptive class, an individual student, or some other specific situation in the school or home. The role of the counselor in this relationship is to help the individual seeking his or her help to acquire new or different ways of dealing with the expressed concern. Kirby (1985) defined the following conditions of consultation:

1. The relationship is voluntary.
2. The focus of attention is the problem situation as articulated by the consultee(s).
3. The consultant is not functioning as part of the structural hierarchy.
4. The power that resides in the consultant's expertise is sufficient to facilitate change.

(p. 9)

Rationale for Consultation

The utilization of consultation by elementary and middle school counselors stems from the understanding that the philosophy of guidance and counseling for all students can only be achieved if some aspects of the guidance program are reached through an indirect approach. This method is indirect in the sense that teachers, administrators, and parents are all guidance functionaries. In this context, the counselor-consultant "gives away" skills to teachers and parents who in turn become better equipped to help children. Obviously, even in small schools, not every child will be able to receive counseling on a regular basis; hence, assisting teachers to become better providers of guidance is crucial (Dinkmeyer, 1971).

Relationships with Teachers

To many adults, the term consultant brings to mind the concept of an "expert" who can *solve* the problems of a group or organization. When the counselor assumes the role of consultant as she or he works with teachers, it is very important that the counselor does *not* take on the "expert" approach to the process. This is true even though there may be some expectation on the part of teachers that counselors will analyze a problem, provide solutions, and direct what should be done. Rather, the elementary and middle school counselor/consultant seeks to help teachers grow in their ability to assist children and others to work out their *own* solutions and action plans.

Relationships with Administrators

There are two important concerns for elementary and middle school counselors in their working relationships with school administrators. The first is clarifying the counselor's role in working with teachers as a consultant, and the second is outlining the counselor's duties in working with school problems as a consultant/cofunctionary to the school administration.

Brown, Pryzwansky, and Schulte (1991) note that most administrators are receptive to consultative models for elementary and middle school guidance, particularly when the objective is one of increasing teacher competence. In addition, some administrators see the use of the counselor as a consultant to be a more efficient use of the counselor's time.

Some administrators, however, may be less enthusiastic about the counselor functioning as a consultant, citing the time demands consultation places on teachers, the effect of the direct service commitments of the consultant, and questions related to accountability. To address these concerns, administrators should be actively involved in the design of the consulting program to ensure that time constraints and other aspects of the program are considered. As with other parts of the overall guidance program, the consulting service should be annually evaluated in ways that address accountability concerns. (Approaches to evaluation are discussed in Chapters 1 and 2)

When the counselor works directly with administrators in a consulting role, he or she must establish a relationship similar to that established when working with parents or teachers. Counselors, as human relationship specialists, have unique skills and knowledge that they bring to the consulting process with administrators. The relationship, then, is one of collaboration, wherein counselors and principals work as a team to understand, analyze, and resolve problems. Together they seek to view all concerns from a holistic point of view, followed by the formulation of a series of tentative hypotheses and possible recommendations. Like counseling, consultation is a process, not a one act play. The term *process* implies an ongoing activity that takes place throughout the school year. At times, additional specialists may join the counselor/administrator team to add a different point of view to the problem at hand. All deliberations should be conducted with the end in sight, which in this case is the building of better worlds for children. The building of these worlds can be accomplished through the use of a number of consultation models.

The Models of Consultation

Mental Health Model

One of the most popular models of consultation and one of particular interest to counselors is the mental health model. Much of the credit for the development of this model must go to Gerald Caplan, who was actively working to develop mental health consultation concepts as early as 1964.

Mental health consultation is, as the name suggests, an attempt to promote mental health in a community through use of the consultation process by direct care givers such as counselors and social workers (Dougherty, 1990). Focusing on current work problems, it is

> a process of interaction between two professional persons—the consultant who is a specialist, and the consultee who evokes the consultant's help in regard to a current work problem with which he is having some difficulty and which he has decided is within the other's area of specialized competence. The work problem involves the management or treatment of one or more clients of the consultee, or the planning or implementing of a program to cater to such clients. (Caplan, 1970, p. 19)

From this definition it is possible to determine the goal of mental health consultation as Caplan views it. The initial goal is that of helping the consultee to improve his or her understanding of a current work situation. The second goal is that of helping the consultee to deal with similar problems that may occur at some time in the future. For example, the elementary or middle school counselor who uses the mental health model may assist teachers (the direct care givers) with problems or concerns they may have about individuals or about their class. Through interaction with the counselor, teachers may be able to resolve immediate issues and also utilize the understandings gained in the process to help them with future, similar concerns.

Caplan (1964, 1970) has devised a system involving two major divisions and four subdivisions. In the first division, the consultant focuses on a "case" or an individual (in schools it could be an individual child) or on an administrative problem with mental health applications (for example, helping teachers implement a new, more humane approach to discipline).

In the second division or approach, Caplan has developed a system wherein the consultant gives a specialized opinion and recommends solutions. In this approach the consultant offers specialized information to help improve the client's problem-solving ability.

From these divisions Caplan has outlined four subdivisions of consultation: client centered with a goal of producing behavioral changes in clients; consultee centered with a target of enhancing consultee performance; program centered or assistance in establishing more effective program delivery; and consultee centered/administrative approaches with a goal of enhanced consultee performance in programming (Dougherty, 1990).

Not surprisingly, Caplan's work has been adapted for use in schools, primarily by Meyers (1981), Meyers, Parsons and Martin (1979), and Parsons and Meyers (1984). Using Caplan's concepts with the variation that the consultant (counselor) does not come from an external agency, these authors have suggested four levels of services with the schools to describe the benefits children may receive from the consultant. Level one is direct consultant services to the child; level two involves indirect services to the child, wherein data is gathered by a person or persons other than the consultant (teachers, aides). Level three involves all forms of direct services to the consultee, and level four includes all services to the organization (school) (Brown et.al., 1988). To illustrate the process, a level two approach will be discussed.

Using steps outlined by Caplan, the elementary or middle school counselor/consultant would first respond to a request for help, perhaps from one of the teachers in the building. In meeting with the teacher, the consultant would pay close attention to the teacher's point of view in order to understand the situation as it is seen by the teacher. Next the counselor would make an assessment of the consultee's setting (school, homeroom). Once completed, the counselor would write a report with some recommendations for action. The teacher would then attempt to implement one or more of the recommendations, and then the counselor and teacher would engage in a follow-up evaluation. In the process, the counselor and teacher operate as peers (in schools this is always the case, or should be). The purpose of this exercise is for the teacher to adopt the *consultant's* insights and inputs to meet his or her needs in dealing with the concern.

The techniques used in this process include the establishment of a relationship (if one does not already exist), clarification of the desired outcomes, and the gathering of data about the concern. Every effort is made to include the teacher in the process, and the pronouns "we" and "us" are more frequently used than the pronouns "I" or "me." Both parties must be active participants. It is useful at the onset to discuss and agree upon confidentiality in order to ensure a free and spontaneous discussion. Similar to the counseling process, during consulsation the counselor/consultant must be empathic and tolerant of feelings in the teacher, and have the belief that by gathering enough information in a systematic manner the human behavior can be understood and assistance provided (Caplan, 1970).

Once good rapport has been established and the counselor feels that the teacher is actively involved in the process, the counselor can begin an examination of the problem or expressed concern. A key technique at this juncture is skillful questioning by the counselor in an effort to have the consultee broaden her or his views of the problem (Brown et al., 1991). Counselors will need to take care in order not to make the questioning become an interrogation. They should ask questions in a way that allows the teacher to think and ponder any of the complexities that may be present. At times, they may suggest some different avenues for the gathering of information (Caplan, 1970).

The responsibility for all action taken with reference to the problem under consideration is the chief task of the consultee. For example, if the teacher came to the counselor for help with a particular child, any direct action taken remains the responsibility of the teacher. The counselor may wish to formulate interventions of both a short- and long-term nature for the teacher to consider.

The fact that the counselor does not directly intervene in the process does not mean that his or her role in the concern is terminated after a course of action has been determined. In school situations, counselors must always follow up with teachers to evaluate the courses of action and perhaps to develop a new strategy if the present one is not succeeding.

These counselors who are going to spend a great deal of their time in consultation should read Caplan's works (1964, 1970) in their entirety for a more detailed description of the mental health approach. They can also expect excellent discussions of the approach in the works of Dougherty (1990) and Brown, Pryzwansky, and Schulte (1991).

Behavioral Models

Behavioral consultation stems from behavioral psychology and learning theory. Behavioral consultants are very much interested in how human behavior is acquired and how it may be changed. As is true in counseling theories that are behaviorally oriented, behavioral consultants operate on the principle that since most behavior is learned, it can also be unlearned and new behaviors acquired (Dougherty, 1990). In essence, the principles of behavior change are combined with an indirect approach to the problem by the consultant (Gutkin & Curtis, 1982). Readers should note that the indirect approach in many behavioral models is similar to the indirect approach advocated by Caplan (1970) in the mental health model of consultation. In addition, many of the techniques utilized by behavioral consultants are also found in some of the cognitive counseling theories of Albert Ellis and William Glasser.

Because of the wide range of techniques used by behavioral psychologists, definitions of behavioral consultation vary. Field, Bergam, and Stone (1987) define behavioral consultation as "a problem-solving endeavor that occurs within a behavioral framework" (p. 185). Keller's (1981) definition came from social learning theory: "Behavioral consultation is based on the theory of change that is derived from a broad-based social learning model encompassing diverse streams of psychological and social science research and theory" (p. 64). Dougherty (1990), in an attempt to arrive at a consensual definition, wrote that all behavioral consultation models have four typical characteristics, as follows:

1. Use of indirect service delivery models.
2. A reliance on behavioral technology principles to design, implement, and assess consultative interventions.
3. A diversity of intervention goals, ranging from identifying problematic situations to enhancing competence to empowering.
4. Changes aimed at various targets (that is, individuals, groups, organizations, communities) in different settings (that is, from single settings to multiple settings).

(Dougherty, 1990, pp. 257–258)

While a single model of behavioral consultation does not exist, there are several approaches that can be examined, according to Brown et al. (1991), Keller (1981), Piersel (1985), and Russell (1978). Readers may want to consult the original sources for more detailed discussions of these approaches.

While some similarities between the mental health approach and the various behavioral approaches do exist, there are also some differences of note. Although the consultee and counselor operating under a behavioral approach still interact in a collaborative relationship, behavioral consultants tend to assume more of an "expert" approach to the process in the sense that more control is in their hands. Behavioral consultants help plan and determine the course or courses of action to be followed and may freely introduce techniques and approaches for the consultee to use. For example, a behaviorally oriented consultant, after working through a problem in classroom management with the teacher, may well suggest that Keller's (1981) approach or a similar one be studied and implemented by the teacher.

In most behavioral approaches, counselors do apply their knowledge and techniques to the process. In some cases, the counselor/consultant may have to "teach the teacher" how to use certain kinds of techniques. Teachers who have communication problems with young children, for example, may be asked to join a study group to learn Piersel's (1985) problem-solving model (Dougherty, 1990).

Even in those instances wherein the counselor assumes more of an active, "expert" role, she or he must be careful not to dominate the proceedings to the extent that the consultee (teacher) no longer "owns the problem. "The primary goal of behavioral consultation is to help consultees solve problems, many of which tend to be work related. In an elementary or middle school, these problems are typically classroom management and individual behavioral concerns for which teachers seek help. The counselor/consultant, through listening, discussing, analyzing, and making suggestions, seeks to bring about changes that will not only help the consultee, but may also have an impact on changing the environment wherein the problem may be occurring. For example, through consultation with a counselor, a teacher may become more sensitive to individual differences of children (Hawryluk & Smallwood, 1986).

To illustrate behavioral consultation for the purposes of this text, the work of Bergen (1977) has been selected because it is a common approach used by many consultants. The selection of Bergen's work does not imply that other behavioral approaches such as those developed by Bandura (1977) and others are not valid. Counselors may wish to study a number of sources as they seek to develop their personal views and approaches to consultation.

In the Bergen model there are four steps in the consultation process: problem identification, problem analysis, plan implementation, and problem evaluation (Bergen, 1977). The initial step involves working with the consultee to determine the objectives that should be met as a result of the interaction. Like most behavioral psychologists, Bergen stressed that all objectives should be measurable in terms of any increases or decreases. Counselor/consultants may use anecdotal records, test scores, teacher observations, and subject interviews to help in the formulation of objectives. Thus a teacher who seeks counselor help because "Mary just will not sit still" would not be handed a reinforcement schedule or some similar approach until there is a more detailed study of the problem (Bergen, 1977).

Problem analysis follows problem identification. A major aspect of this phase is to carefully review all the appropriate variables in the situation. In the aforementioned case of the child who will "not sit still," the counselor and the teacher would examine the context of the child's behavior. When does it occur? What is generally happening in class when it does occur? Are there any identifiable conditions that seem to trigger the behavior? What is taking place at home? What needs are being met? Do they have any information from other teachers who have worked with her? From other adults who know her? What do standardized tests tell them? As they seek a solution, do any remedial steps need to be taken? (Bergen, 1977)

Once the analysis is complete, the counselor and teacher formulate a plan to attack the problem. The plan should have definite objectives, and it should include specific intervention strategies with the child. The plan will also include evaluative standards for each strategy.

The teacher will need to monitor the plan in order to help evaluate whether any progress is being made. The counselor and teacher must remain in close contact while the plan is in effect to determine if the objectives are being met and if changes need to be made.

Suppose the counselor and the teacher decide that the cause of Mary's inability to sit still is her strong need to gain the attention of the teacher and her peers. In reviewing the data that has been gathered, the counselor and teacher discover that the behavior or "misbehavior" generally occurs about mid morning of each day, usually right before lunch, and on some days it occurs again in late afternoon. They then reach an initial goal of reducing the number of times the child will leave her seat by one half. If Mary typically leaves her seat six times a day, a goal of reducing this to three or fewer times per day in a two week period may be appropriate. Next they outline several strategies. These may include ignoring the child when she leaves her seat (that is, don't provide her with the recognition she wants for misbehaving), standing near her seat at the times the behavior is most likely to occur, or perhaps doing the unexpected when she does get up (for example, stop and have the whole class stand up and stretch for a moment, or simply turn out the classroom lights).

The final stage of the process is that of evaluation or the determination of the "degree to which the client's behavior is congruent with specified objectives" (Brown et al., 1988, p. 80). To conduct the evaluation, it is necessary to view the objectives from the initial stages of planning to the end of the process. If the objectives included a reduction of out-of-seat behavior by 50 percent and the number of incidents was indeed reduced by half, the consultation process could be considered successful. Of course, not all plans will work to perfection, and we do not intend to oversimplify what can be a long and difficult process. In fact, counselors may need to try out a number of plans, techniques, and interventions to produce the desired results.

Adlerian Models

A number of authors, including Dreikurs and Grey (1968), Dreikurs and Stoltz (1964), Popkin (1982), and Albert (1989), have expanded upon the original ideas of Alfred Adler. None, however, has made a more significant contribution to the elementary school guidance movement with Adlerian concepts than Don Dinkmeyer. His numerous professional works that explore parent training (Dinkmeyer & McKay, *Raising a Responsible Child* (1973) and *STEP* (1976); Dinkmeyer, McKay, & Dinkmeyer, *STET* (1980); Dinkmeyer, McKay, Dinkmeyer, Dinkmeyer, & McKay, *Step/Teen* (1983), *The Next Step* (1987), and *Early Childhood STEP* (1989)) are just a few of his numerous contributions. One would not find it surprising to learn that Dinkmeyer has also actively been involved in the study of professional consultation from the philosophical base of Adlerian psychology.

Dinkmeyer, in discussing consultation strictly from the perspective of counselors working with teachers, defines the process as a procedure through which teachers, parents, principals, and other significant adults in the life of a child communicate (Dinkmeyer, 1971). Inherent in this definition is the concept that consultation is provided as an indirect as opposed to a direct approach to working with children. In this sense, his model is similar to some aspects of both mental health and behavioral models.

The goals of Adlerian consultation are centered on helping adults increase the effectiveness of their work with children. The emphasis is on joint planning and collaboration, in contrast to working within a superior-inferior relationship. A basic assumption is that increased teacher effectiveness will logically lead to the creation of better worlds for children.

The rationale for Dinkmeyer's work stems from the Adlerian principles that behavior is purposeful and reasonable. Behavior reflects the personal perceptions of the child and is best understood in its unity or pattern. Human motivation stems from each individual's striving for significance, and the behavior that results from this motivation has social meaning for each individual. Of key importance is the concept that belonging is a basic human need (Muro & Dinkmeyer, 1977).

The Adlerian consulting process in an elementary or middle school generally starts with a request for help from a teacher or other significant adult. The Adlerian counselor/consultant initiates a team approach to the problem or concern. Together, the counselor and teacher decide on the kinds of information that may be needed. The teacher provides anecdotes and other samples of the child's work and also provides his or her reaction to the work or incidents and the child's subsequent reaction to the teacher's reaction. This kind of assessment permits the counselor/consultant to gain some understanding of the child's psychological movement, goals, and purposes.

Early in the process, the Adlerian counselor makes a careful attempt to discover kinds of interventions the teacher has attempted up to the time of initiating consultation. The counselor asks the teacher to relate any attempts on his or her part to take corrective action, along with an assessment of how well any of the corrective action worked. Time is also spent discussing the child's perceptions and the child's assets as well as his or her concerns. The discussion of assets is important in that it provides the counselor with some knowledge of the child's self-image as well as providing some clues as to the purposes of the child's behavior.

If necessary, the counselor schedules a visit to the classroom for the purpose of obtaining anecdotal data on child and teacher interactions. As the counselor observes the child and teacher interacting, she or he attempts to identify and describe the social meaning of the child's behavior.

Dinkmeyer, while advocating an indirect approach, has noted that consultants who do not know the child in question may wish to conduct brief interviews to help understand the child's perception of his or her position among siblings and of the family atmosphere. One approach is to ask the child what she or he would do if she or he had three wishes (Muro & Dinkmeyer, 1977).

Once the counselor and teacher have gathered the information needed, they are ready to discuss its meaning and implications. At this time, they will be able to generate some tentative hypotheses and recommendations. All recommendations should be formulated with some understanding of the personality of the teacher and of his or her capacity to carry out these recommendations. At this juncture all recommendations are considered tentative, and, as is the case with other models of consultation, the counselor and teacher should schedule ongoing evaluation meetings.

Organizational Models

There is no single approach to consultation under the organizational model approach. Thus Dougherty (1990) has probably done the counseling profession a service by reviewing a number of approaches and synthesizing them into a unified whole. He offers the following definition:

> Organizational consultation is a process in which a professional functioning either internally or externally to an organization provides assistance of a technical, diagnostic/prescriptive nature to an individual or group from that organization in order to enhance the organization's ability to deal with change and maintain or enhance its effectiveness in some designated way. (p. 187)

Although there are a number of models for organizational approaches to consultation, the education training approach, which is the most common, will be discussed for the purposes of this book. The education/training model is the one that is most commonly in use in educational institutions.

The primary goal of education/training consultation is to help the group in question to increase its effectiveness in an area that is the focal point of the process. Suppose, for example, that a school board in a given district discovers that a significant portion of the school budget is spent on standardized testing. A survey of the teachers reveals that the results are not frequently used to help with instruction, and when they are used, a number of the staff seem to be using them incorrectly. The board may then decide to initiate an organizational consultation process, using an education/training approach. Since external or internal consultants could be used, the board could decide to assign the counselors in the district to perform the consultation or seek the services of an outside individual or agency, perhaps a professor who is an expert in measurement from a nearby university.

Regardless of who does the actual consultation, the goal of the board would probably be improved teacher functioning in the use of standardized tests. The consultant will be expected to have the necessary knowledge and skills to help the staff so that noticeable changes in the use of tests would become evident. The education aspect could be simple or rather complex. The consultant would probably have to begin by teaching the staff basic statistical concepts in order to help them utilize the standardized materials properly.

In this approach, the role of the consultant may take on some aspects of that of an "expert," and this could be problematic if the counselor is providing the consulting to his or her peers. Some teachers may be reluctant to accept "consultation" from a coworker. This is why consultants hired from outside the school district sometimes are more readily accepted than are internal ones in this model.

The steps in this model are similar to those discussed in the other approaches. They include needs assessment, planning and educational activities, performing the educational or training activities, and evaluation (Dougherty, 1990). As the description of step one indicates, the consultant must first conduct a needs assessment, a process familiar to most educators. The consultant would either do the assessment as part of his or her duties or have the task completed by others in the school. Again, if we use the example just given, the consultant would want to have some knowledge of the background of the teaching staff in the area of measurement, to include how many have had courses in testing, and what kinds of experiences each has had with measurement. At times, a single questionnaire will suffice to provide the essential information, but if a more in-depth study is needed, the consultant may decide to interview each teacher.

Once the information has been gathered, the planning phase can begin. In this phase, the consultant must decide what information, techniques, and activities will be utilized to teach the stated goals. The consultant may find, for example, that the levels of understanding of measurement concepts vary widely and that separate sessions may need to be held for different groups. The key aspect of this phase of the process is to ensure that the activities meet the needs of the staff as much as possible. This is why teachers should have maximum input into what they will be learning.

The next step involves direct teaching activities by the consultant, and the activities could include lectures, discussions, role playing, films, videos, and printed handouts. This phase of consultation is similar to a "mini" graduate class.

When this phase is completed, the consultant turns his or her attention to an evaluation of what has transpired. Perhaps the consultant has given the staff a pretest on measurement and, in order to evaluate, decides on a posttest measure to show what gains the teachers have made. The consultant may want to observe actual teacher/pupil interactions involving the use of test scores. He or she may want to gather expressions of opinion on the value of what was done. If the goal is one of increased teacher understanding of measurement concepts, consultants should be able to measure that goal. One of the dangers of this approach if the consultant is also the school counselor is the fact that it tends to place the counselor in the role of an evaluator. Unless done carefully, some teachers may well resent judgements made by the counselor.

Dougherty's Generic Model of Consultation

Because of the overlap among the various models of consultation, Dougherty has appropriately suggested a generic model that he outlines in extensive detail in five chapters of his 1990 text, *Consultation, Practice, and Perspectives*. This model calls for a four-stage process, and the stages can overlap. Some elements in this model are similar to those in other approaches.

Stage one is what Dougherty labels the *entry stage* or the "starting up" of the consultation process. At this time, the consultant enters the school or organization and initiates the necessary relationship with the consultee. Of course, if the consultant is the school's counselor, a relationship may have already been established. Other aspects of this initial stage include a discussion of parameters of the problem and, if necessary, the details with respect to contracts.

Stage two, the *diagnostic stage*, involves further and deeper understanding of the problem presented. At this time goals are discussed and agreed upon and avenues to meet these goals are determined. Dougherty suggested that the use of the term "diagnosis" implies a process rather than a task that is done only once.

Stage three is the *implementation stage* in which a plan is formulated, implemented, and evaluated. Dougherty labels this stage implementation in order to reflect its primary focus on action and its secondary emphasis on planning.

The final phase of this generic model is called the *disengagement phase*, a term that Dougherty prefers over the more commonly used "evaluation." The process now moves toward a conclusion, and while the term is not used, evaluation measures do take place (Dougherty, 1990).

This generic model has appeal for elementary school counselors in that it incorporates many of the characteristics suggested in other models, is easy to use, and lends itself to the role of the elementary and middle school counselor/consultant.

Working with Parents

Consultative efforts with parents are best established through an educational focus, and most parents will welcome school efforts that focus on normal, developmental concerns. This is not to suggest that family counseling is of any less importance, but many professionals feel that counselors must be most actively involved in helping adults with parenting skills. When skillfully done, parent consultation programs will attract adults with a wide range of interests and needs related to parenting and human development.

Goals of Parent Counseling

Muro and Dinkmeyer (1977), identified four goals of parent counseling. They are:

1. Helping parents understand the part they play in influencing their child's behavior.
2. Helping parents learn procedures for improving parent-child relationships.
3. Enabling parents to get feedback on their ideas and methods of training children.
4. Helping parents to recognize that their problems in child rearing are not unique, but are shared in common with other parents, providing them the benefits of group thinking and mutual encouragement.

(p. 334)

Goal four is especially important in that it illustrates a key and very powerful component in group counseling, that of universalization. Learning that one is not alone in one's concerns can be very beneficial to good mental health.

The Parent Consulting-Study Program

Elementary and middle school counselors should initiate a systematic approach or approaches to working with parents. Since some parental involvement can involve sensitive issues, counselors must make a special effort to ensure that the school administration and ultimately the school board are informed. However, much of what counselors do with parents will not involve sensitive and personal issues, and work with parents in an educational stance is an excellent way to help both children and parents. In addition, it can become a very effective public relations tool.

To launch a parent consulting-study program, counselors should start with a single group. While no specific group size is required for parent groups, we recommend a total of ten group members, since more than ten tends to decrease the amount of time any one individual can participate in an hour or an hour and a half session. Groups should meet once a week for an hour or an hour and fifteen minutes.

The parents of the youngest age group of the children in the school are the best candidates for initiating parent meetings. Counselors should remember in early sessions to stress the developmental as opposed to remedial aspects of child development. Any ground rules or other expectations such as willingness to share are best covered in pregroup information sessions or in very early meetings (Muro and Dinkmeyer, 1977).

The approach to all sessions must be flexible, but in general counselors should initiate each meeting by reviewing goals and explaining objectives and procedures that will be used. Do not surprise parents with a technique or exercise that may cause embarrassment. If counselors are going to employ any specialized techniques, they should explain these to parents *prior* to enrolling them in a group. Some exercises, such as "trust walks," that are well understood and accepted by counselors can be threatening to the uninitiated parent.

At the very first session, counselors should use a nonthreatening icebreaker to help parents get to know one another and begin interacting with each other. Groups will become much more productive if they become cohesive, and cohesion is a function of member to member interaction. Icebreakers help initiate the process toward cohesion. Also, counselors should ask parents to give the name or names of their children and to state their reasons for joining a group. Counselors should be certain to assess parental expectations of the meetings, and stress the need for them to read any materials that are presented.

In subsequent meetings, counselors should review the topics covered in the prior session and respond to any questions. (Remember, questions are often expressions of feeling.) A discussion of the content for the session should follow. If counselors are going to teach new skills, then role playing or practicing the skills should follow. Counselors should spend time helping the parents develop some understanding of how the newly learned concepts can be utilized with their children. At the end of the session, counselors should make a new assignment and ask parents to respond to the session by stating, "Today, I learned or I relearned _____."

Sessions will vary in time from three or four weeks to those that last a semester or even longer. If the program receives a favorable reception, counselors may wish to consider training parents to lead additional groups.

Materials for Study Groups

Materials to use in parent study groups are available from a wide variety of sources. Counselors may want to develop their own materials, or they may want to choose from some very good commercial products. At the risk of overlooking some fine material, we would like to suggest some that have been used by the authors. Of course, these programs require a financial investment on the part of the school.

1. *Strengthening Stepfamilies* (1968) by Linda Albert and Elizabeth Einstein. Available from American Guidance Service, Circle Pines, MN.

   This is one of the few programs that deals directly with stepparents. It provides excellent information about the skills needed to deal with potential volatile situations. Topics also include conflict resolution, communication, and the improvement of relationships within the home.

2. *Systematic Training for Effective Parenting (STEP)* (1976) by Don Dinkmeyer and Gary McKay. Available from American Guidance Service, Circle Pines, MN.

   The STEP program has a marked Adlerian point of view and provides a pragmatic approach for parents who wish to raise responsible children. Materials include a wide range of discussion topics, readings, recordings, and activities. Parents are encouraged to practice what they are learning in group sessions. The *Parent's Handbook* includes information on ways to understand behavior and misbehavior, ways to understand children and parenting, communication, encouraging, logical consequences, family meetings, developing confidence, and using potential. The nine chapters lend themselves well to discussion groups. This program is also available in Spanish.

3. *Early Childhood STEP* (1989), *STEP/Teen* (1983), and *The Next Step* (1987) by Don Dinkmeyer, Gary McKay, Don Dinkmeyer, Jr., James S. Dinkmeyer, and Joyce L. McKay. All are available from American Guidance Service, Circle Pines, MN.

   Step/Teen is a program designed to help parents work with specialized concerns of adolescence. It is a logical follow-up to STEP and stresses parent-adolescent communication at a difficult time in a young person's life.

   Early Childhood STEP was written for parents of children under six years of age. It includes seven chapters dealing with understanding children, behavior, building self-esteem, communication, cooperation, discipline, and social and emotional disorders.

   The Next STEP is a program designed to help parents refine skills that were learned in *STEP*. It contains a special focus on the "problem-solving group."

4. *Active Parenting* (1983) by Michael H. Popkin. Available from Active Parenting Inc., Atlanta, GA.

   Popkin's program also has an Adlerian base. It is designed to help parents communicate with their children, and it teaches them how to build mutual respect in families. It has a good approach to the teaching of humane discipline. *The Active Parenting Handbook* has six pragmatic chapters, and the *Active Parenting Guide* has sixty-four pages of suggested practical exercises.

5. *Raising a Responsible Child* (1973) by Don Dinkmeyer and Gary McKay. Available from Simon and Schuster, New York.

   While the printing of the book may seem a bit dated, the concepts are timeless, and as such, it is still a very useful tool for parent study groups. There are eleven chapters in four sections, and much of the material found in the *STEP* series is also found in this book. A plus for this book is that most parents will find it very readable and easy to comprehend.

6. *Raising Kids Who Can* (1989) by Betty Lou Bettner and Amy Lew. Available from Harper/Collins, New York.

   This book describes how parents can use family meetings, encouragement, and logical discipline to raise responsible, self-reliant children. This book is short and easy for most parents to understand and apply. The cartoons and concrete examples provided by the authors make this book fun and enjoyable.

7. *How to Talk So Kids Will Listen and Listen So Kids Will Talk* (1980) by Adele Faber and Mlaine Mazlish. Available from Avon Books, a division of the Hearst Corporation, New York.

   Counselors who are familiar with the work of Dr. Haim Ginott will enjoy this work. The book is a straightforward approach to helping parents communicate with children. It contains some theory and extensive practice exercises. The use of cartoons to teach concepts is a good feature of this book.

The "C Group"

Work with parents using the concepts of the "C Group" spans over two decades. Time tested and widely used by numerous elementary school counselors, the "C Group" remains a viable counselor tool in the 1990s and beyond.

Credit for the creation of the "C Group" concept should be given to Don Dinkmeyer, who wrote about the approach as early as 1971 and developed it more fully in a book with Jon Carlson in 1981. It has also been described in works by Dinkmeyer and Muro (1977) and Muro and Dinkmeyer (1977).

In essence, a "C Group" is a combination of group counseling and parent education, although it is equally effective as a counseling and consulting tool for use with teachers. As a "relative" of a counseling group, the "C Group" operates with many of the mechanisms found in group counseling and group therapy. Altruism, feedback, acceptance, and universalization (see Chapter 7) are all part of the process. In fact, the name "C Group" stems from the fact that three major components of the process, collaboration, consultation, and challenges, are all very much a part of most helping groups. Other "C" components are clarification, congruence, caring confrontation, cohesion, and commitment to change. Counselors who wish to utilize the "C Group" with parents may want to adapt the process to their individual counseling styles while still retaining the essential aspects of the process.

In forming a "C Group" with parents, counselors should focus on the common beliefs and feelings held by parents in their groups. After an initial introduction or icebreaker, the counselor should use a "go round" technique and ask each individual to relate his or her most common concern in rearing children. When each parent has had an opportunity to speak, the counselor seeks to identify any common concerns in the group. For example, two or more parents may have trouble with children at bedtime. This or another common concern is a good way to initiate the group interaction. Counselors may say something like, "Three of you have stated that you have some concerns related to getting your children to go to bed on time. Maybe we could start our group with this issue. Let's start with you, Mrs. Cay. Could you tell us what your daughter Andrea does when you tell her it is bedtime?"

After the parent responds, the counselor should then ask, "Then what do you do?" After the parent responds once again, the counselor asks, "Does what you do work?" If the response is negative, the counselor asks, "How do you feel when this happens?" After hearing any expression of parental feeling, the counselor then asks, "Do you know why Andrea acts as she does?" Generally, parents will provide some response to this question. The counselor should acknowledge these responses and then say, "Yes, you may be right. Let me try out a few more thoughts with you." At this juncture the counselor should refer to one of the four goals of misbehavior: undue attention seeking, rebellion, revenge, or avoidance.

The counselor should attempt to actively involve other parents by sponsoring them, linking their thoughts, clarifying, summarizing, interpreting, reflecting, and using any other appropriate group counseling techniques. Parents are asked to identify approaches they would take to deal with the misbehavior under discussion. From time to time, the counselor provides insights and perhaps some suggestions. For example, if the goal of the child's misbehavior is attention seeking, the counselor may suggest that parents attempt to ignore the misbehavior and give the child attention at times when he or she is not expecting parental attention. With rebellious children, parents may be counseled to "remove themselves from the power struggle" or to "take the sail out of the child's wind." Resentful children who seek revenge should also be ignored and provided positive interactions during times when they are more calm. Children who display inadequacy need parental patience and should be given tasks that ensure success. The counselor can also help parents to understand how to deal with the concept of logical consequences for children's behavior. Each of these "learnings" can be woven into the discussions at appropriate times. (A number of suggestions can be found in the resource material mentioned in this chapter.)

After the members have discussed one concern, the group should be ready to move on to another parent or parents who have expressed a different problem, and the process starts all over again. It is very important in the "C Group" to allow parents to relate how they attempt to solve problems, how successful they have been in dealing with these problems, and their feeling about dealing with them. In all cases, we have found it useful to introduce the goals of misbehavior, allowing the group to make suggestions about how the situation should be handled.

Some counselors have taken the basic "C Group" approach and used it with concepts from Glasser's Control Theory and Reality Therapy. The process is flexible enough to allow a range of counselor behaviors and can be a very effective way to work with parents.

Parent Conferences

Many teachers dread the thought of parent conferences, particularly when the conference is parent initiated, in that most parent-initiated requests for conferences are a signal that something is perceived as being wrong. Counselors may be able to be present for some parent-teacher meetings.

Of course, not all parent conferences are negative in nature, but even those that may not seem tense can become just that if some basic guidelines are not followed. Muro and Dinkmeyer (1977) have provided the following guidelines to help make conferences more effective:

1. Be certain to prepare definite objectives for the conference. Each interview has a purpose.
2. Preplan for all conferences. Have all essential data such as the child's work ready to present to parents. Teachers and counselors should also be prepared to discuss other aspects of the child in school, including his or her self-image, social development, and general behavior.
3. Be sure that all conferences focus on communication. Counselors must hear all that parents are communicating. Empathic responses such as "You are worried about Joey's work habits" will help facilitate communication.
4. Look for nonverbal cues that may be expressed by parents—tensional outlets such as hand wringing, tears, lack of eye contact, and so forth.
5. Use a comfortable setting for the conference. If the counselor's office is used, the counselor should not remain behind the desk.
6. Use language that the parent can understand. Avoid jargon whenever possible.
7. Include positive comments in interactions with parents. Refrain from one-word labels (lazy, slow, etc.).
8. Accept the parent's feelings. All individuals are behaving as well as they can at any given moment. Realize how important children are to most parents.
9. Allow time for the parents to summarize what they have learned from the interview.
10. Close each conference by once more summarizing the child's strengths. While no parent should be given a "sugar coated" report that will gloss over some fundamental concerns, neither should parents leave the session with the feeling that the situation is hopeless. Remember that when children are in elementary school, there are many years ahead of them. What seems like a major problem today may well be resolved in months or a year.

(pp. 337–338)

Working with Teachers

Much of what has been discussed in the consultation models presented in this chapter is appropriate for the elementary school counselor in her or his role as a consultant to teachers. The mental health, Adlerian, behavioral, and generic approaches are now widely used by counselors in schools across the land. In addition, some counselors have used these models to develop their own approach to consulting.

Some counselors may find it useful to initiate study groups with the members of the teaching staff. Through informal discussion or through use of a survey of the staff with an inventory, the counselor should discover a time when interested teachers are willing to meet in discussion groups. Counselors must be certain that the needs of teachers are considered, since elementary and middle school faculty members are generally burdened with heavy schedules. Teachers will hesitate to join any group unless they feel that some personal benefit will occur.

Once counselors have established and set a meeting date and time, they should involve the teachers in determining the information they are interested in studying. It is generally wise to be certain that the building principal and the superintendent are fully informed about the meetings.

We recommend having one meeting a week of no longer than forty-five minutes to an hour in length. Each meeting would include a discussion of any material used, followed by a time for teachers to ask questions and make plans for ways to use any new ideas or concepts that they have learned. At the end of each meeting, counselors may want to ask members to summarize what they have learned.

In this process the counselor is once again a facilitator, not an expert. As in all groups, members tend to become leader dependent in early sessions, and if counselors allow this to happen, they may end up providing lectures rather than assisting the teachers to take ownership of the problems presented.

As is the case with parent study groups, counselors involved with teacher study groups may choose to develop their own materials for group meetings. Others may want to select materials from a wide range of commercially available products. The following materials have been used by the authors or their students and are useful for teacher study groups:

1. *Systematic Training for Effective Teaching (STET)* (1980) by Don Dinkmeyer, Gary McKay, and Don Dinkmeyer, Jr. Available from American Guidance Service, Circle Pines, MN.

   The STET program includes many of the concepts that are found in STEP, only the material has teacher groups as its focus. The fourteen chapters in the resource book for STET are pragmatic and written to allow teachers to use the material in their classrooms. The first eight chapters contain group discussion topics on promoting cooperation and mutual respect. Chapters 9 through 12 contain exercises to help provide students with additional experiences in working together.

2. *A Teacher's Guide to Cooperative Discipline* (1989) by Linda Albert. Available from American Guidance Service, Circle Pines, MN.

   Albert's cooperative discipline program has strong roots in Adlerian psychology. Albert's work is based on the contention that students will respond to positive approaches to discipline if they are provided the opportunity. The work contains seven detailed chapters that discuss the theory of cooperative discipline, followed by a detailed discussion of pragmatic ways teachers can deal with the identification and remediation of misbehavior.

Other useful references for teacher study groups include the following:

1. Baruth, L. G., & Eckstein, D. (1976). *The ABC's of Classroom Discipline*. Dubuque, Ia., Kendall/Hunt.

2. Dreikurs, R., Grunwald, B., & Pepper, F. (1980). *Maintaining Sanity in the Classroom*. New York, Harper.

3. Dreyer, S. S. (1977). *The Bookfinder: A Guide to Children's Literature About the Needs and Problems of Youth, Aged 2–15*. Circle Pines, Minn., American Guidance Service.

4. Gorden, T. (1974). *Teacher Effectiveness Training*. New York, Peter W. Wrydin.

5. Knaus, W. J. (1974). *Rational Emotive Education: A Manual for Elementary School Teachers*. New York, Institute for Rational Living.

6. Sanford, G. (1972). *Developing Effective Classroom Groups*. New York, Hart Publishing Company.

CONCLUSION

One key role for the elementary school counselor is that of consultant to teachers, administrators, and parents. The acquisition of consulting skills should be a vital aspect of all university counseling preparation programs. In fact, developmental guidance goals can only be reached if some guidance services are delivered to consumers (children) indirectly. The consultation process is a way of achieving these goals through an indirect approach.

Definitions of consultation vary, but in essence consultation is a voluntary problem-solving process that seeks to assist consultees to develop attitudes and skills that will enable them to function more effectively with clients. Models of consultation include the mental health approach, the behavioral approach, the Adlerian approach, the organizational approach, and the generic approach. Each of these has concepts useful to the elementary and middle school counselor.

Consultation efforts with parents include parent study groups, "C Group" approaches, and parent conferences. With teacher consultation, efforts focus on teacher study groups, teacher "C Groups," and direct collaborative efforts between counselors and classroom teachers.

REFERENCES

Albert, L. (1989). *A teacher's guide to cooperative discipline*. Circle Pines, MN: American Guidance Service.

Albert, L., & Einstein, E. (1968). *Strengthening stepfamilies*. Circle Pines, MN: American Guidance Service.

Bandura, A. (1977). *Social learning theory*. Englewood Cliffs, NJ: Prentice Hall.

Bergen, J. R. (1977). *Behavioral consultation*. Columbus, OH: Merrill.

Bettner, B. L., & Lew, A. (1989). *Kids who can*. New York: Harper/Collins

Brown, D., Kurpius, D. J., & Morris, J. R. (1988). *Handbook for consultation with individuals and small groups*. Alexandria, VA: Association for Counselor Education and Supervision.

Brown, D., Pryzwansky, W. B., & Schulte, A. C. (1991). *Psychological consultation: Introduction to theory and practice*. Boston: Allyn & Bacon.

Caplan, G. (1964). *Principles of preventive psychiatry*. New York: Basic Books.

Caplan, G. (1970). *The theory and practice of mental health consultation*. New York: Basic Books.

Dinkmeyer, D. C. (1971). The C group: Integrating knowledge and experiences to change behavior. *The Counseling Psychologist, 3*(1), 63–72.

Dinkmeyer, D. C., & McKay, G. D. (1973). *Raising a responsible child.* New York: Simon & Schuster.

Dinkmeyer, D. C., & McKay, G. D. (1976). *Systematic training for effective parenting (STEP).* Circle Pines, MN: American Guidance Services.

Dinkmeyer, D. C., & Muro, J. J. (1977). *Group counseling: Theory and process.* Itasca, IL: Peacock.

Dinkmeyer, D. C., McKay, G. D., & Dinkmeyer, D. C., Jr. (1980). *Systematic training for effective teaching (STET).* Circle Pines, MN: American Guidance Service.

Dinkmeyer, D. C., McKay, G. D., Dinkmeyer, D. C., Jr., Dinkmeyer, J. S., & McKay, J. L. (1983). *Systematic training for effective parenting of teens (STEP/Teen).* Circle Pines, MN: American Guidance Service.

Dinkmeyer, D. C., McKay, G. D., Dinkmeyer, D. C., Jr., Dinkmeyer, J. S., & McKay, J. L. (1987). *The next STEP.* Circle Pines, MN: American Guidance Service.

Dinkmeyer, D. C., McKay, G. D., Dinkmeyer, D. C., Jr., Dinkmeyer, J. S., & McKay, J. L. (1989). *Early childhood STEP: Systematic training for effective parenting of children under six.* Circle Pines, MN: American Guidance Service.

Dougherty, A. M. (1990). *Consultation, practice and perspective.*s Belmont, CA: Wadsworth.

Dreikurs, R., & Grey, L. (1968). *Logical consequences: A new approach to discipline.* New York: Meridity Press.

Dreikurs, R., & Stoltz, V. (1964). *Children: The challenge.* New York: Durell, Sloan, & Pearce.

Engels, D. W., Dameron, J. D., (Eds.) (1990). *The professional counselor: Competencies, performance guidelines and assessment* (2nd ed.). Alexandria, VA: American Association for Counseling and Development.

Faber, A., & Mazlish, M. (1980). *How to talk so kids will listen and listen so kids will talk.* New York: Avon Books.

Field, J. K., Bergam, J. R., & Stone, C. A. (1987). Behavioral consultation. In C. A. Maker & S. G. Forman (Eds.), *A behavioral approach to education of children and youth* (pp. 183–219). Hillsdale, NJ.: Erlbaum.

Gutkin, T. B., & Curtis, M. J. (1982). School based consultation: Theory and techniques. In C. Reynolds & T. B. Gutkin (Eds.), *The handbook of school psychology* (pp. 796–828). New York: Wiley.

Hawryluk, M. K., & Smallwood, D. L. (1986). Assessing and addressing consultee variables in school based behavioral consultation. *School Psychology Review, 15*(4), 519–528.

Keller, H. R. (1981). Behavioral consultation. In J. C. Conoley (Ed.), *Consultation in schools: Theory, research, and procedures* (pp. 59–99). New York: Academic Press.

Kirby, J. (1985). *Consultation, practice and practitioner.* Muncie, IN: Accelerated Development.

Meyers, J., Parsons, R. D., & Martin, R. (1979). *Mental health consultation in the schools.* San Francisco, CA: Josey-Bass.

Meyers, J. (1981). Mental health consultation. In J. C. Conoly (Ed.), *Consultation in schools: Theory, research and procedures* (pp. 35–58). New York: Academic Press.

Muro, J. J., & Dinkmeyer, D. C. (1977). *Counseling in the elementary and middle schools.* Dubuque, IA: Wm. C. Brown.

Parsons, R. D., & Meyers, J. (1984). *Developing consultation skills.* San Francisco, CA: Josey-Bass.

Piersel, W. C. (1985). Behavioral consultation: An approach to problem solving in education settings. In J. R. Bergam (Ed.), *School psychology in contemporary society.* (pp. 331-364). Columbus, OH: Merrill.

Popkin, M. H. (1983). *Active parenting.* Atlanta, GA: Active Parenting.

Russell, J. L. (1978). Behavioral consultation: Theory and process. *Personnel and Guidance Journal 56,* 346–350.

Chapter Thirteen

Crisis Intervention

🌳 Several semesters back, the students in a school practicum class I (T.K.) was teaching had to deal with two student suicides; four accidental deaths of either students, teachers, or parents; one tornado that partially destroyed a portable school building; and sixteen cases of suspected child abuse or neglect. One of the things that truly amazed me was that there were only five people in the class, each of them working for 10 to 12 hours a week in an elementary or middle school. It was shocking to me that there were that many crises that affected elementary and middle school children on a daily basis.

Although the ideal school counseling job allows the counselor to focus on preventative activities and developmental guidance, reality has a way of creeping into most counselors' jobs in the form of crises—"fires" that counselors must help to extinguish. Over the past several years, many practicing counselors have told me that they felt unprepared for dealing with crises, that they went into their jobs assuming "someone else in the school would handle that kind of thing—like the principal or the nurse or someone." While it is true that all school personnel should be prepared to deal with crises, there are many types of crisis situations, like working with suicidal students and children who have been abused, for which the school counselor is the best-trained and most appropriate person to intervene. If you have to put out fires (and you probably will), you will want to be well versed in fire-fighting strategies. This chapter will describe (a) the nature of crisis and stages of crises, (b) a method for using developmental guidance activities to teach children coping skills for dealing with crisis, (c) stages and counseling strategies in crisis intervention, (d) techniques for developing districtwide and schoolwide crisis intervention plans, and (e) specific issues related to working with suicidal children, individuals who have experienced the death of someone close to them, and children who have been abused or neglected.

Crisis Theory

A crisis is a kind of severe stress that negatively affects a person's ability to think, plan, and effectively cope with situations (Allan & Anderson, 1986; Caplan, 1964; Janosik, 1983). Usually individuals in crisis go through a predictable sequence during a crisis: (a) they experience a specific precipitating event, (b) they perceive the event as threatening and anxiety-provoking, (c) their responses to the event are disorganized and ineffective, and (d) they develop a coping strategy for handling the situation and the resultant stress (Parad & Parad, 1990). France (1990) described five elements that characterize crises:

1. Crises are triggered by "specific identifiable events that become too much for the person's usual problem-solving skills" (p. 4). They can be the result of a series of accumulating stressful situations, a generalized inability to cope with situations, or some single devastating event.

2. Everyone has crises in their lives at some time or another, when they feel unable to cope with the stressful situations in their lives.

3. People react differently to life situations—what is stressful for one person may not be for another person. This means that crisis is personal and subjective, depending on the individual's interpretation of the situation and his or her level of anxiety and coping skills.

4. Crises last for relatively short periods of time. Sometimes this is due to the fact that the individual simply cannot sustain the intense stress and the tension level dissipates even though the problem is not solved. Sometimes it is due to the fact that the individual has the added motivation to work hard to resolve the crisis to avoid experiencing such elevated levels of intense stress.

5. There are two types of crisis resolution: adaptive, in which the individual learns new coping or problem-solving skills, and maladaptive, in which the individual becomes progressively more disorganized or defensive.

It is difficult to predict which situations will evoke a crisis response and which will not, because each individual has different coping skills and different perceptions of what constitutes a precipitating event. It is important to remember this when working with children in schools. Many times children will come in to the counseling office devastated by something that the counselor may think is relatively trivial, like someone telling them that they do not want to be friends anymore or that they have freckles or someone calling them a nickname that they do not like. These crises may not seem overwhelming to the counselor, but they are very real and very stressful to young children. The counselor must respect the children's perceptions and not discount the severity of the crisis when working with them.

Different Types of Crises

Crises usually fall into three main classifications: (a) crises related to biology, (b) crises related to the environment, and (c) adventitious crises (Parad & Parad, 1990). Crises related to biology are universal and developmental in nature. The precipitating event in this type of crisis derives from some kind of biological change or developmental task, such as reaching school age or puberty (Allan & Anderson, 1986; Parad & Parad, 1990). Since all of the children in a school will eventually have to respond to normal developmental crises, counselors can best serve them by designing guidance activities to help them prepare for and cope with crises related to biology.

Crises related to the environment are not universal, but they happen frequently and, given enough information, can be predicted (Parad & Parad, 1990). The precipitating event in this type of crisis is usually interpersonal or situational, like the death of a parent, divorce, abuse, moving, or a chronic illness. Counselors can help children deal with crises related to the environment in several different ways. As a preventative measure, since this type of crisis affects many of the students in elementary and middle schools in some way, counselors can incorporate lessons on the issues involved with interpersonal and situational crises in their developmental guidance program. Counselors can use these activities to teach children the coping strategies that are appropriate in dealing with this type of crisis. They can also offer small group counseling for students who are struggling with a particular crisis of this nature. Many times students in crisis benefit from hearing that their experiences are similar to those of other children. They may also learn new ways of dealing with problems from other students who have encountered comparable situations. Other children may need the help and support of individual counseling sessions. Counselors can offer students individual counseling for crisis intervention, but they may choose to refer students who experience ongoing problems related to crises to counselors outside the school setting.

Adventitious crises are events that cannot be predicted in advance and usually involve natural disasters, such as flood, fires, and tornados (Parad & Parad, 1990). In response to this type of crisis, counselors may want to design specific guidance experiences for the entire school or for the group of students that has been most affected. They may also want to offer small group and individual counseling to help students cope with this type of crisis.

Stress Reactions in Children

Sandler and Ramsay (1980) studied stress reactions in children. They found that the most stressful circumstances were those of loss. When students experience the death of a parent, sibling, or friend or their parents divorce or separate, the resultant sense of loss creates a tremendous amount of anxiety for them. Slightly less stressful for children were family struggles, including neglect, abuse, and parental job loss. Farther down the list of stressful events were changes in environment, like moving, changing schools, or a parent who had been at home starting to work outside the home. Conflicts with siblings; physical threats, such as accidents, sickness, and violence; and natural disasters also evoked anxious responses, but were perceived as less threatening by the children in this study than these previously mentioned crisis situations.

While it may be helpful to keep the results of this study in mind as they assess the impact of crisis situations on the children in their school and as they plan their crisis intervention strategies, counselors must remember that each person will have a unique personal interpretation of stressful situations. Counselors should design their crisis intervention plans based on the stress reaction and coping skills of the individual students in their schools and on the overall school and community reactions to crisis situations.

Parad and Parad (1990) listed nine typical reactions to crisis situations:

1. Bewilderment. Individuals manifesting this reaction usually have difficulty understanding what is happening. They do not remember ever having experienced this level of stress before, and they have no idea how to go about handling the situation or their reaction.

2. Danger. People who feel endangered by the crisis situation have a sense of impending doom. They are convinced that they will be irreparably hurt, either physically or psychologically, by the crisis.

3. Confusion. Those people who react with confusion have difficulty reasoning and cannot formulate plans for resolving the crisis due to their distress.

4. Impasse. In this type of reaction to crisis, individuals feel "stuck" and unable to generate alternative coping strategies. They believe that any solution they attempt will fail, and they consequently feel immobilized.

5. Desperation. Desperate people are willing to try anything to resolve the crisis, even methods that they would normally not be willing to use or that do not logically relate to the situation. They begin to "throw" possible solutions at the problem.

6. Apathy. These individuals simply give up. They refuse to try to make changes or to resolve the crisis situation. They believe that their situation is hopeless.

7. Helplessness. People who experience this reaction to crisis situations believe that they cannot possibly help themselves and that they must have someone else come to their rescue.

8. Urgency.   Those who react with urgency want a solution to the problem, and they want it now. They may try their own solutions, or they may urgently seek help from others.

9. Discomfort.   With an uncomfortable reaction to crisis, individuals feel miserable—they have difficulty settling down to think about possible solutions. Their anxiety manifests itself in restlessness and inability to concentrate.

Most individuals do not have "pure" reactions that fit neatly into one of these categories. The children in each school will probably have different combinations of these reactions, depending on their personalities and the circumstances. Knowing the various possibilities will help counselors to reflect their feelings and beliefs and help them formulate their approach. If a counselor is working with Jennifer, who is reacting to the death of her cat with bewilderment and confusion, the counselor will not want to rush her in her grief process. The counselor will be very patient and concrete with her, helping her to understand her feelings and clarify her thinking. The approach would be different if Jennifer reacted with discomfort and urgency. If this was her reaction, the counselor might want to help her to achieve a resolution to her miserable feelings quickly, or the counselor might want to teach her patience with herself because the process of grieving takes time. The counselor might want to try to communicate that she or he understands that Jennifer feels as though she needs to solve this right away, but that the usual cycle of grief requires the passing of time.

It would be helpful if counselors also could teach the teachers in their buildings and the parents of the children in their schools about the different types of reactions to crisis. If they understand the various reactions, they can also try to tailor their interactions with children to accommodate the individual reactions.

Developmental Considerations

Counselors must always take developmental considerations into account when they are trying to understand the crisis reaction of a child. Young children frequently do not have a cognitive awareness of the implications of crises and will react accordingly. Older elementary children may have an intellectual understanding of what has happened, but they tend to be bound to the here and now. Their reactions will usually be based on the present reality and not on an anticipation of future problems that will arise due to the crisis. Middle school children have a much more adultlike set of reactions to crisis. Their responses will be very similar to those manifested by adults, except that they may have more intense feelings of helplessness because they have less power over external factors than do adults in similar situations.

Phases of Crisis

Each person usually experiences different reactions to crisis depending on the phase of the crisis process. The individual usually passes through at least two, and sometimes three, phases of crisis (France, 1990). In the first phase of the crisis, the impact phase, the person experiences his or her initial reactions to the realization that this particular situation has reached crisis proportions. The usual coping strategies the person uses have not resolved the problem created by the precipitating event, and the person may begin to feel helpless, anxious, frustrated, angry, afraid, depressed, or out of control.

Since the impact phase occurs immediately after the precipitating event, this phase is usually relatively brief. Unless counselors are working with a child right after a precipitating event or at the time when the impact of the precipitating event becomes clear to the child, they will probably not encounter many students during this phase. Many times, a child in this phase will appear not to react at all, especially in a situation that he or she has lived with for a long time, but that has just recently begun to overwhelm his or her coping strategies. For example, Jane is a child who has been sexually and physically abused over a period of time and who has decided to reveal this abuse to the school counselor. Jane may appear almost nonchalant during the disclosure. This may be due to the method that she has developed for coping with the abuse—she may have learned to detach herself from reality and not react at all. Other times a child may appear not to react simply because he or she is still in shock during the impact phase. For instance, Lonny may tell the counselor that his mother died over the weekend and then proceed to change the subject and talk about the field trip his class is going to take next week. Lonny may not have fully realized the impact of the event, he may not know how to express his feelings, or he may just be acting like a child.

The second phase of crisis reaction is the coping phase (Caplan, 1964; France, 1990). During this phase, individuals begin to make attempts to change the situation or to change their reactions to the precipitating event. They usually feel an increased level of discomfort or anxiety and/or a sense of desperation or urgency. They may reach an impasse or give way to feelings of apathy. In the coping phase, people are more willing to try new solutions to problems, and they are more open to suggestions and help from others than they are at other, noncrisis times of their lives. In some cases, certain individuals use a problem-focused method of coping and manage to learn new coping skills or to generate a solution using the coping skills they already had in response to the crisis situation (France, 1990). Other individuals use an emotion-focused method of coping, and they try to change their feelings about their situation (France, 1990). They may use an adaptive strategy, like learning to accept the situation, that would give them relief from the pressures induced by the precipitating event. They may use a maladaptive strategy, like trying to deny the problem and the accompanying negative feelings or using drugs or alcohol to cover up their pain. With these people, the crisis reaction ends in the coping phase, either with a positive resolution of the problem or a dissipation of the intensity of the tension.

Because children in the coping phase are more likely to try new approaches to their problems and are more likely to seek assistance, this is the perfect time for counselors to approach them with help and possible solutions. Counselors must pay attention to the types of reactions they are experiencing and the types of coping strategies that they are using and adapt their approach appropriately. For example, Tom, a fourth grader who has been having behavior problems, talks to Mr. Roy, his school counselor, about his upcoming move. Mr. Roy's first response will be to reflect the feelings Tom expresses during the impact stage and help him clarify his thoughts and reactions to the impending move. Then Mr. Roy will evaluate how he can help Tom develop coping strategies. Mr. Roy will listen to the ideas that Tom generates for coping before he makes any suggestions. If Tom tells him that he has some good ideas for making new friends in his school, Mr. Roy may ask him to relate those ideas to him, perhaps adding several ideas to his list. If Tom tells the counselor that he will never be able to make friends, Mr. Roy might want to explore the thinking and feelings underlying this conclusion and then help him explore how he made friends when he started in this school and how he could apply those skills in his new school.

If none of their coping strategies work, individuals move into the third phase of crisis reaction, withdrawal (Caplan, 1964; France, 1990). This happens when people feel that nothing they have tried has helped to alleviate their pain. There are two basic types of withdrawal: voluntary and involuntary. Suicide is a voluntary form of withdrawal, in which individuals end their lives or attempt to end their lives in order to avoid the pain inherent in a continued crisis situation. Involuntary withdrawal usually involves some type of psychological or emotional disorganization. It might take the form of some type of psychotic break involving distorted cognitions, mood swings, and other personality disruptions.

Generally speaking, people do not move into the withdrawal phase unless the crisis has gone on for some time without a resolution or some type of assistance in sight. One of a school counselor's duties is to monitor the children in school to make sure that those who are experiencing crises are receiving support and assistance. In a large school with a high student/counselor ratio, counselors may not be able to consistently make contact with all of the students. When this is the case, they will probably want to enlist the help of the teachers and staff of the school to watch for children who may be falling through the cracks and not getting help. If counselors find children who need help with crisis situations that they are unable to give them directly, counselors must arrange for some kind of mentoring program in the school or refer the children for outside counseling.

A Preventive Guidance Approach to Crisis Situations

Allan and Anderson (1986) developed a classroom guidance curriculum module designed to teach children adaptive coping skills they can use in crisis situations. They suggested that children could learn to cope more adequately with the crises in their lives if they participated in guidance activities designed to teach them: (a) what a crisis event is, (b) what kinds of feelings and thoughts are generated by a crisis event, (c) how feelings and thoughts about a crisis event usually change over time, and (d) the kinds of coping strategies that help in crisis situations.

The module Allan and Anderson (1986) developed consisted of three 40 minute lessons. In the first lesson, the children defined the word crisis and discussed different types of precipitating events. Each of them drew a crisis that might affect them or some other child. In the second lesson, students wrote a story about a crisis that they had experienced or that someone they knew had experienced. The third lesson helped the children explore immediate feelings and long-term feelings about crises. They also discussed possible ways of coping with crises and ways for parents and teachers to help children in times of crisis.

This model has great potential as a preventive intervention tool for school counselors. Counselors might want to consider adapting some version of this guidance module for application in their schools. As the children in a counselor's school acquire more coping skills for dealing with the crises in their lives, the counselor will be able to reduce the amount of time and energy needed to help them put out "fires."

Crisis Intervention in Schools

While school may not be the ideal place for crisis intervention from the perspective of the development of a comprehensive preventive guidance program, there are many reasons why school counselors must be prepared to deliver crisis intervention services. School counselors usually have continuous, immediate access to children. Since time is limited in crisis situations, many times the school counselor is the only person available who can work with children during these brief windows of time (Steele & Raider, 1991). Quite frequently, the precipitating event occurs in school, which puts the school counselor in the position to begin crisis intervention in the impact phase. This allows the counselor to gain a more thorough understanding of the nature of the crisis and the child's perception of and reaction to the precipitating event. Many school counselors take a problem-solving approach, rather than a long-term insight-oriented clinical approach, to children's difficulties (Steele & Raider, 1991). The fact that this orientation is well suited to crisis intervention situations further validates the involvement of school counselors in crisis intervention with children. In order to successfully deliver crisis intervention services in schools, counselors need to develop an understanding of the goals of school-based crisis intervention and explore the skills involved in intervening in a crisis situation in a school.

Goals of School-Based Crisis Intervention

The primary objective of crisis intervention in schools is to replace self-defeating behaviors and maladaptive thoughts and feelings with appropriate and effective coping skills and adaptive thoughts and feelings (Steele & Raider, 1991). In order to do this, the school counselor must help children and their families attain four goals: (a) realize that crises are a normal part of life, (b) gain a different perspective on the precipitating event and the current situation, (c) recognize and accept the feelings associated with the crisis, and (d) learn new problem-solving skills.

Normalizing Crisis Responses

In helping children and their families normalize their responses to crisis situations, the school counselor must assist them in clarifying what the crisis is and why it has occurred (Steele & Raider, 1991). He or she may also help them explore why this particular situation has overwhelmed the coping skills that they presently have. This process serves to normalize the reactions of family members and lets them realize that their behaviors, thoughts, and feelings are not inappropriate under the circumstances.

For example, Jeremy Solomon comes to Ms. Lambert, his school counselor, and wants to talk about his desire to run away from home because of his parents' reaction to finding him smoking marijuana in his bedroom. He believes that he can no longer live in the same house with them and that they will refuse to trust him in the future. First, Ms. Lambert explores exactly what happened in order to clarify the nature of the crisis. She then asks Jeremy to talk about his thoughts, feelings, and behaviors and to consider what his parents are thinking and feeling. Ms. Lambert also asks him to describe what has happened, both with him and with his parents, in other crisis situations in the past. Her purpose is to help Jeremy see that both his own reaction and the reaction of his parents are not unusual in this circumstance.

Reevaluating Crisis Situations

The next goal in the crisis intervention process is assisting children and their families to reevaluate the crisis situation and shift their perception so that they "see the situation for what it is, no more and no less" (Steele & Raider, 1991, p. 11). To achieve this goal, the counselor asks children and their families to explore new information and to reconsider what they already know about the problem. The counselor will challenge negative or distorted interpretations and review alternative positive or neutral interpretations of the situation. He or she might point out that the precipitating event did not create the crisis; rather the interpretation of the precipitating event created the crisis.

Continuing with the example of Jeremy Solomon, Ms. Lambert asks Jeremy what it was in the interaction with his parents that led him to believe that he could not live in their house anymore. She further asks him which of their comments suggested to him that they would never trust him again. Ms. Lambert gently challenges Jeremy's cognitive distortions of the conversation with his parents. She also challenges his belief that the only possible solution to the problem is for him to run away. She suggests that there are many alternative responses to this situation that he has not considered.

Recognizing and Accepting Feelings

The third goal in crisis intervention in schools is the recognition and acceptance of feelings (Steele & Raider, 1991). In addition to distorted perceptions and cognitions, children and their families also experience distorted feelings. Before they can make affective shifts, they must recognize that the feelings they are experiencing are a part of the crisis state and they must express them. This process will dissipate some of the tension inherent in the crisis situation and will allow children and their families a chance to examine their feelings and correct any distortions apparent in their affective states. The purpose in this procedure is to help them gain a sense of control over the feelings they experience in response to the crisis.

Jeremy has many feelings in this particular situation. He feels anxious, desperate, angry, embarrassed, afraid, helpless, and hopeless at various times during this crisis. Ms. Lambert reflects his feelings and helps him to recognize and express his feelings, using conversational and expressive techniques like drawing and writing. As she works with him on understanding his feelings, Jeremy begins to see that he can control his emotional reactions and that he does not have to let his emotions control him.

Developing Coping Skills

The final goal in this process is to help children and their families develop more adaptive problem-solving strategies (Steele & Raider, 1991). This may involve assisting them in reviewing coping techniques they already know and generating ways of applying them in the specific crisis situation. It may also involve teaching them new coping skills, helping them practice those skills, and adapting those skills to their current circumstances.

Ms. Lambert assists Jeremy in considering which of the coping strategies he already knows, such as apologizing, could help him solve this particular situation. She asks him to think about how he can adapt some of his usual problem-solving skills, such as brainstorming, to working out a solution with his parents. Ms. Lambert teaches Jeremy some negotiation techniques that she believes might be helpful in coming to a new understanding with his parents. They practice these skills in her office. She may also suggest that they invite his parents to her office so that she can help the entire family work on dealing with this crisis in a cooperative manner.

These four goals are not as discrete as the preceding example might lead the reader to believe. As counselors work with children and their families in this crisis intervention process, they will find that the different goals and the strategies that they use to achieve them will overlap. Counselors will also find that all of this happens very rapidly. Because the crisis phenomenon is time-limited, there is always a certain degree of telescoping and truncating in crisis intervention that makes the process different than ordinary counseling interaction. In crisis intervention, everything happens more quickly and intensely than it does in other counseling situations.

Stages and Counseling Strategies in Crisis Intervention

The literature on crisis intervention suggests that crisis intervention usually follows a logical sequence of stages (Aguilera, 1990; France, 1990; Steele & Raider, 1991). A frequently used arrangement of crisis intervention progresses through the following stages, which resemble a typical problem-solving paradigm: (a) assessing the crisis and personal resources, (b) increasing emotional clarity and cognitive understanding about the problem, (c) generating possible solutions, (d) deciding on an intervention, (e) planning for the execution of the intervention, and (f) planning for evaluation of the intervention.

Assessment

The first stage involves some type of assessment of the person and the problem. During this first stage, the counselor will want to elicit the child's description of the circumstances leading up to and following the precipitating event(s) and the child's feelings about the crisis. The counselor will want to assess the child's repertoire of coping skills related to this particular situation. The counselor will also want to evaluate the possibility that the child might be a danger to self or others. If the counselor decides that the child is suicidal or dangerous, she or he will need to intervene more directly and make arrangements to ensure the safety of the child. This will involve notifying the child's parents and any other appropriate authority figures. It may also involve helping the parents arrange for some type of hospitalization or other medical intervention.

During this process, the counselor's primary job is to encourage children to tell the counselor about their perspective on the problem, their feelings, and their plans. The primary skills the counselor will need to use to bring this about are reflective listening skills and clarification skills (France, 1990). Many times, people in crisis have difficulty organizing their thoughts and feelings and/or expressing themselves, so counselors may need to ask children to provide more concrete information or to help them focus on a particular aspect of the problem. Counselors should not do a great deal of probing into the underlying interpersonal or intrapersonal dynamics of the students at this time. If there is time and if this type of intervention is within the purview of the school counselor's duties, she or he can do this type of in-depth counseling at a later time, after the crisis point has passed.

Understanding Feelings and Cognitions

The second step involves helping the child reach the goal of increasing his or her ability to comprehend and express feelings about the crisis situation and developing a more positive cognitive understanding of the problem. The counselor will help the child "take ownership" of the problem, recognizing the part that the child plays in the situation and acknowledging that he or she will probably have to make some personal changes in order to resolve the problem (France, 1990).

In order to help the child gain an intellectual understanding of the crisis and the part he or she plays in it, the counselor will usually need to use more active counseling skills, such as reflecting meaning, confronting, and reframing. He or she may need to point out the underlying meaning in the statements the child makes. Because of the confusion inherent in crisis situations, the child may not be thinking very clearly, and the counselor will have to highlight ideas and information that would usually be obvious to the child. There will probably be many discrepancies between what the child is telling the counselor and his or her nonverbals, between the child's perception of the situation and the counselor's perception of the situation. The counselor will use confrontation to point out these discrepancies so that the child can more clearly examine the problem. Because the child is feeling overwhelmed and unable to use routine coping skills, he or she will probably view the entire situation from a negative, hopeless perspective. The counselor may want to use reframing to suggest an entirely different point of view. Sometimes it helps to use a highly exaggerated, absurd reframe to give the child a chance to see the possibilities for using humor as a coping skill. The counselor will probably have to be direct in explaining the nature of crises, the effects that they have on people, and how the counselor views the connection between this particular crisis and how it is affecting the child.

Considering Solutions

In the third stage of crisis intervention, the counselor's primary responsibility is to help the child consider potential solutions and their probable consequences. It is sometimes helpful to break the problem into smaller segments. Quite frequently, one primary element of the crisis mentality is thinking that the entire problem needs to be completely solved in the immediate future. If the counselor can systematically divide the problem into manageable parts, it will seem less overwhelming to the child and counselor and child can generate solutions to each component separately. From the subdivided problem, counselors should choose the segment that is most amenable to change to begin their problem solving. This will give the child a taste of success, which can be very encouraging to the child. When the counselor has picked the part of the problem she or he wants to help the child to tackle first, the following three questions will help structure the problem solving (France, 1990):

1. What has the child already tried in order to deal with the situation?
2. What has the child thought about trying?
3. Right now, what other possibilities can the child think of?

This sequence of questions helps to organize the problem-solving process and give structure to the exploration of possible coping mechanisms. The counselor can use a brainstorming strategy to help the client generate a multitude of possible options in answer to the third question. In brainstorming, the counselor asks the client to simply list potential solutions without evaluation or censorship. The counselor writes everything the client says, no matter whether the solutions are appropriate or possible. This encourages creative thinking and new ways of looking at the situation. The counselor may also want to ask the child how he or she has resolved similar problems in the past. Both of these counseling techniques help build the child's sense of control and self-confidence. They send the message that the counselor believes the client has the capacity to cope with the problem.

The counselor should avoid trying to solve the problem for the child. However, sometimes the counselor may have an idea for a possible solution that the child has not mentioned. When this happens, the counselor may want to subtly add it to the list. France (1990) suggested that the counselor use a metaphoric technique to introduce additional solutions to the child. This would involve saying something like, "In my other school I worked with a sixth grade boy who got beat up by a third grade girl. He was pretty embarrassed, but he figured out a way to deal with it. This is what he did. . . ." Using this method, the counselor can make suggestions to the child without appearing to doubt the solutions he or she has generated and without seeming to want to fix the problem without the child's help.

Evaluating Options

In step four of the crisis intervention process, the counselor helps the client evaluate the potential coping options and choose the one that appears most likely to successfully solve the problem. Although a long list of possible solutions may have been generated during the brainstorming procedure, the counselor will probably want to quickly eliminate all but two or three of the possibilities. In evaluating the remaining options, the counselor will want to help the child consider the advantages and disadvantages of each of them. During this interaction, the counselor will need to remain alert to the child's feelings and the possibility that the child may not be thinking clearly. The counselor will use his or her reflecting skills to help the child gain an understanding of feelings and clarifying skills to help the child think carefully. The counselor may also need to use confrontation if the child tries to convince the counselor that he or she must solve the problem or if the child persists in unrealistic interpretations of the crisis.

Eventually the child will eliminate all but one of the potential solutions. When this happens, the counselor should try probing a bit to make sure that the child believes that this solution will help resolve the crisis, that it has minimal potential negative outcomes, and that the child is willing to commit to the execution of this particular solution. After the child has made this commitment, the counselor can move to the fifth and sixth steps in the crisis intervention process, planning the application of the solution and planning the evaluation of the solution.

Application and Evaluation of the Solution

Because the nature of a crisis is time-limited, the client will need to apply the solution to the problem in relatively short order. In the last two steps of the crisis intervention process, the counselor will need to develop a timetable for the application of the solution, teach any coping strategies that the child does not already know, practice the coping strategies necessary for the solution of the problem, and discuss how the child will know if the solution has worked and the crisis is resolved.

During these two steps, the counselor will again use reflecting and clarifying skills to help the child continue to deepen his or her emotional and cognitive understanding of the problem and the proposed solution. The counselor may also use some teaching techniques to help the child acquire new coping skills. If this is necessary, the counselor should be sure to use a variety of teaching approaches, including modeling, drawing, and demonstrating with toys or other media. This will help the child gain mastery over these skills more quickly than if the counselor simply talks about the coping technique. The counselor will also want to participate in role playing with the child so that he or she can practice these new skills. The counselor may want to have the child play himself or herself and the other parties involved in the crisis situations so that the child can anticipate potential problems and gain insight into the perspectives of the other people involved (France, 1990). A method of evaluating the success of the solution may be obvious. If this is the case, the counselor will just discuss how the child will know that the crisis is resolved. If that is not the case, however, the counselor may want to use brainstorming to generate ideas for how the child can assess progress in dealing with the problem.

This description of the phases and techniques used in crisis intervention will give the school counselor a general sense of the process involved. However, because every crisis situation is unique, there is no guarantee that all of them will proceed in the same manner. The counselor will have to be alert to the variety of possibilities and apply his or her counseling skills according to the needs of each individual client and the particular crisis situation.

Developing a School Crisis Plan

Many authors have written about the need for developing procedures for dealing with crisis situations in the schools (Hunt, 1987; Oates, 1988; Palmo, Langlois, & Bender, 1988; Sorenson, 1989; Zinner, 1987). Traumatic events affect children, their families, school personnel, and entire communities. In order to appropriately respond to crises, the district must have a crisis management policy and procedure already in place. If the district does not have such a policy and procedure, the school counselor should play an integral role in the design of a policy manual outlining crisis management procedures and in the implementation of any crisis interventions.

The school board and district administrative personnel must support this as a necessary and legitimate undertaking (Palmo et al., 1988). In some communities, these individuals may be reluctant to admit that there is a need for a plan for dealing with crises, preferring to deny the possibility of such occurrences in their locale. However, since "school districts and school personnel are held responsible for the appropriate care of the students" (Palmo et al., 1988, p. 95), they have a legal responsibility to plan ahead to mitigate any traumatic effects of crisis situations that might occur in school. Otherwise, individuals negatively affected by the crisis might have a legitimate case for a malpractice suit based on negligence.

The implementation of a districtwide crisis policy will require the cooperation of many people, and the committee to develop the manual should include school guidance counselors, teachers, administrators, school board members, and individuals from the community (HCA Hill Country Hospital, 1989). As community representatives, it is essential to include professionals trained to deal with crisis situations and community mental health practitioners who would be willing to volunteer to provide intervention and assistance to school personnel in a broad-based crisis. This committee will organize available information about the kinds of crises that affect schools; how the different crises impact children, their families, and school personnel; and ways school counselors and other school personnel can intervene to help these populations effectively deal with crises. They will want to consider forming a districtwide crisis response team and an individual school crisis response team. If they decide these teams would be helpful, they may want to make recommendations about who should be included on the teams.

The main task of this committee will be to write a policies and procedures manual outlining step-by-step staff responsibilities for staff members, including the school counselor, the school nurse, and the principal, for specific types of crises that can affect children in schools. In case one of the usual staff members is absent or unavailable, the manual should provide for a backup person for each of the critical staff members. Some of the responsibilities should include arranging for access to rooms, records, telephones, and such; coordinating dissemination of information to staff, students, parents, and other people who need to know details; providing liaison with community mental health agencies; and acting as part of a crisis intervention team. The manual should include descriptions of each type of crisis, the typical responses by an individual who is experiencing that type of crisis, and developmentally appropriate intervention strategies for helping an individual in that type of crisis. Another helpful component of the manual would be a list of community resources, with telephone numbers, addresses, services available, and a contact person.

After committee members have gathered this information and formulated the manual, they will need to create awareness in the schools and in the community about the different kinds of crises, the impact they have on people, and possible intervention strategies (Palmo et al., 1988). They will also need to provide training for specific school personnel, especially school counselors, in strategies for helping individuals in crisis situations. The school counselors will, in turn, want to train teachers, parents, and students about how they can help one another in times of crisis.

On a school level, the counselor will probably want to form a crisis response team and use the district manual as a prototype for developing a detailed plan for dealing with specific types of crisis. Counselors should include themselves, the school principal, the school nurse, representative teachers from each grade level, and anyone else who they think could be helpful in considering the possible impact of and responses to crisis situations. In considering crises that are not confidential, such as the death of a student, counselors will want to designate a single spokesperson who will deal with the media or other people who seek information about the crisis (Oates, 1988). There should also be a plan for informing staff and students about nonconfidential crises that might affect them. Counselors will also want to decide who will notify the appropriate person if a death happens at school and who will deliver personal effects to the family. The team will need to develop a policy for funeral attendance, school remembrance ceremonies, and other such activities.

It is essential to provide emotional support to students and staff following a tragedy. While the various members of the team will have specific responsibilities in this area in accordance with the district manual, counselors may want to refine and add details to the district policy and procedures. They will also probably want to make plans for conducting developmentally appropriate classroom guidance lessons for each grade level in order to help students deal with the particular crisis and how it affected them. It might also be helpful to provide an in-service for teachers, educating them about signs manifested by children when they need additional individual help dealing with a crisis. Counselors might also want to conduct a teacher in-service on crisis intervention strategies and incorporating coping skills into a classroom.

Working with Suicidal Children

Although most adults prefer to think that children do not commit suicide, there is evidence to show that at least 200 children under the age of 14 commit suicide annually in the United States, and experts assume there are many, many more unconfirmed suicides and suicide attempts (Herring, 1990; Stefanowski-Harding, 1990). These numbers continue to increase. While the increasing suicide rates of elementary and middle school children are still significantly less than those of high school children, they are still high enough to cause grave concern. Elementary and middle school counselors must understand the issues that contribute to suicidal ideation and behavior, conduct suicide prevention programs, and assess and intervene with suicidal students.

Contributing Factors that May Lead to Suicide

Researchers have found that certain intrapersonal, cognitive, and environmental conditions are significantly related to suicidal behavior (Blumenthal & Kupfer, 1988). These elements include hopelessness, depression, psychopathology, cognitive rigidity, stress, the family system, and coping strategies (Davis & Sandoval, 1991; Orbach, 1988). Individuals who feel hopeless and depressed frequently have a tendency to act on any suicidal thoughts. Many children who are suicidal suffer from severe psychopathology, especially emotional illnesses that involve losing contact with reality. Another risk factor among children is cognitive rigidity—a lack of flexibility in thinking that prevents individuals from considering alternative solutions to problems and contributes to feelings of depression, helplessness, and hopelessness.

Life stress frequently contributes to suicidal behavior in children and adolescents. Stressors that greatly increase the likelihood of suicidal thoughts and behaviors are issues around sexuality, achievement pressures, family suicide, and personal loss, such as the death of friends or family members. The family system can also serve as a risk factor. The following characteristics of the family system may increase the possibility of suicidal behavior: family hostility and/or scapegoating of a particular child, medical and psychiatric illness, high economic stress, high conflict, and low cohesion. Although all of these risk factors can contribute to suicidal ideation and actions, children and adolescents who have effective coping strategies learn to deal with conditions such as these. Therefore, probably the most essential risk factor is poor problem-solving skills. Children and adolescents who lack problem-solving skills are more susceptible to being overwhelmed by negative intrapersonal, cognitive, and environmental pressures than are those who have adequate coping strategies.

As a school counselor, one of the best methods to use to recognize potential risk factors is to observe the coping techniques manifested by students. Those students who have poor problem-solving strategies will be more likely to succumb to any of the other risk factors. Counselors and the teachers in their schools will need to carefully monitor students for signs of hopelessness, depression, cognitive inflexibility, and severe psychopathology. Counselors should encourage students to discuss the various life stresses they are experiencing with counselors and with their teachers so that both counselors and teachers can recognize those students who are feeling overwhelmed by stress. In talking with students and their parents, counselors may want to explore the family system for risk factors that can negatively affect children. Counselors can include countermeasures to all of these risk factors in their guidance curriculum, and as they learn to recognize children who are at greater risk for suicidal behavior, they can include these children in counseling groups and see them for individual counseling sessions.

Precipitating factors are those actions that trigger the suicidal crisis (Blumenthal & Kupfer, 1988). With adolescents, precipitating factors usually fall into four main categories: disciplinary crises, problems with parents, problems with boyfriends or girlfriends, and problems with friends (Davis & Sandoval, 1991). Frequently the suicidal individual wants to demonstrate the intensity of the emotions evoked by the precipitating event or to get relief from the pressure of the precipitating event. With younger children, the precipitating event can be due to loss or impending loss, especially brought about by death or divorce, child abuse or neglect, family aggression, family crises, or academic pressures (Orbach, 1988).

The main thing counselors can do to prevent precipitating factors from actually prompting a suicide attempt is to increase the protective factors by providing guidance and counseling services to the students in their schools. Counselors will not be able to actually prevent most precipitating events from happening, but they can give children the coping skills they need to deal with these problems as they occur. Counselors can design guidance activities that increase cognitive flexibility, hopefulness, and friendship skills so that students can build strong social support systems. They can suggest that teachers build opportunities for enhancing cognitive flexibility into their lessons. Counselors can also continually advertise their availability as supportive listeners, and they can encourage the teachers in their schools to learn listening skills so that they, too, can provide support to students. Another protective factor that counselors can affect is treatment of psychiatric disorders and personality disorders. Although these maladies are too severe for intervention by most school counselors, they can learn to recognize the symptoms and refer children suffering from serious psychopathology for counseling and psychiatric services in the community. Counselors can also enhance the self-protective qualities of all of the students in their schools by providing a wide-ranging suicide prevention program.

Suicide Prevention Programs

Most experts advocate a school system-wide comprehensive developmental approach to suicide prevention (Davis & Sandoval, 1991; Sattem, 1991; Smaby, Peterson, Bergmann, Bacig, & Swearingen, 1990; Tierney, Ramsay, Tanney, & Long, 1991). As a primary prevention effort, the school counselor should provide a program that helps create a positive school climate, addresses the emotional development and mental health of students, and promotes student awareness about suicide (Tierney et al., 1991). The school counselor should also screen for at-risk students, monitor suicide-prone populations, involve peers in suicide prevention, and promote suicide awareness throughout the school community (Davis & Sandoval, 1991).

Because the atmosphere in the school can affect the mental health of the students, school climate should be positive. Interactions between students and school personnel must be encouraging to both parties. Students should be involved in the discipline procedures, and consequences for behavior problems should be logically connected and in proportion to the transgression. The school counselor can have a tremendous impact on the school climate by acting as a role model for positive interactions with students and providing encouraging feedback to faculty and other school personnel.

Many school counselors have developed guidance programs that focus on suicide awareness and prevention. In designing an awareness program, counselors will want to help students understand their own thoughts and feelings about suicide and those of others (Tierney et al., 1991). As always, they will want to take the developmental level of students into account as they design the program, using concepts and language that their target population will understand. Because many children confide in a peer, rather than an adult, some essential elements of an awareness program are (a) ways to identify the warning signals of a suicidal person, (b) how to talk to a friend who manifests these warning signs, (c) how to get help for the friend, and (d) resources available in the community that can provide intervention for children, adolescents, and their families (Davis & Sandoval, 1991; Tierney et al., 1991).

Before counselors conduct suicide awareness programs with students, they will probably need to make sure that they communicate the importance of such a prevention strategy to parents and other school personnel. There are many people who still believe the myth that discussing suicide may insert the idea of suicide into the mind of susceptible individuals, especially children (Capuzzi, 1988). Part of the counselor's mission in introducing suicide prevention programs into the school guidance curriculum will be to counteract this myth by providing accurate information about the causes and prevention of suicide among children and adolescents. One way to do this is to provide informational programs to teachers, staff, administrators, and parents (Nelson & Crawford, 1990; Tierney et al., 1991). Counselors should include information on myths of suicide, warning signs, and concrete recommendations for how teachers and parents can handle situations with children who may be suicidal (Nelson & Crawford, 1990).

Assessment of Suicidal Students

In order to evaluate a student for suicidal risk, school counselors must know (a) the warning signs that suggest the possibility that a student is contemplating suicide, (b) how to assess potential lethality, (c) how to obtain a commitment from the child not to harm himself or herself, and (d) how to involve the family in the process of protecting the child (Davis & Sandoval, 1991). School counselors must consider all suicidal thoughts and behaviors seriously, even when parents, teachers, and even the counselor believe that the child is mainly seeking attention (Davis & Sandoval, 1991; Hipple, 1993). It is also important for all counselors who are going to work with suicidal clients to examine their own ideas and feelings about death and suicide so that these personal reactions will not sabotage their work with clients.

Students, school personnel, and parents should all be aware of the warning signs that frequently serve as precursors to suicidal behavior. The warning signs usually cluster in several broad categories: (a) behavioral clues, (b) verbal cues, (c) situational clues, (d) cognitive patterns, and (e) personality traits (Capuzzi, 1986; McBrien, 1983). Most children and adolescents who act on suicidal ideas manifest more than one of these warning signs, but there are some suicidal students who never show any of the warning signs.

The most common behavioral clues involve changes in the child's behavior (Capuzzi, 1986). These behavioral shifts might be a sudden drop in grades, a previously unnoticed difficulty in concentrating, or a loss of interest in friends, hobbies, and goals. The child may also manifest changes in sleeping or eating patterns. He or she may begin experimenting with drugs and/or alcohol, running away, or becoming sexually promiscuous (Capuzzi, 1986). Other behavioral clues might include giving away prized possessions; collecting guns, drugs, or other potentially lethal objects; asking questions about the hereafter; maintaining isolation from peers or close family members; and/or showing a sudden interest in church (Hipple, 1993).

Sometimes suicidal children and adolescents express blatant verbal clues, and sometimes they express more subtle verbal clues (Capuzzi, 1986; Hipple, 1993; McBrien, 1983). Common overt verbal warnings include:

- I am going to kill myself.
- I wish I were dead.
- You'll be sorry after I'm gone.
- If I don't get my way, I am going to kill myself.
- Life is hopeless.
- The only solution to this situation is to die.

Indirect verbal warnings usually contain veiled suicide threats like:

- How many aspirins would it take to kill a person?
- What would you do if I were dead?
- I'm tired.
- I'm not the person I was before.
- This is the last time you will see me around here.

The counselor can also consider situational clues as warning signals from a suicidal student (McBrien, 1983). The most common situational clues are obvious or masked depression; an inability to cope with some current crisis, especially a crisis involving loss of some kind; and/or a previous suicide attempt. Another situational clue would be an abrupt shift in a child's life circumstances, such as death, divorce, loss of a pet, or any other highly stressful condition. Counselors and other school personnel should be alert to any type of drastic changes in the life situation of students in the school, because sometimes children and adolescents react to such abrupt changes with suicidal thoughts and behaviors.

Many times young people who are contemplating self-destructive behavior manifest certain specific themes or preoccupations in their thought patterns (Capuzzi, 1986). School personnel should closely monitor the behavior of students who express a pattern of persistently thinking about the following:

- Revenge
- Escape from intolerable circumstances or an unresolvable conflict
- Deserving to be punished
- Avoiding punishment
- Becoming a martyr for a specific cause
- Wanting to punish someone else
- Wanting to meet a friend or relative who is dead
- Wanting to control the time or method of death

If a student has a pattern of talking about these types of topics, counselors will want to consider these cognitive patterns as a warning sign and stay alert to other clues.

Many students who attempt or complete suicide seem to share particular personality traits (Capuzzi, 1986; Hipple, 1993). Quite frequently, students who have poor self-concepts, weak communication skills, inadequate coping strategies, and/or a strong need to achieve are susceptible to suicidal behavior. Other personality traits that may contribute to a tendency toward self-destructive actions include complete devotion to a single ideal or relationship, difficulty dealing with elevated levels of stress, weak social support systems, or extreme feelings of guilt or responsibility. Part of the counselor's job will be to watch for students who manifest these personality characteristics to make sure that they are not exhibiting any of the other warning signs.

If a child evidences signs of being suicidal, the child's counselor will want to evaluate his or her current degree of lethality (Capuzzi, 1988; Hipple, 1993). To do this, the counselor must ask questions about whether the student has considered potential means for hurting himself or herself and whether he or she has access to potential instruments of destruction. The counselor will also want to ask about whether the student has a plan for the suicide, including such specifics as where, when, and how often he or she thinks about this plan. The counselor should ask if the child has ever attempted self-destructive acts in the past and if anything could prevent him or her from hurting himself or herself. As the counselor asks these questions, she or he will be forming an opinion about the potential lethality of the child's suicidal intent. The more concrete the answers to these questions, the more likely the student is to act on suicidal ideations. With children who manifest high degrees of lethality, the counselor will want to contact the child's parents to arrange some type of medical intervention such as hospitalization. This may be the only way to protect the child from harm.

Because it is essential to take a suicidal child seriously, regardless of the potential lethality, the counselor must try to make a no-suicide contract with the child (Drye, Goulding, & Goulding, 1973; McBrien, 1983). In a no-suicide contract, the child signs a statement that says he or she agrees to refrain from any self-destructive act for a certain specified period of time or until he or she has the next session with a counselor. Hipple (1993) suggested that children and adolescents are much more likely to abide by a time-limited agreement than they are to an open-ended agreement, so the contract should contain specific information about the time interval to which they are agreeing.

It is also essential that the counselor get the child's parent(s) involved in some type of suicide intervention strategy. Counselors have a legal and ethical responsibility to make sure that parents understand the gravity of their child's situation and that they have the information they need to provide some kind of professional help for their child. The counselor may not feel qualified to determine whether the child needs hospitalization and may decide to refer the family to a psychiatrist to evaluate the situation (Davis & Sandoval, 1991). If the counselor chooses not to involve a psychiatrist, he or she should always consult a qualified colleague who has experience assessing suicidal intention (Capuzzi, 1988). The counselor may decide that the child is not in imminent danger, but that the family should "suicide proof" their house (Davis & Sandoval, 1991). This means that the family removes all potential tools of destruction from the house and institutes a round-the-clock watch on the suicidal child.

Intervention Strategies

Counselors will need to be prepared to intervene with students who are at the crisis point where they are feeling as though killing themselves is the only viable solution to the problem. The following list provides some suggestions for crisis intervention strategies that have been effective with suicidal children and adolescents (Capuzzi, 1988; Davis & Sandoval, 1991; Hipple, 1993; Orbach, 1988):

1. Maintain a calm, nonjudgemental, and supportive attitude.
2. Encourage the child to self-disclose, especially about the precipitating problem.
3. Do not try to talk the child out of his or her plan, but do ask for a delay and continued exploration.
4. Acknowledge that many students consider suicide as one option, but encourage the child to explore other options and coping skills.
5. Communicate that you care about the child and that you hope that she or he will continue to be safe.
6. Empathically reflect the child's pain, despair, and sense of hopelessness.
7. Explore both the positive and negative aspects of the person's desires—on the one hand, the individual wants to stay living and on the other hand, the individual wants to die. In this process, you will want to encourage the positive view.
8. If you feel that the threat is immediate, do not leave the student alone, even for a minute.
9. If you feel that the threat is not imminent, begin to explore problem-solving strategies.

An in-depth description of long-term intervention strategies is beyond the scope of this chapter. Most of the time, if a counselor has a severely depressed or suicidal student in school, the counselor will want to refer the student for ongoing help from a mental health professional in the community. The counselor should have a list of three or more professionals in the area who have training and experience in working with suicidal children and adolescents. Counselors living in rural communities will want to investigate statewide mental health services. If for some reason a counselor must conduct continuing intervention with suicidal students, she or he should obtain training in specific techniques that have proven successful with this population.

Helping Students Deal with Death

When students experience the death of someone close to them, like a parent, sibling, classmate, teacher, grandparent, or pet, their academic and behavioral performance at school will be affected. Because of this, school counselors must be equipped to help students cope with bereavement and grief.

Developmental Considerations

Although each individual will react to death in a unique manner, there are some important developmental considerations to take into account. Children will have varying ideas about death and what it involves, and they will have differing reactions to death depending on their level of development (Cook & Dworkin, 1992; France, 1990; Krupnick, 1984).

There seem to be three main stages of reaction to death that depend on the developmental level of children (Cook & Dworkin, 1992; France, 1990; Krupnick, 1984). We will only address those stages that might affect children in elementary or middle school. Kindergarten and first grade students may still fall into the preschooler category, which usually consists of children between the ages of about three to five. They see death as reversible, a condition equivalent to sleep. Their sense of loss may be expressed as anger at the person who has "chosen" to leave them, and they may displace this anger to others who remain with them. When a caretaker, such as a parent, grandparent, or teacher, dies, children this age are usually concerned about who is going to take care of them. They may also believe that they are somehow to blame for the death or that they will be the next person to die. They may engage in regressive behavior, such as bed wetting, thumb sucking, or becoming overly dependent. It is important to reassure young children that they will continue to receive care and protection and that they are not responsible for the death. They may need repeated explanations about the death and reassurance that there is a low level of risk to others.

Children in the age range of five to nine have begun to understand that death is final, but they assume that it only happens to other people (Krupnick, 1984). If they ask questions about the death and subsequent events, caretakers should give them factual information. Because their lives have been disrupted to a certain extent, it is important to make sure that they have a set routine to follow during the day. This will help them cope with a sense of being out of control. They may also regress or exhibit their grief through temper tantrums, aggressive behavior, distractibility, discipline problems, or being negative.

After roughly the age of 10, children begin to understand the causes of death, and they perceive death as final, inevitable, and universal (France, 1990; Glass, 1991; Krupnik, 1984). They frequently feel helpless or frightened. Upper elementary and middle school children need to realize that being angry and concerned about themselves are normal responses to grief. They may exhibit intense emotional reactions, such as depression, rage, guilt, and confusion. They may also report problems with sleeping and eating, or they may engage in antisocial behaviors. Quite frequently children in this age group believe that they must control their grief in order to be perceived as an adult. They will not ask for help or comfort because they are afraid that that would be childlike, so they may suppress their feelings. It is important with older children and adolescents to give them permission to express their sadness and to seek support and comfort.

Intervention Strategies

School counselors must be prepared to provide in-service training for teachers and other school personnel on childhood bereavement and to provide direct services to children and their parents. Cunningham and Hare (1989) outlined the elements of a teacher in-service training program on child bereavement. This particular training consists of four modules, each one hour long, on (a) children's bereavement behaviors, (b) children's perceptions of death, (c) teachers' personal attitudes toward death, and (d) practical exercises in helping bereaved children with their concerns. This program also helps acquaint teachers with curricular and community resources for helping children and their families deal with death and loss.

The most important element of helping bereaved children is to teach their parent(s) to provide support and understanding for their children (Krupnick, 1984). Counselors will need to show parents how to listen to their children, how to explain death to them, and how to use art and play to provide a means of communicating about grief and loss. Counselors will also need to teach parents about the developmental considerations that affect children's grief reactions and remind them that children, even bereaved children, still need to run, laugh, and play. The parents may need help and advice in deciding about practical considerations, such as whether children should attend funerals or other family rituals. Experts seem to agree that children should be allowed to participate in funerals and other mourning rites but not forced to attend if they do not wish to do so (Cook & Dworkin, 1992; Krupnick, 1984). If the child decides not to attend, the parent(s) may want to arrange for some type of private memorial service for the child, such as lighting a candle or saying a special prayer or poem.

When counselors are providing direct services to bereaved children, they will want to design their interaction with children based on developmental considerations. With younger children, who have limited abilities to verbally communicate abstract ideas, counselors may want to use art and play techniques (Cook & Dworkin, 1992). Since grief is an individual process, counselors may need to remind themselves not to expect children to move at a specific pace. According to Glass (1991), it would probably be helpful to children if counselors could communicate the following ideas:

1. Grief is a normal process that takes a long time. There is no set timetable for a resolution of sorrow.
2. Everyone who is grieving has both high and low periods—they can be feeling fine one minute and in tears the next.

3. Loss evokes very strong emotions that must be expressed in some way, whether it is through talking, playing, drawing, writing a poem, making up a dance, or some other form of expression.
4. No one can grieve all the time. Children, especially, need breaks from grieving, periods of time in which they can spend time with friends, play, be by themselves, and so on.

Counselors will need to use many of their counseling skills as they interact with bereaved children (Glass, 1991). They must learn to concretely communicate encouragement and hope. Many times bereaved children begin to believe that there is no end to their pain. They will need counselors to communicate that time will gradually diminish the hurt and that they can go on with life. Counselors will need to help children remember positive memories and celebrate the good times. Counselors may also need to help children remember negative memories and cope with the hurt inherent in the bad times. Children sometimes forget to take proper care of themselves, and if their parents are also grieving they may forget too. If this is the case, the counselor will want to encourage children to eat and sleep properly but also reassure them that frequently those who experience grief neglect their physical well-being. Counselors will need to provide support and unconditional positive regard. Children who are struggling with grief need to know that there is someone who will listen to their thoughts, feelings, and reactions without judging them or wanting them to be different than they are.

Working with Abused Children

In 1988, the American School Counselor Association published a position paper that defined child abuse as "the infliction by other than accidental means of physical harm upon the body of a child, continual psychological damage or denial of emotional needs" (p. 262). This would include sexual abuse, physical abuse, emotional abuse, and neglect. Because all fifty states and the District of Columbia have mandatory reporting laws, school counselors should be aware of the symptoms of abuse so that they can monitor the well-being of the children in their schools. All forms of abuse greatly affect children's views of themselves, others, and the world and their performance and behavior in schools. Consequently, school counselors must learn intervention strategies so that they can help students who have suffered from abuse to survive and overcome their experiences.

Sexually Abused Children

According to Sgroi (1982), children who have experienced sexual abuse frequently manifest the following behaviors:

1. Sexual acting out and/or seductive or promiscuous behaviors.
2. Unusual fear of or lack of trust in adults.
3. Detailed knowledge of sexual behavior that is not age-appropriate.
4. Change in eating or sleeping habits.
5. Drop in grades or academic performance.

6. Sudden loss of interest in school activities or diminished ability to concentrate on school assignments.
7. Arriving at school early and reluctant to return home.
8. Angry, hostile, or aggressive behavior.
9. Pseudomature, overly compliant.
10. Regressive behavior, such as thumb sucking, bed wetting, baby talk.
11. Secretive, reluctant to share thoughts and feelings.
12. Expressing excessive shame, guilt, and/or anxiety.
13. Unable to make or keep friends.
14. Running away from home.

Not all sexually abused children will manifest these symptoms, but counselors should pay close attention to those students who do exhibit any of these behaviors.

Treatment of sexually abused children falls into three main categories: (a) crisis intervention; (b) short-term therapy, which usually lasts six months to a year; and (c) long-term therapy, which usually lasts about two years (Porter, Blick, & Sgroi, 1982). Most of the time school counselors will only be able to conduct crisis intervention with students in their schools. With some students who are minimally traumatized by their experience, this may be the sole intervention. Most of the time, however, children who have experienced sexual abuse will need either short- or long-term counseling. In some settings, school counselors may be able to conduct short-term therapy with sexually abused children. They will rarely be able to provide long-term therapy, however, and in cases where it is necessary, they will usually need to refer students to outside agencies or mental health professionals.

When a child discloses that someone has sexually abused him or her, the first step in the crisis intervention process is to attend to the immediate needs of the child (Porter et al., 1982). The counselor must make sure the child is not in pain or immediate danger. After this, the counselor's main function will involve listening, reflecting feelings and content. The counselor will always want to use the same vocabulary for sexual acts and body parts that the child uses. No matter what the child describes, it is important for the counselor to stay relaxed, natural, and nonjudgemental, expressing neither shock nor panic in front of the child.

It is important to tell the child during the disclosure session that the situation is not his or her fault. The counselor will want to reassure the child that it is good to tell a counselor or some other adult about this kind of interaction. Before reporting the abuse, the counselor will need to tell the child that the counselor must talk to some other adults about the situation in order to try to keep the child safe. It might help the child be less frightened if the counselor reassures the child that the counselor will do his or her best to protect and support the child.

It is not the school counselor's job to investigate sexual abuse, so it would be inappropriate for the counselor to probe for details or verification of the authenticity of the child's claim. This is the function of the child protective workers and/or the police. The counselor's job is to provide immediate crisis intervention and ongoing support for the child.

If the alleged perpetrator of the sexual abuse is not part of the nuclear family, the counselor will probably want to inform the parents immediately so that they can do everything within their power to protect their child. The counselor should be prepared for a shocked reaction and denial if the alleged perpetrator is a member of the extended family or a friend of the family. If the alleged perpetrator is within the child's family, the counselor will have to make a decision whether or not to also inform the parents that sexual abuse has been reported. With families where the counselor has already built rapport and with families where the counselor would like to continue to provide ongoing services, the counselor will be more likely to continue the relationship if he or she has informed the parent(s) of an impending investigation. However, the counselor has no legal or ethical obligation to inform parents of the report, and some counselors believe that it is better to try to remain anonymous in order to protect the child and/or to protect themselves. This is a decision counselors will have to make on a case-by-case basis.

If the position as a school counselor affords a person the opportunity to conduct ongoing counseling with sexual abuse victims, he or she will want to design intervention based on the development of the child (Gil, 1991; Sgroi, 1982). With younger elementary children and with some older elementary children, counselors will probably want to use some form of play therapy (Gil,1991; Marvasti, 1989). With most older elementary and middle school children, counselors may want to combine art therapy with some type of activity therapy or group therapy (Hussey & Singer, 1989). In order to provide short-term, in-depth counseling for these children, counselors will need to seek out training and gain experience in working with sexually abused children and adolescents.

No matter what intervention strategies are employed, counselors should be familiar with common counseling issues that affect many sexually abused students (Gil, 1991; Porter et al., 1982). Many of these children feel haunted by guilt and fear. They may feel guilty about the sexual behavior, betraying the perpetrator, and/or disrupting the family. They are frequently afraid that they will experience abuse again or that their parent(s) will abandon them. Many sexually abused children have low self-esteem. They frequently feel that they are "damaged goods" and not worthy of love and respect. These issues will come up repeatedly in counseling, and counselors will have to use the therapeutic relationship to help children in the healing process.

Physically Abused Children

Martin and Rodeheffer (1980) listed the following as behavioral symptoms of physically abused children:

1. Hypervigilance in regard to the behavior of others.
2. Constant anxiety and anticipation of some kind of danger.
3. Inability to interact appropriately with peers.
4. Defensive behavior in social interactions.
5. "Chameleon" behavior, in which they constantly change personality and interactional style according to the situation.
6. Refusal to attempt challenging tasks (learned helplessness).
7. Propensity to take care of their parents' physical and emotional needs.
8. Visibly flinch from physical contact of any kind.

Counselors who see several of these warning signs may want to investigate further by asking the school nurse to physically examine the child. If there is any evidence of physical abuse, such as bruises or burns, or the child reports that he or she is the object of physical abuse, the counselor must report this to the child protection authorities for investigation.

While in most cases counselors will want to refer the entire family for counseling with an outside agency or mental health professional, there may be some cases that a counselor pursues for ongoing counseling. The developmental level of these children must determine the treatment modality used, just as it would with sexually abused children. With physically abused children, counselors will need to use the counseling process to address trust issues, an elevated need for nurturance, a reduced capacity for joy and play, low self-esteem, a limited ability to express feelings, a tendency toward regressive behavior, and weak cognitive and problem-solving strategies (Kempe, 1987).

Emotionally Abused and Neglected Children

Garbarino, Guttman, and Seeley (1986) listed the following as behaviors that characterize children who have experienced emotional abuse and neglect:

1. Behavior disturbances, including anxiety, hostility, and aggression.
2. Emotional problems, including the feeling of being unwanted, unworthy, and unloved.
3. Inappropriate social interactions, typified by an age-inappropriate pessimistic and cynical worldview.
4. Feelings of inferiority and inadequacy.
5. Overly dependent on or avoids interacting with parents.
6. Poor self-esteem.
7. Delinquent or truant behavior.

If counselors observe these behaviors, they should document them. It might also be helpful to schedule short appointments with children who manifest these types of behaviors and to "check in" with them about how their relationship with their parents is progressing. If a child like nine-year-old Joel reports that his mother screams at him, calls him names, and belittles him, it is difficult to establish that the parent(s) are being emotionally abusive. In most cases, even when a counselor reports emotional abuse or neglect to a child protection agency, they can do little to substantiate the child's claims or change the family situation. Protective agencies are most likely to intervene in cases where there is extreme neglect, when parents refuse to provide the proper food, clothing, shelter, or medical care for their children. Because emotional abuse and/or neglect are hard to prove, the school counselor may be the sole source of help for children who live in these situations.

Treatment issues with emotionally abused or neglected children are similar to those of all abused children. These children need to work on establishing and maintaining trust, gaining reassurance that they are worthy of love and support, experiencing a caring, attached relationship with an adult, learning how to express aggression and hostility symbolically instead of physically (Szur, 1987). It is also important to provide help for them in the areas of social skills, problem solving, cognitive functioning, and self-esteem (Szur, 1987).

The treatments of choice for families in which emotional abuse or neglect takes place are family therapy, marital counseling, and/or parent education (Garbarino et al., 1986). However, if the counselor cannot engage the family in one of these interventions, either directly or by referral, she or he may want to work with the child individually or in a group. Again, with younger children play therapy seems to be an appropriate method of increasing self-esteem, managing behavior problems, enhancing attachment, and learning social skills. With older psychologically mistreated children, counselors could teach them social skills and interactional behaviors through behavior therapy, and problem-solving and relationship skills through social skills training (Garbarino et al., 1986).

CONCLUSION

While most school counselors would prefer to focus on developmental and preventive guidance and counseling, they are frequently the people most qualified to help children and their families deal with crises. The primary components in successful crisis intervention are understanding the dynamics of crises, the warning signals that indicate a crisis has developed, and the intervention strategies that can help individuals cope with potentially overwhelming situations. School counselors who arm themselves with this information will have the tools to be effective "firefighters."

REFERENCES

Aguilera, D. (1990). *Crisis intervention: Theory and methodology* (6th ed.). St. Louis, MO: C. V. Mosby.

Allan, J., & Anderson, E. (1986). Children and crises: A classroom guidance approach. *Elementary School Guidance and Counseling, 21,* 143–149.

American School Counselor Association (1988). The school counselor and child abuse/neglect prevention. *Elementary School Guidance and Counseling, 22,* 261–263.

Blumenthal, S., & Kupfer, D. (1988). Overview of early detection and treatment strategies for suicidal behavior in young people. *Journal of Youth and Adolescence, 17,* 1–23.

Caplan, G. (1964). *Principles of preventive psychiatry.* New York: Basic Books.

Capuzzi, D. (1986). Adolescent suicide: Prevention and intervention. *Counseling and Human Development, 19,* 1–9.

Capuzzi, D. (1988). *Counseling and intervention strategies for adolescent suicide prevention.* Ann Arbor, MI: ERIC/CAPS.

Cook, A., & Dworkin, D. (1992). *Helping the bereaved.* New York: Basic Books.

Cunningham, B., & Hare, J. (1989). Essential elements of a teacher in-service program on child bereavement. *Elementary School Guidance and Counseling, 23,* 175–182.

Davis, J., & Sandoval, J. (1991). *Suicidal youth.* San Francisco, CA: Jossey-Bass.

Drye, R., Goulding, R., & Goulding, M. (1973). No-suicide decisions: Patient monitoring of suicidal risk. *American Journal of Psychiatry, 130,* 171–174.

France, K. (1990). *Crisis intervention: A handbook of immediate person-to-person help* (2nd ed.). Springfield, IL: Charles C Thomas.

Garbarino, J., Guttman, E., & Seeley, J. (1986). *The psychologically battered child.* San Francisco, CA: Jossey-Bass.

Gil, E. (1991). *The healing power of play.* New York: Guilford.

Glass, J. (1991). Death, loss, and grief among middle school children: Implications for the school counselor. *Elementary School Guidance and Counseling, 26,* 139–148.

Herring, R. (1990). Suicide in the middle school: Who said kids will not? *Elementary School Guidance and Counseling, 25,* 129–137.

HCA Hill Country Hospital. (1989). *Crisis management manual* (2nd revision). San Antonio, TX: Author.

Hipple, J. (1993, November). Suicide: The preventable tragedy. Paper presented at the meeting of the Texas Counseling Association, San Antonio, TX.

Hunt, C. (1987). Step by step: How your school can live through the tragedy of teen suicides. *The American School Board Journal, 174,* 34–37.

Hussey, D., & Singer, M. (1989). Innovations in the assessment and treatment of sexually abused adolescents: An inpatient model. In S. Sgroi (Ed.), *Vulnerable populations: Vol. 2* (pp. 43–64). Lexington, MA: D.C. Heath.

Janosik, E. (1983). *Crisis counseling: A contemporary approach.* Belmont, CA: Wadsworth.

Kempe, R. (1987). A developmental approach to the treatment of the abused child. In R. Helfer & R. Kempe (Eds.), *The battered child* (4th ed.) (pp. 360–381). Chicago: University of Chicago.

Krupnick, J. (1984). Bereavement during childhood and adolescence. In M. Osterweis, F. Solomon, & M. Green (Eds.), *Bereavement: Reactions, consequences, and care* (pp. 99–141). Washington, DC: National Academy.

Martin, H., & Rodeheffer, M. (1980). The psychological impact of abuse on children. In G. Williams & J. Money (Eds.), *Traumatic abuse and neglect of children at home* (pp. 205–212). Baltimore, MD: Johns Hopkins University.

Marvasti, J. (1989). Play therapy with sexually abused children. In S. Sgroi (Ed.), *Vulnerable populations: Vol. 2* (pp. 1–42). Lexington, MA: D. C. Heath.

McBrien, R. (1983). Are you thinking of killing yourself? Confronting suicidal thoughts. *The School Counselor, 31,* 75–82.

Nelson, R., & Crawford, B. (1990). Suicide among elementary school-aged children. *Elementary School Guidance and Counseling, 25,* 123–128.

Oates, M. (1988). Responding to death in the schools. *TACD Journal, 16,* 83–96.

Orbach, I. (1988). *Children who don't want to live.* San Francisco, CA: Jossey-Bass.

Palmo, A., Langlois, D., & Bender, I. (1988). Development of a policy and procedures statement for crisis situations in the school. *The School Counselor, 36,* 94–102.

Parad, H., & Parad, L. (1990). Crisis intervention: An introductory overview. In H. Parad & L. Parad (Eds.), *Crisis intervention. Book 2: The practitioner's sourcebook for brief therapy* (pp. 3–66). Milwaukee, WI: Family Service America.

Porter, F., Blick, L., & Sgroi, S. (1982). Treatment of the sexually abused child. In S. Sgroi (Ed.), *Handbook of clinical intervention in child sexual abuse* (pp. 109–146). Lexington, MA: D. C. Heath.

Sandler, I. R., & Ramsay, T. (1980). Dimensional analysis of children's stressful life events. *American Journal of Community Psychology, 8,* 285–302.

Sattem, L. (1991). Suicide prevention in elementary schools. In A. Leenaars & S. Wenckstern (Eds.), *Suicide prevention in schools* (pp. 71–82). New York: Hemisphere.

Sgroi, S. (Ed.). (1982). *Handbook of clinical intervention in child sexual abuse.* Lexington, MA: D. C. Heath.

Smaby, M., Peterson, T., Bergmann, P., Bacig, K., & Swearingen, S. (1990). School-based community intervention: The school counselor as lead consultant for suicide prevention and intervention programs. *The School Counselor, 37,* 370–377.

Sorenson, J. (1989). Responding to student or teacher death: Preplanning crisis intervention. *Journal of Counseling and Development, 67,* 426–427.

Steele, W., & Raider, M. (1991). *Working with families in crisis: School-based intervention.* New York: Guilford.

Stefanowski-Harding, S. (1990). Child suicide: A review of the literature and implications for school counselors. *The School Counselor, 37,* 328–336.

Szur, R. (1987). Emotional abuse and neglect. In P. Maher (Ed.), *Child abuse: The educational perspective.* Oxford, England: Basil Blackwell.

Tierney, R., Ramsay, R., Tanney, B., & Long, W. (1991). Comprehensive school suicide prevention programs. In A. Leenaars & S. Wenckstern (Eds.), *Suicide prevention in schools* (pp. 83–96). New York: Hemisphere.

Zinner, E. (1987). Responding to suicide in schools: A case study in loss intervention and group survivorship. *Journal of Counseling and Development, 65,* 499–501.

Chapter Fourteen

Appraisal in School Counseling

Robert J. Drummond, Ed.D.
University of North Florida

🌳 Alan was referred to the counselor because he was showing poor progress in class. He was failing all subjects in the third marking period in his self-contained second grade class.

Alan has two brothers and sisters and is the "baby" of the family. His father was laid off nine months ago when the company he worked for downsized. He has not been able to find employment during this period. His mother works at McDonald's as a shift supervisor.

Alan had bruises on his face and could not adequately explain their presence. The teacher suspects child abuse and will follow school procedures in reporting the incident.

Alan is a friendly boy and was at first shy when he met with the counselor but quickly warmed up. The counselor had a difficult time understanding what he was saying. Alan had difficultly expressing himself and would cover his mouth with his hand or look down when speaking. His teacher reports that Alan has a great deal of difficulty with the work required of him and does not understand what he is asked to do. Often his responses have nothing to do with the questions he is asked. He wants to please his teacher and will fill his papers with attempts to respond. When writing, he has a tendency to reverse and transpose letters or numbers.

The counselor reviewed Alan's portfolio of work and found that Alan succeeds better in mathematics than in reading and can do simple addition and subtraction. The counselor observed Alan in class and found that he was quiet then and kept to himself. He tries to do his assignments. The teacher allows Alan to copy from other children when he does not understand. He smiles broadly when he receives teacher or peer recognition.

On the basis of the teacher's concern, the counselors's observation, and preliminary test results, the counselor and teacher decided that Alan would be referred to a child study team. Public Law 94–142 and its amendments guarantee disabled students like Alan appropriate educational opportunities in the least restrictive environment and spell out procedures that have to be followed in getting parental consent and involvement. There are strict requirements for how the tests are to be selected and used.

After consultation with and approval of Alan's parents, the counselor administered the Peabody Picture Vocabulary Test-Revised, the Woodcock-Johnson Test of Achievement, and the Draw a Person Test. Later the school psychologist administered the Wechsler Intelligence Scale for Children-III (WISC-III) and the Test of Nonverbal Intelligence (TONI). The child study team assembled to review Alan's scores determined that he had a verbal IQ of 70 on the WISC-III, a performance IQ of 86, and a full scale IQ of 76. His drawing mental age was 7.6. His score on the Peabody was 54. On the Woodcock-Johnson he scored at the 1 percent level on the reading cluster, at the 5 percent level on the arithmetic cluster, and at the 2 percent level on the knowledge cluster. His score on the TONI was 76.

Why Use Tests?

In the case of Alan, test information can be important in helping school counselors make decisions on how to best help him. School counselors are many times the chair of child study teams. Test information is one source of information that can help educational personnel describe Alan's behavior and identify the best type of learning environment for him. The test information supplements data provided by his teachers regarding Alan's level of ability and achievement. The test information on Alan helps educational personnel describe Alan's behavior and place him in the best learning environment for him. The test information provides another source of information to evaluate Alan's level of ability and achievement.

The American Counseling Association (1980, 1989) (formerly the American Association for Counseling and Development) has published two position statements on how counselors should use tests. The reports emphasize four major uses of tests. Tests are oftentimes used for placement and selection of individuals. The test results for Alan will help provide information for where he should be placed. A related use is that tests are sometimes used to select students for gifted and other special programs. A second major area of test use is when tests are used to describe an individual. The Woodcock-Johnson provided a description of Alan's achievement. The WISC-III provided a description of the level of Alan's intellectual and cognitive skills. These tests are also used to describe an individual's personality type and traits, and test results can be used to assist helping professionals in diagnosing the strengths and weaknesses of the individual. In Alan's case the teacher would be aided in writing Instructional Educational Plans (IEPs) for Alan by knowing what his strengths and weaknesses were in reading or mathematics.

A third area of test use is when tests are used to predict success in schools or in training or educational programs. For example, the Scholastic Aptitude Test (SAT) is used to help predict whether students will be successful in college, and the Graduate Record Examination predicts success in graduate school. Tests might be used in middle school to predict whether a student would be successful in a special mathematics program or modern language program.

A fourth area of test use is when tests are used to help counselors measure growth, for example in achievement or in motivation for school. If counselors are running small groups to help students in developing positive self-concepts or in lowering anxiety, the difference in tests scores at the beginning and end of the program would provide the counselor information on how the students changed over time. Assessments provide useful information to evaluate programs.

How Not To Use Tests

Anastasi (1992) points out that most popular criticisms of tests are clearly identifiable as criticisms of test use (or misuse) rather than criticisms of the tests themselves (p. 610). She concludes that whether a test is an instrument of good or bad depends upon how the test is used. Counselors misuse tests when they opt for shortcuts, quick solutions, and clear-cut answers to their questions because they are often overworked, have too many students, and sometimes have the tendency to want to ship the responsibility to "objective test results."

Counselors need to remember that a test is just one source of information. It provides a sample of behavior at a given moment of time with a sample of items measuring the domain, or area of sampling (Drummond, 1992). Anastasi (1992) identifies four common assessment hazards that lead to misuse of a test. The first is using a single score to represent the test performance rather than looking at the score band with the aid of the standard error of measurement. The second hazard is the single time period of a score. The counselor may tend to label old scores in the student's cumulative folder as not valid anymore. Counselors need to restrict score interpretation to the fact that a score represents a student's performance on a specific test at a given date. Anastasi reminds counselors that the third hazard is focusing on a single indicator without collaborating and qualifying the data from other tests or from other sources of information about the student. Illusory precision is the fourth hazard. For example, counselors may be able to come up with a scoring system on a projective test that gives a quantitative score which in turn may create the illusion of objectivity. Some of the common misuses of tests by counselors are as follows:

- using a test for some purpose other than the purpose for which the test was developed
- using a test for a minority group member when the test did not include any minority group members in its standardization sample
- assuming a test will be culturally fair if it is translated into the language of the student
- assuming a widely used test developed for normal students will also be appropriate for handicapped students
- failing to translate the results of a test into language that students and parents understand

Achievement Tests

Elementary school counselors work with the following six major types of achievement tests:

- survey achievement batteries such as the Comprehensive Test of Basic Skills, the Metropolitan Achievement Test, the Stanford Achievement Test, and The Iowa Test of Basic Skills
- subject area achievement tests in subjects such as PreAlgebra, Algebra I, World Geography, and the like
- criterion-referenced tests such as tests on subtraction, addition, multiplication, reading comprehension, and other subjects
- minimum level skills tests such as the Survival Skills Test and other tests that measure the minimum level and essential skills that students have to achieve in order to pass from one grade to the next or to graduate from school
- individual achievement tests such as the Wide Range Achievement Test, the Wechsler Individual Achievement Tests, the Peabody Individual Achievement Test, and the Basic Achievement Skills Individual Screener
- diagnostic tests such as the Key Math Diagnostic Arithmetic Tests, the Woodcock-Johnson Psycho-Educational Battery, and the Gates-McKillop-Horowitz Reading Diagnostic Test

The following cases give examples of the different types of achievement tests and their uses.

Review the profile for this seventh grader who took the Stanford Achievement Test (SAT) on April 1 of the school year. (The maximum grade equivalent score for this time in the school year is 7.8.)

Tests	Raw	Percentile Rank	Stanine	Grade Equivalent
Reading Comprehension	26	11	3	5.2
Vocabulary	19	14	3	5.9
Listening Comprehension	21	9	2	4.9
Spelling	29	30	4	6.8
Language	35	37	4	6.5
Concepts of Number	16	29	4	7.0
Math Computation	21	32	4	7.5
Math Application	15	21	3	6.3
Social Science	32	22	3	5.6
Science	33	30	4	6.4
Using Information	25	39	4	7.0
Total Listening	40	12	3	5.3
Total Language	63	34	4	6.6
Total Mathematics	52	27	4	7.0
Basic Battery Total	32	27	4	7.0

Questions/Activities

1. Role play or discuss how you would interpret the scores on the SAT to this student.
2. Role play how you would interpret the scores to the parents of this seventh grader.
3. Are there other types of information you would want to have to be able to analyze the achievement of his student? If so, what are they? If not, why not?

Case of Betty

Betty is ten and in third grade. She repeated first grade and is currently repeating third grade. She has two sisters, age 11 and 7, and one brother, age 6. Betty's mother and father are separated, and she is living with her mother. Her mother is working in the food service industry as a waitress.

Although Betty attends school regularly, her grades have been mostly Ds and Fs.

Grade	Test	Score
1	Stanford Achievement Test	4% (Basic Battery Total)
1R	Stanford Achievement Test	20%
2	Stanford Achievement Test	14%
3	Stanford Achievement Test	4%

Essential Skills Test (criterion referenced—must get 75 percent of items correct)

Grade	Test	Result
1	Reading	failed
1	Mathematics	failed
1R	Reading	passed
1R	Mathematics	passed
2	Reading	passed
2	Mathematics	passed
3	Reading	failed
3	Mathematics	failed

Betty's third grade teacher rated the following behaviors as severe problems on the Behavior Problem checklist:

Exhibits "I don't know" or "I quit" behavior.
Is very quiet.
Is shy, bashful.
Has feelings of inferiority.
Has a short attention span.
Is distractible.
Lacks self-confidence.
Is reluctant to try new tasks.
Achieves below seeming potential.

Other assessments:

Test	Grade Score	Age Score
Woodcock-Johnson	1.7	6–10
Wide Range Achievement	2.5	7–8
Key Math	2.2	7–5

The school psychologists found that Betty's weak areas were:

fund of factual information
verbal concept formation
visual organizational skills
eye/hand coordination
self-concept

Questions/Activities

1. Role play or discuss what you would discuss with her mother about Betty's test results.

2. What other information would you like to see to have a more complete picture of Betty?

3. On the basis of the information you have on Betty, what is your tentative diagnosis? How would you advise her third grade teacher to help Betty?

Tests of Behavior/Personality

Personality tests can help elementary counselors describe students systematically, diagnose their problems, and give indications of growth or changes in behavior. They can be used to predict behavior as well as help identify personal problems and diagnose psychopathologies. Anastasi (1988) identified four major ways personality tests have been constructed. First is the logical content approach, in which, for example, items are based upon typical behavior for a given stage of development or on research findings across several studies. The classic behavior checklist, the Mooney Problem Checklist, is an example of a test using this approach. The second approach is the theoretical method, where the scales represent dimensions of behavior described by the theorist. The Measures of Psychosocial Development, a test based upon Erickson's eight stages, is an example of a test of this type. The third approach is empirical and uses the criterion group approach. An example of this approach is the Million Adolescent Personality Inventory. The fourth type of approach is the factor analytical approach used in tests such as the Early School Personality Questionnaire and the Children's Personality Questionnaire.

Koppitz (1982) categorizes personality tests according to the technique being utilized, that is, verbal, visual, manipulative, objective, and other. These categories will be examined in the following sections.

Verbal Techniques

Verbal techniques are those methods that involve a verbal stimulus and require a verbal response. One technique counselors use often is asking projective questions.

Example: Who is the person you would most like to be?

*   My aunt—because she is nice, smart, pretty, and special. (F, 12)
*   Michael Jordan—because he is a great basketball player and he can slam good. (M, 11)
*   Me, myself . . . I'm smooth. (M, 12)
*   All the counselors. They are great people! (F, 12)

Example: If you had three wishes and could wish for anything, what would you wish for?

- Three more wishes.

    a. Me to have a good life.
    b. For kids to grow up to be successful.
    c. For me to have a good husband who is rich.

- For no more pollution.
- For no more drugs. (F, 12)

Another popular type of item that counselors find they can use to assess attitudes toward family, peers, school, anxiety, and the like is the sentence completion item.

Example: Finish these sentences.

Education is *to learn.* (M, 11)

Education is *a nice thing to get if you want it.* (F, 13)

My parents expect me *to try hard.* (M, 12)

My parents expect me *to be good in school and respect other people.* (M, 12)

Visual Techniques

Visual stimuli are given to children by the counselor, and the children then are asked to make a verbal response. The classics in this category are the Children's Apperception Test and the Children's Apperception Test—Human Figures. The first test presents pictures of animals in human social contexts through which the child becomes involved in conflicts, identities, roles, and family structure. The child is asked to tell a story about each picture. The test is a projective type of test which provides insight into how children view people in their environment, their motives, their needs, and the defense mechanisms they use. The second test uses human figures to provide children with the same opportunities.

Other picture story tests the counselor should be familiar with are as follows:

- The Children's Apperceptive Story Telling Test (CAST) by Mary Scheider, published by ProEd. This test can be used for children ages 6–13. It provides profiles for children with attention deficit disorders, conduct disorders, anxiety disorders, oppositional disorders, and childhood depression.
- The Roberts Apperception Test for Children by Glen Roberts and Dorothea McArthur, published by Western Psychological Services. This test can be used for children ages 6–15. The child is asked to make up stories about the situations presented in the pictures. The test measures conflict, anxiety, aggression, depression, rejection, punishment, dependency, support, closure, resolution, unresolved problems, maladaptive outcome, and deviation response.

- The Roberts Apperception Test for Children: Test Pictures for Black Children, also published by Western Psychological Services. This test measures the same constructs as the test just described but features black rather than white individuals in the situations pictured.

Drawing Techniques

There is a wide variety of drawing tests used to assess the personality of elementary school students, including the House-Tree-Person Test, the Draw-a-Person Test, the Draw-a-Family Test, and the Kinetic Family Drawing Test. In these tests, drawing is viewed as a way in which children share their perceptions and reactions to the world around them. Groth-Marnat (1984) reminds us that how children approach drawing reflects how they approach life situations.

The Draw-a-Person test is one of the classics; it was originally developed by Goodenough to assess the intelligence of children but was expanded by Machover (1949) to include a guide for evaluating personality from the drawings. Koppitz (1968) identified thirty emotional indicators that were significant in interpreting the drawings. For example, poor achievement of a student might be reflected in the drawing by poor integration, monsters, and omission of body parts. Children showing aggressive behavior might draw big figures, crossed eyes, teeth, big hands, and long arms.

Family drawings provide insight into how children view their place within the family. The Kinetic Family Drawing Test (KFD) requires children to draw the whole family doing something. What is important in interpretation of the drawing is the size of the figures, their position, their distance from each other, and their interaction with one another.

Manipulative Techniques

Koppitz (1982) recommends the use of material such as puppets, toys, play dough, or clay to assess children who have trouble expressing their feelings or attitudes verbally or through drawings. This approach works well with children who also have social, language, or physical disabilities. There are many kits available, but many appropriate objects can also simply be purchased at store toy counters.

Objective Techniques

The most widely used technique to assess personality is the personality inventory. Students are asked to respond to each item on a 2 to 6 point scale. For example, some tests require children to mark "Yes" or "No" or "True" or "False" to the item. Others use Likert or Guttman type of scales. There are questionnaires to measure just about every dimension of personality conceivable. Some of the most widely used personality inventories are the following:

- The Children's Personality Questionnaire (CPQ), authored by Rutherford Porter and Raymond Cattell and published by the Institute for Personality and Ability Testing, can be used to assess personality traits of children ages 8–12.

- The Early School Personality Questionnaire, authored by Raymond Cattell and Richard Coan and published by the Institute for Personality and Ability Testing, can be used to assess children ages 6–8, the test measures similar constructs to the CPQ.

- The Children's State-Trait Anxiety Inventory by Charles Spielberger and others, published by Consulting Psychologists Press, can be used to assess anxiety in children in grades 4–8.

- The Junior Eysenck Personality Inventory, authored by Sybil Eysenck and published by Educational and Industrial Testing Service, is used to measure extraversion-introversion, neuroticism-stability, and distortion (lie scale) of children ages 7–16.

- The Personality Inventory for Children, authored by Robert D. Wirt and others and published by Western Psychological Services, is used to identify psychopathologies, developmental problems, and social disabilities of children ages 3–16.

Ratings by Others

Examining ratings by others, such as counselors, teachers, and psychologists, is another way of assessing the personality of children. Sometimes the child being observed is incapable of completing a self-report inventory. Factors such as social desirability and defensiveness may also interfere with the validity of self-report instruments. Children as well as adults tend to either consciously or unconsciously say (or check off on forms) good things about themselves, so they select socially desirable alternatives on self-report inventories, using defense mechanisms to block revelation of their true behaviors. Sometimes, of course, children behave in just the opposite way and are "overly truthful," exaggerating their negative behaviors. In the case of Betty, the teacher used a behavior rating scale to describe her behavior. The behavior has to be observable and measurable for self-report instruments to be valid and reliable tools for counselors.

The following are some of the most widely used scales:

- Burks' Behavior Rating Scales by Harold Burks, published by Western Psychological Services, are used to identify patterns of behavior in children. There is a form for kindergarten and preschool for use with 3–6 year olds, and one for students in grades 1–9. There are eighteen scales for measuring behaviors such as excessive self-blame, anxiety, withdrawal, dependency, and the like.

- The Child Behavior Checklist and Revised Child Behavior Profile are authored by Thomas Achenbach and Craig Edelbrock and published by the Department of Psychiatry of the University of Vermont. There's a four page Child Behavior Checklist, the Teacher Report Form, the Direct Observation Form, and the Youth Self-Report Form, and all of which can be used with children ages 2–16. The scale assesses the behavioral problems and competencies of children and adolescents.

- The Child Behavior Rating Scale by Russell Cassel, published by Western Psychological Services, measures the behavior and personality adjustment of children and is used to counsel normal as well as handicapped children.

- The Children's Problems Checklist by John Schinka is published by Psychological Assessment Resources and is completed by parents of children ages 5–12. It covers areas such as emotions, self-concept, peers/play, school, language, and thinking.

Intelligence Tests

The conceptualization of intelligence is changing. Sternberg (1980, 1985) has a model which is based upon cognitive and information-processing theories. He identified ten metacomponents as being important in intellectual functioning. Sternberg (1990) argues that memory and analytical reasoning are important operations necessary for success in school, but that tacit, informational knowledge rather than explicit, formal knowledge is required to be successful at work. He points out that most traditional tests are contextualized with respect to the school; the problems are relatively short, have single correct answers, and contain no real-world content.

Gardner (1983), on the other hand, postulated a theory of intelligence that focuses on a system approach and combines both factor analytical and information-processing models. Gardner proposes that there are seven types of intelligence: linguistic, logical mathematical, spatial, musical, body-kinesthetic, interpersonal, and intrapersonal.

Even though these theories offer practical application to the work of the counselor in the school system, three major tests are most likely to be used by counselors and psychologists to assess children: the Stanford Binet (Fourth Edition), The Wechsler Scale for Children-III, and the Kaufman Assessment Battery for Children (K–ABC) (Aylward, 1991). Normally these tests are administered by the school psychologist and require special training and internship to learn to use them. There are some individual tests that counselors can learn to administer, score, and interpret without extensive training. Two of the most widely used are the Peabody Picture Vocabulary and the Slosson Intelligence Test. These tests can give the counselor a quick appraisal of a child's level of intellectual functioning. The Peabody Picture Vocabulary Test measures receptive vocabulary and provides estimates of the child's verbal ability and academic aptitude. The child has to point to the picture of the word being said by the examiner and make a selection from a plate containing four pictures. The Slosson Screening Intelligence Test-Revised can be used to measure the mental age, IQ, and reading level of children.

Self-Esteem

Battle (1992) defines self-esteem as the perception individuals possess of their own worth which includes a composite of their feelings, hopes, thoughts, and perception of who they are, what they have been, and what they might become. There are some differences in how test authors conceptualize the construct. Coopersmith (1967) postulated the global nature of self-esteem. Brown and Alexander (1991) believe that there is sufficient evidence to view self-esteem as having distinct dimensions. Piers (1984), through factor analysis, identified six distinct dimensions of self-concept.

Battle (1992) includes five scales in the form developed for elementary students in grades 2 through 9: general, social/peer-related, academic/school-related, parental/home-related, and lie (to measure defensiveness). Coopersmith has general, social, school, and family/parents categories on the school version of his self-esteem inventory. Brown and Alexander have four scales: perceptions of academic competence, perception of familial acceptance, perception of peer popularity, and perception of personal security. The Piers-Harris Children's Self-Concept Scale has identified behavior, intellectual and school status, physical appearance, anxiety, popularity, happiness, and satisfaction as categories for measuring self-esteem.

Self-esteem inventories are given to help counselors identify students who might be in need of psychological assistance because they are believed to have self-esteem or behavior problems, to be emotionally disturbed, or to be experiencing personal and social adjustment problems. The profile on such tests will help counselors plan appropriate interventions and to target goals for behavior change.

The following are some of the major instruments for measuring self-esteem:

- The Self-Esteem Inventories, School Form by S. Coopersmith, published by Consulting Psychologists Press
- The Piers-Harris Children's Self-Concept Scale by E. V. Piers, published by Western Psychological Services
- The Culture-Free Self-Esteem Inventories by J. Battle, published by Pro-Ed
- The Self-Esteem Index by L. Brown and J. Alexander, published by Pro-Ed
- The Self-Concept Adjective Checklist by Alan J. Politte, published by Psychologists and Educators, Inc.

Learning Style

Learning style is an important construct for counselors to understand. It is defined as the composite of characteristic cognitive, affective, and physiological factors that serve as relatively stable indicators of how a learner perceives, interacts with, and responds to the learning environment (Keefe & Monk, 1988). Cognitive styles are defined as intrinsic information-processing patterns that represent a student's typical mode of perceiving, thinking, remembering, and problem solving (Messick, 1969). There are a number of different conceptual ways of organizing the construct of learning style. Curry (1987) points out four dimensions that help broaden our concept of learning style: personality, information processing, social interaction, and instructional preference.

Griggs (1991) feels that knowing learning styles of students is extremely valuable because "counseling is fundamentally a learning process that, if successful, involves positive changes in the attitudes and behavior of the counselee" (pp. 33–34). She states that if counseling approaches are compatible with the individual learning style preferences of the student, the counselor has a better chance of achieving the goals of counseling, since each student is unique and learning styles are central to the counseling process.

Griggs recommends the following five steps when counseling children for their individual learning styles:

1. Assessing the developmental needs of students.
2. Developing a comprehensive, developmental counseling program based upon the needs assessment.
3. Assessing the individual learning styles of students, counselors, teachers, and staff members.
4. Planning teaching and counseling interventions that are compatible with the learning style needs of students.
5. Evaluating teaching and counseling outcomes to determine the extent to which program objectives and counseling objectives have been achieved.

Griggs concludes that utilizing a learning styles approach in teaching and counseling results in improved teaching and counseling, which in turn results in improved academic achievement, more positive attitudes toward schools, and selected developmental gains.

There are a number of learning style tests that counselors should be familiar with, including the following:

• The Group Embedded Figures Test by P. Oltman, E. Raskin, and H. Witkin, published by Consulting Psychologists Press, assesses cognitive style in perceptual tasks, primarily field independence-field dependence.
• The Learning Style Inventory by R. Dunn, K. Dunn, and G. Price, available from Price Systems, Inc., measures preferences of students toward the immediate environment, sociological needs, and emotional and physical needs.
• The Learning Style Identification Scale by P. Malcom and others, published by the California Test Bureau, is used with children to assess the extent to which a student relies on internal sources of information and external sources. In addition, five learning styles based on the student's preferred manner of reacting to situations and solving problems are assessed.

Brain preference is another dimension that is sometimes included in learning style assessment. Grady (1984) concludes from research that there are two hemispheres of the brain. The left hemisphere is responsible for linear and sequential operations, and the right hemisphere is responsible for simultaneous and visual functions. The Style of Learning and Thinking (SOLAT) test (Torrance & Reynolds, 1980) has a version for children and provides scores for left brain, right brain, and integrated ways of functioning.

The Myers-Briggs Type Indicator (MBTI) provides a way of looking at learning from a personality type perspective. The Murphy-Meisgeier Type Indicator for Children (1987) is a downward extension of the MBTI designed to measure the psychological type of children in grades 2–8. There are separate manuals available to help teachers and parents understand personality types of children.

Modality assessment is viewed as another dimension of learning style by many theorists. Students have to discriminate visually, aurally, tactilely, or kinesthetically to receive, store, recall, and integrate stimuli into memory.

There are instruments to measure visual acuity and perception such as the Snellen Eye Chart, the Frostig Developmental Test of Visual Perception, and the Bender Visual Motor Gestalt Test, among others. Tests of auditory assessment include the Wepman Auditory Discrimination Test, the Goldman-Fistoe-Woodcock Test of Auditory Discrimination, and the Oliphant Auditory Discrimination Test.

Tests are also available to assess children's motor abilities, such as the Bruininks-Oseretsky Test of Motor Proficiency, the Purdue Perceptual Motor Survey, and the Lincoln-Oseretsky Motor Development Scale. The Swassing-Barbe Modality Index (1979) is used to assess a student's visual, auditory, or kinesthetic preference.

Other Tests and Assessment Procedures

Attitudes toward school are also a concern for the school counselor. The School Attitude Measures (SAM), Second Edition, has five forms that cover grade 1 through grade 12. SAM has five subscales: Motivation for Schooling; Academic Self-Concept, Performance Based; Academic Self-Concept, Reference Based; Student's Sense of Control Over Performance; and Student's Instructional Mastery.

There a number of guidebooks to help school counselors in identifying child and adolescent mental disorders. Samuels and Sikorsky (1990) have identified fifteen symptoms whose presence or absence should be considered in diagnosing children with potential disorders. These are inattention, implusivity, abnormal activity level, aggressiveness, violation of rules, isolation/withdrawal/avoidance, inability to form/maintain relationships, disturbances of affect or moods, anxiety, depression, delusions/hallucinations, somatic complaints, oddities of behavior, language impairment, and impaired cognition. They have developed a twenty-item questionnaire to help sharpen the diagnosis and ask questions such as whether the child has repeatedly run away from home, whether the child is a pathological liar, and so on. A student who, for example, shows aggressiveness, violation of rules, isolation/withdrawal/avoidance, and inability to form and maintain relationships and also exhibits inattention, anxiety, and impaired cognition would show symptoms for having a Conduct Disorder, Solitary Aggressive Type.

CONCLUSION

There are many types of assessment procedures available for elementary counselors. This chapter provides just a brief introduction to some of the major areas. Even though most counselors have taken courses in appraisal procedures, there are new instruments and techniques coming out all the time. Counselors need to be proactive and work at early identification and prevention of problems, and the use of the tests and procedures mentioned in this chapter will help toward achieving this goal.

REFERENCES

American Association for Counseling and Development & Association for Measurement and Evaluation in Counseling and Development. (1989, May). The responsibilities of test users. *AACD Guideposts,* 12–28.

American Association for Counseling and Development. (1980). *Responsibilities of standardized test users.* Falls Church, VA: Author.

Anastasi, A. (1988). *Psychological testing* (6th ed.). New York: Macmillan.

Anastasi, A. (1992). What counselors should know about the use and interpretation of psychological tests. *Journal of Counseling and Development, 70,* 610–615.

Aylward, E. (1991). *Understanding children's testing.* Austin, TX: Pro-Ed.

Battle, J. (1992). *Culture free self-esteem inventory* (2nd ed.). Austin, TX: Pro-Ed.

Brown, L., & Alexander, J. (1991). *Self-esteem index.* Austin, TX: Pro-Ed.

Coopersmith, S. (1967). *The antecedents of self-esteem.* San Francisco, CA: Freeman.

Curry, L. (1987). *Integrating concepts of cognitive or learning styles.* Ottawa, ON: Canadian College of Health Services Executives.

Drummond, R. J. (1992). *Appraisal procedures for counselors and helping professionals* (2nd ed.). Columbus, OH: Merrill.

Gardner, H. (1983). *Frames of mind: A theory of multiple intelligence.* Cambridge: Cambridge University Press.

Grady, M. P. (1984). *Teaching and brain research.* New York: Longman.

Griggs, S. A. (1991). *Learning styles counseling.* Ann Arbor, MI: ERIC/CAPS Clearinghouse.

Groth-Marnat, G. (1984). *Handbook of psychological assessment.* New York: Van Nostrand Reinhold.

Keefe, J. W., & Monk, J. S. (1988). *Manual to learning style profile.* Reston, VA: National Association of Secondary School Principals.

Koppitz, E. M. (1968). *Psychological evaluation of children's human figure drawing.* New York: Gruen and Stratton.

Koppitz, E. M. (1982). Personality assessment in the schools. In C. R. Reynolds & T. B. Gutkin (Eds.), *The handbook of school psychology.* New York: Wiley.

Machover, K. (1949). *Personality projection in the drawing of the human figure.* Springfield, IL: Charles C Thomas.

Meisgeier, C., & Murphy, E. (1987). *Murphy-Meisgeier Type Indicator for Children.* Palo Alto, CA: Consulting Psychologists Press.

Messick, S. (1969). *The criterion problem in the evaluation of instruction.* Princeton, NJ: Educational Testing Service.

Piers, E. V., & Harris, D. B. (1984). *Piers-Harris Children's self-concept scale.* Los Angeles, CA: Western Psychological Services.

Samuels, S. K., & Sikorshy, S. (1900). *Clinical evaluations of school-aged children.* Sarasota, FL.: Professional Resources Exchange.

Sternberg, R. J. (1980). Factor theories of intelligence are all right almost. *Educational Researcher, 9,* 6–13.

Sternberg, R. J. (1985). *Beyond IQ: A triarchic theory of human intelligence.* Cambridge: Cambridge University Press.

Sternberg, R. J. (1990). T & T is an explosive combination: Technology and testing. *Educational Psychologist, 25* (3 & 4), 201–222.

Swassing, R. & Barbe, R. (1979). *Swassing-Barbe Modality Index.* Columbus, OH: Zanev-Bloser.

Torrance, E. P., & Reynolds, C. R. (1980). *Your style of learning and thinking.* Athens, GA: Georgia Studies of Creative Thinking.

Chapter Fifteen

Career Counseling in the Elementary and Middle School

Robert J. Drummond, Ed.D.
University of North Florida

🌲 The early experiences of elementary school students do tend to influence initial career decisions. Children in elementary school are not only influenced by television and school experiences but by their family and socioeconomic background, their community, and the significant adults in their life (Super, 1990). Programs in developmental and career counseling during this period tend to focus on self and career awareness. Middle school students are coming to an end of childhood and are entering adolescence. Middle school students have important decisions to make about what courses they should take, and these decisions can affect the educational and career decisions they will have to make later. Programs in developmental and career counseling during this period tend to focus on decision-making skills and increasing career awareness through exploration and planning.

Career Development Theories

Ginzberg, Ginsberg, Axelrad, and Herma (1951) proposed a developmental model of career development and called the period from birth to age 11 the fantasy period. Super (1981) labels the period of 4 to 14 the tentative period. Both developmental theories cited are characterized by children using fantasy in their play to act out a variety of adult career roles. The children identify with different people whose behavior they model. As children reach the end of grade five, their interests become more differentiated.

During the middle school years, students, according to Ginzberg (1972), pass through the early phases of the tentative period. They begin to consider what they like and are interested in doing and see that they also have to consider their aptitudes. They may excel in verbal areas, for example, rather than mathematical/logical, psychomotor, or mechanical areas. Super (1990) identifies this period as a growth stage. In middle school, students are exploring their interests and aptitudes, and they begin to make important educational decisions which will affect their career decisions in the future.

Role of the Counselor in Career Preparation

Counselors assume the roles of facilitator, consultant, coordinator, information giver, and liaison person between school and business and industry. Miller (1989) defines the elementary counselor's role in career guidance more specifically: counselors have as objectives enhancing children's self-awareness, promoting self-skills such as planfulness and cooperation, and providing students with information about the world of work and occupational fields.

Many times counselors are responsible for coordinating the career choice with the academic components of the curriculum. They also consult with teachers on how career concepts can be infused into the curriculum. Students are more motivated to learn if they can see how what they are learning relates to their experiences in the real world as well as to the career fields they may choose. The counselor works with small groups and large classroom groups to help students develop emotional, physical, and social awareness of themselves and others to ensure healthy development.

Career Preparation Competencies for Grades K–5

The goal for career preparation of kindergarten through fifth grade students is to help them develop awareness of self, and of the value of work and to provide them with exposure to careers and technology. One such program, the Florida Blueprint for Career Preparation (Florida Department of Education, 1989), calls for a career development program which infuses self, career, and technology awareness into the curriculum. The career development competencies are included in Table 15.1

Table 15.1

Career Development Competencies K–5

Self-Knowledge

Acquiring knowledge of the importance of concept to career development

Developing skills for interacting with others

Developing awareness of importance of emotional and physical development in career decision making

Education Vocational Development

Developing awareness of the importance of educational achievement to career opportunities

Developing awareness of the relationship of work to learning

Developing awareness of the interrelationship of personal responsibility, good work habits, and career opportunities

Acquiring skills for understanding and using career information

Acquiring awareness of how careers relate to the needs and functions of society

Career Planning and Exploration

Developing awareness of interrelationship of life roles, life styles, and careers

Developing awareness of different occupations and changing male/female roles

Source: From Florida Department of Education (1990) and *Insights: A Self- and Career-Awareness Program for the Elementary Grades.* (Based on Florida's Guide to Career Development: Student Competencies Kindergarten through 12th Grade, no date).

Activities for K–3 Career Awareness

There are many activities that can be done in grades K–3 to help students gain greater career awareness. A traditional activity is to have students invite their parent(s) in to class to discuss what they do at work. Another is to take field trips to local businesses, industries, and governmental agencies. A popular field trip is to visit the police, fire, and rescue departments. Other activities that have been successful are the use of the following:

* outside speakers from different businesses and industries in the community
* audiovisual materials to introduce new career fields
* role playing and drama
* games and simulations
* puppets

One school that had a closed-circuit television station with a 10–15 minute opening program produced by students had a career segment every day. Students showed pictures of parents and siblings and discussed the work they did. Most states have available curriculum guides, best practices, and computer guidance systems to help teachers and counselors with designing career preparation programs.

Lessons for K–3 students are more effective when students are actively involved in the class rather than being passive listeners. The following sample lesson plans include activities to help students explore career choices.

Sample Lesson Plan for Kindergarten or Grade 1

Goal: To have students see the importance of making a plan.

Objective: To make an ABC book of careers as a class.

Materials needed: Construction paper, markers, crayons, scissors, paste, activity sheets with pictures of occupations.

Script:

Today, girls and boys, we are going to make an ABC book of jobs as a class. Each of you will be responsible for helping get the booklet done. What is the first letter of the alphabet? (Response "A") Now, how many jobs can you think of that begin with the letter"A"? Look on your activity sheets and see if you can find the pictures of jobs that begin with an "A . . ." Yes, actor and actress begin with an "A." Where do actresses and actors work? . . . Do you know how you become an actor or actress? . . . Who is your favorite actor? actress? . . . Do you see any other pictures of a job that begins with the letter "A"? . . . Architect, that's right. What do architect do? . . .

When we are finished, each person will be assigned a letter and have to print the name of the job on the bottom of the page, cut out the picture, and paste it on the page. Or, if you want, you can draw a picture of your own of the jobs beginning with the letter you were assigned.

Wow, we got through to the letter "Z." Now you can draw your assignment from the basket I am bringing past everyone in each row. Some of you will have assignments of making the cover, others of collecting the pages and putting them in alphabetical order. Each of you will have an assignment.

End Phase:

Did everyone complete the assignment? If not, why not?

What steps did we use to make our ABC book?

Was it important to work as a team to make the booklet?

Summary:

We have learned about many careers today and followed a plan to complete our ABC book. We worked well as a team. Everyone participated. It is good when you have a project to do, to make a plan to get it done. It is also less work for everyone if we all cooperate and help. Think of some activities we could do better if we did them as a group or team.

Sample Lesson Plan for Grade 4 or 5

Goal: To have students demonstrate knowledge of various occupations.

Objective: To have students complete a job analysis questionnaire about a job performed by a family member, neighbor, or relative.

Sample form:

NAME OF JOB _____

DESCRIBE WHAT THE PERSON DOES DURING A TYPICAL DAY.

_____

_____

_____

WHAT EDUCATION OR TRAINING IS REQUIRED TO DO THIS JOB?

_____

_____

ARE THERE ANY SPECIAL REQUIREMENTS FOR THE JOB? PHYSICAL
ABILITIES, APTITUDES, SKILLS, ETC.

_____

_____

_____

HAVE YOU OBSERVED THE INDIVIDUAL AT WORK? IN WHAT KIND OF
ENVIRONMENT DOES THE WORKER DO HIS OR HER JOB? (EX. OUTSIDE,
INSIDE, OFFICE, HOSPITAL, ETC.)

_____

_____

_____

WOULD YOU LIKE TO DO THIS JOB WHEN YOU COMPLETE SCHOOL? WHY
OR WHY NOT? IF YES, HOW WOULD YOU PREPARE FOR THIS JOB?

_____

_____

_____

Sharing could take place by playing a game like twenty questions. Have a panel
of three or four students ask questions that can only be answered by "YES" or
"NO."

An alternative is to have students pantomime, show and tell, or in some other
way dramatize the job they studied and have the rest of the class guess what the
job is.

Discussion Topic: What did you learn from this interview? How would your
parents feel if you chose the job that you just studies for your future career?

Summary: We learned about some of the skills and requirements of jobs in our
community which you may want to study further.

Career Competencies for Middle School Students

The career development goals for students in the middle school are to continue developing self-awareness and to begin more formal career orientation and exploration. Specifically, programs should emphasize assisting students with the assessment of their personal aptitudes, abilities, and interests prior to focusing on orientation and exploration of careers. Students need to be guided to evaluate career information in relation to their personal assessment. Students also need to learn the basic concepts of technology. Competencies for sixth graders include:

- enhancing and fostering positive self-concept and self-efficacy for career development
- understanding the cognitive, affective, and psychomotor development required for career decision making
- learning the value of personal responsibility and good work habits and of planning for career and education opportunities
- showing technological literacy and identifying career fields related to technology

(Florida Department of Education 1989)

Seventh and eight grade students need to begin to identify career and educational goals that they are striving for and translate these tentative plans into a four-year plan for grades nine to twelve. These plans need to be reviewed each year by not only the students and counselors but by the parents of the students. Competencies for seventh and eight graders include:

- relating achievement/grades in school to career and education opportunities
- recognizing that there is a relationship between one's attitudes and success in school and work
- knowing where to locate career and educational information and how to interpret and use it
- identifying types and levels of work performed across a wide range of occupations
- seeing how careers are a function of the economy and needs of society
- choosing alternatives and making decisions to plan and pursue tentative educational and career goals
- being aware of how sex-role stereotyping and discrimination can have a negative effect on career choice and achievement
- assessing personal aptitudes, interests, abilities, and achievement relative to the nineteen career clusters, Holland's six types, or some other system of classification*

The career preparation competencies for middle school by category are presented in Table 15.2.

*Holland has identified six types of work environment: realistic (R), investigative (I), artistic (A), social (S), enterprising (E), and conventional (C). He classifies careers by looking at the makeup of personality types normally found in each field. For example, a counselor is classified as SAE (social, artistic, enterprising). The dominant personality type is signified by the first letter, S, for social.

Table 15.2

Career Preparation Competencies

Component	Competency
Self-Knowledge	Develop and use a positive self-concept for career development
	Practice skills for career development
	Understand the importance for cognitive, affective, and physical development required for decision making
	Develop and use skills for coping with physical and emotional decisions that can impact decisions
Educational and Vocational Development	Demonstrate knowledge of relationship of educational achievement to career opportunities
	Relate educational achievement to career opportunity
	Demonstrate technical literacy
	Identify career opportunities in the field of technology
	Locate, understand, and use career information
	Identify types and levels of work performed across a broad range of occupations
	Comprehend significant technology in the world of work
	Relate careers to the needs and functions of society
Career Planning and Exploration	Demonstrate knowledge of skills necessary to obtain and maintain a job
	Understand the skills needed in making decisions and choosing alternatives in planning for and pursuing tentative education and career goals
	Understand the process of career exploration and planning
	Assess personal attitudes, interests, and abilities relative to career clusters
	Demonstrate a knowledge of the relationships of life roles, life style, and careers
	Understand how sex role stereotyping, bias, and discrimination can limit career choice, opportunity, and achievement

Source: Based on Florida Blueprint for Career Preparation and Florida Department of Education (1990). *Insights: A Self- and Career-Awareness Program for the Elementary Grades.*

Activities for Middle School Programs

Career guidance programs should meet the needs of the middle school student. The counselor, in planning activities for the career program, must make an assessment of the community resources as well as the resources in the school. Bergmann (1991) advocates involving students in community service and providing them opportunities to do problem solving in a wide range of situations. Career days are popular in middle schools. There are computerized guidance services, such as CHOICES and DISCOVER, that students can access on PCs. Teachers and counselors can provide valuable experiences for students if students can be involved in volunteer programs. Some guidelines are as follows:

- Have students identify future jobs and places where they can find volunteer work.
- Tell students that many important services depend on volunteer help to maintain them.
- Discuss the roles and functions of volunteers.
- Brainstorm and have the students list as many examples of volunteer work as they can.
- Have students who have been volunteers discuss their experiences and the value of those experiences in selecting occupations or careers.

Many schools use older students to help younger students who need one-on-one help in mathematics or reading. Fifth and sixth graders often work with students in kindergarten, first, and second grade. Other schools use students to show new parents and students and visitors around the school campus. Students also are used to help in physical education activities and in supervising games and other recreational activities.

Peer Facilitator Programs

A formal way of having students work with other students is the peer facilitator program. Peer facilitators are trained in one-on-one and group skills, and are involved in both academic and nonacademic situations. They are able to be in contact with their peers in class, out of class, and even out of school. Students involved in these programs gain first-hand, realistic experience in what careers in the helping professions would be like.

Portfolios

The use of portfolios in career counseling by middle school counselors is becoming more common. Portfolios are a way of assessing whether the program of career education was successful in the school. The teacher or counselor can review the folder and evaluate the degree of reflectivity and planfulness of the student regarding his or her educational and vocational plans. The portfolio provides a systematic process for students to collect and analyze information and record progress toward accomplishing developmental tasks appropriate to their age and grade. Students can see where they were, where they are now, and where they may be able to be. Students can file different worksheets that they complete in their folder along with their test results, grades, and projected schedule of courses. They can be guided to collect information on their learning styles, personal competencies, current interests, and parent expectations for their future education and career decisions.

Gender Stereotyping

Zunker (1994) pointed out that career exploration programs can be useful in promoting self-esteem, and achievement motivation, but that they also should focus on discouraging gender stereotyping. Kranweiler (1984) recommends that counselors work with teachers to show students women and men in nontraditional career fields. Discussions should focus on recognizing and overcoming discriminatory practices in the career decision process as well as the work environment. Both women and men from the community can be invited to speak to middle school students about their nontraditional career fields. Since the middle school years are a period of exploration, more hands-on experiences should be designed to provide girls positive experiences in doing mathematics and science activities. Fitzgerald and Crites (1980) suggest that counselors become more actively involved in questioning the values and choices of their students by helping students compare and contrast their choices, especially between traditional and nontraditional occupations. In selecting assessment instruments and career information materials, counselors need to review the materials for gender bias.

Working with Minority and At-Risk Groups

Minority and at-risk students need special help in making their career and educational plans. Because many minority and low socioeconomic group members become school dropouts, the middle school career guidance program must attempt to meet their needs. In order for members of these groups to be competitive, they need to recognize the trends in the labor market. The U.S. Department of Labor projections (1992–93) show that the numbers of labor force entrants will be much larger than the labor force growth. The educational and technical requirements for entering the work force have increased, with many jobs requiring at least a grade fourteen or some technical education. There has also been a surplus of college graduates in recent years, and these graduates compete with high school dropouts and graduates for positions that require a high school diploma or less.

There are a number of special programs that have been developed to help at-risk middle school students to see the need for completing high school and plan for some post-secondary education to achieve better career goals. Many states have College Reach Out Programs. Some of the key elements that have been successful in changing attitudes, increasing motivation, and keeping students in school have been to:

- have students meet, talk with, and listen to role models from their culture and community who have been successful but still have maintained their cultural identity.

- have prominent city and school officials talk to the groups and interact with the students and parents.
- visit colleges to hear about admissions requirements and financial aid. Visits by African-American students to black colleges have worked well.
- provide individualized help in areas where the student is weak or needs practice.
- involve parents in sessions so that they can see and understand the need for their children to finish school.
- provide structure for the students, including having them develop goals and objectives, decide upon strategies and activities, and set target dates for completing the tasks.

Learning About Going to College

The College Reach Out Program was designed to encourage at-risk and minority students to include college or some postsecondary education in their education and career plans. Another aid to students comes from the State of Virginia, which has published a booklet entitled "Middle School Guidebook to College," designed to help all middle school students understand the steps needed for them to prepare for college. Some of the topics covered are testing, the advanced academic diploma program, study skills, interests, sources of information, leadership skills, communication skills, the college experience, interpersonal experiences, and financial aid. The booklet requires students to read, reflect, and write, set plans, and assess their strengths and weaknesses.

The Outlook: 1990–2005

Even elementary school counselors need to be familiar with the labor market outlook projections developed by the Bureau of Labor Statistics and published in the *Occupational Outlook Quarterly* and the *Occupational Outlook Handbook*. Some of the factors that are mentioned in *Outlook, 1990–2005* that are of importance to elementary counselors are as follows:

- Workers with the most education and training will have the best opportunities for obtaining higher-paying jobs.
- Although there will be jobs available for those without training beyond high school, the jobs will be low paying.
- Students who drop out of school or complete high school without obtaining basic reading and mathematics skills will be at a great disadvantage in the workplace.
- Technology will continue to change the structure of employment and how work is done.
- More workers will have to be computer literate than in the past.
- The manner in which businesses operate is changing so that greater analytical skills are needed. Schools will have to provide more than the 3 R's.

Table 15.3

Fastest-Growing Occupations, 1990–2005

College Degree	Postsecondary Training	High School Diploma or Less
Systems analysts	Paralegals	Home health aides
Physical therapists	Medical assistants	Personal home care aides
Operations research analysts	Radiological techs	Human service workers
Medical scientists	Physical and corrective therapy assistants	Medical secretaries
Psychologists	Data processing equipment repairers	Subway or street operators
Computer programmers	EEG technologists	Travel agents
Occupational therapists	Occupational therapy assistants and aides	Corrections officers
Managerial analysts	Surgical technologists	Flight attendants
Marketing/advertising/ public relations managers	Medical records specialists	Child care workers
Podiatrists	Nuclear medicine technologists	Receptionists and information clerks
Teachers in secondary/ preschool/special education	Respiratory therapists	Nursing aides
Security and financial services representatives	Electromedical and biomedical equipment repairers	Detectives Gardeners and groundskeepers

Source: From "Projections 2005" in *Occupational Outlook Quarterly*, vol. 35, no. 3, Fall 1991; and J. M. Berman and T. A. Cosca, "The 1990-2005 Job Outlook in Brief" in *Occupational Outlook Quarterly*, vol. 36, no.1, 1992, pp.6-41.

The fastest-growing occupations requiring a college degree, post-secondary training, and a high school diploma or less are presented in Table 15.3.

CONCLUSION

The career and life-style development of students is an important facet of the work of the elementary school counselor. The basic building blocks of career development and career decision making are self-awareness and knowledge, educational and career awareness, and career planning and exploration. The counselor needs to work with teachers, administrators, parents, and community members to help students develop their potential. Students' career development is not the sole responsibility of the counselor, but counselors are often made responsible for developing, structuring, and infusing the program into the curriculum.

REFERENCES

Bergmann, S. (1991). Guidance in the middle school level: The compassion component. In J. Capellute & D. Stokes (Eds.), *Middle level education: Policies, practices, and programs.* Reston, VA: NSSP.

Florida Department of Education (1989). *Blueprint for career preparation.* Tallahassee, FL: Author.

Ginzberg, E. (1972). Toward a theory of occupational choice: A restatement. *Vocational Guidance Quarterly, 20,* 169–176.

Ginzberg, E., Ginsberg, S. W., Axelrad, S., & Herma, J. L. (1951). *Occupational choice: An approach to general theory.* New York: Columbia.

Kranweiler, J. B. (1984). Career development of women. In H. D. Burck & R. C. Reardon, *Career development interventions.* Springfield, IL: Charles C Thomas.

Miller, M. J. (1989). Career counseling for the elementary school child. *Journal of Employment Counseling, 26,* 169–177.

Super, D. E. (1981). A developmental theory: Implementing a self-concept. In D. H. Montros & E. J. Shinkman (Eds.), *Career development in the 1980's: Theory and practice.* Springfield, IL: Charles C Thomas.

Super, D. E. (1990). A life-span, life-space approach to career development. In D. Brown, L. Brooks, & Associates (Eds.), *Career choice and development* (2nd ed.). San Francisco: Jossey-Bass.

U.S. Department of Labor. (1992–93). *Occupational outlook handbook.* Washington, DC: U.S. Government Printing Office.

Zunker, V. (1994). *Career counseling: Applied concepts of life planning* (4th ed.). Pacific Grove, CA: Brooks/Cole.

Chapter Sixteen

Ethics and Legal Issues for School Counselors

🌳 A third grade girl comes to you and tells you that her fifteen-year-old uncle is selling marijuana to students at the high school. What would you do? What should you do?

A divorced mother calls you and wants to know what her son thinks about his father who has custody of him. What do you tell her? What should you tell her?

The principal at your middle school comes to you and wants to know which of the children you counsel has been cheating on tests. What do you tell her? What should you do?

Every day in your job as a school counselor, you will be faced with situations like these. You must have a firm grasp of ethical and legal issues that pertain to the field of elementary and middle school counseling so that you will have some guidelines about what to do and say in these kinds of circumstances. In this chapter, we have attempted to explain important ethical issues and legal concerns in order to help counselors protect themselves in both of these areas. We have provided specific examples that apply to situations faced by counselors in elementary and middle schools to give readers a practical sense of these sometimes abstract and confusing concepts.

Ethical Codes—What Are They and Why Have Them?

Ethical standards are general guidelines that provide a basic framework for professional conduct and responsibility (Huey, 1987; Mabe & Rollin, 1986). As such, professionals can use their code of ethics as a guide to help them make decisions. Professional codes of ethics delineate:

> (a) the specific duties or rights that differ from ordinary ethical requirements, (b) the specific duties or rights that may simply be the application of general ethical principles in a particular professional area, (c) a reiteration of certain ordinary ethical requirements that need emphasis for some reason, (d) aims or general goals that the profession should aspire to realize, (e) requirements that relate to coordinating or protecting the interest of members of the profession, and (f) a statement of the responsibility of members of the profession for reporting code violations or other violations (Mabe & Rollin, 1986, p. 294).

An ethical code provides general guidance in making ethical decisions, but it does not provide hard-and-fast rules that dictate exactly what to do or say in a particular situation (Van Hoose, 1986). In some cases, counselors have ethical dilemmas "because there are good but contradictory reasons to take conflicting and incompatible courses of action" (Van Hoose, 1986, p. 168). Since ethical standards tend to avoid specificity, counselors must *interpret* the code and apply it to the specific dilemma. In most circumstances, counselors will have to make a decision about how to handle ethical dilemmas based on their understanding of the context and the individuals involved. Other factors that may affect the interpretation of the ethical standards are counselors' personal needs, beliefs, values, and attitudes (Huey, 1987).

It is important for counselors to be aware that these elements may influence their thinking about the situation. By remaining conscious of the effects of the various factors that can interfere with clear thinking about ethical dilemmas, counselors can make informed, wise decisions. Counselors may also want to consult with professional colleagues before making choices about ethical dilemmas. When counselors confront an issue that they are uncertain about, the ethical code allows for consultation with other professionals (DePauw, 1986). By explaining the case without using names and specifics of the situation, counselors can obtain objective feedback on both ethical and clinical issues without violating confidentiality.

Ethical Codes for School Counselors

Three different ethical codes guide the actions and judgments of school counselors: the *Ethical Standards* of the American Counseling Association (ACA) (1988), the *Ethical Standards for School Counselors* of the American

School Counselor Association (ASCA) (1992), and the *Ethical Guidelines for Group Counselors* of the Association for Specialists in Group Work (ASGW) (1989) (see Appendix K). The basic ethical guidelines for all professional counselors are included in the *Ethical Standards* (1988) of the ACA. This code covers general principles of ethical practice and ethical guidelines for practices and procedures of counseling relationships, measurement and evaluation in counseling, research and publication, consulting, private practice, personnel administration, and preparation standards.

The ASCA *Ethical Standards for School Counselors* (1992) provides more specialized guidance for counselors who work within the structure of a school providing individual counseling, developmental guidance, and small groups to children and their families. The ASCA standards have described specific responsibilities to pupils, parents, colleagues and professional associates, the school and community, self, and the profession. They also include suggestions for maintenance of the ethical policies.

Since many elementary and middle school counselors work with students in small groups, the ASGW *Ethical Guidelines for Group Counselors* (1989) may also contain helpful wisdom for them. This document outlines the group leader's responsibility in providing information about group work to clients, delivering group counseling services to clients, and safeguarding ethical group practices.

Specific Ethical Issues for School Counselors

School counselors have different ethical responsibilities to each of the populations they serve and to themselves. The overriding ethical concern that touches all of these groups of people is confidentiality.

Confidentiality

The ASCA Position Statement on the school counselor and confidentiality states that it "is the professional responsibility of school counselors to fully respect the privacy of those with whom they enter counseling relationships" (ASCA, 1986, p. 1). By ensuring confidentiality, the counselor provides students, parents, faculty, staff, administrators, members of the community, and colleagues with a relationship in which they can talk about their concerns without being afraid of disclosure (ASCA, 1986).

As we explain in the section of the chapter on legal issues, children do not have legal rights to privacy. However, none of the ethical code for counselors acknowledges an age restriction to the confidentiality standard (Zingaro, 1983). Many counselors consider this to mean that the child's right to confidentiality is more binding than the parents' right to know what happens in a session (Zingaro, 1983). When this is the case, at the beginning of the counseling relationship with a child, the counselor usually tells the child that he or she will not tell anyone the specific information revealed by the child unless the child has given permission for sharing that information (Ferris & Linville, 1985). The counselor might also add that she or he may want to help other people, especially parents and teachers, better understand the child. In order to do this, the counselor may share a general sense of the child's concerns, feelings, attitudes, and the like with other people in order to help them gain enhanced comprehension and ability to make changes in their interactions with the child (Ferris & Linville, 1985).

The only ethically sanctioned exceptions to the confidentiality guideline are when (a) the client requests that the counselor reveal a confidence, (b) there is "clear and present danger to the student and to other persons" (ASCA, 1986, p. 1), and (c) the courts demand information (Zingaro, 1983). The counselor must always act to protect the child from harm, especially in cases of child abuse or neglect. The school counselor may want to discuss these three reasons for breaking confidentiality with the child at the beginning of the relationship. Although very young children may not understand all of the implications of these exceptions, many counselors believe that it is appropriate to explain reasons for breaking of confidentiality when they are just starting the counseling. This prevents the necessity for suddenly introducing possible exceptions after the child has started revealing some information that would invoke an exception to the rule.

There are counselors who tell the child that their interactions are confidential and then choose to reveal information to concerned adults. They may base this decision on the belief that sharing this information could help the child, on the belief that the parents' legal right to information supercedes the child's ethical right to confidentiality, or some other rationale. Quite frequently parents, teachers, and/or principals will request information about what transpires in counseling sessions. Some counselors comply with these requests. Wagner (1981) conducted a survey of elementary, middle, and high school counselors, asking them how they handled confidentiality with their child clients. This survey uncovered a general pattern in which counselors tend to be more likely to disclose confidential information to parents of younger children than they do to parents of older children. This would mean that middle school and elementary counselors frequently make the decision to share information about their clients with parents or guardians and abrogate their younger clients' right to confidentiality. Counselors who decide to provide other adults with information from counseling sessions seem to assume that young children do not have the same rights to privacy that older children and adults have in a counseling relationship. Wagner (1981) also found that school counselors were more likely to answer parental requests for confidential information if they believed that the sharing would not hurt their clients, even when children had requested that no information be revealed to parents. These counselors seemed to believe that they had the right to make decisions for children without regard to the children's concerns or requests for privacy.

It is extremely important for elementary and middle school counselors to ponder the results of this survey when making decisions about the confidentiality of children. Rather than making unconscious assumptions about children and their rights to privacy, it is important for counselors to examine their beliefs about the rights and privileges of children, parents, and school personnel before they make choices about revealing or not revealing information they receive in counseling relationships. They must also consider how their choice will affect the ongoing interactions with both the child and the concerned adults.

Zingaro (1983) suggested that whenever the counselor receives a request for confidential information about a client, he or she first thinks about how best to preserve the client's privacy. The counselor may decide that other people have a need for a certain amount of information about the child. When this is the case, the counselor can protect the child's confidentiality but also convey useful information to the concerned adults. The counselor, rather than disclosing the details of specific conversations, can make suggestions to the adults about ways they can help the child. Most adults will respect the counselor's wish to preserve confidentiality at the same time that they appreciate any information they can use to help the child.

The following sequence is an example of an interaction between a parent and a school counselor in which the counselor reflects the parent's feelings, explains confidentiality, and begins to make some suggestions for addressing the parent's concerns:

Mr. Snopes: I know that my son has been coming to see you in your office. I'm wondering what he thinks about my new wife and her son moving in with us.

Mr. Lake: It sounds as though you might be kind of worried about how Joey feels about his new stepmother and stepbrother.

Mr. Snopes: Yes, I am. Joey hasn't really acted very friendly since the wedding. I would like to know what he's been talking to you about.

Mr. Lake: Well, as you know, what Joey and I talk about in counseling sessions is private, just like what you and I talk about in our sessions is private. It might be a good idea for you and Joey to talk about what he thinks about Mrs. Snopes. What do you think would happen if the two of you talked about his feelings about the new situation?

Mr. Snopes: I don't know if he would be willing to talk to me about that.

Mr. Lake: You're afraid that he wouldn't want to discuss this topic. How could you go about talking this over with him? I have some suggestions about ways for you to help Joey talk about things that are hard for the two of you to discuss. . . .

If counselors choose to limit the information they share or choose not to share any information with the concerned adults in a child's life, it is advisable to be empathic and tactful in the refusal. Simply telling a parent or teacher, "It is unethical to tell you anything and I am not going to do it" may hurt the counselor's chances of influencing the adult to make changes in his or her interaction with the child. Instead, the counselor will probably want to reflect the adult's concern and other feelings, then gently explain the reasons for confidentiality in counseling relationships. With teachers, principals, and other school officials, if this does not satisfy them, the counselor can resort to telling them that she or he is ethically and legally bound to preserve confidentiality. However, with parents who are not mollified, counselors will have to decide which is more important: the child's ethical right to confidentiality or the parent's legal right to have information.

The standard of confidentiality also applies to the counselor's therapeutic or consulting relationships with parents, teachers, administrators, school staff members, and individuals from the community. Any time counselors enter into an interaction in which they are the "helper" and another individual is the "helpee," counselors have an ethical obligation not to share the contents of their conversations with that person. This protects the sanctity of the helping relationship and encourages people who come seeking help to trust the counselor and share information about themselves and their interactions that they might not normally divulge.

One way to prevent inappropriate attempts to gain information is to provide training for concerned adults about the ethical considerations around confidentiality. In the authors' experience, the amount of time the school counselor puts into developing and presenting in-service programs for teachers, administrators, and staff and programs for parents about the purpose and practice of confidentiality is well worth the investment.

The counselor also has an ethical responsibility to make sure that all school personnel handle school records in a confidential manner (ASCA, 1986; Walker & Larrabee, 1985). In order to help make the requisite safeguards possible, the counselor should encourage school administrators to develop written policies regarding records and confidentiality and provide in-service training related to the legal and ethical guidelines of record-keeping for school staff members (ASCA, 1986; Walker & Larrabee, 1985).

Responsibility to Students

The primary ethical responsibility of the school counselor is to provide respect and loyalty to the students in his or her school (ASCA, 1992). This responsibility has several components. The counselor must holistically consider the needs of all students in the school. This entails encouraging students to grow in four main areas: (a) educational, (b) vocational, (c) personal, and (d) social. In designing counseling groups and guidance activities, counselors should include elements from all four of these areas. Quite frequently, elementary and middle school counselors tend to focus on their students' personal and social development, and they may neglect the other two areas, especially the vocational. While counselors must keep their interactions developmentally appropriate, it is possible to include educational and vocational elements in a guidance and counseling program, as described in the previous chapter.

The counselor also has a responsibility to students to inform their parents and appropriate authorities if students represent a clear and present danger to themselves or others. If the counselor, after careful thought, decides that this breach of confidentiality is necessary, it is important to inform the student that he or she is going to take this action. The counselor can use this preliminary discussion with the student to work on preserving the student's trust, clarify his or her expectations, and discuss options for prevention of the danger and for continuation of the counseling relationship. While this happens more often with high school students, elementary and middle school counselors must be prepared to deal with suicidal and/or dangerous students. The following is an example of a possible interaction with an elementary student:

Jason: My mom doesn't love me anymore. She likes my baby sister, but she doesn't ever pay attention to me.

Ms. Craig: You're afraid that your mom doesn't love you anymore because she seems to pay more attention to your sister than you.

Jason: Yeah. I bet she'd be sad if I were dead.

Ms. Craig: So, you're feeling like she would be sorry that she hadn't paid enough attention to you if you were dead.

Jason: Yeah. If I killed myself she'd be sad.

Ms. Craig: Sounds like you're feeling pretty sad that she's not paying attention to you, and you think maybe you've figured out a way for her to be sorry about that.

Jason: I could run out in front of a car, and she would cry.

Ms. Craig: Have you thought about when you might do something like that?

Jason: No, but I could do it whenever I wanted to.

Ms. Craig: You know Jason, I'm feeling kind of worried that you might decide to do that. One part of my job is to make sure that you're as safe as you can be. In order to make sure you're safe, I am going to need to talk to your mom about how you're feeling and what you're thinking.

Jason: No, don't tell her. She'll be mad.

Ms. Craig: You're kind of scared that she might be angry at you and you don't want me to talk to her about this, but it's my job to try to keep you safe. I am going to talk to her this afternoon about this. Would you like to be here with me when I talk to her, or do you want to wait with your teacher while I talk to your mom?

If the student participates in any school-based assessment procedures, the counselor has an obligation to explain the procedures, purposes, and results of the tests in a way that the student can comprehend (ASCA, 1992). The counselor also must adhere to appropriate standards in selecting, administering, and interpreting any assessment instruments used with students. When using standardized tests, it is important to choose tests that have strong reliability and validity and that have standardization samples that are compatible with the population of students in a given school.

Most tests that counselors administer in elementary and middle schools are standardized tests. With these instruments, counselors will have a set method of describing the test procedures. With nonstandardized tests, the best approach to describing procedures is simply to tell the child what to expect in the test administration and what he or she will have to do. This would include comments such as, "I will show you some colored blocks and ask you to make some designs" or "I'm going to ask you to draw some pictures and answer some questions."

With middle school children and older elementary children, explaining test purposes and results is relatively straightforward. Counselors just adjust the explanation provided by the manual to developmentally appropriate vocabulary. With younger elementary children, counselors should probably limit their explanation to one or two sentences, such as, "These will help your teacher decide what you still need to learn in math" or "I'm going to ask you some questions to help me figure out how you get along with other kids." When reporting results to younger children, counselors should make sure to present results in a simple, positive manner, stressing the child's strengths. Counselors should make statements like, "I can tell that you like to read and that you really understand what the stories are all about" or "You can be really proud of the way you can add and subtract. I bet your teacher can help you figure out how to use those skills to help you with your multiplying."

Another factor in the counselor's responsibility to students is to provide informed consent for counseling services (ASCA, 1992). The counselor must explain the procedures, goals, and strategies involved in counseling to students before they enter into a counseling relationship. This informed consent must include an explanation of confidentiality, privileged communication, consultation with other professionals, and exceptions to confidentiality. It is important to discuss all of these things with students in the first session in developmentally appropriate language. Counselors might say something like, "In here what you say is important to me. What we talk about is private, and I will not tell anyone else about the things you say or the things you do in here with me. If there's something I don't know how to help you with, I might ask another counselor for help. When I do that, I will tell you that I am going to do it, and I will not tell the other counselor your name or who you are. The only time I will need to tell someone about the things we talk about is if someone is hurting you or I think you might hurt yourself or someone else." This is a long speech to deliver to very young children, so counselors might want to break it up into smaller ideas and present them one at a time at intervals during the first session.

One way to make the explanation more concrete is to provide a professional disclosure statement to clients (Gill, 1982). For elementary and middle school students, this would, of necessity, be a rather simple document. When working with very young children, counselors might even consider using pictures or pictographs to explain these concepts in a way that lower elementary children could comprehend. The following is an example of a professional disclosure statement for children in the intermediate grades:

> As your school counselor, I am here to help you. I can help with things that happen at school and things that happen at home. We can talk about what happens with your teacher, your friends, your pets, your neighbors, your family, or anything else that you want to talk about. I would like to help you with school work, study habits, what you want to be when you grow up, friendships, or anything else you think you need help with. When you come and talk to me in my office, what you do or say is private—between the two of us. If somebody asks me what we talked about, I will tell them that I can't tell them because it is private.

The only time I will not do this is if I think you are going to hurt yourself or someone else or if I think someone is doing something to hurt you. If I think you are going to hurt yourself or someone else, I will need to tell your parents and some other grownups to try to make sure that you are safe, because I care about what happens to you. If someone else is hurting you, I will need to tell some grownups who are in charge of trying to make sure that kids are safe. They will ask you some questions to see how they can try to protect you. The other time I would have to talk about what happens when we talk is if a judge tells me that I have to. I would ask the judge to let me keep what we talk about private, but the judge might tell me that I have to tell. If any of these things are going to happen, I will tell you before they do, and we will talk about what you think the best way for me to do this will be.

Sometimes I might not be sure about the best way to help you. If this ever happens, I may talk to a different counselor about how to help. If I do this, I will make sure that the counselor does not know who you are. I will give them a pretend name for you so no one will know who you are, and I will ask for ideas on how to help. If I am going to do this, I will let you know before I do it.

In the process of relating to students, the counselor must not consciously impose his or her values, plans, decisions, or beliefs on them (Huey, 1986). School counselors must be aware of their own values, attitudes, and beliefs and monitor how they communicate these views to the students in their schools. Counselors must be sure that they never try to direct students' decisions based on their own personal definitions of right and wrong. At the same time, they cannot simply ignore their own values and beliefs. Counselors will need to constantly examine their own beliefs and their interactions with students to make sure that they are not unconsciously conveying biases that could influence students.

In many situations, it may be appropriate for the counselor to express his or her attitudes and to explain that he or she has formulated these ideas after much consideration and that students have the right and responsibility to make their own decisions about what is valuable and important to them (Huey, 1986). If the counselor feels so strongly about certain issues that it is impossible for him or her to avoid attempting to influence students, the counselor must refer students who are struggling with those issues to other professionals for help.

The following is an example of a conversation between a middle school student and a counselor in which the counselor explains her values without trying to impose them on the student:

Jenny: My mother smokes marijuana, and she says that it's all right if I try it with her some time.

Ms. Brown: You sound like you're thinking about whether you should take your mom up on her offer.

Jenny: Well, she has a good time when she smokes dope, and I'm thinking it might be fun. I never tried it before, but if she says it's O.K. I guess it must be. What do you think?

Ms. Brown: You think that she has a good time, and you might have a good time, but you haven't really decided yet. You sound like you want my opinion about what you should do.

Jenny:	Yeah. I respect you, and I'd like your advice about this.
Ms. Brown:	Well, it's important that you decide things for yourself, and it isn't right for me to tell you what to do. For myself, I have thought about this issue a lot, and I think that people should really think about the possible bad things about doing drugs as well as the good things. What do you think about it?

Ms. Brown had strong beliefs about drug use, but it would have been unethical for her to try to impose them on Jenny. She tried to lead Jenny to consider her own thoughts on the subject and to make a decision based on those thoughts, rather than on Ms. Brown's beliefs.

The counselor should also avoid being the vehicle for imposing the values and beliefs of any other person or organization on students as well. If a principal or parent suggests that a counselor use his or her influence to persuade a student to make a certain decision or take a specific direction, the counselor must decline to do this. The counselor may want to explain tactfully that using the counseling relationship in this manner would be inappropriate and unethical.

In the following interchange, a principal asks a middle school counselor to impose certain values on a group of children, and the counselor must tactfully explain why this violates his code of ethics:

Dr. Jennings:	I'd like you to work with these six girls who are always in trouble and teach them the value of right and wrong. These girls are going to go to prison if they keep on dressing in short skirts and wearing so much makeup. I saw them down the street after school smoking cigarettes and cursing. I want you to get that idea across to them— they are just bad, and they better shape up or they're going to have a tough time surviving life.
Mr. Goldstein:	I can design a group to deal with their behavior and attitude problems in school, but I don't think it would be helpful to threaten them or judge them. I can't really address their behavior after school or when they are not on the school grounds.
Dr. Jennings:	What do you mean? Everybody knows that kids who act like they do wind up in jail or dead by the time they're in high school!
Mr. Goldstein:	You sound like you're feeling really frustrated by these particular girls and their behavior.
Dr. Jennings:	Yeah. I want you to convince them to dress decently and start studying. That's the way to get ahead in this world. You need to get them to want to go to college so they can get a good education.
Mr. Goldstein:	Well, it would be unethical for me to try to impose someone else's values on the girls. I can't tell them how they should act outside of school or what they should strive for in life. Let me tell you what I can do. I can design a counseling group to help the girls explore their motivations and the consequences of their present behavior. We can explore their goals in life and the various pathways that are available to them.

In this interaction, Mr. Goldstein, the counselor, declined to conduct a group designed to impose the principal's values and beliefs on students, but he did make some suggestions about what he could do to help the students. This was more tactful than simply telling the principal that his request was disrespectful to Mr. Goldstein and to the students and unethical as well.

The ASCA code of ethics states that the counselor must avoid dual relationships. A dual relationship is one in which the counselor has an already established relationship with a person and then adds a counseling relationship to that relationship. Examples of dual relationships would be (a) counseling members of one's own family, (b) counseling close friends, (c) counseling children of close friends, (d) counseling children of one's hairdresser, minister, and so on. The reason this practice is considered unethical is that the previous relationship can easily get in the way of the counselor maintaining an objective perspective. In a dual relationship, the client frequently discounts the counselor's perspective because of their previous relationship, which undermines the counselor's therapeutic effectiveness. In these cases, counselors must arrange for some other type of service provision, either an alternative counselor available through the school or a referral to outside counselors. In some situations, like working in a small school district in which everyone knows everyone else in the town or situations in which there are no other counselors available to work with clients, it is impossible for the school counselor to avoid a dual relationship. In these situations, counselors must try to make sure that the dual relationship does not interfere with the counseling relationship. Counselors may want to seek out additional consultation and/or supervision to ensure that they are being objective with the client in such cases.

In the following scenario, a counselor must inform a parent that he cannot work with her child because this would constitute a dual relationship:

Sally Whitmire:	Hello, Jake. I have filed for divorce from Charles, and I would like for you to work with Sue to make sure she isn't traumatized by the divorce.
Mr. Chance:	Sally, I would really like to work with Sue, but I feel as though the fact that I have been friends with you and Charles for years would get in the way of my working with her on this issue.
Sally Whitmire:	What do you mean? You know that Charles and I haven't gotten along for a long time now and we just can't work this out.
Mr. Chance:	I understand that you and Charles have decided that you need to get a divorce, but I don't think it would be fair to Sue for me to try to work with her. I have known her outside of school since she was a very little girl, and I think that it would be hard for her and for me to try to switch from my role as friend of the family into school counselor with her. I think she would be very confused by this. If you are worried about her adjusting to the divorce, I have a counseling intern who could work with her, or I can give you several referrals to counselors who work in the community.

Not all dual relationships are this cut-and-dried. Sometimes counselors will not be sure that their previous relationship with a person is close enough to constitute a potential threat to a counseling relationship. Counselors who are uncertain about the degree to which a prior interaction would interfere with a counseling relationship might want to consult with a colleague to discuss whether this particular situation would fit into the category of dual relationship.

School counselors must also keep in mind their own personal and professional limitations and competencies. If counselors feel that students need more help than they can adequately provide, it is an ethical obligation to make informed, appropriate referrals for services (ASCA, 1992). If counselors are in doubt as to whether they are qualified, they may want to consult with another counselor. However, generally speaking if a counselor is not confident of his or her competence, it is probably advisable to refer counselees elsewhere.

Counselors should know their own issues and be aware of how those issues could potentially interfere with their ability to be objective and helpful to children and their families. For instance, if a counselor's father was an alcoholic and the counselor does not feel as though she or he has dealt sufficiently with the impact of this relationship on his or her own life, the counselor may want to avoid working with children whose parents are alcoholics. Of course, counselors who have personal limitations that prevent them from working with students in their school should seek out professional help to resolve these issues so that the issues do not continue to interfere with the counselors' job.

As part of professional self-awareness, counselors will need to maintain an ongoing assessment of their counseling and guidance skills. Counselors must be sure to refuse to offer services for which they have not received appropriate training and supervised experience. Suppose, for example, a counselor attended a three-hour workshop on play therapy and two weeks later a parent requested that he conduct play therapy with her child. With such limited training, the counselor would not be qualified to competently use this counseling approach, so he would have to decline this request and refer the child to a counselor trained in this modality.

Responsibility to Parents

The ASCA ethical code (1992) outlines the following obligations of the school counselor to parents. The counselor must:

1. Try to establish a cooperative relationship with parents in which the adults work to maximize the development of students. It is essential that the counselor respect the rights and responsibilities of parents, both custodial and noncustodial.
2. Explain the role of the school counselor to parents, emphasizing to parents that the counseling relationship between the student and the counselor is confidential.

3. Balance the confidentiality of the child, the parents' need to know, and the parents' legal right to know information about their children. The counselor must give parents "accurate, comprehensive and relevant information in an objective and caring manner, as appropriate and consistent with ethical responsibilities to the counselee" (ASCA, 1992, p. 3).
4. Maintain the parents' confidentiality as well as the child's.
5. Make sure that the parents or legal guardians have given written permission before sharing any information about a student with anyone else.
6. Provide appropriate assistance and referrals for family difficulties that are interfering with students' functioning in school.

The counselor has to maintain a difficult ethical balancing act between the responsibilities to students and the responsibilities to parents. The need to provide confidentiality to children and information to parents presents a potential ethical conflict. Counselors will often have to choose which of these responsibilities to honor. They will have to weigh each case individually to make a decision about whether to preserve the student's confidentiality or provide information to parents that they have gained in a counseling relationship. Counselors may want to consult other counselors before they make a professional judgement about how to proceed.

Responsibilities to Colleagues and Professional Associates

The school counselor also has ethical responsibilities to faculty, staff, administrators, and other professionals. The primary obligations in this area involve establishing and maintaining professional relationships in which counselors work cooperatively with colleagues and associates to help students. In order to do this with maximum effectiveness, counselors will want to educate other educators about the counselor/student relationship and confidentiality. Counselors should also discuss the advantages and guidelines for professional consultation.

Whenever possible within the limits of confidentiality, counselors should provide colleagues with information that will assist them to understand and interact with students. For example, Ms. Chaim, the school counselor, is working with Jessica on enhancing her self-concept and improving her behavior in school. Mr. Lee, Jessica's second grade teacher, is convinced that Jessica's parents and their discipline procedures are the main source of Jessica's problem. Although Ms. Chaim has explained client confidentiality, Mr. Lee frequently asks Ms. Chaim for information about what goes on in Jessica's home. Ms. Chaim declines to provide Mr. Lee with anecdotes about Jessica's family, and she firmly brings the conversation back to what school personnel can do to help Jessica change her behavior in the classroom. Based on her interactions with Jessica, Ms. Chaim shares her views on the motivation for Jessica's behavior and suggests different methods for Mr. Lee to try to work with her.

Counselors will also want to establish a network of outside professionals and organizations that they can use as referral sources for students who need help they cannot provide in their role as a school counselor. Since counselors must ethically provide at least three referral sources, it is helpful for them to meet counselors they might want to refer students to. Many service providers will be willing to visit schools or to make an appointment for counselors to come to their offices, meet them, and discuss the services they provide. Establishing a wide-ranging professional network can also provide counselors with different sources of expertise when they need to consult about a particular case.

Responsibilities to the School and Community

According to the ASCA ethical standards (ASCA, 1992), the school counselor has the following obligations to the school and community. The counselor must:

1. Guard the school program from any eventuality that could hurt the best interests of the students. If counselors become aware of a problem that might hurt students, like illegal activity, drug dealing, and such, they will have to weigh their primary responsibility of confidentiality to students and their obligation to prevent harm. In such a case, the best course might be to inform administrators of the existence of potentially harmful activities without revealing one's sources or the culprits' names. If counselors decide to do this, they must weigh the potential damage such a revelation could have on their credibility with the students in the school.

2. Give appropriate officials any information about conditions that could damage or disrupt school procedures, events, property, or personnel. This would involve situations such as vandalism, plans to disrupt school functions, and other similar activities. Again, counselors must balance the need for preserving confidences against this responsibility to their school and community.

3. Disseminate information about the school counselor's role and function and notify appropriate officials about conditions that could disrupt the delivery of services. Potential disruptions of the counselor's provision of services frequently center around conflicts between counselors and parents about the role of the school counselor. The counselor's primary responsibility in this area is to keep school officials informed and involved in any type of interaction that could potentially threaten the counselor's ability to provide guidance and counseling to the students in the school.

4. Participate in developing curriculum and school conditions suited to the locale. One of the counselors's ethical obligations to the school and community is to help ensure that the guidance curriculum, the academic curriculum, and the climate in the school are consistent with the local social and academic realities. For instance, it might be perfectly appropriate to have a guidance lesson on how to avoid getting involved with gangs in Los Angeles, California, but that lesson would probably not be appropriate in Pottsboro, Texas.

5. Ensure that the school's programs and procedures, especially in the area of guidance, meet the needs of the students who attend the school. Each school has its own unique blend of students. The counselor's job is to match his or her services to the population in the school so that all children have access to

guidance and counseling programs that provide helpful support and information to them. Special needs students and regular education students all need to have access to counselors and the services they provide.

6. Develop and carry out systematic and comprehensive evaluation of the guidance and counseling services and personnel. In order to make sure that they are effectively meeting the needs of the students in their school, counselors should be conducting ongoing needs assessment and evaluation of the guidance program, both on a process basis and an outcome basis. In order to gather information on a process basis, counselors would use a systematic interviewing process to keep informed about school and community attitudes toward the program and the efficacy of the services provided. To collect data on an outcome basis, counselors would conduct follow-up studies on children who have attended their school, using questionnaire/survey instruments.

7. Maintain ongoing professional relationships with local individuals, organizations, and agencies in the school and community that can provide services for students.

While there is, of course, an ethical obligation to keep consumers informed in order to provide for accountability for counseling programs, there are other reasons for counselors to devote significant time to establishing strong relationships with people from the local area. Keeping members of the local community and the other people in the school informed about what counselors are doing to help children will build a support system that becomes invaluable. If the continuation or integrity of the counseling is in danger—either because of criticism or budget cuts—having established links in the community with people who know the program can protect the program from being eliminated or reduced.

Responsibilities to Self

School counselors also have responsibilities that relate to themselves and their ability to perform their duties (ASCA, 1992). Counselors must make sure that they are aware of their own strengths and limitations and not take on professional duties that exceed their professional competence. Counselors must know themselves and their patterns of interacting with others well enough to evaluate any possible negative effects of their own personal characteristics on the students they counsel. School counselors must also be aware of their own level of functioning and effectiveness and ensure that their own issues or personal problems do not interfere with counseling relationships or have any potential negative effects on students. It is important for counselors to be aware of differences among students (for example, with regard to gender, race, religion, sexual orientation, socioeconomic status, and ethnic background) because they may need to obtain advanced training to competently work with certain populations of students. Counselors also have a professional obligation to continue their own education and personal growth.

Responsibilities to the Profession

The final area of responsibility outlined by the ASCA code of ethics (1992) is the school counselor's obligations to the profession. These include maintaining professionally appropriate conduct, participating in research and reporting findings to other professionals, participating in professional organizations, adhering to ethical standards, abiding by relevant laws, and sharing skills, ideas, and expertise with other professionals. These responsibilities to the profession involve counselors making a conscious decision to act in a professional manner, to support professional activities, and to monitor other counselors to make sure that they conduct themselves as professionals as well.

Special Considerations in Working with Groups

School counselors who work with students in counseling groups must remember that there are unique ethical considerations that apply to group counseling. It is important for school counselors to be competent in group procedures (ASCA, 1992; Terres & Larrabee, 1985). They must also assess the appropriateness of the students to be included in the group—for group work and for inclusion in this particular group (ASCA, 1992; Terres & Larrabee, 1985). Counselors must provide information about the purpose of the group, the leader's qualifications to lead this particular type of group, and any other information that relates to the group process to students and to parents (Corey, Corey, Callanan, & Russell, 1982). Counselors must decide how much information they want to provide to parents about ongoing group dynamics, weighing parents' legal rights and students' rights to confidentiality (Terres & Larrabee, 1985).

Confidentiality tends to be more difficult to maintain in group counseling than it is in individual counseling because in group counseling it is not just the counselor who must keep silent. Elementary and middle school counselors who wish to lead groups must devote a significant portion of pre-group screening interviews and the first session to helping students understand the concept of confidentiality (Terres & Larrabee, 1985). Counselors should also be aware of this as an ongoing concern that they will need to continue to stress with the children in the group. Because children have specific needs and abilities at different ages, counselors must also take developmental concerns into consideration when designing a counseling group.

In order to meet his or her ethical responsibility to provide the optimal growth experience for each student, the school counselor needs to think about the developmental level of group members when establishing space, number of participants, the amount of structure, the length of sessions, and the purpose of the group. For instance, first grade students have shorter attention spans than do sixth grade students, and they need more attention and more structure than older children. When designing a group for first graders, counselors should keep the group small (usually with five children at the most) and the sessions short (twenty minutes or less), and they should provide a lot of highly structured activities. When designing a group for sixth graders, counselors could include a greater number of children (even up to eight or ten), have longer sessions (up to forty minutes or an hour), and devote at least part of the session to free-form processing.

Legal Issues for School Counselors

As we have explained, school counselors must understand legal issues and how these issues impact schools and school counselors. In order to find this information, they can look to the Constitution of the United States, federal statutes, state statutes, local policy manuals, and legal briefs (Schmidt, 1993). Many school administrators subscribe to publications summarizing current legal rulings that pertain to education, and most states produce publications explaining statutes that pertain to education and schools (Schmidt, 1993). School counselors usually have access to the school board's attorney for specific information about testifying and current legal interpretations. Whenever possible, school counselors may also want to attend workshops that deal with topics concerning state and local laws and the practical implications of statutes and testifying.

Students' Rights/Parents' Rights

The area of children's legal rights in our society is fraught with uncertainty (Remley, 1985). While children are guaranteed some of the rights that adults are guaranteed, in many cases the protection of these rights depends on the interpretation of parents, guardians, or the courts (Remley, 1985). There is an ongoing legal debate about whether children have the capacity for making sound decisions and whether parents should have the exclusive right to make decisions about children and their lives (Remley, 1985; Schmidt, 1993).

The main issue under contention in this arena is confidentiality. As we have indicated earlier in this chapter, most authorities believe that children do not have the legal right to privacy (Remley, 1985). In order to balance the parents' legal right to know what is happening with their children and the children's ethical right to have privacy, Remley (1985) suggested school counselors avoid describing exact comments or behaviors of students to parents. Instead of saying, "Johnny said he hates your new wife and he wishes she was dead," the counselor could say, "I understand there are some problems between Johnny and his stepmother. What is going on in that relationship at home?"

School counselors should inform children before they disclose any information to another person and try to help students gain age-appropriate control in any ongoing decision-making process that involves them and their lives. If parents or other adults make decisions that concern children without their input, counselors should be sure that the children know what those decisions are and how they were made (Remley, 1985; Schmidt, 1993). For instance, if a mother calls to tell the counselor that she is going to enroll her fourth grade son in a private school for the next year, the counselor might ask if mother and son have talked about this decision. If it seems that the child has had limited input, the counselor might even want to offer his or her services as child advocate in a family conference by saying, "If you would like some help talking this over, I would be glad for the family to come to my office and discuss the situation."

One other disputed issue that relates to students' and parents' rights is situations in which parents object to children participating in various school activities, including guidance lessons, small group counseling, and individual counseling (Schmidt, 1993). In some instances, the parents are opposed to any kind of counseling and guidance services because they believe that those services conflict with their family values and beliefs. In some instances, the parents have objections to a particular counseling program, such as AIDS education or drug education, or they may have objections to particular commercial guidance curricula used by the counselor. While the courts have stated that parents do not have the right to deprive their children of an education (Alexander & Alexander, 1985), they have not specifically addressed children's rights to participate in counseling and guidance services versus parents' rights to decide whether those services are appropriate for their children (Schmidt, 1993). Since this subject is increasingly controversial, counselors should pay close attention to future court cases that might address the legal implications of whether school counseling services are vital to educational programs and student development.

Duty to Warn

One of the main exceptions to the ethical obligation to keep client information confidential is when the client is a danger to self or others. While this is not a frequent occurrence at the elementary and middle school levels, counselors should be familiar with the legal ramifications of the duty to warn and the practical procedures required if they work with a suicidal or dangerous student.

When a counselor has a student who has given indications that he or she is seriously thinking about suicide or other harm to self, there is a clear precedent for breaking confidentiality and contacting parents (Thompson & Rudolph, 1992). Even if counselors feel that a suicidal threat or discussion of suicidal ideation is simply a way of getting attention, they must always respond to such remarks by notifying parents and suggesting to them that they consult with a psychiatrist or other mental health professional who is thoroughly trained in suicide prevention (Thompson & Rudolph, 1992). There is legal precedent to support this course of action, and courts have found school counselors who have neglected to follow this procedure liable (Henderson, 1987; Pate, 1992).

In 1976, a California court ruled that mental health professionals who treat potentially dangerous or violent clients have a legal obligation to do everything reasonable in their power to protect potential victims from harm

(Tarasoff v. Regents of University of California, 1976). This would include warning the potential victims, warning the potential victim's family and friends, and notifying police and other appropriate authorities (Kelleher, 1984). In several subsequent cases (Brady v. Hopper, 1983; Davis v. Lhim, 1983; Leedy v. Harnett, 1981; McIntosh v. Milano, 1979), courts at the state and federal levels have decreed that there must be an identifiable potential victim before the counselor has a duty to warn (Herlihy & Sheeley, 1988). Contradicting these rulings, other courts (Lipari v. Sears, Roebuck, & Co., 1980; Peterson v. State, 1983) have found that mental health professionals also have a duty to make sure that a client does not have the power to harm others, even when the danger is to the general public rather than to a specific individual (Herlihy & Sheeley, 1988).

Until recently, court cases have not specifically addressed the issue of school counselors and their obligations to warn victims of a potentially dangerous client. In October 1991, a Maryland Court of Appeals ruled that school counselors do have a duty to attempt to prevent student suicide if they can foresee a potential danger (Pate, 1992). Future court decisions will establish further precedents in this area, and school counselors must keep informed about court rulings that specifically apply to school counselors.

Reporting Child Abuse

The other legally mandated exception to the ethical guideline of confidentiality is child abuse. All fifty states and the District of Columbia have laws that mandate reporting and investigating suspected cases of child abuse (Camblin & Prout, 1983). These laws require that school personnel report physical abuse, sexual abuse, general neglect, psychological and emotional abuse, abandonment, and inadequate supervision (Camblin & Prout, 1983; Schmidt, 1993). While each state legislature decides who must report and the guidelines for reporting, most states stipulate penalties for failing to report suspected abuse (Morrow, 1987; Schmidt, 1993). Just as with all other legal matters, it will continue to be important for counselors to stay current about issues regarding child abuse and state and federal legislation in this area. Each school district should have a policy describing the policies and procedures for dealing with sexual abuse. School counselors do not have to investigate abuse, as that is the job of a designated state agency, but they may have to work with children and the parents of children who have been abused.

Privileged Communication

Privileged communication is a right granted by law that allows counselors and other professionals to refuse to disclose client communication (Remley, 1985; Schmidt & Meara, 1984). Every state has its own method of defining the extent to which professional relationships are privileged (Remley, 1985; Thompson & Rudolph, 1992). In a limited numbers of states, the courts have granted school counselors the right to privilege (Sheeley & Herlihy, 1987).

In states that do not specifically include school counselors in the list of professionals who have the right to privileged communications, school counselors should not assume they will be allowed to claim immunity from discussing client confidences if so ordered by a court of law.

Counselors who live in states without privileged communication protection have several options for handling the ethical dilemma of being asked to disclose client communication in court testimony (Sheeley & Herlihy, 1987; Stude & McKelvey, 1979). They can explain the confidentiality guidelines in the code of ethics to the judge and ask the court to extend privilege to them. They can also make arrangements to become an agent of the client's attorney by confiding the confidential information to the attorney (Stude & McKelvey, 1979). In some instances, this act of becoming a designated agent of the attorney extends the attorney-client privilege to the counselor. If the counselor cannot persuade the judge to extend privilege to him or her, it is sometimes possible to limit who hears the confidential information by asking the judge to allow testimony *in camera*. If the judge grants this request, the counselor can provide testimony in the judge's chambers or in open court without spectators (Sheeley & Herlihy, 1987).

Access to School Records

The Family Educational Rights and Privacy Act (FERPA), also known as the Buckley Amendment, is a federal law that affects all school personnel, including school counselors (Schmidt, 1993). School counselors should familiarize themselves with the regulations of this act so that they remain in compliance with the laws when dealing with student records (Gibson & Mitchell, 1990). FERPA guarantees students eighteen and older and the parents of minor students the right to review all official school records pertaining to their children. The law also provides a vehicle for the parents or students to challenge the accuracy of any information in these records and to register disagreements that the school must subsequently include in the records. While the law delineates many of the records included under FERPA guidelines, it is not yet clear whether parents and students can demand confidential information from counseling notes, tape recordings of counseling sessions, and other counseling-related activities (Schmidt, 1993). So far, the general interpretation seems to be that counselors may keep private, personal notes on counseling relationships, because the FERPA regulations do not apply to personal files (Thompson & Rudolph, 1992). The legal definition of personal files, however, precludes anyone other than the counselor seeing or discussing the contents of these notes. Remley (1990) pointed out that there are no legal or ethical rules that counselors keep notes about their sessions. He also suggested that counselors who choose to include subjective material in their notes remember that the contents may eventually become public record. The enforcement of this important law seems open to change and subjective definition. Therefore, it would be prudent for counselors to stay informed about current rulings and interpretations of the Buckley Amendment.

Noncustodial Parents

Current laws and regulations give little guidance in the area of counselor communication with noncustodial parents (Aiello & Humes, 1987). There are, however, legal precedents in case law—based on findings in actual court cases— that can provide some help in determining action in regard to non-custodial parents' access to school records and counselor contact with non-custodial parents (Aeillo & Humes, 1987). Case law interpretations of the FERPA (Mattie v. Johnston, 1976; Page v. Rotterdam-Homonasen Central School District, 1981) suggest that "either parent of a student has access to the records of that student, in the absence of a court order or other official instrument prohibiting that access" (Aiello & Humes, 1987). Even when the custodial parent has requested that the noncustodial parent be denied access to the school records, the courts will not uphold such a request and the school is obligated to allow the noncustodial parent access to records (Aiello & Humes, 1987).

Case law also supports school counselor contact with noncustodial par-ents when the counselor believes that such communication would be in the best interest of the child (Aiello & Humes, 1987). In Weiss v. Weiss (1981), the court ruled that school personnel could make professional judgments about whether to discuss a child's educational concerns and progress if such contact would enhance the physical and emotional well-being of the child. The implication of this ruling is that the counselor is not obliged to notify the custodial parent about the decision to contact the noncustodial parent (Aeillo & Humes, 1987). However, in the spirit of continued cooperative re-lationships with both parents, the school counselor may decide to discuss the need for support and communication from all parties concerned with the welfare of the child with both of them.

In the authors' experience, the best way to establish and maintain suc-cessful interactions with parents is for counselors to honestly and openly communicate about their intentions before they act. However, in some situa-tions this is inadvisable or impossible. In those cases, counselors may feel re-assured to know that presently there is no legal mandate for this advance no-tice. However, just as in all other legal issues, counselors should continue to stay abreast of current developments in legislature or case law that could af-fect their decision-making process in this area.

Malpractice and Potential Liability

Although there are few malpractice suits brought against school counselors, it is important for counselors to understand their legal liability (Henderson, 1987; Pate, 1992; Remley, 1985; Schmidt, 1993). Malpractice results when a professional practices negligently (Beis, 1984; Picchoini & Bernstein, 1990) and can involve civil liability or criminal liability (Schmidt, 1993). In a civil malpractice suit, the plaintiff must bring evidence that proves someone (usu-ally the plaintiff or the plaintiff's child) was harmed physically or emotionally as a direct result of the counselor's inappropriate behavior or omission

(Remley, 1985; Schmidt, 1993). The plaintiff must also prove that other counselors who work in that community or in similar communities would have handled the situation in a different way (Remley, 1985). In a criminal malpractice case, the state attempts to prove that the counselor behaved in an unlawful manner, such as disobeying laws, contributing to the delinquency of a minor, or being an accessory to a crime (Hopkins & Anderson, 1985; Schmidt, 1993).

Several authors (Picchioni & Bernstein, 1990; Remley, 1985; Schmidt, 1993; Woody, 1988) have suggested the following precautionary measures to limit counselors' potential liability:

1. Make sure that you have an accurate description of your job and your school counseling program and that you do not deviate from the dictates of this description. This job description should be endorsed by the school board and should be well publicized so that the consumers of your services know what you are supposed to be doing and what you are doing in your job. If you stray from the duties outlined in the job description or you do not provide services described in the job description, you could be leaving yourself open for lawsuits.

2. Establish a reliable network of fellow professionals—both in your school district and in the community. This network can provide you with potential referral sources and with peers available for consultation about appropriate behavior. By referring when the level of need exceeds your expertise, you can avoid attempting to provide services for which you lack competence or training. By consulting with other professionals, you can insure that the course of action you take is consistent with the current practice in your community.

3. Know and understand all of the codes of ethics that apply to school counselors—this includes the ACA, ASCA, and ASGW codes. Follow the guidelines outlined in these codes in your interactions with students, parents, school personnel, and community members.

4. Stay current in relation to all of the laws and legal rulings that apply to the field of counseling, especially those that concern school counselors. Since these change rapidly, this may take some time and effort on your part, but it can provide protection for you.

5. Attend classes and workshops in the field of school counseling in order to stay informed about current developments.

6. When in doubt about a particular ethical or legal situation, consult a lawyer familiar with school law and/or with laws pertaining to counseling or an official from your professional organization. They can frequently provide current information on interpretations that might affect your decisions and behavior.

Many counselors have immunity from malpractice suits due to their employment by a government agency or are protected by their school liability insurance policy (Remley, 1985). However, it is important for counselors to investigate their liability protection. Depending on the level of security with the limits of coverage provided by the school, counselors may also want to obtain individual professional liability insurance through a professional organization or as a rider to their personal liability insurance policy.

Testifying in Court

School counselors sometimes have to testify in court cases involving child custody, child abuse, or other matters concerning children in their schools. Whenever counselors must testify, it is important that they remember that their role in the courtroom is as an educator, rather that as a child advocate (LaForge & Henderson, 1990). It will be the counselor's job to educate the judge, jury, and other participants about the counseling profession and about the child's current condition and how that can affect future functioning (Deutsch & Parker, 1985; LaForge & Henderson, 1990). A counselor may testify as a "fact" witness or as an "expert" witness (La Forge & Henderson, 1990). A fact witness simply testifies about information that he or she knows to be true—based on direct observation—or believes to be true—based on professional judgement and knowledge. For example, if a counselor was testifying as a fact witness, the court might ask her to describe an interaction between her and a child or to describe a bruise that she observed on a child's body.

An expert witness usually renders an opinion based on an analysis of the case, including a review of case records, interviews with involved parties, and other relevant information. The purpose of having an expert witness testify is to help the judge and/or jury understand the situation from a mental health perspective. For example, if a counselor testifying as an expert witness, the court might ask him, based on his interactions with a child and the child's parents, whether the child's mother or father would be the most appropriate custodial parent.

Before the actual court testimony, there are usually several pretrial procedures, which might include preparing case records, having a deposition taken, and/or requesting a pretrial conference (Dorn, 1984; LaForge & Henderson, 1990). The court can subpoena counseling records for a case, so counselors will want to consider the kinds of records they keep, knowing that they may become part of a permanent court record. Counselors may decide to keep limited records, relying on their memory of conversations or events, or they may decide to keep extensive records, documenting all aspects of the interactions or occurrences. The counselor's decision in this matter will depend on the school district's policies and the individual's own philosophy and attitude toward testifying.

When a counselor has been asked to testify by an attorney, she or he may want to request a pretrial conference with the attorney who has requested the counselor's presence (LaForge & Henderson, 1990). This will give the attorney a chance to explain procedures and strategy to the counselor. The attorney can go over possible questions the opposing attorney may ask, and the counselor can make suggestions about questions that he or she thinks the attorney should ask.

A deposition is a sworn statement that is made in an office with both sides' attorneys and a court stenographer present (Dorn, 1984; LaForge & Henderson, 1990). The deposition provides an opportunity for lawyers from both sides to gather information. As in court testimony, both sides have a chance to ask as many questions as they want. In preparation for making a deposition, counselors will want to review any notes they have made on the situation.

During the deposition and in court testimony, counselors should remember the following suggestions (Neff, 1982):

1. Speak in a loud, clear voice so that all members of the court can hear you.
2. You will want to use your usual professional vocabulary, but without a great deal of jargon.
3. Make sure you understand each question before you answer it. If you do not understand a question, you have the right to ask for the attorney to rephrase it.
4. Answer each question in a direct, simple way, avoiding elaboration.
5. If you know something is true, be assertive in your presentation. If you are not sure, do not try to act as if you are. You can say, "I do not know."
6. If there is no court subpoena for your records or case notes, do not bring them.
7. Remain polite and unruffled during cross-examination.
8. Avoid stating personal reactions or opinions unless asked directly for them.

By following these guidelines, counselors can maintain their professional credibility and dignity. Although most school counselors do not seek opportunities to testify in court, those occasions when they cannot avoid this experience do not have to be unpleasant or traumatic.

CONCLUSION

School counselors look to their professional codes of ethics for guidelines on ethical practice, but they will still have to examine their own personal values and beliefs in making decisions about how to conduct themselves professionally. While the primary ethical responsibilities in school counseling are owed to the students, counselors also have ethical obligations to parents, colleagues and other professionals, schools and communities, themselves, and their profession. Counselors must also attend to legal decisions and court cases that could affect their guidance and counseling practices. While many counselors would not choose to testify in court, when they must do so there are strategies that they can use to present themselves as competent professionals who can offer insights into understanding and helping children.

REFERENCES

Aiello, H., & Humes, C. (1987). Counselor contact of the noncustodial parent: A point of law. *Elementary School Guidance and Counseling, 21,* 177–182.

Alexander, K., & Alexander, M. (1985). *American public school law* (2nd ed.). St. Paul, MN: West.

American Counseling Association (ACA). (1988). *Ethical standards* (rev. ed.). Alexandria, VA: Author.

American School Counselor Association (ASCA). (1986). *ASCA position statement: The school counselor and confidentiality* (rev. ed.). Alexandria, VA: Author.

American School Counselor Association (ASCA). (1992). Ethical standards for school counselors. *The ASCA Counselor, 29(3)*, 13–16.

Association for Specialists in Group Work (ASGW). (1989). *Ethical guidelines for group leaders* (rev. ed.). Alexandria, VA: Author.

Beis, E. (1984). *Mental health and the law.* Rockville, MD: Aspen Systems.

Brady v. Hopper, 570 F. Supp. 1333 (D. CO 1983).

Camblin, L., & Prout, H. (1983). School counselors and the reporting of child abuse: A survey of state laws and practices. *The School Counselor, 30*, 358–367.

Corey, G., Corey, M., Callanan, P., & Russell, J. (1982). Ethical considerations in using group techniques. *Journal for Specialists in Group Work, 7*, 140–148.

Davis v. Lhim, 335 N.W. 2d. 481 (MI App. 1983).

DePauw, M. (1986). Avoiding ethical violations: A timeline perspective for individual counseling. *Journal of Counseling and Development, 64*, 303–305.

Deutsch, P., & Parker, E. (1985). *Rehabilitation testimony: Maintaining a professional perspective.* New York: Matthew Bender.

Dorn, F. (1984). The counselor goes to court. *Journal of Counseling and Development, 63*, 119–120.

Ferris, P., & Linville, M. (1985). The child's rights: Whose responsibility? *Elementary School Guidance and Counseling, 19*, 172–180.

Gibson, R., & Mitchell, M. (1990). *Introduction to counseling and guidance.* New York: Macmillan.

Gill, S. (1982). Professional disclosure and consumer protection in counseling. *Personnel and Guidance Journal, 60*, 443–446.

Henderson, D. (1987). Negligent liability and the foreseeability factor: A critical issue for school counselors. *Journal of Counseling and Development, 66*, 86–89.

Herlihy, B., & Sheeley, V. (1988). Counselor liability and the duty to warn: Selected cases, statutory trends, and implications for practice. *Counselor Education and Supervision, 27*, 203–215.

Hopkins, B., & Anderson, B. (1985). *The counselor and the law* (2nd ed.). Alexandria, VA: American Association for Counseling and Development.

Huey, W. (1986). Ethical concerns in school counseling. *Journal of Counseling and Development, 64*, 321–322.

Huey, W. (1987). "Ethical standards for school counselors:" Test your knowledge. *The School Counselor, 34*, 331–335.

Kelleher, M. (1984). Psychotherapists and the duty to warn: An attempt at clarification. *New England Law Review, 19*, 597–617.

LaForge, J., & Henderson, P. (1990). Counselor competency in the courtroom. *Journal of Counseling and Development, 68*, 456–459.

Leedy v. Hartnett, 510 F. Supp. 1125 (M.D. PA 1981).

Lipari v. Sears, Roebuck & Co., 497 F. Supp 195D (NE 1980).

Mabe, A., & Rollin, S. (1986). The role of a code of ethical standards in counseling. *Journal of Counseling and Development, 64*, 294–297.

Mattie v. Johnston, 74 F.R.D. N.D. (MS 1976).

McIntosh v. Milano, 403 A.2d. 500 (1979).

Neff, W. (1982). Testifying as a competent and credible witness. *Journal of the College and University Personnel Association, 33*, 42–45.

Page v. Rotterdam-Homonasen Central School District, 441 N.Y.S. 2d 323, 109 Misc. 2d 1049 (NY 1981).

Pate, R. (1992). Are you liable? *American Counselor, 2*, 15–19.

Peterson v. State, 671 P.2d.500 (WA 1983).

Picchioni, T., & Bernstein, B. (1990). Risk management for mental health counselors. *Texas Association of Counseling and Development Journal, 18*, 3–18.

Remley, T. (1985). The law and ethical practices in elementary and middle schools. *Elementary School Guidance and Counseling, 19*, 181–189.

Remley, T. (1990). Counseling records: Legal and ethical issues. In B. Herlihy & Golden (Eds.), *Ethical standards casebook* (pp. 162–169). Alexandria, VA: American Counseling Association.

Schmidt, J. (1993). *Counseling in schools: Essential services and comprehensive programs.* Boston: Allyn & Bacon.

Schmidt, L., & Meara, N. (1984). Ethical, professional, and legal issues in counseling psychology. In S. Brown & R. Lent (Eds.), *Handbook of counseling psychology* (pp. 56–96). New York: Wiley.

Sheeley, V., & Herlihy, B. (1987). Privileged communication in school counseling: Status update. *The School Counselor, 34,* 268–272.

Stude, E., & McKelvey, J. (1979). Ethics and the law: Friend or foe? *Personnel and Guidance Journal, 57,* 453–456.

Tarasoff v. Regents of University of California, 17 CA 3d 425, 551 P.2d 334, 131 CA Rptr. 14 (1976).

Terres, C., & Larrabee, M. (1985). Ethical issues and group work with children. *Elementary School Guidance and Counseling, 19,* 190–197.

Thompson, C., & Rudolph, L. (1992). *Counseling children* (3rd ed.). Pacific Grove, CA: Brooks/Cole.

Van Hoose, W. (1986). Ethical principles in counseling. *Journal of Counseling and Development, 65,* 168–169.

Wagner, C. (1981). Confidentiality and the school counselor. *Personnel and Guidance Journal, 59,* 305–310.

Walker, M., & Larrabee, M. (1985). Ethics and school records. *Elementary School Guidance and Counseling, 19,* 210–216.

Weiss v. Weiss, 52 N.Y. 2d 170, 418 N.E. 2d 377 (NY 1981).

Woody, R. (1988). *Fifty ways to avoid malpractice: A guide for mental health professionals.* Sarasota, FL: Professional Resource Exchange.

Zingaro, J. (1983) Confidentiality: To tell or not to tell. *Elementary School Guidance and Counseling, 17,* 261–267.

The Counseling Story*

I. Introduction of the counselor.
   A. Introduce yourself.
   B. Provide a little of your professional background and experiences.

II. Introduction of the counseling program.
   A. Explain the need for guidance.
   B. Discuss the organization of the program, to include counselor duties.
   C. Discuss the comparative costs of counseling vs. those of specialized external agencies.

III. Explanation of the need for guidance and counseling.
   A. Point out that guidance and counseling are needed for all children. Stress the fact that most children need help with normal development tasks.
   B. Discuss the impact of changing family lives, the mobility of families, and the potential impact of these moves on children's learning.
   C. Show how counseling can help in achievement and assist in the development of positive self-images and self-understanding.
   D. Discuss the potential impact of television, and the possible concerns of students over increased social pressures at an early age.
   E. Discuss the importance of good (and continuous) early study habits.
   F. Without being overly dramatic or a "dooms sayer" show how children of today face some unique pressures that their parents did not have to face. Stress the fact that a comprehensive counseling program can help prevent some of these problems:
      1. Depersonalization in large schools.
      2. Loneliness.
      3. School failure.
      4. Delinquency.
      5. Dropouts (use local figures or get statewide data).
      6. Chemical abuse.
      7. Mental health.
   G. Present a brief case study of an actual case, and show how counseling helped a child with a normal concern. Discuss both individual and group counseling. Always try to show how guidance and counseling are consistent with the school's objectives.

IV. Presentation of counselor duties.
   A. Prepare a chart with a figure of the counselor in the middle. Draw arrows that show all the tasks the counselor performs. Stress guidance objectives.
   B. Outline counseling in detail. Show how counseling differs from therapy. Be sure to include a section on counseling that is available for all students. Show a videotape of a simulated role-played counseling session. Allow time for questions.

*Adapted from Muro, J. J., & Dinkmeyer, D. C. (1977). Counseling in the elementary and middle schools. Dubuque, IA: Wm. C. Brown.

      C. Outline the philosophy of your programs. Be sure to include basic guidance concepts.

      D. Describe how your program is evaluated.

V. Explanation of counseling program costs.

      A. Prepare a chart to show guidance costs. Include salaries, materials, and the like. Break total cost down to a yearly per pupil cost.

      B. Obtain figures from state departments of education on the yearly costs of:

          1. State support of mental institutions.

          2. State support of individual prisoners per year, and the overall costs of maintaining prisons.

          3. State support of special training centers for juvenile offenders.

      C. Be certain to point out that a counselor would more than "earn" his or her annual salary by simply preventing two or three children from commitment to one of the above institutions.

*Coloring Book for Orientation to Counseling**

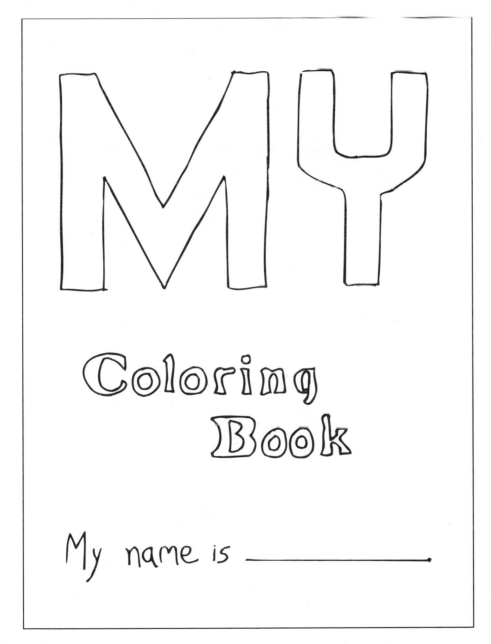

*Adapted from Muro, J. J., & Dinkmeyer, D. C. (1977). Counseling in the elementary and middle schools. Dubuque, IA: Wm. C. Brown.

This is my school

Draw a picture of you.

This is my guidance counselor.
Her name is _____.

This is my guidance counselor's office.

Sometimes we play together.

Sometimes we talk together.

The guidance counselor talks to my teacher.

The guidance counselor talks to my parents.

The New Helper and My Coloring Book
Written By
Charlotte LaRochelle and Gail Higgins

Illustrated by Art Marcho
Monroe, Maine

Student Introduction to Counseling*

I. Introduce yourself. Use a coloring book that explains who you are to children in grades one through three.

II. Give a brief overview of the overall guidance program. Make it a point to highlight counseling.

III. Define counseling using terms and concepts that children will understand:
   A. Emphasize that counseling is available for all students.
   B. List some typical concerns that children bring to counselors (making friends, school work, etc.).
   C. Be sure to present yourself as a friend and helper. Explain confidentiality in simple direct terms.
   D. Encourage self-referrals. Explain how appointments with the counselor may be made.
   E. Explain the counseling process; tell students what they can expect from a visit to the counselor.

IV. Make a VCR recording of a counseling session. Use a student to role play for the tape. Stop the tape at appropriate points to explain what is happening.

V. For children who are able to write, pass out 3″ by 5″ cards and ask that they put down any questions they may have about counseling. Also ask them to list any topics that they may want to discuss with the counselor. Do not require them to sign their names to the cards unless they want to do so (this will avoid embarrassment for some). Collect the cards and respond to the questions. With younger children, take the questions orally.

VI. End the meeting by asking the children, "What have you learned about counseling today?" (This will allow you to assess how well you are conveying your message and whether or not you need to make modifications for a particular age group).

Experienced elementary counselors support the contention that if given the opportunity, elementary school children will refer themselves for counseling. In fact, some children will refer their friends for counseling, particularly if the "friend" is either doing or saying something that the referring child does not like! As one might expect, many of the self-referrals that seem to have a sense of urgency are really minor developmental matters. What is minor to an adult, however, is often major to a child. An effective referral system is important to the counseling program.

In setting up a referral system, counselors should provide some form of box at a location that is accessible to many children. A simple card that asks for the student's name and his or her home room number should be

*Adapted from Muro, J. J., & Dinkmeyer, D. C. (1977). Counseling in the elementary and middle schools. Dubuque, IA: Wm. C. Brown.

provided for student use. You may want to encourage younger students to ask their teachers for referral help. You will also need to provide special times for impromptu walk-in appointments by students. Physically appearing in the lunch room or on the playground from time to time will encourage students to seek you out for brief counseling sessions.

Some counselors have had success by setting up a "counseling information booth" near the lunch room. You can train older middle school students to provide information about counseling and about how to see the counselor to those who may be shy or feel embarrassed seeking counseling help directly. In addition, those students who work in these information booths, if carefully selected and trained, can become part of a cadre of a peer counseling program. You can assign these same children as big brothers and big sisters to children who need daily help in some aspect of school life. For example, counselors should request the names of all new and transfer students to the school and assign each to a big brother or sister. One of the tasks of the big brother or sister would be that of meeting the new student and introducing him or her to the counselor.

Of course, some of the very best orientation activities take place within the context of a comprehensive guidance program. No presentation can take the place of the physical presence of the counselor in the various classrooms working with the teacher on a wide range of guidance activities. If for example, the teacher is reading a story from DUSO, the counselor can be present and part of the discussion of the story, or he or she can take the opportunity to move from seat to seat with a smile or word of encouragement. The point here is that counselors must go beyond saying that they are helpers. Children must see them in a wide range of helping situations.

Life-Style Guide

Date _____

Student's Name _____ Birth Date _____

Grade _____ Sex: M _____ F _____ Chronological Age _____

Teacher _____ Building _____

Family Constellation

1. List all siblings in descending order, including the child in his or her position within the family.

Name	Age	Education
_____	_____	_____
_____	_____	_____
_____	_____	_____
_____	_____	_____
_____	_____	_____
_____	_____	_____
_____	_____	_____
_____	_____	_____

2. Who is most different from you? _____

   How? _____

   _____

   _____

3. Who is most like you? _____

   How? _____

Functioning at Life Tasks

1. If you had your choice of going to school or staying home, what would you do?

   _____

   Why? _____

    a. What do you like about school? Why? _____

    _____

    b. What do you dislike about school? Why? _____

    _____

    c. What is your favorite subject? Why? _____

    _____

    d. What subject do you like the least? Why? _____

    _____

2. Who is your best friend? At school? _____

   _____

    a. Who are some of your other friends? _____

    _____

    b. What do you usually do when you are with your friends? _____

    _____

    c. When you play a game, are you usually picked first, last, or in the middle?

    _____

d. Suppose you and your friend wanted to play a game where four people are needed to play, but the other kids want to play another game—what would

you do? Why? _____

_____

Family Atmosphere

1. If you needed special permission to go somewhere, who would you ask—your

   mother or father? Why? _____

   _____

2. If you got in serious trouble at school and needed help, would you ask your

   mother or father for help? Why? _____

   _____

3. When you misbehave, who disciplines you—your mother or father? Why? _____

   _____

   _____

4. What do you like to do best with mom or dad? Why? _____

   _____

5. What do you like to do least with mom or dad? Why? _____

   _____

6. Do you get an allowance? How much? _____

7. What kinds of jobs do you do at home? Do you usually do them without being

   reminded? _____

8. Which of the children in the family act most like dad? How? _____

   _____

9. Which of the children in the family act most like mom? How? _____

_____

_____

_____

10. Rate the highest and lowest sibling for each trait:

		Highest	Lowest	I am more like
a.	Intelligent	_____	_____	_____
b.	Best grades	_____	_____	_____
c.	Athletic	_____	_____	_____
d.	Prettiest	_____	_____	_____
e.	Strongest	_____	_____	_____
f.	Hardest worker	_____	_____	_____
g.	Helps around the house	_____	_____	_____
h.	Selfish/shares	_____	_____	_____
i.	Cares about other feelings	_____	_____	_____
j.	Feelings easily hurt	_____	_____	_____
k.	Gets own way	_____	_____	_____
l.	Most friends	_____	_____	_____
m.	Bossiest	_____	_____	_____
n.	Blamed most often when things go wrong	_____	_____	_____
o.	Gets in trouble most often	_____	_____	_____
p.	Easiest to get along with	_____	_____	_____

Alaska

1. If you were going to Alaska and could take only one person with you, who would

   it be? Why? _____

   _____

   _____

2. What are some of the things you would take to Alaska? Why? _____

   _____

   ·

   _____

Animal

1. If you could be an animal, which would you choose? _____

   _____

   _____

2. Which would you *not* want to be? Why? _____

Three Wishes

1. _____

2. _____

3. _____

Early Recollections

_____

_____

_____

_____

_____

Basic Mistakes

_____

_____

_____

_____

_____

Recommendations

_____

_____

_____

_____

_____

_____

_____

_____

_____

_____

_____

_____

_____

_____

The Children's Interaction Matrix

The Test

The Children's Interaction Matrix (Intermediate and Primary forms) has been designed to identify the preferred work and content styles of children in group situations. These factors aid the researcher, teacher, and counselor in understanding the individuals' preferred mode of behavior in groups, and indicate the students' reactions to group situations. The information can be particularly useful to the counselor or teacher in structuring group composition or providing group experiences. When researchers, teachers, counselors, or psychologists have evidence of children's characteristic modes of response in a variety of group situations, they are better equipped to guide them to and through group experiences and to help the individual student experience situations conducive to social and personal growth and adjustment.

Both the Intermediate and Primary forms of the Children's Interaction Matrix are based on the conceptual framework of the Hill Interaction Matrix (HIM) (Hill, 1965). This is a two-dimensional matrix which describes a person's preferred content style and work style modes of group behavior. The HIM is presented in Figure E.1, and the descriptions of the categories of the interaction are given in Table E.1.

The Intermediate and Primary forms of the Children's Interaction Matrix are primarily research instruments. Clinical judgments of psychologists, counselors, and teachers should also be utilized in structuring and organizing experiences.

Construction of the Tests

The Children's Interaction Matrix Intermediate and Primary forms are based on the 20 cells of the Hill Interaction Matrix, but the responsive category is omitted, so there is a total of 16 cells. Four items were included for each cell, for a total of 64 items. The pool of original items on the HIM-B (Hill, 1965), as well as the cell labels, were used as criteria for development and selection of the items. The structure of the items and the wording were simplified to be appropriate for children in the respective grade levels. The items were rated by three judges as to their appropriateness for each cell. The Cahall and Lorge formulas for readability of test items were computed as a check on the verbal level of the tests (Cahall, 1958; Lorge, 1944).

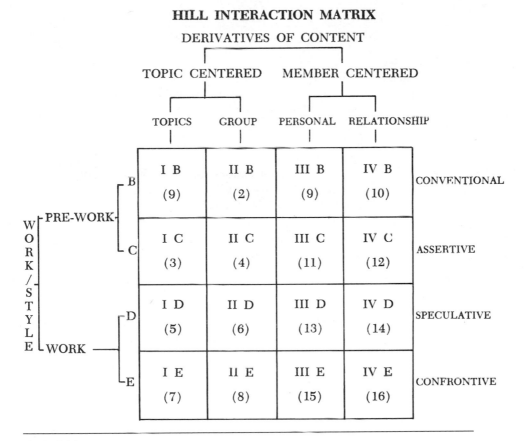

Figure E.1
Hill Interaction Matrix showing content and work style categories.

The response format was also simplified, from a six-position Guttman Scale to a two-position "Yes-No" format for the Primary form and a three-position "Usually, Sometimes, Not Often" format for the Intermediate form.

Sample

The subjects of the testing program which led to the development of the Children's Interaction Matrix were 1,049 students from five communities representing rural and urban, middle and lower class, and white and black populations in three states.

Table E.1

Categories of Interaction in the HIM

Category	Description
Work Style (row)	
B—Conventional	Behavior that is socially appropriate for any group. The interaction may be so socially oriented to be devoid of any content and may be no more than pleasantries and amenities.
C—Assertive	Argumentative, hostile, or assertive statements.
D—Speculative	Speculative, intellectual, or controlled approach to pertinent therapeutic issues.*
E—Confrontive	Penetration to the significant aspects of a discussion. Because of this penetration, these statements confront members with aspects of their behavior which are usually avoided.
Content Style (columns)	
I—Topic	Statements about any one of an infinite number of topics of general interest, exclusive of the group or its members.
II—Group	The speaker identifies with the group as an entity, and personal reactions to the group are probed for or are given in answer to such probes.
III—Personal	Interaction having as its topic a group member; usually a member's actions, problems, or personality.
IV—Relationship	The speaker demonstrates (acts out), alludes to, or discusses a relationship between members or between a member and the group.

*In our thinking we substitute the word *developmental* for *therapeutic.*

Reliability

From the pilot testing of the Children's Interaction Matrix, split-half coefficients were computed for both forms of the test. The reliability coefficients are reported in Table E.2. The total acceptance scale, based on responses to all 64 items, has sufficient reliability for use with individuals. The work style scales tend to have higher reliabilities than the content scales and appear to be more useful for individual assessment. The reliabilities of the content scales are sufficiently low that cautious interpretations are suggested.

Additional reliability studies have been conducted. Information on the coefficient of stability based upon test-retest results was made available in June 1975. The test has been cross-validated on other samples, and reliability coefficients have been computed for the factor scale as well as the theoretical scales proposed by Hill.

Table E.2

Corrected Split-Half Reliability Coefficients for Children's Interaction Matrix

Scale	Level	
	Primary (N = 304)	Intermediate (N = 745)
Conventional	.69	.71
Assertive	.49	.72
Speculative	.67	.72
Confrontive	.58	.75
Topic	.55	.61
Group	.60	.67
Personal	.64	.58
Relationship	.60	.48
Total acceptance score	.89	.85

Validity

Two types of analysis have been conducted with the Children's Interaction Matrix. The validity was studied by comparing the test with the Children's Personality Questionnaire as well as with peer and teacher nominations. The construct validity was also examined by a factor analysis and by analyzing the scores based on teacher and peer nominations.

Concurrent Validity

Teachers in grades 1 and 2 were asked to identify students who demonstrated clearly one of the four work styles. Students nominated for each work style were then compared with other students in the same classes not nominated. Significant differences were found between the means of students nominated in two work styles, assertive and confrontive, and students in general. No significant differences were found between the two groups on the Conventional and Speculative scales.

Teacher nominations were also sought from grade 4–6 teachers. Students nominated for each category were compared with those nominated for each of the other three. Significant F values were found on the Conventional and Speculative scales. An F value of 4.56 (3/203 df), significant at the .01 level, was found on the conventional scale. Those nominated as Conventional had significantly higher means than those nominated as Assertive, according to Duncan's Multiple Range Test. An F of 2.67 with 3/203 degrees of freedom was found on the Speculative scale. Duncan's Multiple Range Test indicated significant differences between the students nominated as Speculative and Assertive and Conventional and Assertive.

Norms

Primary Form

The Primary form of the Children's Interaction Matrix was based on the responses of 304 students in grades 1–3 from three different school districts, one rural, one inner city, and one large suburban city. Students included 151 girls and 153 boys.

Analysis of the means of the scales by the T test revealed significant differences at the .05 level between the means of grade 3 boys and girls on three of the scales. Third-grade girls had significantly higher means on the Conventional, Speculative, and Personal Scales. Analysis of variance of the scores by sex and by grade revealed that the third-grade group of girls had significantly higher scores than girls in lower grades on seven of the nine scales. This was true for only two out of the nine scales for boys.

Intermediate Form

The Intermediate form of the Children's Interaction Matrix was based on the responses of 689 fourth- through eighth-grade students from five different districts located in three states. The sample contained students from urban, rural, and suburban districts, as well as an urban inner-city group. The sample consisted of 348 boys and 341 girls. Sex differences were found on only one scale for each of the fourth- and fifth-grade groups. There were sex differences on five of the scales for the eighth-graders. No significant differences were found for the male groups, but differences were found on five of the scales for females. The scores tended to be higher primarily for the eighth-grade groups.

Scoring

Children's Interaction Matrix—Primary Form

The item responses from the test booklet should be transferred to a profile sheet. "Yes" responses are given a weight of 2 and "no" responses a weight of 1.

Specific scale scores are obtained as follows:

Conventional Scale. Add the scores in the four cells of the first row—Topic, Group, Personal, and Relationship—to get the total Conventional scale score.

Assertive Scale. Add the scores in the four cells of the second row—Topic, Group, Personal, and Relationship—to get the total Assertive score.

Speculative Scale. Add the scores in the four cells of the third row—Topic, Group, Personal, and Relationship—to get the total Speculative score.

Confrontive Scale. Add the scores in the four cells of the fourth row—Topic, Group, Personal and Relationship—to get the total Confrontive score.

Topic Score. Add the scores of the items in Column 1.

Group Score. Add the scores of the items in Column 2.

Table E.3

Profile Sheet for Scoring Children's Interaction Matrix

Name _____ Grade _____ Sex _____

School _____ Age _____

	Topic	Group	Personal	Relationship
Conventional	24 _____	9 _____	1 _____	11 _____
	26 _____	19 _____	15 _____	38 _____
	48 _____	25 _____	41 _____	49 _____
	63 _____	37 _____	64 _____	58 _____
	T _____	T _____	T _____	T _____
Assertive	13 _____	14 _____	4 _____	7 _____
	27 _____	20 _____	32 _____	10 _____
	51 _____	22 _____	55 _____	16 _____
	57 _____	39 _____	59 _____	40 _____
	T _____	T _____	T _____	T _____
Speculative	3 _____	17 _____	18 _____	5 _____
	6 _____	30 _____	31 _____	44 _____
	29 _____	52 _____	36 _____	53 _____
	54 _____	60 _____	43 _____	61 _____
	T _____	T _____	T _____	T _____
Confrontive	28 _____	8 _____	12 _____	2 _____
	33 _____	21 _____	35 _____	23 _____
	45 _____	34 _____	56 _____	42 _____
	50 _____	46 _____	62 _____	47 _____
	T _____	T _____	T _____	T _____

T _____   _____   _____   _____

Personal Score. Add the scores of the items in Column 3.

Relationship Score. Add the scores of the items in Column 4.

Total Acceptance Score. Add the sum of the topic scores. Add the sums of the work style scores. These sums should be the same if you have added correctly. This number is the total acceptance score.

Children's Interaction Matrix—Intermediate Form

The item responses from the test booklet should be transferred to a profile sheet (see Table E.3). "Usually" responses are given a weight of 3, "Sometimes" responses a weight of 2, and "Not Often" responses a weight of 1.

First compute the scores for each of the 16 cells. Example: Add the Topic-Conventional items (24, 26, 48, 63) and record the same by T. Add the Group-Conventional items (9, 19, 25, 37) and record the sum by the T directly under the set of items. Personal-Conventional items are 1, 15, 41, 64. Relationship-Conventional items are 11, 38, 49, 58. Work style and content scores are then obtained by the procedure described for scoring the Primary form.

Total Acceptance Score. Add the sums of the Topic scale, Group scale, Personal scale, and Relationship scale. Add also the scores of the four work style scales. The sums of both should be the same if you have added correctly. This number is the total acceptance score.

The Children's Interaction Matrix: Intermediate Form

This form is intended for use with students in grades 4–8. Read the questionnaire to yourself before giving it.

The test can be administered in groups in three different ways:

1. Students, after being given directions for taking the inventory, can read the test themselves and respond on the test booklet or separate answer sheet.
2. The teacher can read the test to the students or use a tape recording of the items and have the students make their responses on the separate answer sheet.
3. The teacher can read the items aloud while the students read them silently and the students mark their responses on the test booklet.

Allow at least 35 minutes for the test. Slow readers will tend to take longer. Fast readers will take shorter periods of time.

The directions should be read to the students.

Children's Interaction Matrix: Intermediate Form

Date _____

Name _____ Age _____ Sex _____

Grade _____ School _____

This questionnaire contains 64 items describing how kids act or feel when they are with their friends. Read each item and decide how you normally act or feel. There are no right or wrong answers. Your best answer is the one that first comes to mind.

In answering the items on this questionnaire read each item and then decide how you normally act or feel. You are asked to respond whether you "usually" do this or feel this way, "sometimes" do this or feel this way, or "rarely" or "not often" do this or feel this way.

Now look at the first item on the test. It says: I like to talk to other kids about my family, my school, my homework, and my hobbies. Below the item you see three choices, "Usually," "Sometimes," and "Not Often." Circle the choice which best describes how you normally act or feel. For example, if you talk to kids all the time about these things you would circle "usually."

Now begin with item 1 and circle the response which best describes how you normally act or feel when you are with your friends. Do this for all the items on the questionnaire.

1. I like to talk to other kids about my family, my school, my homework, and my hobbies.

Usually   Sometimes   Not Often

2. When they ask me, I tell other kids what I think of them.

Usually   Sometimes   Not Often

3. I like to talk with other kids about the way people think, fell, and act.

Usually   Sometimes   Not Often

4. I like to take the side of a classmate who is being picked on.

Usually   Sometimes   Not Often

5. In a group I like to ask questions about how individuals feel about each other.

Usually   Sometimes   Not Often

6. I like to know why people do the things they do.

Usually   Sometimes   Not Often

7. Kids need to be "told off" a lot.

Usually   Sometimes   Not Often

8. When a group of my friends are not getting along well, I try to help them get along better.

Usually   Sometimes   Not Often

9. I ask people to repeat what they have said when I don't understand them.

Usually   Sometimes   Not Often

10. I like to say unkind and mean things to other kids.

Usually   Sometimes   Not Often

11. I try to say and do things that will help others.

Usually   Sometimes   Not Often

12. When others tell me that I am misbehaving, I try to learn from what they say.

Usually   Sometimes   Not Often

13. Even though other kids don't like my ideas, I stick to them anyway.

Usually   Sometimes   Not Often

14. I like to take the side of boys or girls who disagree with the group.

Usually   Sometimes   Not Often

15. I like to know something about the families, the homes, and the hobbies of other kids.

Usually   Sometimes   Not Often

16. I let others know what I think of them.

Usually   Sometimes   Not Often

17. I like to tell my friends how they might do things better.

Usually   Sometimes   Not Often

18. I ask other people for help when I have a personal problem.

Usually   Sometimes   Not Often

19. I like to plan and start group discussion, games, and things like that.

Usually   Sometimes   Not Often

20. Boys and girls don't know how to help each other with their problems.

Usually   Sometimes   Not Often

21. If kids can't agree on what they are going to do, I ask them why they can't agree.

Usually   Sometimes   Not Often

22. Kids talk about everything except what they start out talking about.

Usually   Sometimes   Not Often

23. I try to get kids to think about how they feel and act toward each other.

Usually   Sometimes   Not Often

24. I like to talk about things that are going on in the world today.

Usually   Sometimes   Not Often

25. I like to help to plan what the group does in its meetings.

Usually   Sometimes   Not Often

26. I like to talk with other kids.

Usually   Sometimes   Not Often

27. I like to complain about my parents, my teacher, and the principal to my classmates.

Usually   Sometimes   Not Often

28. I like to try to help others see how each person has good and helpful ideas.

Usually   Sometimes   Not Often

29. I like to talk about why other kids get upset and angry.

Usually   Sometimes   Not Often

30. I try to figure out if friends I'm with are better or worse than friends I've had before.

Usually   Sometimes   Not Often

31. I try to help kids when they have problems with their parents or other kids.

Usually   Sometimes   Not Often

32. When kids tell me that I don't do something very well, I tell them they have faults too.

Usually   Sometimes   Not Often

33. When my friends talk about their problems, I like to talk about why they have those problems.

Usually   Sometimes   Not Often

34. I tell others how I think they are doing and where they are making mistakes.

Usually   Sometimes   Not Often

35. When people say one thing and do the opposite, I tell them about it.

Usually   Sometimes   Not Often

36. I like to have other kids help me to know what I am really like.

Usually   Sometimes   Not Often

37. In a group I'm the one who asks what we are going to do and how we are going to do it.

Usually   Sometimes   Not Often

38. I like to praise my friends when they do a good job.

Usually   Sometimes   Not Often

39. I disagree with the way kids I'm with do things.

Usually   Sometimes   Not Often

40. I like to make fun of others.

Usually   Sometimes   Not Often

41. I like to know all about my classmates.

Usually   Sometimes   Not Often

42. I tell other kids how I feel toward them, even if it may hurt their feelings.

Usually   Sometimes   Not Often

43. I am willing to tell others all I know about myself.

Usually   Sometimes   Not Often

44. When I tell my friends what I think of them, I try to do it in a way that doesn't hurt their feelings.

Usually   Sometimes   Not Often

45. I try to help others understand a problem when they are having trouble figuring something out.

Usually   Sometimes   Not Often

46. If one person is keeping us from doing what we want to do, I complain to the others.

Usually   Sometimes   Not Often

47. I try to find out how other kids feel about the things that I say and do.

Usually   Sometimes   Not Often

48. I like to hear and tell gossip.
Usually   Sometimes   Not Often

49. I like to tease other kids.
Usually   Sometimes   Not Often

50. I try to get my friends to talk about the way they think and feel about things.
Usually   Sometimes   Not Often

51. Kids don't really understand much about most of the problems they see and hear.
Usually   Sometimes   Not Often

52. I like to tell others my ideas about what the gang is doing.
Usually   Sometimes   Not Often

53. I like to get boys and girls to talk about how they feel about each other.
Usually   Sometimes   Not Often

54. People need to know more about why they think, feel, and act the way they do.
Usually   Sometimes   Not Often

55. I get angry when my friends tell me I am not the kind of person that I should be.
Usually   Sometimes   Not Often

56. I try to get my classmates to do something about their problems even if they don't want to.
Usually   Sometimes   Not Often

57. I like to argue with other kids.
Usually   Sometimes   Not Often

58. I like to be close friends with other kids.
Usually   Sometimes   Not Often

59. People who talk about their troubles make me mad.
Usually   Sometimes   Not Often

60. I tell the gang how I think it is doing.
Usually   Sometimes   Not Often

61. When someone asks me if I like them or not, I usually tell them.
Usually   Sometimes   Not Often

62. I try to find out what my friends really think about me.
Usually   Sometimes   Not Often

63. I like to be with groups of kids.
Usually   Sometimes   Not Often

64. I like to meet new people and find out about them.
Usually   Sometimes   Not Often

The Children's Interaction Matrix: Primary Form

Directions for Administration

This form is intended for first-, second-, and third-grade students. The test is to be read to students by the examiner or teacher. It is suggested that the test be administered to the students at two separate periods, since children at this age level cannot sustain interest for 64 questions at one sitting.

Preparation

Read the inventory to yourself several times before giving it. It may be wise to record the items of the test on a recorder so that you will be free to supervise the testing and answer any questions that arise. The students will circle their answers on a separate answer sheet. It is usually desirable for you to write the names of students on the answer sheets.

Pupils will need a pencil, crayon, or marker. You will need to allow at least 25 minutes for each half of the inventory. Repeat each item twice when reading the test to the students. Have the students cross out unwanted responses with an X so you can identify the items for which they have changed their minds.

Draw an example of the response box for the sample item on the board.

Procedure

Distribute the answer sheet and pencils. Read:

This is a set of questions about how you act or feel when you are with other kids. Listen carefully to the questions I read to you (or which are read to you on tape) and decide whether you usually act or feel this way. If you do, circle YES on your answer sheet in box 1. If you do not act or feel this way, circle NO on your answer sheet.

Everyone find the answer box in the first column with a ball in the center. Now let's try a practice question. The question is: Do you like to do things with other kids? If you do, circle YES, Y-E-S, with your pencil. If you don't like to, circle No, N-O, with your pencil.

Now that we have finished the practice question, find the box with the square right under the one with the ball (square no. 1). Do you like to talk with other kids about your family and school?

Children's Interaction Matrix: Primary Form

Square	1.	Do you like to talk to other kids about your family and school?
Star	2.	Do you like to tell kids what you think of them when they ask you?
Car	3.	Do you like to talk to other kids about why they act the way they do?
House	4.	Do you "stick up" for a friend who is being picked on?
Diamond	5.	Do you like to ask kids how they feel about each other?
Flower	6.	Do you like to know why people act the way they do?
Glasses	7.	Do you think some kids in your group need to be told off by the other kids?
Hat	8.	Do you like to try to figure out why some kids don't get along with each other?

Now find the triangle at the top of the page.

Triangle	9.	When kids say something to you and you don't understand what they mean, do you ask them to repeat it?
Tree	10.	Do you like to say mean things to other kids?
Boat	11.	Do you like to do and say things that will help other kids.
Wagon	12.	Do you try to learn from people when they say you are doing wrong?
Plane	13.	Do you like to stick up for your ideas even if other kids don't like them?
Clock	14.	Do you like to stick up for kids that others don't like?
Truck	15.	Do you like to find out about the family and homes of your friends?
Scissors	16.	Do you like to let other kids know what you think of them?
Heart	17.	Do you like to tell kids how they can do things better?

Turn to the next page. Find the box with the ball in the first column.

Ball	18.	Do you ask people for help when you have a problem?
Square	19.	Do you like to be the one who plans and starts games?
Star	20.	Do you like to help other kids when they have problems?
Car	21.	Do you think it is wrong for kids to argue with each other when they can't agree?
House	22.	Do you tell your friends when they're not paying attention?
Diamond	23.	Do you like to get kids to think about how they act toward their friends?
Flower	24.	Do you like to talk about what's going on in the world today?
Glasses	25.	Do you like to plan what other kids will do?
Hat	26.	Do you like to talk with other kids?

Go to the top of the page and find the box that contains the triangle.

Triangle	27.	Do you like to disagree with your teachers and your parents?
Tree	28.	Are you interested in what other kids say in class?
Boat	29.	Do you like to talk about why other kids get mad?
Wagon	30.	Do you compare friends that you've had before with friends that you have now?
Plane	31.	Do you try to help when kids have problems with their parents or with their friends?
Clock	32.	When kids tell you you're wrong, do you tell them off?
Truck	33.	Do you like to talk about why kids have the problems they do?
Scissors	34.	Do you like to tell kids how well they are doing?
Heart	35.	When kids say one thing and do another, do you tell them?

Turn the page and find the box with the ball at the top of the page.

Ball	36.	Do you like your friends to tell you what you are like?
Square	37.	Do you like to ask other kids what you should do and how you should do it?
Star	38.	Do you like to tell other kids when they do things right?
Car	39.	Do you like to disagree with the way kids do things?
House	40.	Do you like to make fun of other kids?
Diamond	41.	Do you like to know about other kids?
Flower	42.	Do you tell other kids how you feel about them even if it may hurt their feelings?
Glasses	43.	Do you like to tell your friends about yourself?
Hat	44.	Do you try not to hurt kids' feelings when you tell them what you think of them?

Go to the top of the page and find the box that contains the triangle.

Triangle	45.	Do you try to help kids when they need help?
Tree	46.	When one kid disturbs the other kids, do you try to make him stop?
Boat	47.	Do you want to know how other kids feel about you?
Wagon	48.	Do you like to hear your friends' secrets?
Plane	49.	Do you like to joke with people?
Clock	50.	Do you like to get kids talking about how they act and how they feel?

Truck	51.	Do you think that your friends have problems you don't know about?
Scissors	52.	Do you like to tell other kids your thoughts about them?
Heart	53.	Do you like to get kids talking about how they feel about each other?

Turn the page. Find the box with the ball at the top of the page.

Ball	54.	Do you feel that kids need to know why they act the way they do?
Square	55.	Do you get mad when friends tell you you're doing something you shouldn't?
Star	56.	Do you like to get kids to do something about things that bother them even when they don't want to?
Car	57.	Do you like to argue with other kids?
House	58.	Do you like to be close friends with other kids?
Diamond	59.	Do kids who talk about their problems make you mad?
Flower	60.	When you are doing group work, do you like to tell the kids how you think things are going?
Glasses	61.	When kids ask you if you like them, do you tell them?
Hat	62.	Do you try to find out what other kids think about you?

Go to the top of the page and find the box with the triangle.

Triangle	63.	Do you like to be with other kids?
Tree	64.	Do you like to find out about other kids?

Name _____ Boy _____ Girl _____

Age _____ Grade _____ Teacher _____ School _____

YES ⬡ NO	YES △ NO 9
YES ⬜ NO 1	YES 🌳 NO 10
YES ✦ NO 2	YES ⛵ NO 11
YES 🚗 NO 3	YES 🛒 NO 12
YES 🏠 NO 4	YES ✈ NO 13
YES ◇ NO 5	YES ⊕ NO 14
YES 🌷 NO 6	YES 🚙 NO 15
YES 👓 NO 7	YES ✂ NO 16
YES 👒 NO 8	YES ♡ NO 17

Name _____ Boy _____ Girl _____

Age _____ Grade _____ Teacher _____ School _____

YES ⬭ NO 18			YES △ NO 27		
YES ▢ NO 19			YES 🌳 NO 28		
YES ☆ NO 20			YES ⛵ NO 29		
YES 🚗 NO 21			YES 🛒 NO 30		
YES 🏠 NO 22			YES ✈ NO 31		
YES ◇ NO 23			YES 🌐 NO 32		
YES 🌷 NO 24			YES 🛻 NO 33		
YES 👓 NO 25			YES ✂ NO 34		
YES 👒 NO 26			YES ♡ NO 35		

Name _____ Boy _____ Girl _____

Age _____ Grade _____ Teacher _____ School _____

YES	⭕	NO
36		

YES	🔺	NO
45		

YES	▢	NO
37		

YES	🌳	NO
46		

YES	⭐	NO
38		

YES	⛵	NO
47		

YES	🚗	NO
39		

YES	🛒	NO
48		

YES	🏠	NO
40		

YES	✈	NO
49		

YES	◇	NO
41		

YES	🙂	NO
50		

YES	🌷	NO
42		

YES	🚙	NO
51		

YES	👓	NO
43		

YES	✂	NO
52		

YES	👒	NO
44		

YES	❤	NO
53		

Name _____ Boy _____ Girl _____

Age _____ Grade _____ Teacher _____ School _____

YES ⭕ NO 54	YES △ NO 63
YES ▢ NO 55	YES 🌳 NO 64
YES ⭐ NO 56	YES ⛵ NO 65
YES 🚗 NO 57	YES 🛒 NO 66
YES 🏠 NO 58	YES ✈️ NO 67
YES ◇ NO 59	YES 🌐 NO 68
YES 🌷 NO 60	YES 🛻 NO 69
YES 👓 NO 61	YES ✂️ NO 70
YES 👒 NO 62	YES ♡ NO 71

References

Cahall, J. S. (1958). *Readability: An appraisal of research and application.* Columbus, OH: Ohio State University Press.

Hill, W. F. (1971). The Hill Interaction Matrix. *Personnel and Guidance Journal, 49,* 619–622.

Lorge, A. (1944). Predicting readibility. *Teachers College Record, 45,* 404–419.

Muro, J. J., & Dinkmeyer, D. C. (1977). *Counseling in the elementary and middle schools.* Dubuque, IA: Wm. C. Brown.

The Group Counseling Game

Playing Data

Age level: Fourth-, fifth-, and sixth-grade levels.

Special prerequisite: Some knowledge of group counseling leadership skills is helpful to both counselor and teacher.

Number of players: Five or six children plus the counselor.

Playing time: Approximately 45 minutes to one hour.

Materials:

1. A board with 37 to 41 "jumping" spaces (see Figure F.1). Almost any board commonly utilized in a children's game can be adapted for use by the counselor. The moves on the board should be color coded so that approximately one third are colored red, one third are colored blue, and one third are colored yellow. Three spaces on the board should be colored green.

2. A marker for each child to show his or her movement on the board.

3. Four packs of cards that direct the player to speak or behave in a specific way. The cards should be colored red, yellow, blue, and white on one side; the opposite side should contain the directions to the child. The cards developed for this game are as follows:

Yellow Cards (Use these first!)

1. Select the nicest kid in the group and tell why.
2. Pick another group member who shows off and give him or her some examples.
3. Choose a member of the group and tell what you like most about him or her, and why.
4. Pick out a member of this group who acts most like a police officer and tell him or her what you mean.
5. Tell another group member why he or she is well known in school.
6. Stand up and tell the group which things you need to do to be more adult.
7. Tell about school when you think it is worst.
8. Tell the group why you're well known in school.
9. Pick out another group member and pretend that you're him or her meeting with this group.
10. Tell the group how you could act more grown-up.
11. Select a group member who will win this game and tell why he or she will win.
12. Pick out the name of a person that you admire most and tell why you would like to be him or her.

Source: The Group Counseling Game was adapted from the Group Therapy Game developed by Park Plastics.

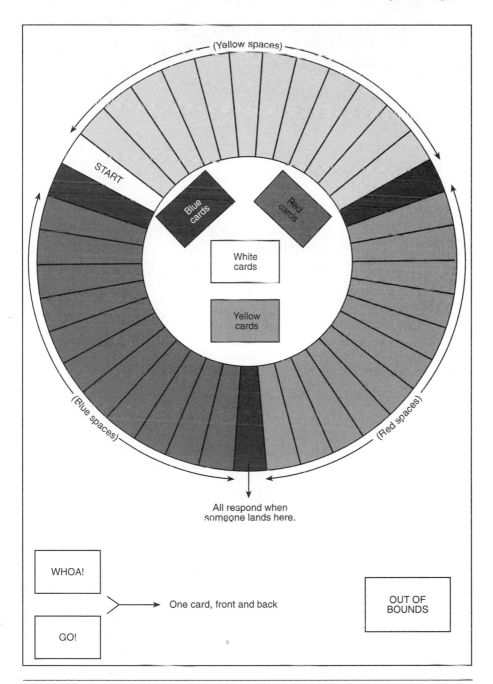

Figure F.1

Playing board for the Group Counseling Game.

13. Go around the group and tell each member why you like him or her.
14. Tell a group member why he or she isn't well known in school.
15. Tell how you show off and why.
16. Tell the kind of people you least like to be with.
17. Pick out a group member and pretend he or she is an adult. Ask this member to do something for you.
18. Tell the group how you are going to do in this game.
19. Pick out a member of this group who needs to laugh more. Help him or her find ways to laugh.
20. Tell the group how you think you look to them.
21. Tell what you like about the group.
22. Tell what you do well in school and why.
23. Tell the group which things are most important to you and why.
24. List the ways in which you could do better in school.
25. Finish this sentence. Happiness is _____.
26. Tell what you like to do best and why.
27. Tell about the happiest day in your life.
28. Tell the group how you treat your friends.
29. Pick out a person from a story you have read and tell how you are like him or her.
30. Tell the group all the good things about you.
31. Tell the group what kind of people you like to be with.
32. One at a time, tell the members of this group what you like most about them.
33. Stand up and tell the group what makes you grown-up.
34. List the things that keep you from doing what you want to do most.
35. The person on your left wants to be with you and you want to be left alone. What do you say?
36. Tell the member of your group whom you know the least what you would like to give to him or her.
37. Tell about school when you feel it is best.
38. One at a time, tell each member of this group how you are most like him or her.
39. Tell what you want to be when you grow up and what you will have to do to be what you want.
40. Tell each member of the group a way in which you would like to know him or her better.
41. Tell a member of the group that you want him or her to like you.
42. Tell what is wrong with this group.

Red Cards (Use these second!)

1. Pick out a group member to be part of your basketball team. Tell him or her why.
2. Tell a member of the group what he or she does on the playground and why.
3. Tell the way that you are when others like you best.

4. Tell the ways that you make your class a good place to be.
5. Go around and ask the group to tell what they would like to be. Tell each one if you think it can be done.
6. Tell a member of the group how he or she has helped you.
7. Tell the group how you would change if you could.
8. Name a famous person you think would really like you and tell why.
9. You are going to place an ad in the school paper to tell who you are. What does the ad say?
10. Help one member of the group to be less shy.
11. Tell about yourself when you like you best.
12. Which group member is a cop-out? Tell him or her what you mean.
13. Tell how you act tough.
14. Tell the group why you want to stay in it.
15. Tell a group member what he or she needs to do to get better grades.
16. You are walking down a street and meet a member of this group. Tell him or her how you feel.
17. Tell how you are when teachers like you best.
18. One at a time, tell each member what you are that he or she doesn't think you are.
19. Pick out a member of the group who needs to be cheered up. Tell him or her what to do to be cheered up.
20. Tell a member of the group what he or she does in class and why.
21. Pick out a member of the group to help you with math and tell why you picked that person.
22. Tell each member of the group what you think he or she would like to change in you.
23. Tell the group how you will get what is really important to you.
24. Talk for a while about how bright you are.
25. Tell the group about your favorite brother or sister.
26. Tell the group how you are boring with people you don't like.
27. Do an impression of the person sitting on your right.
28. Pick out a member of the group and ask him or her to give you something.
29. What group member is most with it? Tell why.
30. Tell what you can do to make more friends.

Blue Cards (Use these third!)

1. Who works hardest in this group? Why?
2. Who gets angry the easiest? Why?
3. Who is easiest in the group to talk to? Why?
4. Pick out the most bossy group member and tell him or her how you feel about it.
5. Tell how you feel when you get angry.
6. Pick out a group member who would like to tell the group something and can't. Say it for him (or her).

7. What person in the group would you like to have fun with? Why?
8. Who would you like to have as a friend in the group?
9. Close your eyes. Tell what is most important to you.
10. In a nice way tell the person who pays the least attention to you to pay more attention to you.
11. Pick out a member of the group you liked least when we started. Tell why you like him or her now.
12. You are told that you're "not with it" in this group. Respond to that charge.
13. Tell the group who is most unlike you and why.
14. Tell each member something you have learned about him or her since we started.
15. Pick out someone who talks too much in the group.
16. Tell what really makes you laugh.
17. What makes you most uncomfortable here? Why?
18. Who wants the group to like him or her most? Why?
19. Who is the hardest to talk to in the group? Why?
20. Show how you feel when you get angry. Don't use any words.
21. Pick out a member of the group who likes you most and tell him or her how that makes you feel.
22. Pick out as many members of this group as you want and ask them to tell something good about you.
23. Tell the group how you have been faking it so far in this game.
24. Tell why girls and boys get lonely.

White Cards (To be used when someone lands on green. All members do what the card says!)

1. Make a plan for doing better. Tell the group.
2. Say something about you that is hard for you to say.
3. Give some member of the group a small plan that will help him or her do better.
4. Tell how you try to help others.
5. Stand up and tell the group why you like it.
6. Tell the group how you have changed, if at all, since you have been coming here.
7. Tell each member how he or she has helped you.
8. Tell a quiet member what he or she can do to be noticed more.
9. Tell the group how you'll be different in the future because you have been in the group.
10. Who most wants the attention of the group? Why?
11. Who most wants the counselor's attention? Why?

4. A set of two 5″ x 8″ cards for each player. Card 1 should read "OUT OF BOUNDS." Card 2 should have the word "GO!" on one side and the word "WHOA!" on the other.

Process

Start the game by having one child select a card from the yellow pack of cards. It is very important to have the top cards of the pack be ones that are essentially positive in nature. In establishing rapport and developing group cohesiveness, it is essential that member-to-member interactions be on a positive basis. While none of the cards could be considered negative or confrontive, some are more positive than others. We have found it beneficial to place cards such as "Tell a member of the group how he or she has helped you" or "Tell the group the good things about you" so that they are selected early in the game—especially during the first session. Cards like "List the ways you could do better in school" or "Tell how you show off and why" could have negative connotations and are better utilized when the group has spent more time together and shared positive feelings.

After the first student selects a card, he or she reads it aloud to the group. (Caution: Be sure to check for nonreaders, to prevent embarrassment.) Then the student responds according to the directions on the card. When the student has completed the assigned task, all group members, including the counselor, judge the performance in terms of whether he or she was trying to "tell it like it is." If other group members feel the first player is "telling it like it is," they hold up a GO! card; if they feel the player is not responding adequately, they hold up a WHOA! card. The player thus moves along the board according to the number of GOs minus the number of WHOAs. For example, if six people were playing, a total of four GOs would mean that the child is permitted to move two spaces forward on the board. Conversely, four WHOAs and two GOs would mean that the child loses two spaces. In general, you as group leader should quickly glance at the "votes" prior to holding up your own card. To prevent the group from scapegoating a child who may initially be unpopular by giving him or her all WHOAs, you may want to lend your support and acceptance of such a child by a GO vote. Some shy children and some who have difficulty interacting tend to respond with minimal dialogue and can be voted down easily. In such instances, counselor support may be needed.

The time immediately following the voting is of vital importance to the game, for it is at this juncture that the counselor can encourage spontaneous interaction. Leading questions like "Why did Joe say 'Whoa' to John?" or "I wonder why Mary said she likes Sue best?" tend to lead the group into explaining the whys of their selection. Frequently five or even ten minutes of "free" discussion will follow an active lead on the part of the counselor. In addition, some children will often receive positive feedback after a WHOA vote. For example, shy John may not be able to tell many "good" things about himself and another group member who voted WHOA may say something like: "I voted 'Whoa' because there are a lot more good things about John than he is telling us."

As might be expected, the children tend to focus on the number of moves that they make on the board, and interest and enthusiasm are generally high. This should not be discouraged, but the counselor, of course, is more concerned with promoting member-to-member interaction than with who "wins." In fact, the counselor should not make specific references to the winning of the game. As the game progresses, the children move from the yellow spaces to the red and blue. If a child lands on a blue space, he or she selects a blue card: on a red space, a red card. At least three spaces on the board should be painted green. A player who lands on any of the green spaces takes a white card. Then all the players, including the counselor, follow the directions on the white card.

The reader will note that a number of these white cards ask for some type of behavioral or developmental commitment on the part of the child and the counselor. For example, one card may read, "Make a plan for doing better. Tell the group." A useful technique at this juncture is to write up the plan on a behavioral or developmental contract; each group member and the counselor should sign the form. At the next group session, each member can give a progress report on how well he or she is meeting his or her personal objectives prior to starting a new session of the game. Generally, these contracts are honored seriously by the children.

The "OUT OF BOUNDS" card was introduced into the game when we discovered that some children had difficulty with the task behavior required by the game. If a child is disruptive, any member of the group may hold up the OUT OF BOUNDS card and halt the interaction. The player who holds up the card then states the nature of the infraction and presents his or her case. For example, in a session led by one of the authors with a group composed of acting-out and shy fourth-graders, one child constantly pushed another's "marker" back one or two spaces at every given opportunity. The child whose marker was moved often was unaware of the behavior of the more aggressive boy; even when he did discover what was happening, he seemed too timid to do anything but move his marker back to its original space on the board. After this event was repeated three or four times, another group member held up his OUT OF BOUNDS card and related to the offender why he felt that his actions were unjustified. After a short discussion, the group decided that the aggressive boy was indeed "wrong," and he subsequently lost his next turn (the usual penalty). The OUT OF BOUNDS card will generally provide focused member-to-member behavior, and the skillful counselor can use such interaction to provide positive group and individual benefits.

The US Game

Playing Data

Age level: Used with second- through fourth-grade levels (and, in some cases, fifth and sixth grades).

Special prerequisites: Knowledge of the Hill Interaction Matrix.

Number of players: The game may be played with the counselor and one child, or with the counselor and from two to six children.

Playing time: From 20 minutes to one hour, depending on the age level of the children. Generally, more than one session is required to complete a round of the game.

Materials:

1. Spinner (see Figure G.1).
2. US Game board (see Figure G.1).
3. Six or appropriate number of toy plastic cars to use as markers.
4. Five packs of cards (see Figure G.3).
5. One package of clay.
6. One package of crayons and a supply of plain white paper.

Construction and Process

US was developed as a group counseling game for use with second-, third-, fourth-, fifth-, and even sixth-grade children. Designed as a device to be utilized in initial group counseling sessions, the game fosters directed interactions while diminishing the tensions or uneasiness that often accompany such interaction.

The game board for US is sectioned off into squares that correspond to the four derivatives of the content of the Hill Interaction Matrix. The matrix is a configuration of 20 cells that are utilized to characterize group interaction among children and adults in the dual dimensions of work style and content style categories. The matrix (see Figure G.2) contains four content style categories that represent the four possible content areas for topics that may be discussed in games: (I) general topics; (II) the group itself; (III) personal, or discussions of the individual; and (IV) relationship, or the effect that one member of the group may be having on another.

Source: The US Game was devised by Ann Dadaleares.

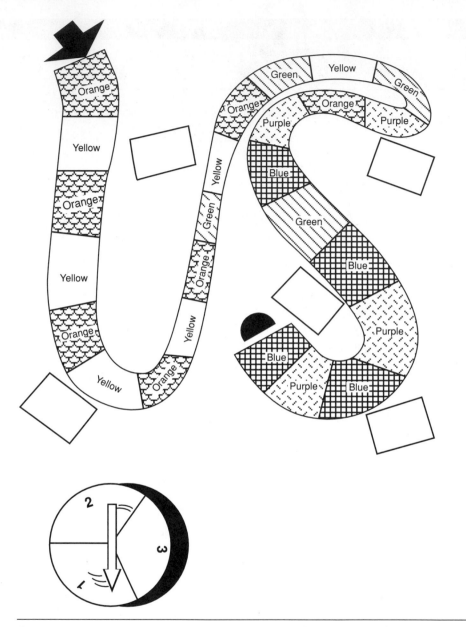

Figure G.1
US Game board and spinner.

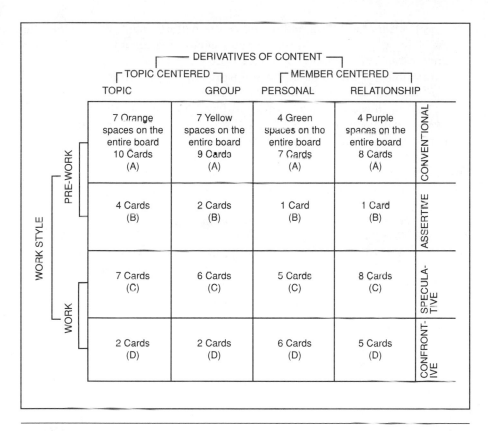

Figure G.2

Content style derivatives of the Hill Interaction Matrix as adapted for the US Game.

Along the right-hand side of the matrix are four of the five work style categories of group life. The responsive work style is omitted because it represents only answers to questions. Therefore there are 16 cells in this matrix, not 20 as in the HIM. An explanation of the work style categories is as follows:

1. *Conventional.* In this style of interaction the group discusses one of the four topic areas in a style that is characteristic of ordinary, everyday conversation.
2. *Assertive.* Assertive interaction is characterized by verbalizations that deny the other group members as a source of help.
3. *Speculative.* Speculative interaction relates to those verbalizations wherein the individual asks questions and formulates hypotheses about presented problems.
4. *Confrontive.* At this level, individuals confront each other, not necessarily negatively, with their behavior.

For a full discussion of the Hill Interaction Matrix, see W. F. Hill, *Hill Interaction Matrix* (Los Angeles: Youth Studies Center, University of Southern California, 1965).

The US Game was designed to follow the patterns suggested by the Hill matrix, although the game does *not* stress negative interaction because it was designed for use by children.

The squares on the game board correspond to the four derivatives of content on the Hill Interaction Matrix: orange represents the topic level, yellow the group level, green the personal level, and purple the relationship level. Work style categories, enabling the group to deal with the various cells in the matrix, are obtained by the use of color-coded cards.

All cards utilized in the game contain a number and letter designation. The letter represents the work style categories. Therefore, all A cards should be placed on top of the pile, then the B cards should be next, and finally the C and D cards. This ensures that the initial interaction will be on the conventional level, as opposed to the more difficult speculative and confrontive categories. The reader will note that the assertive cards do not truly represent the type of interaction that Hill (1965) describes, since this interaction by definition is a denial of the group as a source of help and, as such, is considered a less desirable work style for children's groups. By using conventional style interaction cards first, you minimize threat and anxiety and help promote cohesion.

Figure G.3 represents the color coding utilized. Among the orange cards there is an A, B, C, and D order, and a like order exists for the yellow, green, and purple cards. At no times should these colors be intermingled.

The numbers on the cards direct the child to a specific course of action. A number 1 requires that the child respond to the card him- or herself; a number 2 asks that the child answer the item and ask someone else in the group also to respond to the card. A number 3 card indicates that the child must answer the item and ask *two* other group members to respond to the card. A card numbered 4 asks the entire group, including the counselor, to respond to the item. Through utilization of this number arrangement, interaction is gradually increased from one person sharing a thought to a sharing process within the entire group.

In the game, emphasis is placed on the conventional and speculative work style categories to maintain a positive set. Assertive and some confrontive style interaction may promote negative "encounter" style behavior that is neither essential nor desirable in children's groups. Stress is also placed on the *topic* and group derivatives at all levels to foster the directed interaction that is the big element of the game. As the game progresses, interaction can occur in the green (personal) and purple (relationship) categories in the matrix.

In the game board originally developed for the US Game, the orange and green squares have pictures accompanying them (these pictures are not shown in Figure G.1). Those next to the orange squares show details of scenes which may be hard to identify. Such "nonsense" pictures or similar ones may be cut from any magazine and tend to brighten the board, nurture children's curiosity, and enable them to utilize their imaginations in speculating what these pictures might be. The illustrations adjacent to the green squares ask the child to relate to the feelings of the pictured children and are similar to the concept of "feeling" pictures used by many counselors.

DECK 1–TOPIC (Orange Cards)

____ If you were a building, what building would you be? ____ If you were a game, what would you be? ____ If you were something to drink, what would you be? ____ If you were an animal, which animal would you be? ____ If you were a piece of candy, what kind would you be? ____ If you were a color, which color would you be? ____ If you were a TV person, who could you be? ____ If you were a food, which would you be? ____ If you were a day of the week, which one would you be? ____ If you were a holiday, which one would you be?	Conventional
____ Unhappiness is _____ . ____ Loneliness is _____ . ____ Sadness is _____ . ____ Boredom is _____ .	Assertive
____ Think of a title or name for this picture. ____ If you had one of these, what would you do with it? ____ If you had one of these, where would you put it? ____ What does this picture remind you of? ____ What do you think this picture is? ____ How would you use one of these? ____ If you had one of these and wanted to give it away, who would you give it to?	Speculative
____ If you had a million dollars, what would you do with it? ____ If you did not have to go to school, what would you do?	Confrontive

DECK 2–GROUP (Yellow Cards)

____ Say everyone's name in the group. ____ Tell what color eyes everyone has. ____ Ask everyone what their hobby is. ____ Ask everyone their middle name. ____ Ask everyone what their favorite school subject is. ____ Ask everyone what they would like to be when they grow up. ____ Ask everyone what their favorite sport is. ____ Tell what color hair everyone has. ____ Try to remember and say everyone's name and their hobby.	Conventional

Figure G.3

Question cards for the US Game as adapted from the Hill Interaction Matrix.

The purple squares were designed to be both behavioral and concluding in the sense that the child may, after thinking about his or her behavior, feelings, and thoughts, act to modify his or her behavior in some positive way. Questions such as "Think of a way you can make another friend" may provide a vehicle for children to make a developmental commitment in terms of their behavior, yet it does not force them to respond in this manner if they do not wish to do so.

DECK 2–GROUP (Yellow Cards)

_____ How would you improve this group?
_____ What is unusual or different about this group?

Assertive

_____ If we meet next week, when will it be?
_____ Why is this group meeting?
_____ What do you suppose we can talk about in future meetings?
_____ If we meet next week, where will it be?
_____ Make a group picture.*
_____ Make a clay sculpture.**

Speculative

_____ Choose someone in the group, and tell him or her one thing you like about him/her.
_____ Who seems to be the happiest in the group?

Confrontive

DECK 3–PERSONAL (Green Cards)

_____ If you felt like this, who would you go to?
_____ How is this person feeling?
_____ Would you like to feel this way?
_____ Where would you be if you felt this way?
_____ What is this person feeling?
_____ What would you do if you felt this way?
_____ Have you ever felt like this?

Conventional

_____ I am afraid of _____ .

Assertive

_____ Would you say that you were:
    _____ a good student, a fairly good student or a poor student?
    _____ a helper or one that gets helped?
    _____ good, pretty good, or not so good?
    _____ neat, fairly neat, or not so neat?
    _____ healthy, fairly healthy, or not so healthy?

Speculative

_____ What does this group think you might be when you grow up?
_____ Ask everyone in the group how they feel most of the time.
_____ What do you think is the best thing about you?
_____ How would you describe yourself in one word?
_____ How do you feel most of the time?
_____ Tell, in a minute, about the happiest experience of your life.

Confrontive

* By taking turns, someone start drawing and each person can add on. What would you call the finished picture?

** Take the clay and give everyone a piece. Make a group sculpture by taking turns, each person adding on to what the other one did. Discuss the results.

Figure G.3 continued.

DECK 4—RELATIONSHIP (Purple Cards)

____ What is more important to you:
    ____ candy, a good teammate, or working hard?
    ____ an "A" in math, a friendly animal, or being honest?
    ____ a favorite dessert, good parents, or winning a game?
    ____ a new coat, a friendly classmate, or doing well in school?
    ____ money, a pet dog, or good sportsmanship?
    ____ a new toy, a sister or brother, or friendship?
    ____ a soda, a good teacher, or love?
    ____ an ice cream cone, a good friend, or happiness?
	Conventional

____ What person makes you feel unhappy or angry?	Assertive
____ Tell about the person that has helped you the most. ____ If you were an adult, who would you be? ____ If you could be another person, who would you be? ____ Tell something you would like others to know about you. ____ How do you usually treat others? ____ What describes a good teacher? ____ What person makes you the happiest? Why?	Speculative

____ Choose people from the group to play act:
    ____ a scene where you have done something good for someone.
    ____ a scene where someone is doing something good for someone in school.
    ____ a scene where someone is being good to you.
    ____ a scene of concern you might be having.
    ____ Put your hand in the center of the group and invite others to stack theirs on top.
	Confrontive

DECK 5—BEHAVIORAL—CONCLUDING (Blue Cards)

There are seven behavioral items and seven concluding fill-in-the blank statements.

____ Think of a way:
    ____ you could make your mother or father happier.
    ____ you could be happier.
    ____ you could help your teacher.
    ____ you could cheer someone up.
    ____ you could help someone.
    ____ you could help yourself to do something you want to do.
    ____ you could make another friend.
	Behavioral

____ I wonder _____ . ____ I wish _____ . ____ In the future, I would like to _____ . ____ I dream that _____ . ____ I hope that _____ . ____ I would like to _____ .	Concluding

Figure G.3 continued.

In terms of group size, the US Game is designed for a maximum number of six students and one counselor. A minimum number of two is a possibility (assuming that more than one is a group), thus providing a one-to-one counseling situation for a counselor and counselee. A complete set of cards would be too numerous for groups of less than four, but an adaptation may be made for a small group by removing a proportionate number of cards from each cell of the matrix. There are 83 cards for a total group of seven (including the counselor), but readers may wish to modify the cards presented or substitute for them. Figure G.4 gives the proportions of cards that are suitable for use with various sized groups:

To play the game, a counseling group of no larger than six children should be formed. The following rules should be clearly explained and used in the game:

1. Each child selects his or her vehicle and places it on the red arrow. After determining who starts, this initiator spins the spinner.

2. The child moves his or her car the number of spaces indicated by the spinner.

3. In order to stay there, the child must pick up a corresponding color-coded card and respond to the item.

4. If the child does not respond, he or she must return to the place where he or she was prior to spinning.

5. If the card the child picks up has a 1 on it—the child must answer it him- or herself. A 2 on the card indicates that the child must answer it himself or herself and, in addition, ask one other person to answer it. If this person does not answer, the first child must ask someone else. If no one else will respond to the question, the first child is not punished in any way and the next child has a turn at spinning. A 3 on the card indicates that the child as well as two others (of his/her choosing) must answer this item. The same rules of nonresponse of the other children apply as in a 2 card. A 4 on the card indicates that all students answer the item, starting always with the child to whom the original question was directed. The same rule of nonresponse applies.

6. The child who enters the final red half-moon first is the winner, and it may be the counselor's choice to reward the winner by allowing him or her to keep the vehicle or some other treat. An arbitrary ending point may be assigned by the counselor in order to be able to complete this game and make a closure in one session. Yet another session might produce an arbitrary starting point in order to complete the game.

As the game progresses, the counselor should pay close attention to the process, since the game itself becomes secondary to the interaction. Because there may be a number of long discussions, the game may take more than one session, and the counselor may have to make a note of the places that the children occupy on the board.

Group Size*	Number of Cards	Methods of Withdrawal**
6	83	Use the entire set as it is.
5	71	Withdraw one card from every cell in the matrix other than topic (B); personal (B); group (D); relationship (B).
4	59	Withdraw two cards from every cell except: all (B) and (D) cells. From these, remove only one card.
3	47	Withdraw two cards from every cell except remove three cards from topic (A); and three from group (A).
2	36	6 cards from topic (A) 6 cards from group (A) 5 cards from personal (A) 6 cards from relationship (A) 2 cards from topic (B) 3 cards from topic (C) 3 cards from group (C) 3 cards from personal (C) 3 cards from relationship (C) 1 card from topic (D) 1 card from group (D) 4 cards from personal (D) 4 cards from relationship (D)
1	24	Take one card from every cell plus: 1 card from topic (A) 1 card from group (A) 1 card from personal (A) 1 card from relationship (A) 1 card from topic (C) 1 card from group (C) 1 card from personal (C) 1 card from relationship (C)

*The group size here obviously excludes the counselor in its count.

**Consult Figure G.2 as a guide in withdrawing these cards. This chart can be used in lieu of looking at the cards in selecting which cards to withdraw.

Figure G.4

Numbers and kinds of cards to use with varying size groups playing the US Game.

Behavior Modification Adaptation

At times, you as a counselor may find that you must deal with an individual or group of children who tend not to listen or who lack motivation to become involved in the game task. With such groups of children, you may decide to announce that an additional "car" will be given to those individuals who respond to the item and (in instances where one child is requested to speak to another) one will also be given to the child who responds. These cars may be placed in an imaginary "garage" and not used in the game except that they will be "repossessed" by the "car dealer" (counselor) at the conclusion of the game. The counselor should announce to the children whenever this technique is utilized that the children with a certain number of "cars" in their "garages" will receive a prize (candy, choice of small car, etc.). In this way, the emphasis is shifted from a position of punishment for misbehaving to a position of positive feedback for becoming involved in the game.

Comment

US has been extremely useful to practicing counselors in their efforts to establish rapid rapport with children. In addition, it is a useful tool in guiding directed interaction while erasing tensions and lessening the strain of encounter.

Children seem to be very enthusiastic about US, and the behavioral modification technique suggested above works well with disruptive groups.

As in the Group Counseling Game, the interaction provides many opportunities for the counselor and the group to deal with the normal developmental concerns of children. For example, one will encounter the child who is losing and does not like to lose, or the impatient child who interrupts the "turn" of another. The skillful counselor may capitalize on these situations and, in fact, they may be much more important than the directed interaction of the game cards.

Orientation to Counseling Using Puppets

Counselors may wish to orient students to guidance services through use of puppetry. A short story describing the guidance services can be developed and the puppets may be brought into a classroom to relate the details to the children. This is a very effective approach for initiating counseling.

Counselor-Developed Guidance Activities

Cooperative Problem Solving
Developed by Carolyn Helfman

Objectives

Students will:

1. Learn the STEP method of problem solving.
2. Role play steps in problem solving.
3. Work in a group to solve a problem.
4. Work in pairs to solve several problems.

Experiences

1. The counselor explains the STEP method of problem solving; (a) State the problem. (b) Think about solutions. (c) Evaluate the consequences for yourself and others. (d) Proceed to complete the task.
2. The counselor leads the students through the steps to practice using the STEP method of solving problems:

    a. Very carefully define the problem.

Example: Should I try out for the soccer team?

    b. Think of all the ways you can solve the problem. Get more information if you need it.

Example: Before I try out for the team, I need to know when the team practices, the cost of taking part in the team, the skills I need to have, and when and where the games are played. Then I need to check with my parent(s) about all of these things.

    c. Talk with someone about the two sides of the problem or write down the "yes" reasons and the "no" reasons.

Example:

YES	NO
• I like to play soccer.	• I'm already busy.
• I want to play better.	• I won't have time to play.
• My friend is on the team.	• My mom has too many carpools.
• It is good exercise.	• I have too much homework.

Consider the consequences of the decision.

Example:

- If I decide to join the team, I will have to give up some activities that I enjoy.
- If I do not join the team, I will have to find other ways to improve my soccer skills.
- If I join the team, I will have to figure out ways to keep up with my schoolwork.

    Make a decision.

Example: I really want to be on the team, but I'm already busy with other things. Maybe I will have more time and would enjoy it more in the summer.

    d. Proceed with the course of action.

3. The counselor divides the class into pairs and asks the students to role play using the STEP method to solve the following problems:

    - You are at a friend's house. You are supposed to go home now, but you are having such a good time that you don't want to leave. How will you decide what to do?
    - You have invited a friend to your house. Another friend calls and wants you to go to the movies. How will you decide what to do?
    - You and a close friend are having a very good time playing. Another person comes along and obviously wants to join you. How will you decide what to do?
    - You and your friends are playing on the same team in a softball game. Your best friend tags a player out, but the umpire calls it safe. You believe that the player was out. How will you decide what to do?

Publication and Process   The counselor leads the class in a discussion of the ways they used the STEP method to make decisions.

Generalization   The counselor reminds the class that they can use the STEP method when they encounter problems at home and in school. To solve a problem, they will need to understand the problem, brainstorm for solutions, consider the consequences of possible decisions, choose a course, and follow through with action.

Application   The counselor gives the members of the class an assignment to use the STEP method at least once during the week to solve a problem at home and at least once during the week to solve a problem at school. He/she indicates that they will discuss what happened next week when they meet for a guidance activity.

Identifying Personal Strengths and Positive Behaviors
(Grades K–3)
Developed by Janet Froese

Objective

Students will identify a personal strength or positive behavior.

Experiences

1. The counselor asks children to draw a picture of something they do well or something helpful they have done in the past month. Each of the children uses the picture as a visual aid in describing to the rest of the class what they do well or the helpful deed they did. The counselor asks each child how he/she feels when he/she does something well or does a good deed.

2. The counselor asks the children to make up a story about themselves, emphasizing their positive qualities, in which they do something to help someone else. The students use art materials to make puppets that represent themselves.

Publication   The students act out the stories they have made up. The counselor asks them to describe the positive qualities they were acting out in the story.

Process   The counselor leads the children in a discussion of their feelings during the puppet shows. He/she might also ask other members of the class to describe their favorite part of each child's story.

Generalization   After the puppet shows and the processing, the counselor asks the class to give one another encouraging feedback about strengths and positive behaviors.

Application   The counselor suggests that the children take their puppets home and tell the stories to their families.

Working Together in a Group
(Grades 3–8)
Developed by Sue Bratton, Ph.D.
University of North Texas

Objective

Students will experience sharing and cooperating in a group effort.

Experiences

1. The counselor will need to gather materials, including magazines, scissors, glue, and construction paper, and divide the class into groups of 4 students each.

2. The counselor begins by saying, "What things are important in order for a group to work together?" Students brainstorm for a few minutes, with the counselor writing their responses on the board. The counselor should be sure to list cooperation, sharing, acceptance, no put downs, and encouragement.

3. The counselor tells the students, "I want each group to make a collage of people sharing and working together. Find some pictures in these magazines that show people sharing or doing things together. Cut them out and paste them on construction paper. You may share the materials, share the work to be done, or both."

Publication and Process   After the collages are completed, the counselor leads a discussion using the following questions:

- How did you go about deciding on ways to share the materials and the work to be done?

- How did you go about deciding what pictures to use and how to accomplish the goals of the assignment?

- How did your group determine the way members were to share and cooperate in your group?

Generalization   In the process of their discussion, each group may report a different way of going about completing the group project and varied methods of achieving a sense of group cooperation. The counselor will want to emphasize that there are many different ways of coming together as a group and accomplishing a task. The counselor can also engage the class in a discussion about other times they have been in a group and how they learned to work together.

Application   The counselor asks the class to notice during the week when they are working in various groups how the groups interact and how the members work out ways of cooperating and establishing and achieving group goals. He/she tells students they will discuss these ideas the next time they have a group guidance experience.

Individual Differences
(Grades K–2)
Developed by Tami Stutz

Objective

Students will increase their awareness of the various ways in which people are alike and people are different.

Experiences

1. The counselor tells the students, "Today we are going to talk about ways we are alike and ways we are different." He/she distributes hand mirrors for each child and lets the children explore the mirrors for several minutes. The counselor asks the children to specifically describe what they see in the mirrors as they look at themselves. (For example, "I see red hair.") After each student has given a specific description of one physical characteristic, the counselor asks the other students if they see the same thing. He/she might ask all of the children who share that attribute to stand up. It is important to emphasize that in many ways we are alike, but in some ways we are different.

2. The counselor leads the children in a discussion about physical similarities and differences. Some questions could be, "Do we all look alike?" "How are we different from one another?" "How are we the same as one another?"

3. The counselor asks the students to think of other ways, besides physical appearance, that they are alike and different. These ideas can include things they like to do, things they like to eat, things they are good at, and so on.

4. The counselor introduces the book *Leo the Lop* (by S. Cosgrove) by saying, "I have a story to read about a rabbit named Leo. He was a lot like the other rabbits, but he was different too. Please listen and see if you can think of how Leo was different and how he was the same as the other rabbits." The counselor reads *Leo the Lop*.

Publication and Process   After the story, the counselor leads the children in a discussion about how Leo and the other rabbits were the same and how they were different. He/she asks the students to tell one specific way in which they are different from or the same as the other students. The counselor asks the children to draw a picture illustrating how they are different from or the same as the other students.

Generalization   The counselor summarizes by explaining that each person has some ways in which he or she is different from all the other people in the world and some ways in which he or she is like many of the people in the world.

Application   The counselor asks the children to look at the members of their families and their neighbors to see the ways in which each of them is like other people and different from other people. He/she suggests that they will discuss the individual differences they have observed the next time they have a guidance lesson.

Alcoholism and the Family
(Grades 3–6)
Developed by Faye Wedell

Objectives

Students will explore the following ideas:

1. All families experience conflict, but that in families in which one or more members are alcoholics, roles get "mixed up," and conflict is not always resolved in positive, appropriate ways.
2. People can help themselves, even though they may not be able to change their situations.

Experiences

1. The counselor explains what alcoholism is. In order to demonstrate how families of alcoholics function differently than other families, the counselor asks the children to perform the following exercise:
   - Off balance: The counselor divides the class into groups of six or eight students. Each group of students gets in a circle and holds hands, and the members try to stand on one foot. They help one another trying to achieve balance and equilibrium. The counselor points out that this is how some families work together. The counselor then appoints one member of each group to be the "alcoholic member," whose job is to pull everyone "off balance." The students then repeat the exercise with this member not cooperating with the rest of the group. The counselor may ask the groups to repeat this activity with various group members serving as the "alcoholic member."
2. The counselor leads the class in a discussion of how these two experiences were different, focusing on feelings and reactions of both the "alcoholic member" and the other group members.
3. The counselor reads "A Wise Word About Alcoholism" (see attached) to the class.

Publication   The counselor asks the students to discuss the following questions:

- How are some ways that your family works out conflicts?
- What are some ways that your family helps one another in difficult situations?
- In what ways did the members of the Squirrel family think they were helping Father? Each other?
- In what ways were they really helping Father? Themselves? Each other?
- If you were in a family like the Squirrel family, what were some ways you could have helped yourself? Others in the family?
- If you are part of a family with an alcoholic in it or in any situation that you cannot change, what are some ways you can help yourself?

Process   The counselor summarizes the themes of this discussion and emphasizes the ways students can help themselves and the fact that they cannot control or change other people.

Generalization   The counselor suggests that the students think about the following concepts:

- Conflicts are not negative in and of themselves, but the way they are resolved is important. People in the family of an alcoholic can unknowingly contribute to the problem.
- A person can improve and change himself or herself even if he or she cannot "fix" the situation.

Application   The counselor asks the students to choose one of these two assignments:

1. Write a short account of something you cannot change in your life right now, and describe some ways you can help yourself.
2. Draw a picture of your family working on something together, making sure that each member is doing something constructive to positively contribute to the family.

The counselor invites students to discuss feelings and reactions to these experiences with him/her outside of class if they wish to do so.

"A Wise Word About Alcoholism"
By Faye Wedell

The M. T. Squirrel family lived in the hollow of a huge oak tree. They had everything a family could want—a safe, sturdy tree for a home, plenty of nuts to eat, and lots of squirrels in nearby trees to be friends with.

There was just one problem—Father Squirrel was an alcoholic. He stayed out all night sometimes, and then the next day, he would feel so awful that he would "sleep in" all day. If anyone disturbed him, he would screech, "Shut up!" Other times he would awaken the Squirrel children with his loud chattering and quarreling with Mother Squirrel. The Squirrel children would feel very scared, crouching down in their nests and pretending not to hear.

Everyone in the family wanted to help Father Squirrel—they loved him! Mother Squirrel would try to "fix" everything by making "excuses" for Father Squirrel. She would say to the Squirrel children, "He's been working so hard! He's so worried about this year's nut harvest!" She would say to the other male squirrels with whom he worked, "I'm sorry. He can't come out to work today. He's sick!"

Jeremy Squirrel, the oldest son, would try to "fix" everything by doing a lot of work his father was supposed to do. He would finish his school work and then be out till dark trying to do Father Squirrel's share. Mother Squirrel depended on Jeremy too. Jeremy watched the younger Squirrels while she gathered leaves to prepare the nest for winter. He didn't get to play much. There wasn't very much fun in his life.

Joshua Squirrel was next oldest in the Squirrel family. He stayed in trouble most of the time. He tried hiding Father Squirrel's booze. Then he poured water in it. One day, he even poured it out. Sometimes he would skip school to try to find Father Squirrel when he was missing from home. Father Squirrel blamed everything on him—*especially* his drinking! Sometimes Joshua felt guilty and angry. He wondered if he *was* the cause of Father's problem. He thought maybe he could "fix" everything by running away, so he tried that, but it didn't help either.

Jenny Squirrel was clownish and cheerful. She thought that she could "fix" Father Squirrel *and* their family problems just by joking around and keeping everyone happy. She would try to tease her father out of his grouchy moods, but it didn't usually help and sometimes she got so tired of pretending to always be happy. Deep inside she knew that Father's drinking and the family problems were *no joke!*

Jill Squirrel was the youngest. She thought she could "fix" things for Father Squirrel just by staying out of his way. She stayed in her nest out of sight most of the time. That way she didn't have to worry about getting yelled at. If she were quiet and didn't upset Father, she wouldn't cause him to drink. He *always* drank when he was upset.

Everyone in this family thought that he or she was helping Father Squirrel by making it easier on him. They were all "walking on nutshells" trying not to upset him.

But do you know what? Just the opposite was happening. Father Squirrel was getting weaker and weaker. He was feeling worse and worse about himself, and he felt useless.

One night, when Father Squirrel hadn't come home by midnight, the entire Squirrel family decided to go out looking for him. Just as they stepped out on the tree limb, a Wise Old Owl on the limb above said, "Wait a minute! Wise up! Accept things the way they are! Nothing you're doing *to* or *for* Father Squirrel is going to help him. He needs help from a doctor, a counselor, or Alcoholics Anonymous *and* from *himself.* The best way you can help *him* is to help *yourselves.* Each of you needs to start doing something nice for *you!*"

You know what? They did. Mother Squirrel started working in a campaign to send nuts to hungry squirrels who survived a forest fire, going to Al-Anon meetings, and visiting with her friends each day. Jeremy Squirrel started playing "Chase" with his friends instead of working all the time. Joshua Squirrel started listening in squirrel school, doing his homework, and making good grades because he was enjoying school. Jenny Squirrel got a part in "Nuts to You," the new school play. Jill Squirrel made a best friend in the very next tree, and they took gymnastics together.

You know what? Pretty soon, Father Squirrel noticed that no one was doing all his work or making up excuses for him anymore. He was still feeling terrible inside, but there was no one he could blame it on. Soon he decided to "fix" himself. He went to Alcoholic Anonymous meetings in Pecan Hall and to a doctor who knew how to help people who were alcoholics.

You know what? By the next winter, the Squirrel family was able to spend a cozy time together—each being himself or herself!

Selected References on Specific Populations

Adopted Children and Their Families

Barth, R. (1991). Adoption of drug-exposed children. Special issue: Research on special needs adoption. *Child and Youth Services Review, 13,* 323–342.

Berry, M. (1991). The effects of open adoption on biological and adoptive parents and the children: The arguments and the evidence. *Child Welfare, 70,* 637–651.

Brodzinsky, D., & Schechter, M. (Eds.). (1990). *The psychology of adoption.* New York: Oxford University.

Brodzinsky, D., & Steiger, C. (1991). Prevalence of adoptees among special education populations. *Journal of Learning Disabilities, 24,* 484–489.

Helwig, A., & Ruthven, D. (1990). Psychological ramifications of adoption and implications for counseling. *Journal of Mental Health Counseling, 12,* 24–37.

MacIntyre, J. (1990). Resolved: Children should be told of their adoption before they ask. *Journal of the American Academy of Child Adolescent Psychiatry, 29,* 828–832.

Melina, L. (1986). *Raising adopted children.* New York: Harper & Row.

Melina, L. (1987). *Adoption: An annotated bibliography and guide.* New York: Garland.

Melina, L. (1989). *Making sense of adoption: A parent's guide.* New York: Harper & Row.

Munsch, A. (1992). Understanding and meeting the needs of adopted children and families. *Child Care Information Exchange, 88,* 47–51.

Myer, R., & James, R. (1989). Counseling internationally adopted children: A personal intervention approach. *Elementary School Guidance and Counseling, 23,* 324–328.

Myer, R., James, D., & Street, T. (1987). Counseling internationally adopted children: A classroom meeting approach. *Elementary School Guidance and Counseling, 22,* 88–94.

Ramos, J. (1990). Counseling internationally adopted children. *Elementary School Counseling and Guidance, 25,* 147–152.

Rosenberg, E., & Horner, T. (1991). Birthparent romances and identity formation in adopted children. *American Orthopsychiatric Association, 61,* 70–77.

Sandmaier, M. (1988). *When love is not enough: How mental health professionals can help special-needs adoptive families.* Washington, DC: Child Welfare League of America.

Schaffer, J. (1991). *How to raise an adopted child: A guide to help your child flourish from infancy through adolescence.* New York: Plume.

Childhood Depression

Bauer, A. (1987). A teacher's introduction to childhood depression. *Clearing House, 61,* 81–84.

Downing, J. (1988). Counseling interventions with depressed children. *Elementary School Guidance and Counseling, 22,* 231–240.

Hart, S. (1991). Childhood depression: Implications and options for school counselors. *Elementary School Guidance and Counseling, 25,* 277–289.

Kazdin, A. (1989). Childhood depression. In E. Mash & R. Barkley (Eds.), *Treatment of childhood disorders* (pp. 135–166). New York: Guilford.

Lasko, C. (1986). Childhood depression: Questions and answers. *Elementary School Guidance and Counseling, 20,* 283–289.

Maag, J., & Forness, S. (1991). Depression in children and adolescents: Identification, assessment, and treatment. *Focus on Exceptional Children, 24,* 1–19.

Rutter, M., Izard, C., & Read, P. (Eds.). (1986). *Depression in young people: Developmental and clinical perspectives.* New York: Guilford.

Schloss, P. (1983). Classroom-based interventions for students exhibiting depressive reactions. *Behavioral Disorders, 8,* 231–236.

Stark, K. (1990). *Childhood depression: School-based intervention.* New York: Guilford.

Stiles, K., & Kottman, T. (1990). Mutual storytelling: An alternative intervention for depressed children. *The School Counselor, 37,* 337–342.

Children with Disabilities

Bello, G. (1989). Counseling handicapped students: A cognitive approach. *The School Counselor, 36,* 298–304.

Berry, J. (1987). A program for training teachers as counselors of parents of children with disabilities. *Journal of Counseling and Development, 65,* 508–509.

Brooks, R. (1987). Storytelling and the therapeutic process for children with learning disabilities. *Journal of Learning Disabilities, 20,* 546–550.

Crnic, K., & Reid, M. (1989). Mental retardation. In E. Mash & R. Barkley (Eds.), *Treatment of childhood disorders* (pp. 247–285). New York: Guilford.

Hadley, R., & Brodwin, M. (1988). Language about people with disabilities. *Journal of Counseling and Development, 67,* 147–149.

Hulnick, M., & Hulnick, H. R. (1989). Life's challenges: Curse or opportunity? Counseling families of persons with disabilities. *Journal of Counseling and Development, 68,* 166–170.

Jenkins, E. (1985). Ethical and legal dilemmas of working with students with special needs. *Elementary School Guidance and Counseling, 19,* 202–209.

Lombana, J. (1992). Learning disabled students and their families: Implications and strategies for counselors. *Journal of Humanistic Education and Development, 31,* 33–40.

Newson, C., & Rincover, A. (1989). Autism. In E. Mash & R. Barkley (Eds.), *Treatment of childhood disorders* (pp. 286–346). New York: Guilford.

Omizo, M., & Omizo, S. (1988). Group counseling's effects on self-concept and social behaviors among children with learning disabilities. *Journal of Humanistic Education and Development, 25,* 109–117.

Parette, H., & Hourcade, J. (1984). The student with cerebral palsy and the public schools: Implications for the counselor. *Elementary School Guidance and Counseling, 18,* 141–146.

Parette, H., & VanBiervliet, A. (1991). School-age children with disabilities: Technology implications for counselors. *Elementary School Guidance and Counseling, 25,* 182–193.

Post-Kammer, P., & Nickolai, S. (1985). Counseling services for the siblings of the handicapped. *Elementary School Counseling and Guidance, 20,* 115–120.

Seligman, M. (1985). Handicapped children and their families. *Journal of Counseling and Development, 64,* 274–277.

Stoll Switzer, L. (1990). Family factors associated with academic progress for children with learning disabilities. *Elementary School Guidance and Counseling, 24,* 200–206.

Taylor, H. G. (1989). Learning disabilities. In E. Mash & R. Barkley (Eds.), *Treatment of childhood disorders* (pp. 347–380). New York: Guilford.

Willians, W., & Lair, G. (1991). Using a person-centered approach with children who have a disability. *Elementary School Guidance and Counseling, 25,* 194–203.

Eating-Disordered Children and Adolescents

Bauer, B., & Anderson, W. (1989). Bulimic beliefs: Food for thought. *Journal of Counseling and Development, 67,* 416–419.

Fallon, P., Friedrick, W., & Root, M. (1986). *Bulimia: A systems approach to treatment.* New York: Norton.

Faust, J. (1987). Correlates of the drive for thinness in young female adolescents. *Journal of Clinical Child Psychology, 16,* 313–319.

Fosson, A., Kinbbs, J., Bryan-Waugh, R., & Lask, B. (1987). Early onset anorexia nervosa. *Archives of Disease in Childhood, 62,* 114–118.

Hendrick, S. (1984). The school counselor and anorexia nervosa. *The School Counselor, 31,* 428–432.

Jacobs, B., & Isaacs, S. (1986). Pre-pubertal anorexia nervosa: A retrospective controlled study. *Journal of Child Psychology and Psychiatry, 27,* 237–250.

Latimer, J. (1988). *Living binge-free: A personal guide to victory over compulsive eating.* Boulder: Livingquest.

Morrill, C., Leach, J., Radebaugh, M., & Shreeve, W. (1991). Adolescent obesity: Rethinking traditional approaches. *The School Counselor, 38,* 347–351.

Nassar, C., Hodges, P., & Ollendick, T. (1992). Self-concept, eating attitudes, and dietary patterns in young adolescent girls. *The School Counselor, 39,* 338–343.

Peters, C., Butterfield, P., Swassing, C., & McKay, G. (1984). Assessment and treatment of anorexia nervosa and bulimia in school age children. *School Psychology Review, 13,* 183–191.

Sacker, I., & Zimmer, M. (1987). *Dying to be thin.* New York: Warner.

Sandbek, T. (1986). *The deadly diet: Recovering from anorexia and bulimia.* Oakland, CA: New Harbinger.

Schactel, B., & Wilborn, B. (1990). A phenomenological approach to bulimia. *TACD Journal, 18,* 21–30.

Winkler, M., & Vacc, N. (1989). Eating-disordered behavior of girls. *Elementary School Guidance and Counseling, 24,* 119–127.

Gay and Lesbian Youth

Borhek, M. (1988). Helping gay and lesbian adolescents and their families. *Journal of Adolescent Health Care, 9,* 123–128.

Cass, V. (1984). Homosexual identity formation: Testing a theoretical model. *The Journal of Sex Research, 20,* 143–167.

Coleman, E. (1982). Developmental stages of the coming out process. *Journal of Homosexuality, 7,* 31–43.

Dworkin, S., & Gutierrez, F. (Eds.). (1992). *Counseling gays and lesbians: Journey to the end of the rainbow.* Alexandria, VA: American Counseling Association.

Gonsiorek, J. (1988). Mental health issues of gay and lesbian adolescents. *Journal of Adolescent Health Care, 9,* 114–122.

Hetrick, E., & Martin, A. (1987). Developmental issues and their resolution for gay and lesbian adolescents. *Journal of Homosexuality, 14,* 25–43.

Hunter, J., & Schaecher, R. (1987, Spring). Stresses on lesbian and gay adolescents in schools. *Social Work in Education,* 180–190.

McFarland, W. (1993). A developmental approach to gay and lesbian youth. *Journal of Humanistic Education and Development, 32,* 17–29.

Troiden, R. (1988). Homosexual identity development. *Journal of Adolescent Health Care, 9,* 105–113.

Urbide, V. (1991). *Project 10 handbook: Addressing lesbian and gay issues in our schools.* Los Angeles, CA: Friends of Project 10.

Ethical Standards

Ethical Standards

American Association for Counseling and Development
(As Revised by AACD Governing Council, March 1988)

Preamble

The Association is an educational, scientific, and professional organization whose members are dedicated to the enhancement of the worth, dignity, potential, and uniqueness of each individual and thus to the service of society.

The Association recognizes that the role definitions and work settings of its members include a wide variety of academic disciplines, levels of academic preparation, and agency services. This diversity reflects the breadth of the Association's interest and influence. It also poses challenging complexities in efforts to set standards for the performance of members, desired requisite preparation or practice, and supporting social, legal, and ethical controls.

The specification of ethical standards enables the Association to clarify to present and future members and to those served by members the nature of ethical responsibilities held in common by its members.

The existence of such standards serves to stimulate greater concern by members for their own professional functioning and for the conduct of fellow professionals such as counselors, guidance and student personnel workers, and others in the helping professions. As the ethical code of the Association, this document establishes principles that define the ethical behavior of Association members. Additional ethical guidelines developed by the Association's Divisions for their specialty areas may further define a member's ethical behavior.

Section A:
General

1. The member influences the development of the profession by continuous efforts to improve professional practices, teaching, services, and research. Professional growth is continuous throughout the member's career and is exemplified by the development of a philosophy that explains why and how a member functions in the helping relationship. Members must gather data on their effectiveness and be guided by the findings. Members recognize the need for continuing education to ensure competent service.

2. The member has a responsibility both to the individual who is served and to the institution within which the service is performed to maintain high standards of professional conduct. The member strives to maintain the highest levels of

professional services offered to the individuals to be served. The member also strives to assist the agency, organization, or institution in providing the highest caliber of professional services. The acceptance of employment in an institution implies that the member is in agreement with the general policies and principles of the institution. Therefore the professional activities of the member are also in accord with the objectives of the institution. If, despite concerted efforts, the member cannot reach agreement with the employer as to acceptable standards of conduct that allow for changes in institutional policy conducive to the positive growth and development of clients, then terminating the affiliation should be seriously considered.

3. Ethical behavior among professional associates, both members and nonmembers, must be expected at all times. When information is possessed that raises doubt as to the ethical behavior of professional colleagues, whether Association members or not, the member must take action to attempt to rectify such a condition. Such action shall use the institution's channels first and then use procedures established by the Association.

4. The member neither claims nor implies professional qualifications exceeding those possessed and is responsible for correcting any misrepresentations of these qualifications by others.

5. In establishing fees for professional counseling services, members must consider the financial status of clients and locality. In the event that the established fee structure is inappropriate for a client, assistance must be provided in finding comparable services of acceptable cost.

6. When members provide information to the public or to subordinates, peers, or supervisors, they have a responsibility to ensure that the content is general, unidentified client information that is accurate, unbiased, and consists of objective, factual data.

7. Members recognize their boundaries of competence and provide only those services and use only those techniques for which they are qualified by training or experience. Members should only accept those positions for which they are professionally qualified.

8. In the counseling relationship, the counselor is aware of the intimacy of the relationship and maintains respect for the client and avoids engaging in activities that seek to meet the counselor's personal needs at the expense of that client.

9. Members do not condone or engage in sexual harassment which is defined as deliberate or repeated comments, gestures, or physical contacts of a sexual nature.

10. The member avoids bringing personal issues into the counseling relationship, especially if the potential for harm is present. Through awareness of the negative impact of both racial and sexual stereotyping and discrimination, the counselor guards the individual rights and personal dignity of the client in the counseling relationship.

11. Products or services provided by the member by means of classroom instruction, public lectures, demonstrations, written articles, radio or television programs, or other types of media must meet the criteria cited in these standards.

Section B:
Counseling Relationship

This section refers to practices and procedures of individual and/or group counseling relationships.

The member must recognize the need for client freedom of choice. Under those circumstances where this is not possible, the member must apprise clients of restrictions that may limit their freedom of choice.

1. The member's primary obligation is to respect the integrity and promote the welfare of the client(s), whether the client(s) is (are) assisted individually or in a group relationship. In a group setting, the member is also responsible for taking reasonable precautions to protect individuals from physical and/or psychological trauma resulting from interaction within the group.

2. Members make provisions for maintaining confidentiality in the storage and disposal of records and follow an established record retention and disposition policy. The counseling relationship and information resulting therefrom must be kept confidential, consistent with the obligations of the member as a professional person. In a group counseling setting, the counselor must set a norm of confidentiality regarding all group participants' disclosures.

3. If an individual is already in a counseling relationship with another professional person, the member does not enter into a counseling relationship without first contacting and receiving the approval of that other professional. If the member discovers that the client is in another counseling relationship after the counseling relationship begins, the member must gain the consent of the other professional or terminate the relationship, unless the client elects to terminate the other relationship.

4. When the client's condition indicates that there is clear and imminent danger to the client or others, the member must take reasonable personal action or inform responsible authorities. Consultation with other professionals must be used where possible. The assumption of responsibility for the client's(s') behavior must be taken only after careful deliberation. The client must be involved in the resumption of responsibility as quickly as possible.

5. Records of the counseling relationship, including interview notes, test data, correspondence, tape recordings, electronic data storage, and other documents are to be considered professional information for use in counseling, and they should not be considered a part of the records of the institution or agency in which the counselor is employed unless specified by state statute or regulation. Revelation to others of counseling material must occur only upon the expressed consent of the client.

6. In view of the extensive data storage and processing capacities of the computer, the member must ensure that data maintained on a computer is: (a) limited to information that is appropriate and necessary for the services being provided; (b) destroyed after it is determined that the information is no longer of any value in providing services; and (c) restricted in terms of access to appropriate staff members involved in the provision of services by using the best computer security methods available.

7. Use of data derived from a counseling relationship for purposes of counselor training or research shall be confined to content that can be disguised to ensure full protection of the identity of the subject client.

8. The member must inform the client of the purposes, goals, techniques, rules of procedure, and limitations that may affect the relationship at or before the time that the counseling relationship is entered. When working with minors or persons who are unable to give consent, the member protects these clients' best interests.

9. In view of common misconceptions related to the perceived inherent validity of computer-generated data and narrative reports, the member must ensure that the client is provided with information as part of the counseling relationship that adequately explains the limitations of computer technology.

10. The member must screen prospective group participants, especially when the emphasis is on self-understanding and growth through self-disclosure. The member must maintain an awareness of the group participants' compatibility throughout the life of the group.

11. The member may choose to consult with any other professionally competent person about a client. In choosing a consultant, the member must avoid placing the consultant in a conflict of interest situation that would preclude the consultant's being a proper party to the member's efforts to help the client.

12. If the member determines an inability to be of professional assistance to the client, the member must either avoid initiating the counseling relationship or immediately terminate that relationship. In either event, the member must suggest appropriate alternatives. (The member must be knowledgeable about referral resources so that a satisfactory referral can be initiated.) In the event the client declines the suggested referral, the member is not obligated to continue the relationship.

13. When the member has other relationships, particularly of an administrative, supervisory, and/or evaluative nature with an individual seeking counseling services, the member must not serve as the counselor but should refer the individual to another professional. Only in instances where such an alternative is unavailable and where the individual's situation warrants counseling intervention should the member enter into and/or maintain a counseling relationship. Dual relationships with clients that might impair the member's objectivity and professional judgement (e.g., as with close friends or relatives), must be avoided and/or the counseling relationship terminated through referral to another competent professional.

14. The member will avoid any type of sexual intimacies with clients. Sexual relationships with clients are unethical.

15. All experimental methods of treatment must be clearly indicated to prospective recipients, and safety precautions are to be adhered to by the member.

16. When computer applications are used as a component of counseling services, the member must ensure that: (a) the client is intellectually, emotionally, and physically capable of using the computer application; (b) the computer application is appropriate for the needs of the client; (c) the client understands the purpose and operation of the computer application; and (d) a follow-up of client use of a computer application is provided to both correct possible problems (misconceptions or inappropriate use) and assess subsequent needs.

17. When the member is engaged in short-term group treatment/training programs (e.g., marathons and other encounter-type or growth groups), the member ensures that there is professional assistance available during and following the group experience.

18. Should the member be engaged in a work setting that calls for any variation from the above statements, the member is obligated to consult with other professionals whenever possible to consider justifiable alternatives.

19. The member must ensure that members of various ethnic, racial, religious, disability, and socioeconomic groups have equal access to computer applications used to support counseling services and that the content of available computer applications does not discriminate against the groups described above.

20. When computer applications are developed by the member for use by the general public as self-help/stand-alone computer software, the member must ensure that: (a) self-help computer applications are designed from the beginning to function in a stand-alone manner, as opposed to modifying software that was originally designed to require support from a counselor; (b) self-help computer applications will include within the program statements regarding intended user outcomes, suggestions for using the software, a description of the conditions under which self-help computer applications might not be appropriate, and a description of when and how counseling services might be beneficial; and (c) the manual for such applications will include the qualifications of the developer, the development process, validation data, and operating procedures.

Section C:
Measurement & Evaluation

The primary purpose of educational and psychological testing is to provide descriptive measures that are objective and interpretable in either comparative or absolute terms. The member must recognize the need to interpret the statements that follow as applying to the whole range of appraisal techniques including test and nontest data. Test results constitute only one of a variety of pertinent sources of information for personnel, guidance, and counseling decisions.

1. The member must provide specific orientation or information to the examinee(s) prior to and following the test administration so that the results of testing may be placed in proper perspective with other relevant factors. In so doing, the member must recognize the effects of socioeconomic, ethnic, and cultural factors on test scores. It is the member's professional responsibility to use additional invalidated information carefully in modifying interpretation of the test results.

2. In selecting tests for use in a given situation or with a particular client, the member must consider carefully the specific validity, reliability, and appropriateness of the test(s). General validity, reliability, and related issues may be questioned legally as well as ethically when tests are used for vocational and educational selection, placement, or counseling.

3. When making any statements to the public about tests and testing, the member must give accurate information and avoid false claims or misconceptions. Special efforts are often required to avoid unwarranted connotations of such terms as IQ and grade equivalent scores.

4. Different tests demand different levels of competence for administration, scoring, and interpretation. Members must recognize the limits of their competence and perform only those functions for which they are prepared. In particular, members using computer-based test interpretations must be trained in the construct being measured and the specific instrument being used prior to using this type of computer application.

5. In situations where a computer is used for test administration and scoring, the member is responsible for ensuring that administration and scoring programs function properly to provide clients with accurate test results.

6. Tests must be administered under the same conditions that were established in their standardization. When tests are not administered under standard conditions or when unusual behavior or irregularities occur during the testing session, those conditions must be noted and the results designated as invalid or of questionable validity. Unsupervised or inadequately supervised test-taking, such as the use of tests through the mails, is considered unethical. On the other hand, the use of instruments that are so designed or standardized to be self-administered and self-scored, such as interest inventories, is to be encouraged.

7. The meaningfulness of test results used in personnel, guidance, and counseling functions generally depends on the examinee's unfamiliarity with the specific items on the test. Any prior coaching or dissemination of the test materials can invalidate test results. Therefore, test security is one of the professional obligations of the member. Conditions that produce most favorable test results must be made known to the examinee.

8. The purpose of testing and the explicit use of the results must be made known to the examinee prior to testing. The counselor must ensure that instrument limitations are not exceeded and that periodic review and/or retesting are made to prevent client stereotyping.

9. The examinee's welfare and explicit prior understanding must be the criteria for determining the recipients of the test results. The member must see that specific interpretation accompanies any release of individual or group test data. The interpretation of test data must be related to the examinee's particular concerns.

10. Members responsible for making decisions based on test results have an understanding of educational and psychological measurement, validation criteria, and test research.

11. The member must be cautious when interpreting the results of research instruments possessing insufficient technical data. The specific purposes for the use of such instruments must be stated explicitly to examinees.

12. The member must proceed with caution when attempting to evaluate and interpret the performance of minority group members or other persons who are not represented in the norm group on which the instrument was standardized.

13. When computer-based test interpretations are developed by the member to support the assessment process, the member must ensure the validity of such interpretations is established prior to the commercial distribution of such a computer application.

14. The member recognizes that test results may become obsolete. The member will avoid and prevent the misuse of obsolete test results.

15. The member must guard against the appropriation, reproduction, or modification of published tests or parts thereof without acknowledgement and permission from the previous publisher.

16. Regarding the preparation, publication, and distribution of tests, reference should be made to:

    a. "Standards for Educational and Psychological Testing," revised edition, 1985, published by the American Psychological Association on behalf of itself, the American Educational Research Association and the National Council of Measurement in Education.

    b. "The Responsible Use of Tests: A Position Paper of AMEG, APGA, and NCME," *Measurement and Evaluation in Guidance*, 1972, 5, 385–388.

    c. "Responsibilities of Users of Standardized Tests," APGA, *Guidepost*, October 5, 1978, pp. 5–8.

Section D:
Research and Publication

1. Guidelines on research with human subjects shall be adhered to, such as:

    a. *Ethical Principles in the Conduct of Research with Human Participants*, Washington, D.C.: American Psychological Association, Inc., 1982.

    b. Code of Federal Regulation, Title 45, Subtitle A, Part 46, as currently issued.

    c. *Ethical Principles of Psychologists*, American Psychological Association, Principle #9: Research with Human Participants.

    d. Family Educational Rights and Privacy Act (the Buckley Amendment).

    e. Current federal regulations and various state rights privacy acts.

2. In planning any research activity dealing with human subjects, the member must be aware of and responsive to all pertinent ethical principles and ensure that the research problem, design, and execution are in full compliance with them.

3. Responsibility for ethical research practice lies with the principal researcher, while others involved in the research activities share ethical obligation and full responsibility for their own actions.

4. In research with human subjects, researchers are responsible for the subjects' welfare throughout the experiment, and they must take all reasonable precautions to avoid causing injurious psychological, physical, or social effects on their subjects.

5. All research subjects must be informed of the purpose of the study except when withholding information or providing misinformation to them is essential to the investigation. In such research the member must be responsible for corrective action as soon as possible following completion of the research.

6. Participation in research must be voluntary. Involuntary participation is appropriate only when it can be demonstrated that participation will have no harmful effects on subjects and is essential to the investigation.

7. When reporting research results, explicit mention must be made of all variables and conditions known to the investigator that might affect the outcome of the investigation or the interpretation of the data.

8. The member must be responsible for conducting and reporting investigations in a manner that minimizes the possibility that results will be misleading.

9. The member has an obligation to make available sufficient original research data to qualified others who may wish to replicate the study.

10. When supplying data, aiding in the research of another person, reporting research results, or making original data available, due care must be taken to disguise the identity of the subjects in the absence of specific authorization from such subjects to do otherwise.

11. When conducting and reporting research, the member must be familiar with and give recognition to previous work on the topic, as well as to observe all copyright laws and follow the principles of giving full credit to all whom credit is due.

12. The member must give due credit through joint authorship, acknowledgement, footnote statements, or other appropriate means to those who have contributed significantly to the research and/or publication, in accordance with such contributions.

13. The member must communicate to other members the results of any research judged to be of professional or scientific value. Results reflecting unfavorably on institutions, programs, services, or vested interests must not be withheld for such reasons.

14. If members agree to cooperate with another individual in research and/or publication, they incur an obligation to cooperate as promised in terms of punctuality of performance and with full regard to the completeness and accuracy of the information required.

15. Ethical practice requires that authors not submit the same manuscript or one essentially similar in content for simultaneous publication consideration by two or more journals. In addition, manuscripts published in whole or in substantial part in another journal or published work should not be submitted for publication without acknowledgement and permission from the previous publication.

Section E:
Consulting

Consultation refers to a voluntary relationship between a professional helper and help-needing individual, group, or social unit in which the consultant is providing help to the client(s) in defining and solving a work-related problem or potential problem with a client or client system.

1. The member acting as consultant must have a high degree of self-awareness of his/her own values, knowledge, skills, limitations, and needs in entering a helping relationship that involves human and/or organizational change and that the focus of the relationship be on the issues to be resolved and not on the person(s) presenting the problem.

2. There must be understanding and agreement between member and client for the problem definition, change of goals, and prediction of consequences of interventions selected.

3. The member must be reasonably certain that she/he or the organization represented has the necessary competencies and resources for giving the kind of help that is needed now or may be needed later and that appropriate referral resources are available to the consultant.

4. The consulting relationship must be one in which client adaptability and growth toward self-direction are encouraged and cultivated. The member must maintain this role consistently and not become a decision maker for the client or create a future dependency on the consultant.

5. When announcing consultant availability for services, the member conscientiously adheres to the Association's Ethical Standards.

6. The member must refuse a private fee or other remuneration for consultation with persons who are entitled to these services through the member's employing institution or agency. The policies of a particular agency may make explicit provisions for private practice with agency clients by members of its staff. In such instances, the clients must be apprised of other options open to them should they seek private counseling services.

Section F:
Private Practice

1. The member should assist the profession by facilitating the availability of counseling services in private as well as public settings.

2. In advertising services as a private practitioner, the member must advertise the services in a manner that accurately informs the public of professional services, expertise, and techniques of counseling available. A member who assumes an executive leadership role in the organization shall not permit his/her name to be used in professional notices during periods when he/she is not actively engaged in the private practice of counseling.

3. The member may list the following: highest relevant degree, type and level of certification and/or license, address, telephone number, office hours, type and/or description of services, and other relevant information. Such information must not contain false, inaccurate, misleading, partial, out-of-context, or deceptive material or statements.

4. Members do not present their affiliation with any organization in such a way that would imply inaccurate sponsorship or certification by that organization.

5. Members may join in partnership/corporation with other members and/or other professionals provided that each member of the partnership or corporation makes clear the separate specialties by name in compliance with the regulations of the locality.

6. A member has an obligation to withdraw from a counseling relationship if it is believed that employment will result in violation of the Ethical Standards. If the mental or physical condition of the member renders it difficult to carry out an effective professional relationship or if the member is discharged by the client because the counseling relationship is no longer productive for the client, then the member is obligated to terminate the counseling relationship.

7. A member must adhere to the regulations for private practice of the locality where the services are offered.

8. It is unethical to use one's institutional affiliation to recruit clients for one's private practice.

Section G:
Personnel Administration

It is recognized that most members are employed in public or quasi-public institutions. The functioning of a member within an institution must con tribute to the goals of the institution and vice versa if either is to accomplish their respective goals or objectives. It is therefore essential that the member and the institution function in ways to: (a) make the institutional goals explicit; and public; (b) make the member's contribution to institutional goals specific; and (c) foster mutual accountability for goal achievement.

To accomplish these objectives, it is recognized that the member and the employer must share responsibilities in the formulation and implementation of personnel policies.

1. Members must define and describe the parameters and levels of their professional competency.

2. Members must establish interpersonal relations and working agreements with supervisors and subordinates regarding counseling or clinical relationships, confidentiality, distinction between public and private material, maintenance and dissemination of recorded information, work load, and accountability. Working agreements in each instance must be specified and made known to those concerned.

3. Members must alert their employers to conditions that may be potentially disruptive or damaging.

4. Members must inform employers of conditions that may limit their effectiveness.

5. Members must submit regularly to professional review and evaluation.

6. Members must be responsible for inservice development of self and/or staff.

7. Members must inform their staff of goals and programs.

8. Members must provide personnel practices that guarantee and enhance the rights and welfare of each recipient of their service.

9. Members must select competent persons and assign responsibilities compatible with their skills and experiences.

10. The member, at the onset of a counseling relationship, will inform the client of the member's intended use of supervisors regarding the disclosure of information concerning this case. The member will clearly inform the client of the limits of confidentiality in the relationship.

11. Members, as either employers or employees, do not engage in or condone practices that are inhumane, illegal, or unjustifiable (such as considerations based on sex, handicap, age, race) in hiring, promotion, or training.

Section H:
Preparation Standards

Members who are responsible for training others must be guided by the preparation standards of the Association and relevant Division(s). The member who functions in the capacity of trainer assumes unique ethical responsibilities that frequently go beyond that of the member who does not function in a training capacity. These ethical responsibilities are outlined as follows:

1. Members must orient students to program expectations, basic skills development, and employment prospects prior to admission to the program.
2. Members in charge of learning experiences must establish programs that integrate academic study and supervised practice.
3. Members must establish a program directed toward developing students' skills, knowledge, and self-understanding, stated whenever possible in competency or performance terms.
4. Members must identify the levels of competencies of their students in compliance with relevant Division standards. These competencies must accommodate the paraprofessional as well as the professional.
5. Members, through continual student evaluation and appraisal, must be aware of the personal limitations of the learner that might impede future performance. The instructor must not only assist the learner in securing remedial assistance but also screen from the program those individuals who are unable to provide competent services.
6. Members must provide a program that includes training in research commensurate with levels of role functioning. Paraprofessional and technician-level personnel must be trained as consumers of research. In addition, personnel must learn how to evaluate their own and their program's effectiveness. Graduate training, especially at the doctoral level, would include preparation for original research by the member.
7. Members must make students aware of the ethical responsibilities and standards of the profession.
8. Preparatory programs must encourage students to value the ideals of service to individuals and to society. In this regard, direct financial remuneration or lack thereof must not be allowed to overshadow professional and humanitarian needs.
9. Members responsible for educational programs must be skilled as teachers and practitioners.
10. Members must present thoroughly varied theoretical positions so that students may make comparisons and have the opportunity to select a position.
11. Members must develop clear policies within their educational institutions regarding field placement and the roles of the student and the instructor in such placement.
12. Members must ensure that forms of learning focusing on self-understanding or growth are voluntary, or if required as part of the educational program, are made known to prospective students prior to entering the program. When the

educational program offers a growth experience with an emphasis on self-disclosure or other relatively intimate or personal involvement, the member must have no administrative, supervisory, or evaluating authority regarding the participant.

13. The member will at all times provide students with clear and equally acceptable alternatives for self-understanding or growth experiences. The member will assure students that they have a right to accept these alternatives without prejudice or penalty.

14. Members must conduct an educational program in keeping with the current relevant guidelines of the Association.

For Further Information Write:

American Association for Counseling and Development
5999 Stevenson Avenue, Alexandria, VA 23304
Formerly American Personnel & Guidance Association

Ethical Guidelines for Group Counselors
Preamble

One characteristic of any professional group is the possession of a body of knowledge, skills, and voluntarily, self-professed standards for ethical practice. A Code of Ethics consists of those standards that have been formally and publicly acknowledged by the members of a profession to serve as the guidelines for professional conduct, discharge of duties, and the resolution of moral dilemmas. By this document, the Association for Specialists in Group Work (ASGW) has identified the standards of conduct appropriate for ethical behavior among its members.

The Association for Specialists in Group Work recognizes the basic commitment of its members to the Ethical Standards of its parent organization, the American Association for Counseling and Development (AACD) and nothing in this document shall be construed to supplant that code. These standards are intended to complement the AACD standards in the area of group work by clarifying the nature of ethical responsibility of the counselor in the group setting and by stimulating a greater concern for competent group leadership.

The group counselor is expected to be a professional agent and to take the processes of ethical responsibility seriously. ASGW views "ethical process" as being integral to group work and views group counselors as "ethical agents." Group counselors, by their very nature in being responsible and responsive to their group members, necessarily embrace a certain potential for ethical vulnerability. It is incumbent upon group counselors to give considerable attention to the intent and context of their actions because the attempts of counselors to influence human behavior through group work always have ethical implications.

The following ethical guidelines have been developed to encourage ethical behavior of group counselors. These guidelines are written for students and practitioners, and are meant to stimulate reflection, self-examination, and discussion of issues and practices. They address the group counselor's responsibility for providing information about group work to clients and the group counselor's responsibility for providing group counseling services to clients. A final section discusses the group counselor's responsibility for safeguarding ethical practice and procedures for reporting unethical behavior. Group counselors are expected to make known these standards to group members.

Ethical Guidelines

1. *Orientation and Providing Information:*
   Group counselors adequately prepare prospective or new group members by providing as much information about the existing or proposed group as necessary.

- Minimally, information related to each of the following areas should be provided.

   (a) Entrance procedures, time parameters of the group experience, group participation expectations, methods of payment (where appropriate), and termination procedures are explained by the group counselor as appropriate to the level of maturity of group members and the nature and purpose(s) of the group.

   (b) Group counselors have available for distribution, a professional disclosure statement that includes information on the group counselor's qualifications and group services that can be provided, particularly as related to the nature and purpose(s) of the specific group.

   (c) Group counselors communicate the role expectations, rights, and responsibilities of group members and group counselor(s).

   (d) The group goals are stated as concisely as possible by the group counselor including "whose" goal it is (the group counselor's, the institution's, the parent's, the law's, society's, etc.) and the role of group members in influencing or determining the group's goal(s).

   (e) Group counselors explore with group members the risks of potential life changes that may occur because of the group experience and help members explore their readiness to face these possibilities.

   (f) Group members are informed by the group counselor of unusual or experimental procedures that might be expected in their group experience.

   (g) Group counselors explain, as realistically as possible, what services can and cannot be provided within the particular group structure offered.

   (h) Group counselors emphasize the need to promote full psychological functioning and presence among group members. They inquire from prospective group members whether they are using any kind of drug or medication that may affect functioning in the group. They do not permit any use of alcohol and/or illegal drugs during group sessions and they discourage the use of alcohol and/or drugs (legal or illegal) prior to group meetings which may affect the physical or emotional presence of the member or other group members.

(i) Group counselors inquire from prospective group members whether they have ever been a client in counseling or psychotherapy. If a prospective group member is already in a counseling relationship with another professional person, the group counselor advises the prospective group member to notify the other professional of their participation in the group.

(j) Group counselors clearly inform group members about the policies pertaining to the group counselor's willingness to consult with them between group sessions.

(k) In establishing fees for group counseling services, group counselors consider the financial status and the locality of prospective group members. Group members are not charged fees for group sessions where the group counselor is not present and the policy of charging for sessions missed by a group member is clearly communicated. Fees for participating as a group member are contracted between group counselor and group member for a specified period of time. Group counselors do not increase fees for group counseling services until the existing contracted fee structure has expired. In the event that the established fee structure is inappropriate for a prospective member, group counselors assist in finding comparable services of acceptable cost.

2. *Screening of Members:* The group counselor screens prospective group members (when appropriate to their theoretical orientation). Insofar as possible, the counselor selects group members whose needs and goals are compatible with the goals of the group, who will not impede the group process, and whose well-being will not be jeopardized by the group experience. An orientation to the group (i.e., ASGW Ethical Guideline #1), is included during the screening process.

- Screening may be accomplished in one or more ways, such as the following:

    (a) Individual interview,
    (b) Group interview of prospective group members,
    (c) Interview as part of a team staffing, and
    (d) Completion of a written questionnaire by prospective group members.

3. *Confidentiality:* Group counselors protect members by defining clearly what confidentiality means, why it is important, and the difficulties involved in enforcement.

    (a) Group counselors take steps to protect members by defining confidentiality and the limits of confidentiality (i.e., when a group member's condition indicates that there is clear and imminent danger to the member, others, or physical property, the group counselor takes reasonable personal action and/or informs responsible authorities).

    (b) Group counselors stress the importance of confidentiality and set a norm of confidentiality regarding all group participants' disclosures. The importance of maintaining confidentiality is emphasized before the group begins and at various times in the group. The fact that confidentiality cannot be guaranteed is clearly stated.

(c) Members are made aware of the difficulties involved in enforcing and ensuring confidentiality in a group setting. The counselor provides examples of how confidentiality can non-maliciously be broken to increase members' awareness, and help to lessen the likelihood that this breach of confidence will occur. Group counselors inform group members about the potential consequences of intentionally breaching confidentiality.

(d) Group counselors can only ensure confidentiality on their part and not on the part of the members.

(e) Group counselors video or audio tape a group session only with the prior consent, and the members' knowledge of how the tape will be used.

(f) When working with minors, the group counselor specifies the limits of confidentiality.

(g) Participants in a mandatory group are made aware of any reporting procedures required of the group counselor.

(h) Group counselors store or dispose of group member records (written, audio, video, etc.) in ways that maintain confidentiality.

(i) Instructors of group counseling courses maintain the anonymity of group members whenever discussing group counseling cases.

4. *Voluntary/Involuntary Participation:* Group counselors inform members whether participation is voluntary or involuntary.

(a) Group counselors take steps to ensure informed consent procedures in both voluntary and involuntary groups.

(b) When working with minors in a group, counselors are expected to follow the procedures specified by the institution in which they are practicing.

(c) With involuntary groups, every attempt is made to enlist the cooperation of the members and their continuance in the group on a voluntary basis.

(d) Group counselors do not certify that group treatment has been received by members who merely attend sessions, but did not meet the defined group expectations. Group members are informed about the consequences for failing to participate in a group.

5. *Leaving a Group:* Provisions are made to assist a group member to terminate in an effective way.

(a) Procedures to be followed for a group member who chooses to exit a group prematurely are discussed by the counselor with all group members either before the group begins, during a pre-screening interview, or during the initial group session.

(b) In the case of legally mandated group counseling, group counselors inform members of the possible consequences for premature self termination.

(c) Ideally, both the group counselor and the member can work cooperatively to determine the degree to which a group experience is productive or counterproductive for that individual.

(d) Members ultimately have a right to discontinue membership in the group, at a designated time, if the predetermined trial period proves to be unsatisfactory.

(e) Members have the right to exit a group, but it is important that they be made aware of the importance of informing the counselor and the group members prior to deciding to leave. The counselor discusses the possible risks of leaving the group prematurely with a member who is considering this option.

(f) Before leaving a group, the group counselor encourages members (if appropriate) to discuss their reasons for wanting to discontinue membership in the group. Counselors intervene if other members use undue pressure to force a member to remain in the group.

6. *Coercion and Pressure:* Group counselors protect member rights against physical threats, intimidation, coercion, and undue peer pressure insofar as is reasonably possible.

(a) It is essential to differentiate between "therapeutic pressure" that is part of any group and "undue pressure," which is not therapeutic.

(b) The purpose of a group is to help participants find their own answer, not to pressure them into doing what the group thinks is appropriate.

(c) Counselors exert care not to coerce participants to change in directions which they clearly state they do not choose.

(d) Counselors have a responsibility to intervene when others use undue pressure or attempt to persuade members against their will.

(e) Counselors intervene when any member attempts to act out aggression in a physical way that might harm another member or themselves.

(f) Counselors intervene when a member is verbally abusive or inappropriately confrontive to another member.

7. *Imposing Counselor Values:* Group counselors develop an awareness of their own values and needs and the potential impact they have on the interventions likely to be made.

(a) Although group counselors take care to avoid imposing their values on members, it is appropriate that they expose their own beliefs, decisions, needs, and values, when concealing them would create problems for the members.

(b) There are values implicit in any group, and these are made clear to potential members before they join the group. (Examples of certain values include: expressing feelings, being direct and honest, sharing personal material with others, learning how to trust, improving interpersonal communication, and deciding for oneself.)

(c) Personal and professional needs of group counselors are not met at the members' expense.

(d) Group counselors avoid using the group for their own therapy.

(e) Group counselors are aware of their own values and assumptions and how these apply in a multicultural context.

(f) Group counselors take steps to increase their awareness of ways that their personal reactions to members might inhibit the group process and they monitor their countertransference. Through an awareness of the impact of stereotyping and discrimination (i.e., biases based on age, disability, ethnicity, gender, race, religion, or sexual preference), group counselors guard the individual rights and personal dignity of all group members.

8. *Equitable Treatment:* Group counselors make every reasonable effort to treat each member individually and equally.

   (a) Group counselors recognize and respect differences (e.g., cultural, racial, religious, lifestyle, age, disability, gender) among group members.

   (b) Group counselors maintain an awareness of their behavior toward individual group members and are alert to the potential detrimental effects of favoritism or partiality toward any particular group member to the exclusion or detriment of any other member(s). It is likely that group counselors will favor some members over others, yet all group members deserve to be treated equally.

   (c) Group counselors ensure equitable use of group time for each member by inviting silent members to become involved, acknowledging nonverbal attempts to communicate, and discouraging rambling and monopolizing of time by members.

   (d) If a large group is planned, counselors consider enlisting another qualified professional to serve as a co-leader for the group sessions.

9. *Dual Relationships:* Group counselors avoid dual relationships with group members that might impair their objectivity and professional judgement, as well as those which are likely to compromise a group member's ability to participate fully in the group.

   (a) Group counselors do not misuse their professional role and power as group leader to advance personal or social contacts with members throughout the duration of the group.

   (b) Group counselors do not use their professional relationship with group members to further their own interest either during the group or after the termination of the group.

   (c) Sexual intimacies between group counselors and members are unethical.

   (d) Group counselors do not barter (exchange) professional services with group members for services.

   (e) Group counselors do not admit their own family members, relatives, employees, or personal friends as members to their groups.

   (f) Group counselors discuss with group members the potential detrimental effects of group members engaging in intimate inter-member relationships outside of the group.

   (g) Students who participate in a group as a partial course requirement for a group course are not evaluated for an academic grade based upon their degree of participation as a member in a group. Instructors of group counseling courses take steps to minimize the possible negative impact on students when they participate in a group course by separating course grades from participation in the group and by allowing students to decide what issues to explore and when to stop.

   (h) It is inappropriate to solicit members from a class (or institutional affiliation) for one's private counseling or therapeutic groups.

10. *Use of Techniques:* Group counselors do not attempt any technique unless trained in its use or under supervision by a counselor familiar with the intervention.

    (a) Group counselors are able to articulate a theoretical orientation that guides their practice, and they are able to provide a rationale for their interventions.

    (b) Depending upon the type of an intervention, group counselors have training commensurate with the potential impact of a technique.

    (c) Group counselors are aware of the necessity to modify their techniques to fit the unique needs of various cultural and ethnic groups.

    (d) Group counselors assist members in translating in-group learnings to daily life.

11. *Goal Development:* Group counselors make every effort to assist members in developing their personal goals.

    (a) Group counselors use their skills to assist members in making their goals specific so that others present in the group will understand the nature of the goals.

    (b) Throughout the course of a group, group counselors assist members in assessing the degree to which personal goals are being met, and assist in revising any goals when it is appropriate.

    (c) Group counselors help members clarify the degree to which the goals can be met within the context of a particular group.

12. *Consultation:* Group counselors develop and explain policies about between-session consultation to group members.

    (a) Group counselors take care to make certain that members do not use between-session consultations to avoid dealing with issues pertaining to the group that would be dealt with best in the group.

    (b) Group counselors urge members to bring the issues discussed during between-session consultations into the group if they pertain to the group.

    (c) Group counselors seek out consultations and/or supervision regarding ethical concerns or when encountering difficulties which interfere with their effective functioning as group leaders.

    (d) Group counselors seek appropriate professional assistance for their own personal problems or conflicts that are likely to impair their professional judgment and work performance.

    (e) Group counselors discuss their group cases only for professional consultation and educational purposes.

    (f) Group counselors inform members about policies regarding whether consultations will be held confidential.

13. *Termination from the Group:* Depending upon the purpose of the participation in the group, counselors promote termination of members from the group in the most efficient period of time.

   (a) Group counselors maintain a constant awareness of the progress made by each member and periodically invite the group members to explore and reevaluate their experiences in the group. It is the responsibility of group counselors to help promote the independence of members from the group in a timely manner.

14. *Evaluation and Follow-up:* Group counselors make every attempt to engage in ongoing assessment and to design follow-up procedures for their groups.

   (a) Group counselors recognize the importance of ongoing assessment of a group, and they assist members in evaluating their own progress.
   (b) Group counselors conduct evaluation of the total group experience at the final meeting (or before termination), as well as ongoing evaluation.
   (c) Group counselors monitor their own behavior and become aware of what they are modeling in the group.
   (d) Follow-up procedures might take the form of personal contact, telephone contact, or written contact.
   (e) Follow-up meetings might be with individuals, or groups, or both to determine the degree to which: (i) members have reached their goals, (ii) the group had a positive or negative effect on the participants, (iii) members could profit from some type of referral, and (iv) as information for possible modification of future groups. If there is no follow-up meeting, provisions are made available for individual follow-up meetings to any member who needs or requests such a contact.

15. *Referrals:* If the needs of a particular member cannot be met within the type of group being offered, the group counselor suggests other appropriate professional referrals.

   (a) Group counselors are knowledgeable of local community resources for assisting group members regarding professional referrals.
   (b) Group counselors help members seek further professional assistance, if needed.

16. *Professional Development:* Group counselors recognize that professional growth is a continuous, ongoing, developmental process throughout their careers.

   (a) Group counselors maintain and upgrade their knowledge and skill competencies through educational activities, clinical experiences, and participation in professional development activities.
   (b) Group counselors keep abreast of research findings and new developments as applied to groups.

Safeguarding Ethical Practice and Procedures
for Reporting Unethical Behavior

The preceding remarks have been advanced as guidelines which are generally representative of ethical and professional group practice. They have not been proposed as rigidly defined prescriptions. However, practitioners who are thought to be grossly unresponsive to the ethical concerns addressed in this document may be subject to a review of their practices by the AACD Ethics Committee and ASGW peers.

- For consultation and/or questions regarding these ASGW Ethical Guidelines or group ethical dilemmas, you may contact the Chairperson of the ASGW Ethics Committee. The name, address, and telephone number of the current ASGW Ethics Committee Chairperson may be acquired by telephoning the AACD office in Alexandria, Virginia at (703) 823–9800.

- If a group counselor's behavior is suspected as being unethical, the following procedures are to be followed:

  (a) Collect more information and investigate further to confirm the unethical practice as determined by the ASGW Ethical Guidelines.

  (b) Confront the individual with the apparent violation of ethical guidelines for the purposes of protecting the safety of any clients and to help the group counselor correct any inappropriate behaviors. If satisfactory resolution is not reached through this contact then:

  (c) A complaint should be made in writing, including the specific facts and dates of the alleged violation and all relevant supporting data. The complaint should be included in an envelope marked "CONFIDENTIAL" to ensure confidentiality for both the accuser(s) and the alleged violator(s) and forwarded to all of the following sources:

1. The name and address of the Chairperson of the state Counselor Licensure Board for the respective state, if in existence.

2. The Ethics Committee, c/o The President, American Association for Counseling and Development, 5999 Stevenson Avenue, Alexandria, Virginia 22304.

3. The name and address of all private credentialing agencies that the alleged violator maintains credentials or holds professional membership. Some of these include the following:

   National Board for Certified Counselors, Inc., 5999 Stevenson Avenue, Alexandria, Virginia 22304

   National Council for Credentialing of Career Counselors, c/o NBCC, 5999 Stevenson Avenue, Alexandria, Virginia 22304

   National Academy for Certified Clinical Mental Health Counselors, 5999 Stevenson Avenue, Alexandria, Virginia 22304

   Commission on Rehabilitation Counselor Certification, 162 North State Street, Suite 317, Chicago, Illinois 60601

   American Association for Marriage and Family Therapy, 1717 K Street, N.W., Suite 407, Washington, DC 20006

   American Psychological Association, 1200 Seventeenth Street, N.W., Washington, DC 20036

American Group Psychotherapy Association, Inc., 25 East 21st Street, 6th Floor, New York, New York 10010

Approved by the Association for Specialists in Group Work (ASGW) Executive Board, June 1, 1989

Ethical Standards for School Counselors
American School Counselor Association

Preamble

The American School Counselor Association (ASCA) is a professional organization whose members have a unique and distinctive preparation, grounded in the behavioral sciences, with training in clinical skills adapted to the school setting. The school counselor assists in the growth and development of each individual and uses his/her specialized skills to ensure that the rights of the counselee are properly protected within the structure of the school program. School counselors subscribe to the following basic tenets of the counseling process from which professional responsibilities are derived.

1. Each person has the right to respect and dignity as a unique human being and to counseling services without prejudice as to person, character, belief or practice.
2. Each person has the right to self-direction and self-development.
3. Each person has the right of choice and the responsibility for decisions reached.
4. Each person has the right to privacy and thereby the right to expect counselor-client relationship to comply with all laws, policies, and ethical standards pertaining to confidentiality.

In this document, the American School Counselor Association has specified the principles of ethical behavior necessary to maintain and regulate high standards of integrity and leadership among its members. The Association recognizes the basic commitment of its members to the *Ethical Standards* of its parent organization, the American Association for Counseling and Development [Author's note: The name of this association was changed to the American Counseling Association (ACA) in July of 1992 after publication of these standards.], and nothing in this document shall be construed to supplant the code. The *Ethical Standards for School Counselors* was developed to complement the AACD standards by clarifying the nature of ethical responsibilities for present and future counselors in the school setting. The purposes of this document are to:

1. Serve as a guide for ethical practices of all professional school counselors regardless of level, area, population served, or membership in this Association.
2. Provide benchmarks for both self-appraisal and peer evaluations regarding counselor responsibilities to students, parents, colleagues and professional associates, school and community, self, and the counseling profession.
3. Inform those served by the school counselor of acceptable counselor practices and expected professional deportment.

A. Responsibilities to Students

The school counselor:

1. Has a primary obligation and loyalty to the student, who is to be treated with respect as a unique individual, whether assisted individually or in a group setting.

2. Is concerned with the total needs of the student (educational, vocational, personal and social) and encourages the maximum growth and development of each counselee.

3. Informs the counselee of the purposes, goals, techniques, and rules of procedure under which she/he may receive counseling assistance at or before the time when the counseling relationship is entered. Prior notice includes confidentiality issues such as the possible necessity for consulting with other professionals, privileged communication, and legal or authoritative restraints. The meaning and limits of confidentiality are clearly defined to counselees.

4. Refrains from consciously encouraging the counselee's acceptance of values, lifestyles, plans, decisions, and beliefs that represent only the counselor's personal orientation.

5. Is responsible for keeping abreast of laws relating to students and strives to ensure that the rights of students are adequately provided for and protected.

6. Avoids dual relationships which might impair his/her objectivity and/or increase the risk of harm to the client (e.g., counseling one's family members, close friends or associates). If a dual relationship is unavoidable, the counselor is responsible for taking action to eliminate or reduce the potential for harm. Such safeguards might include informed consent, consultation, supervision and documentation.

7. Makes appropriate referrals when professional assistance can no longer be adequately provided to the counselee. Appropriate referral requires knowledge about available resources.

8. Protects the confidentiality of student records and releases personal data only according to prescribed laws and school policies. Student information maintained through electronic data storage methods is treated with the same care as traditional student records.

9. Protects the confidentiality of information received in the counseling relationship as specified by law and ethical standards. Such information is only to be revealed to others with the informed consent of the counselee and consistent with the obligations of the counselor as a professional person.

    In a group setting the counselor sets a norm of confidentiality and stresses its importance, yet clearly states that confidentiality in group counseling cannot be guaranteed.

10. Informs the appropriate authorities when the counselee's condition indicates a clear and imminent danger to the counselee or others. This is to be done after careful deliberation and, where possible, after consultation with other professionals. The counselor informs the counselee of actions to be taken so as to minimize confusion and clarify expectations.

11. Screens prospective group members and maintains an awareness of participants' compatibility throughout the life of the group, especially when the group emphasis is on self disclosure and self-understanding. The counselor takes reasonable precautions to protect members from physical and/or psychological harm resulting from interaction within the group.

12. Provides explanations of the nature, purposes, and results of tests in language that is understandable to the client(s).

13. Adheres to relevant standards regarding selection, administration, and interpretation of assessment techniques. The counselor recognizes that computer-based testing programs require specific training in administration, scoring and interpretation which may differ from that required in more traditional assessments.

14. Promotes the benefits of appropriate computer applications and clarifies the limitations of computer technology. The counselor ensures that (1) computer applications are appropriate for the individual needs of the counselee, (2) the counselee understands how to use the applications, and (3) follow-up counseling assistance is provided. Members of the underrepresented groups are assured of equal access to computer technologies and the absence of discriminatory information and values within computer applications.

15. Has unique ethical responsibilities in working with peer programs. In general, the school counselor is responsible for the welfare of the students participating in peer programs under his/her direction. School counselors who function in training and supervisory capacities are referred to the preparation and supervision standards of professional counselor associations.

B. Responsibilities to Parents

The school counselor:

1. Respects the inherent rights and responsibilities of parents for their children and endeavors to establish a cooperative relationship with parents to facilitate the maximum development of the counselee.

2. Informs parents of the counselor's role, with emphasis on the confidential nature of the counseling relationship between the counselor and counselee.

3. Provides parents with accurate, comprehensive and relevant information in an objective and caring manner, as appropriate and consistent with ethical responsibilities to the counselee.

4. Treats information received from parents in a confidential and appropriate manner.

5. Shares information about a counselee only with those persons properly authorized to receive such information.

6. Adheres to laws and local guidelines when assisting parents experiencing family difficulties which interfere with the counselee's effectiveness and welfare.

7. Is sensitive to changes in the family and recognizes that all parents, custodial and noncustodial, are vested with certain rights and responsibilities for the welfare of their children by virtue of their position and according to law.

C. Responsibilities to Colleagues and Professional Associates

The school counselor:

1. Establishes and maintains a cooperative relationship with faculty, staff, and administration to facilitate the provision of optimal guidance and counseling programs and services

2. Promotes awareness and adherence to appropriate guidelines regarding confidentiality, the distinction between public and private information, and staff consultation.

3. Treats colleagues with respect, courtesy, fairness, and good faith. The qualifications, views, and findings of colleagues are represented accurately and fairly to enhance the image of competent professionals.

4. Provides professional personnel with accurate, objective, concise and meaningful data necessary to adequately evaluate, counsel, and assist the counselee.

5. Is aware of and fully utilizes related professions and organizations to whom the counselee may be referred.

D. Responsibilities to the School and Community

The school counselor:

1. Supports and protects the educational program against any infringement not in the best interests of students.

2. Informs appropriate officials of conditions that may be potentially disruptive or damaging to the school's mission, personnel and property.

3. Delineates and promotes the counselor's role and function in meeting the needs of those served. The counselor will notify appropriate school officials of conditions which may limit or curtail their effectiveness in providing programs and services.

4. Assists in the development of (1) curricular and environmental conditions appropriate for the school and community, (2) educational procedures and programs to meet student needs, and (3) a systematic evaluation process for guidance and counseling programs, services and personnel. The counselor is guided by findings of the evaluation data in planning programs and services.

5. Actively cooperates and collaborates with agencies, organizations, and individuals in the school and community in the best interest of counselees and without regard to personal reward or remuneration.

E. Responsibilities to Self

The school counselor:

1. Functions within the boundaries of individual professional competence and accepts the responsibility for the consequences of his/her actions.

2. Is aware of the potential effects of her/his own personal characteristics on services to clients.

3. Monitors personal functioning and effectiveness and refrains from any activity likely to lead to inadequate professional services or harm to a client.

4. Recognizes that differences in clients relating to age, gender, race, religion, sexual orientation, socioeconomic and ethnic backgrounds may require specific training to ensure competent services.

5. Strives through personal initiative to maintain professional competence and keeps abreast of innovations and trends in the profession. Professional and personal growth is continuous and ongoing throughout the counselor's career.

F. Responsibilities to the Profession

The school counselor:

1. Conducts herself/himself in such a manner as to bring credit to self and the profession.

2. Conducts appropriate research and reports findings in a manner consistent with acceptable educational and psychological research practices. When using client data for research, statistical or program planning purposes, the counselor ensures protection of the identity of the individual client(s).

3. Actively participates in local, state, and national associations which foster the development and improvement of school counseling.

4. Adheres to ethical standards of the profession, other official policy statements pertaining to counseling, and relevant statutes established by federal, state, and local governments.

5. Clearly distinguishes between statements and actions made as a private individual and as a representative of the school counseling profession.

6. Contributes to the development of the profession through the sharing of skills, ideas and expertise with colleagues.

G. Maintenance of Standards

Ethical behavior among professional school counselors, association members and nonmembers, is expected at all times. When there exists serious doubt as to the ethical behavior of colleagues, or if counselors are forced to work in situations or abide by policies which do not reflect the standards as outlined in these *Ethical Standards for School Counselors* or the AACD *Ethical Standards,* the counselor is obligated to take appropriate action to rectify the condition. The following procedures may serve as a guide:

1. If feasible, the counselor should consult with a professional colleague to confidentially discuss the nature of the complaint to see if she/he views the situation as an ethical violation.

2. Whenever possible, the counselor should directly approach the colleague whose behavior is in question to discuss the complaint and seek resolution.

3. If resolution is not forthcoming at the personal level, the counselor shall utilize the channels established within the school and/or school district. This may include both informal and formal procedures.

4. If the matter still remains unresolved, referral for review and appropriate action should be made to the Ethics Committees in the following sequence:

   - local counselor association
   - state counselor association
   - national counselor association

5. The ASCA Ethics Committee functions in an educative and consultative capacity and does not adjucate complaints of ethical misconduct. Therefore, at the national level, complaints should be submitted in writing to the ACA Ethics Committee for review and appropriate action. The procedure for submitting complaints may be obtained by writing the ACA Ethics Committee, c/o The Executive Director, American Counseling Association, 5999 Stevenson Avenue, Alexandria, VA 22304.

H. Resources

School counselors are responsible for being aware of, and acting in accord with, the standards and positions of the counseling profession as represented in such official documents as those listed below:

Code of Ethics (1989). National Board for Certified Counselors. Alexandria, VA.

Code of Ethics for Peer Helping Professionals (1989). National Peer Helpers Association. Glendale, CA.

Ethical Guidelines for Group Counselors (1989). Association for Specialists in Group Work. Alexandria, VA.

Ethical Standards (1988). American Association for Counseling and Development, Alexandria, VA.

Position Statement: The School Counselor and Confidentiality (1986). American School Counselor Association. Alexandria, VA.

Position Statement: The School Counselor and Peer Facilitation (1984). American School Counselor Association. Alexandria, VA.

Position Statement: The School Counselor and Student Rights (1982). American School Counselor Association. Alexandria, VA.

Ethical Standards for School Counselors was adopted by the ASCA Delegate Assembly March 19, 1984. This revision was approved by the ASCA Delegate Assembly, March 27, 1992.

Credits

PHOTOGRAPHY

Chapter Openers

Chapter 1, 11 © David Young Wolff/Photo Edit; Chapter 2 © Michael Siluk; Chapter 3, 4, 6, 7, 9, 10, 12, 13, 15, 16 © James Shaffer; Chapter 5 © Paul Conklin/Photo Edit; Chapter 8 © Jean-Claude LeJeune; Chapter 14 © Michael Newman/Photo Edit.

TEXT

Chapter 10

Questionnaire (p. 220) reprinted from C. Strangeland, D. Pellegreno and J. Lundholm, "Children of divorced parents: A perceptual comparison" in *Elementary School Guidance and Counseling, 23,* pp. 167–73, February 1989. © ACA. Reprinted with permission. No further reproduction authorized without written permission of the American Counseling Association.

Appendix E

The Children's Interaction Matrix (Intermediate and Primary Forms) (p. 410) was developed by Drs. Robert Drummond and Donna B. Brown of the University of North Florida, Jacksonville, Dr. Walter McIntire of the University of Maine, Orono, and Dr. James J. Muro of the University of North Texas. It is used with their permission.

Appendix I

(p. 446) Reprinted with permission from Carolyn Helfman, Janet Froese, Sue Bratton, Tamara Stutz, and Faye Wedell.

Appendix K

Ethical Standards (p. 458) from American Counseling Association (formerly American Association for Counseling and Development), as revised by AACD Governing Council, March 1988. © ACA. Reprinted with permission. No further reproduction authorized without written permission of the American Counseling Association. Ethical Guidelines for Group Counselors (p. 469) from the Executive Board of the Association for Specialists in Group Work (ASGW), June 1, 1989. © ACA. Reprinted with permission. No further reproduction authorized without written permission of the American Counseling Association. Ethical Standards for School Counselors (p. 478) reprinted from *The ASCA Counselor,* 29(4), April 1992, pp. 13–16. © ACA. Reprinted with permission. No further reproduction authorized without written permission of the American Counseling Association.